UNDERNEATH THE MANGO TREE

Very little is needed to make a happy life; it is all within yourself,
in your way of thinking.

Marcus Aurelius

Max Michell
6 June 2017

*This book is dedicated to my children Daniel and Toni.
I am sorry that I have been unable to tell you some of
these things before. The truth is I was never able to for
a multitude of reasons that you will read about.*

Veritas vos liberabit.

Table of Contents

Prologue

Everyone has got a story to tell; this is mine. My primary motivation for writing this book was to leave behind my story for my children, Daniel and Toni, and in turn, for their children and so on. It will be my legacy, something left behind so that future generations will know what at least one of their forefather's life and times was like. I suppose it is also an attempt to put the record straight and to try and make sense of my own existence.

I never met my father's parents and know very little about them. It should be a given that in writing an autobiography one would aim to portray events as accurately as possible. Sometimes it is disconcerting to be honest, but I think honesty is a perquisite to writing such a book. I want to tell my children things that I have never been able to, for a multitude of reasons. Not surprisingly this puts me in a vulnerable position, but I have chosen this path. Some of the invidious statements in this book are not palatable but I can assure you that I do not intend to hurt anyone. If there is harm done, than alas it is to none but me. I'm no hero that's for sure. There are no medals to pin upon my chest for military service or any other kind of service for that matter. I am at heart just a quintessential Aussie country bloke who might have been in some unusual situations. I tend by nature to be self-effacing and polite. I remember once a good friend told me that he thought that I was too nice a bloke to have been a cop, especially in the NSW Criminal Investigation Branch. Let's put it this way; I don't stand out in a crowd.

Another reason for wanting to write this book is to let people know about the difficulties a person who suffers from severe clinical depression has to navigate throughout their lives. Depression is like a virus in that it never leaves you. Perhaps in some small measure this book may assist a victim of this insidious and potentially fatal disease. Make no mistake; it is a 'killer' disease. It probably would be the major cause of suicide; not to mention its victims who commit violent crimes like serious assaults, rape and murder. I can say with clarity that for nearly all of my adult life I have to some degree suffered from depression. At one stage I became so desperate with it I contemplated suicide. This book details how all that came about and how I have managed against the odds to survive, and to lead a relatively normal life.

I am going to take you on a journey telling my story chronologically. It is not all doom and gloom. There are many positive and encouraging moments throughout the odyssey. At the beginning of each period I insert some important historical facts pertaining to that time so the reader can keep in touch with major events that affected the world such as the dropping of the atomic bomb on Hiroshima on 6 August 1945. My narrative starts in 1944 when I was born and ends in mid 2017, a period of 73 years. It begins with my separation and abandonment when I was sent to a Catholic boarding school at the age of five and I stayed in that education system for the next ten years. After leaving school I faced the tribulations of parental abuse during my adolescence years, coupled with what I saw then, and still do, as child labour exploitation, rural social isolation and the short comings of a dysfunctional family.

After finally being able to break away from the shackles of my family, I started to roam and did all sorts of things that I write about. The next onerous and most dangerous period of my life was the surfacing of severe mental illness. At this stage I write about my critical depression and on-going hospitalisation. I try to articulate how horrendous it was and how desperately lonely, introverted and isolated I had become. It was a period of appalling low self esteem and utter sadness. I write about how the depression got so dreadful that I had a loaded cocked .45 Colt pistol in my hand and went 'within an inch' of putting the weapon to my head and delivering the final coup de grâce. I don't know what stopped me but that was exactly fifty years ago and a lot of water has flowed under the bridge since then. It goes without saying that I'm pleased I didn't. I'm hopeful that anybody with severe depression who may read this book will be influenced to seek medical help.

After this period that I refer to as the 'Days of Darkness', I went through a time of rehabilitation and managed to a large degree to control the clutches of mental illness and went on to lead a relatively normal and successful life. I married and had two children and at the time of writing, I have three grandchildren and these are the people that I am writing this book for. I talk about my time as a nurse and how I graduated with high distinctions in my hospital finals. After I graduated, I never nursed again but instead joined the NSW Police Force. After leaving the police I got into the international hotel business and was also very successful, but became a victim of internal corporate politics as many of us do. I talk the reader through all three of these great experiences I had and include a lot of stories; some of which have a humorous side, some sad but all true.

Next I had to face the second biggest challenge of my life when I went into business and made some 'near-death' decisions. In the final wash-up I lost everything and I mean everything including my family. I had to navigate the tremendous challenges of bankruptcy, divorce and spousal illness simultaneously. Paradoxically I never wavered and simply could not afford to have a relapse of my mental illness. Under no circumstances was I prepared to put my children into a situation where they did not have their own roof over their heads. During this time I believe that I did what very few people could do and showed extraordinary strength and resilience. This period was without doubt my Everest. If it weren't for the 'Lady in the Sauna' (Chapter 12), I don't know how I could have survived it.

Survive I did, and in 1997 I went to Singapore and stayed there on and off for the next fifteen years. I travelled the world as a Security Risk Management Consultant and worked at such prestigious events as the Beijing Olympic Games, the South African Football World Cup and the Winter Olympic games at Vancouver. In 2012, I came back to Australia (Sydney) and in

2013, I appeared before the Royal Commission into Child Sexual Abuse and gave evidence relating to my physical, psychological and sexual abuse at the hands of the teaching clergy of the Catholic church. At the same time I addressed the issues of parental abuse in my adolescence years and spoke about how and why I believe I developed severe mental illness.

In summary I suppose, my story grapples with dark subjects: the abandonment, separation and abuse of children in the Catholic boarding school system of the 1950s and the inconceivable lack of parental support against the power and influence of the clergy. The abuse, both at school and at home, precipitated profound on-going mental illness, substance dependency, social isolation, financial deprivation, and relationship collapses. Not withstanding that, the story is not a narrative of despair, but one of ultimately overcoming insurmountable odds leading to redemption and hope.

I think it is a story that portrays the human spirit and the will to survive.

Chapter One: Those Terrible Michell Boys
1944 - 1956

In 1944 - The Allies invaded Normandy on D-Day on June 6 and the Bretton Woods Conference created the International Monetary Fund and World Bank. The US, British Commonwealth and USSR proposed the establishment of the United Nations. The Battle of the Bulge began as the Germans penetrated the Allied front in Belgium on 16 December to 16 January 1945. Franklin Delano Roosevelt (FDR) was re-elected President of the USA. Oscars awarded in 1944 included the Academy Award for Best Picture to *Casablanca*.

In 1945 - Germany surrendered on 7 May. The US dropped atomic bombs on the Japanese cities on Hiroshima and Nagasaki. Harry S. Truman became President of the USA. The ENIAC (Electronic Numerical Integrator and Calculator), the first all-electronic computer, was completed. Sir Alexander Fleming, Ernst Boris Chain and Sir Howard Florey (all UK) won the Nobel price for the discovery of penicillin. The Academy Award for best picture was 'Going My Way'. Movies released in 1945 included *The Lost Weekend, Mildred Pierce, National Velvet, A Tree Grows in Brooklyn* and *Spellbound*. John Steinbeck's book *Cannery Row* became available. Notable deaths during 1945 included those of Ernie Pyle, George Patton and Franklin Delano Roosevelt.

In 1946 - The Philippines gained independence from the United States on 4 July. Twelve Nazi leaders (including 1 tried in absentia) were sentenced to hang, 7 imprisoned and 3 acquitted in the Nuremberg trials. Winston Churchill's "Iron Curtain" speech warned of Soviet expansion. The Academy Award for best picture was *The Lost Weekend*. The Cannes Film Festival debuts in France. Movies released in 1946 were: *It's a Wonderful Life, The Best Years of Our Lives* and *The Razor's Edge*. The book, *'All the King's Men'* by Robert Warren was also released. Notable deaths included those of W.C. Fields, Gertrude Stein and H.G. Wells

In 1947 - Britain nationalised coal mines. The Marshall Plan proposed to help European nations recover economically from World War II. India and Pakistan gained independence from Britain. The Dead Sea Scrolls were discovered at Qumran. The microwave oven was invented by Percy Spencer (US). John Bardeen, Walter H. Brattain, and William B. Shockley (US) developed the transistor. Movies released were, *Gentleman's Agreement*, *Miracle on 34th Street*, *Great Expectations* and *The Bishop's Wife*. Notable deaths included those of Henry Ford and Max Planck.

In 1948 - Gandhi was assassinated in New Delhi by a Hindu militant on 30 January. The nation of Israel was proclaimed. Berlin airlift began on 21 June and ended 12 May 1949. Columbia Records introduced the 33 1/3 LP ("long playing") record at New York's Waldorf-Astoria Hotel. Edwin Land (US) invented the Polaroid Land camera. The Academy Award for the best picture was *Gentleman's Agreement*. Movies released in 1948 were, *The Treasure of the Sierra Madre*, *Hamlet*, *I Remember Mama*, *Johnny Belinda* and *The Snake Pit*. Notable deaths included those of D.W. Griffith, Babe Ruth and Orville Wright.

In 1949 - The Communist People's Republic of China was formally proclaimed by Chairman Mao Zedong. South Africa institutionalises apartheid. Britain recognised the independence of the Republic of Northern Ireland and it remained a part of the United Kingdom. Cable television debuted in the US, bringing better reception to rural areas where the conventional television signal was weak. 45 rpm records were sold in the US. The Soviet Union began testing atomic weapons. The academy award for the best picture of 1949 was awarded to *Hamlet*. Movies that were released included *All the King's Men*, *Twelve O'clock High*, *Sands of Iwo Jima*, *She Wore a Yellow Ribbon* and *The Third Man*. Notable deaths included those of James Forrestal, Bill Robinson and Richard Strauss.

In 1950 - The Korean War began when North Korean Communist forces invaded South Korea. British atomic physicist Klaus Fuchs was convicted of spying for the Soviet Union. Life expectancy for the western developed world was 68.2 years. President Truman ordered the development of the hydrogen bomb. The first Xerox machine was produced and the first self-service elevator was installed by Otis Elevator in Dallas. Richard Lawler (US) performed the first successful kidney transplant at Loyola. The academy award for the best picture was awarded to *All the King's Men*. Movies released during 1950 included *Sunset Boulevard, All About Eve,* and *Born Yesterday*. Notable deaths included those of Al Jolson, George Orwell and George Bernard Shaw.

In 1951 - Yul Brynner made his first appearance as the King of Siam in Rodgers and Hammerstein's *The King and I*. Colour television was introduced in the US. UNIVAC (Universal Automatic Computer), the first business computer to handle both numeric and alphabetic data, was introduced. Gregory Pincus, Min Chuch Chang, John Rock, and Carl Djerassi (US) developed the first oral contraceptive pill. The first nuclear power plant was built by the US Atomic Energy Commission. The Nobel Prize in Chemistry was won by Glenn T. Seaborg and Edwin H. McMillan (both US), for discovery of plutonium. The Academy award for the best picture went to *All about Eve*. The books *A Catcher in the Rye* by JD Salinger, and the Caine Mutiny by Herman Wouk, were released, as were the movies: *The African Queen, A Streetcar named Desire, An American in Paris* and *A Place in the Sun*. Notable deaths included those of John Alden Carpenter and Dorothy Dix.

In 1952 - George VI of England died and his daughter became Queen Elizabeth II on 6 February. Britain announced its development of atomic weapons. The US exploded first thermonuclear bomb at Enewetak Island. Jonas E. Salk (US) developed the first experimentally safe dead-virus polio vaccine. The first plastic artificial heart valve was developed at Georgetown Medical Centre. The Academy Award for best picture went to *An American in Paris*. Movies released in 1952 included *Singing in the Rain, High Noon, The Greatest Show on Earth* and *Moulin Rouge*. Ernest Hemingway released his book,

The Old Man and the Sea. Who would ever forget Gary Cooper in *High Noon* and Spencer Tracey in *The Old Man and the Sea*? Notable deaths included John Dewey, Hattie McDaniel and Maria Montessori.

In 1953 - Joseph Stalin died on 5 March and Georgi Malenkov became Soviet Premier. The Korean Armistice was signed on 27 July. Moscow announced explosion of hydrogen bomb 20 August. Dwight D. Eisenhower was inaugurated President of United States on 20 January. Playboy magazine hit news stands and the first edition displayed a nude Marilyn Monroe gracing the cover. Rosalind Franklin (England), Francis Crick (England), and James Watson (US) discovered the double-helical structure of DNA. Edmund Hillary of New Zealand and Tenzing Norgay of Nepal reached the top of Mt. Everest on 29 May. First successful open-heart surgery was performed in Philadelphia. The movie *The Greatest Show on Earth* won the academy award for best picture. Movies that were released in 1953 included *The Robe, From Here to Eternity, Shane* and *Roman Holiday*. Sir Winston Churchill won the Nobel Prize for Literature. Notable deaths included those of Queen Mary, Eugene O'Neill and Jacques Thibaud.

In 1954 - The Geneva Conference was convened to bring peace to Vietnam. The country was divided at the 17th parallel, pending democratic elections. Dien Bien Phu, the French military outpost in Vietnam, fell to Viet Minh Army on 7 May. Algerian War of Independence against France began on 31 October. The USS Nautilus, the first atomic submarine, was commissioned at Groton, Connecticut. Boeing tested the 707, the first jet-powered transport plane. The Academy Award for best picture was *From Here to Eternity* and the Nobel Prize for literature was awarded to Ernest Hemingway. Movies released in 1954 included *On the Waterfront, Rear Window, The Caine Mutiny, Sabrina* and *The High and the Mighty*. Notable deaths included those of Lionel Barrymore and Henri Matisse.

In 1955 - Argentina ousted dictator Juan Perón on 19 September. US started sending $216 million in aid to Vietnam. Rosa Parks refused to sit at the back of the bus, breaking Montgomery, Alabama segregated seating law. Martin Luther King, Jr., led 381-day black boycott of Montgomery bus system; desegregated service began 21 December 1956. Narinder Kapany (England) developed fiber optics. The corticosteroid prednisone was developed. *On the Waterfront* won the Academy Award for best picture in 1955. Other movies released in this year included *Rebel without a Cause, Marty, East of Eden, Bad Day at Black Rock* and *Picnic. Gunsmoke* debuted on CBS, and would go on to be television's longest-running western. James Dean died in a car accident at age 26. Other notable deaths included those of Albert Einstein, Alexander Fleming, Thomas Mann, Carmen Miranda and Charlie Parker.

In 1956 - Egypt took control of Suez Canal. Israel launched an attack on Egypt's Sinai peninsula and drove toward Suez Canal. British and French invaded Egypt at Port Said. Cease-fire forced by US pressure stopped British, French, and Israeli advance. Soviet troops and tanks crushed anti-Communist uprisings in Hungary. US tested the first aerial hydrogen bomb over Namu islet, Bikini Atoll with the force of 10 million tons TNT. With many hit singles (including 'Heartbreak Hotel'), Elvis Presley emerged as one of the world's first rock stars. Felix Wankel (Germany) developed the rotary internal combustion engine. The DNA molecule was first photographed. *The Wizard of Oz* had its first airing on TV. The movies *The Seventh Seal, Giant, The Searchers, Around the World in 80 Days, The King and I,* and *Friendly Persuasion* were released. Notable Deaths included those of Tommy Dorsey, Connie Mack and Jackson Pollock.

I was born at Inverell in the north-west of New South Wales, exactly one month before D-day, on 6 May 1944. I have two sisters Patricia and Margaret and one brother, John. Patricia is three years older than me and John is 14 months older. Margaret is three years younger so that puts me third in line. I mentioned I have never met my grandparents on my father's side but I understand that they came out from Kent in England in the early 1900s and settled at Kew in Melbourne. Mum used to tell us that they came from an aristocratic background in England and she insisted that Dad was named after the Earl of Fenton who was allegedly a direct descendant of Lord Kitchener. She said that my grandfather had been booted out of England by Kitchener because of his loose morals and was an embarrassment to the family. She added they paid him to leave and go to the antipodes as far away from England as you could get. I don't know, and have never investigated the authenticity of these claims but they could be true. On my mother's side, there is much more detail. My Mum's Mum (my grandmother Eva) lived from 1877-1952 and my Mum's Dad (my grandfather Cornelius) lived from 1870-1954. My grandmother's parents were Frank Coggan and Annie Nias. Frank was 3 years old when his family migrated out to Australia in 1856. Before they came to Australia they were farmers from Somerset in England. Annie's parents were John Gore and Elizabeth Hyde who were from Northern Ireland. John owned and captained his own ship, and it was on this ship that Annie was born in 1857 as they entered Australian waters at Sydney. My grandfather Cornelius was also born in Australia, so on my mother's side I am a fourth generation Australian and on my Dad's side, a second generation Australian. I do recall fondly referring to Mum's parents as Minnie and Da in my early years.

Mum finished nursing at St Vincent's Hospital in Sydney in 1938 and came home to Inverell to live with her family on a pastoral property in the district. She was lonely as one might understand, bored and 'beaten by circumstances' as she put it, after having lived in the metropolis of Sydney in the 1930s. She wanted to further her studies in nursing but her traditional father would not allow it. However he did allow her to work at the Inverell hospital providing she came home when she was not at work. She used to go to the local balls with her brother Max and it was at one of these that she met Dad. She says that he was a great dancer and a persistent suitor and they drifted into a friendship. They were married on 3 November 1938 at the Sacred

Heart Church in Inverell. That date was nearly one year before the start of WW2 when Prime Minister Chamberlain declared war on Germany (1 September 1939) after Hitler attacked Poland. In Mum's memoirs, she referred to her marriage day as that fateful day that she said, "I do." She explained that further and made it very clear that she considered it a major mistake. She added, "I'd be lying if I said I approached my wedding with the usual enthusiasm and excitement associated with brides. I felt trapped! I dreaded the 'until death do us part." I have a lot to write about this subject and its impact on me later on. The name given to me was Maxwell Cornelius Michell. Mum named me after her father Cornelius (Neil) and her favourite brother, Maxwell (Max). Mum always thought that her brother Max was a saint and she absolutely idolised him. She also thought that her father was the greatest man who ever lived. So you can see that right from the start I had some big shoes to fill. Unfortunately (or fortunately, depending how you look at it) you will learn that I was never able to do that. Dad was a farmer that grew wheat and wool and because of this, was exempted from war service. Their property 'Narine' just outside Bingara in north-west New South Wales was where I spent the first five years of my life.

On 'Narine' there was one of those older style country houses that had a verandah three parts of the way around it. In the kitchen there was a stone sink and a wooden draining board with a cold water tap underneath. The kitchen water that they used for washing up was boiled in a large iron kettle that was permanently on the internal wooden stove. The hot water that was needed for personal washing was boiled in a copper that was outside in the laundry and bought into the bath when hot water was needed by bucketing it in. If there was ironing to be done, these old iron irons would be heated on the stove and when considered hot enough, the ironing would be done, but not surprisingly there was little need for ironing in country life at that time. Outside there was a box like a safe that was filled with charcoal in the outer walls and had fine mesh inside for the lining. They were called the charcoal boxes and they were used to keep food cool; if you like, a type of refrigeration. In those days there were no televisions, or hand phones, or the personal computers that we all take for granted now. There was also no electricity on the property and we used kerosene lamps for lighting. Whenever there was a cricket test on, Dad would come home and spend five days lying on the couch and listening to the cricket commentary on the ABC radio. For a telephone we were connected with other cockies (farmers) on a shared party line and that was considered very modern at the time. In fact we had this type of telecommunications system for many years to come. Outside the house we had what you call the colloquial dunny (toilet). It was a big hole in the ground with a wooden seat built over it and enclosed within a tin shed. That's what we called the dunny and I will write more about that shortly when I am writing about the crimes of the terrible Michell kids. A mailman used to come to the house twice a week. Apparently he normally drove a horse with a buggy but if the roads had been too damaged by the rain, he would ride a horse and lead a pack-horse with all the mail and bread on it. Bingara is not far from Inverell and I recall it as just a small farming community. My brother John spent the first six months of his life in a Sydney hospital because he suffered from the terrible skin disorder, eczema. This was a very itchy disease so he had to be tied down to a bed to stop him from scratching himself. Consequently Mum had to spend most of her time down in Sydney looking after him, so I was sent to my Aunty Joan's place on their pastoral property named 'Willowie' which was near Graman, just outside Inverell. It was Aunty Joan that bought me up for the first six months of my life, as I understand it.

John and I developed a fearsome reputation within the district, and I really don't know how much is based on fact and how much on fiction. I feel that a certain amount of embellishment may have taken place over the years, and that we were not as bad as we were portrayed. Nevertheless, in Mum's memoirs, she has alluded to all of the stories I mention, but I still have my doubts as to their authenticity. I really can't believe that we actually did these terrible things. At least I hope that is the case, otherwise we were really just insufferable and demented children. An example of our nefarious behaviour was when we were supposed to have put the hose into the living room of our local priest's house in Bingara and flooded his house. I have no recollection of that; nor does John. Another thing we were credited with was to spray paint over the white goods in some retail store in Bingara, so Dad was forced to buy the damaged goods. Again, I have no recollection of that. The other incident I can't recall is that we were alleged to have stolen the tools from the local policeman's bike. I just can't imagine that one either but Mum insisted we did and I will take her word for it. However, there are certain unfortunate incidents that I do remember.

For some unexplained reason, John and I could not talk coherently even when I was four and John was five. To compensate, we developed a language whereby we were able to communicate with each other, but not with anybody else. We were called 'Bilbar' and 'Gardee' (or something like that). With four young ones Mum must have had a handful, no doubt, when she was there. I believe that for most of that time she did have some form of domestic help but country life gave us a lot of freedom with the wide open spaces and little supervision. If even any of these stories are true, we must have been a nightmare for our carers. To try and have some control over us, Mum wrote that she used to shut us up in some sort of a cage with a top on it that she could lock. I imagine that would have been effective in one sense but perhaps damaging in another. It may have had some serious ramifications in later life and I will explain all that later. However, I don't blame her for that; she would have had to do something. We were said to be out of control and Dad would not take any action. What was she to do? Another 'locked in' moment might have been when I very nearly drowned when I was toddler; maybe about two years of age. One cold winter's morning in Inverell the story goes, Mum went to the dentist and left me in Dad's care. Dad's laconic temperament and lack of responsibility meant that he was not cut out for fatherhood. He took me down to the park on the Macintyre River which ran through Inverell. As he was reading the paper he heard screaming from people on the bridge that traversed the river and suddenly he realised that I was gone and that I must have fallen into the river. The people on the bridge were pointing to where I was under the water and he dived in and rescued me. I was fully clothed for winter and so was Dad so it must have been a harrowing experience for him as well. When he got me back to Minna's place, she told Mum that Dad should never have been a father. On the basis of this account, I will take it that I very nearly drowned and sometimes I wonder if this incident contribute to my anxiety regarding being on my own in the dark, which I have had to deal with for the majority of my life but that's just speculation.

There are three incidents that I do have a recollection of. One was when we allegedly tried to saw the head off a live sheep with a cross-cut saw. I know that's very hard to imagine but I have a recollection of that. I think it was the sheep that Dad had put in the shearing pen ready for slaughter. In this instance we had the sheep down so we must have tied it legs and rendered it immobile. We were ready to do the business with the saw when Mum caught up with us, stock whip in hand, and she very quickly put an end to it. Mum was by nature 'highly strung' and quick to lose her temper. We deserved a flogging with the whip, and maybe we got one. Dad should have given us a belting for that, but he never hit us. I never heard my father swear and he lived to be 71. He was a real gentleman, a man of the land, born to English parents. Although he was not educated, he had those gentlemanly values and behavioural traits of the English gentry. The worst I ever heard him say was 'God spare my days' and that was the extent of his use of foul language.

The discipline side of things was left to my mother and being 'highly strung,' she was quick with the rod. Fortunately in this incident we never went through with killing the sheep. As I write this I wonder if this incident was blown up to be more than it actually was. Could it be possible that we were just fooling around and just pretending to do it? Country kids are brought up to kill animals; it is second nature to them. I hasten to qualify that by saying that they didn't do it the way that I have just described. Perhaps that is why country boys make such good soldiers. Cutting the throat of a sheep for our meat was something I did for years, but interestingly enough, I couldn't do it now. I would say that I would have slaughtered, skinned and cut up my first sheep around the age of twelve or thirteen. Since that time, I have killed hundreds of them and have an interesting story later about how I got the sack over the killing of a sheep when I was working in the shearing sheds. Nor could I shoot an animal now, any animal. More about that later! But how could two little kids about four years of age, do such a thing or in this case, even attempt to? I just don't understand it. Another incident I clearly remember is throwing the chooks (hens) down into the outside dunny. The paper we used in the dunny was usually the old newspaper and the biggest threat when going to use one of these was being bitten by a red back spider. They used to hibernate underneath the seat and you had to be careful because they are very poisonous, characterised by a red strip down their back. Anyway John and I threw a few chooks down there. I don't know why, but I think Mum might have locked us away for a stint in the cage for that one. Another incident that occurred around about this time was when we lit a fire in the stove in the shearers quarters. Nothing too bad about that except we had a live chook in the oven. Crikey, that's a bit over the top I think. You have to keep in mind we were only about 4 and 3 years of age when we were doing these things.

The next one and probably the worst was when we burned Dad's wheat crop. I remember this like it was yesterday. We were sitting in this old style military blitz truck out in the wheat field whilst Dad was harvesting the wheat. When wheat is ready for harvesting it is very dry and as such, flammable. We started playing with matches that were in the truck. Somehow a lighted match got out of the truck and well, you can imagine what happened. I remember clearly that John was on the outside near the door, and I was in the middle. Unfortunately my parents are long passed and I have no way of verifying the extent of the damage. John doesn't remember it but I do, and it scared the living daylights out of me. Again, I can't be precise about what damage was done but I would feel the story may have been embellished and maybe made to look worse than it actually was. Mum had a tendency to seek sympathy from others, and maybe this was one way of doing that: telling people about her terrible boys, and how much trouble they gave her. The point is that I do remember that we started a fire but the rest is a bit hazy. It is possible that it was quickly put out but as we so often repeat, don't let the truth get in the road of a good story. Referring back to Mum's memoirs, she said that we adapted easily to the cages (that is what she called them) and wrote that we could do quite remarkable athletic exercises swinging by our toes on the top bars of the cage. She added that we never resented being locked in them. I wonder about this and like the drowning, I wonder what influence, if any, this had on my developing personality.

Perhaps all this undue behaviour on our part acted as a catalyst for Mum to decide to send us to boarding school and saw this as our only hope. Get the Catholic nuns to sort us out may have been the prevailing thought; they certainly had that reputation. It worked and we were sent to a preparatory boarding school for little boys at St Joseph College at Aberdeen. They did sort us out. I was five and John was six. It is clearly implanted on my mind that at one time John and I were taken to the railway station and put on a train by ourselves, to be picked up by the nuns when the train reached Aberdeen. This is a very significant point because I believe that the baseline for my troubles in later life may have had its genesis in what I would now see as rejection, separation and abandonment. John and I catching the steam train is very clear to me but again, John has no recollection of it. I am not sure where it was but it may have been Tamworth. Later on when I describe the onset of mental illness, I refer back to this type of abandonment and the Catholic Church's rigid discipline at the time. I can never recall either of my parents coming to see me at St Joseph's College; or in fact to any of the colleges I went to, with one exception. Mum did come down to St Brendan's once when I was 13. It was normal for the parents of the children to come down to the college and see their kids from time to time. That statement contradicts what Mum has written in her memoirs as she stated that she used to regularly come to see us but I don't remember it. Parents might do this once a week or once a month and bring some goodies, like cookies and lollies, with them; but not our parents. Strangely though I remember catching the steam train with John but I don't remember him being with me at St Joseph's in Aberdeen. I suspect I was mostly there on my own.

I do have recollections of the nuns at St Joseph's being cruel to me. Of course you have to remember that this was in the late forties. 'Don't spare the rod' was the accepted disciplinary measure in the Catholic school system at the time. It was considered natural that we used to get a flogging now and again. These days we refer to it as a corporal punishment and it is a criminal offence for teachers to strike children. I do recall that I had this nun screaming at me one day to eat this awful food that was put in front of me. Remember Oliver Twist telling Mr Bumble "Please Sir, I want some more". A bit like that but in reverse; I wanted less. The nun was furious and screamed at me like a maniac, and told me in no uncertain terms that I would stay there until I had finished it. She also told me that if I gave her anymore trouble I would get a 'damn good thrashing'. They use to give us what we called 'frogs eyes' most of the time for food and I think it was either sago or tapioca. Mass produced and probably nutritious, but certainly not tasty and we got it what seemed like every day. I was recently talking with my sister Margaret about the nuns flogging us. She told me that once when she was at the Range College in Rockhampton, she was flogged so badly on the legs that she suffered massive bruising and had trouble walking for a few days. Can you believe this? Make no mistake, these nuns were not averse to giving you a damn good flogging. It does not take someone of Freud's genius to work out that this type of behaviour could leave a profoundly adverse imprint upon a young child's personality and subsequent behaviour.

I think that some of these Catholic boarding schools were breeding grounds for anti-social behaviour and I will write more about that when I write about St Brendan's. I would say that the abuse I suffered at boarding school, amongst many other things, made me a follower, an appeaser, and easily led. I was the youngest and smallest boy at school for most of the time I was at the various schools and I was bought up with a fear and mistrust of authoritarian figures. I developed a behavioural pattern of appeasement and acquiescence towards authority. I found that this was the best way to survive. My father was like this so that should not have been surprising. A culture permeated throughout the schools that allowed for excessive physical and psychological abuse. This must have had an effect on some of the children that would surface for good or bad in later life. I don't really remember much else about St Joseph's. The things that I do remember were the catching of the steam train, abandonment by my parents, the brutal enforcement of discipline by the nuns, the horrible food, not seeing my parents and the incident with the shorts that I have yet to describe to you. If I was asked to describe the school I would not be able to. I have no recollection of the class rooms, dormitories or any of the recreational areas. I do remember that a 'big' river ran by the school and I suppose that must have been the Hunter River. I also remember that one time my shorts were so soiled with urine and the inside of my legs so chaffed that I had to secretly get rid of the shorts. I remember going to the outskirts of the school and throwing them in the bushes. I don't know why my shorts were in that state but it does throw up some disturbing possibilities. What is interesting for me now, is to try to understand why it had to be so secretive? That's about all I can remember about St Joseph's and I sometimes wonder what sort of influence the school, and in particular the nuns, had upon my upbringing. How could they not have had at the age of five?

I can understand that my parents had to do something as it seems that we were behaving very badly at home and we were sent there to be brought under control. That is understandable to some degree I suppose, but look at the potential damage that process could inflict upon little children. Who better than the Catholic nuns of the 1940s to sort out mischievous little boys?

What is more difficult to understand is why our parents, at least Mum, never came to see us. Patricia was at a boarding school at Lochinvar and I am really stretching my memory now but I think it was also called St Joseph's College. It is just outside the town of Maitland in the Hunter Valley and not far from Aberdeen. I spoke with Patricia about the cruelty of the nuns and she told me that she never had any trouble with them and could not recall any beatings. On that basis then, we are not talking about all of them being cruel; just some of them. I would also suggest it might be that the behavioural characteristics of a pure OCD (obsessional compulsive disorder) that I went on to develop like avoidance behaviour and reassurance-seeking behaviours, had their genesis at this school. I have suffered from this disorder for nearly all of my adult life and will go into more detail about it later. I think also that my fear of authoritarian figures was inherited at St Joseph's and stayed as an indelible part of me, much to my detriment with later career and business opportunities.

Early in 1951 when I was six, my parents sold Narine and bought a forty acre block about six kilometres from Inverell on the road to Glen Innes. This property had a lovely big old house on it and now that Mum was cashed up from the sale of Narine, she spared no expense in making the house beautiful and expensively furnished. Nevertheless, the move from Narine to Torrendorra (the name of the lifestyle block outside Inverell) did not allow me to escape boarding school. From St Joseph's College John and I went to an all-boys Catholic teaching boarding school at De La Salle College (DLS) in Armidale in 1952, so on that calculation we were in Aberdeen for three years. Armidale is a city in the New England district of Northern NSW. This particular De La Salle College was the first school of the DLS brothers in Australia and was established in 1906. As at St Joseph's, I was the smallest and youngest boy there. Perhaps it is time to tell you that as a young person I was considered very 'pretty'. I had golden red curly hair and people used to frequently say I should have been a girl; always women! "Oh Mary, he's too pretty to be a boy, he should have been a girl, what a shame" I would hear them say to Mum. Not too good for the self-esteem and sexual identity I'd suggest. 'Too pretty to be a boy' was not an unusual comment. I also remember at one time my mother dressing me up as a girl at Walgett. I don't recall the circumstances around it but there is a photo included in this book that shows it. I think it was only done for a lark but you know; the devil is in the detail. When I start writing about my child sexual abuse at St. Brendan's, I'm going to detail the relevance of this. Johnny Cash can sing about a boy called Sue but I can tell you that life was pretty tough for little 'pretty' red headed kids, especially in the Catholic boarding system in the fifties. I don't want to sound contradictory but paradoxically enough, I don't have a lot of bad memories about DSL College. After some time I was accepted by the older boys and adopted one of them as my hero. He was the Captain of the school's rugby team. What better man to get onside with? I had the honour of looking after his kit whilst we were playing the annual rugby game against Downlands College from Toowoomba. But take my word for it, the teachers were sadistic bastards. The same system was in place for boys for seeing their parents. But for us, it just never happened. The only time I ever got to see my parents was when we went home on school holidays.

Armidale is on top of the Great Dividing Range in NSW, and very cold in winter. We boys used to wear shorts all year round. Beltings were regular and getting the 'jack' was often seen as a badge of honour. Sometimes you got it on the legs. You can imagine what it was like wearing shorts in the middle of winter. In class one day, a very unfortunate incident took place and I believe that the teacher was Brother Benedictine. He was flogging this kid in the front of the class, probably for nothing much at all, and that was not unusual. The victim (the boy) would have been all of 10 or so. This boy had a sort of nervous breakdown. He started bawling and then swearing, yelling at the teacher. He told him he was a f****** big fat c*** and a bully and he should try and pick on someone his own size. We boys were shocked. The teacher offered to give the boy the strap and told him he could thrash him. The boy took it and he laid into the teacher as hard as he could for a couple of straps but then completely broke down. That boy had to leave the college after that and of course I don't know what happened to him. When we used to go back to school at DLS, my brother John would have an allergic action. His eyes and mouth would swell up and he looked an awful sight. I think I was at DLS for about four years but for at least one of those years, John had injured his knee and went home to Torrendorra to recuperate. We had some good teachers at DLS, even though they could be ferocious. In particular the principal, Brother George; bejesus, could he lose his temper and when he did, everybody froze; even the other teachers. However I remember them as generally being fair, unlike those later at St Brendan's. You'd get the jack now and then but not often. They taught us to play good rugby and cricket and the school grounds were quite beautiful. Magnificent grounds with big pine trees on the boundaries where we used to have our hideaways, and built little tree houses. It's interesting that the nuns used the cane and the brothers used a leather strap. I don't know why the Catholic Church did not standardise the procedure throughout its schools. You know, have a standard operating procedure for belting the kids. It was always great to go home for holidays. We would be planning what we would do when we got home — go and see Roy Rogers, Hop-along Cassidy and the like at the old Inverell Hoyts for their Saturday matinee. It was really good fun. Mum used to talk about going to the pictures. I had this mental image that the pictures were a series of pictures that you looked at on the wall. You can imagine my amazement when I saw my first motion picture, which was Davy Crockett. It was really great being home and I loved it and I loved my mother very much at this stage of my life. Before leaving school to come home we would count off the days and there was always great excitement in the air. We even had our own rhymes. One such rhyme was in part:

> Two more weeks and I'll be free,
> Out of the gates of misery.
> No more pencils, no more books,
> No more teacher's dirty looks.

Mum was great because she was happy. She used to say that she would pray every day that I would become a Catholic Priest; she would call me her littlest angel. She had taken a job at the Inverell Hospital as the Deputy Matron and in that role she was able to form a strong social network of doctors and senior nurses. We had all sorts of animals on the lifestyle block; horses, cows, sheep, pigs, turkeys, chickens, dogs, cats, and whatever else. One day John and I found an old discarded buggy in the creek down by the river and we cajoled Mum to get it restored and we would then have a horse and buggy. Mum got someone out to help us break in our little pet pony Bessie to pull the buggy and off we went into the sunset, so to speak. We three children, John, Margaret and myself with Mum's help, used to go all over the countryside in it. It was incredible and we had so much fun. We'd go all over the place without any supervision, and we had a bit of a catch-cry that sounded like this, 'Cheers to the red road and to the top of the hill'. I have no idea now what that meant but I do remember it. I don't recall hearing about John and I misbehaving in a damaging way during this time so maybe the Catholic clergy had sorted us out. We had this great big house and most importantly Mum was happy. The family car was a black Ford Mercury and Mum named it Bertha. Bertha was the very first car that I got behind the wheel of. Dad was away share-farming at a place called Myall Creek and everything at home was good. There is a very interesting and sad story about Myall Creek. On 10 June 1838 a group of eleven white men brutally murdered about twenty-eight Aboriginals who were camped near the homestead of the Myall Creek cattle station. At that time the killing of Aboriginals was not unusual but what set this one apart was that this was the only massacre where white men were charged and hanged for murder. The killers waited until the tribe's men were away from the camp for work when they tied up 28 women, children and elderly men and took them to a gully not far from the homestead and beheaded them with their swords. For this crime, seven of the men were hanged.

After Dad sold Narine in 1951, he bought a property about 30 miles outside of Lightning Ridge. The property ran about 7000 fine merino sheep so it was a significant place. It was the right time for Dad to be buying a sheep property because the price of wool dramatically increased due to the Korean War which started in 1950, creating a huge demand for wool. It went to a pound for a pound; that is that one pound (weight) sold for one pound sterling (currency). This was their big breakthrough but when Dad went to settle, the cocky pulled out of the deal, which was his option. This intending purchase must indicate that they were reasonably well off at the time but Mum states that Dad invested all their money into some engineering firm which collapsed and they lost everything. She does not give any more detail about that so I am unable to elaborate.

Mum had this special relationship with a Catholic priest, Father Conroy. I think he might have been the parish priest at Walgett. I have recollections of Fr. Conroy staying over in our house at Torrendorra and I do recall him being in Mum's bedroom in his pyjamas. I could not describe what Fr. Conroy looked like, but I can tell you that he was wearing; blue and white striped pyjamas. Isn't that amazing? That was over sixty years ago. Isn't it interesting what young children hold on to? I am not inferring anything was untoward. He was not in the bed, nor on it. He was just in the room as I was at the time. That's why I know. Even if I knew something was untoward, I wouldn't say anything, but it wasn't that I know of. The last thing I would do is to try and tarnish my mother's moral reputation publicly. She had very high standards of morals; too high I think. Although I must say that it was hardly appropriate behaviour for a man of the cloth to be in a lady's bedroom in his PJs. Fr. Conroy was very kind to John and I and used to regularly send comic books to us at De La Salle College. These comic books made us very popular with the other boys as you could well imagine. I think they were comics about the Phantom, Dennis the Menace, Archie; that type of thing. Mum also formed some sort of a relationship with one of her patients; a bloke named Archie Marsh. Archie had a bad accident and had to be immobilised in bed in the Inverell Hospital. I seem to remember that he had a broken hip, amongst other injuries and was on traction. Archie was a land owner who had a property named 'Rio Grande' up Mungindi way, near the Queensland border. Again, I am not inferring anything was untoward. He would regularly come to Torrendorra with his two children, Rodney and Kathy. I fell in love with Kathy Marsh. I was 11 years of age and she was my first true love. The day Archie and his kids left to go back to Mungindi was the saddest day of my life up to that point in time. I was inconsolable and cried for three days. I didn't think that I could live without being with her. I had trouble understanding why she had to leave me and was very deeply saddened by it. Mum was very supportive and I sort-of got over it. I do wonder what impact that had on me. It seems now such an insignificant event but at the time it had a very profound effect on me. I still have trouble all these years later saying goodbye to someone that I truly love. Interestingly enough, my daughter Toni also has a lot of trouble saying goodbye. Perhaps it is a case of 'chip of the old block.' I feel that Toni may have felt abandoned by me when Sue (her mother) and I separated, and that it has left its imprint on her. I'll write more about that later. It seems that I was developing a major problem with separation and abandonment early on in life.

Sometime between De La Salle College and going to Queensland, we went to a little country school at a place called Brodies Plains. It was just a little village school and I think we were all more or less in the same class, but we loved it. Primarily because we could come home every night and go for a ride in the buggy, or some other country thing. Life was good. I cannot imagine kids having a better life than we did. One of my fondest memories was when Mum would let me drive her little Hillman car (the other car). I'd say I was about ten at the time. I was driving home from Inverell to Torrendorra. Naturally Mum was at my side but I was driving it on my own. Not too many mothers would do that. This lorry sped past us going up a hill and stopped in front of us. He claimed that he was a cop and gave Mum a very stern lecture about letting me drive the car on a public highway. Mum apologised and told him something like that I had been sick and she was trying to cheer me up a bit and asked him if he could overlook it on this occasion. He did and let us go. That gives you an idea of how good a mother Mum was at this time in my life, but perhaps not such a good example of being a responsible parent. Let's keep the negatives out of it at this stage as there are plenty of them later on in the story.

Actually having just written that John and I had largely reformed, we did get up to a bit of mischief which I am embarrassed to admit to. We used to play doctors and nurses. Of course, John and I were the doctors and poor Margaret, all of about 7 was the nurse. It involved playing with each other and simulated sex. We were about eleven, ten and seven respectively. Mum found out and my God, the proverbial s*** hit the fan; and so it should have. Straight into the confessional box to confess our crimes to the Catholic Priest before God and receive absolution. I cannot explain why we did such things. I just can't. I know that because John was 14 months older than me, he was the leader. Mum used to say that John loaded the gun and I fired it. I can say that there was never any actual sex involved but still, it's not healthy for kids to be behaving like that. You wonder why. It almost seems like we were in some sort of a feckless state. Dad was away in the bush at Myall Creek share farming and he really didn't care about us. He was happiest when he was alone; Mum was working in the hospital. Of course it might be a bit unfair to blame our parents but their absence, particularly Dad's, may have been the catalyst for precipitating such things. I can never remember my father showing me any affection, ever. I suppose you can't blame him after we burned down his wheat crop and damaged his truck. I look back and feel immensely guilty that we were 'those terrible Michell boys' but still wonder why. It's a question that I have never been able to answer.

Dad had a peculiar habit and had it all his life; at least the part I knew. He used to talk to himself, out loud. You would hear him talking and you would ask him who he was talking to. He would simply say himself. The parts I remember were in the form of questions and answers. He might ask himself (aloud and alone) for example, quote, "Fenton, do you think it is going to rain today?" Then he would answer himself (aloud), "Nah, I don't think so, maybe in the next couple of days". It never worried him, and from memory it never worried us. I'm just pleased that I did not inherit this unusual and to my mind, peculiar characteristic.

Then came the news we were going to Queensland. At some time during my DLS period Mum and Margaret took a trip up to Cairns and Innisfail. On their way back to Inverell, they passed through a place called Emerald where Mum caught up with her brother Les, who was the uncrowned prince of the area. It was Uncle Les who told Mum about blocks of land in the area that the Queensland Government were going to ballot out to potential cockies free. In case you don't know what a cocky is in this terminology, it means a small scale farmer and could also refer to larger landowners; really anyone who owned land but generally smaller farmers. You can have wheat cockies, cow cockies, sugar cane cockies, wool cockies and so on. Mum got onto this and got all the applications to enter the ballot in on time and on 18 August 1956 the Department of Lands in Brisbane notified my parents that they had won a 5,546 acre block of prime farming country near Capella (not far from Emerald) in Central Queensland. Mum was now leaving everything she cherished behind, including her work at the hospital and her strong social network. She was also leaving her extended family where she had lived all of her life and of course, so were we children. Nearly all of her brothers and sisters lived in the Inverell district and Mum had very strong ties to them. At the Torrendorra auction at Inverell, her heart was broken. All her valuable artefacts, crystal, paintings and accessories went for next to nothing at the auction. The carpetbaggers moved in and cleaned her out. Dad of course was in his usual imperturbable manner; he took it in his stride. Mum was bitter and that bitterness never left her. You can imagine packing up and leaving a really nice lifestyle, good standard of living, friends and relatives, to go to a block of land in the middle of nowhere, not knowing anyone, and with nothing on it. I don't know what happened to Bessie and our buggy. Probably given away to somebody! I think that Bertha was sold at auction for next to nothing. If you have ever read *The Grapes of Wrath* by John Steinbeck, you might better understand what I mean by undertaking a migration. We were just like the 'Oakies' migrating from the dust bowl lands of West Texas, Kansas and Oklahoma going to greener pastures in California. We packed up, put all the gear on Dad's comer truck tray and in Mum's car, and took off for Emerald, across the Carnarvon Ranges. That's 938 kilometres and the roads were not too flash in those days of the mid-fifties. When we camped overnight on the Carnarvon Ranges, it was the first time I heard the howl of a dingo. I thought that they were wolves and that we were in a bit of strife. We arrived in Emerald and stayed with our cousins, the McCoskers. They were anything but poor. My main memory of that first encounter in Queensland was using mosquito nets; I'd never encountered them before. A short time later, after being given all the leftover school uniforms from them, John and I were packed off to the Christian Brothers College named St Brendan's at Yeppoon. Patricia (my older sister) was sent to the Range Catholic College in Rockhampton and Margaret stayed at home with Mum and Dad. I was 12 years of age at this time.

What happened next was pivotal to my well-being and personal development. Up to this point I have spoken about what I perceived to be abandonment and separation and the harsh discipline of our Catholic teachers. I believe that the damage done by this earlier separation and abandonment was largely mitigated by my coming home to a loving home environment with some stability in our lives when we were able to go to a local village school and come home every night. It was a squaring of the ledger so to speak. The wrong that was done by sending me away at such a young age may have been compensated by bringing me home to Torrendorra and giving us a loving home life where we were with Mum and the surrounds of a lovely lifestyle block to live on. Not to mention the enormous amount of fun we had with Bessie and the sulky going all over the countryside without a care in the world.

When we get older I think we all tend to reflect on our lives and certainly when you are writing a book about your life, it is essentially a time for reflection. I think by nature we all want to be positive rather than negative but when you are telling a non-fiction story it is not realistic if it's all a 'bed of roses'. Nevertheless, I would say that the period when I lived on the lifestyle block outside of Inverell was the happiest period of my life. The Inverell district is wonderful farming country with beautiful undulating terrain that grows high quality merino wool and wheat. I would often go to one of the properties of my extended family and spend part of my holidays with them. I recall with great fondness and clarity how I used to love going to Cherry Tree Hill and spend time with a family of Mum's cousins, Jack McCosker family. Jack had joined the Australian Light Horse Brigade and served in Palestine during WW1. I used to go riding with him and marvel at his ability to control his sheep dogs with whistling and his skills with the stock whip. His daughter Doris (or Dora), not sure which, treated me like a son and I cannot articulate enough how much I loved them. I think that it was Jack's family that was related to Rick McCosker who went on to become an International test cricketer, and personified what courage was all about in test cricket.

Another extended family property I used to enjoy visiting immensely was my cousin's John McCosker's, just outside Inverell. I used to go to boarding school with John at DLS College and he was a wonderful companion for me. We both had this love of the country hillbilly music and we would get up early morning and listen to these fellas with all the yodelling and singing mainly about the land and its people. Blokes like Slim Dusty and Tex Morton come to mind. One time when I went to John's father's place, Nigel McCosker (Mum's brother and my Uncle) he offered John and I a job to help him with the wheat harvesting. We were about 11 years of age at the time. My recollection is not that good that I can describe our job description, but it centred round the harvest, filling bags of wheat, maybe sowing the bags; that type of thing. I did not expect any money for what we were doing and just saw it as a bit of fun. It would have been great playing grown-ups I imagine and having a sense of self-worth. We were just little kids sort of helping. However at the end of harvest he took us into town to a cafe, bought us each a soda pop in one of those American style diners of the 1950s and gave us a quid each for our labour. We could not believe it and we felt that we were really cashed up. I told Nigel (we always called our uncles and aunties by their christian name) that I couldn't take it but he insisted, saying that a fair day's work deserves a fair day's pay; so I took it. I can't remember what I did with mine but have a thought that I may have bought a watch and this was the first money I had ever made.

There were many other examples that highlight the wonderful life that I had at that time and many of them involved the land and my immediate and extended family. Mum had one sister and five brothers and three of them (all boys) lived on pastoral properties in the Inverell district that Da had left them. If I wasn't at one of these places, I'd be at another. Unfortunately the wonderful life was to come to an end and that all changed after we went to Queensland in late 1956, early 1957. That is when the rot really started and later manifested itself with serious repercussions for me.

Chapter Two: Underneath the Mango Tree
1957 - 1958

In 1957 - The USSR tested its first successful ICBM. The temporary artificial heart was invented by Willem Kolff. Interferon was invented by Alick Isaacs and Jean Lindemann (England and Switzerland). Clarence W. Lillehie and Earl Bakk (US) invented the internal pacemaker. Leonard Bernstein's West Side Story debuted on Broadway and brought violence to the stage. The Movies released included *The Bridge on the River Kwai, Twelve Angry Men, Sayonara, Peyton Place* and *Witness for the Prosecution*. Notable deaths included those of Humphrey Bogart, Richard E. Byrd, Joseph McCarthy and Arturo Toscanini. The most notable event of 1957 was that Russia launched Sputnik I, first earth-orbiting satellite — the Space Age begins.

In 1958 - The European Economic Community (Common Market) became effective. Khrushchev became Premier of The Soviet Union as Bulganin resigned. Gen. Charles de Gaulle became French Premier and remained in power until 1969. The existence of the Van Allen Belt, a radiation belt surrounding the Earth, was confirmed by the Explorer I satellite. NASA initiated Project Mercury, aimed at putting a man in space within two years. *The Bridge on the River Kwai* won the Oscar for best picture. The movies, *Vertigo, Gigi, Cat on a Hot Tin Roof* and *The Defiant Ones* were amongst those released. Truman Capote released the book *Breakfast at Tiffany's* and Leon Uris released *Exodus*. Notable deaths included those of Robert Donat, Norman Bel Geddes and Alfred Noyes.

They say that life is great in the sunshine state. Well, it didn't turn out that way for me. The Queensland Government had opened up vast amounts of land at Peak Downs, Retro and Magenta, just outside Capella in Central Queensland. These were massive pastoral stations that were virtually not being used and the Queensland Government wanted to settle them. After winding up the Queensland British Food Corporation, the government subdivided Peak Downs, Retro and Magenta into farming blocks of approximately 5000+ acres and opened these up for selection in 1956. It was one of these blocks that my parents won in the ballot that I mentioned previously. It was beautiful virgin country with these magnificent peaks in the background, hence the name Peak Downs. Capella is situated between Emerald and Claremont in Central Queensland. It's about at the half way point between these two towns. When Dad won one, he and Mum were elated, but unbeknownst to me at that time; this was the beginning of the end for me. We moved up to Queensland in late 1956, early 1957. There was absolutely nothing on these blocks. No buildings, fences, windmills, roads, nothing. It had never really been settled. The first thing my parents had to do was put a roof over our heads. They did this by building a shearing shed that we used to live in until they could build a house, a couple of years later. The land was riddled with wildlife; wild pigs, kangaroos, wild turkeys, foxes, emus, dingoes, to name a few. For a long time there was no electricity, no phone, no showers, no kitchen to cook in, etcetera. If you know what a shearing shed looks like, you'd know. We used kerosene lamps for light and an open fire for cooking. We had a bucket with holes in the bottom for a shower and frequently bathed in the local Arbor creek that ran through the property. I recall reading about the life of Abraham Lincoln and the dire circumstances in which he was bought up in as a subsistence farmer (a cocky), first in Kentucky and then in Indiana. The shack that he was bought up in during his very early years had a dirt floor. It was not until his father married a second time, that his new wife made his father build a floor to cover the dirt for the shack. When he was nominated as a candidate for President of the United States, a Chicago newspaper man interviewed him about his childhood and Lincoln explained it this way "Poverty was our constant companion. That was my life, and that is all you or anyone else can make of it". If a one room shack was good enough for Abraham Lincoln, I reckon a shearing shed (with a floor) was good enough for us. Over time, my parents got a diesel generator that provided electricity; built a three bedroom house, shearing quarters, sheep yards, cattle yards, a machinery shed, and so on. Dad had bought up his farming machinery and he started cultivating the land. My brother John and I, when we were home on holidays, would keep that tractor going 24/7 cultivating the land. Any money that they did have had to go into buying all the materials required for the fencing; strainers posts, still posts, gates, grids, wire netting and barb wire. This had to be done before we could buy any livestock because they would wander off the property and who knows where they would end up. They were now very poor and relied on the advances that were provided by the pastoral company Dalgety, out of Rockhampton. These advances were also paying to keep four children in private boarding schools which would have been an incredible strain on their resources. This must have taken a terrible toll on my mother. She was used to comfort and the finer things of life and all of a sudden, here she is in the middle of Central Queensland living in a shearing shed and pretty much living a life of social isolation. She must have thought at times that she was a long way away from the glamour life she used to lead in both Sydney and Inverell. It must have been brutal for her and I am sure that this affected her adversely. No doubt it was one of the main catalysts for the significant negative changes in her behaviour towards me a short time later.

In the meantime John and I were sent to St Brendan's Christian Brothers College in January 1957 at Yeppoon near Rockhampton in Queensland. We left Inverell on 6 January 1957 so it would appear that we went straight from Emerald to St Brendan's. We were very badly bullied at St Brendan's during that first term of 1957, very badly indeed. Not so much by the brothers but by the other kids. The bullying was terrible. We were outsiders and were referred to by the other boys as the ugly red headed kids from NSW. They frequently bashed us. If you were in a line to get something, they would push you out and make you get to the end of the queue. It was not unusual for one of the boys to give you a good kick on your backside, just for the fun of it and everybody else would laugh. We became the butt of their jokes. We had to get to the end of the queue for everything. We had a cousin there, Billy McCosker, one of the Emerald mob. Billy was a sort of minder for us and did what he could but that was limited. In those first three months of the first year at St Brendan's an awful lot of damage was done to me. You could compare it with the behaviour of wild dogs. You will have seen on wildlife documentaries on TV how the pack can isolate the weakest and most vulnerable members of the pack. The alpha positions were reserved for the older boys with the omega roles reserved for the boys lower down in the pecking order. My brother and I, unlike the animal world, were not even in the pack. We were made to feel total outcasts. The role of protectors should have been fulfilled by the brothers and the older boys but they did not do that, so we were essentially being treated like lepers. To further complicate things, our parents did not come to check on us and the reason for that could well have been that they simply could not afford to make the trips. It was 226 miles (361 kilometres) from Capella across to Yeppoon and they were very ordinary roads in those days. The truth is that Mum and Dad were living 'on the smell of an oily rag' and I understand their terrible financial predicament. Like I said, just like John Steinbeck's 'Oakies.'

I was only 12 years of age at the start of 1957. When I spoke with John about it for this book he did not seem to have been as effected by it as I was, but then again, he was fourteen months older than me and he had a very different personality to mine. I recall this 3-month period as one of almost total alienation and abandonment, with a constant fear of violence and complete marginalisation. I can remember being too frightened to even go into the locker room for fear of being belted by the other kids. I would say that for that first term period in 1957, I lived in an almost constant state of fear of the other boys. It was not an option for us to go to school at Capella. I don't even know if there was one there. If memory serves me correctly the population of Capella at that time was only about 150 people. However, in the second term the bullying eased up. Perhaps they just got sick of bullying us and by the second term of the scholarship year we got in with the 'bad boys' of the school. In Queensland at that time, scholarship was the last year of primary school. The 'bad boys' accepted us and we became members of their pack, if I can use that analogy but of course, only at the omega level. We became valued members of the school's wood cutting team, under the guidance of a grand old man, Irishman Brother Fitzpatrick. He was truly a lovely man. I make this point because I don't want you to think they were all scumbags. I suppose there were some decent men amongst them. We used to go with Brother Fitzpatrick on the school's old Ferguson tractor out into the scrub and pick up all the wood that the school needed for its energy requirements. The school was situated in bushland outside of Yeppoon so it was easy for us to get as much wood as the school needed. We would then bring the wood back on a trailer and cut it up at the school's saw mill. It was great; country kids working hard. We were rewarded afterwards with a cup of tea and sandwiches. Although Br Fitzpatrick would say a little prayer and cross himself before we started the electric saw, he never made us do it. I think by now we were all budding atheists anyway; at least I was. The other kids would be at their sports. This was a good fit because we had no interest in that unfortunately. Naturally enough I suppose the school's administration must have liked it because of all the cheap labour they were getting. It was a win-win situation for everybody. Seems even at this early stage my labour was very much appreciated but not paid for.

Our teacher that year was another reasonable bloke, a fella by the name of Brother Higgins. However sometime during this year, perhaps the latter part, a very unfortunate incident occurred. By this time at the age of thirteen we were smoking. Maybe you remember the old log cabin tins and champion cartons of tobacco. I don't know where we got the money from to buy it but we most certainly had it. One Sunday Brother Higgins noticed that John, Paste (Fisher - a boy from Longreach, you get it, fish paste?), and I were not at mass. He bailed me up in the locker room and asked me if I was at mass and I told him I was. You are not going to admit to a grievous mortal sin are you? Well, this hitherto reasonably minded brother could not restrain himself. He slapped me so hard across the face it lifted me off my feet which slammed me against the lockers and knocked me to the floor. I will hasten to add that he did not punch me. He could not contain his anger and he pulled me up onto my feet and told me to empty my pockets. Out fell the tin of log cabin tobacco. He soon got it out of me who was with me and rounded us up. We had committed three very serious crimes. Firstly, we had missed mass on a Sunday, a cardinal sin in the Catholic Church at the time; I think it still is. Two, we had been smoking. An act strictly forbidden within the school and three, I had lied to him. I think he discussed it with the principal Brother Duffy and the punishment was that we would each receive six strokes of the jack (the strap) in front of the entire class on the backside. We are going back to the days of penal settlement now and that's what happened. Br. Higgins assembled the whole class and flogged us in front of it but we were not expelled. To be truthful, I think it hurt Brother Higgins as much as it hurt us and he stopped the punishment after he had reached three or so. For the rest of the year he was good and we had truly learnt our lesson. Although the smoking continued, we were sure not to miss mass at all anymore. Would you believe we had to go to mass every day, first thing after getting up? If that flogging happened today Brother Higgins would be charged with assault with actual bodily harm and Brother Duffy with being an accessory. You will hear a lot more about the 'jack' as we go on. The school had pineapple farms on one of its boundaries. It was common for us to sneak out of school, have a smoke and steal some pineapples. The farmer was forever having to contend with this menace but I think in the end he had a word with the Principal and he put an end to it. Like it was at De La Salle College, the food was lousy. If you dished it up in prison, you'd have a riot on your hands. My memory is not good enough to tell you what it was but I can tell you that this is where I learnt to gobble down my food quickly. Once a week we would get fresh bread and we boys loved it. Once you finished your table plate of bread you were allowed to put your hand up and they would bring another plate. However, you were strictly forbidden to put your hand up until the plate was empty and the dining room staff would monitor it. The quicker you ate this beautiful fresh bread, the sooner you would get more.

The Christian Brothers were mostly religious bigots, fanatics and completely indoctrinated. They wanted us to be the same. Here is a breakdown into the religious agenda that we had to adhere to; you had no choice in this:

- Mass every morning (except one day - I think Mondays);
- A standing prayer before and after every meal;
- A standing prayer before and after every lesson;
- A religious lesson every day (you were never belted in that lesson);
- Rosary in the chapel every night;
- Novena of the Perpetual Succour every Thursday night;
- Benediction every Sunday night;
- We all had a turn at being altar boys (I have some good stories about this one);
- One three day silent retreat throughout the year.

Certainly I was a non-believer by the time I went to St Brendan's. My mother's prayers were not being answered, it seemed. What a disappointment for her! The Novena to the Lady of the Perpetual Succour (OLPS) is the Madonna. We would write out petitions each week and place them in a locked box at her shrine. The Priest would collect these petitions and on Thursday nights he would read them out to the congregation (us). It was said that if you asked OLPS she would always grant a request. You know, a bit like asking the Godfather for something on his daughter's wedding; he couldn't refuse. Ask and you shall receive; seek and you shall find; knock and it shall be open unto you; all that sort of thing. Then we had to say nine Hail Mary's followed by the usual sermon. Well, you can imagine what happened. All sorts of petitions were secretly put into the box and I know for a fact, one boy asked her to get rid of Br. Broderick; our mathematics and physics teacher in our sub junior year. I know it was a fact because I was that boy. My the Lord works in mysterious ways, doesn't he? Boys used to put all sorts of rubbish into the box and of course the brothers could never find out which boy put in what petition. I suppose these days that they could put up a camera and watch it on their mobile phones but couldn't do that in the 1950s. The Benediction was about the only religious ceremony I liked and I'm sure that I would still like it. Not for its religious significance but rather for the Latin dialogue that was used and the beautiful hymns that were sung. There was a certain magic about the Benediction that captivated me. To this day, I would be prepared to go to Benediction if it was held in Latin, but of course it isn't anymore.

John was faring poorly scholastically, and was the 'dunce' of the class. Strange because he is a fairly intelligent man. So he left and I went back to St Brendan's on my own the following year (1958). Going back to school rarely involved my parents taking me back but on this occasion Dad took me as he had to pick up supplies in Rockhampton. He 'dumped' me at the main entrance to the administration block, shook my hand and left me there. Normally going back to school was on the train from Capella to Rockhampton. At this stage of my life I was very happy at home. I loved helping Dad and Mum. Everywhere we went we'd run into wild pigs, mobs of kangaroos, foxes, wedge tail eagles, wild turkeys and so on. Mum was generally good to me although she could be erratic at times. You never knew if she was going to hug you or give you a clip behind the ear. For many years I used to duck instinctively when she raised her hand. By now Dad had fully fenced in the property so it was time to get the livestock in. I must point out that we all got on pretty well during this period. When Dad bought in a few thousand sheep from 'Terrick Terrick' at Blackall the dingoes came. They were a real menace. They did not kill sheep for the meat but just played with them. They'd bite the sheep in the kidney area and of course the sheep would die but the dingoes did not eat them. Instead of losing just one or two for the dingoes' food, you might lose twenty or thirty in a single night. A group of Cockies got together and hired a dogger (a dingo hunter) to eradicate the menace. He'd live under the stars and would start howling them up. We could not tell which one was howling, the dogger or the dingo. He was very good and he would bring them right up to where he was, set the telescopic sight up squarely between the eyes and put a bullet neatly between them. He actually got rid of all of them. My brother John also became adept at catching them. He learnt how to set traps and had a fair bit of success tracking them down. I became somewhat competent with shooting and Mum bought me my first rifle when I was 13 whilst I was home on holidays from St Brendan's. It was single shot .22 calibre rifle and I shot a lot of kangaroos and pigs with it during my school years. She also bought a 24/20 Winchester rifle like the type you see in the American cowboy movies; that was for John. She got it second hand from old Mrs Brown, who had drawn another block in the ballot. Dad and I used to go to the local firing range and we did a lot of target shooting using the military style .303 rifles with aperture sights. Over time, I became a very good shot. John had this great pig dog and we used to go hunting pigs with him. We didn't have to go far, anywhere on the property and you'd find them. He (the dog) would grab the wild pig, sometimes big boars, by the ear and we would either shoot the pig at point blank range or stab it in the heart with a big hunting knife. When you think about it, this can be quite a dangerous occupation. We were only about 13 or 14 at the time. You can imagine, especially if the pig was a big boar, what would happen if the dog let go of the ear but he never did and we always got our pig. We'd cut off the snout and the tail and take them to the local council who would give us a small sum of money for them. John was at home working full time now but of course, he did not receive any payment. I guess that was fair enough since my parents were broke at the time but even when they did have it the practice continued.

Fast forwarding a bit, probably my best shooting story was the story about the slaying of my Uncle Lionel's pet emu on his property at 'Cullin-la-Ringo,' near Springsure. He had this one emu on his property which was about 10,000 acres. It wasn't a pet but he used to call it that and strictly forbade me, or anybody else, to shoot it. One day we were out laying baits in dead lambs that had been killed by wedge tail eagles. These eagles were huge and they would swoop down and pick up the lambs by their hind quarters and take them for a ride a couple of thousand feet up, or whatever it was and let them go. We would put strychnine in the meat around the loins of the lambs. When the eagles came back, they'd eat the meat and that was it for them. Sometimes we would come along in Lionel's old Land Rover and these very sick eagles would be trying to take off but couldn't get off the ground. It was a hunting bonanza for me as Lionel would let me carry out the coup de grâce on these killer birds. I shot a lot in this manner and we were able to eventually kill them all and wiped them out, getting rid of that menace. Back to the emu. We saw this emu yonder. I really don't know how far it was but I used to say seven hundred meters so let's stick to that. It certainly was a long way away. I again badgered Lionel to let me take a shot. He told me that I could on the express proviso that I was never to ask him again if I could shoot it. I agreed and took the shot with this old sporting hard bore . 303 rifle I used to cart around with me. After the shot, the bird darted away at a million miles per hour and Lionel said that I was now to honour the agreement. Would you believe that as we were watching the bird dropped. We drove over and saw that the bullet had just about blown its neck off. The neck of an emu is about as thick as your forearm. To hit that, at 700 meters was just a total fluke. It just wasn't the bird's day. Lionel was very angry but he could not do much about it as he had agreed and that was the end of it. This incident happened when I was about sixteen so I am getting ahead of myself a bit.

During holidays from school, life was good away from that prison at St Brendan's. Going back to school was highly traumatic for me; I mean really traumatic. I was inconsolable as Mum put me on the train. I doubt that Dad even came. There was no doubt all the parenting was left to my mother, and later very much to her detriment and also to mine. I'd catch the old steam train at Capella and off I'd go to Rockhampton (Rocky), and I really can't remember how I got from Rocky to Yeppoon. Year 1958 was my first year of high school as we started our sub senior year. As soon as we got back to St Brendan's rumours started to float around that the school had bought in some 'heavies' to clean us up and they were going to get stuck into the deadwood. Little did we know at the time how right that proved to be. On the first day of the first term we met our new teachers. This brother who we had never seen before walked into the classroom, stood at the podium and never said a word. He reached into his pocket and pulled out his black jack. With one sweeping motion, he whirled it about his head and landed a thunderous blow on the podium. He now most certainly had our attention. He then spoke and said, quote, "Boys, my name is Brother Mc Sweeney. I am here to teach you Latin and let me make it very clear from the start, nobody is going to fail". For the record, he carried out his promise and nobody did fail Latin. He bashed it into us and we spent hundreds of hours learning it off by heart to avoid getting a flogging from him. I vividly recall him asking me one day in class to stand up and read a passage of Latin into English. I read it word perfect and he was dumbfounded. He thought I must have been cheating. He made me stand, keep the book in my hand whilst he came to the back of the class to see if I was cheating. I wasn't but he never apologised or said sorry for calling me a cheat. He was just a f****** c*** and an extremely cruel man. I got so good at learning Latin parrot fashion I could say the Confession in Latin verbatim and in part can still do that until this day. Here it is but I confess (pardon the pun) that I had to look up the spelling:

Confiteor Deo omnipotenti, beatae Mariae semper Virgini,
beato Michaeli Archangelo, Beato Joanni Baptistae,
Sanctis Aspostolis Petro et Paulo, omnibus Sanctis, et vobis,
fratres (et tibi pater), quia peccavi nimbus cogitatione,
verbo et opere: mea culpa, mea culpa, mea maxima culpa.
Ideo precor beatam Mariam semper Virginem,
beatum Michaelem Archangelum, beatum Joannem Baptistam,
sanctos Apostolos Petrum and Paulum, omnes Sanctos, et vos,
fratres (et te, pater), orare pro me ad Dominium Deum
nostrum. Amen.

Imagine being forced to learn that at 12 years of age.

Another teacher was Brother Broderick (I think that was his name). His ubiquitous influence was felt by all of the kids, even the goodie goodies. He was an ogre and a sadist; worse than McSweeney. Broderick would belt you for the simplest of mistakes. If you didn't know the answer to a question, he'd belt you. If you got something wrong in your homework, he'd belt you. He was forever belting the kids and I believed he enjoyed it. Even though it was generally accepted at the time that there were times you needed to use corporal punishment, this was way over the top, even for a Catholic school. Later in the year we learnt that Broderick was killed whilst on holidays in North Queensland. Apparently he had a mishap with a marine creature, stood on it, or was stung, whatever the case, and got poisoned or something to that effect. We boys were elated, justice had been done. As I said before the lord works in mysterious ways. Our Lady of the Perpetual Succour had indeed responded to my petition and got rid of Broderick, although I had not asked her to kill him; just to get rid of him. She might have misunderstood me. When it was announced at the school assembly by the principal, Br. Duffy said to us, quote "Boys, I have some very sad new for you. Brother Broderick has passed away". There was a section of the assembly that clapped quietly. That's an absolute true story. He was a f****** tyrant and got what he deserved.

There is no doubt in my mind that both McSweeney and Broderick were sadists and enjoyed inflicting pain upon the boys. I would not go so far as to say that it was a sexual gratification thing but would not discount it either. I have now admitted for the first time that I put a letter in the OLPS petition box thanking her for dealing with Broderick. I wonder what the Priest thought when he was going through the petitions. I know one boy put in a petition that he would like to f*** one of the young female workers in the dining room. She was a pretty little girl and he drooled over her. In this case, I don't believe his wish was granted but it strikes me as odd that you would have a young pretty girl working in the dining room that would have been full of some very horny young boys. Anyway, that was the story about OLPS and our happenings with her.

I found solace and companionship in the wood gang and we were basically the misfits of the school. We expressed our displeasure at the way we were treated in the class room in a passive-aggressive manner. Things like never going to confession, never going to communion and generally doing anything that we could, without getting a belting, to let the Brothers know we were very unhappy with them. There is a great deal of talk in the press at the moment about the radicalisation and marginalisation of the young people that are signing up to go to ISIS in Syria and Western Iraq. I can see the parallel here. You have to experience it to know what it is like to be marginalised and an outcast. When you are being treated like this, you look for a home, any home. You need to have a sense of belonging, somewhere you are accepted and treated as a member of the family. Having said that I don't condone for a minute what ISIS do. I'm just making the point that kids that are treated badly as children, are much more likely to turn out 'bad'. I found my home with the wood sawing gang.

Some of the methods of punishment at St Brendan's lacked a great deal in creativity and innovation. I imagine that these punishments were the norm for any Catholic school at the time. A few come to mind:

- You were made to listen to the pictures (movies) but you couldn't watch it. You had to sit behind the screen. This happened to John and I during that first term of the first year that I described to you. He actually remembers this one.
- Write out five hundred times, I must not speak during class; or whatever;
- Eat your meals standing up (that was an easy one);
- Stand up in class in a corner for the whole lesson, facing the wall;
- Stand up in front of the class and tell the class what an idiot you were ("Miss Australia, tell the class you are an idiot");
- Be made to miss a meal;
- Be made to go to your meal place but not allowed to eat. That was really tough;
- Stay in class at the end of the day and do extra work;
- Stand on the spot with your arms held outwards for X number of minutes;
- And of course, their favourite, getting the jack.

The other teacher I need to tell you about was Brother Walsh and I have deliberately left him to last. He was a pedophile. He proved to be my nemesis and he made my life hell. John missed out on all of this because he had left school which is a shame because then he could have corroborated my assertions. Walsh was a very ugly man who had some sort of deformity with one leg, perhaps from polio. He used to 'chew his cud' and nearly always sat underneath the mango tree after school. This tree was strategically placed between one of the dormitories and the main building, which housed the dining room and chapel. Initially nothing happened. I don't even remember what he taught us but it wasn't latin, maths or physics, that's for sure. At this stage of my life I still very much had my girlish looks, red curly hair, fair skin, freckles and so on. He told me in front of the whole class that I should have been a girl and he started humiliating me publicly by calling me 'Miss Australia'. That became my name from him for the rest of the year. He would not refer to me as Max but rather Miss Australia. Initially the other boys, from my perspective, reacted badly to this. They started to call me the same name and they used to ask me to drop my pants and prove I wasn't a girl. That sort of thing happened, but I still had my friends from the sawmill. I petitioned OLPS but this time, I did not get a result. I asked her not just to get rid of him but to kill him like she did with Broderick. She did not answer my calls. One day in class he thought that he had noticed that I was feeling myself. Boys do this at aged 13 or 14. In fact they usually do it for the rest of their lives; I know I have. He picked up his black board duster and threw it from the front of the class to my seat which was at the back of the class. He hit me clean between the eyes. He obviously felt that it was wrong for boys to be 'feeling' themselves in class. Imagine if it had hit me in the eye and permanently damaged it. What a c***! I imagine that he would have been sexually inept but this fella really had a thing about me.

An incident like I have just described was all very normal in the Catholic boarding school environment of the 1950s. There was nothing unusual about a teacher throwing a black board duster at you and hitting you bang in the middle of the frontal lobe. There was nothing unusual about a boy having to stand up, put his arms out straight with one palm under the other and getting two, four or even six strokes with the jack. It was normal. The question is, given what we now know, was it sadistic behaviour or did they honestly believe that the boy got the jack because he deserved it. I'll create a scenario whereby you might get the jack. Say Broderick asked you to quote the Pythagorean theory. This theory states 'that the square of the hypotenuse (the side opposite the right angle) is equal to the sum of the squares of the other two sides. The theory can be written as an equation relating the lengths of the sides a, b and c, often called the "Pythagorean equation". This is the answer he would expect and if you got one word out of place, bang, that was it. Stand up, put your hands out and cop it. It was not unusual for him to keep a record of who he was going to give the jack to. He'd write the names down and the number you were to get. He'd get all the boys that were going to be punished to stand up and go from one to the next, with his bit of paper in his hand telling him how many to deliver. If there were forty boys in the class and he had a record of twenty that had to be punished, he'd do you all at the same time, one after the other. It is very hard for me to believe that he did not enjoy it and I imagine that he must have had a very strong right hand from doing this and other things!

At times Br. Walsh adopted a more friendly persona towards me. As he sat underneath the mango tree he would call me over, and quite openly and blatantly, put his hand on the inside of my thigh, running his hand up and down touching my scrotum. We always wore shorts. He would sit on the wooden bench that surrounded the mango tree with his back to the tree. You could not see what he was doing from behind and on his right would be the passageway up to the chapel and the dining room. On his left would be the dormitory and swimming pool. He could easily choose his timing to make sure that no one would see him doing it. He always got you on the right side of him, underneath the mango tree. The first time he did it I was shocked but did not realise at the time its full implications and brushed it off. The second time I began to realise that it was me he wanted to touch and that he enjoyed doing it. He used to tell me how pretty I was and that I should have been a girl. Hadn't I heard that before? I think this would be akin to touching a girl's vagina. Just by way of comparison, I lived in Singapore for about fifteen years. If somebody touched a child indecently like I have described, he would be jailed for many years plus given a flogging with the rattan. Food for thought. Paradoxically he used to call me Michell, not Max or Miss Australia in these little episodes. Did that have anything to do with Michelle being a girl's name? I can't explain to you how I felt at the time. He was just a f****** animal who really should have been locked up. He had a dichotomy of behaviour towards me. In class it was all about humiliating and embarrassing me but underneath the mango tree it was the opposite behaviour. This would be all about affection and warmth. How on earth did the Christian Brothers allow this sort of thing to happen? How could you have a man like Brothers Fitzpatrick and Higgins mixing with sadists like Brothers McSweeny and Broderick and a pedophile like Walsh? It is my view that this collectively amounted to severe physical, sexual, and psychological abuse from these men that was later to have some very serious ramifications for me.

When I gave evidence at the Royal Commission, they agreed that what Walsh was doing was sexual abuse and what the other two were doing was psychological and violent physical abuse. I believe in my heart that these men, particularly Br. Walsh, were responsible to a significant degree, for the serious mental illness I developed. The mango tree scenario played out a number of times. No one did anything about it; I didn't do anything about it. I couldn't complain. Who would I complain to? Certainly not the other brothers! Parents' maybe? There was no such thing at the time as using a telephone for the boys. In any event my parents did not have a phone at this stage. Write to them maybe. I don't know if I told my parents about the physical sexual abuse by Walsh but they wouldn't have believed me anyway. Don't be silly, Mum would likely say, he was just being friendly and besides he didn't really touch you, did he? Of course, I did my best to avoid him and took the long way around to the dormitory to do so. There is no doubt that my parents knew about the psychological sexual abuse (the Miss Australia thing) and they did nothing. Can you believe that? Can you imagine the damage to a young boy's confidence, self-esteem and worth, when he is being told in front of all his peers that he should have been a girl? To compound it a hundred times over, to then give him a girl's name in front of the entire class in a boys only school. Even if it stops, the damage has been done. What sort of people do these things? Then you have to ask yourself, why did the parents not intervene? Would you, as a parent, intervene if it were your son? I'm sure that the vast majority of parents would. We keep making excuses for our parents claiming that they were simply a product of their times. That they believed in the Catholic Church and would not countenance under any circumstances that the clergy would do anything wrong. My parents knew he was calling me Miss Australia and must have known that it greatly affected me. They knew that by their own admission and they did nothing. Some parents are just not suited to the job of bringing up children. There was no father role model. I will say they did a fair enough job with the girls but we are not talking about them. Mum told me many years later that my problem was I never had a father. In a sense that was true. It is also equally true that after I turned fourteen, I never had a mother either. They were all tarred with the same Catholic brush where they only believed in the one holy Catholic apostolic church and that was all you needed to do. They believed that no man of God could or would ere in administering his duties. They had this unshakeable belief in the church and nothing would convince them otherwise. I go into this in more detail when I come to the Royal Commission on Child Sexual Abuse (RC-CSA).

I will tell you this. When my Dad passed in 1974 I was very upset, especially when I heard his dogs crying. You may not believe this but his dogs were actually crying. They were as sad as I was. When Mum passed, I didn't shed a tear. It hurts me so much to admit to this. There has to be some message in that.

Please don't get me wrong. I am not saying that my mother was a bad person, nor Dad. They were good people in very difficult circumstances, and should never have been together. What I am saying is that from a boy's perspective, they were bad parents. It was a union that was not conducive to bringing up boys. Mum would have been much happier, as she so often used to say, if she had become a nursing nun. Dad would have had a happy life if he had been on his own or with some sweet angelic woman, who wasn't so 'highly strung'. It is one of my greatest regrets that I had an estranged relationship with my mother after I was 14. I deeply regret that I was unable to repair the damage that was done. I think it is very dangerous to any man's mental health to have a poor relationship with his mother. I feel that I missed out on a lot. I would have had a better attitude to women generally had this relationship been sounder. I have to some degree moved on from the feelings of guilt that she used to bestow upon me almost on a daily basis during this era, (which I have not written about yet). Mum even told people that I would be the death of her before she reached fifty. Isn't that strange? She lived to be 96. Another big regret that I have, is that I am an atheist. I would dearly love to be able to believe in the teachings of the Catholic Church and specifically the resurrection of Jesus of Nazareth. The deal that the church offers you can't be bettered. All you have to do is follow a few simple rules like attend Mass on a Sunday, and you are guaranteed that when you die, you will automatically go to paradise and sit at the right hand of the father and experience everlasting happiness. Who in their right mind would reject such an offer? The problem is that it's not an offer based on fact and I think any reasonable and intelligent person would reject it. Having said that, many reasonable and intelligent people don't reject it and believe that when they die, they will experience everlasting happiness. Well, no one has ever come back from the dead to tell us for sure, and no one ever will.

The next big discovery in my life was masturbation. This is how it all came about. One of the boys discovered that if you keep pulling your penis, white stuff would come out and it felt really good. We told him that he was full of s*** and was talking rubbish. He offered to give us a demonstration and so we took him up on it. One day out in the scrub he gave us that demonstration. Sure enough, it worked and out it came. That's how I learnt about masturbation. So we all had a try at it. A funny way to bond together and form a comradeship. I did not witness any homosexuality between the boys at school; other than what I have just mentioned about the masturbation but I wouldn't refer to that as homosexuality. I recall that we were all fairly focused on girls. I even had a picture of Jayne Mansfield with my school books. I can say with hand on heart (with the exception of the group masturbation) that I never saw any homosexual behaviour other than that displayed by Br. Walsh and I think in this case, we are talking more about pedophilia than homosexuality.

It's difficult to summarise the effects that the period of boarding school from the ages of five to fourteen and a half, had on me. When searching for positives, they are hard to find. We were isolated from our family for long periods of time without visitation from them. Maybe some of the good values I have today were reinforced by these schools but I doubt it. On the negative side, there are many. The Catholic boarding schools were institutions where any form of assertive behaviour from the younger boys was suppressed. Consequently I grew up learning at a very early age that you had to bow to authority. I never developed a sense of self-worth and generally always had low self-esteem. These clergy were generally putting you down and keeping you there. I don't remember the reinforcement of any positive behaviour. I believe that I developed good values as I got older and inherited these from my parents, especially my father; but not from school. It was an incredibly rigid and negative environment for the most part. The younger you were, the more that is going to affect you. Many of them were fanatically religious, brutal, sadistic and bigots. If you didn't toe the party (church) line, then you were automatically considered a rebel and had to be stamped on. At St Brendan's, we all had to serve our time being altar boys. When I had my turn, I convinced one of the kids who I sawed wood with to go to Holy

Communion; just for a lark. When I put the plate under his chin for him to receive Holy Communion, I deliberately hit his Adam's apple. He half spurted out the bread that had been placed on his tongue by the priest. For those people that don't understand the sacrament of the Holy Eucharist, this is the ultimate sacrilege within the Catholic Church.

The Church explains it this way. The Holy Eucharist is a sacrament and a sacrifice. In the Holy Eucharist, Jesus Christ is contained, offered, and received in the form of bread and wine. They try to sell us the concept that the whole Christ is really and truly present in the Holy Eucharist. They use the words "really and truly" to describe Christ's presence in the Holy Eucharist to distinguish Our Lord's teaching from that of mere men who falsely teach that the Holy Eucharist is only a sign or figure of Christ, or that he is present only by his power. All Christians, with but a few minor exceptions, held the true belief of the real presence from the time of Christ until the Protestant Revolution in the sixteenth century. This is referred to as the period of Reformation where we started to wake up to ourselves and question the authority and moral right of Rome. The word "Eucharist" means "Thanksgiving." So, you see it has such reverence it is not to be fooled around with; but we did. I got a good dressing down from the priest about hitting the boy's Adam's apple but what could he do. I told him it was an accident and I did not mean to do it; but that was a mistruth. I meant it, no doubt. The Brothers couldn't do anything about it because they never really knew what was going on. There was another incident, again with the Holy Eucharist. Just as the priest lifted the chalice to commemorate the blood of Christ, an altar boy would ring the bell three times. This is probably the most revered period during mass. This is the time when the body and blood of Christ is consecrated. On this one occasion as the priest lifted the chalice one of the boys farted just as the bell rang and the priest held high the chalice with the blood of Christ. Many of the other boys could not contain themselves. Muted laughter burst out in this holiest of holy of times. Crikey, what a ruckus that caused. The priest gave us a severe dressing down as he should have done. The brothers never perused which boy it was, probably because they did not like to punish boys for religious infractions. We felt that it was incredibly funny and we were glad that it caused so much embarrassment to the priest and the brothers. I think that gives you a level of understanding of the amount of respect we had for them. They were our jailers; not our guardians. That pretty much sums it up. I was in a Catholic prison in 1958 and like any other prison, the only thing you want to do is to get out of it. The only real positive to take out of 1958 was that John was not subjected to any of this, and in any event, he was not as pretty as me. The farting story is 100% true but I have heard other people speak of it.

One time a brother came up to me and asked me to try and go to confession and get a couple of the boys to go to confession as well. Why I wondered? I think it is the law of the church that you had to go once per year but I am not sure of that. Anyway, there were a few boys there who never went and I was one of them. Going to confession and having to go to holy communion were two things the brothers could not make you do. I told the boys about the approach and they told me to tell him to go and get f***** . They never went. One of them even put a petition in the box at the Novena asking her to reprimand the brother for making such a request. Of course the priest never read out petitions that transcended the Christian values but we'd put them in anyway because we knew he had to at least read them and he would no doubt discuss the more contentious ones with the Principal, especially about wanting to kill one of his brothers.

I have absolutely no doubt that St Brendan's in particular left some deep psychological scars within me. The excessive bullying and marginalisation by the other boys in that first term left its mark. You can't compare it with getting a flogging; that leaves physical scars on you but once they heal, you don't feel it anymore. Not so with psychological scars. Even when the bullying had stopped, the scars do not heal. The continual floggings by the teachers in 1958 left their mark. But by far the most damaging marks were the ones that were left by Br Walsh. He sexually, physically and psychologically abused me. It took me fifty-six years to tell anybody about all this and I did that when I attended the 'Royal Commission into Child Sexual Abuse' in 2013. Now I am telling everybody who happens to read this book. I did mention that I told my mother about the Miss Australia bit but apart from that, I never mentioned it to anybody. They say that sticks and stones will break your bones but names will never hurt you. Don't believe it. Like any good cocktail you have to have all the ingredients to get it right. The cocktail I am referring to here is my appointment with severe mental illness. Let's just call it the mental illness cocktail. All it needed now to get the end product right was the last ingredient, and that unfortunately was supplied by my own mother. That was just around the corner.

I know that boarding school prevented me from learning to be assertive and left me with a deep seeded inferiority complex. It needs to be kept in mind that I first went there when I was five and I have told you that for many years I was the smallest and youngest boy at school. It was not hard to bully me. I recall that I had a real fear of being seen in the shower because I was worried that the other boys would see what a little penis I had. All the showers were open and you didn't have your own cubicle. I used to make sure that I would go last and could have my shower without being stared at. It is important that all of us learn to communicate in an assertive, non-aggressive manner. You were not encouraged to have an opinion. Little boys should be seen and not heard. Not to assert your rights because you really didn't have any. Consequently I never learnt assertive skills because when I left, I really got more of the same from my mother. I had a real fear of authority and could not relate properly to people in senior positions. I did not know how to relate to people generally. Especially when there was a difference of opinion and things would get heated. I either backed down or took them on fully as I will explain later when I was being bullied by people in the work place. It was not until I worked as a cop that I learned to be assertive and it is a real power to have. I think that the assertive behaviour as a cop was more about exerting the authority vested in me by having a police badge, rather than any transformation on my part; but at least it proved I could do it.

When I came home after the end of school year of 1958, I began a concerted effort to persuade my mother not to send me back to St Brendan's. John was working at home now and was a big help to Dad. I supported my argument to stay at home by saying that I could do just as much as John and collectively we could really get this property into order and make something out of it. I basically begged them not to send me back to St Brendan's College and now you know why. Eventually I won the argument and Mum agreed that I would not have to go back to school and would stay home and help Dad on the property. I think that day may have been one of the happiest of my life. I left school in November 1958 and went to work on my parent's property. I was now fourteen and half years old. Unfortunately for me this turned out be a case of 'jumping out of the frying pan and into the fire'. It will be equally difficult for me to articulate the damage that I feel was done to me by my mother during this period but I will give it my best shot, and await the criticism I expect to get for doing it.

I don't know if the near drowning as a toddler in the McIntyre River at Inverell left its unconscious imprint upon me. Perhaps that had been repressed into my sub-conscious and played its part later in my illness. I don't think that this would be an unreasonable consideration. I don't know if the screaming and beatings of the Nuns at St Joseph's College left their psychological mark, especially my attitude towards women, but again, I would not discount it and think it likely. However what is very clear to me is that I suffered a serious case of separation anxiety and abandonment when sent to boarding school at five years of age; of that I am certain and it has affected me for the rest of my life. I write later about how I had a very disconsolate breakdown at Sydney airport when I had to say goodbye to my children who were on their way to NZ after my separation from my wife. I don't think it would take someone of the brilliance of learned psychiatrists to see the connection between that incident and my own abandonment. The thought that comes to mind as I write this is our catching the train to Aberdeen that I have written about when I was a little fella. My children were aged eight and five at the time. But to balance it out and in the interest of fairness, there were some positives and I mentioned our life on the lifestyle block. I describe how happy I was there and what a great life I had with Mum and my brother and sisters and reinforced the great love I had for my mother at this stage.

What is equally certain was the psychological damage that was done to me at St Brendan's College in Yeppoon when I was twelve to fourteen years of age. I talked about the serious bullying that took place in that first term of the first year at this school and cannot articulate strongly enough how that affected me. It doesn't not matter that the bullying stopped after the first term; the damage had been done. I went from being a 'normal' kid at De La Salle College in Armidale to one that lived in a state of fear for three months and was treated like a leper and an outcast at St Brendan's. It is very hard for a twelve-year old boy to comprehend what is going on; why he is being treated like this? Where were my parents, my guardians? It is little wonder that you grow up not trusting people. I went into detail about what some of the brothers did to me, especially Br Walsh. There's no need to repeat that. I can think of a few other defining moments that significantly impacted upon my mental health later on in life and I will mention them later. What I took away from St Brendan's College was an even greater sense of not trusting people especially those in authority; a deep sense of anger about the brutality by adults upon children and the reinforcement of a serious (perhaps pathological) lack of confidence and self-esteem into my personality. I was totally humiliated by Brother Walsh on an on-going basis with his calling me Miss Australia in front of the entire class. Here I am, a 'beautiful' 13-year old child, flaming locks of golden red hair, rosy fair skin and being told by him that I should have been a girl (and all the other boys agreeing with him). This and the touching of my genitals by him underneath the mango tree has affected me all of my life. I even thought about making 'Miss Australia' the title of this book. The church did nothing, the brothers did nothing and my parents did nothing. Who could you trust? I see red when I think about it and not surprisingly, I developed an abhorrence against people that mistreated children, which I will write more about when I talk about my time in the Police Force.

Footnote: When describing my time at St Brendan's College, I am only referring to my time there (1957 and 1958). I have spoken to other blokes who went to this college long after I did and they spoke very favourably about the school. In the interest of fair play and balance, I would not want to infer that the college is now what it was when I was there. My research has indicated to me that it a fine college and they are doing a fine job of teaching the boys from country western Queensland. I think I was unlucky. I was in the wrong place, at the wrong time, and became a 'victim of circumstances'. It was just a situation where I had no control over what was happening to me and could not do anything to prevent it.

Chapter Three: Torrendorra Capella
1959 - 1964

In 1959 - Cuban President Batista resigned and fled; Fidel Castro assumed power. Alaska and Hawaii became the 49th and 50th states of the USA. Jack S. Kilby of Texas Instruments (US) supervised the development of the first integrated circuit. Severo Ochoa and Arthur Kornberg (both US), were awarded the Nobel prize in Medicine for discoveries related to compounds within chromosomes that play a vital role in heredity. The Oscar for the Best Picture was Gigi. Frank Sinatra won his first Grammy Award; best album for 'Come Dance with Me'. Movies that were released included *Some Like It Hot, North by Northwest, Ben Hur, Anatomy of a Murder*, and *Room at the Top*. Boris Pasternak released *Doctor Zhivago*, and DH Lawrence released *Lady Chatterley's Lover*. Notable deaths included those of Lou Costello, Cecil B. De Mille, Mel Ott and Frank Lloyd Wright.

In 1960 - An American U-2 spy plane, piloted by Francis Gary Powers, was shot down over Russia. Top Nazi murderer of Jews, Adolf Eichmann, captured by Israelis in Argentina was executed in Israel in 1962. Senegal, Ghana, Nigeria, Madagascar, and Zaire (Belgian Congo) gained independence. John F. Kennedy defeated Richard Nixon in a closely fought presidential race. Ben Hur won the Oscar for best picture. Seventy-million people watched the presidential debate between Senator John F. Kennedy and Vice President Richard Nixon. Ninety percent of US homes had a television set. The first working laser was built by T. H. Maiman (US). Alfred Hitchcock's *Psycho* terrified movie-goers and became one of the year's most successful films. Other movies released were *The Apartment, The Sundowners*, and *Sons and Lovers*. Harper Lee released her best seller book *To Kill a Mockingbird*. Notable deaths included those of Boris Pasternak, Emily Post, Lawrence Tibbett and Clark Gable.

In 1961 - US broke diplomatic relations with Cuba. 1,200 US-sponsored anti-Castro exiles invaded Cuba at the Bay of Pigs and the attackers were all killed or captured by Cuban forces. East

Germany erected the Berlin Wall between East and West Berlin to halt the flood of refugees. USSR detonated a 50-megaton hydrogen bomb in the largest man-made explosion in history. The first US Astronaut, Navy Commander Alan B. Shepard, Jr., rocketed 116.5 miles up in 302-mile trip. Moscow announced putting its first man in orbit around Earth, Major Yuri A. Gagarin. Alan B. Shepard became the first American man in space aboard the Freedom 7. Jack Lippes developed the contraceptive intrauterine device (IUD). The Oscar for the best picture was *The Apartment. West Side Story* was adapted for the big screen. Audrey Hepburn delighted as Holly Golightly in *Breakfast at Tiffany's,* but Henry Mancini emerged as the real star. He won two Oscars and four Grammy Awards for the score, which included the hit 'Moon River.' The Movies *West Side Story, The Hustler, Judgment at Nuremberg* and *La Dolce Vita* were released. Joseph Heller released his book *Catch 22.* Notable deaths included those of Sir Thomas Beecham, Ty Cobb, Carl Jung and Chico Marx.

In 1962 - The USSR was to build missile bases in Cuba. President Kennedy ordered a Cuban blockade and lifted the blockade after Russia backed down. Burundi, Jamaica, Western Samoa, Uganda, Trinidad and Tobago became independent. The movie West Side Story won the Oscar for the best picture of the year. Marilyn Monroe died of a drug overdose at age 36.The first transatlantic television transmission occurred via the Telstar Satellite, making worldwide television and cable networks a reality. Lt. Col. John H. Glenn, Jr., was the first American to orbit Earth (3 times in 4 hours 55 minutes). The Nobel prize in Medicine was awarded to James D. Watson (US), Maurice H. F. Wilkins, and Francis H. C. Crick (both UK), for determining the structure of deoxyribonucleic acid (DNA). The movies *Lawrence of Arabia, To Kill a Mockingbird, The Manchurian Candidate* and *Divorce-Italian Style* were released. Ken Kesey released his book *One Flew Over The Cuckoo's Nest.* Notable deaths included those of Niels Bohr, William Faulkner, Ernie Kovacs and Eleanor Roosevelt.

In 1963 - British Secretary of War John Profumo resigned in the wake of an affair with Christine Keeler, a teenage showgirl who was also involved with the Soviet Naval Attaché. The Washington-to-Moscow "hot line" communications link opened, designed to reduce the risk of accidental war. Michael E. De Bakey implanted an artificial heart in a human for the first time at Houston hospital. Martin Luther King delivered his "I have a dream" speech on 28 August. US President Kennedy shot and killed in Dallas on 22 November and Texan Lyndon B. Johnson became President the same day. *Lawrence of Arabia* won the Oscar for best picture. Beatle mania hits the UK. The Beatles, a British band composed of John Lennon, George Harrison, Ringo Starr and Paul McCartney, take Britain by storm. The sedative Valium (chlordiazepoxide) was developed by Roche labs. Movies that were released included *Tom Jones, Lilies of the Field*, and *America, America*. Notable deaths included those of John Fitzgerald Kennedy, W.E.B. Du Bois, Robert Frost, Rogers Hornsby and Aldous Huxley.

In 1964 - Nelson Mandela was sentenced to life imprisonment in South Africa. China detonated its first atomic bomb. Three civil rights workers — Schwerner, Goodman, and Cheney were murdered in Mississippi. The movie *Tom Jones* won the Oscar for best picture of the year. Folk musician Bob Dylan became increasingly popular during this time of social protest with songs expressing objection to the condition of American society. US Surgeon General Luther Terry affirmed that cigarette smoking causes cancer. The movies released included *Red Desert, Dr Strangelove, My Fair Lady, Mary Poppins, Zorba the Greek* and *Becke*. Notable deaths included those of Herbert Clark Hoover, Douglas MacArthur and Harpo Marx.

A consequential point to mention when we talk about my relationship problems with my mother was an incident that occurred one day when we were out mustering sheep. We all used to go; a sort of family affair. I had just left school and at this point everything was fine between my mother and me. I have mentioned that Mum was a great horsewoman and spent little time in the house as she was not the domesticated type. Dad, Mum, Margaret and I would all go mustering to get the sheep in for whatever reason. On this occasion the horse that I was riding reared over on the top of me and gave me a compound fracture of my left humerus (the bone where your biceps are). Mum was great and got me off to hospital in Emerald. She was always good in a crisis and just the sort of person you need in the trenches. At the hospital they reset the bone under general anaesthesia; not what we use today, but with chloroform. Crikey, I remember that like it was yesterday; it really was terrifying. When the drug started to take effect little stars started appearing in my brain and then as the drug took hold they became huge stars and they started banging into each other and I started panicking. They held me down on the table and I must have been screaming; then I was out. I really thought that as I was going under I was going to die. After the procedure Mum and the Matron of the hospital decided that I should stay in hospital until the plaster came off. This was because it was the beginning of the wet season and the Doctor wanted to see me every week. Many of our roads were black soil and if it rained heavily it could be many days before you could travel on the roads. Consequently the decision was made that I should stay in hospital and I loved it. Great food and I enjoyed the company of the other patients.

I was now fourteen and a half and well into adolescence. The incident that I am about to tell you about was the turning point in my relationship with my mother. We all look for defining moments in our lives and in my case this was one of them. Hitherto, I loved my mother but after this incident she changed and so did my attitude towards her. It was well known that I was an affectionate boy and was not backward in showing that affection. One day Mum and Margaret came to see me in hospital and on my bed were some magazines and an old pipe that one of the patients had given me. I think Pix, People or something in that order. These magazines showed attractive women in swimwear but they were considered quite acceptable for the time. I am sure that Matron would not have allowed them in the hospital if they weren't. I can't be any more specific about them but I'm sure you get the idea. They were nowhere near pornographic and were available in any newsagent. Mum picked up these magazines and threw them across the floor, in front of the other patients, exclaiming, "Don't you dare read this rubbish, it's sinful". That was that. I was shocked, as were the other patients and a little humiliated by her display of indignation and self-righteousness. The seed for a negative relationship change with my mother had now been sown, maybe now 'the die was cast'. Eventually I went home and did my own physiotherapy. I made a billy out of a tin and filled it up with dirt and used that in much the same manner that you would use a dumbbell, contracting and relaxing the bicep muscle. For vertical exercise I would gradually learn to crawl up the wall with my left hand on it. I did my exercises and got my arm back to normal and it has been good ever since. Maybe I was now physically back to normal but the magazine throwing had a profound effect on me and I suspect, also on my mother. I am sure that in life we all experience incidents that seem at first to be trivial and have little significance, but can have broader and more sinister implications later on. I think that this incident represented my changing from a child into adolescence and onto the road to manhood.

Mum's attitude changed dramatically towards me. The strain of living in the circumstances she now found herself in became too much for her. She turned on me and used the same strategy that the Catholic Church has used for many centuries; that is making you feel guilty about yourself. I have no doubt that she did not like me and could see that I was turning out to be just like my father. As I have written she was a naturally volatile person and could get angry very easily. I did not know until very recently when my brother John told me, that she was known in the district as 'bloody Mary' and that wasn't just because of her red hair. I never knew that. Hitherto Mum's anger was not loaded with malice but now it was and with real venom. It was about this time that Mum began to suffer badly from migraines. She would have to stay in bed many mornings with severe headaches and dry retching. As for me, Dad would have me up before daylight and I would jump on the John Deere tractor and spend the next twelve hours cultivating the fields, whether it be ploughing, scarifying, or sowing the seed. Mum always felt herself superior to most other people. I have told you she came from a well-to-do pastoral family in the Inverell district in North Western NSW. They were deeply religious people and totally committed to the teachings of the Catholic Church. In Mum's case, she really was a total religious bigot. I don't mean that in a slanderous sense. If you look at the meaning of the word bigotry it means having an obstinate belief in the superiority of one's own opinions and a prejudiced intolerance of the opinions of others. That described Mum's religious beliefs to a tee. She really had that obstinate belief in the superiority of her own opinions and often a prejudiced intolerance in the opinions of others, especially mine and especially, when it came to religion. Nothing could shake Mum's belief in the Catholic Church and perhaps more saliently, the righteousness of the clergy. In her eyes they were God's representatives on earth and they could do no wrong. I think it was good that Mum died during 2010 because she would have had difficulties facing up to the realities of the findings of the Royal Commission into Child Sexual Abuse. I think it would have devastated her to learn the extent of the physical, sexual and psychological abuse that was rampant in the Catholic Church and had been going on for many decades. To make matters manifestly worse, it was covered up by the Church's hierarchy, as high as the Vatican itself.

I mentioned earlier that Mum went to St Vincent's hospital in Sydney in the thirties and graduated as a Nursing Sister. I have seen photos of her at this time and she was a very attractive women. During this time she formed relationships with some quite influential people that lasted a lifetime. Many of them were well connected people in the social elite of Sydney. Some of them remember Mum riding in the Sydney Royal Easter Show or riding around Centennial Park, and winning major equestrian events. Not only was she a great horsewoman, she was very socially well mannered, well versed and an educated lady. She was very much in demand when the suitors came. Mum used to say with some bitterness in later life that she wished she had become a nursing nun and never got married. My brother John told me that in her autobiography Mum wrote she admitted that the day she got married was the saddest day of her life. I found that hard to believe and sought to locate her memoirs to find out if that was right, which I did. He was not far off the mark as I explained earlier when she referred to it as that fateful day and was particularly graphic when she said that she did not take too kindly to the 'death do us part' bit. It was very clear that Mum was not a happy person and one wonders why she ever agreed to marry my father with in the first place.

One reason she accepted his proposal was that he was willing to convert to the Catholic Church and agree to all the rules the church imposed. She said in later life that she felt he was a good man and she felt sorry for him. She insisted that he begged her to marry him and that may well be right; although it does not sound like Dad's behaviour to me. Whatever! It was the bringing together of a passive, reliable, benevolent, courteous, good natured, hardworking, passive, independent, stoic, humble, calm, punctual, easy going, laid back, apathetic, phlegmatic, uneducated, and faithful man with the exact opposite. Mum was an assertive, attractive, charismatic, energetic, confident, decisive, dogmatic, bigoted, superior, volatile, 'highly strung,' successful, intelligent, educated, strong-minded, and deeply religious woman. Mum and Dad stayed together until Dad died in 1974, at the age of 71. Mum would never countenance a divorce and regularly used to preach that no matter how bad things got, you didn't just walk away from it; you stayed the course. She thought that it was dreadful that people were getting divorced and believed that they should see their marriage through 'thick and thin'; as the saying goes. Apart from anything else, it was against the law of God and as far as Mum was concerned that was the end of the argument. Just because you were desperately unhappy did not mean that you ended it. You stuck at it and if you had to lead an unhappy life, so be it. That's what Mum did and that did not work in my favour. I believe that Mum was very unhappy with life after she went to Queensland and that is very easy for me to understand and accept. She more than likely suffered from clinical depression herself. I think that is very likely but she would never countenance that either. Mum had amazing recuperative powers. She could be bed ridden in the morning and up working her horses in the afternoon. That is why I think that stress may have been a large part of the migraine pathology. Dad was very much 'a run with the fox, hunt with the hound' kind of person. He believed in peace at any price. He could not understand the point in arguing all the time but did little, if anything, to stop it. In fact he could not see the point in arguing at all, about anything.

They were almost the exact opposites. How could two people who were so very different get married? I think it might have worked if my Dad had Mum's characteristics and vice versa. In that scenario I would have grown up loving my mother and perhaps had a distant relationship with my father. Perhaps some Sociologists are right in saying, 'opposites attract' like the law of physics on positives and negatives. Whatever the reasons, they did marry. My own view is that Dad should never have married and that he was not cut out to be a husband or father. I never saw my father kiss or show any affection towards my mother or any of his children, never. When pushed on the subject, he would say it a private thing. I never knew my father to show any affection to me either. He was almost incapable of showing his feelings and that is why I have added the phlegmatic and apathetic characters in his profile. I feel sure that he would have had them but was incapable of showing them. But please don't misunderstand me. He was a very good man in his own right and who knows if he had married a nice 'softer' lady, things might have been different for him. I would be a very proud man if I could say that I was as decent a person as my Dad was, but I can't make that claim and the reasons for that will become clearer as you read on. Yet in spite of his decency and high standards of morals, Dad was not a father to me and that had serious repercussions. Yet he was a very popular figure wherever he lived. You would have to travel many a mile to find a person that did not like my father. Mum used to remind us that he was so popular because he was so agreeable and that she had to do all the dirty work. There was a bit of truth in that, but she did not have to broadcast it to the world. Both of my sisters accused Dad of being a weak man and one of them was on record as saying that he was the weakest of all men. Yet Dad adored his girls. Out of the four of us, I was his least favourite and yet I was the one that turned out to be most like him. He never caused arguments. It was my father's philosophy that you never complained, not matter what. You just got on with it, no matter the circumstances. At his funeral (1974) at Tara in Queensland, the whole town turned out to farewell him. He had an extraordinary medical history. If the medical profession had to rely on people like my father for business, they would go into bankruptcy quickly. I can't remember in my time with Dad that he ever went to see a Doctor. Of course, at times he must have done but I never saw it. When he got the flu, he reckoned the best cure was to take a bottle of rum to bed and sweat it out. Having said that, Dad was a very moderate drinker but a prolific taker of bex headache medicine. They used to say in the old days, "Have a cup of tea, a bex and a good lie down". Bex was recommended for headaches, neuralgia, sciatica, lumbago, cold and flu, all nerve pains, rheumatism. It also claimed to calm people down. They came in a yellow box with great big blue letters of BEX written on them. They were loaded up with some quite good chemicals, aspirin, phenacetin, and caffeine. No wonder Dad liked them but I have not seen a packet of bex since the 60s.

Dad used to boast that he would outlive Mum easily as Mum had so many medical aliments. You would expect that from a person who was living a life she hated and was desperately unhappy. At my sister Patricia's wedding (which I never went to), the priest (Father Dunlea, the one I mentioned earlier who started Boys Town in Sydney) told the congregation that Dad had such a calm manner, that if his house had burnt down, you might find Fenton (Dad) some distance away, asleep under a tree. Perhaps it might have been Mum who had to clean the mess up. It was not unusual on the hot Queensland summer days when we were ploughing the fields to find Dad asleep under a tree in the paddock. Sometimes it might be the only tree in the paddock.

If the tractor was stopped, you knew where to find him. But he was an incredibly hard worker and would be up and light the kitchen fire before dawn every day and I would go to work as the sun was coming up. Father Dunlea first came to us when we were living at Inverell. After having just started Boys Town he became a bit of a socialite around Sydney. He started drinking at all the social events he had to attend and apparently it got to him and he became an alcoholic. He was Irish after all! Mum said that he came to our place to get off the booze and I understand that he was successful in doing that.

Dad went to work one day, I think on the 26 November 1974 and did his usual twelve hours on the tractor, sowing wheat at the time. He woke in the middle of the night and told Mum that he had a bit of indigestion and that it was worse than normal. Mum persuaded him to let her take him to town to see the local Doctor who was a friend of Mum's. He admitted Dad to the Tara Hospital and hours later, on the 27th, he was dead. Unbelievable! How could this happen? Why no autopsy? At the time I was in my second year of nursing at the Prince Henry Hospital in Sydney, working in the cardio thoracic theatres. Margaret was in the UK and John was over in Western Australia managing some big cattle station. Patricia was now married to a great bloke named Ian Walker and living in Bundaberg. I got three days bereavement leave from the hospital, flew up, went to the funeral, came back and continued with my nursing diploma. It was quite incredible the outpouring of grief that the local people showed towards Dad. I did sense hostility towards me and had heard from my brother John that Mum had been less than fair in her assessments of both of us in front of other people in the district. That is just the way she was. Remember I told you that she referred to John and I on more than one occasion as 'her useless bloody boys'. I suppose it was only natural the locals formed an opinion on us. Mum used to tell people that they only bought the property for the boys but that is a long way from the truth. It was the talk of the district that Fenton had to work the property himself while his boys were doing this and doing that. Most of it was all about Mum garnishing sympathy and that was very unfair to me particularly as I was doing it very tough with the nursing course that I will tell you more about as we go along. I would say that if I had not have been bullied and abused by my mother, especially at Capella, I would have stayed on the property and lead my life as a man of the land. I also believe that if this abuse had not have taken place, I may not have, on the balance of probability, progressed to developing severe clinical depression that I will explain in detail shortly. This is a very profound statement to make and points the finger clearly in one direction. More about that later!

After the broken arm incident, Mum 'upped the ante' and really took parental abuse to a new level. My brother John had gone out to be a Jackaroo on a station near Quilpie, called Retreat. A Jackaroo is a young man working on a sheep or cattle station to gain experience to become a Manager. In reality it was just cheap labour and a touch of 'squatters' snobbery. At the time it was managed by a bloke that everybody called Sack-em-Jack. Mum was over the moon. She wanted her sons to be somebodies, not just working class types and there's nothing wrong with that I suppose. Here John would learn to be a grazier, following along in the footsteps of her own people, the gentry on the land. She was immensely proud of him and felt the opposite about me. In the meantime, as well as working at home, I started to work in the shearing sheds. Mum did not like that at all. She did not want her son mixing with the 'riffraffs'. Dad, of course, was all for it because when the shearing time came at home, guess who one of the shearers would be? And to make it much more attractive, for nothing. So, I'd do a shed here and there as a roustabout and gradually learnt to shear. I held a bit of a record in the district as being able to shear 100 sheep per day at the age of 16. That is really something. If I were to use a cricket analogy it would be like scoring a century in first grade cricket at 16. I understand now where Mum was coming from but didn't then. There was a social gap between the gentry of the land and the working class; no doubt about it. Dad sort of had a foot in each social group. Whilst he had been a respected farmer in the Bingara district, he was considered a grazier (a sort of upmarket cocky). He did however do some shearing of his own during the great depression of the late 1920s and early 1930s. Mum had never been exposed to the working class and was bought up to believe that she was better than them. This was especially so in the early days and the gentry had a real superiority complex. Whereas the working class, like the shearers, were usually uneducated, urban dwellers, who some would say, did not know how to speak the Queen's language correctly, didn't dress nicely and had bad manners. It was all just about feeling superior. For some reason that I have never fully understood some people need to feel superior to others. Especially country women and specifically women of the land that came from generations of large land owners who were perhaps the worst.

Mum's malevolence grew towards me when I was responsible for an accident involving my younger sister Margaret. We were coming home late at night in the truck which had the horse float on the back. Margaret and I were in the back with bags of horse feed. We were playing, and her leg got twisted between the bags of feed and she badly dislocated her knee. It was an accident, completely. The sort of thing that could happen to any kids playing. She really bawled me out over this like I did it deliberately. I was slowly beginning to really resent and dislike her and the anger was building up within me. I saw the abuse as just an extension of what I had to endure at St Brendan's and most of all I saw it as unjust and unwarranted. I was after all was said and done, putting in 12-hour working days, 7 days a week at home and not even getting any pocket money for it. That is worth thinking about that.

Now I was openly rebellious about the religious thing. Mum used to make us all say the family rosary every night. Just what you need after you have done twelve hours on the tractor or been out fencing all day or shearing all day or whatever. God, we used to have some fights about that. Her view was that families who pray together, stay together. Again, her prayers were not answered. Her dreams for me were fading. Not only did I not accept Catholicism, I wanted to be a shearer. I will point out that at this time I wanted to leave home and made a big effort to achieve that. A shearing contractor from United Graziers, Max Johnson, offered to take me out to Western Queensland, out Longreach way, and make me a gun shearer. As a point of interest, Longreach is about 197 kilometres from Winton. Winton is famous for a number of things, most notably the place where Qantas first operated (Queensland and Northern Terrority Aerial Services) in 1920. It is also the place where the poet Banjo Paterson wrote the words to *Waltzing Matilda* in January 1895 while staying at Dagworth Station, a sheep and cattle station near Winton. Everybody told me I would become a gun shearer. Just for your information a gun shearer is somebody that can shear 200 sheep a day. This was driving Mum nuts. She just could not abide the thought that one of her sons would become a shearer. I knew of course that by now they could not afford to lose my free labour so she wouldn't let me go. Notice I say she wouldn't let me go. Dad really had nothing to do with it. That might be a bit unfair but let's remember that she was very strong in her views and always got her way. To be fair there may have been some parental instinct there as well, especially on Mum's part. Anyway, I didn't go out to the back country shearing as you read about in one of old Henry Lawson's poems and I often reflect how I might have turned out had I done so. At this stage of my life I was fifteen years of age; it was 1959. I wonder what would have happened if I had rolled my swag and went shearing out west. One of the things I would like to do before I pass on is to go to Dagworth Station and see the billabong that Banjo Patterson wrote about when he penned *Waltzing Matilda*. In fact, I have mentioned to a friend of mine that I would like my ashes to be taken out to this billabong and planted underneath a large coolabah tree. I think you can see from this that I am a very patriotic Australian, and a bit nationalistic. Nothing wrong with that and you might be able to pick up that I have a profound love of the Australian bush. Later I will be able to explain why I never settled in the bush, but never lost my love for it either.

I have since rationalised that Mum's behaviour was related to her displacement mechanism. She was so regretful during this period with her lot but she could not take it out on my father because he did not respond. Most days she would lie in bed suffering chronic migraine pain and dry retching. It was one such day on my 16th birthday, that she called me into her room to wish me a happy birthday. She said, "Happy birthday Max. Oh the trouble I had having you sixteen years ago; you nearly killed me you know". I think that these are the words of someone who is clearly not in a happy place. Unfortunately I was not able to rationalise it at the time. I now believe that she took out her anger, bitterness and frustration on me as she got no response from Dad, hence the displacement. She just did not want me to turn out like Dad and I understand that now. Usually I was the only one at home. John was now on a very big pedestal and I was at the other end of the spectrum. "Why can't you be like your brother John?" was something I heard regularly during this time. Patricia came home on holidays sometimes but that was rare. After she finished school she went nursing in Brisbane. When she graduated she got on a ship and went to England. Margaret followed a similar path.

The abuse I am referring to at this time did not involve anything physical although I felt trapped; there was nowhere else I could go unless I just took off and that was easier said than done. That is perhaps what I should have done with having the wisdom of hindsight. My mother further stripped me of any self-esteem that was already in short supply and it just made me more full of self-loathing with no self-esteem or confidence and real anger. During this period John perfectly fitted the stereotype of what they admired most; that he was a squatter's son and developing as a man from the gentry and the land. He epitomised the class difference between the landowners and the working man. He was what Mum wanted and I was the exact opposite. I can tell you that thinking changed dramatically in the years ahead. Most of all Mum made me feel incredibly guilty. One of her favourite expressions was that I was a 'useless bloody coot'. Not sure what coot means but the message is clear enough. If this happens to you in those early formative adolescent years, it's conceivable that you might never get over it. The truth is that when it comes from your own mother you end up believing it. You end up believing that you are a no-hoper and not surprisingly, you run the real risk of becoming one. I did not grow up the way that she wanted me to and she was very hurt by that. I was too much like my father. She wanted her sons to be devout Catholics and successful graziers. She was bitterly disappointed with how her life had turned out and I believe that she took it out on me. There was no one else around that she could take it out on.

I also believe that Mum's behaviour had its genesis in the Catholic Church. I do recall in the following years that when John's star started to fade, he too got the brunt of Mum's anger. The animosity towards Mum from both of us was so bad that an incident at the Emerald Agriculture show epitomises the level of feeling both John and I had towards our mother. Mum was riding in the ladies hack event and had a fall from her horse. She badly dislocated her shoulder and would have been in a great deal of agony, as you would be with a total dislocation. Of course the ambulance attended to her but John and I just held our ground. I am really, really ashamed to admit it now but we never did anything. It was our own mother out there lying on the ground and we never lifted a finger. We should have, no matter what, but our non-reaction does underpin the enormous resentment we had towards her and that was a terrible shame for all of us. This incident highlights the depths of anger that we both had towards her and I will believe until the day I die, that Mum behaviour towards me at this time played its part in my developing mental illness. I am unshakeable in that belief. No doubt the sense of abandonment I would have felt being sent to St Josephs as well as what the brothers at St Brendan's had done to me put the bullet in the chamber, but my own mother pulled the trigger. I must say that it hurts me so much to have to say this and on the face of it, without knowing the background, a person could rightly refer to me as a pretty ordinary sort of a character for saying it and I would understand that. The thing is I am just relaying it the way that I saw it at the time and still see it the same way today, some fifty-five years later. I would have dearly loved to have had a supportive mother in my adolescence years in the real sense and deeply regret that I didn't. There is no point in sugar-coating it and I felt a deep sense of betrayal. In her memories, Mum skirted around these formative years by basically leaving everything out about me for that period from 1958 until 1963. She simply wrote that Max set off to see the world; mainly hitch hiking, and that's a very practical way of doing it. However it is not correct. I never started hitch hiking until after I went to Sydney in 1965. The truth is that I spent most of the time from late 1958 until 1963 at home working for Mum and Dad working for nothing. Later I refer to this as slave labour and write about how dangerous rural social isolation is for adolescent boys in distant communities.

One of the things I enjoyed about working in the shearing sheds was that I did get respite from the psychological abuse at home. Mum and Dad's defence against this was that I was a difficult adolescent teenager just growing up and that one day I would 'come good.' There were a couple of interesting stories that came out of the shearing sheds I worked in. When I was 15, I did a shed at a place called Solferino, out of the town of Claremont in Central Queensland. Solferino was a six stand shed, meaning it had six shearers. Shearing by nature is hard work but in central Queensland, it is very, very hard work. The merino sheep are wrinkled and often riddled with spear grass, bathurst burr, matted wool and/or fly blown wool with maggots. Anyway, the boss of the board, Max Johnson, came up to me on a Friday afternoon and told me that I was to finish up that day. In other words, he sacked me. I thanked him saying, "Yes, Mr. Johnson." I told the lead shearer, Dave Watkins (a great bloke) that Mr. Johnson had sacked me. He rang the bell which was a sign that shearing was to stop immediately; even if the sheep was half shorn, the shearer was not to finish it if he heard the bell calling for a stop work meeting. The shearers quizzed me about being sacked and I told them I didn't know why. Dave approached Johnson and asked him why the boy (me) had been sacked. He said he didn't know, only that the cocky had told him to. So the shearers had a meeting and Dave told Johnson and even after all these years I can quote it verbatim, "Mate, you get in your f****** tilly (utility), go and see the f****** cocky, and find out why he sacked the boy. There will be no more shearing until you come back and tell us." Well, that's what happened. Johnson got into his tilly, went and saw the cocky and came back with the news. He told the shearers that the cocky claimed I never washed the blood off the killing block after having killed the sheep. The shearers were very angry about this. They told Johnson that he could tell the cocky to get f***** and that I had to be reinstated immediately. They pointed out to him that it was not my job to wash down the killing block; it was the cook's. All I was doing was helping the cook in my own time and that it was a totally unfair dismissal. They also told him that if I was not reinstated, they would walk off the job immediately. This had real leverage as there were only a couple of days left to finish the shed. So, Johnson had to get back into his tilly and go back and see the cocky. One of the shearers thought that Johnson was pulling a swift one and that the cocky didn't have anything to do with it. Johnson had just bought a new automatic zephyr car and he was using it as a taxi service to transport those shearers and shed hands that did not have their own transport. This shearer put forward that all Johnson was doing was looking for a long distance fare to take me to town which was about 100 kilometres away. Maybe this argument had some merit but in the end it didn't matter. The end result was that I got put back on with a guarantee that I would also go to the next shed, which was an eighteen stand shed at Gordon Downs near Emerald. I had to join the AWU (Australian Workers Union) and from that day since, I have always had an affiliation with the injustices suffered by the working man. Perhaps that is why I am a great fan of the American folk singer, Woody Guthrie. Imagine what it must have been like in the early days of settlement and through the great depression. I wonder in bewilderment when you hear the politicians (mostly Liberal) degrading the unions. If it were not for the unions and/or Labour Prime Ministers there would be no sick leave, no eight-hour working day, no minimum wage, no paid vacation leave, no overtime pay, no 40 hour working week, no workers' compensation, no superannuation, no holiday pay, no maternity leave, no aged pensions, and a host of other working benefits. Of course, some of the unions went too far and they are still going too far. There is corruption is some of them and the shock jocks get a lot of mileage out of it. To my mind it is nothing compared to the wrong-doings of our politicians at both local, state and federal level; and the corruption within our political establishment is nothing compared to the corporate greed in this country. Major multinational establishments like Apple, Google and Microsoft pay little or no tax in this country; sending billions of dollars offshore to avoid paying tax. Give me the unions any day over that lot.

So at fifteen years of age, I inadvertently caused a strike in a shearing shed. I sort of felt that I had some sort of a family with the shearing team. Soon after I was involved in two other incidents. We were at a place called Diamond Downs, actually not far from Solferino. It was an eight stand shed and the shearers had been on the grog in Claremont over the weekend. It rained a bit on Sunday night and the cocky didn't have the sheep undercover. The shearing team which included me as a roustabout rolled up to start shearing on Monday morning. I think kick off time was 7.30am. On the first sheep being shorn, one of the shearers (with a massive hangover) reckoned that the sheep were wet. In that scenario, the shearers have to have a vote. The vote went something like 5 wet, 3 dry. So, no shearing for the first shift. The cocky put the sheep out in the boiling hot Queensland sun and by law, another vote was taken at 10.00am. This time the vote went 6 wet, 2 dry. One of the shearers reckoned the sheep were wetter after they had been out in the sun for a couple of hours. The cocky sacked the entire team and the contractor had to start all over again with a new team. The union did not back the men on this occasion because they were clearly in the wrong. The sheep were not wet enough not to shear in the first place. Most of the boys just wanted to have Monday off to get the booze out of the system. The year was 1959, just three years after the great shearing strike of 1956 which the shearers won. This was wonderfully portrayed by Jack Thompson in the movie, 'Sunday Too Far Away'. If you wonder what a roustabout would do in a shearing shed; this is portrayed through the character Michael Simpson in the movie. So, if you have not been in a shearing shed and want to understand it better, this movie is absolutely spot on. You can watch it on Youtube. It is almost exactly what it was like. I saw it when I was nursing in the early seventies and it brought tears to my eyes. I don't know where Jack Thompson learnt to shear but he looked like he could. Perhaps it was the cameras doing some of their neat tricks but it looked persuasive to me. This movie portrays a large part of my early life when I was 15, 16 and 17. I have not been in a shearing shed since I'd say the late 1960s. I would also say that I have not ridden a horse for forty plus years. I think that if I had not developed mental illness with some of its phobias I would have stayed on the land. I do regret that this never eventuated. I have a special love for animals, particularly horses and dogs. There is something very special about the Australian bush, hard for me to describe. As I continue with this book I talk about the time we hitchhiked around Australia, and that just endorsed my love of the land. I will also tell you about why I left the land, even though I had a strong affinity with it. As Dorothy McKellar says in her poem, 'I love a sunburnt country, a land of sweeping plains, of rugged mountain ranges, of droughts and flooded rains. I love the far horizon, I love the jewel sea and a treasure to my heart, is this wide brown land for me.' I think that is close to quoting it right without having to look up google to make sure.

The third incident that resulted in grief for the cocky was on my own Uncle Les's property 'Codenwarra' just out of Emerald. He owned vast tracks of land in the area as well as sawmills and butcher shops. He was truly a wealthy man and an early pioneer to this part of the world. He was another bloke who had this reputation for sacking people as if this were his hobby. Well, one of the shearers there reckoned the sheep were scabby mouthed. This disease is a viral disease of sheep that causes pustules and scabs around the mouth and face of the sheep. Shearers won't shear them because they believe that they contain contagious dermatitis. They had a vote and agreed that there would be no more shearing. Uncle Les would have to put his sheep out to graze and wait for the sheep to get rid of this disease, which would take weeks before they could be shorn. He had no choice and had to accept their decision. Of course, no other shearers would be allowed to shear them either. If he organised another team, there would almost certainly be a reception committee awaiting their arrival. Similar to the reception committee that were waiting for the scab shearers in 'Sunday Too Far Away'. I couldn't be blamed for this one. We actually went back there some weeks later after the scabs had cleared up and got all the shearing done to my uncle's satisfaction.

Shearers are an interesting group of men. I say men because I have never seen a female shearer. They say that cutting sugar cane and shearing are the two hardest jobs men can perform. It depends a lot on the condition and breed of the sheep. If you are shearing cross bred sheep that have course wool and no wrinkles, like they are in New Zealand and Tasmania, it is much easier. On the other hand there are the wrinkled fine wool merinos that bring with them all the baggage. Shearers are away from home and the living conditions in my time were awful. I recall that at my Uncle's property, we had to pump our water by hand pumps up from the river, just to have a shower. No such thing as hot water; we had paper thin mattresses, no heating, no electric lighting or air conditioning. Nothing like that; just very basic stuff. We used those old style carbide lights and did not even have kerosene lighting. The water was freezing cold of course but old Uncle Les was determined that he was not going to do anymore that the barest minimum he had to for the shearers. That was typical of the larger land owners. Then the shearers had to go and work their butts off. The one redeeming feature was that they were now well paid and the cockies resented it. They knew however that they could not shear their own sheep and were totally dependent upon the shearers. The shearers knew that as well. As I have alluded to before there was a great deal of animosity between the graziers and the shearers. Remember that it was just after the 1956 shearers strike. There is much more to it than that and I saw it in my own parents. Land owners, large and small, saw themselves as the gentry; a throwback to the colonial days. Many of the landholders got their land from inheritance and it can often be traced back to the early settlement of the land with the migration to Australia of people from Great Britain. This happened pretty much around about the time that the transportation of the convicts stopped; I think about 1853. Some of these people were given vast tracts of land simply because they were the first there and made their claims. At that time many of the working men came from convict stock who were later given their freedom. They did not have the resources and know-how (there are some exceptions) to obtain this land. This created a social underclass and with that comes a social upper-class, to which the graziers belonged. This is wonderfully discussed in the book, *The Fatal Shore*, written by Robert Hughes. It is one of the best books, certainly the best non-fiction one, that I have ever read. Every Australian and anyone from the United Kingdom should read it. It is a masterpiece. It is a history of the birth of Australia which came out of the suffering and brutality of England's infamous convict transportation system. The main themes of the book are the historical, political and social reasons that led to the transportation of convicts to Australia and the hardships of the voyage and of the early years of the colony. Hughes goes on to write about the makeup of the convict population, the secondary detention centres such as Norfolk Island, and the established colonies. He finishes his work with the opening up of the interior for pastoral settlement, the bushrangers, and the early pioneers. These early pioneers became the wealthy landholders and were called squatters and later graziers.

I will divert away from the shearers for the moment. When I was last in Sydney I went to my old place of work, which is now the Four Seasons Hotel at The Rocks in George Street. When I worked there it was called the Regent Sydney Hotel. The Rocks is where the first settlement took place in Australia (apologies! I mean by white men) on 26 January 1788. Just for a historical point of reference, that is one year before the French

Revolution. As I walked around the hotel I noticed a plaque had been erected on the southern west corner of the hotel. It is not a big plaque; about the size of a small dinner plate. It reads that on this site in 1789, a 19 year old convict had been hung for stealing provisions from the store. Crikey, maybe I should not complain so much about the Christian Brothers after all.

Back to the shearers. I think that the animosity between the graziers and the shearers had its genesis in this early environment and society was not at all egalitarian in those days. In truth, it never really had been; a bit of a myth really. There was a scene in 'Sunday Too Far Away' where the producers dealt with this. The owner of the property came into the shed and introduced himself as Mr Dawson, the owner of the property. That's waving a real flag, calling himself Mr to start off with, denoting his feelings of superiority. I think it automatically assumes superiority and it's not a smart thing for a cocky to do. He asked the shearers to take special care with the rams as they were valuable stock and were used for breeding. He offered to pay extra and the shearers accepted. The problem was he was walking up and down the board, making a nuisance of himself, telling the shearers to be careful; that sort of thing. The shearers got sick of it and had a vote. They barred him from his own shed whilst shearing was taking place. Dawson, sorry Mr Dawson, took to peeping through cracks to keep an eye on them and Foley (Jack Thompson) caught him doing it. Foley then pretended to cut off the pizzle of a ram by calling for the tar boy. The tar boy was also the roustabout and when you cut the sheep and it needed stitches, you'd call for the tar boy to put a bit of crude antiseptic on the cut. Mr Dawson was beside himself and raced outside to look at the shorn sheep to see which one had been badly wounded and missing his pizzle. The shearing contractor had to tell him that they were just taking the 'mickey' out of him and Foley hadn't done any damage at all. That was a serious loss of face for Mr. Dawson. That night in his luxury homestead when he was talking with his daughter, he said that he had forgotten how much he hated the shearers.

In 1960 I organised the shearing for Dad; I was 16. I got the gun shearer Dave Watkins and a well-respected wool classer, Yappy Douglas. He was called Yappy for obvious reasons. He talked a lot but he knew his wool. I took the other stand; it was a two-stand shed. Dad did the wool pressing, penning up and I think we had another shed hand. Dave and I shore between us between four to five thousand sheep that year. He was shearing three to my every two so on that estimate I would have shorn about 40% of them, so that makes it somewhere in the vicinity of about 2000 sheep. Not only was Dave fast but he could also take the fleece off very cleanly without cutting the sheep very much. Now, don't you think that shearing 2000 sheep gratis at 16 years of age was quite an effort for someone who was just a boy and probably should have been at school? I was not given one penny for it. Dad had a lot of good points but one of them was not generosity. I will say that he was probably the meanest man I ever met and I don'y like saying that. When Dave and I finished the shearing, we all came over to the house to have a beer and settle up. It is customary at shearing time when the shed is finished, the cocky shouts a few beers for the boys; a sort of job well done type of thing. It was there that Mum said, quote, "Well with all the money we have saved with Max shearing, we might be able to buy another Kubelick". Kubelick was a racehorse they owned and raced in the district. That statement broke my heart. I thought my contribution to the effort was phenomenal but there was no suggestion of any remuneration for me. I should have just rolled my swag there and then and just took off.

I loved the shearing sheds, the comradeship, the smell of the wool, the hard work and being treated as an equal. I didn't experience any bullying in the sheds. I know the shearers would not stand for it. I recall the 'Shearer's Dream' all too well. One night in the pub after we had finished a shed we were all getting drunk (even me at 16-17) and one of the shearers got up on the bar and recited the 'Shearer's Dream,' much to the delight of everybody there. I should not have been there as I was underage, but the shearers reckon that if I could work like a man, I should be able to drink like one. I loved being with them and felt like I had a home with them. The other thing is that I only needed a couple to get me intoxicated but I got better as time went on. Here it is in verse: (apologies for any foul language but I wanted to leave it intact)

I was shearing outback be a wayside track,
what a c*** of a place bejesus,
Where the trees are small and the grass ain't tall,
and there's f***all there that pleases

The roustabout was a pommie lout
The boss was a hungry bastard
The expert c*** with his tools all blunt,
Oh Christ, what a bastard

I struck a blow at a big black yoe
and the skin of her gut was rotten,
I cursed and swore as the shit bag tore
and reached for my needle and cotton.

I was run-arse first, as we f***** and cursed,
To the sheep, to the shed, to the engine,
But I kept my place in that louse-bound place,
And kept pace with the southern cross engine.

The presser 'Slim' had a mind of quim
His bales were all buggered and busted,
I hamstrung more than me pen-mate shore,
And it was 'all go', while it lasted,

The greasy cook had a sore-eyed look,
All covered in scabs and rashes,
He stuffed our mouths with his half-baked rolls,
And would have poisoned Christ with his hashes.

So, if I ever go back to the wayside track
I'll be broke to the wide and cringing
You can jam the lot, up your big fat blot,
And I'll start with a southern cross engine.

To think that I can still remember this after nearly 55 years. Years later when I was in the cops and we had our choir practice, I used to recite the shearers dream. Talking about shearing and food, Mum was not the type to spend much time in the kitchen, except at shearing time. It was well known that when shearers come they'd have to pay for their food. This too was portrayed in the movie, "Sunday Too Far Away". The shearers decided they were going to sack the cook, but because he was such a big bastard, no one had the courage to tell him. They had to get him drunk on lemon essence and Foley was the one designated to take him on. When they considered that he was drunk enough with the essence, Foley told him his food was s*** and he could stick it up his a**. Foley ended up beating him and they put his drunken body on the mail truck and that was the last we saw of the cook. Since shearers have to pay for the cook out of their own wages, they demand a fairly high standard of food. Getting back to Dad's shed, it turned out that Mum was a good cook. In fact, a very good cook. No one wanted the shearers to talk about the lousy food they got at a particular shed. I can tell you during shearing, it was spot on. I can recall at one time my brother John throwing his food out of the window saying he would not eat it anymore. Perhaps that is why even today I will basically eat anything and never complain about the food. I would have been well educated to do that with a decade of boarding school behind me and to give Mum her due, she did an enormous amount of work on the property centred around horse riding, so I think it reasonable that she did not have the time to be cooking. I did Dad's shed twice more, once again in Torrendorra and again at his property at Tara, as well as other properties in the district. It was at about this time, that I had a very bad total dislocation of my left shoulder, whilst playing league for Capella against Emerald. It happened in a scrum and was incredibly painful. Like all things, dislocations have degrees to them. I got the full monty with this one. In those days, they would take you up to the local hospital and put it back into place. Then you would wear a sling for a few days and it would all be back to normal. This turned out to be the wrong treatment for dislocations. They are now treated like fractures and I should have immobilised it for up to six weeks; but that was the prevailing treatment at the time. Not surprisingly it came out regularly after that; once in my sleep and once when swimming in the dam near the house. Sometime thereafter I went to Brisbane and saw an Orthopaedic Surgeon, Dr Anthony McSweeny. He did what you call a putti platt operation at the Mater Hospital and after that I went back home to Capella. I think that I was about 17 at this time. This shoulder problem story had some interesting side stories but not for years later. I'll tell you about that when we come to it. It was also about this time that I got the fright of my life when my shoulder dislocated in my sleep. Naturally enough I was screaming out in pain in the early hours of the morning and Mum and Dad came running. By now it would pop back in fairly easily. The next time I was yelling out they thought that it was just another dislocation but this time there was a snake in my bed. Mum thought that I was dreaming but there was a snake in my bed, between the sheets. God, it scared the daylights out of me. Of course we killed it but for a long time after that I would have a peep inside the bed before I got into it. In Mum's memoirs she tells the story and describes the snake as a big brown one but in fact I think it was a simple carpet snake and not too dangerous. Nevertheless!

After the first time I shore at Torrendorra, I went with the transport driver with our wool, or rather my parents' wool, to Tweed Heads. It was close to a 1000 kilometres. He had a Thames truck with a 34 foot trailer. It was strange but in those days, to get the wool to Brisbane, you had to first take it to Tweed Heads, across the border in NSW. Then bring it back again to Brisbane, where you unloaded it at the wool store for auction. I don't really know why but I think it had something to do with protecting the railways. This trip was an eye opener for me; seeing the big smoke. I couldn't get over it, seeing the ocean, all the satellite towns on either side of Brisbane. I can you tell you it was quite an experience for a boy from the bush. Later on I heard that the owner of the transport company, Mr Richardson, committed suicide. Apparently he took off all his clothes, left them on the beach and kept swimming in one direction until he eventually drowned. It was known around the cocky sheds that he was in deep financial trouble with his trucks breaking down all the time. He didn't buy big enough trucks for the type of work they had to do and he got into trouble. Some said that he probably created a smoke screen and didn't commit suicide at all; just made it look like he did. Who knows?

You need to understand that it was my 'duty' to help my parents. From a very early age it had been drummed into me that we were to obey the fifth commandment; 'Honour thy father and thy mother'. My parents regularly reminded me what a lousy son I was and repeatedly reminded me that the property would one day be ours. Mum always felt aggrieved that she was essentially left very little from her parents' estate. This was the prevailing thinking at the time. The men were the providers and the women were the home makers. She was left out because she was a woman, not because of any animosity in the family. Mum was very close to her family and was largely the major carer of her father in his later years when he needed a lot of help. He died in 1954 and Mum was disappointed when very little was left to her and her sister, Eva. Her brothers were all left substantial pastoral properties in the Inverell district; that is, all except one. His name was Athol, and he was the black sheep of the family. Athol subsequently went the legal route and successfully sued his brothers, claiming that he should have been entitled to something. To his credit he was one of the 'Rats of Tobruk'. They used to say that he was never the same after the war. It is therefore food for thought that Mum herself did what her father did, but in reverse. She left her boys out of her will and left it all to her girls. I think there is enough evidence there to show how mean-spirited and ill-disposed she was towards John and I. They always insisted that we would all have equal shares in the will. That did not happen by a long shot. Therefore I was really working for myself and that was their argument. The money I had earned was from the shearing sheds and kangaroo shooting.

I can give you a good example of the different ways that Mum and Dad handled things. Around about this time, they entered their racehorse Kubelick into the Emerald Cup. I'm not sure what year but suggest that it could have been 1960 or 1961. Kubelick was looking good and his trainer thought that he might be a good thing to win it and he did. However even though Kubelick won by three lengths the jockey of the horse that came second lodged an appeal and it was upheld. Most people that were at the races thought that it was a set up and that Kubelick had won the race fair and square. Dad walked over and congratulated the connections of the second placed horse, now the winner. He accepted the umpire's decision and left it at that. Mum was very different. She thought that the decision to uphold the appeal was wrong and would not accept the umpire's decision. She was furious and she got my Uncle Les (who I told you was the uncrowned Prince of Emerald) to speak with the person who made the decision. I suppose he'd be the race supervisor or something like that. Uncle Les got stuck into him on Mum's behalf but it did not alter the decision. It stayed and Mum and Dad went home losers when we should have gone home winners. There seemed little doubt that Mum was right as the vast majority of people at the races agreed with her but right is not always might. I leave it to you to judge what the more appropriate behaviour in this instance was. However I think I would back her on this one. They got into horse racing and there were other horses to follow. I just could not reconcile how they could afford to have race horses and not pay me anything. I still can't reconcile it but I do understand that it was their enjoyment and they needed something to look forward to. Let's leave it at that.

As well as doing the shearing at home, I would also do the crutching and wigging. Like shearing, it is back breaking work but is over much quicker. The crutching is done to mitigate the risk of sheep getting fly blown. I have shorn some awfully fly blown sheep and it's no fun holding the hand-piece (what you shear the sheep with) full of maggots. Fly blown sheep are a major problem for the cockies. They lose a lot of sheep this way. So a few months out from shearing when the flies are breeding, you crutch and wig the sheep. The crutching part of it is done by taking off the wool between the hind legs and around the rear end of the sheep. The wigging is removing wool around the eyes because sometimes the wool grows over the eyes and they can't see. There was another way, a very cruel way of preventing sheep from getting fly blown. It was called mulesing. Merino sheep tail areas are wrinkled much like the rest of the sheep. In this rear end area it all becomes wet with urine and contaminated with faeces. Blowflies lay their eggs which become maggots. The maggots start living off their host by eating the flesh of the sheep. There were times when I was shearing as a boy that I wondered how I was going to see out the next day. Sometimes the sheep would be so flyblown you get a handful of maggots just shearing them around the crutch. Often these fly blown sheep would be covered in spear grass and/or Bathurst burr and your hands would be so sore from where the spear grass and burrs pounded them. After work sometimes I would get some hot water and antiseptic and just bathe them. I'd often be asleep before the sun went down, totally exhausted. I was just a kid but could work as hard as any man.

Mulesing involves cutting flaps of skin from around a sheep's rear end and tail to create an area of bare, stretched skin. Because the scarred skin has no folds or wrinkles to hold moisture and faeces, it is a lot less likely to get flyblown. It is a very cruel way of doing it and I would doubt that it is legal now to do this to animals. Another cruel but necessary procedure with the lambs, was castration. Dad was an old fashioned man and did things the old fashioned and inexpensive way. One of us would hold the lamb on a table (or something similar) by holding all four legs together. Dad or I, if I was doing it, would cut the top off the scrotum. Than squeeze one testicle out of the pouch and pull it out with your teeth, then cut it off at the cord. Similarly with the other one! Then slap a bit of tar (a form of crude antiseptic) on it and let them go. Within minutes they would be eating the grass. If one of the sheep dogs was nearby he/she would be the lucky recipient of the testicles. They loved them and they always knew when it was on. We did many thousands of lambs like this but towards the end of my tenure with Dad, he did start using the rings. This was a plastic ring you would put at the base of the scrotum and make it very tight. Over time, everything would just simply fall off. It was considered a lot more humane. Whilst we were doing the castration procedure, we used to also ear mark them. This is done by taking a big piece out of their ear in the shape of whatever was your registered sign was. Say it was an M. Then that is the shape you want to leave in the ear and you'd do this by taking half their ear off.

It was more brutal with cattle. Young male cattle (bulls) would be pushed up into a collapsible ramp. Before ramps came into vogue, we used to wrestle them to the ground, one around the head, another holding his hind leg back, and the other doing the castration. The ramps made it a lot easier. Once secured in the ramp, the first thing we would do is dehorn the beast. That means cutting of most of their horn so they don't gore one another. This really used to make them bellow. Then you would collapse the ramp and the steer would now be immobile on the ground. This is when you would castrate them. Similar as with a lamb but with a young bull you wouldn't use your teeth. They are much too big for that and besides, it would not be practical. Cut the scrotum, pull one testicle out at a time, cut the cord and maybe throw it to a dog, and then do the other. Put a bit of tar on it; no stitching or injections or anything like that. Just cut them out and that was that. After the castration, you would ear mark them in the same manner as lambs. Then for the 'piece de resistance,' the branding. You would get a red hot iron and imprint your brand into the steer's hide, usually on the rump. Crikey, that would really make them bellow even louder than the dehorning and you could well imagine how painful it would be. Pretty gruesome stuff really but we took it in our stride and it seems, so did the animals. It was as normal to us as having a cup of tea. You could no sooner get me to do that now than fly. Same with shooting animals! Funny how you change when you get older. I just couldn't be so cruel now. But that is the way it was at the time. The strange thing is though, these beasts and lambs would be out grazing within minutes of having this done to them. They are amazingly tough animals. Dad got this crazy idea once that we should cut the tail of one of our dogs because this dog was forever chasing its own tail. He thought that the poor thing might have had a mental problem; so we cut the tail off. The dog was not apprehensive because it had no idea what was going to happen. We gave him a bit of meat and then put his tail across the chopping block and with the meat cleaver, the same one we used to cut the sheep up, took it off in one chop. Well, the dog took forever to stop yelping. He viewed us with very deep suspicion for a long time after that. It took ages for him to regain his trust in us but it solved the problem. With no tail, the dog never chased it. Perhaps in the final wash-up, the end justified the means. Mum was furious with us but in the end, we all had a big laugh about it; one of the few times we did during this period of time.

Talk about work. Dad would have me up before daybreak and I'd be on that tractor as the sun was coming up and I wouldn't come home until after dark. I'd take a water bag and a tucker box with me of sandwiches of cold meat (always lamb) and tomatoes. I hated it. Because of Dad's meanness, we did it tougher than we had to. For example, in those days you had to grease the plough discs fairly regularly throughout the day to stop the ball bearings overheating. He had this old plough and this old grease gun that you had to fill up by hand. It would get air pockets in it and the grease would not come out. It was an awful piece of equipment and I asked him to buy one that was sort of automatic and would make life a lot easier, but he wouldn't. I argued that all the other cockies had one. Everything always cost too much; but they could own and train racehorses. So you'd have to grease the plough and get grease and dirt all over your hands and clothes and there was no way of getting it off until you got home. One time I got so angry with the grease gun not working properly I lost it and continually smashed it up against the plough, then spent half an hour trying to fix it up but couldn't. I remember that I exhausted myself with smashing this awful bloody grease gun and I told Dad that I accidentally ran over it with the plough. Dad never got angry. He just replaced it with another one but would not get the one that would make life a lot easier, for both of us. Another example of his lack of innovation and creativity was trying to get him to put an umbrella on the tractor so that I would have some shade in the hottest part of the day. A very inexpensive item but again as always, he said it cost too much. You can imagine how hot it is in a cultivated field in the middle of summer in the middle of Queensland. Perhaps his highlight for meanness was when he ordered an engineering company to make him a grain bin. The bin would be fitted on the back of the truck to take the grain to the railway siding. The norm, even in those days, was to fit an auger at the bottom of the bin attached to a little motor or to the driveshaft of the truck and it would empty the grain. Some cockies had tip trucks that would dump the grain over the grid simply by raising the bin. Not Dad! All he had fitted was chutes at the side of the bin that had an inverted 'V' shape in the middle. The end result was we had to get up into the bin and shovel part of the load out by hand. This had the effect of a lot of extra hard work and held up the other cockies, who used to get up and help us from time to time. I really had a problem with Dad over his meanness not to spend a quid on making life a bit easier. As I have said he was an incredibly resilient individual and could put up with woeful conditions. It was said, although I didn't see it, that Dad scooped out maggots out of a leg of lamb once and then started eating it. I wouldn't doubt it. He would not waste anything. Absolutely nothing! I never knew him to wear socks; he reckoned they were dirty. To Mum's eternal credit, it was she that gave me a positive sense of personal hygiene and cleanliness. If it was left to Dad, I'd hate to think. However if Dad was anything, he was a perfect gentleman. He would always stand up when a woman entered the room. He would never call a woman by her christian name unless he knew her really well. If he met a woman in the street he would tip his hat and always open the car door for them. Dad had little to no education. He could really not write very well and I suspect that he never got past primary school. Interestingly enough, I know very little about his upbringing and feel disappointed about that. I knew all about Mum's side of the family but very little about

Dad's. As I mentioned at the beginning, I never met my Dad's parents. Nor did I meet most of Dad's brothers and sisters, my uncles and aunties, but Dad did have that something of an English gentleman about him. Most of all I never heard Dad say a bad word about anybody and I have told you that I never heard him use foul language, ever. Can you believe that? He was indeed a true gentleman. I just wished that he could have been more assertive and stopped Mum from her constant bullying when she ran off with her tantrums but in my heart, I know that he couldn't. It just wasn't in his makeup.

I'll give you an example of his passive manner and how it worked in my favour. One night we were driving home from the pictures at Capella. I was driving and it was about a 20 mile drive; in those days we were still on the old mileage system. About half way home I had to take a right hand turn off the main road and onto another road. Now this was black soil country and there had been a lot of rain about. He told me to be careful with the corner but I wasn't careful enough and I bogged the truck. It was about ten or eleven at night. Another thing that Dad was; he was fiercely independent. We could have gone into a number of people's properties and sought help. They would have taken us home. Next day we would have come back with the tractor and pull it out. But Dad would not do it. He would rather walk ten miles in the middle of the night, than wake someone up to help us. He never raised a voice against me. He said that these things happen and not to worry about it. Well, I did duck into see one of the neighbours, a fella named Charlie Kraus - a German immigrant who had won one of the blocks. Of course, he offered help. Not just any help but he drove his tractor down with Dad and I hanging on to pull us out in the middle of the night. That's what we did. Charlie would not have it any other way but Dad was very stubborn about this sort of thing. He lost this one. We got out of the bog and drove home. The whole thing was totally my fault but Dad never raised his voice against me. He was the exact opposite of my mother and I think I have made that point a number of times already. Dad's credits far outweighed his negatives and I think it fair to say that he was a very good decent man. If you leave behind that legacy, you are doing well enough.

Around this time, a noteworthy incident occurred whereas I could've ended up in jail. It's strange how kids do silly things. Mum, Dad and Margaret had gone for a 3-week holiday, up to Cairns and left me in charge of the property. Of course one thing I must do Mum instructed, was to pick John up and go to mass on Sunday. That I must do; whatever you do don't miss mass on Sunday she said. Come this Sunday, John and I were on the way to mass and we spotted a brand new council grader on the side of the road, just outside Murphy's block. Well, I don't know how it came about but John was probably the creative one who loaded the bullet and I was the easily led one who fired it. I got up on the grader and managed to start it. It was one of those big Caterpillar graders that was used for road maintenance. I got it started and off I went and John followed in the truck. I parked it in the scrub a couple of miles down the road and then we went to mass. Well, all hell broke loose when the council driver came out on Monday (the following day) and couldn't find his grader. Of course he went straight to the police and old Sergeant Grace handled the investigation. All sorts of theories abounded and the most popular one was that interstate thieves had driven up in a semi end loader and taken it interstate, probably to Victoria where they would hide it on some property. In due course, naturally, they found the grader parked in the scrub with no damage. Now they had to find who took it and they had no idea. I suppose when you are looking to solve a crime like this, you look for motivation, opportunity and having the means to do it. Maybe it was someone with a grudge against the council; maybe friends of the driver having a joke with him. It was the talk of the district. In those days, a group of cockies, say about five families, would share the same telephone line. Each person had a special ring and that's how you knew if it was for you. I think our call was two long rings and one short one. Another might have been say three short rings. We were on the same party telephone line as the Murphy family. Basically they built a telephone line from our place into Capella, about 20 miles I think. I overheard

Murphy telling someone about it. You were not supposed to listen in but remember I was 16, alone, bored and just did it, probably for a bit of human interaction. Anyway, now I knew there was a full scale police investigation into the matter. I had to make a decision and I talked to John about what to do. I decided to fess up. He wasn't so keen as he thought that if we kept quiet they would never find out who did it. But my conscience got to me and I decided to fess up.

I recall my confession like it was yesterday. That is my going into see Sgt Grace. I asked him if he was looking for the fellas that stole the council grader and he told me that their lives would not be worth living after he caught up with them, or words to that effect. I thought crikey, I better not fess up after all. In the end after some small talk I told him that he didn't need to look any further and that it was my brother John and I that did it. He called me a f****** idiot and he was going to lock me up. I thought for a moment that I was going to get another back hander like I got from Br Higgins when he caught me smoking. I don't remember why he didn't lock me up but when Dad came back they interviewed him about it. They were seriously thinking of charging both of us as juveniles but wanted to talk with Dad first. It blew over. We were told that because of Dad's good standing in the community, the council had voted not to press charges and the police agreed. This was primarily because they accepted that we did it just for a lark, there was no malice in it, no damage was incurred and I owned up to it. It remained the talk of the district for many years thereafter. If I had been charged, I would never have been able to join the NSW Police Force. I am reminded of Banjo Patterson poem 'The man from Ironbark' when he wrote, "And when at last the barber spoke, and said, `Twas all in fun, Twas just a little harmless joke, a trifle overdone'. I think this describes our stealing of the grader, a harmless joke that was a trifle overdone. I'd reckon up there in the Capella district that they would still be taking about the time those young Michell boys stole the council grader. I think that it is worth repeating that I believe that the dynamics between John and I were that he was the leader, came up with the good (bad) ideas and silly me, carried them out. A legacy from the Bilgar and Guardee days perhaps! There were other silly things that we did. It's probably a good thing that he was not home all the time. In Mum's memoirs she talked about the grader incident and said that when they came back from their northern Queensland holiday, I told them about it first thing so that they did not get it second hand from somebody. As Mum describes it, she says that John and I were both left on the property to look after it whilst they were away but that was not the case. John was working on a property next door for a fella by the name of Robbie Donaldson and would have been at least a 15-20 minute drive from our home. The truth is that I was left on my own with no one within cooee. I was 16 years of age.

We had a practical problem at this time. Because I was still only 16, I couldn't get a driver's licence until I was 17; so lawfully I was not allowed to drive. I did anyway and took a lot of grain to the silo in this 'bloody bin' that Dad had made. This year my parents got a bumper wool clip and a bumper sorghum crop. Sorghum is a cereal crop that is usually used for grain feed. You would therefore think that I would have been paid some wages out of this, but no, 'we can't afford it' was all I ever heard. I would reply, "You can afford bloody racehorses but you can't pay me". It was around this time there were discussions about me doing some share farming with Dad and we actually put something in place. The next year I received a small portion of the crop revenue but was encouraged to put that money back into buying some farm equipment, for the future. You know, the sort of build up your assets philosophy that parents teach, especially if it is something that will benefit them as well. Emanating out of that philosophy I bought an 18 disc John Shearer plough. Isn't it funny how you can remember the small details? Dad bought a new John Deere tractor, fully imported from the USA. There is a follow-up story with the plough that I will come to later.

On a social level we used to get invited to the locals' private functions on their properties and they were wonderful people. However there was a fly in the ointment. In this part of the world, these very good country people used to like to be called by their first names, even by the children. Dad's name was Fenton and Mum's, Mary. Well, Mum could not abide this. She hated anybody who she did not know really well and especially children, calling her Mary. She hated the working men calling my dad Fenton. She felt superior in spite of her financial downgrade and would not let us call the older people by their first names. It was always Mr this and Mrs that, not John and Annie. Of course, this caused resentment. Why did we have to be different to all the other kids I used to ask? Because we were better Mum would tell me; that's why and that was the end of it. She had a pet dislike for people that used improper grammar, which was not uncommon in that part of the world at the time. For example using them, when you should use those; them people instead of those people. Of course, she was right but that was not the point. Mum did not want her children growing up like that. That's fair enough I suppose but it did ostracise us to a certain degree and I felt that there should have been some leeway with it. We were the only kids that called the older people Mr and Mrs and that made us different. They were wonderful people, real salt of the earth Queensland country people but to be truthful, after I left Capella in 1964, I have never been back and don't intend to. Too many unhappy memories at 'Torrendorra' Capella for me and there is no reason for me to revisit them; although I am doing that in part I suppose by writing this book.

Mum would scream at Dad but that was water off a duck's back. I mentioned before that he had this phlegmatic character. It just didn't seem to worry him whereby it really got to me. I hated being yelled at. I got plenty of that at school and had developed a real aversion to it. Mum was relentless; she constantly nagged me about my table manners and my speech. Hold the fork this way, put the knife here, don't put your elbows on the table, don't speak when you are eating, keep your mouth closed when you are eating, wash your hands before you eat, say grace before the meal, make sure you help with the washing up, etcetera. All good things to do but she'd be yelling them at me day after day after day after day. It applied to everything I did. If we went mustering, I wasn't sitting properly on the horse. I wasn't holding the reins correctly, stop slouching and on and on it went. She even had the audacity to get into me claiming I slept too much and was lazy. Regularly she would say that I would never be able to do a nursing course like the girls have done because I could just never stick at it. I think her inference was pretty clear. On and on it went, day after day after day. Here they are getting free labour, including the shearing and crutching and this is the way I am treated. With me Mum found an outlet for her anger and frustrations and it made life almost unbearable for me. Mum should have seen a Psychiatrist but it's doubtful that she would ever have done that. She used to say that if she needed to see anybody it would be a Priest in a confessional box. When John was home, he and I would badger Dad to pull her into line but she had total control over him. If all people were like Dad, there would be no wars. If they were like Mum, there would never be peace. I think I sit somewhere in-between.

Years later, in fact in 2013 when I made my submission to the Royal Commission into Child Sexual Abuse, I offered to give a copy of it to John and my sisters. I told them that they were not to discuss it with anyone else and to destroy the digital copies I sent them as soon as they had read it. They all wanted it but I warned them in advance that I would be saying less than flattering things about Mum. Patricia was aghast saying. "What Mum, what on earth did she do?" There you go, Patricia was unaware of the abuse that Mum was putting upon me during this time. Not surprising I suppose since she was rarely home. Margaret was more understanding and said that she would not prejudge me and I was entitled to say what I felt was the truth. John of course was fully aware of it as he had been on the receiving end of it quite a lot himself and ironically, the worst for him was yet to come. The worst for me was during these hard days when Mum was really doing it tough herself. I suppose, to encapsulate it, I was caught up in a very negative environment where I really did not have my father's protection and guidance, and the abject senses of loneliness and social isolation were exacerbated by my mother's tirades against me. I became an even more socially isolated, introverted and self-loathing individual during this difficult time.

Eventually, as you would expect, the continual abuse got to me. I developed a psychosomatic illness that manifested itself as severe diarrhoea. It just would not stop so Mum took me into see the local doctor in Emerald; the same one that had put my arm in plaster a couple of years before. He could not find anything wrong and suggested we see a physician in Rockhampton, which we did. We saw the specialist doctor and he too found nothing physically wrong with me. After the physical examination he asked me if there was anything troubling me. Mum was also present at the consultation. I broke down and told him that I was sick of being bullied, abused by my mother and not protected by my father. I told him I was not getting paid, saw myself as basically a slave and that I couldn't handle it anymore. He asked me if I had been in the cadets at school and I told him I had because it was compulsory. He then asked me if the RSM (Regimental Sergeant Major) had ever yelled at me. When I answered that he had, he then asked me the most extraordinary thoughtless question. He asked me, "What's the difference between the RSM yelling at you and your mother yelling at you?" He qualified that by saying that surely they were one and the same thing. Of course that was the end of it. He told me to go home and basically sided with my mother, suggesting tacitly that I pull my socks up. I often reflect on this. I reckon that I would have been about 17 at the time, so that would make it 1961. I now believe that if the doctor had recognised that the chronic diarrhoea was a physical symptom of a psychological problem and that I was crying out for help, things may have turned out differently. He would have, and should have given very different advice and my future might have taken a different direction. I was in a situation that I had no control over. Just think about it. I am working really hard seven days a week for no pay, being abused by my mother and reminded on a daily basis about how useless I was, and had absolutely no social connections at all. I was stuck out on the property and apart from everything else I was also regularly reminded that it was my duty to help my mother and father. It was never mentioned that I had reciprocal rights. We all lost a golden opportunity because of this very poor assessment by this doctor.

Mental disorders were still in the dark ages and those that suffered from them were shunned and considered inferior beings. Things were kept very hush, hush. People didn't want to know about it. Consequently the medical profession did not have the knowledge to deal with it. Thank goodness much of that has changed as we have become a more liberal, educated and tolerant society. Although I did not know it at the time, things for me could only go from bad to worse. Boarding school had made me an introverted shy type, uncomfortable in people's company, with poor social skills and very low self-esteem and almost no confidence. My parents just made it that much worse. I think it is very sad for any young man to have to grow up, especially in a rural environment, with a mother that is an abuser and to really compound it, get no protection from his father. I feel deeply regretful that my relationship with my mother soured the way it did. If I can get one message across it is to try to make sure that the relationship between mother and son is strong, based on genuine love, affection and respect. In my case, after the scene in the hospital, there was none of that. Instead of getting better, it got worse. The most overwhelming influence that the Catholic clergy teachers and my mother left me, was *this unrelenting feeling of guilt.* I had this woeful opinion of myself and felt very guilty about almost everything I did. That I was a bad Catholic; that I was lazy; that I was never going to be anything; that I was going to be the cause of an early death for my mother; that I was a terrible son; that I should be totally ashamed of myself, and on it went. I was so ashamed of myself and should not have been. If I had committed suicide, Mum would have said that I was a weak person who rejected God and that she wasn't surprised. Well, you will learn that weakness is not part of my character as we go on and perhaps in a perverse way I did get some of that strength from my mother. Isn't that a paradox?

When I broaden my scope of inquiry further about the relationship difficulties between my parents and myself, I hold the Catholic Church primarily responsible. Mum in particular had these Catholic bigoted beliefs that greatly influenced her behaviour. She saw what most reasonable people would think as normal adolescent behaviour as sinful and must be punished. I mentioned earlier that Mum use to pray every day that I would become a Catholic priest. She held the church in the highest possible esteem even while I was being abused at St Brendan's. In Mum's eyes mother church was the epitome of everything that was good. When Mum lived in the city in later life she would go to Mass every day and she never went to bed without her rosary beads in her hand. I guess therefore that you can imagine how the animosity towards me festered when I rejected the church and everything that she believed in. I don't know that I would have developed mental illness if it weren't for those terrible days of parental abuse at Torrendorra, Capella. Notwithstanding the traumas I suffered at boarding school, and in particular at St Brendan's, if I had come home to a loving home environment with a father showing the way and a loving, supportive mother, I feel that there would have been a good chance that I would have been spared what was to come. Fanaticism of any sort is dangerous, maybe even evil, and what I am trying to say is that this religious fanaticism played its part in my mental illness. I have no doubt about it.

Just as an interesting side story, not related to what I am talking about I suppose, but I'd like to write about it: a story about how some mothers really care for their children. When I was in the Police I would do a cruise of the pacific islands on the cruise ships once per year. The cruise was free and they'd give you ten dollars a day to spend, in return you had to keep the peace on the ship and one of the many good things about cruise life was that the booze was very cheap. I'll talk more about that when we get to that time space but an incident occurred on board one day. It highlights a mother's true love for her son. For a few days I noticed that a couple were staring at me and it got to the stage where I was being unnerved by it. When the opportunity came to get the husband on his own I took it. He told me that they both believed that I was their son. He walked out on them many years before in England and came to Australia. He became estranged from them and never contacted them. They decided they would come to Australia to look for him. She in particular, firmly believed her prayers had been answered. I agreed for both of them to talk with me providing I had my work partner with me. When she saw me she threw her arms around me and started sobbing. I handled them very gently and told them who I was, where my mother could be contacted and that as a Policeman I had been fully vetted to join the Police Force. I firstly persuaded him and finally got her to understand that I was not her son. Now how's that for a mother's devotion? Apparently when the boy left his home in England to come to Australia he was a tall gangly red headed youth who had the physical features and looks that exactly matched mine. I had another incident of being mistaken for someone else, though not so dramatic. I had just come out of hospital in Brisbane after having had my putti platt operation, so I was about 16 and all strapped up in plaster to protect the wound. I was walking down the street in Brisbane when I was pulled up by a couple of Demons (Detectives). In those days they wore hats so you couldn't miss them. They started questioning me about who I was, what was wrong with me and so on. They asked me to (sort of made me) accompany them to the house of an Italian immigrant who had her house broken into a few days earlier. Apparently, according to the detectives, I fitted the description down to a tee. Well, the Italian lady had a good look at me and told them that I had too much of the carrot. That is to say, I was too much of a redhead. The cops were good but disappointed. They thought that they had their man.

Back to Torrendorra, Capella. Other things happened during this era. One day I very nearly shot myself (accidentally). It could have been disastrous. I was out with my cousin Billy McCosker on their property 'Codenwarra'; not far from Emerald. That's the same property I mentioned where we refused to shear the sheep because they had scabby mouth. Billy was the one that

I told you about at St Brendan's who acted as a bit of a minder in that first term at school in 1957 when John and I were being put through the ropes of school bullying. We were driving around in Billy's father's utility and behind the seat was a rifle. Nothing unusual about that, but unbeknown to me, Billy's father always kept a bullet in the chamber (according to Mum's memoir) and put the rifle into a safety catch mode. In this way he'd always have it ready in an emergency. That doesn't make any sense at all to me as doing this is an absolutely no-no thing to do with a rifle for obvious reasons. You never carry around a loaded rifle unless you are getting ready to use it. I put my hand in the area where the rifle was and somehow pulled the trigger. The safety catch was not on and it blew a massive hole in the side of the vehicle, just behind the passenger seat where I was sitting. It missed me by a few inches. God, can you imagine the fright we both got? I don't know how Billy explained that to his father but Mum really gave it to me over this and claimed that it was all my fault. However in her memoirs she does not accuse me of loading the rifle so that is some consolation I suppose. She made me feel totally inadequate and was unrelenting in her attack on me over this incident. To be fair to all of us I think if I had accidentally shot myself and there was a subsequent coronial inquiry, the Coroner would have found that whoever loaded the rifle would have to accept the majority of responsibility. But in Mum's court she condemned me for it and reacted accordingly.

Another time at Torrendorra, we bought in a bloke to do the contract harvesting of our sorghum. It was night time and he was filling up the auto harvester (a machine that strips the wheat) with petrol. I walked over with a kerosene lamp in my hand and there had been a trail of petrol somewhere because the lamp caught fire quite some distance away from the harvester. The contractor suffered burns to his legs and had to be hospitalised. This could have been catastrophic but I didn't feel that it was my fault. I suppose with the wisdom of hindsight, I should not have taken a naked flame anywhere near flammable material like petrol but I was some distance (perhaps 12-15 metres away from him) when it happened. He must have left a trail of petrol for it to happen and maybe I should have been aware of that, maybe! Anyway I really copped it (again) from Mum who went on with her vitriolic abuse. The bush is a bit of a dangerous place actually. A good example of that is that when the new owners of Torrendorra took over from my parents (early 1964), they had a fatal accident on the property within weeks of taking over. Apparently the new owners (father and son) were working in an underground well on the property to try and get some water to the surface. They took an engine down the well with them but didn't think about where the poisonous fumes would exhaust out of the well. Because there was no exhaust they were overcome by the fumes of the engine and died from carbon monoxide poisoning. That's kinda like putting a hose on the exhaust pipe of your car and locking it inside the vehicle with the windows up. I couldn't be blamed for that one.

Between 1958 and 1963, I spent a lot of time with my uncle Lionel on Cullin-la-Ringo. He was an interesting man who went off to war in WW2 and served as a transport driver in North Africa and Palestine with the AIF (Australian Infantry Forces). He had a mate named Norm that also served with him in Palestine and Norm was often there and actually did some work for Mum and Dad at Capella. Later when Mum and I would go to help Lionel, we would play the card game 500. There would only be the three of us so we had a hand we called Norm's. I guess that indicates that were periods of relative harmony between us to be able to play cards together and have some fun. You may recall I told you about having a .45 colt pistol. It is interesting how I got this .45 in the first place. I told you about Mum nursing Archie Marsh at the Inverell hospital. He gave it to me (through Mum) when I was still at Inverell; so I must have been no more than 12 years of age. Nice present for one so young! In any event, Mum passed it onto Lionel for safe keeping as it was considered I was too young to own such a weapon. I think we can all agree on that. In the middle part of 1967 when I went back to Emerald for my cousin's Margaret McCosker's wedding, we stayed at Cullin-la-Ringo. I got the weapon there. When I say we, I went with my beautiful girlfriend Pauline and her friend Judy and my brother John. Nobody knew it but I was severely clinically depressed at this time and I have no recollection of Pauline, Judy or John being with me. Thank God (metaphorically speaking) I did not blow my brains out on the veranda that day, overlooking the massacre cemetery. I have already written that I went 'within an inch' of doing it. I should have been happy because I was with Pauline but I will explain to you later why I wasn't. I was always downcast, miserable and gloomy during this period. That veranda and Cullin-la-Ringo are long gone and now buried in history. It is all under water and I don't know what they did with the cemetery. I will go into more detail about the mental illness in the section I refer to as 'Days of Darkness'.

I was also doing a lot of kangaroo shooting in the early sixties. I bought a 22 hornet and fitted it with a high powered telescopic sight. I would reload my own bullets and that significantly cut down on the costs of ammunition. We would go out spotlighting at night and find the roos eating the crops. Once you got the animal in the spot light, it was usually curtains for them. It was more often than not, one shot - one kill. The key to doing that was to make sure that you had the telescopic sights sighted correctly and had it well protected. The hornet bullet did not leave a big hole and that was important because you did not want any damage to the skin. I would try and hit them in the middle of the chest for a front on shot or through the neck if it was a sideway shot. Then we would skin them, take the skins home and peg them out to dry; then sell the skins. It was a tough life; hard work, a lot of blood and guts but I was used to it. Not as tough as shearing though! I made quite a bit of money doing this and really got to be an expert shot. Isn't this now a massive contradiction? I could not shoot any animal now. I just couldn't do it; but that was then. After the kill you would often find the joeys (baby kangaroos) still in their mother's pouches. There was little benefit in skinning them so all we did was pull them out of the pouch and bash their heads against a tree. If no tree, then against the side of the vehicle we were using, usually up against the bull bar. It saddens me to have to admit to such cruelty. I just think now how terrible this type of behaviour is but that was then and that is what we did. It was considered normal behaviour for people of the land. I imagine that it would still be but for my part I am ashamed of it now and find it a bit hard to admit to such barbarity. Many years later when I was having a psychotherapy session with a learned psychiatrist at the Prince of Wales hospital in Sydney, I told him this story. He was shocked and got really angry with me. He said that if I wanted to shoot something, why not get a camera and shoot with that. I remember once when I was going to NZ, the friendly immigration bloke asked me what I was going to do in NZ and I flippantly said that I was going to go down south deer hunting. That wasn't the right thing to say to him but it was the first thing that came to my head, but I picked the wrong man to say that to. I think that he was a staunch environmentalist and he gave me a stern lecture about killing defenceless animals and basically suggested that I should bugger off back to where I came from. If it's any consolation I agree with him now and have done for a long time. Shooting and killing animals was in our DNA; wherever we went on the property we'd usually take a rifle with us. It was considered essential kit for the man on the land. We had a 'shoot at anything that moves' mentality.

There was another shooting incident when Mum accused me of nearly shooting John or Billy when we were out shooting pigs one day. I have explained to you how we used to do it. John's dog would grab the pig by the ear and one of us would either shoot the pig at point blank range or stick it with a knife. On this occasion John and Billy had hold of the pig while the dog kept hold of the ear and I shot the animal in the heart with my . 22 rifle and killed it. That was all normal and the way that we did it. Mum got hold of the story and in her version of events (she wasn't there) had me galloping full pace by on a horse shooting at the pig whilst it was being held by the boys and concluded that I could have shot one of them. I will give her credit for something; she at least gave me kudos for being an expert marksman. My side of the story is the correct one.

At home they now had the infrastructure in place to run a rural property. Homestead, shearing shed, machinery shed, shearers quarters, sheep yards, cattle yards and so on. Dad had selected the site because it was on top of a red hill and he figured it would be better placed there for pragmatic reasons than on the rich black soil that covered most of the property. He chose well but had some bad luck trying to get a water supply for it. He was a firm believer in the water divining system. With this system you get a forked twig and walk about with it at a horizontal level to the ground. When the twig pulls towards the earth there is said to be water there. Dad was convinced of its accuracy and called in the drillers to dig a bore and we would have all the water we needed. Not so! I think we went down a couple of hundred feet. You pay the contractors per foot of drilling. As some stage you have to make a decision as to whether or not you continue. Eventually Dad admitted defeat and gave up on it. Instead he got the bulldozers in and built a dam right near the house and put a windmill on it. After that, we had all the water we needed because the dam was kept full from the run-off water on the hill.

I moved into the shearer's quarters at about this time so I could be out of the house. You can probably guess why. It was an incredibly lonely life for me on the property and I think that I have more or less explained that. I sometimes wonder what part social isolation and loneliness played in my mental illness. If you can just imagine living at home out in the bush isolated. Most of the time with no brothers or sisters for company. There was no social life for me at all. We'd go to Mass every Sunday and there would be a ten minute gossip session afterwards and that was that. I had no contact with girls at all in this part of my life and I longed for it. If you can just imagine I rarely went to anything. I don't know how it came about but I found an old gramophone player with a couple of records. One was, 'Noah found grace in the eyes of the Lord' and the other, 'Cigarettes, whisky and wild, wild women'. If memory serves me correctly, you had to change the needle after every record or at least very frequently. This device became a source of companionship for me in the shearer's quarters. At this stage there was still no outward indications of any mental illness although the repetitive playing of these records might have been one. I was considered just another awkward, introverted teenager who was having problems with adolescence. Amongst the many criticisms that my parents were levelling at me was that I was wasting my life and should never have left school. This went on indefinitely until I announced that I was going back to school to get qualified to gain entrance into the medical school at St Lucia in Brisbane. Mum claimed that the brothers at St Brendan's had told her that I could be whatever I wanted to be, but was just too lazy. Mum wanted me to be somebody that she could be proud of and held the medical profession in very high regards, as most of us do. So, she kind of badgered me into going back to school which I did in 1963. I actually went back to St Brendan's would you believe at 19 years of age but now I know that it was just an act of appeasement. I believe that I did this because I was believing all the negatives levelled at me at the time and wanted to do what I saw as the right thing (my duty) by my parents. I don't remember who the brothers were but I think the 'heavies' and Walsh had gone. I couldn't adjust and the principal ended up giving me the sack after I went out with my Uncle Lionel one weekend and didn't come back when I was supposed to. The principal made the right decision. I was a square peg in a round hole and we all knew it. I think that I was only there for a month or so. I realise now that I was now mentally ill at this time but didn't realise it then. The next term I went to the public school in Emerald and boarded with an old lady, Mrs Daniels, in town. Again I couldn't fit in. I was incredibly introverted, shy and although a bit older than the other kids, just couldn't cut it on a social level. A simple thing like getting up in class and reading a paragraph used to create a great deal of anxiety. I did not have any social skills to speak off and carried with me this awful burden of guilt. It's probably true to say that I withdrew into myself because I was always that way after coming to Queensland in 1957. I'd go home on Friday nights, work the weekend on the property and go back to school on Monday morning.

I did avoid interaction with others because I felt inferior to them and had a preference for solitude. Whenever we would go to the rare ball in Capella or Emerald, I sensed that the girls were not interested in me and I had absolutely zero confidence in approaching them. When I look back on this period, it should have been clear that I was developing mental illness and anything could have happened. Whilst staying at Mrs Daniels place (my boarding house), I met a couple of travelling salesmen from Victoria who were selling kitchenware door to door. They were in their mid-twenties or so and doing this just to have a look around Australia. One of them was a larger than life character, Ron Andrew. They only stayed a week or so but they left their mark. Both of them were handy Australian Rules footballers and could punt or drop kick a league ball well over fifty meters. The local league footy club wanted them to stay and play football (league) for Emerald. Of course they didn't but I only mention these blokes because Ron features more in my story later.

It was around about this time and perhaps not that long after I saw the doctor in Rockhampton, that it was decided by Mum that I should see a psychiatrist. She contacted a cousin of hers Monsignor McCosker, who was a priest and lived in Sydney. The Monsignor arranged for me to see a Dr. Nuffield (I think that was his name) at the Royal Prince Alfred Hospital in Sydney. The good doctor assessed me and told me that I would be fine but I needed to cut the umbilical cord and get away from my mother. He suggested I pack my backpack and do what I always wanted to do and go and see the world. Unfortunately I did not do that but went back to school instead.

Looking back at those times I think that I was starting to outwardly show signs of mental illness that came to the surface in 1967 but no one, including me, realised it. I was socially withdrawn, unable to learn, introverted, shy, lacked confidence and very low self-esteem. I believed that I was useless, lazy and basically good for nothing. God knows, I had been told it enough times. I left this school as well and badgered my parents to let me go to Hubbard Academy in Brisbane. This was a school that specialised in teaching kids to get their matriculation to go to university. I did much better there and worked hard. This was also the year the Beatles came out to Australia. I thought that I had a chance to get the grades to go to University but had a weakness in physics and mathematics.

More importantly, I found that socially I was much better with this group. I was becoming almost normal, or so I thought. I was good at English, Latin, logic, zoology and chemistry. Silly me! I spoke to a friend of mine at school who arranged for a bright spark to attend the Latin exam for me. He assured me that he would pass with flying colours. We agreed on a fee and the logistics. You can probably guess what happened. This bright spark never turned up and I failed Latin because of it. I probably would have passed if I had attended myself. I also failed in physics but passed everything else. As bad luck would have it, they presented us with the hardest physics paper that had ever been presented for a senior examination in Queensland and I failed it. It became clear that I did not have the high intellect that my mother insisted I had (or more pertinently wished I had) and I blame the St Brendan's brothers for misleading her and indirectly misleading me about my academic capabilities. As an aside to that, I went to a vocational guidance centre in Brisbane and undertook psychological testing which included aptitude and intelligence evaluation. It was determined that I had an IQ of about 110-115 so any of the glamour university courses, especially medicine, were not within my reach.

In January 1964 my parents sold Torrendorra for delivery in March. After this happened they bought a caravan and hit the road so to speak. They had earned it after having completed the compulsory seven years on the property which was one of the conditions imposed upon successful applicants for the ballot. I was studying for my senior examinations in Brisbane; John was jackerooing out west somewhere; Patricia was working as a hostess at the Philadelphia Hotel in Amman, Jordan - and Margaret was doing her nurse training in Brisbane. I did not start to wander until after 1965. In fact for most of the time from 1958 (end of) until they sold Torrendorra at Capella, I was at home. I think they took delivery of their new property, Moonie Park which is near Tara in SE Queensland in October 1964.

I want to say more about the Church at this point. The Catholic Church is about putting the fear of God in you, literally. The Reformation was bought about in an effort to correct the excess and wrong doings of the Church and to some extent it did. Throughout the Church's history the driving factors have always been the fear of death, the fear of the devil, and the fear of hell. The Church is an institution that has fear as its central core. The Church has been somewhat discredited in recent times because of the incredible advancement of scientific information and people using more rational thinking. Just look at the theory of evolution. I will mention more about Charles Darwin later on when talking about depression. However, even today the church is still teaching little children that heaven and hell exist. What rubbish and couldn't this be a risk factor to a child's mental health? They still teach that if you die in a state of mortal sin (like missing Mass on Sunday: remember the Br Higgins story), you would be damned to the everlasting fires of hell. So the smart thing to do they preach is to get in step and toe the line. The consequences of not obeying the Church are unimaginable and catastrophic according to them.

I recall that during one of our daily religious lessons at St Brendan's we were told a story by one of the teachers. It may even have been that b****** Walsh. He said that during the Roman persecution of the early Christians one of the punishments was to throw them into boiling water. If they recanted they would be taken out and put into cold water and this would revive them. We were expected to believe this; they appeared to. Here an example of Christianity's cruel brainwashing of the innocent. This quotation is from an official approved Catholic children's book (Tracts for Spiritual Reading, by Rev. J. Furniss). Quote: *'Look into this little prison. In the middle of it there is a boy, a young man. He is silent; despair is on him. His* *eyes are burning like two burning coals. Two long flames come out of his ears. His breathing is difficult. Sometimes he opens his mouth and breath of blazing fire rolls out of it. But listen! There is a sound just like that of a kettle boiling. Is it really a kettle which is boiling? No; then what is it? Hear what it is. The blood is boiling in the scalding veins of that boy. The brain is boiling and bubbling in his head. The marrow is boiling in his bones. Ask him why he is thus tormented. His answer is that when he was alive, his blood boiled to do very wicked things'.* In reply, the Catholic Church gave a rousing endorsement to this. William Meagher, who was the Vicar-General of Dublin, stated in his approbation: *"I have carefully read over this Little Volume for Children and have found nothing whatever in it contrary to the doctrines of the Holy Faith; but on the contrary, a great deal to charm, instruct and edify the youthful classes for whose benefit it has been written."* A great deal of charm; f***, what is it with these religious bigots.

How much more violent can you describe a situation than this? It's worse than a description of the Nazi SS exterminating the Jews. In my view it ought to be a crime to write such rubbish, and the perpetrators of such trash should be jailed. The Church is based on a lot of things that most intelligent and educated people reject. An interesting one is that the Church, even though it is riddled with homosexuals and pedophiles, is homophobic. We know now from the Royal Commission that this is 100% true; there is no denying it now. Wow, that's a paradox if ever there was one. The biblical basis for this homophobia lies in the story of Sodom in Genesis, and in Leviticus. Leviticus 18:22 reads, quote, "You shall not lie with a male as one lies with a female; it is an abomination," and Leviticus 20:13 reads, quote, "If a man lies with mankind as he lies with a woman, both of them have committed an abomination; they shall surely be put to death; their blood shall be upon them." So am I correct in saying that the bible is advocating death for homosexuals? That's the way I read it. The Catholic Church is also misogynistic. That is why women are not allowed to be ordained as priests in the church. Even though it is generally women that are the carers of children, they are not allowed to be God's representatives on earth.

I believe that the Catholic Church is based on a lie. The big lie is the story of the resurrection of Jesus of Nazareth from the dead. Where is the proof that this ever happened? There seems to be historical recordings that there was a man named Jesus of Nazareth, who was a teacher in Galilee. A good man who preached positive things but may possibly have had mental illness; delusions of grandeur and hallucinations. Love your enemies, do good to those who hate you, bless those who curse you and pray for those that abuse you. To one who strikes you on the cheek, offer the other and as you wish for others to do to you, you also must do to them. Impossible to live like this of course, but nevertheless all very noble and inspirational. I even believe that Jesus said such things as recorded. That does not mean he was the Messiah. I have had many arguments about the resurrection, starting with my mother in the early days and many others since. No one has ever been able to give me an answer. If this went to a court of law it wouldn't even reach the stage of prima facie. This is one of the main reasons why I am an atheist. The other main reason is because of the theory of evolution. The church offers everlasting eternal life at death in a place called Heaven. Why wouldn't you do everything possible to get there? It is quite literally just too good to be true and I believe it is not. I also believe that the majority of intellectuals and modern day scientists believe that as well. If the Church wants to persuade us to 'see the light' it must change from being an arrogant, authoritarian, hierarchal institution to one that uses the power of logic and reasoning. They can't do that because it is not logical in the first place and therefore reasoning is not within its capabilities. It must provide evidence and not ask us, or threaten us more likely (with this nonsensical idea of the fires of hell), of the existence of God. The answer to the question of 'Was Jesus of Nazareth the Christ' has never been proven, not even remotely. Other religions like Islam, Judaism, Hinduism, Buddhism and a host of others, don't believe the Christian Church's belief that Jesus of Nazareth was God. There is a wonderful book entitled, Zealot by Reza Aslan who does an in-depth study into this and his conclusions are more than interesting.

It is said that Jesus walked on water, turned water into wine, raised Lazarus from the dead, fed thousands with one loaf and one fish, etcetera but where is the proof? The story of Jesus was told two thousand years ago and could be a stockpile of myths surrounding what appears to be an extraordinary man. His persona attracted stories at a time when they were all under Roman occupation. The ordinary people needed a hero and that is what he became. He preached non-violence and love but that proves nothing other than he was a peaceful and truly remarkable man. The history of science is the history of one religious superstition after another being debunked by rational reasoning and due logical process. For me the final nail in the coffin is that the theory of evolution disproves God. When I was a young boy, my people thought that anyone who was not a Catholic was an inferior being to be pitied and prayed for. There was this arrogant superiority permeating throughout the church. At school we used the pray for the conversion of Russia. At the time, Catholics thought everybody else was going to burn in everlasting hell indefinitely. Do you know that more people have been killed in the name of religion than for any other cause in the history of mankind?

In 1095, Pope Urban 11, started 'Holy Jihad' with the First Crusade. He believed, in God's name, that the Christians had the right to start war against the non-believers, the Muslims, who the church considered heathens or if you'd prefer, infidels. At Claremont in France he declared that any person that took up arms against the Muslims would obtain 'Salvation through Slaughter'. It was considered an act of purification. If a crusader was killed in battle, it was an automatic ticket to heaven. He/she would automatically become a martyr. This was the religious bigotry that led to the crusades and was responsible for the mass killings of hundreds of thousands of people. In one daily occurrence alone in 1191, Richard the Lionheart ordered the beheading of over 3,000 Muslims. One of the reasons for this was that Saladin, the Muslim leader would not hand back the holy cross, the holy grail. Hundreds of thousands of Muslims were killed during the holy crusades. That is definitely what the

Catholic church was like in those times and it has a great deal to answer for. I believe that the vast majority of people reject Catholicism outright and so they should. When you start talking like this you hear them shouting from the rooftops that you are a Communist, but that is far from the truth in my case. I'm just as opposed to Communism as I am to Catholicism.

I recall that during the dry spells at home, the Parish Priest would implore us to have faith and keep praying for rain. The church used to tell us that if you asked from God, you would receive. Seek and you shall find; knock and it shall be opened unto you. So, we prayed week after week but the rain never came. Of course, eventually it did; it always does. What would the priest say when it finally did rain? "You see I told you, your prayers have been answered". The only evidence that I can give you off God's existence was when the Madonna of Our Lady of Perpetual Succour at St Brendan's answered my request to get rid of Br Broderick and she did; at least that is one way of looking at it. That's as close as I have come to witnessing a miracle in my lifetime.

Having said all that, my old Dad used to say that religion may not be right but what they preached was good for society. If we all followed the ten commandments, it would be a better place. I agree with that. To do that however all you have to do is follow the laws of the land. Don't steal, don't cheat, don't kill, and all the other do's and don'ts. Just do the right thing; we don't need the church to tell us what is right. I don't think there is any room in modern society for religion. When I was in the cops, we used to use a bit out of the bible. Do unto others as they would do to you but we added a bit to that and it read, 'Do unto others as they would do to you but do it to them first'.

So it was against this religious Christian background, that I was bought up. These people were my teachers and guardians. Religious bigots, authoritarian, hierarchal, homophobic, misogynistic, cruel, some were sexual predators, racists and probably a lot of other things. Make no mistake about it, racism was the norm out in redneck country in the 1950s. We may not have had the Ku Klux Klan, but when I was growing up indigenous Australians were not allowed to vote and were not allowed to go into pubs. It wasn't good form to be seen speaking to a black man. In any of the schools I went to there were never any Aborigines. This book is not about the treatment of Aborigines but suffice to say that our past treatment of them was disgraceful and abominable. Some would argue that it still is. For me to have a better understanding of modern day treatment of Aborigines, I watched the documentary *Utopia* by John Pilger. He believes that nothing has improved.

I went back to Moonie Park, Tara after I finished school in Brisbane and began working for my parents again. When my parents sold the property in Capella, they had an auction and sold everything; no doubt for next to nothing. Not unlike what they did seven years earlier at Inverell. This included my 18 disc John Shearer plough but they never forwarded the money onto me. My birthday is in May so the only barometer I have as to where I was at this time is what was I doing for my 21st birthday. I recall that I was at Moonie Park and Mum gave me a small reading lamp for my 21st birthday present. At this point in time I was still very unsure of myself with women but I think my year at Hubbard Academy did have a positive effect on me even though I did not get the grades to graduate to go to the university. I had hitherto suffered rejection from women from as far back as I can remember and I definitely developed a complex about women. I have explained how I had grown up as a guilt ridden, introverted young man and had obtained a type of incertitude about my actions. I was very uncomfortable in the presence of women. I think in the very little bit of social interaction I had with them up until this point in time, they generally viewed me as fairly ordinary. I would not say that I thought I was ugly, but definitely in the 'just ordinary' class. I explained earlier how I had been ridiculed at school and I think that this is why I presented in this way. Instead of being bought up to be confident, self-assured and proud of myself, I had been bought up the opposite. That much is very clear. This rejection by women went on for years. I think that is fair to say that I developed a fear of social situations generally and certainly had symptoms of social phobia. Later in the Police Force this came to the forefront when I was required to give evidence in court. The irony of that situation was that I'd fret about it for days before but when required to do it, I'd perform very well. This fear had the effect of me doing my best to avoid any court case situations where I had to give evidence. The anxiety was in the lead up to it. My anxiety and self-consciousness arose from a fear of being closely watched, judged, maybe criticised by others. Maybe even laughed at; made fun off. An interesting point is that I was not always like this. I recall that once we had a concert at De La Salle and the boys were allowed to vote for the best performance. Our group of three did an act centred around advertisements with a bit of a twist to them. I loved being up on the stage and we ended up getting second prize. The point is that I had no fear of being on display then. What changed? My theory is that perhaps a throw-back to the days of boarding school and the 'Miss Australia' thing. Maybe it had something to do with Br. Walsh telling the class how pretty I was and that I should have been a girl. Then to add salt to the festering wound going on to naming me Miss Australia publicly. I can barely contain my anger when I think about it. Paradoxically though, I turned out to be quite a good presenter and public speaker. I will explain later that I have spoken at international conferences. I also had some long term meaningful relationships with some very attractive women but that was later on, much later on.

At the end of 1964 I had finished school. I first left in my sub junior year at the age of 14 years of age and went back in 1963 at the age of 19. For most of that time, I was at home working gratis with intermittent work in the shearing sheds and kangaroo shooting in the winter. I have described the introversion and probably got ahead of myself with going through my depression and contemplation of suicide at Cullen-La-Ringo in May 1967. Up until this point in time, there were no obvious outward signs of severe mental illness. However, when I look back there were red flags (e.g., the Rockhampton doctor incident) indicating that something was abreast; we just did not know it. I have given you a detailed historical account of my schooling concentrating on the physical, psychological, mental and sexual abuse that I suffered at all of the three boarding schools but overwhelmingly at the Christian Brothers School at St Brendan's at Yeppoon. I have also written about the abandonment and rejection I felt at St Joseph's College in Aberdeen and this picture of me catching the steam train from home to Aberdeen is firmly implanted in my mind. I have gone through the difficult time I had at Capella from 1958 until 1964 and tried to analyse and explain how lonely, socially isolated, and entrapped I felt during this period. When I was taking about what type of picture to put on the cover of this book, I eventually settled for having one of a brother dressed in whatever you call it that they wear, sitting under a mango tree with a little boy. The brother of course was Brother Walsh and the little boy is me. At one time I was thinking of making it a picture of two little boys standing on a railway platform waiting to catch a steam train to Aberdeen. I even thought that a title like, 'Goodbye my Son' might have been appropriate signifying the separation and abandonment of us as little children but in the end, Br Walsh won the day and I settled for 'Underneath the Mango Tree'.

Things seemed to be improving at the turn of 1965. Outwardly I was fine and looking forward to a life away from home. I had no outward signs of mental illness and was starting to feel better about myself. I was even getting on better with my mother who, while she still had a lot to say, wasn't as vitriolic and harsh as she had been in my teenage years. However we all knew that it was best for me to not be at home and to go and see the world. Nevertheless it is far to say that the damage had been done and mental scars don't heal so easily. They fester like a virus and can surface later on in life after what appears to be some seemingly innocuous event. That's what happened to me.

Chapter Four: Hitting the Road
1965 - 1966

In 1965 - The Byrds recorded 'Mr Tambourine Man' and Bob Dylan released 'Like a Rolling Stone'. The first US combat troops arrived in Vietnam. Malcolm X the black-nationalist leader was shot to death at a Harlem rally. Muhammad Ali knocked out Sonny Liston in round 1 of the heavyweight title rematch. LBJ was sworn in as the 36th President of the USA. Soviet cosmonaut Aleksei Leonov performed the first spacewalk on March 18. Edward White II became the first American to walk in space. The 1st Battalion, Royal Australian Regiment left for Vietnam on HMAS Sydney and the first drawing of the national service conscription lottery in Australia took place. The movies released included Dr. Zhivago, The Sound of Music, A Thousand Clowns and Darling. Notable deaths included those of Winston Churchill, Nat King Cole, T.S. Eliot and Adlai Stevenson.

In 1966 - Simon & Garfunkel's "Sounds of Silence" reached No 1. President Sukarno left office in Indonesia and Suharto assumed power. Movie actor Ronald Reagan was elected Governor of California and the US began bombing Hanoi in Vietnam. Botswana, Lesotho, and Guyana become independent states within the British Commonwealth. The Food and Drug Administration declared "the Pill" safe for human use. Massachusetts Institute of Technology biochemist Har Khorana finished deciphering the DNA code, Insulin was first synthesised in China. The movies *A Man for All Seasons, Who's Afraid of Virginia Woolf, Alfie* and *A Man and a Woman* were released and Truman Capote wrote the book *In Cold Blood*. Notable deaths included those of Montgomery Clift and Walt Disney.

I can say that sometime early in 1965 I settled in Sydney. I arrived there with next to nothing and stayed initially at some cheap run down hotel in the CBD area and I met this girl by the name of Robin. At the time we were both applying for work on the Sydney buses and she told me she had friends at Manly and that they were looking for a flat mate. We went over to Manly and I met these fellas who were all surfers from Jersey Island. I moved in with them and got a job at the Canopus (the Can) room at what is now the Manly Pacific Hotel. Just prior to that I had tried my hand as a lounge room waiter at the Steyne Hotel on the Manly waterfront but got the sack after a few weeks. The head waiter told me that I should go back to shearing as I was not cut out for this type of work. Mum just could not get her head around a man as a drink waiter. She thought that men that did this type of work were not real men. The real men were the doctors and graziers. This was just the stereotypical redneck thinking that permeated the country at the time. She is not to be condemned for that. Many right wing conservative people of the land thought this way at that time. At the Can I started off picking up glasses, sometimes helped on the door and sometimes delivered drinks. Max Merritt and the Meteors were playing there and the place was really heaving. The system for serving the customers was that the waiter paid for the drinks when you ordered them from the bar and then you would collect the money from the customer. To keep up with the demand you would have to load your tray with the beers all partly on the rim of the tray leaning inwards. Then you had to carry this tray to at least shoulder height to be able to navigate the traffic. I don't know how we did it but very seldom would a waiter drop anything and we could make good money. Some of the waiters used to overcharge but if you keep it to just a few cents each time no one complained. All service was by waiter only so we had the upper hand.

The boys that I lived with were really good looking surfing types and the women loved them. I'd often find myself back at the flat listening to all of the sexual activity taking place but unfortunately they (the women) weren't interested in me. I was not the bronze type Aussie you see on the lifesavers brochures but these fellas were. They were all quite good surfers and they worked in the various clubs around the Manly area. This way they could go surfing during the day time hours. One time, one of them came home and told us that he had pissed into a customer's beer because he had complained that it wasn't cold enough. He said that he asked the customer if the beer was all right now and he replied it was good. Not to be undone, the waiter's mate, also working there, had a complaint about the food. Wasn't hot enough or something like that. He decided to load the sandwich up with some very hot spice sauce and sent it back. Just the way the customer wanted it. Make it hotter was the customer's request, nice and hot. There was a hell of stink about it and the customer went off his head and got management involved. The waiter denied that he put it in the sandwich and said that all he did was deliver what the kitchen had given him. The cook denied he did it and wanted to know why he would do such a thing; so they couldn't resolve the matter. I think management wiped the bloke's bill for the night or something like that. I admit I can see the funny side of that. But it does make you wonder how often this type of thing happens in restaurants. Maybe better not to complain in the first instance. One of these blokes was a lot different to the others and I hooked up with him; his name was Stewart Collings.

I believe that I went home sometime late in 1965 and did my usual thing. Worked there for a couple of months gratis, got lonely and took off back to Sydney. I recall that I was back in Sydney in late 1965 because Stewart and I started on our hitch-hiking journey in December 1965. The Jersey boys had hit the road and were travelling Australia looking for the best waves. Stewart stayed behind. He was not a surfer and we both sort of had the same interests. We planned to hitch hike around Australia and after that hitch hike around New Zealand. We both worked in the same clubs. Sometimes he was the barman dispensing the drinks and I would be the waiter or visa versa. You can imagine what happened. I'll tell you more about Stewart later.

From there I got various jobs, working in clubs mainly. I worked for a while at the Manly Warringah Rugby League Club and others clubs. Once Stewart and I had what we thought was enough money, we took off on what turned out to be quite a long and arduous journey. We caught the train from Central Station in

Sydney out to outer western suburb of Sydney, Liverpool and started hitching from there. This was the first time I had ever hitch-hiked. We were well dressed at this stage and initially didn't have too much trouble getting rides. I don't remember when we got to certain places or even many of the people that gave us rides, but we did see a lot of country. We crossed the NSW border at Albury and I remember sleeping under a bridge that night. We had sleeping bags so that was not a problem. The following day we ended up near Geelong and stayed with this lovely woman who had picked us up. She had an Italian name and was very generous to us. From there we found our way over to Kingston in South Australia. I had an Uncle (Angus) and Aunt (Beverley) there and we stayed with them on their property. As it turned out they were just in the final stages of shearing. The shearers told us that when they finished this shed they were heading back home to Perth in Western Australia in their EK Holden sedan. We accepted their offer of a ride and went on this 2985 kilometres journey across the Nullarbor Plains, from Kingston in SA to Perth in WA. In those days there were no tar sealed roads and the existing road was full of bull dust holes. These were dangerous because you couldn't see them. They were holes in the road that filled up with dust and you could not tell that it was in fact a hole. This had the effect of sometimes smashing the undercarriage of the cars. On the trip across the side of the road was littered with vehicles that were damaged and could go no further. I don't know when they tar sealed the highway but it is all tar sealed now, so that problem no longer exists. The Nullarbor has the Great Australian Bight on its southern aspect and the Great Victoria Desert on its northern aspect. Another interesting aspect of the Nullarbor plains is that it has the longest single straight railway line in the world. It is a 478 kilometres stretch of rail that extends from Ooldea to Loongana. It can be seen in relative comfort now by crossing it in the Indian Pacific rail that will take people from Sydney to Perth. I think it is about a three day trip and I know that my Mum did it after Dad died in 1974.

Once we lobbed up in Perth we decided that we should get a job for Stewart to experience the outback. We both got jobs with the Western Australia Wheat Board at a place called Norseman. Our jobs were to help the wheat cookies unload their wheat. We got the job because I was a cocky's son and was familiar with the procedures when I used to deliver our own grain that I told you about and knew the ropes. We also had to take some samples of the wheat in each load and arrange for them to be analysed. I seem to recollect it was to measure the moisture content in the grain. This environment was a real turn up for Stewart. He'd gone from being a hotel trainee at the Savoy in London to unloading wheat from cocky trucks in the outback of Australia. Good for him! He had not really been out of Sydney since he came to Australia and here he was in the middle of nowhere. But he did well. One day he was starting an engine to drive one of the augers and had an accident. To start the engine you had to do it by cranking it like you did with the old southern cross engines. It backfired and he was not holding the handle correctly. It cracked him across his skull, just above his left eye. Fortunately it turned out not to be too serious although he had to get stitched up by the Flying Doctor who was stationed at Norseman. It was quite an experience for a Jersey boy. It was in the summer and temperatures were getting up to 40 degrees Celsius and bejesus it was hot. Australia can be a very hot country, with most of the continent being semi-desert. The highest recorded temperature in Australia was 53 degrees at Cloncurry in Queensland. Years later when I went to the Australian Open tennis (2002) the temperatures in Melbourne rose to 43 degrees and Adelaide recorded a temperature of 47 degrees. Stewart was finding it hard to adjust to the inland heat and wondered what the hell he was doing unloading wheat in the middle of the Aussie outback for some red neck wheat cockies who incidentally were great blokes. We stayed until the wheat harvest was finished and all the grain was delivered. I think it was about 2-4 weeks. Than we hitched back to Perth and from there, we headed north into the vast wilderness of Western Australia. We stayed for a couple of days in Perth and slept on beaches in the area. To give you an idea of the size of this country, it is 2240 kilometres from Perth to Broome and still in the same state.

Our plan was to go to Broome and maybe find a bit more work. We had no trouble getting to Port Headland. The bloke that gave us the lift was going into Port Headland and let us off on the desert highway that went straight up to Broome. We could have gone into Port Headland with him but we wanted to keep going. We went a whole day and rarely did anyone go by and when they did they wouldn't pick us up. Pricks! We had to sleep under the stars that night but by then we were getting used to that. We were starting to get worried as we had no food and in this context limited water. Late on the second day, we had some luck. A diamond drilling team came along and told us that we were f****** mad and that we could die out in the desert. They said that we could get up on the back of the semi and travel with them. They were going to Mt Isa in Queensland. That is a distance of 3583 kilometres. Can you believe that? Hitching a ride for 3583 kilometres! We decided that we were no longer going to look for work in Broome. We went with them all the way to Mt Isa, on the back of the semi and thought we were in heaven. We didn't want any more of that being stuck in the desert thing and any ride was a good ride. With all our lifts we made sure that we were able to provide for ourselves and never scrounged meals or drinks from them. Once they became aware of that, we got on well with all the people that gave us lifts. We went through Broome and stayed overnight on Cable Beach. Broome is a really interesting place. In 1688, William Dampier visited the Broome area "New Holland" as the area was known to the rest of the world at the time. So you see, it was not Captain Cook that first discovered Australia. In the early days of the pearling industry of Broome it was considered as the source of the world's finest pearls. Just for historical information, a Dutch ship, 'Duyfken' captained by Willem Janszoon, made the first documented European landing in Australia in 1606 off the West Australian coast. Ten years later in 1616 another Dutch explorer landed on islands just off the coast of Western Australia and in 1630 a Dutch cartographer Hendrick Hondas published the first world map showing part of Australia that was chartered. Again in 1642 it was another Dutch explorer, Able Tasman that discovered Tasmania and New Zealand. That was about 128 years before Captain James Cook discovered the East coast of Australia. What extraordinary sailing skills these European sailors from countries like England, Portugal, Spain, Holland, not to mention the Vikings from the Scandinavian countries, must have had. Fast forward to the year 2000 when I had a bar in Singapore, I used to do a trivia night once a week and I was the Quizmaster. Two of my favourite questions were one: who was the first (white man) to discover Australia, and two: where was Christopher Columbus born? You have the answer to the first and Columbus was born at Genoa in Italy in 1451, and died in 1506 in Spain.

From Broome we went to Fitzroy Crossing into the Northern Territory. Fitzroy Crossing is a small town in the Kimberley region of Western Australia, 400 kilometres east of Broome and 300 kilometres west of Halls Creek. It is approximately 2,524 kilometres from the state capital of Perth. Previously on our journey we had either been travelling south, west or north but now we are traveling in an easterly direction for the first time. One of the first European explorers of the Kimberly area was a bloke by the name of Alexander Forrest in 1879. Following his exploration, around 1882, the first cattle stations were established around the mouth of the Fitzroy. The area was finally settled in 1886 by a bloke named McDonald when he set up the Fossil Downs cattle station. This was following a three-year, 5,600 kilometres trek from Goulburn, New South Wales. My God, you have to admire these early pioneers. What incredible fortitude, resilience, and vision they must have had.

From Fitzroy Crossing, we went through one of the biggest cattle stations in the world: Wave Hill Station. Wave Hill is 13,500 square kilometres in size; that is 3,335,922 acres. That's small compared with the biggest cattle station in Australia which is Anna Creek station in South Australia; although we did not pass through this one. This station is 23,677 square kilometres or

5,858,714 acres. To put that in perspective, Dorset in the UK is 2653 square kilometres or 655,570 acres. You could fit nine Dorsets into Anna Creek station. Wave Hill property is best known as the place where there was a strike by the indigenous people who were the workers on the station. I remember this strike well. They staged a walk-off demanding better pay and conditions. This happened in 1966 not long after we had passed through and this action later had a profound influence on indigenous land rights in Australia. Wave Hill is about 600 kilometres south of Darwin in the Northern Territory. The traditional owners of the lands are the Gurindji people, who have lived in the area for approximately 60,000 years. 60,000 years, my God, can you believe that? The area was first explored by Europeans in 1854 by Augustus Charles Gregory, and later in 1879 by Alexander Forrest during his journey from the coast of Western Australia to the Overland Telegraph Line. Both Wave Hill and Victoria River Downs were established in 1883. The original station owner of Wave Hill was Nathaniel Buchanan, who took delivery of 1,000 head of cattle in May 1884. Buchanan took delivery of another 3,000 head in late 1885 that had been overlanded from Cloncurry in Queensland, up through the channel country. By 1907 Wave Hill was stocked with an estimated 58,000 head of cattle. There have been many books written about the early pioneers that opened up this country and bought stock in. One that I have read is *We of the Never-Never*. Another book that fascinated me was *The Cattle King*. This was a book about the life of Sir Sidney Kidman who became known as the Cattle King. When he was 13 he was said to have run away from home with only five bob (shillings) in his possession. It's what I should have done. At one time Kidman was supposed to be the biggest cattle owner in the world and a completely self-made man. He created an incredible empire and at one stage he had more than one hundred cattle stations in his name. How does one go from having five bob to billions? It is just mind boggling! This is an incredible story and I read once that he was asked by a reporter why he always travelled second class, which he allegedly did. His reply was because there was no third class.

After Wave Hill we went to Tenant Creek which is on the main highway leading to Darwin. Tenant Creek is approximately 1,000 kilometres south of the territory capital, Darwin and 500 kilometres north of Alice Springs. This region encompasses the junction of the highways the Barkley and the Stuart, also known as the Overlander and Explorer's Ways. The Overlander's Way retraces the original route of early stockmen who drove their cattle from Queensland through the grazing lands in the Northern Territory. Like we did at Fitzroy Crossing and Wave Hill cattle station, we camped overnight. At Tenant Creek we shouted ourselves and our travelling companions a beer. Stewart wanted to have a drink in a good old country outback pub — so we did. A bit of a difference to the Savoy in London, but he was becoming a man for all seasons. We got into a bit of chat at the pub with some ringers and they were taking the 'mickey' (making fun off) out of Stewart because of his posh English accent but it was water off a duck's back. In case you don't know what a ringer is; it's an Australian cattle stockman, or a cowboy if you like to use the American terminology. From Tenant Creek, we headed straight to Mt Isa which was only about 661 kilometres away. So all up we did over 3,500 kilometres on the back of a semi with the diamond drillers and we parted good friends in Mount Isa. Mount Isa is a mining town, which mines for copper, lead, silver and zinc, and has got a nickname by locals as 'The Isa'. Today Mount Isa is one of the largest producers of both lead and silver, in the western world. It is located just 200 kilometres from the Northern Territory border and 1,829 kilometres from Brisbane. The nearest major city is Townsville, which is on the eastern coast seaboard and about 883 land kilometres from Mount Isa. We stayed in Mt Isa for a couple of days and slept in our sleeping bags at the Isa show grounds. It was at Mt Isa we committed our first crime of the journey.

By now we looked the part of vagrants. We made an approach to the Salvation Army for a feed but they basically told us to f*** off explaining that they only helped needy people. I think they were frightened by us. You can well imagine how one would look after spending days on the road and not sleeping in a bed for ages. We had just come all the way from Port Headland on the back of a semi-trailer and we were in a ragged state, no doubt. We were tired, worn out and our money was running out. So we 'jumped' a passenger train, the Inlander that runs from Mt Isa to Townsville. The trip is a twenty hour journey and you travel 977 kilometres. I don't know how we were not caught but the crime we committed was I suppose fare evasion. We had to sit in the sitting cabins and when the conductor came, we went to the end of the carriage. He must have seen us and did nothing. We actually went all the way like this and when we got to Townsville we just walked off the train and onto the street. Just like that. We soon found our way to the highway going south and headed for Brisbane. By good fortune, we got a ride with a simple minded chap who was driving a mini minor and travelling by himself. We did take advantage of this fella and accepted his offer of meals during the journey. But that was all we did. He took us to the city of Toowoomba, a distance of 1366 kilometres on the Warrego highway. We therefore avoided going to Brisbane. We actually stayed in Toowoomba, freshened up and looked forward to the final stretch of the journey. Toowoomba is also an interesting place. Toowoomba's history can be traced back to 1816 when English botanist and explorer Allan Cunningham arrived in Australia from Brazil where he had been searching for native trees and plant life that would be suitable for the Australian climate. In June 1827, he was rewarded for his many explorations when he discovered 4 million acres of rich farming and grazing land that was bordered on the east by the Great Dividing Range and about 160 kilometres west of the settlement of Moreton Bay, which later became Brisbane. Cunningham named his find Darling Downs after Ralph Darling (later Sir Ralph), then Governor of New South Wales. At the heart of the Darling Downs is a town named Dalby. It was this town that I was taken to when my jaw was shattered after I got worked over in a brawl that I will tell you about that happened at Tara. The Darling Downs is magnificent farming country and it reminded me a great deal of the country I saw when we drove from Pretoria to Bloemfontein in South Africa in 2008. In fact Toowoomba is just 172 kilometres from Tara but it would never cross my mind to detour and take Stewart to meet my parents. In any event by this time we were keen to get back to Sydney. From there we went down the New England Highway and ended up back in Sydney. From Toowoomba to Sydney it is 868 kilometres. We travelled this with multiple lifts going through towns and cities like Armidale, Tamworth, Aberdeen and Newcastle. You will recall St Joseph's College at Aberdeen and De La Salle College at Armidale. I think we were away for a couple of months and both of us walked straight back into jobs as barmen at the RSL club in Manly. We started saving again and we were going to go and do the same in the land of the long white cloud, New Zealand.

In Australia, we started at Sydney and ended in Sydney. By my estimates, a distance of over 12,500 kilometres. All of that except 997, when we jumped the train, was by hitch-hiking. Australia is such a vast country with nearly all of the population living on the eastern seaboard. It is so vast that you can travel hundreds of kilometres without seeing a sign of any human being as you do when you cross the Nullarbor Plains. At least, that was the case when we did it. The Aborigines were able to live in this hot arid dry interior of the land. Their instincts and abilities to find food and water in these desolate places is an extraordinary feat of human initiative and endurance. I suppose the most interesting part of it for me was walking (or rather driving) in the footsteps of those early pioneers that opened up the area known as the outback in the mid to late 1880s and understanding better the incredible hardships and feats of endurance that they must have undertaken. Imagine taking a large herd of cattle thousands of kilometres up through Eastern Australia to the Kimberley's and the Northern Territory. There is a folk song that deals with the subject called 'The Over-landers'. These were the men that we call the drovers that took the herds to wherever they had to go. Let me see if I can remember some of the 'The Over-landers' without the benefit of Google. 'There's a trade you all know well, it's bringing cattle over, from every track to the gulf and back, men know the Queensland drovers.

Pass the grog around boys, don't let the bottle stand there for tonight we drink to the health of every Over-lander'.

Now it was time for a change of scenery. I can't be too specific about when we went to New Zealand but I think it would have been early to mid-1966. We caught the Greek cruise liner 'Australis' to the capital city Wellington and stayed at the YMCA before we hit the road. Wellington is the capital of New Zealand and quite an interesting city. It is well known for being very windy and the city is often buffeted by strong gusts that are funnelled through Cook Strait. The local people often refer to it as windy Wellington. In 1839 it was chosen as the first major planned settlement for British immigrants coming to New Zealand and several ships arrived there in 1840. What we found when we were there was a windy cold city and we were reasonably glad to move on.

New Zealand (NZ) was very different to Australia. It was cold, windy and wet for a lot of the time but then again, we were there in the winter time. Perhaps not such good planning by us but NZ is truly a beautiful country. We hitched north to Rotorua and sampled the wonderful sulphur baths and the Maori culture. From there we went to Auckland and back to Wellington via the East coast to Hamilton, Whakatane, Tolaga Bay, Napier and Masterson. On the way back from Auckland, we were involved in what could have been a fatal car accident at Hamilton. We had hitched a ride in one of those old Vauxhall cars and we were traveling south from Auckland on the highway. At one stage this old man drove onto the highway on our left side without looking for oncoming traffic. Our driver served to miss him, hit the medium strip and onlookers said we rolled three to four times and the car slammed into somebody's garage. I was sitting in the front passenger seat and Stewart was asleep in the back. No one was hurt expect me and that was not much but I was admitted to the Waikato hospital. They put some sutures in one of my fingers and also in a cut on the scalp. I stayed overnight and left the next day. That really was a close shave and we were ever so lucky that it was not much worse. The car was a complete write off and that could well have been the end of it for me; there'd be no more waltzing Matilda for me, or for Stewart.

We passed through the town of Napier in the Hawkes Bay area on the East Coast. We had been travelling with some Maoris and they were filling us in on some of the historical points of interest. What was really interesting was to learn about the large Napier earthquake which occurred at Napier on 3 February 1931, killing 256 and devastating the Hawke's Bay region. It still remains as New Zealand's deadliest natural disaster. From Napier we came back to windy Wellington. In Wellington we found jobs at what is now the Imperial Tobacco cigarette factory at Petone, just outside Wellington. I think then it was WD&HO Wills but am not sure. It was interesting to note the differences between the job we got in the 40 degree heat at Norseman in Western Australia for the Wheat Board to the cold, drizzle and grey skies of working at Petone in New Zealand. In WA it was shorts and T-shirts; in NZ you really had to be rugged up for it. We stayed again at the YMCA in Wellington and worked at the factory under assumed names. We did that just for a lark; there were no other sinister reasons. We weren't running from the law or anything like that. In all our time hitch hiking we never committed any crimes (except jumping the train at Mt Isa). Stewart went under the French name of Pierre Petite Souris (little mouse) and I was Michael James Flanagan; he went French and I went Irish. I hate to admit it but our job was making cigarettes. Another thing I would never do again because I have long been an ardent opponent of cigarette smoking. I became an addicted chronic smoker, smoking between 40-50 a day. The very first thing I did of a morning was to light up as soon as I woke up (in bed) and the very last thing I did at night was to have a smoke before I switched off the bed side lamp. I was well and truly hooked and strangely enough this is one thing my parents did not complain about. Neither of them smoked and I stopped smoking when I was 28. It came about when I was studying for my diploma in nursing at the Prince Henry Hospital. I had been trying to give up for ages as it was made very clear to me during my nursing training, the damage that smoking does to a person.

You may remember that I mentioned in the 1964 historical highlights that the US Surgeon General Luther Terry affirmed that cigarette smoking causes lung cancer.

Diverting from our NZ trip for a moment. As part of our nurse training I attended a post mortem and the Pathologist showed us the lungs of a chronic smoker. They were near black; it did the trick. That night I went down to the golf club at Prince Henry and threw my near full sack of drum tobacco into the rubbish bin. This was in 1973 and I have not had one since. That is forty-three years ago. Do the math on that. 40 (per day) x 365 (days per year) x 43 (number of years) = 627,800 cigarettes. I think it very unlikely that I would be alive today if I had not have stopped smoking. I worked in the respiratory and the coronary care units and saw first-hand, the damage that smoking does to the human body. I even looked after one patient who was smoking through his tracheostomy. (A tracheostomy is an incision in the windpipe made to allow the patient to breathe who has an obstruction.) Would you believe that? The other thing of course, is the money that I have saved. If we take the present price of a packet of twenty cigarettes, the results are staggering. 627,800 divide by 20 = 31,390 (packets) x $20 (price per packet) = $627,800 or $1 per cigarette on present day costs. That in itself should be an incentive for people to stop smoking.

We often ask ourselves what are the best things we have done in life. In fact some interviewers for employment ask this question to obtain a better understanding of the applicant. I don't hesitate for at least one of them and that was to give up smoking. I think I have said enough about smoking but it is interesting how Stewart and I found ourselves working in a cigarette making factory at Petone in New Zealand. Incidentally, we both smoked at the time so you can imagine our smoking costs went down to zero during this period. We use to distribute quite a few to our Maori friends as well and they loved the idea that they did not have to pay for their cigarettes whilst their Aussie friends were working at the factory.

As usual, Stewart and I didn't stay too long at Petone. We were well and truly wandering nomads by now. When we were there we made some good friends, especially with the Maoris. I thought that they were wonderful people but could get a bit aggressive when drinking alcohol. We really enjoyed their company and went to their houses for BBQs and parties. I got on well with one girl in particular and if we had not headed south, I may have taken up with her; but we did head off to the South Island. We caught the overnight ferry down to Christchurch. Little did I know how big a part Christchurch would play in my later life when I first went there with Stewart. In Christchurch we slept our first night under a tree opposite the Christchurch General Hospital, in Hagley Park and nearly froze to death. Even though we had sleeping bags, it was freezing. The next day we bought the local newspaper and looked up the classified jobs section. There was an advertisement in it for hospitality positions at a place called Gore. Gore is towards the southern end of NZ in the midst of some great farming country in the province of Southland. They were looking for a sous chef and a cocktail barman. Stewart's background had been in hospitality and as I have told you before, he came from a rather well to do hotel family in Jersey Island and studied at the great Savoy in London so hotels were in his DNA. He reckoned he could pull off the Sous Chef's job. The Managers of the tourist hotel/motel, a husband and wife team, were desperate and hired us over the phone without even seeing us or one on interviews.

We hitched on down to Gore, met this husband and wife management team and were soon housed up in one of these new suites in the motel section. We had really upgraded ourselves. From sleeping under trees in the desert or on beaches, under bridges, in parks, show grounds, on the side of the roads and the like, and the YMCA, we were now doing it in luxury. The job went well. I knew how to be a normal barman and they gave me a book on how to make cocktails; but they were mainly a beer and wine crowd. The clientele were mainly cockies from the local farming community. They were good people and Stewart and I really enjoyed our time there. Everybody loved Stewart's cooking and we could have stayed there as long as we liked. I did find out later after we left that there was an expensive statute missing from the Lodge and unfortunately they figured that we took it. I found this out when I applied to join the NZ Police Force and the recruiting Sergeant told me that this was the reason I was rejected. I can assure you we never stole anything; that was not part of who we were. In the end it didn't matter. I joined a more interesting and rewarding Police Force in NSW.

Also working there were some girls from Christchurch. One was Pauline and she had a friend, Judy. I fell hopelessly in love with Pauline. She was a beautiful girl, a devout Catholic and any man would have been proud to have been with her. Nothing happened at Gore and after about three months we left and continued our journey around NZ. We should have stayed longer but we were the restless nomadic types. Pauline and I promised to catch up the following year when she came to Australia, so I had something to look forward to. From Gore we went across to Queenstown, Milford Sound and Te Anau. Queenstown and its surrounds are the most beautiful part of the world that I have ever been to and that includes the Swiss Alps. It took my breath away when I first went there. I can't tell you how beautiful the bottom part of the South Island of NZ is. It is quite extraordinarily beautiful. We stayed in Queenstown for a few days and saw the Remarkable Mountains covered in snow, took a jet boat ride on the Shotover River which had only recently started and a lot of other outdoor things. You could see these magnificent towering mountains over the landscape and descending into beautiful lakes and rivers. I have travelled much of the world since and I have not seen anywhere as beautiful as the areas around Queenstown and Arrowtown in the winter time. Queenstown has been over commercialised now but in the 60s it was still in its infancy as a tourist destination. Yes, I'd rate it as the most beautiful part of the earth that I have seen. It sits on the shore of the Lake Wakatipu, set against the magnificent Southern Alps. The surrounding Central Otago area is known for its pinot noir and chardonnay vineyards, and for adventure sports. In fact a fella from Queenstown by the name of Hackett started bungee jumping in Queenstown. I would recommend Queenstown as the place people must go and see for the adventurous and active young people anywhere in the world. I have been back many times since but when I first saw it in 1966 I just could not believe how beautiful it was; even though we were hitch hiking, doing it rough and it was freezing cold.

Then we moved onto the West Coast. This was an interesting and different place; largely it existed because of the mining industry. We walked on the Fox and Franz Josef glaciers and flew over Mount Cook. From the Franz Josef we moved on and stayed at a town named Greymouth which is the largest town in the West Coast region. Because we had worked in Gore for some time, we had money and could afford to stay at budget priced accommodation. However in recent times Greymouth had become internationally known for a tragedy that occurred there in 2010. On 19 November of that year, there was an explosion at the Pike River Mine that trapped 29 miners. The mine is about 46 kilometres northeast of Greymouth and all of the miners were killed and entombed in the mine. Attempts to rescue the trapped miners were repeatedly delayed due to high levels of methane gas until a second explosion on 24 November was believed to have dashed all hope of survival for the miners. This left an indelible mark on the locals of the West Coast. My son Daniel knew one of the miners. I really liked the Kiwis and have had a lot to do with them since this time. When I was drinking with a mob of Kiwis and the question comes up, what is the biggest mistake you have made in your life, I say (tongue in cheek) after much disingenuous thought, that I married a Kiwi. I did this in 1979 and after my marriage separation in 1997, my ex-wife and children went to live in Christchurch and they have been there ever since. My little Aussie kids have become Kiwi adults. One time when I had a pub in Singapore, a group of us of all nationalities was having a discussion about where one's loyalty lies. One of them asked me who my kids would support in the rugby world cup, Australia or New Zealand. I believe that it would be NZ. My son was playing a bit of rugby league at the time for the Kaiapoi Bulldogs and was doing ok with it. The same bloke persisted with his questioning about loyalty and asked me who I would support if my son was playing for NZ against the Wallabies. I didn't hesitate. I would support who I have always supported, the Wallabies. We took a show of hands with the group and only one other fella, coincidentally also an Australian, agreed with me. The group of about eight of us mostly supported the concept that we should support whoever our children were playing for, not our country. The two of us that didn't were the older members of the group so we decided that it was a demographic thing. Older people stay with the flag, younger people go with the family. This was a discussion that became ongoing and we had many a beer over it. Often when rugby people came into the bar that we knew we'd ask them and generally speaking the 6:2 ratio prevailed. If I was asked the question today, I would still have the same answer which would be, "Well of course, I hope that my son has a great game but I hope the Wallabies will win".

After finishing exploring the West coast, we made our way back to Picton which is a town in the Marlborough region of New Zealand. The town is named after Sir Thomas Picton, the Welsh military associate of the Duke of Wellington, who was killed at the Battle of Waterloo. Interesting! We caught the ferry to Wellington which was about 92 kilometres and took 3 hours. I think we stayed in Wellington, again at the YMCA, for a couple of days and caught up with our old friends from the cigarette factory and then flew home to Australia from there. We had by now hitched hiked around Australia and NZ, a distance of maybe about 18,000 kilometres. They are both very interesting countries. Australia with it cruel history as a convict settlement and the harsh rugged outback that is strangely beautiful in its own way. Compare that to the soft green fields and great beauty of New Zealand. I used to say that I had never really seen green grass until I went to NZ. We travelled around in anything but comfort for most of the time. We were only 21 and doing it tough was not a problem for us and we still had our sense of adventure. Stewart had a fascination for the outback and another one of my significant disappointments is that I lost contact with him after we came back from NZ and haven't heard from him since. Australia is a vast continent with a small population and it is not really until you start travelling the vast outback that you get a sense of the enormous distances and rare natural beauty. I remember reading a book about Australia and it began by saying that white people were not meant to live in this harsh continent. We have all read about the heroic exploits of people like Shackleton's trip to the Antarctica; Roald Amundsen's search for the Northwest Passage; Sir Edmund Hillary and Tenzing Norgay's conquest of Everest; Ferdinand Magellan and the first circumnavigation of the earth; the travels of Marco Polo; Stanley's search for Livingstone; Lewis and Clark and the Expansion into the American West; Christopher Columbus' discovery of the New World and of course, the latest one, with Neil Armstrong's first steps on the Moon. All extraordinary achievements but we only need to look into our own back yard to learn about what our own explorers did. You get a sense of this when you travel the vastness of the outback. People like Burke and Wills who in 1860 led an expedition of nineteen men with the intention of crossing Australia from Melbourne in the South, to the Gulf of Carpentaria in the North (near Darwin), a distance of around 3,250 kilometres. That's a little short of the distance we travelled on the back of the semi from Port Headland in WA to Mt Isa in Queensland. At that time most of the inland of Australia had not been explored by non-indigenous people and was completely unknown to the European settlers. The south-north leg was successfully completed but both Burke and Wills died on the return journey. Only one man, an Irish soldier named John King, crossed the continent with the expedition and returned alive to Melbourne. One survived out of nineteen; that is not a good survival rate. There were other people like John Stuart who led the first successful expedition to traverse the Australian mainland from south to north and return, and the first to do so from a starting point in South Australia. His experience and the care he showed for his team ensured he never lost a man, despite the harshness of the country he encountered. When you travel around like we did, you get a deep appreciation of just what these fellas did under terribly harsh circumstances.

As I mentioned earlier, in the summer time in Australia the temperatures regularly go well over 40 degrees Celsius (104F) and you won't last long without water in the outback. The Australian outback has claimed many lives and some of these need not have happened if proper precautions had been taken. Perhaps in our own romantic way we saw ourselves as explorers conquering the vastness of the great Australian outback. Stories about Burke and Wills and Stuart resonated with me and we crossed some of the same country in somewhat different circumstances, but they were still challenging. You can imagine sitting on the back of a semi-trailer travelling thousands of kilometres across the desert and thinking we were in heaven.

I did a little research on what some Australians have done in terms of exploration. This came about because when I had the bar in Singapore you will recall that I was the Quizmaster and had to come up with the questions and answers. Many of our patrons were Australians and New Zealanders so naturally enough some of the questions centred around them. This is how I learnt what some Aussie explorers had achieved. There are many examples and I used them for my trivia questions. It never ceased to amaze me that some people would get them right. Examples were, "Who was the first person to fly solo from the USA to Australia?" Answer - Charles Kingsford Smith. "Who was the first person to fly a helicopter solo around the world?" Answer - Dick Smith. There were many others questions that came up and the trivia became in part at least, a history and geography lesson. Other useful information I learnt from my trivia was that John Muir was the first person to walk across our vast continent solo and Greg Mortimer was the first Australian to climb Mt Everest, K2 and Mt Vinson (Mt Vinson is the highest peak in Antarctica). Another regular question I had and one of my favourites was to name the highest peaks on the seven continents? Astoundingly, people used to get some of these right and it was just extraordinary how much knowledge some people have. There was Douglas Mawson who was the first to reach the South magnetic pole and I had read a book about that. What an incredible man he was and very few Australians know about him but he was one of the world's great explorers. I think that Australians and New Zealanders have a bit of explorer DNA in them and maybe that is a throwback to the early pioneering days and the exploits of men like Burke and Wills and Stuart.

What is also very interesting about this harsh country is that of the top ten deadliest snakes in the world, seven are found in Australia. The most poisonous snake in the world is the Australian inland taipan and it is said to have enough toxin to kill over 100 people. Following on from the taipan, is the common brown snake which is considered the second most toxic snake in the world. Then there is the costal taipan (a different one, found more on the costal fringe). The tiger snake kills more people in Australia than any other snake. Of course we mustn't forget to mention the deadly death adder who can finish you off pretty quickly if it has a mind to. That's just five, there are plenty more. What about Australia's deadliest spider; there are a handful? The Sydney funnel web spider is thought by some experts to be the deadliest spider in the world and there are others. Earlier I talked about how the red back spider that hung around the bush dunnies was very dangerous. These are the Australians that you don't want to meet. Nor do you want to meet the Great White shark and for that matter any of the other sharks that inhabit our costal shoreline and if you think coming inland alleviates the danger, then you have the massive and very dangerous crocodiles. I haven't yet mentioned the box jelly fish and it could be the worse of all. So I can see what the author of that book I mentioned was thinking when he said that white people were not meant to live in Australia.

New Zealand was a different experience. Interestingly enough, there are no snakes in NZ. We went from temperatures of up to 40+ down to below freezing when we hit the bottom part of the South Island of New Zealand. In NZ we mostly stayed at youth hostels and met a lot of what we now call backpackers from all parts of the world. Many of them were attractive young women but the age of promiscuity had not really taken off yet so sex was not readily available. It would not have been to me anyway but I was improving dramatically socially and I found once I left home that people actually liked me and that I was not as bad as I thought that I was. I found out that I was not the no-hoper that I had been led to believe I was and I gained a bit of confidence. There were some very rugged landscapes in NZ but of a different nature to the outback. Milford Sound and the great Southern Alps are truly a sight to be behold. We actually flew around Mt Cook in the middle of winter in a small plane with skis on it and landed on it. You felt like you could put your hand out and touch the snow on the side of the mountain. I don't think I have ever, before or since, experienced anything so beautiful. Coming from the land like I did, I just couldn't believe the farming country that I saw on the Canterbury Plains could look so good. It seemed to me that they never had droughts in this part of the world and everything looked so orderly. I thought they only had hedge fences in good old England but I saw plenty in NZ (any many other places since). The contrast to Australia was intriguing and I am pleased that Stewart and I did what we did. I'm also pleased with the way we did it but would not advise young people these days to hitch hike. It is too dangerous and there are many stories about how hikers come to a sad end at the hands of people that have picked them up. The one that most readily comes to my mind is the case of the serial killer Ivan Milat who was convicted of the murders of seven hitchhikers in what became known as the backpacker murders. The bodies of seven missing young people aged 19 to 22 were discovered partly buried in the Belanglo State Forest, south west of the New South Wales town of Berrima. Five of the victims were foreign backpackers visiting Australia (three German, two British), and two were Australian travellers from Melbourne. This happened in the late 80s and early 90s. Stewart and I passed by this place after we left Liverpool en-route to Albury on the NSW-Victorian border in 1965.

For me at this stage, there was still no indications outwardly of any signs of mental illness. I had definitely improved from my late teenage years. I was now 22 years of age. After NZ, I came back to Tara and started working for Dad -

again. The relationship with my parents was better and they enjoyed my stories about where I had been and what I had done. Mum's abuse more or less had subsided and it was gratifying that we got on better, although still far from perfect. There was a very unfortunate incident at the local hotel/motel in Tara one day. This happened early on in the piece before my illness, so it must have been shortly after I came back from NZ. John and I had been drinking for most of the day at the local horse race track and ended up back at the Tara Hotel and Motel. John had an argument with a couple of working people at the pub and they went out the back to sort it out. One of the cockies came over to me and told me that John was outside and I better go out and see what was going on. The upshot of it was that I intervened to try to stop the fight and ended up having to fight this bloke. I think I was getting the better of him and his mates got involved. I understand in total that there were four of them and they gave me a terrible beating. I do recall being held up against a car with one on each arm and another flogging me. I don't know what happened to John. I also remember being kicked in the head while on the ground. The cocky took us home and Mum flew into a rage. She got stuck into John (rightly so) and kept telling us that we boys gave her so much trouble and grief. I was the one that was badly injured and I did not do anything to provoke it. I simply came to my brother's rescue to stop a fight. There was no aggression on part. They took me to the Dalby Hospital and found that I had three fractures to the jaw; two on either side of the mandible and one in the maxilla. My face was blown up like a balloon and very painful. I was transported to the Royal Brisbane Hospital in Brisbane and had my jaw reset and wired. They had a pair of pliers on the bedside table in case I started vomiting and they had to undo the wire in an emergency. There is absolutely no doubt that I could easily have been killed. As it was, it was an assault with GBH (grievous bodily harm). The local police did nothing and I don't really know why. I think it was generally felt that John started it and we had been drinking heavily. The bashing had a serious psychological effect on me and contributed to my future bad behaviour when I went back to NZ. It left an indelible mark on me and I think this might have been my way of fighting back. I needed a gut full of booze first though! Whether or not it contributed to my mental illness, which was just around the corner, I don't know. I have never thought that it did but maybe there is a connection. It's an interesting thought and who knows. Interestingly enough though I spoke with John about this incident many years later and he had a completely different version of it, portraying me as the instigator of the fight. He has no recollection that we were ever at the race track and he feels that it happened because of my mental state. However this all happened before my mental illness surfaced and I'm fairly confident that my side of the story is the right one. He does have this propensity to see and believe things that in some instances, are just not true. Nevertheless, he's a good man who has had a hard life himself.

About this time, I experienced a bad case of bullying against me in my workplace. I believe that it would have been before I got the beating of my life in that Tara brawl whilst working at my parent's property at Tara. This incident therefore must have been before the mental illness surfaced, so I would estimate it to be in late 1966 or early 1967. I started a job as a Jackaroo on a station called 'Victoria Downs' out at Morven on the way to Charleville in Western Queensland. Victoria Downs was a stud merino property and about 30,000 acres. They had magnificent stud rams there and were well known in the merino stud community. It was a tough job. We had breakfast at 6.30am every day and before breakfast we two Jackaroos had to milk the cows, cut the sheep up and get the horses in. After breakfast on most days we would have a packed lunch and go mustering all day. It was always dark by the time we finished work. Because we were Jackaroos we had to clean up and dress properly for dinner. We ate with the boss and his family, which is something the ordinary station hands would never do. As always hard work never bothered me but the Overseer of the property took a dislike to me. He made the mistake of starting to bully me badly and it became the norm with him and his specialty was humiliating me in front of others. Eventually I called him out on it. I wanted to settle it, out the back so to speak, but he wouldn't be party to that. Perhaps he was showing better judgement than me. Because of this I more or less had to leave. It was a pity because I loved working with sheep and being around real quality livestock. I could have learnt a lot at Victoria Downs but it wasn't to be. I ended up just simply catching the mail truck into town and made my way down to Tara and started work for Dad again.

My life at this period in time centred around working at home and doing some shearing for some of the local cockies. Mum and Dad would regularly go to the agriculture shows in the area and I would look after the property whilst they were doing that. I can't be sure if they had racehorses at this time, but I think they did. I had no problem being on my own and was always comfortable when I had dogs around me and work to do. Everywhere Dad went he would always wear a big Texan style Stetson cowboy hat so you couldn't miss him; a bit like Bob Katter does. I did quite a few shearing sheds in the district but I did not have any plan for what I was eventually going to do. Of course I helped Dad with his shearing and spent countless hours on that tractor, not the John Deere that we had at Capella but it was a Chamberlain this time. Even though Dad never paid me for my work, it is fair to point out that he never asked me to come home either. John would come home to Tara from time to time, as too would the girls. John had lost favour completely with Mum and Dad and he was no longer viewed as the squatter's son. John is very different to me. He was much more like Mum and I more like Dad. He was one of these ready-fire-aim men. He'd do things impulsively without thinking it through. Like I have told you, he'd load the chamber and I'd fire the bullet. John has had a hard time of it himself and I have urged him to write an autobiography. It was not very long after this period that he had a very bitter falling out with Mum and Dad, as well as with his sister Patricia. I don't know the details but he left and to this day he carries grudges. I don't know if they are without foundations or not, however I did witness some appalling behaviour towards him and his family by Mum and the two girls later. That much is true at least.

The black dog is now just around the corner and I am about to go into the most despairing, inconsolable and onerous period of my life.

Chapter Five: The Days of Darkness
1967 - 1971

In 1967 - Ronald Ryan became the last man hanged in Australia. Prime Minister Harold Holt disappeared while swimming in heavy surf at Cheviot Beach. The Six-Day War ended with Israel occupying Sinai Peninsula, Golan Heights, Gaza Strip and The West Bank. Dr. Christiaan N. Barnard and team of South African surgeons performed the World's first successful human heart transplant. The patient died 18 days later. The movies released in 1967 included *The Graduate, Bonnie and Clyde, Guess Who's Coming to Dinner, In the Heat of the Night* and *Cool Hand Luke*. Notable death included those of Ernesto "Che" Guevara, Spencer Tracy, Woody Guthrie, Alice B. Toklas and John Coltrane.

In 1968 - Dr Martin Luther King and Robert Kennedy were assassinated. John Gorton was sworn in as Prime Minister of Australia after the disappearance of Harold Holt. British comedian Tony Hancock committed suicide in his Sydney hotel room. American soldiers massacred 347 civilians at My Lai. Czechoslovakia was invaded by Russians and the Warsaw Pact was forced to crush liberal regime. Amniocentesis was developed. The movies released in 1968 included *2001: A Space Odyssey, Romeo and Juliet, Funny Girl, The Lion in Winter,* and *Oliver*. Other Notable deaths included those of John Steinbeck, Marcel Duchamp, Helen Keller and Upton Sinclair.

In 1969 - Richard Nixon succeeded Lyndon Baines Johnson (LBJ) as the 37th President of the United States of America. The Boeing 747 made its maiden flight. Midnight Cowboy, an X-rated, Oscar-winning John Schlesinger film, was released. The lunar module Eagle landed on the lunar surface. An estimated 500 million people worldwide watched in awe as Neil Armstrong took his historic first steps on the Moon, the largest television audience for a live broadcast at that time. Apollo 11 astronauts—Neil A. Armstrong and Edwin E. Aldrin, Jr, took first walk on the Moon on 20 July. Lieutenant William Calley was charged with 6 counts of premeditated murder, for the 1968 My Lai Massacre deaths of

109 Vietnamese civilians in My Lai, Vietnam. The movies released included *Midnight Cowboy, Butch Cassidy and the Sundance Kid, The Wild Bunch, Easy Rider* and *Anne of the Thousand Days*. Notable deaths include those of Dwight David Eisenhower and Joseph P. Kennedy.

In 1970 - IBM gave the world the floppy disc. Concorde made its 1st supersonic flight (700 MPH/1,127 KPH). Apollo 13 announced "Houston, we've got a problem!" as Beech-built oxygen tank exploded en-route to Moon. Pope Paul VI visited Australia. Earthquake killed more than 50,000 in Peru. Bar codes (computer-scanned binary signal code) were introduced for retail and industrial use in England. Lithium was approved by the FDA for the treatment of manic-depression. Jimi Hendrix and Janis Joplin both died of drug-related deaths at age 27. *Midnight Cowboy* wins the Best Picture Oscar, the first and only time an X-rated movie received the honour. The movies *M*A*S*H, Patton, Love Story*, and *Airport* were released. Notable deaths included those of Jimi Hendrix, Janis Joplin and Sonny Liston.

In 1971 - Mao Zedong invited the US ping-pong team to visit Beijing. Joe Frazier beat Muhammad Ali in 15 rounds and retained heavyweight boxing title at Madison Square Garden. Don McLean's 8 plus minute version of "American Pie" was released. Jim Morrison died in Paris at age 27. Intel introduced the microprocessor. Mariner IX, orbited Mars, taking revealing pictures of the planet's surface. The movies released in 1971 included *A Clockwork Orange, The French Connection, The Last Picture Show, Fiddler on the Roof* and *McCabe and Mrs Mille*. Notable deaths included those of J.C. Penney and Igor Stravinsky. The population of the world was 3.3783 billion.

From mid 1967 on until about late 1971, it all gets a bit nebulous for me and I cannot remember exact times or details. In some instances, I'm not even able to accurately detail incidents as they actually happened. Normally I have a very good memory; however during this time I have had to reply on accounts for some of the information from people that were about at that time. I am referring to the period of time from mid 1967 until 1971 and I refer to that period as, 'The Days of Darkness' period. Dates that I can confirm help me to some degree sort out some of the missing time frames in this part of my life.

6/5/65 - My 21st birthday - I was at home at this time and had not yet started my travels. I started travelling around Australia and NZ in December 1965 and was back before my cousin's wedding; so nearly all of the travelling was in 1966.

21/5/67 - My cousin's Margaret McCosker's wedding
The depression manifested itself not long before going to this wedding. It seems that I got hit with it in the early part of 1967. The suicide incident occurred at this time so I was critically depressed at this point in time but still had not seen anybody about it.

20/7/69 - The landing on the moon; I was definitely working as a night auditor in Christchurch at this time because we were all watching it on TV at the hotel I was working at.

1/3/72 - I left my family's home permanently. This is an approximate date only.

October 1972 - I started my Nursing Diploma in Sydney

An analysis of these dates indicates that my hospitalisations occurred between the second half of 1967 and sometime in 1971 - that's about 4 years. Four years of hell is the best way to describe it.

I feel that the first real indication of mental illness were the psychosomatic symptoms that I exhibited when I saw the doctor in Rockhampton in the early 60s when I was about 16 or 17. I have mentioned how disappointing it was that we did not take advantage of that and maybe help stem the flow of what was to come. There was another incident where there was further evidence of mental illness around about 1965, maybe a bit later.

Mum and Dad went on one of their regular show excursions. It never bothered me. I actually liked being on my own and I loved the land. However on this occasion, it hit me the first night they had left and I can only describe it as a type of panic attack. I was about 21 now. I developed a fear of being alone in the dark. I was fine in the daytime but at night I went into a state of panic and this had never happened before. I had to keep the lights on and sleep was out of the question. I even got the dogs into the house to keep me company. This came out of the left field completely. It got so bad that I had to put my tail between my legs and go to my parents. I really had no one else I could turn to and to say that Dad was very disappointed with me is an understatement. Here he had a son he couldn't even leave on the property anymore, alone for a week or so. Mum was more understanding and put it down to 'Max doesn't like to be alone; he gets lonely'. Of course it wasn't that at all but at the time we didn't act on it. Another opportunity was lost but no one is blame for that, least of all Mum. Years later during psychotherapy it came to light that it may have been associated with my near drowning incident when I was a toddler. It also came out that it might have been related to being locked up in the cages when we were misbehaving at Narine. Who knows, but the medical people thought that there may be a connection. For many years after that I had trouble staying alone but only at night time. In fact I still have it but it has to be in a situation where I am really on my own. It would not for example happen if I was staying in a hotel on my own. My understanding of this phobia, which is called achluophobia, is that it is not the darkness we fear, but rather we fear possible dangers that are hidden by the dark. There is a suggestion by some psychoanalysts that the fear that I am describing is a manifestation of a separation disorder. That could make some sense because it never happens if I am with someone or even have access to someone. It is like being locked in with no escape. In any event Dad was really peeved about it and it meant that if they wanted to go somewhere, they have to make other arrangements and that would cost money. Even today, as much as I love the land, I doubt that I could stay on a farm by myself.

You see how childhood trauma can effect you for the rest of your life.

I have an apartment on the Gold Coast and found that I had difficulty sleeping in the bedroom. I have these nightmares that I was being stared at by others (people) whilst I am asleep. In my sleep I'll be dreaming that there was someone else in the room staring at me. I'd see an object like a coat hanging on the back of the door and in my sleep induced state, that coat would take the shape of a human being and he/she was staring at me. Sometimes I would lash out at the figure or figures and on more than one occasion found myself out of the bed when I woke up. One time I banged my fist so hard when I punched the wall, thinking I was punching the figure, I thought I had broken my knuckles. A number of times I would swipe everything off the bed side table swinging at the offender/s. I'd scream at them to come and face me, man to man but these figures were never identifiable but they were always human. I'd be screaming, "Come on you f****** scumbag, I'm fed up with this". Then I would wake and realise I had this bad dream again. I suppose I have learnt to live with it but would love to have a deeper understanding of it. In fact I'd like to have a deeper understanding of a lot of other things as well but in my psychotherapy sessions, I have never been able to find out. I found that if I moved the bed into the lounge room and could see my escape route it was a lot better. I needed an escape route that I could see, even in the dark. This has never really left me and I do my best to avoid situations where I am left in dark places on my own.

Pauline and her friend Judy came over from Christchurch in early 1967 and we got a flat in Victoria Street, Manly, in Sydney. Both the girls got jobs and I worked at my old place 'The Can'. I picked up the glasses initially and then graduated to serving drinks. It was an even busier place than before. I think that Max Merritt and the Meteors were still playing at the time and their most popular song was 'Mr Tambourine Man'. I just continued doing what I had done before we left to hitch hike around Australia. Pauline and I had a fight one night and she said that she could never live with me because I could kill her. She said that she was going to go home and was leaving the next day. This had an immediate and very profound effect on me. It was a defining moment. It totally gutted me and the sense of rejection and abandonment was overwhelming. It was too much for me to bear at the time and I felt she had no reason to say these things. I never touched her and never threatened to and never would. The die was now cast for me. This was the catalyst that triggered the mental illness and bought it to the surface. Hitherto I had been fine, seemingly normal if you like. I think I saw Pauline's rejection of me in such a brutal way as the same sort of betrayal as I had experienced by being sent to boarding school at 5 years of age. In any event the black dog (depression) surfaced almost immediately after that and I can tell you I was in for some rough times ahead.

It did not make any difference that she recanted the next day and told me that she could never leave me and was very sorry for saying what she had said; but it was too late, the damage had been done. The trust had been broken and it had hit a really raw nerve with me. Let's be clear that this in no way infers that Pauline was responsible for my mental illness. The damage had been done long before I had ever met Pauline but it needed a catalyst to trigger it. It is very clear to me now that my teachers and parents played a major part in my developing mental illness. I very much believe that my illness was brought about by environmental causes. I believe that I would have been better off if I had been brought up in an orphanage; I really mean that. It is clear that I could not handle abandonment and all I wanted to do now was to get away from Pauline. I felt a terrible sense of betrayal. She had, in my weakened psychological state, hurt me too much with the threat to leave. I felt that she had betrayed me just like my parents and teachers had done. It seemed to me that no one could be trusted. Her wholehearted and sincere apologies could not erase the betrayal I felt. I truly loved this girl and acknowledge that it was my damaged personality that did not know how to deal with it, rather than anything that Pauline had done. It is just another glaring paradox; maybe a blessing in disguise, and I will explain that later.

Shortly thereafter the depression was starting to take a grip on me and I can't describe the level of melancholy and sorrow that overcame me. It was to get worse. I couldn't function properly but it was not apparent to anybody else, except Pauline and Judy. I was just seen as an introverted quiet sort of bloke and nobody picked up that I was suffering from severe depression. One night at the Can the boss spotted that I was crying and asked me what was wrong. This was not long after the incident with Pauline. I told him that the chlorine in the swimming pool had irritated my eyes and made them 'watery'. He believed me and I kept going. That is another thing that is worthwhile mentioning. You become very good at covering up your illness and because you can't actually see diseases of the mind, you can get away with it. Just look at how many of these killers behave. They are so hard to catch because they appear to be so normal. You become in essence quite a good actor. Where I came from in redneck Catholic right wing rural conservative territory it was considered poor form for anyone to get depressed, especially men. The prevailing thinking at the time was that if you were in this position it was time to 'pull your socks up' and get on with it'. I know because that is basically what the Doctor in Rockhampton told me to do in 1961. Consequently the best strategy (or so I thought) was to keep it to myself and hope that it would blow over.

Sometime soon after this rejection incident, we went to Emerald in Queensland for my cousin's Margaret McCosker's wedding on 21/5/67. I had just now turned 23, so I can be very clear as to when the illness surfaced. As I have told you we stayed at my Uncle's property Cullin-la-Ringo near Emerald. You know, the place where I shot Uncle Lionel's pet emu. I have also told you about the .45 Colt incident overlooking the cemetery. This is when that happened. I had the pistol in my hand, loaded, cocked and seriously contemplated suicide. I could not see how I could live like this any longer and I had the means to end it immediately, in my hand. All I had to do was put the gun to my temple or underneath my chin and pull the trigger and my unhappiness and melancholy would go away forever. Major depression takes away all your capabilities to feel better, to have your good moments; there aren't any. Pauline knew that I was very different now but put it down to the fight that we had and thought that it was a transient thing. I never told her how badly I was feeling. I did not know how to terminate the relationship. Pauline was a part clone of my mother; beautiful, a religious bigot, assertive, dogmatic and very influenced by the Catholic Church. I think now that I was sub-consciously attracted to somebody just like my own mother, who I had very good feelings for pre-adolescence but inherently negative feelings towards thereafter. Wow, that's a bit of a twister and a bit hard to fathom. It's hard to fathom that I would want to marry somebody like my mother after all the abuse I had endured from her but I think there is merit in this suggestion. It may be that subconsciously I felt trapped and needed to find a way out of it and did not have the necessary assertive skills to terminate it in a normal manner. Maybe the mental illness was part of that, a type of defensive mechanism if you like. I didn't pull the trigger (obviously) and Pauline and Judy went back to NZ and I went home to Tara. Pauline and I made arrangements that I would come over and live in Christchurch and we would get married, all things being equal. This is exactly what would have happened I believe, if she had not have told me that night that she was going to leave me. Was it a blessing in disguise? Maybe it was. It is very difficult for me to try and explain this to you. It is ever so hard to articulate how I felt.

I know that it may appear to be contradictory at times; it probably is. On the one hand I loved this girl and wanted to marry her. On the other hand, I was fearful that I would be marrying a woman that dominated me and ended up treating me just like my mother had done. It that were true, then the depression, as bad as it was, could have been a defence mechanism protecting me. That's just a theory but it seems to make a bit of sense. I must say if it were a subconscious defence mechanism, that it is a hell of a way to go about protecting yourself. I think that I learnt my father's passive characteristics and traits and never learnt to be assertive. Perhaps there is a genetic connection there? Dad believed in peace at any price and would never get involved in an argument. That is one of the reasons why people liked him so much. He just did not know how to be assertive and was just a peace loving man. I do wonder if I was more assertive with Pauline if I could have sorted it out. The other consideration is that if I was a more assertive character, perhaps she would never have fallen in love with me in the first place. It all gets a bit complicated doesn't it?

These days I have a partner who is a lot like my father. She does not like confrontation of any sort and rejects aggressiveness and anger out of hand. We have what you would call a steady good relationship and it works. Marrying someone like Mum was a very big mistake for me but being with somebody like my father is the best thing I have ever done; it works. There has to be a lesson here. Clearly I am not aggressive with people in general but I have learnt to be assertive and have a clear division between being aggressive and being assertive. I found when I was in the Police I had no problem being assertive but generally I'd take the softly, softly approach with criminals in the first instance at least. I believed then, and I still do, that the best detectives that I worked with were the ones that took this approach. I think it is a basic human need to want to be treated decently and to be seen as just that, a human being with dignity.

The first time I went to hospital would have been shortly after we came back from the wedding at Emerald in 1967 and Pauline and Judy went home to NZ. My parent's property was a relatively small property of about two to three thousand acres but very good farming land. They said they wanted a place 'for the boys' but also where Mum could continue with her equestrian work. Actually I think the latter was much more the case. She got into dressage and even bred yearlings for the horse sales in Brisbane. I always found my way back home after my travelling and would continue to work for nothing when I was there. At times I would go shearing in the Tara district. I was doing a shed for a local shearing contractor. I had just finished one shed and started another. I was shearing about 120 a day and they were really tough sheep so that wasn't too bad but I was doing it under extreme mental pressure. The other shearers and the rest of the team just saw me as an introverted quiet bloke who didn't talk much, in fact didn't talk at all. There was apparently no outward sign of the turmoil I was going through otherwise I suppose it would have been mentioned. There were no tears and outwardly I could do my work satisfactorily. We were shearing these tough merino sheep, as they always are in that part of the world. I knew that I had to get medical attention urgently or else I might either go mad (people do you know), or commit suicide, out of desperation. I also knew that it was pointless to take it up with my parents. Mum probably would have wanted me to go and see the local parish priest and Dad just would not have been able to get his head around it. Somehow I had the good sense to realise that suicide was not the answer and that I must go and seek specialist help quickly. So, I concocted this story for the shearing contractor to get out of it. I was aware of the very negative stigma that was associated with mental illness at the time and I did not want anybody to know that this was the problem. Even today there is stigma towards people with mental illness although it was not as bad as it was in the 60s, particularly out in the conservative rural areas of Australia. You only have to listen to one of the remarks made by our former Prime Minister, Tony Abbott when he was talking about a former liberal NSW politician who had a breakdown and suffered very badly from depression.

In any event, I told the shearing contractor that my shoulder was giving me a lot of pain when we were shearing the rams. It was not of course but I told him that. I told him that I thought that my shoulder might improve once we got into the normal sheep; so I hadn't mentioned it. Then I said to him I couldn't shear anymore; the pain was unbearable and even started to drag my arm feigning injury. It was true that I was suffering unbearable pain, but I lied about the source of the pain. I had the scar from the putti platt shoulder operation which I had in 1963, so it was a plausible story. Of course he was pissed off and angry about it. To lose a shearer in the middle of the shed caused him a lot of grief but there was not much he could do. He had to let me go and I went into town and saw the local doctor in Tara, who was a friend of Mum's. Once I started talking about it to another human being, I completely broke down in his surgery. I asked him to keep it to himself as I was now an adult and could rely upon his professional confidentiality. Actually he was a good bloke and he knew I was in big trouble. He got on the phone straight away and rang a Psychiatrist at a Brisbane Hospital that he knew from his internship days. He arranged for me to go the Psychiatric Unit (called Lowson House) at the Brisbane General Hospital and see a Dr Proctor. He gave me a sedative to get through the night and I stayed at the local hotel. Another reason I never told my parents was because they were so anti anything of a psychiatric nature. I got a ride from Tara with the local transport company to Brisbane. It is about 300 kilometres and I don't think I spoke a word to the driver the whole way. When I got to Brisbane I went and saw Dr Proctor at Lowson House. He interviewed me and told me that I would have to be admitted immediately. He told me that I was suffering from severe depression but he did not think that I was suicidal. He also did not thing there were any indications at this early stage of the investigation of psychotic illnesses. Because of this, I was put into a standard psychiatric ward with freedom within the rules, and not restrained in any way. He told me that he would arrange for me to have a 'needle' the next day that would probably make me feel better. Of course, I had no idea what he was referring to when he talked about a needle. Now I was entering a new world; the world of the mentally ill.

I would describe the depression as the action of accusing myself, stemming from feelings of guilt. Remember I have told you that all my life I was made to feel guilty by the Catholic clergy and by my religiously bigoted mother. The depression was further characterised by a severe lack of self-esteem and serious self-accusation. These early formative years collectively made me feel guilty of things that I never should have been. I look back and realise that I was made to feel guilty just for being alive. There is no doubt that the Catholic Church used to rule by fear and put the guilt complex on you, and therefore it is not surprising that devout Catholic parents would do the same. In that sense they are also victims also of the Catholic Church intransigence. You can imagine how impressionable a young five-year old child would be. You would believe that whatever they told you were true. Later in life, my mother in general conversations with people, would tell them that she hoped that one day I would 'come good'. Now of course I understand that I was never bad. I just had these religious bigots telling me I was and I believed it. I think I told you that even in our twenties, Mum used to refer to us as her 'useless bloody boys'. I told you about those terrible things that John and I did as little boys. I don't remember what the punishment was but I can well imagine that it was rammed into us what terrible boys we were and God would punish us. The interesting question is why were we like this in the first place and I don't have the answer. Why on earth would two little boys aged three and four burn their father's wheat crop? What could possibly motivate them to do that? I have mentioned how the nuns used to scream at me from age five onwards for not eating my food and would give me the cane for the slightest infractions. I suppose a synopsis of this is that the Catholic Church creates an environment of fear and uses threats and fear as a weapon to get people to conform. When you don't, according to them, the consequences can be catastrophic like burning in hell for eternity. Eternity! My God, that's a terrible threat to have hanging over a 5-year old child. No wonder so many of we boys grew up having a severe guilt complex. You have to question who these neanderthal people really were and what was wrong with them.

The next day I had 'the needle' and found out later it was an injection of the so called truth drug, sodium thiopental. This drug was meant to induce me to talk and give the medical staff a deeper insight into what might have been bothering me. Then they could work out a treatment program. With me, it worked a miracle (or so I thought). Of course, I don't know what I told them. I remember well the procedure, who did it but not the actual conversation. They seem to put you in a state of complete relaxation but not asleep. It is at this stage they'd ask the questions and you give the answers. Perhaps something that you have repressed into the sub-conscious will come out. I felt like a new person; just like that. The medical staff were happy with my progress and sent me home without any medication or follow up support. Whilst I was at the hospital I was happy. I felt safe and secure and could easily have become dependent upon it. It is easy for me to understand how people become institutionalised. I didn't have people yelling at me, I was being fed decent food three times a day and did not have to work like a dog. Anyway it was good at the hospital. The staff were really good and I reckoned that I could easily get used to being treated properly. That's the catch! Sooner or later you are going to have to leave and stand on your own two feet. The world can be a very threatening place to the mentally ill and it is easy to become dependant on the safe and secure environment of a hospital.

I could not believe it when I saw one of the wards men there; it was Ron Andrew. Remember the two travelling salesmen I told you about that were pretty good at Australian Rules Football in Emerald. He was working there and he sort of took me under his wing. He had access to all my medical notes and he reckoned that all I needed was some good sex and to get away from my mother. Ron reminds me now of the character R.P. McMurphy, played by Jack Nicholson in the movie, 'One Flew Over the Cuckoo's Nest'. He was giving me the same sort of advice which basically translated that the psychiatric ward was no place for me and that I should get out and have some fun. The major redeeming feature for me was that I showed no signs of psychosis. I saw a lot of Ron over the next couple of years and had a lot of admiration for him. He was a type of misfit, I suppose. His passions were women, physical fitness and body building. He had so much energy and fortunately for me, totally heterosexual. He once showed me a hole he had in his foreskin and he reckons that an indigenous lady in Cairns sunk her teeth into him. True or not I don't know, but I would not doubt it. This fella was full of life and lived for the day and did not worry about tomorrow. He got permission from the Doctors to take me out on Moreton Bay to do some fishing. Maybe you remember the scene in the movie when R.P. McMurphy took all the patients out fishing one day. Well, this was much the same but the big difference was that Ron had permission and I had only been in hospital a couple of weeks. He just felt that all I needed was some male heterosexual company and get out there and have some fun. He felt that I had been starved of human contact because of my rural social isolation and lack of parental intimacy. Most of all, he felt that I should get away from my mother who he pinpointed as the major source of my problems. He also thought that my father was a significant part of the problem because he was not a father protector. This was long before the movie came out but Ron was definitely an R.P. McMurphy character and I was a bit like the timid Billy Bibbit. Ron was telling me to do what McMurphy told Billy to do; go out and eat burger, drive Chevrolet and bang beaver. That's all you gotta do he said. Billy had major hang-ups with his mother so maybe Ron was a bit more perceptive than they thought he was. In the immediate years that followed I hung around with Ron a lot. He became a sort of older brother figure and mentor. He was rough around the edges and not a man to pick a fight with but he had a heart of gold and really cared about people. He moved to Auckland and in my dark years I actually stayed with him there for a while. He worked as a wards-man at the Auckland General Hospital and got me a job there, doing much the same thing. His outgoing personality, coupled with his natural charm, always meant that he had a beautiful woman with him. I lost touch with him after I came back to Australia around about mid 1971 and have not heard or seen of him since.

One interesting character, who was a friend of Ron's, was a fella named David Galbraith. David was a rampart homosexual, chain smoker, drug addict and an absolute drunk. He was very well known in NZ and was a bit of a celebrity. Anyone meeting David for the first time would probably have seen him as just another homeless drunk. He certainly looked and acted the part. But he was in fact one of NZ's top piano concerto players and to listen to him play was something to behold. If I am not mistaken he had played in Royal Albert Hall in London. He lived in reasonable circumstances and had a small apartment in Parnell, an inner suburb of Auckland. He never made any overtures of homosexuality towards me but used to boast that he had f***** quite a few Chief Petty Officers. He seemed to have had something for Navy blokes. One time David came to Christchurch and gave a concert in the Town Hall. He was given a standing ovation and the crowd was demanding more. His playing of Tchaikovsky 1812 overture and the piano concerto No 1 were something I will always remember. He invited me back to his hotel to meet with some of the orchestra and once he got on the booze, he became his usual arrogant and belligerent self. He upset one of the members of the orchestra who threatened to punch him. David responded by telling him that because he could not afford to damage his hands he would not fight him but assured him that with all things being equal, he would have no problem giving him a 'father of a hiding'. He would deliver these sorts of statements in his upper class English accent and that would irritate his antagonist even more. Later that night David went missing and no one could find him. He had collapsed on the outside fire escape stairs, completely drunk and not far from being in a coma. But I liked David and I gave him some insight into what I was going through. He was a very humanitarian person as you might reasonably expect from someone who could play music so beautifully. In his approach towards me he wanted me to see a gay Doctor friend of his who specialised in depression but I never did. I had grown to believe that they could not do anymore for me and just kept on the medication and battled on so to speak. I never felt my sexuality threatened in David's company and I regret, like I did with Ron, that I never kept in contact with him. One time years later, I make enquiries about him when I went to Auckland for the rugby and I was told that he had passed on. When I pushed as to what he died from the bloke telling me said that he didn't know, but thought that it would be either Aids, a drug overdose or cirrhosis of the liver, or a combination of all three. That sounds very much like my friend David Galbraith. I hope he rests in peace.

Back to Lowson House on my first admission there. After my discharge I went home and not surprisingly, I almost immediately had a relapse. This time it was worse, a lot worse. I could not eat, could not sleep and basically was sobbing most of the time. I now know that I should not have been sent back to the root cause of the problem. I also now knew that I was very ill and the future looked very bleak indeed. They admitted me again, this time into the locked ward, thinking that I may be suicidal. It was obvious that the injection was just a band aid solution. Initially Dr. Proctor was disappointed I was back but he quickly changed his attitude when he saw the state I was in. I was lying on the bed in the locked ward, in the foetal position, sobbing. I would say that this was the saddest day in my life; the day that I was readmitted to Lowson House the second time. I was in a ward with a lot of seriously disturbed people. I saw patients do things that you wouldn't see anywhere else. Adults throwing their food on the floor, urinating in the ward, throwing faeces about, that type of 'psychotic' behaviour. The ward was full of psychotics and I wondered how I came to be in this predicament. A couple of days later, Dr. Proctor got me out of the locked ward and put me in the general one that I was at before. The diagnosis was the same but this time they were calling it critical depression and thankfully again there was no evidence of psychotic illness, such as schizophrenia. They decided that the depression was so severe this time that they would have to give me a course of ECT (electro convulsive therapy). I think it was a course of six treatments. It started to work slowly for me but after a few treatments I started to feel better. I responded very well to it and I think I was in the hospital for about six to eight weeks. The only side effect I had from the ECT was temporary memory loss. They don't really know why ECT works but there are several theories. One theory indicates that the seizure activity that is induced causes an alteration of the chemical neurotransmitters which are the messenger transmitters in the brain. Another theory is that the induced seizures adjust the stress hormone regulation in the brain which may affect mood. In any event, it doesn't really matter how it works but rather that it did work and for me and that was a miracle (but nothing to do with God).

In my discussions with Dr. Proctor I don't know if I expressed any reservations about my going to NZ and getting married. I can't be sure if I felt trepidations about that whilst I was still at Lowson House or if it only hit me after I left to go to the airport. Finally the medical team realised that I should not go back home but should proceed with my plan to go to New Zealand and marry Pauline. I didn't understand at the time, nor did the medical people, that subconsciously I did not want to do that. I agreed to it and I recall catching the Qantas flight over the Tasman. I have gone through with you how my feelings for Pauline had changed but I still went. If I didn't express those feelings to the staff at Lowson House, I don't know why I didn't. If I did, I don't know why they would have let me go. I was like a man with no home, no family, no support, no job, no nothing; a complete unknown, going into a type of abyss and a total loser. We all made mistakes at this point. I should never have gone to NZ in the state that I was in, and it was very clear that going home was not an option either. What should have happened in hindsight, is that I should have been put into a half way house and got a part time job in Brisbane. My family as such should have been there for me and I could have continued on as an outpatient and went through some extended treatment. I can assure you that my 'family' were never there for me and did very little to help me though this period. Perhaps they felt that there was little they could do. The medical team should have realised that I was in no fit state to go to NZ and certainly I too should have realised it as well.

I think that the most relevant point that I can make here in an effort for you to better understand me, is that I do not recall my parents ever coming to the hospital on the three occasions I was a patient at Lowson House. Dad also never mentioned anything about it to me in the following years. He never came to see me at school and never showed any affection towards me. Yet in an extraordinary paradoxical and contradictory way, I loved him and felt that it was Mum that contributed at least in no small part to my mental illness, rather than my Dad. That may well be an unfair analysis and I one hundred percent acknowledge that. I do wonder sometimes if I am being grossly unfair to my mother but one thing we can be certain about is that Dad never abused me, never, and my mother did, badly, very badly.

Once I left the safe and secure environment of the hospital, I didn't know what to do. I cannot explain to you why I went to NZ under these circumstances only to suggest I had nowhere else to go. I couldn't go home and Pauline was the only person in the world that cared about me. Clearly going to New Zealand was a huge mistake on my part but at this stage of my life, I was incapable of making sound decisions as my judgement was seriously impaired. I should have spoken with a social worker and arranged for a suitable place to stay in Brisbane and found some part time work. This way I could have had the psychiatric support that I so desperately needed at that time. You have to realise that this is the 1960s and psychiatry was still in its infancy, relatively speaking. I just did not have the good sense to back out of going to NZ and I really didn't have any other options. I had to live somewhere so I went to be with Pauline in Christchurch. Any normal man would have been happy with Pauline, but I was not a normal man, far from it. In fact I didn't even consider myself a real man at this time. You must be able to see now the mistakes I am making and the poor decision processes. Keep in mind that I had no support base and found the world a terrible place to live in. It was an embarrassment for my family for me to be in a psychiatric ward and it was all kept very hush, hush like I had committed some devious crime and was a serious criminal.

The plane trip to Christchurch was unbelievably despairing. I almost cry when I think about it, even now. I was terrified. I was quietly sobbing for the entire three hour journey. I was back to square one within the space of a couple of hours. We are all wise in hindsight and there are a lot of ifs and buts in our lives. You have to take it and deal the hand that you have been served. Unfortunately the hand dealt to me was a very poor one. I don't know how much of this illness was due to my own weaknesses but I felt that I was almost worthless at this time. To meet me now, it would be almost incomprehensible to believe that I was once like this. But I was a total loser and a complete failure at this point and could not see that I was going to get out of it. As I have said before, I felt that I had two options only. One, commit suicide or two, get institutionalised. Neither of them were very appealing but I felt that I could never be normal again. It was at this stage that I could quite easily have become institutionalised and got myself admitted permanently to a mental hospital. The outside world to me was one of betrayal, rejection, abandonment, abuse, hostile and threatening. I would have been much better within the walls of an institution where these things did not occur. Yes, even the mental hospitals of the 60s would have been better for me than being in normal society. Terrible thing to admit to, isn't it?

The reaction I experienced from my second discharge from Lowson House was immediate on my discharge. Pauline and her wonderful family came to pick me and I stayed with them. I tried to hide my melancholy but I couldn't hide it anymore. Pauline knew that I had just come out of hospital but no doubt expected that I would be back to my normal self. They were not wealthy people and they put me in a caravan in the back yard. The very first night I completely broke down. This time I even got locked jaw, couldn't speak, sobbing uncontrollably. It must have been terrifying for Pauline and her family as I had not gone into the finer details with her about my hospitalisation; another mistake on my part. They took me to their local Doctor the following morning. Pauline's parents must have been thinking what on earth had their daughter bought home. He told Pauline's mother "You are surely not going to let your daughter marry this bloke are you?" This was the beginning of my life taking prescribed medication for depression, OCD and anxiety. Lowson House did not prescribe any medication for me and I feel that they should have done. It was around this time that I developed obsessional neurosis and chronic anxiety. I'm sure that you would not want your daughter to marry such a man — that is completely understandable. The obsessional neurosis usually took the form of unwanted unpleasant thoughts of violence and sexual deviancy and these in turn created the anxiety. It was deeply distressing for me. The more I tried to ignore them, the more I couldn't. So I had the trifecta — depression, obsessional neurosis and anxiety. Imagine how awful this would have been for Pauline and her family. Here she would have been talking me up and getting so excited about my coming to New Zealand. She would have been telling people what a great bloke I was and how she could not wait to introduce me to them. God, what a mess I made of it. Somehow I survived this period. I saw different Psychiatrists in Christchurch. I started work as a service station attendant, shared a house with some fellas who I don't even remember and got by on a day to day basis. The medication allowed me to function (sort of) and showed I could hold down a job and live seemingly normally in the community. The medication was helping me survive; that is the best way to put it. It was 'softening the blow' in the severity of the depression but not ending the suffering. I would say that I was depressed all the time, but not critically and at times, not even severely, but always depressed to some degree.

I couldn't make New Zealand work for me and eventually got the courage to break it off with Pauline. I have never seen nor heard from her since, but she was a great girl. I lost everything but most of all I lost any sense of purpose and self worth. I considered myself worthless and this is not the first time that I have said that. My understanding of a defence mechanism is that it is a mental process initiated unconsciously to avoid experiencing conflict or anxiety. The key word in the sentence is unconsciously. There are a number that I can recall from my nursing days during our psychiatric lectures. Denial, regression, acting out, dissociation, compartmentalisation, repression, displacement, rationalisation, sublimation, compensation and assertiveness are the ones that come to mind. In my case I know that I lacked assertiveness; just as my father did. My mother had no in-between and would explode at the 'drop of a hat' rather than try to be constructively assertive. If you can imagine, when you went to a Catholic boarding school in the late 1940s at a very early age, without any parental support, you learnt at a very early age, it was very unwise to take an assertive approach. I think with Pauline I was seriously lacking assertiveness. If I had a reasonable level of assertiveness I would have discussed my concerns with her and maybe we would have found a solution. I needed to find a way out of the relationship and did not have the interpersonal relationship skills to deal with it in a rational and assertive manner. Put simply, I just did not know how to do it. I wonder if this is a hint that there may be a genetic and/or behavioural connection to Dad's non-assertive approach? I think likely. Much of me was still like the boy child that I was at school and I never learnt how to communicate effectively and have adult relationships. They say don't they, that men often marry a girl like their mother and girls marry men like their father. Anyway Pauline and I were finished and I hope that she found a normal man and led a happy and fruitful life. I still think about her and the good times we had and how things could have been different. She was a very beautiful girl that's for sure. There's no doubt that she and her family were the big winner in our relationship breakup. I stayed on and off in Christchurch up until 1971 when I returned to Australia permanently. I'd actually love to see Pauline again just to let her see that in the end, I turned out to be an ok man and lead a reasonably successful life. If Pauline had not acted as the trigger with threatening to leave me, it would have been someone else later on. Perhaps if you look at it this way, it may have been a blessing in disguise.

I made my way back to Australia, and ironically I always seemed to end up going home. I know that I had another stint at Lowson House and went through the ECT program again but I can't remember when, nor the circumstances. The Psychiatrists in Christchurch had me on massive doses of anti-depressants and sleeping tablets. They tried to sort me out but we just couldn't get past the post. They more or less admitted that. I think the

ECT I had at Lowson House took me from a critical stage to a medium stage and the truth is that you can function when you are not in the critical stage. During all this time I never received any welfare benefits and managed to earn my own living. For years I used to take two Mandies (Mandrax) every night just to sleep. When I went on a binge, I'd feel good with the combination of Mandies and booze. I'd also go a bit crazy. I recall that during this period I would have these great dreams and life was so good when you were dreaming. When I woke up I would feel that melancholy that I have described almost immediately and would have liked to have slept indefinitely. I was basically depressed all the time except when I was asleep or when I was high on the Mandies and booze. It was always a day of feeling depressed. Any level of happiness eluded me for most of this period except for the intermittent periods of drug and booze induced happiness.

I had all sorts of other drugs prescribed for me, mainly the tetracyclic and monoamine oxidase inhibitors anti-depressants and sleeping tablets. For a number of years I was 'bombed out' on this medication. I'd say from 1968 until 1971. Perhaps they did make me feel marginally better and probably was the reason that I was able to at least survive and work. I was very unhappy and depressed but I could work; I could function, sort of. I was not as depressed as when I first went to hospital or when I first landed in New Zealand. That was just indescribable and debilitating so I improved from that position and worked. I had a job at what was then the White Heron Lodge near the airport in Christchurch. I started off as a room service waiter and was promoted to the overnight clerk whose primary function was to do the daily audit and sign off on it. I lived with a lovely woman, an Australian lady. She was a great girl and I had a good relationship with her (relatively speaking) but at some time she had to go home. I had a few friends that I had lived with when I first got to Christchurch and they were a good bunch of blokes but I ruined all the friendships I made. I won't mention their surnames but blokes like Johnny, Jack, Jim, Ron and Howard were good friends but they all ditched me; they really had to. I'd get on the booze and become a Mr. Hyde, away from my normal persona of Dr. Jekyll. I was a complete idiot and would do stupid things. No wonder when you consider that I was bombed up with Mandies, anti-depressants, anti-anxiety drugs and booze. They didn't know that.

One time I jumped up on top of the bar on a busy Friday night and offered to fight anybody in the bar at the Carlton Hotel in Christchurch. For that one, I got barred for life by the publican, old Joe Booth. Another time, I went into a store, and pretended to stick up the proprietor with a carrot and stole a box of frozen hamburger-patties. My flat mate at the time and I lived on hamburgers patties for weeks afterwards. I was a loose cannon when I was on the mandy/booze cocktail and strangely, I was fearless. At first the boys I knocked around with thought it was all funny but that soon wore off. I remember once when on my cocktail, I chopped down some poor fella's mail box with a tomahawk. Another time, I jumped the counter of one of my best mate's bottle-shop and made off with a bottle of whiskey. The young fella behind the counter chased me and I turned to meet the challenge. He must have seen the madness in my eyes and backed off. My mates found out about it and basically all of them ditched me. You would never know what I was going to do. There was another time at a wedding that I took offence to what one of the young fellas in a particular group was doing and invited him outside to discuss it in front of everybody. Fortunately he did not accept the offer but this really was outrageous behaviour and I was running off the tracks big-time. In fact its fair to say that during these episodes I was 'mad' and not in control of myself. Blame the mandies you might say. Of course if I didn't have the cocktail these things would not have happened, but it's not as simple as that. I think also the brutal attack I suffered at Tara and the excessive bullying at St Brendan's might also have had something to do with it.

Fortunately I never did anything really bad, mainly stupid things like I have described that just alienated me more from my friends. When I was sober I was good and could masquerade my depression but when I got on the booze and mandies, I could explode. We would get out on the lawn at the back of the flat we rented and I would drink to a stage where I could not walk, literally. There was once a photo floating around of me in a paralytic state crashed out on the lawn in my own vomit and a cat was licking it up. I hope it is still not floating around. I often vomited but would always be able to front up for work. It is amazing how when you are young what your body can endure. Sometimes when I was doing day shift as a breakfast room service waiter I would go to work drunk, without any sleep and get away with it. The combination of the drugs, especially the mandies and alcohol could have been lethal. If I had not have mixed the two I feel that the bad behaviour would not have occurred. At the end of the day I was the big loser. I really don't know how I came out of this period alive. I regularly used to ride my motor bike when I was in this high fuel injected state and ride the bike like a crazy bastard. God, I wonder how I did not get killed. I was doing most things wrong but at least I was earning an honest living and paying my own way. Maybe that was my saving grace.

One time a friend of mine, a fella called Campbell, and I got on the booze and we ended up in some bar at a hotel in the square of Christchurch. We were told to go and wouldn't. I told the bouncer to 'f*** off'; so they threw us out, literally. I was thrown down the stairs and badly damaged my ankle. I had to go to the Christchurch General hospital and get x-rays. The knee was very badly bruised and swollen, but I was cleared of any fractures and left on a pair of crutches. We ended up at a Maori party and a big Maori and I got into an argument over the rugby league. I told him that the Kiwis were rubbish and would never beat the Kangaroos. One thing led to another and he got stuck into me. I was unable to get up off the chair but in this state, I had no fear. I told him he was a weak c*** to hit a man on crutches and that his punches were like him, 'weak as piss'. Well, now he really went berserk and others had to restrain him. There was blood everywhere but they were all superficial wounds and I repeated to him my assertion that he was as weak as piss and as soon as I got my ankle fixed up I'd sort him out. One of the females at the party cleaned me up and got me a taxi and I went home. It was soon after that I came back to Australia. Totally ashamed of myself, friendless, and my self-esteem and respect was rock bottom. If you have listened to Bob Dylan's song, 'Like a Rolling Stone,' it is apt. He sings about 'when you got nothing, you got nothing to lose.' This was me at the time. Completely on my own, with no direction, no home and a nobody. I was like a rolling stone. I started off with a good circle of friends in Christchurch, met and lived with a lovely woman and should have made some serious inroads into getting my mental health in order. Instead I blew it all and I blame the depression for that. I lost all my friends and ended up with nothing. As a point of interest one of these good friends went onto become one of the richest men in NZ. On the positive side and you always should look for the positives, if I had not have taken the medication, I might have been institutionalised permanently.

Somewhere in between all this, I had another trip to Lowson house. It must have been before 1971 as I am very clear on events from that point on. Whenever it was, my brother John took me down from my parent's property at Tara. I cannot really remember what happened this time. This was a bit like the Melbourne scenario; I can't remember anything about it except John taking me there. There was more ECT, certainly medication reviews but at the end, there was not much they could do. I really don't know what happened after this. I spoke with my brother John, who told me that sometime in late 1968 we both went to Melbourne. We got jobs for Murphy's transport company delivering sugar around Melbourne. How I was in any state to drive a truck I truly don't know. I have no recollection of this, nor where we lived. He told me that I stayed for about three months and then hitched hiked somewhere. He doesn't know where and nor do I. I suppose it must have been back to New Zealand or to my parents in property at Tara. I did spend quite a bit of time at 'Moonie Park' on and off but I think it was more likely to be New Zealand. If it was, I'd go back to the White Herron Travelodge and they would find something for me to do.

I understand that it must have been terrible for my parents to see me in this state. It is not that hard for me to understand now how there was a period of amnesia around the Melbourne period. It was before I met the Australian lady so it was before I became a night clerk so 1968/69 would appear to be right. This was also the time that I had the ECT and that may have contributed to the amnesia over a longer period than I realised but until I spoke with my brother John, I did not remember what happened in Melbourne. I remember going there. We called into see our Uncle Athol, who had a poultry farm on the NSW coast at Dempsey I believe. He was the uncle that successfully sued his brothers over being left out of the inheritance. I remember staying at a hotel in Sydney and going out with one of Mum's friends, a Chemist named Eric Drew. But after that, it's more or less a blank. Fancy driving a truck around Melbourne for three months and not being able to remember anything about it or even staying in Melbourne. Incredible! I have no recollection of the apartment we stayed in; what it looked like or where it was — nothing. John tells me I got the sack after I backed the truck into a car. That might or might not be right. He said that I told everybody that I was going to hitchhike somewhere and just left. It is like I was in a coma for the period of time that I was in Melbourne. That's what depression can do to you.

Between 1967 and 1971, I interchanged from being at home working with Dad gratis or being in hospital in Brisbane, or in New Zealand. I cannot tell you much more than that. I do recall that one time I went back to New Zealand, saw my old boss and asked him if I could have my old job back. When I was not drinking I was well liked and people generally thought well of me. My employers at the Travelodge liked me because they didn't know about the mental illness, the drug taking and they never saw my bad behaviour. He couldn't give me my old job back as naturally they had made other arrangements. However he offered to let me paint the hotel, the entire hotel and that is what I did. It was a two storey wooden resort with about 130 rooms; so I had a job on my hands. Perhaps that precipitated me coming back to Australia and I ended up back home, because I had nowhere else to go. Now it all becomes clear again.

During this period I did a lot of different jobs and was going from one place to the next. I can't be sure of when I did what, only that I did do it but cannot remember the specifics. One time when I was discharged from Lowson House, the Social Worker got me a job in Brisbane at a Hardies (James Hardie & Co) factory. The factory was making fibro sheets and my job was when a sheet came off the assembly fine, I would grab hold of one end of it and put it on a stack. You would stand in the one spot doing this all day. I started my employment with them one morning and worked the first shift and found it too dusty. At the smoke break I just walked out of the factory and never went back. Now we know that may well have been a blessing in disguise. These fibre sheets made by Hardies contained a material called asbestos. It was a very common building material until they found out how dangerous it is. Asbestos is directly related to a few life threatening lung and abdominal diseases. Some of these diseases include asbestosis and mesothelioma which are fatal lung diseases and peritoneal mesothelioma which is a fatal abdominal disease. People were contracting these diseases by inhaling the asbestos fibres through the dust that is floating around in the air in the factories where it was being made and on building sites where it was being installed. Although I did not know at the time that I was working in a time bomb factory, this is the way that it turned out. Of course, asbestos has long been banned and great care has to be taken when handling it. Every cloud has a silver lining perhaps!

At another time I worked for an armoured car company picking up and delivering cash around Auckland. We were armed and I would often be the driver. Not much more to say about that other than I got to know Auckland pretty well and that the blokes I was working with were pretty good blokes, even though they were kiwis! I'd say that I probably stayed there for a few months before moving on. I worked in a few bars in Auckland as well. Usually as a barman, sometimes on the door but would usually start off picking up glasses. Some of these places were pretty rough and you had to have your wits about you. I do recall I worked at the big 'I' which was the Intercontinental Hotel in Auckland. I am reminded a lot of my work in the bars in Auckland when I see the movie, 'Once Were Warriors'. This was close to the mark and it looked at the behaviour of the indigenous people and their lives generally and particularly in the bars. They were not people to get on the wrong side off and when I was doing the door (usually relieving for meal breaks), I'd be worried. I knew that if I got into a situation with a big Maori, I'd be the loser, that is for sure.

I think that I have made it abundantly clear a number of times, that during this period, the days of darkness, I was in a confused and muddled state most all of the time; so I could be contradicting myself sometimes. I do know that I was working at the White Heron in Christchurch when Neil Armstrong and Buzz Aldrin landed on the moon because we were all watching it on TV at the hotel so that put me there on 30 July 1969. It certainly is a bit of jigsaw puzzle working out my movements during 1967-1971. Somewhere in between all of this I ended up back in Sydney. I don't know when it was but I think it was before I did my 9-month stint at home at Tara. If that is correct than it would have been late 1970 or early 1971. I started nursing in Sydney in October, 72. I arrived in Sydney after one of my jaunts to New Zealand and I found a boarding house at McMahons Point, not far from the Sydney Harbour Bridge. They charged $19 at the time for bed and breakfast per week. My first assignment was to go to Centrelink and I think at that time it was located at Crows Nest. I told the lady that I was going to pawn my watch but she told me not to. She said that before the day was out she would probably be able to get me a job. She did. I got work as a builder's labourer at a building site in Archer Street, Chatswood. I got on well there and I remember getting my first pay. It was something like $80 and I thought that I was a millionaire. I stayed with the builders for a couple of months until we finished the building, made some money and then inexplicably, drifted back home to Tara. I really don't know why I did that.

From this point on I can be very clear and precise about my movements. For nine months I stayed at home with Mum and Dad in 1971. I stopped all the drugs and went cold turkey. There is no doubt that I responded better with the hard work at home and getting off the drugs. I was also getting on better with Mum and Dad. Mum even told me that Dad was impressed with the work that I was putting in but there was no talk about wages. It was no trouble for me to do twelve hours on the tractor, day in day out. I even did the shearing for Dad (again). He would shear every fourth one so I was getting frequent rests. At the time he couldn't get shearers because he did not have a shearing shed and we used to shear the sheep with a little portable shearing unit. At least at home I had a roof over my head and always had something to eat. Mum had stopped her abuse to a large extent and that created a much 'nicer' environment. It is fair to say that her attitude towards me was better, a lot better. However she did have some major problems with my brother John. He had come home to do so some share farming with Dad. He now had a wife and twin children. I don't know what happened but at some point Patricia and Margaret had come home for a while. The three girls really gave John a hard time and made life hard for him. They behaved like an alpha pack of animals towards him with Mum being the alpha female. For some reason he was no longer in favour and I never heard my parents say to me again, "Well, why can't you be like your brother John." Of course there is more to it than that but the end result is that he just walked off vowing never to come back and he never did. He took his wife and family and went to Western Australia. I thought that Mum and the girls treatment of John and his new wife was absolutely appalling and maybe even possibly pathological in nature. I recall an incident at the Catholic Church in Tara when Mum was introducing John's wife to somebody when she referred to Katherine as the wife of one of her 'useless bloody boys.' Something is not right there.

I stayed on after John and the girls left to wherever they went and lived in the caravan. I worked hard for Dad and was a very big help to him and as I wrote Mum acknowledged that.

Once I got my energy back I found that I could keep working from basically daylight until dark. If I wasn't ploughing, I'd be doing something with the stock. Whenever there was nothing to do, I'd go out to pick up all the trees that had been knocked down years before and stack them into bundles for burning. There was always something to do and it was important that I was kept busy. I was living a life of social isolation but by choice and completely got off the drugs and booze. Smoking was still part of me but I tried with some success to limit myself. One way I had of doing this would be to limit myself to one smoke for one round of the paddock. If it was a small paddock, I would do two rounds. Would you believe that when I left after nine months to go to Sydney, they gave me $300 plus Margaret's little car, which she had in Sydney. I'm sure that this would all have been Mum's doing. Dad was not one to dip his hand into his pocket. Margaret was going over to London and didn't need the car anymore. Things were improving it seemed.

This is the first and only time I was given anything for my labour. You might very well say, well that's not much but at least it was something and I deeply appreciated it. Margaret's little car was wonderful for me when I starting working as a student nurse and it served me very well. I did not see my father again until I viewed his body in the hospital morgue at Tara in November 1974. After this long stint at home, I decided once again to leave and go back to Sydney and as it turned out, this time it was for good. I did not have a plan but without the drugs I was finding my energy again and the depression was inexplicably better. Could I be getting better without the medication? I would say during this 9-month period I never had a serious blow up with my mother and that is really saying something. I was no longer handicapped with the effects of the drugs. I was starting to find my feet again and I give my parents some credit for that. They provided an environment whereby the influences like excessive drinking and drug taking did not exist. In all of this nine-month stint, I did not have a drink of alcohol and completely got myself off prescribed medication. Of course I still suffered depression but not as bad, nowhere near it. They, particularly Mum, were a lot better with me and I think that helped a lot. I want to give her credit for that.

At the beginning of 1972 I told them that I was leaving, this time for good. I did not have a plan but agreed to keep in contact and let them know what I was doing. My relationship with them was better. However I still harboured a deep seated animosity towards them, especially Mum, but I found it became more manageable. I hitchhiked to Sydney and started work with Grace Bros Removals, operating out of Artarmon. This was a great job. We worked very hard as you could imagine. Lugging pianos, refrigerators, all that sort of stuff up and down stairs. All the furniture vans were contract driver owners so they really kept you going but I liked it.

In summary, the jobs I have had during my life included:
• Farmhand (Central Queensland and Tara)
• Ringer, Jackaroo, and Stockman (Central and Western Queensland)
• Roustabout and Shearer (Central and South East Queensland)
• Truck Driver (Brisbane, Sydney, Christchurch)
• Factory Hand (James Hardie & Co, Fibro Factory, (Brisbane)
• Store man (Brisbane)
• Service Station Attendant (Christchurch)
• Cocktail Barman (Gore, NZ)
• Barmen (Several clubs in Sydney and bars in Auckland)
• Assistant Carpet Layer (Sydney)
• Builder's Labourer (Sydney)
• Waiter and Relief Doorman (Outlets in Sydney, Gold Coast and Auckland)
• Room Service Waiter and Night Clerk (Christchurch, Auckland, Brisbane and Sydney)
• Armoured Car Driver (Auckland)
• Furniture Removals (Artarmon, Sydney)
• Wheat Grain Attendant (Norseman, Western Australia)
• Wards man (Auckland)
Jobs that I had after 1972 were:
• Nursing (Sydney)

- Police Officer (NSW)
- Soldier (No 1 Commando Co - part time, based in Sydney)
- Hotel Security Officer, Director of Security, Assistant Hotel Manager and Executive Housekeeper (All in one Sydney hotel)
- Contract Commercial Cleaner (Sydney and Wollongong)
- Contract Carpet Cleaner (Sydney)
- Fitness Instructor and Personal Trainer (Sydney)
- Hotel Security Manager (Sydney)

The jobs I had after 1997 were:

- Owner, Managing Director and General Manager of Bars and Restaurants (Singapore)
- International Hotel Security Risk Management Consultant (Singapore, Malaysia, Thailand, Maldives, Hong Kong, Spain, Australia, India, China, Japan, USA, Canada and South Africa)
- Olympic Games Security Coordinator (Beijing Olympics)
- Security Risk Management Consultant (Global)
- Loss Assessor (EQC-NZ-Christchurch)
- Crowd Controller (Sydney)

We are all different and I wonder if it is just a little bit too convenient to say that clinical depression is caused by a chemical imbalance in the brain. There certainly seems to be some evidence to support this and this is why the SSRIs generation of drugs (Selective Serotonin Re-uptake Inhibitors) have been so successful. I don't know what caused the obsessional component of my illness but it is interesting to note that this came upon me after the depression surfaced and that makes me think that it is probably a by-product of the depression. Although there may be a genetic component as well. I see it primarily as a defence mechanism. We all know that the mind does funny things that we don't understand, but I can tell you that if I don't want to do something the obsessions are worse. A good example of that was the difficulty I had when I was working at the hospitals as a student nurse. If I am in a happy comfortable environment everything is better. I know that when I am gainfully employed I feel good about myself. My self-esteem goes up and so does my confidence levels. When I am not, I go the other way and get a bit depressed, obsessional and anxious.

For me I believe that people generally have an inner strength and resilience that does not come to the fore until they have to overcome a 'sea of troubles'. This is required when dealing with severe depression and if you have a faith like religion to support that, then that at least gives you a prop to believe in and hold onto. A possible negative of having a strong religious belief is that it can well be your faith in this religion that is making you feel incredibly guilty about things that you have done and that in turn, could be the major cause of your depression. I am grateful that I was never considered psychotic although at times in those dark days, I probably wished that I had been.

My summary of my life between 1967 until 1971 was that it was a very inconsolable and depressing one but the important thing is that I survived. I really, really don't know how I did it. I was bogged down and handicapped with severe and critical depression and in trying to deal with it, I took massive amounts of strong medication. By my accounts I had four spells in Lowson House and had probably seen half a dozen different Psychiatrists but none were able to cure me. I basically wasted those years but as I have said, the most important thing is that I got through it and was able to go on and lead a productive life, free from any medication or medical help. I look back and wonder how on earth I came out alive from the 'Age of Darkness'. To be perfectly honest I get sad just writing about it. It is amazing what human beings can endure and the resilience we have. It was not the end of mental illness for me, that will never come. I wrote at the beginning of the book that mental illness is like a virus in that it never leaves you. I get depressed sometimes for sure, but nothing like what I did during this period. I can have a laugh and a joke just like most people and I think I now have a relatively good head-space. I will always suffer from obsessional neurosis and an anxiety disorder but I have it under control. I have accepted that's part of me and I have just got on with things. It is now 2017 and I have not been in a psychiatric ward of a general hospital since around about 1970/71 (something like that); that's forty-six years. I think that is my climbing of Mt

Our house in North Randwick
that I bought for $300,000 in 1989.
It is now worth $3.8 million but I
lost it in bankruptcy in 1996

Father and son Dan - 1986

Max (9) & Marg (6) with Bessie in cart
"Torrendorra" Inverell

My driver and I stop for lunch on
the way to Bloemfontein doing
reconnaissance work for the 2008
Football World Cup. On our long
drives he taught me the RSA
national anthem — a great bloke

The old Darlinghurst Police
station that features a lot in my
story about the Police. I think it's
just as well that the walls can't
talk. I did a lot of my plain
clothes work at this station. Had
a serious allegation made against
me here.

No, it's not Lawrence of Arabia. It's me in Jordan on the way to the Dead Sea on the River Jordan where Christ was baptised.

MM as a guest speaker at the Hotel Terrorism Conference in Singapore in 2006

A Police photo taken of me (1979) at a political demonstration by the Special Branch who could not identify who this was. Opposite - Mum and Dad in 1938

My mother at 93 years of age with my niece Rachael in 2007. Mum passed in June 2010.

Everest. In the early days the doctors did not have a good prognosis for me. In fact, according to my mother, one of the doctors told her that I would probably lead an institutionalised existence as he felt this would be the only way that I could cope with life. Although he proved to be wrong but I understand his thinking and it certainly looked like it could have been the case between 1967-71. Since I was last in hospital in 1971 I have obtained a nursing diploma with hospital high distinctions in the final examinations. I was accepted and served in the NSW Police Force and left with distinguished service. I served in the Reserve Army in the Commandos and only left because of injury. I rose to senior executive positions in the international hotel business and successfully built and ran my own restaurant, bar and night club in Singapore. I was successful as a global security risk management consultant working at the Beijing Olympic Games, the Football World Cup in South Africa and the Winter Olympics in Vancouver. I have worked as a security consultant in many countries on five continents, usually on my own and managed well enough to satisfy some very high profile global clients. I have been a guest speaker at a number of conferences, including in Chicago, Thailand and Singapore. I married and had two children that have both been successful and I have had the same partner for the last nineteen years. I also now have three grandchildren. So not only was I not institutionalised, I also became independent of medical help having not seen anybody about my demons from 1975 until the time of writing this book; some forty-two years. I suppose the obvious question is how did I do this? How did I manage to climb Mt Everest?

I think I at least in part, know the answer. I finally woke up to the fact that I was not the person that my teachers and my parents led me to believe that I was. I know now that I am a decent and honourable man and probably have been all my adult life. Sure I have done things that I regret doing and made mistakes that I regret but don't we all have regrets about things we have done. Isn't that just being human? Going to the Royal Commission was of tremendous therapeutic value for me, as is the writing of this book. I had never discussed before some of what I discussed with the Royal Commission until now. I would have liked to have sat down and talked about it with my wife and children and my present partner but felt that it was too risky and it could stimulate misunderstanding and that would threaten the relationships. I guess all that will be exposed once this book gets published but I am up for it and ready to deal with that. Clearly I have had an enormous struggle to find some normality in my life. My teachers were wrong about me but teachers are not like them anymore so we can move on from that. We hope that the Royal Commission will make recommendations that will ensure that teachers of the future in these clergy schools conform to a set of decent values and standards. There should be no more dinosaurs like Brothers Walsh, McSweeny and Broderick. They will become what they are, the dinosaurs of the past and we can all move on. My parents were wrong about me but I am not wrong about them. They just were not made for one another and I believe that I became a 'victim of circumstances' of a 'perfect storm'. It is what it is; none of us are perfect. Human beings are capable of incredible feats of resilience. I give myself a pat on the back for being able to do what I did with the handicaps (demons) I had.

I am saying that people generally can do anything (provided it is a realistic goal) they want to. You have to believe in yourself (self-belief) and not be influenced by those that want to put you down, especially during those early formative years. A good and simple example of human inner strength is the strength that is required to give up smoking. People tell me they can't stop. Poonam, my partner, tells me that, but you can. I know I did and millions of others have. Yet some can't, why is that? It was easier for me to stop smoking than it was for me to carry on life riddled with melancholy and depression. I think it is a myth that mentally ill people are weak. I know that I am not. Actually I think the opposite. Look at Churchill and the great man himself, Abraham Lincoln, who both suffered from the black dog as Churchill called it. In many cases I think it is just the opposite. You just have to have that special human quality of resilience and inner strength to do it. You can beat critical depression but in some cases, it is indeed a very, very hard road to go down. You need all the help you can get.

When I look back over the whole episode, I feel that I can more of less figure out what went wrong for me. Why did this happen to me for example, but not to my brother John who incidentally has his own demons to deal with but unlike me, he doesn't discuss them? Also unlike me, he has never been treated for mental illness; at least that I know off. So why was it me and none of my brothers and sisters? You might answer that by asking me why is it I am a diabetic (which I am) but none of the others are. I think that's the biological argument. I think the bulk of the mental problems that I suffered came from behavioural and environmental factors. I believe that I was a victim of the various environments that I found myself in as a young person. I mean seriously what parents in their right mind would send their five year old boy to a Catholic boarding school hundreds of miles from home, where they know the Nuns use corporal punishment for discipline? I went into great detail about St Brendan's college and tried to articulate the toxic environment that I was exposed there. At that time, St Brendan's had no comprehension of what providing a 'duty of care' meant. I have detailed the incredible bullying that took place against John and I in that first term of 1957. The worst part of all was what happened in the following year - 1958; the year that John was not with me. What possesses a grown adult man to put a little 13-year old boy up in front of the class and humiliate and degrade him in front of his peers by telling them that he was too pretty to be a boy and should have been a girl and then proceeded to call him Miss Australia for the rest of the year. What an absolute c*** and then to follow that up with a physical sexual contact on a number of occasions. How could this not damage you psychologically? I keep asking the same question, where were my parents?

I feel that my separation anxiety that I still carry with me stems from being abandoned by my parents at a very early age. I recall very vividly the pitiful scenes at the railway station in

Capella when my parents were sending me back to boarding school, especially in 1958. I had a real problem with it and I think now you can understand why. That in turn made me unable to handle rejection in early adult life, like the time that Pauline rejected me. I do believe that if we had not have gone to Queensland I may not have developed mental illness. If we as a family had a normal life, then I feel confident that this would not have happened. The abuse that I got at home after I left school leaves the deepest wound. When a parent start abusing you, you develop a deep sense of betrayal that stays with you for life. The damage had mostly been done at the schools but the domestic abuse was the catalyst for bringing the depression to fruition. We need to also take into account that since John was not with me at school in 1958 he did not suffer the sexual abuse that I did. He was not called Miss Australia in front of the whole school and humiliated like I was. Even though neither of my parents were ever treated for mental illness, that is not to say that they never suffered from it. I believe that my mother suffered from depression and that manifested itself with the awful and debilitating migraines that she used to get. Not surprisingly, in the latter part of her life the migraines disappeared. I believe now that if my Mum was still alive, I would be able to reconcile with her. I am what I am and she was what she was, but the fact remains that in those early days (up until fourteen) she was a great Mum and I loved her dearly.

I think that the word that comes out of these and hits me in the face the most is GUILT. I was made to feel incredibly guilty about myself by my teachers and parents alike at a very young age. For many years I was unable to look into the mirror even to shave. I'd get a 'weird' sensation as if I could see myself all too clearly. When I looked into the mirror I basically saw somebody who was an unworthy scumbag and I was ashamed of myself. I wonder if this had anything to do being told I was that pretty much for most of my life and actually believed it or was it in the subconscious? I actually could not hold my gaze in the mirror, I'd have to turn away. I have spoken about this with my medical therapists but have not been able to get a clear handle on it.

Having said this, it has not happened to me for quite some years now but at one stage it was very bad. I even found myself shaving without looking into the mirror. The mirror was making me too aware of myself and it was an insightful frightening feeling. I thought maybe it was a type of depersonalisation but the medical people did not think so, but could not tell me what it was.

The other thing that I had for years was what they refer to as sleep paralysis. I spoke with Mum about this and she told that she used to get it as well. I have not had it for a long time now but basically what it is, is that when you wake up, you are paralysed and can't move your body but you are awake or at least you think you are. Then it becomes a battle to force your body to wake up as your mind has already done. In my mind I used to try to throw myself out of bed to wake up but couldn't move. Eventually you'd wake up and feel completely drained and exhausted. I experienced this first in my teenage years and really thought that I was dying when it first happened. It stayed me for the next two or three decades. At the beginning I found it fairly terrifying but gradually learnt to deal with it by recognising what it was and not trying to fight it. I don't know if there is any relationship with the sleep paralysis I used to get and the mental illness but feel that there could be.

For me to get better, I had to get rid of this guilt. Perhaps it all started when we did those awful things as little kids, like burning Dad's wheat crop. Perhaps! I don't know but I do know that I was made to feel terribly guilty from a very early age. When I am writing this I have this image of this Nun screaming at me with a cane in her hand telling me to eat my sago at St Joseph's. Do I still feel guilty now? I don't know. I can say that I don't but unconsciously maybe I do. I think a more realistic stance to take is that rather than feel guilty, I prefer to feel regretful. I regret we burnt Dad's wheat crop; I regret that as little kids we experimented with things sexual; I regret that I was unable to see the light of God; I regret that I had those terrible battles with Mum; I regret developing mental illnesses, I regret getting involved in the drug scene, and so on and so on it goes. I don't have anything to feel guilty about but for many, many years I felt guilty, ashamed and unworthy. There was a great need for me to seek atonement and I wonder if unconsciously that is the real reason why I went nursing. I wanted to punish myself and do something really good and wholesome where I could cleanse my soul, so to speak. I'm looking at it as a type of absolution. Interestingly enough, nearly all of these negative feelings left me after I joined NSW's finest. If I felt guilty before I joined the Police Force, I should have felt a damn side guiltier after serving in the Police, but I didn't.

I think that people like me that have experienced guilt on a chronic basis, mistakenly believe that we have harmed other people when we haven't. I have mentioned to you a few times in this book, it was our teachers and my parents that made me feel this way. The theory is that if you can change your thoughts, you can change your emotions. I have worked hard over the years on not feeling guilty. The overwhelming culprit here is the Catholic Church. I have told you that it is an organisation that is based on fear and you can imagine that little five-year old children being sent to their care, could suffer from guilt complexes. My mother in a sense was a victim of the Church as well. She believed unequivocally in what the church preached and lived her life accordingly. She in turn expected that her children would do the same and when they didn't, we were all heading on a collision course. I think the key for me to get better with the depression, OCD and anxiety, was to mitigate to some degree the risks associated with the guilt complex. To a significant degree I have done that. The Catholic Church teaches that it is a mortal sin to masturbate and made you feel very guilty about it. I told you the story about when Br. Walsh threw the black board duster at me when he thought that I was just touching myself; yet he had no problems running his hand up the inside of my thigh and touching my genitals.

The foundation for a good relationship had been established early but clearly I felt I was treated badly by my mother for the abuse that she handed out to me and the lack of protection afforded by my Dad to counteract that. Having lauded the possibility that a reconciliation may have been possible, Mum's final act was an act of vindictiveness and unfairness when she left John and I out of her will. That was inherently very unfair and these days you can challenge that in court and I would have been successful but that legislation was not available at the time of her passing. There is no doubt that a court would take into account the years of work that I did for them when I received no pay. Mum overlooked the enormous work contributions I made as a young man on their properties. I would estimate that if I were to add up the time that I worked at home gratis, between 1958 until 1972, it would come to about six to seven years. Start doing your maths and you will find that it adds up to a pretty penny. The Church influenced my mother to be totally inflexible on the issue of religion and gave her a warped perception of male adolescence and puberty. You will recall the story I told you about with her and the magazines when I was in hospital. That type of thinking can only come from a profound indoctrination by some religious order or of course the other alternative could be mental illness but I am not suggesting that was the case with Mum. Mum was adamant that the Church could do no wrong and took that to her deathbed. I think it made her a dogmatic, inflexible and a very judgmental person and the truth was, she often got things wrong. Mum died with her rosary beads in her hand and died the way that she lived: with an inexpugnable faith in the Catholic Church. The thing that would have made my mother very happy would have been having a son that people referred to as Father Max.

I have no doubt that the ECT saved my life, literally.

Chapter Six: Depression, Obsessional Neurosis and Anxiety

The last chapter dealt a lot with my mental issues. This chapter deals more with the subject in general. The statistics for severe depression are horrifying. If we had the number of deaths from some other physical diseases, there would be no question the enormous support that could be solicited from governments at all levels, local, state and federal. Just because you have 'the black dog,' doesn't mean you will commit suicide. However I feel sure, without really knowing, that the vast majority don't. It also doesn't follow that if you commit suicide, you are depressed I suppose. Just have a look at what happened in Guyana in 1978 when more than nine hundred followers of the Reverend Jim Jones took part in a mass suicide in Jonestown. They all died knowingly drinking a flavoured drink that was poisoned with cyanide. In other words they all committed suicide. Were they all depressed as well? However I would think most people that commit suicide were suffering from depression at the time of committing the act.

The leading cause of death for Australians aged between 15 - 44 is suicide.

Many extraordinary and famous people have committed suicide. Just to name a few. Mark Antony, Socrates, Marcus Brutus, Hannibal, Erwin Rommel, Heinrich Himmler, Herman Goring, Henry V11, Cleopatra, Hannibal, Tchaikovsky, Prince Alfred of Edinburgh, Robert FitzRoy, Marilyn Monroe, Vincent Van Gough, Merriwether Lewis, Ernest Hemingway, Charles Boyer, Cheyenne Brando, Sergei Yesenin, Adolf Hitler, Alan Turing, Robin Williams, Hart Crane, Tony Scott, Melvin Purvis, Kurt Cobain, Virginia Woolf, Chris Benoit, David Wallace, Tom Lewis, Phillip Seymour Hoffman, Lee Thompson Young, Amy Winehouse, L'Wren Scott, Whitney Houston, Hunter S. Thompson, Hart Crane, Mindy McCready, Freddy E, Jonathan Brandis, Johnny Lewis, Freddie Prinze, Aaron Swartz, David Foster Wallace, Sylvia Plath, Don Cornelius, Lucy Gordon,

Alexander McQueen, Christine Chubbuck, Michael Hutchinson, and James Whale

Equally, many extraordinary people have been known to suffer from major depression. Just to name a few. Buzz Aldrin, Woody Allen, Christian Bale, Jim Carrey, Charles Darwin, Charles Dickens, Bob Dylan, Stephen Fry, Graham Greene, Anthony Hopkins, Angelina Jolie, John Kiran, Stephen King, Abraham Lincoln, Michelangelo, Vincent van Gough, Mozart, Isaac Newton, Brad Pitt, J.K.Rowling, J.D.Rockefeller, Britney Spears, Rod Steiger, Leo Tolstoy, Mark Twain, Winston Churchill and Virginia Wolf. Isn't it interesting to see Rockefeller's name there; the richest man in the world at the time and he suffered from depression. It's also interesting to see all the names of the actors in the movie industry - I wonder why they have such a high representation?

I think you'd agree that those of us who admit to suffering from depression are in fairly illustrious company. Churchill's story is very interesting. Around about 2006, a British mental health charity put in place a statue of Churchill with him in a straitjacket. Of course this upset a lot of people and the charity defended its action by saying that they wanted to get the message out to the public that it is possible to overcome bipolar depression and that the great man himself was an example of that. Some people even suggested that his great leadership during those terrible war years was because of his bipolar, not in spite of it. That's an interesting thought. In the book Black Dog, Kafka's Mice and Other Phenomena of the Human Mind the author, who is a psychiatrist, wrote that had Churchill been a stable man, he could never have inspired the nation. The author further states that when Britain was on its knees a 'normal' man might have thrown the towel in thinking that there was no hope and he wanted to save unnecessary carnage; not Churchill. He was known to have said that he did not like standing near the edge of a platform when an express train was passing through. He wanted to stand right back from the platform edge and get a pillar between himself and the train. He said that he did not like standing by the side of ship and look down into the water. He said that a second's action could end everything. Was he describing obsessional neurosis here? Churchill made frequent references to his depression which he called his "black dog". His depressive periods tended to be intense and prolonged. Sometimes they were connected with traumatic external events such as his dismissal from the Admiralty after the Dardanelles disaster in WWI. We all remember the disaster at Gallipoli and many historians consider that Churchill was largely responsible for that. His depressions came and went throughout his long and remarkable life and commenced in his youth. When Churchill was almost 80, his personal doctor, Dr Moran prescribed some speed to give Sir Winston enough of a boost to make a final speech in Parliament. Churchill's favourite drink was whisky and soda and he would often start drinking after breakfast. It seems clear that he was an alcoholic and he is on record as having once drunk eleven whiskies and sodas during a single meal. When Churchill travelled to the US during the prohibition era, he obtained a doctor's note to certify that he had to drink alcohol regularly as it was necessary for his health and well-being. His heavy drinking was no secret and President Roosevelt complained that Churchill was drunk half the time. Isn't it a staggering thought that the man most responsible for defeating the Nazis during WW2 was a manic depressive, an obsessive and an alcoholic? I think on this basis, we could agree that we need more people like Churchill amongst our global leadership ranks. Perhaps when we are assessing our leaders like they have just done with the US elections, it might help a candidate if he can show that he is bi-polar, like Churchill or a depressive like Lincoln.

Another famous figure who suffered from clinical depression was Abraham Lincoln (AL). I regard him as probably the greatest US President ever with FDR coming a close second. AL suffered from clinical depression and severe melancholy. Historians have speculated that AL's depression encouraged him to painfully look at the very 'core of his soul'. It is even suggested that when he developed the techniques to deal with his depression, it helped him make the incredibly hard decisions that had to be made during the US Civil War. It is perhaps why he had such a strong sense of compassion and understanding that few could compare with. I think that people that have suffered severe depression do have a sense of compassion and understanding that others don't have. They know what suffering and disability is and this makes them have more empathy for those less fortunate. AL was such a man. He frequently commuted death sentences for deserters from the Union Army and in this book, I have included his Gettysburg address. When you read through that you can see that there is an almost spiritual understanding of just how horrible war was and the terrible suffering resulting from it. When he said that, "We cannot dedicate, we cannot consecrate, we cannot hallow this ground. The brave men, living and dead, who struggled here have consecrated it, far above our poor power to add or detract". This could only be said by a man that felt extreme pain with the sorrow and suffering that goes with it. It is said that AL's depression was characterised by a marked decrease in pleasure, agitation, fatigue, feelings of worthlessness, and even thoughts of suicide. It is not hard to imagine the enormous stress of having to deal with the American Civil War between 1861 to 1865. This was a war where, for the first two plus years the Union Army had no real successes and were losing many tens of thousands of men. He felt, unfairly, responsible for their deaths, most of them just young men in uniform. Domestically he had to deal with the unbalanced mind of his wife Mary Todd, and with the early deaths of his sons, particularly the death of Willie (William) from typhoid fever in 1862. It is recorded that in the US Civil War the fatalities alone were over 600,000 in a country with a population of just 32 million. Isn't it interesting that Winston Churchill wrote an acclaimed book entitled The American Civil War?

It is also interesting when you look at some other famous people that suffered mental illness and there are many of them. I have mentioned Churchill and Lincoln thus far. Another famous person who changed modern thinking on the origins of mankind was Charles Darwin. Some may argue that he was one of the most influential people that ever lived. I sometimes go on the Charles Darwin walk in the Blue Mountains outside Sydney and walk in his footsteps, so to speak. Yet it is said that Darwin was seriously mentally disturbed. Historians have concluded that he suffered from several serious and incapacitating psychiatric disorders, including severe depression, anxiety and agoraphobia. Agoraphobia is an extreme fear of open spaces which seems odd when you consider that he spent five years on board HMS Beagle travelling around the world studying specimens that led to his theory of evolution and the process of natural selection. Bejesus, you can imagine what the Catholic Church thought of Charles Darwin! A study by Barloon and Noyes of Darwin's mental condition concluded that he suffered from many anxiety disorders that impacted upon his ability to function normally and bordered on psychosis. There is a biography book entitled 'Darwin: the Life of a Tormented Evolutionist' that details the problems he had with mental illness. Amongst his many symptoms he had terrible insomnia, sobbing episodes, nausea, vomiting, de-personalisation and even hallucinations. It was suggested at the time that much of Darwin's poor health was attributed to his ambiguity that although he had devoted his life to something that many regarded at fantasy, he worried that he might be wrong and that there was in fact a divine creator. Apparently this weighed heavily on his mind and may have been the major contributing factor towards his mental illness. Is that the guilt complex raising its ugly head again?

Yet look at the legacy these three men left behind. Churchill is regarded at the greatest British statesman ever and as I have stated, the person most responsible for stalling Hitler's advance on global domination. If it were not for Abraham Lincoln, the USA would never have become what it is today; the world's only hyper power. He saved the Union, thereby saving the USA, and in so doing, freed the slaves and united the confederacy back into the Union. Could anybody other than AL have done this? Darwin's legacy is that he discovered that living organisms descended from species that lived before them and that natural selection explains how evolution occurred. Darwin's thinking changed how we think about life itself.

I don't suppose it serves my purpose any more to keep writing about famous people that developed mental illness. My god, you could write a book just about that. Look at what Michelangelo, Vincent van Gough, Isaac Newton, Beethoven, Edvard Munch, Charles Dickens and Leo Tolstoy, just to mention a few more. Michelangelo is regarded as the most famous artist of the Italian Renaissance. Among his works are the "David" and "Pieta" statues and the Sistine Chapel frescoes. He suffered from depression and many historians have concluded that he may have been an autistic. Vincent van Gough was one of the greatest artists the world has known but he was mentally flawed. Perhaps that is what made him a genius. He was so unbalanced he once cut off part of one of his ears and gave it to a woman. He suffered badly from depression and ended up committing suicide. Isaac Newton was one of the greatest scientists of all time and he suffered badly from bipolar depression disorder and may also have been autistic. It did not stop him from giving us calculus, the theory of gravity and the telescope. Beethoven wrote magical symphonies and concertos and he often did this when he was on a high with his manic depressive disorder. Edvard Munch use to suffer from severe panic attacks and it was one of these that inspired him to paint possibly the most valuable painting of all times, 'The Scream'. "The Scream" sold for more than $119 million in 2012—setting a new world record. Who has not read the work of Charles Dickens, the great English novelist? Dickens suffered badly from depression in his lifetime. Russian author Leo Tolstoy suffered badly from depression later in his life but still left us his great work, the acclaimed novels *War and Peace*, *Anna Karenina* and *The Death of Ivan Ilyich*.

All these great people suffered from mental illness and with most of them that included depression. It is easy to understand how depression in many cases, is married to people who are gifted, creative, innovative and scientific. I think that most people would not be aware that there are many great and famous people that suffered badly from depression. That is a staggering thought when you think about it. I can't imagine how a 'normal' (whatever that is) person would have struggled to deal with the dreadful and painful events of the US Civil War as Abraham Lincoln did. It does make me wonder what would happen if we had one of these 'unbalanced' people in charge of a country (maybe a rouge state) that had a nuclear capability. He might be going through a bipolar high episode and tells his generals, "Let's nuke them." A sobering thought.

Of course I am not suggesting that I am a genius like the people that I have written about. But it is interesting and even comforting to learn during my research that there were some very famous people who suffered mental illness. It is impossible for me to articulate the level of melancholy I felt. I think only a person who has suffered from severe depression can have any 'real' empathy with it. You are caught in an enigmatic situation, between the devil and the deep blue sea. You don't want to live but on the other hand, you don't want to die. You just want to feel happy and at peace with yourself.

In subsequent psychotherapy, I was able to understand that the obsessional thinking and anxiety were probably a by-product of the depression. Psychiatrists disagree amongst themselves on this point. We must accept that psychiatry is not an exact science and opinions can vary greatly between practitioners. The Psychoanalysts take a different approach, based on Sigmund Freud's findings. In my case, I think that the obsessional thinking is interlinked with some sort of defence mechanism and is probably heredity, probably from my father. Now it gets complicated. This is experienced as guilt, regret and anger over the mistakes I have made. I think that if only things had been different; if only I didn't go to St Brendan's; if only I had decent parents; if only I had left home when I was fifteen; if only Dad could have been a father; if only Mum could have been a real mother; if only (and so on and on). My mind was full of negative thoughts and I could not get any positivity into my life. When I was a student nurse, I worked for a time in the psychiatric ward at the Prince Henry Hospital. I had by this stage made very significant inroads into getting better. I met patients will all these problems. I met a really nice man who suffered from obsessive compulsive disorder (OCD). It was awful. He just could not stop washing his hands, repeatedly. His hands were almost red raw. Yet, he knew it was totally irrational but could not stop doing it. He had to act the compulsion out but he was not considered psychotic (mad). It totally controlled his life. He was an invalid pensioner, highly intelligent person, unable to live and work in the normal world. Sometimes I think it would just be easier for people that were so disadvantaged as this, to just go crazy. Better to adopt another personality, go crazy and be happy at least.

I met Jesus of Nazareth. Please, I am not trying to be funny. He offered me a job in Jerusalem as one of his apostles and he truly believed it. He felt that we were the fools for not believing him. He felt sorry for us (the staff) for not believing him. He would remind us of the story of Saint Thomas and his doubting that Christ had resurrected from the dead. This patient felt that he was on a mission to save mankind and that he was the only normal person on earth. He assured us that one day we would realise that he was telling the truth. The mental hospitals are full of people like this and I don't believe that this person suffered anything like the man with the OCD I mentioned. I met homosexuals who were having treatment, just for being gay. I think they were having some sort of aversion therapy. These were the times we lived in. Of course I met the depressives. These were the majority. All sorts — bipolar or manic depressives, paranoid schizophrenic depressives (psychotic depression) and major depression. As part of my training, I had to assist in the administration of ECT, or shock treatment as the layman calls it. The most miraculous successful psychiatric treatment I saw at Prince Henry was the treatment of people that had uncontrollable stuttering. They would come (the patients) into the nursing lecture room when they first arrived for treatment carrying a tape recorder. I think they were outpatients and they could barely put two words together. After a few short weeks or so, they would come back and speak to us. Maybe 100 people in an auditorium type room. It was truly amazing. The program was run by a Psychiatrist named Dr. Gavin Andrews and he got worldwide recognition for his work. This was an example of the wonderful work that the staff did in the psychiatric unit at the Prince Henry hospital in the early seventies.

Depression affects many millions of people worldwide and is considered by the WHO (World Health Organisation) to be one of the leading causes of disability. It is said that in western society that up to 30% of the population have had or are suffering from clinical depression. That would mean that many of your friends would fit into that category or even maybe you. That's almost one in three people are either clinically depressed or have been. As with all things, there are degrees of severity. A person can be mildly depressed, moderately depressed, severely depressed or critically depressed. I would think that the majority of the 30% that I talk about would be bracketed in the mildly to moderately depressed category and that is where I would put myself in the present day. When I was in Lowson House the first and second time there is no doubt that I was critically depressed. It is therefore easy for me to understand why a critically depressed person would take his or her own life and I talk more about that later. Suicide is a horrifying statistic. Electroconvulsive therapy is a well-established treatment for severe depression. Intravenous anaesthetic medication is used to minimise the patient's unpleasantness and the adverse side effects of the induced seizure. In this stage, small electrodes are placed on the patient's temples and a device put into their mouth, to stop them swallowing their tongues. Than the doctor dials a type of telephone dial and a small amount of electricity goes into the patient. The patient gives no more than a little shudder, like he was having a mild seizure and that's it. The patient wakes up and is no worse for wear. It is a huge mistake to call it 'shock' treatment and completely misleading. This view was distorted and augmented by the movie, 'One Flew Over the Cuckoo's Nest.' You may remember that RP McMurphy was given 'shock' treatment as a form of punishment without the anaesthesia. That is rubbish, they never did that but it made for some dramatic film making I suppose. It was totally off the mark and just part of Hollywood sensationalism and distortion. ECT is nothing like that and in many cases, such as myself, it has proven to be a life saver, literally. There is nothing wrong with having ECT and nothing to be afraid off. I would have assisted in this procedure on at least twenty or so occasions. It was a miracle to see severely depressed patients come into hospital in a suicidal state and within a couple of weeks go home, 'new' people. My advice to the severely depressed patients who cannot see any light at the end of the tunnel is to see a Doctor that specialises in depression. There are other, better options than harming oneself and they just might work; it is certainly worth a try. ECT seemed to work in most of the cases that I was involved in at Prince Henry Hospital. Having said that, I am aware that there is medical opinion in some quarters that it does more harm than good.

Of course it's hard for the severely depressed to be positive: by its very nature it is negative thinking. Negative thinking is the depressive world. I can assure you that if you are suffering from critical clinical depression, you are not capable of doing anything positive and I mean anything in a constructive manner. Anti-depressive medication is the most widely prescribed drug in western society today. So where are all these depressed people? Imagine the USA with a population of 319,000,000 people. If a quarter of them suffer from clinical depression, that would mean there are nearly eighty-million depressives in the USA. No wonder, they make all the mistakes they do. I am saying that in a 'tongue in cheek' manner of course. Just making a point!

I read recently where Scientists have discovered that there are seventeen separate genetic variations that increased the risk of an individual developing depression. They believe that genetic and environmental factors are major contributing factors towards the development of depression and that the interaction between these two factors have significance. It seems now that a section of the medical world accepts that depression is in fact a brain disease and that it is more about biology than anything else. Professionals now believe that there are three key motivational aspects which contribute to suicide. They are: 1) a sense of not belonging, of being alone, 2) a sense of not contributing, of being a burden and 3) a capability for suicide, not being afraid to die. It is thought that these motivations or preconditions must be in place before someone will attempt suicide. Clearly there is something very wrong if seven Australians are committing suicide every day. I have all three of these motivational aspects which contribute to suicide. I do have that feeling of being alone because I am alone. I write that I have never fulfilled my potential and therefore do feel that I could have contributed a lot more. On the third aspect, I am on record saying that I am not afraid of death.

Murder/suicides are always distressing to hear about but one that occurred in September 2014 is particularly sad. This relates to the murder of the Hunt family; mother and their three children, followed by the suicide of their father. They came from a place called Lockhart near Wagga Wagga in the southern western part of NSW. Geoff Hunt was a grain farmer in the area and his wife Kim was a trained registered nurse. They had three children, Phoebe, Fletcher and Mia. The family were well respected in the community and Geoff Hunt was a third generation farmer. Geoff was very popular in the community and had lots of mates that he caught up with regularly. At times they were doing it tough but that is often the farmer's lot and it was said that the Hunt family weren't doing it any tougher than any other farmers in the district. What appears to have happened was that Geoff shot his wife first at the back of the house and then systematically shot his three beautiful children in the house. He then went to a dam not far from the homestead and shot himself. Five people dead; just like that. People that had seen Geoff just days before said that he looked completely normal and nothing seemed to be untoward. The family was said to be well integrated into the community — social, productive, well-loved citizens. Geoff Hunt seemed to have everything to live for and outwardly, nothing to die for. His wife Kim had a bad car accident a couple of years earlier and that bought about behavioural changes in her which included finding fault with her husband and putting him down, belittlement maybe. So, what happened? That will be up to a Coroner to determine but it could be that he was pushed beyond his limit and 'snapped'. Pushed by who? I think it likely that he was suffering from severe depression and under a lot of pressure in some aspects of his life since his wife's disability. Perhaps he just couldn't cope with the pressure and in some sort of egocentric deranged state of mind, went and got a gun, shot his wife and three kids dead and then shot himself. How terrible is that? All this being done by a 'salt of the earth' Aussie farmer who never raised his voice in anger to his family and from all accounts loved them dearly. My guess is that Greg Hunt would have been a really good bloke but 'snapped' and lost control of himself. It's a very sad story and I wonder if it could have been prevented by some type of earlier intervention.

Maybe Greg Hunt was suffering from depression and had made the decision not only to take his life, but that of his entire family; so that they could all die together; that sort of thinking. I'm sure we all remember the death of Luke Batty who was killed by his mentally disturbed father, Greg Anderson in February 2014. Luke was bashed with a cricket bat and then stabbed to death by his estranged father. It was later revealed that Greg had a history of mental illness and was the subject of an AVO (apprehended violence order). Luke died in front of some of his mates after a cricket training session in the little town of Tyabb, outside of Melbourne. Greg Anderson was shot by Police at the scene and died a short time later. I believe that Anderson told Police that his son was in a better place now and he wanted to join him. I image that he gave the Police no option but to shoot him so that he could join his son in wherever they believe they go. I find it appallingly sad.

Cases like these two repeat themselves far too often in our communities. I think it highlights the way that some people handle stress. In the case of Greg Hunt it may have been a case of his inability to admit to feeling depressed. He was a third generation farmer and it goes against the very core of what male rural people believe. They may think that getting mentally ill is weak and whatever they do, they must not admit to weakness. I have described that to you when I was shearing how taboo it was to be suffering from mental illness. In my case, I fabricated a story that I knew would be acceptable. Greg Hunt may have taken another option and saw through his darkened egocentric depressed mind, that the only solution was to end it all; for all of them. Maybe to send them to a better place. Maybe he thought that if he only killed himself, who would look after his family. What a terrible shame that whatever was the catalyst for this dreadful occurrence, he did not seemingly feel that he could go and talk with a medical professional in the first instance. The question has to be asked that if they had professional psychiatric help in Lockhart at that time, would Geoff Hunt have used it? Maybe not; maybe he would have. What is needed in the community is an education program that make people aware that mental illness is like any other human illness. We need to move away from that medieval rubbish we have been influenced by in the past and understand that depression is a sickness of the brain (biology) which is part of the body and needs to be treated just as any medical illness does. We have seen all too often, the consequences of neglect in this area and these consequences can be extraordinarily devastating and catastrophic.

What is depression? I don't know why but I find it very difficult to answer this question. When I went through my 'annus horribilis' that I have yet to tell you about, in 1995-1996, I had periods of sadness, unhappiness and almost total despair; but I don't believe that I was clinically depressed. When you are severely depressed, you go into a different condition of feeling that is very hard to articulate. It seems to come from within, hence some medical people call it endogenous depression. 'Endogenous' is the Latin word meaning 'from within'. It's almost like you are beset with something that is evil, something that is trying to destroy you. Severe depression is characterised by feelings of guilt, worthlessness, hopelessness and anhedonia. Anhedonia is the inability to feel pleasure from normally pleasurable things, such as sex. Reactive depression is said to be caused by stressful events in one's life. For example, you can imagine the mother in the story I will tell you about when I get to the Police section, who lost her son to a heroin overdose could have experienced depression as a result of his death. It might be reasonable to suggest that as a result of that awful news, she might have developed depression. You would at least know what the cause was and the medical people could go to work on it. With endogenous depression something very sinister and debilitating enters your system and attempts to destroy you. That's the best I can come up with.

Religious people might say, indeed used to say, it is the devil inside you. You lose your capacity to experience joy or happiness. I can honestly say that if you had told me that I had just won a million dollars in 1967, it would not have made one iota of a difference. You are in a constant state of melancholy and hopelessness. Abraham Lincoln confided in one of his cabinet colleagues after the death of his son Willie that he doubted that he would ever be happy again. Perhaps he wasn't. Behind it all I think, at least in my case, is that you have these terrible feelings of guilt and sense of failure; a sense of worthlessness and loss. Put simply, it is a feeling that you are not a worthwhile human being. Recovery depends on a host of factors. High on the list of these is that they seek professional help. We are talking about over two thousand suicides in Australia every year. An interesting comparison is Japan, which has about 30,000 per year with a population of 127 million. If Australia were to have the same rate as Japan, we would have 10,000 per year. Over one million people die by suicide worldwide each year. The main reason I never told anybody about my mental illness was that I felt ashamed of myself. For a very long time, I felt worse than a criminal. I felt that I was so weak and inadequate that it was an embarrassment to have to admit to being hospitalised for depression. This belief was not without foundation. People generally, especially in the 60s, had mental illness at the bottom of their respect ladder. If you were mentally ill you were an inferior being and treated accordingly. Strange when you consider that people like Churchill, Lincoln, Beethoven, Dickens, Newton, Mozart, Michelangelo and van Gough all had it.

Part of my later success in life would not have come had I admitted to mental illness. I would never have been accepted into the Police Force. It's doubtful that my wife would have wanted to be with me if I had explained to her what had happened to me. Most people would see you as just a weak and inadequate person, so why tell them? Indeed one psychiatrist told me once that I had a weakness in my personality. Imagine that. I wonder how most people would have handled my 'annus horribilis' the way that I did. I showed incredible strength and staying power, both mentally and physically through that period with no support whatsoever from any quarter, but didn't have a relapse into clinical depression. How many people would have declared bankruptcy if they were in the dire financial circumstances that I was? The vast majority would I'd suggest. How many people would have paid off the deed of arrangement like I did? How many people would have sent $2000 per month for their family like I did but kept nothing for himself? What's my point? My point is that rather than feel that I was an inadequate person, it was now time to see myself for what I really was; a good, strong, decent and honourable man. Paradoxically it was an opportunity to show people, especially myself, how stoic and resilient I really was. Even though I had a terrible time in that 1995/96 period that I will get to shortly, I was given an incredible opportunity to show people, especially myself, just what sort of a person I really was. Every cloud has a silver lining and I can assure you God had nothing to do with it.

I have made a conscious effort to bring up my children up in the opposite manner in which I was bought up. I never hit them and regularly reminded them of how good they were. I constantly sought to use positive reinforcement with them and so did Sue. Hitting the children was pretty much forbidden in our place. If my son came home and told me that the teachers had been bashing him, I would have approached them about it and may have reported it to the Police. If he came home and told me that one of the teachers was making fun of him in front of the other kids, I would be up to that school so quickly to sort it out. The problem was that my father was not that type of man and deep down I think he was pleased to be rid of me. Parents have this awesome responsibility in bringing up their children and I have to say, my parents failed their sons, me in particular. I paid a fairly hefty price for that and it affected me for the rest of my life. There will be those that say that I should not blame the church and my parents in this manner. That I should accept responsibility for what happened to me. They are wrong; so very wrong.

An interesting question might also be, "Where did you get the strength and character you showed during the 'annus horribilis' crisis of 1995/96?". To be fair and balanced, could it be that I also got that from my parents? I'd like to think that I did. I know that my parents faced an incredible amount of adversity when dealing with their own financial collapse, the migration to Queensland, living for years on the 'smell of an oily rag,' the severe droughts, the floods, my mental illness, and all the other obstacles that were placed in their path, but they kept going; they never faltered. You could imagine the hardships when they first went to Queensland living firstly in a tent and then in a shearing shed with no running water, no electricity, no sewerage, no telephone, and no cooking or washing facilities and most of all, no money. My parents were essentially pioneers who were doing it just as rough as the early pioneers of the 1850s would have done. The criticisms I have levelled at them centre around religious bigotry, domestic abuse, salve labour, exploitation, and no protection towards me. Nevertheless, they were in fact very resilient, hard-working and durable people who could face adversity and often did, in a very honourable manner. I believe that the strength of character that I showed during that very challenging period of 1995/96 I inherited from my parents and I must thank them very much for that. It's not a perfect world and it is a shame that I have to tarnish our relationship with the negative statements about them but I must not shy away from the truth, no matter how distasteful it may be.

There are many websites that people can be referred to if they think they suffer from depression and/or are suicidal. Generally speaking the starting point is to see your GP. This is what I did instead of telling my parents about it. I was lucky and I got a good one. I have told you about my experiences with the specialist physician in Rockhampton and the GP that inferred I was a loser in Christchurch. They were clueless about mental illness; but this was the 60s. Have things improved? I don't know. My intuition tells me that a lot of GPs are not switched on with mental disorders and know little about them. On the other hand, I imagine that some are really good with it. I suppose it's a matter of asking them how competent they feel in this area. There are many organisations that can help people as well. Places like Beyond Blue and The Black Dog Institute come to mind that offer a 24/7 consulting service.

There has been some very troubling occurrences in recent times. People suffering from depression, committing murder and suicide using aircraft. Take the case of the German-wings aircraft that flew into the French Alps. On the 24 March 2015 a German-wings Airbus A320 crashed in the French Alps while travelling from Barcelona to Dusseldorf. The plane was carrying more than 140 passengers. The co-pilot Andreas Lubitz, deliberately flew the Airbus A320 with 149 other people on board into the mountain range on March 24. He had his mental health questioned by aviation chiefs as far back as 2010. America's Federal Aviation Authority (FAA) debated whether to grant the rookie pilot a license to fly in the country following an episode of depression. A freedom of information request revealed Lubitz's German doctors convinced the FAA he had recovered. The fresh information proves authorities were aware the pilot potentially posed a danger and raised fresh questions over whether more could have been done to prevent the disaster. According to the documents released in America, Lubitz was being treated for severe depressive episodes with two drugs - Cipralex and

Mirtazapine — between January and October 2009. (As a matter of interest, Mirtazapine is the drug that I take, but only a small dose of it to help me sleep.) He required a US pilot's license to complete his Lufthansa pilot training, which includes several months' flying at a training centre in Arizona. The FAA was ultimately reassured by Lubitz's doctors but warned he could be barred from flying if his depression returned. As early as January 2009 he was prescribed antidepressants and being treated with psychotherapy. His German doctors said that his modified living conditions caused the onset of a depressive episode. So, was it depression that made Lubitz fly his plane into a mountain and kill 149 souls?

I mentioned earlier that clinical depression is rampart in western society, 25-30% of people have or are currently experiencing, clinical depression. Does that mean that of all of our pilots, 25-30% are clinically depressed? Probably not but it does indicate that at least some of the active pilots flying today would suffer from clinical depression. Of course that does not mean they are homicidal/suicidal, but the fact remains some could be. There's been quite a few murder and suicide cases involving pilots. I researched this and went to Wikipedia to find the answers. It is pretty scary stuff. On September 26, 1976, the pilot of an Aeroflot aircraft flew an Antonov An-2 from Novosibirsk-Severny Airport and crashed the aircraft into an apartment complex where his ex-wife lived. His ex-wife was not killed in the crash but twelve other people were; the pilot and eleven on the ground. On January 5, 1977, a disgruntled former employee of Connellan Airways flew a Beechcraft Baron into the Conn-air complex at the Alice Springs Airport killing himself and four on the ground. On August 22, 1979, a 23-year-old aircraft mechanic working at Bogota El Dorado Airport stole a Hawker-Siddeley HS-748 and crashed it into a Bogota suburb. There were four fatalities, the pilot and three on the ground. On February 9, 1982, a pilot on a commercial flight, Japan Airlines Flight 350, engaged numbers 2 and 3 engines thrust-reversers in mid-flight. The first officer and flight engineer were able to partially regain control; there were twenty-four fatalities. On 21 August 1994, the pilot of a commercial flight, Royal Air Maroc Flight 630 crashed the plane intentionally killing 44 people. On 19 December 1997, the pilot of a Commercial flight SilkAir Flight 185, crashed the plane intentionally, 104 dead. I remember this one well because my boss at the time narrowly missed putting his wife on this flight when I was in Singapore. On 31 October 1999, the first officer of a Commercial flight Egypt Air Flight 990, deliberately crashed the aircraft into the ocean after the captain left the cockpit, while repeatedly saying, "I rely on God" in Arabic, killing 217. On 18 April 2002, a pilot crashed into the Pirelli Tower in Milan killing three. On 29 November 2013, the pilot of a commercial flight, LAM Mozambique Airlines Flight 470, intentionally crashed the plane; the co-pilot was locked out of the cockpit, according to the voice recorder; 33 were killed. On March 8, 2014, a commercial flight Malaysia Airlines Flight 370, the pilot is thought to have committed suicide, killing 239 people.

I wonder how many of these people were clinically depressed when they carried out these horrendous acts. I wonder if any of these pilots could have been prevented from flying. Just how responsible are Psychiatrists that allow people like Lubitz to fly a commercial aircraft. If we accept that 30% of our population are or have been clinically depressed, then on average, that would mean that of the 16,000 serving members of the NSW Police Force, that close to 5000 are suffering clinical depression. In my day we were all armed and took our firearms home every night and I suppose that is still the case. I don't think we even handed them in for holidays. Yet I never heard of a cop wiping out his family or anybody else's for that matter. I have heard of many cops that committed suicide with their service revolver and I will tell you about three of them that I knew well when I come to the section on my Police days. It seems to me that it is too easy to say that depression caused Lubitz to fly that aircraft into the French Alps. To my mind, there could be a lot more to it. I recall reading in the Sydney Morning Herald about the murderer, Daniel Kelsall (2015). He had told his GP a year before he murdered Morgan Huxley in 2013 that he was having thoughts about following someone on their way home from work and stabbing them just 'for the thrill of it'. He was also said to have told his psychiatrist before the murder that he wanted to murder someone saying, "It would probably be a total random, with a knife. I could hide a body". Yet during a sentencing hearing the prosecutor told the court that a psychiatrist had found that Kelsall was not suffering from any mental disorder that explained his crime, but that he did have a personality disorder with 'psychopathic traits'. Isn't that a contradiction? It seems to me that the medical profession is letting society down a bit here but I don't have the answers; it is far too complex for me.

What worries me as a father and grandfather is that great young people find that the only way out of their depression is to commit suicide. We as a society must be failing them and probably thousands of others. If well over 2,000 people are committing suicide each year, this is a major problem. Look at the massive resources we pour into road safety, including the top heavy levels of staff in the Police Highway patrols in all of the states. Then again, this is a good revenue stream for the government; cynicism perhaps! Yet the road toll is much less than suicide. In 2012 the road tool in Australia was 1,310 deaths and that's a very sad and a sobering statistic. Suicide was nearly double that. All governments, local, state and federal, have to do much, much more to tackle this problem of depression, PTSD and suicide. I consider myself one of the lucky ones and managed to escape to some degree at least, its life-long evil clutches. A good starting point would be to implement the recommendations of the Royal Commission into Child Sexual Abuse when they are released. I believe that will be towards the end of 2017.

One recommendation I'd make is that medical students should be given more focused training in psychiatric medicine and this training needs to be supplemented with extra training for GPs. They are the people at the coalface. We don't want GPs asking severely depressed patients what is the difference between your mother yelling at you and a Regimental Sergeant Major; or we don't want a GP telling a young lady whose fiancé he is treating, that she ought to move on and find someone else worthwhile. We have to do a lot better than that.

On the issue of obsessional neurosis, this has been my unwanted companion for many years. I cannot be specific about when I first experienced unwanted thoughts but I can be clear that it was after the depression, although not long after. Does that mean that they are related, along with anxiety disorder and the depression? Are they interlinked and kinda married to one another? This is a source of a lot of conjecture with the medical people. Some say definitely yes; some say definitely no. Who do you listen to? I do know that when I am doing well in my professional and social life, everything is much better. The depression is almost non-existent but the obsessional thinking and anxiety can prevail. I know that my obsessional thinking was much worse when I was nursing and I rationalised that this was because I hated what I was doing. The obsessional thinking might include things like doing harm to a patient, like turning off the drip or injecting a drip with an overdose of insulin. Or something much simpler like punching the Charge Sister in the mouth or doing some other horrendous thing to her. Another unwanted thought was that you would masturbate a male patient in the washing process who was immobilised. Imagine! It was that sort of thinking that created a great deal of anxiety. I could not and still can't understand why I had to have such awful thoughts and medicine did not know how to treat this in the early 70s. My research indicates that the causes of OCD (obsessional compulsive disorder) are not fully understood. Research shows that OCD may be related to chemical, structural and functional abnormalities in the brain. Genetic and hereditary factors may also play a role in the development of OCD. There we go again; blame our genes. It is likely that each person's OCD is the result of several interacting factors and is affected by stressful life events, hormonal changes and personality traits. That's saying a lot without say much at all. What they do know is that about 3% of all Australians will develop OCD. Do the maths, 3% of 23,000,000 is 690,000 people.

There is some good news. There is now effective treatment, which was not available in my younger days but I won't be pursuing it, because it is not like it used to be. What they generally do now is put you on medication (I think usually one of the SSRIs anti-depressives) and couple that with CBT (cognitive behaviour therapy) and psychotherapy. The medications help the brain restore its normal chemical balance which in turn helps to control the obsessions and compulsions. I suppose I was lucky that I did not have the overt compulsions so it was never obvious to anybody, only me. CBT helps you challenge and overcome automatic thoughts, and uses practical strategies to change or modify their behaviour. The result hopefully is more positive feelings, which in turn leads to more positive thoughts and behaviours. That's the theory; easier said than done I should think but I am told, the medical people have a lot of success with it.

Taking an entirely different angle, I wonder if it may be that the obsessional thinking escalated during my nursing days could have been an unconscious defence mechanism protecting me against having to continue with it. It was distressing as you can imagine. You knew you would never do it (or did you) but at the same time you could not control the thoughts entering your mind. If you knew that you were not going to carry out your thought, why would you have the thought in the first place? I really needed help with this. I seldom had any of these thoughts when I was doing the removal work and I felt that its severity was related to my doing nursing when I really did not want to do it. I have told you how much I hated it and that is why I see it as a likely unconscious defence mechanism.

I spoke to my flat mate Gary about it and he put me onto a clinical psychologist that was doing work in this area at the University of New South Wales; a fella named Dr. Ron Farmer. He was a great bloke and he worked with me to at least learn to cope with it. He used to record the conversations on a tape and give me the tape to go over so that I was reminded of the issues and how I was going to deal with them. He tried aversion therapy. The idea was that I would put an elastic band around my wrist and every time I had an unpleasant thought, I would hit myself with the band, inflicting a bit of pain. The theory was that your mind would start registering that unpleasant thought would bring pain to you and ultimately you would stop having them. All very well in theory but it did not really work. I think that these days it has largely been discredited. An example given to me by a psychiatrist was of a priest who would get the thought that when he got up in the pulpit, he would tell his congregation to get f***** and that they were all a bunch of c****. I must admit I could not stop laughing when he told me this and he wondered why I found it so funny. Of course it is anything but funny and it's far from being a laughing matter. Just imagine how terribly uncomfortable that would be for the poor priest and how much anxiety it would cause before the event. I can truly identify with this priest and my heart goes out to him. I first came across aversion therapy for the homosexuals at the Prince Henry but was not directly involved in it.

My OCD is referred to as Pure Obsessional OCD. Pure OCD is when you report experiencing obsessions without observable compulsions. For people like me with pure obsessional OCD, these thoughts can be frightening and torturous precisely because they were so antithetical to my values and beliefs. That is it in a nutshell; they are so antithetical to one's beliefs. The obsessional thoughts are directly opposite those that you would want and that's why they hurt so much. I think the medical profession, at least at the general practitioner level, generally don't have a clue what to do with this sort of thing. They may take the view that because the patient is not going to hurt anybody that he/she is likely to be depressed and just put them on antidepressant medication and hope for the best. Of course they'd be depressed and in this case, the doctor knows why. What he doesn't know is how to treat it. What they should be doing, is to send the patient to a specialist psychiatrist. I think the term Pure Obsessional OCD is somewhat inaccurate. While it may at first appear that people like me experience obsessions without compulsions, they say that a careful assessment almost always uncovers numerous compulsive behaviours, avoidant behaviours, reassurance-seeking behaviours, and mental compulsions. These behaviours are not as easily observed as other, more obvious OCD symptoms, such as hand-washing and checking the gas is turned off, but they are clearly compulsive responses to unwanted obsessions. For many years it was thought that pure obsessional OCD was next to impossible to manage because there were no behaviours (compulsions) to treat, only thoughts. However, a specific type of Cognitive-Behavioural Therapy (CBT) known as "Exposure and Response Prevention" (ERP) has proven to be very successful in the treatment of pure obsessional OCD. Using ERP, you learn to directly face your fears of specific thoughts, and to proactively challenge the compulsive and avoidant behaviours you have been using to cope with these thoughts. Another CBT technique that is said to be extremely valuable is called Cognitive Restructuring, in which you learn to challenge the validity of the unwanted thoughts that are causing you so much distress. You can imagine how difficult it would be to discuss one's OCD with your partner, especially if the unwanted thoughts included violent thoughts towards her. When I write this I am reminded of Sir Winston Churchill's problem with OCD where he had to have a pillar on the station platform between him and a speeding train. I think we can speculate reasonably what unwanted thought was going through his head. Modern thinking on the subject seems to be suggesting that most sufferers of OCD, if not all, have a history of OCD in the family giving evidence that it is hereditary, therefore physiological. Isn't that interesting? I wonder if my Dad (or Mum) suffered from it. I know for sure that if either of them did, they would keep it to themselves; that is for sure. I don't think that this is too hard to understand.

We all have different ways of coping with stress. In my Mum's case, she used to get very severe migraines and that was terrible. Some people like my Dad never showed it; some get boisterous and loud, some get aggressive, some get violent, some people just get moody, some get angry, some go on a drinking binge, some take to drugs, whatever, we all have our own ways of dealing with stress. Unfortunately some of us have chosen sinister methods to deal with it and that is what we need to change. If we want to get rid of whatever is ailing us, we need to find ways to deal with the stress. We need to be better equipped to identify the red flags, intercept them and put in place methods that will mitigate the stress. We can call that stress management. Perhaps that's why people that practice yoga and meditation report that once they do, they are less bothered by mental disturbances.

In my case, the doctors rationalised that if you could successfully treat the depression, you would also be treating the OCD and anxiety. I think to a large degree that is correct. I am told that there is a group of psychiatrists that do not adhere to this view. With treating depression there has been major developments with the advent of the SSRI drugs. SSRI is an acronym for selective serotonin re-uptake inhibitors. I think that I cope pretty well and coming from the position where I was in 1967, I think I have done amazingly well. F*** it, I am going to take some credit for that. I did try SSRIs once and I had a very bad reaction with them. I really thought that I was going mad and stopped taking them after a couple of days. They made me very agitated. I now know that you have to be very careful prescribing these drugs to patients and GPs need to have a better understanding of the side effects, which can lead to homicidal behaviour, especially in adolescents. I now take a drug named Mirtazapine (generic), commonly called Remeron (brand). The normal dose is 30 mg per day but can be shot up to 60 mg per day for the severely depressed. I take 15 mg per day and have done for the last fifteen years. It has served me well. It has two well-known side effects, one good, one bad. I get them both. The good one is that it can create drowsiness and in that sense, it helps me to sleep better. In fact the first time I took it, I took 30 mg and slept for fifteen hours. The second one is that it can increase the appetite and that makes you eat more. They actually give it to people sometimes as an appetite stimulant. Consequently, you can gain weight and over the past fifteen years I have done just that. Nevertheless, I have decided to stay with this one as the side effects of the SSRIs were just too much for me to deal with. It totally killed my libido, not to mention the agitation that it caused in me. However, many millions of people have benefited by taking the SSRIs for their depression and for some, they are miracle drugs. The most common are Prozac, Paxil, Lexapro, Celexa and Zoloft. With the depression, OCD and anxiety, it's very much a what came first, the chicken or the egg!

There are some who think that an individual's brain chemistry is the defining factor in their happiness. It doesn't matter what else you are. You may be a multi-millionaire or a bum but if you are not getting the right doses of serotonin, oxytocin and dopamine circulating in your brain, you can be pretty miserable. There is an interesting book that talks about it named 'Sapiens: A Brief History of Humankind.' The author Yuval Harari writes that when a person experiences a sense of euphoria as a result of some type of stimulus (e.g., being successful with examination results) that they are not really reacting to that result but rather to the release of certain hormones that are released due to that stimuli. Imagine if he is right!

There are the drugs I discussed, but I have learnt that one in three people don't respond to medication. For those people with severe depression who don't respond then ECT can be used. That's what happened in my case and I have said that ECT saved my life. People with OCD and anxiety now have good options to treat their disorder. They have recently come up with something called Trans-cranial Magnetic Stimulation (TMS) and they are using this at the Monash Alfred Psychiatry Research Centre in Melbourne. In 2008 the Food and Drug Administration in the US approved TMS as a treatment for people with major depression who have failed to respond to at least one antidepressant. It must be noted that I am not qualified to write about what depression/ OCD/anxiety are in the medical sense. However, I think from my own experiences, I am able to talk a bit about what caused it in my case and I have done that. I mentioned some significant traumas that I have experienced, especially in early childhood, but there may be others that are embedded into my subconscious. I don't know. I don't know how much of a part genetics played in it. I think that most medical professionals think that there is a generic risk with a family history of mental illness as they do with most other illnesses. They are certainly saying that about OCD. No doubt this is one of the reasons for writing this book. I want my children to know about it and what to do should if it visits them in their lifetimes. Dad certainly had a lot of avoidance habits, as well as burying his head in the sand, the 'emu phenomena' and the talking to himself was different. Mum had her severe migraine, very aggressive behaviour and lived a very stressful life after we migrated to Queensland.

I think it is fair to say that good mental health starts at home and it is just so important that parents give their children the strong foundations in their youth, starting from being a toddler to their adolescence years. To do that, the parents have to be the right role models. Where our family went wrong in simplistic terms, was that Mum wore the pants and she was not equipped or able to carry out the function of the man. She was must too 'fiery' and needed to be controlled, but unfortunately there was no one around to do that and you know who took the brunt of that. Still there is much to admire about both of them though and we must not lose sight of that. My overall assessment of my mental illness is that it resulted from childhood and adolescence trauma.

However, the true cause of depression has not been settled even though many experts suggest that chemical imbalances in the brain or genetic disposition are largely to blame. However, a growing body of pre-eminent global researches think that there is growing evidence that in many cases of depression, it is our own immune system that is blame. Imagine that. It could after all be a physical disease, just like diabetes. They think that trauma suffered in childhood (e.g., being sent to boarding school at the age of 5 years), could create inflammation in the brain. In adulthood, this group of people when under severe stress, develop inflammation in the brain and it is this inflammation that causes the depression which does not respond to conventional medication. Certainly I didn't respond to the SSRI's (the miracle drugs) and it is said that about a third of depressives fall into this category. Could it be in my case that the childhood and adolescence trauma I have described caused inflammation in the brain? When I was rejected by Pauline in adulthood, the momentary stress of it caused the inflammation and I was unable to recover from it, even though she did her best to reconcile the following morning. That in turn lead to severe depression. I wonder; it makes sense to me.

There's hope yet!

Chapter Seven: POW and PH Hospitals, Sydney
1972-1975

In 1972 - President Nixon made an unprecedented eight-day visit to Communist China and met with Mao Zedong. US Supreme Court ruled that the death penalty was unconstitutional. CAT (Computerized Axial Tomography) scanning was developed in England. The compact disk was developed by RCA (US). The antidepressant Prozac (fluoxetine) was developed by Bryan B. Malloy (Scotland) and Klaus K. Schmiegel (US). The video disk was introduced by Philips Company (Netherlands). Electronic mail was introduced. The Movies released included *The Godfather, Deliverance, Cabaret, Sleuth,* and *The Discreet Charm of the Bourgeoisie*. Notable deaths included those of Edgar J. Hoover and President Harry Truman.

In 1973 - A ceasefire was signed ending involvement of American ground troops in the Vietnam War. US bombing of Cambodia ended, marking the official halt to 12 years of combat activity in Southeast Asia. Egypt and Israel signed US-sponsored cease-fire accord. Nuclear Magnetic Resonance (NMR), the technology behind MRI scanning, was developed. Skylab, the first American space station, was launched. At the 1972 Academy Awards, Sacheen Littlefeather stood in for Marlon Brando and refused his Best Actor Oscar for his role in *The Godfather*, to protest the US Government's treatment of Native Americans. Movies released included *The Harder They Come, American Graffiti, The Exorcist, The Sting,* and *Last Tango in Paris*. Notable people that died included those of Betty Grable, Pablo Picasso and President Lyndon Baines Johnson.

In 1974 - OPEC ended the oil embargo that began in 1973 during the Yom Kippur War. India successfully tested an atomic device, becoming the world's sixth nuclear power. US President Nixon announced his resignation; the first President to do so. Vice President Gerald R. Ford of Michigan was sworn in as 38th President of the US. The movies released included *Chinatown, The Godfather Part II, Day for Night, Blazing Saddles* and *The Towering*

Inferno. Notable deaths included those of Bud Abbott, Dizzy Dean, Duke Ellington, Charles Lindberg and Ed Sullivan.

In 1975 - Pol Pot and Khmer Rouge took over Cambodia. The city of Saigon surrendered and remaining Americans were evacuated, ending the Vietnam War. John N. Mitchell, H. R. Haldeman and John D. Ehrlichman were found guilty of Watergate cover-up and sentenced to 30 months to 8 years in jail. President Ford escaped assassination attempt in California. Home videotape systems (VCRs) were developed in Japan by Sony (Betamax) and Matsushita (VHS). The Altair home computer kit allowed consumers to build and program their own personal computers. *One Flew Over the Cuckoo's Nest*, swept the top Oscars, winning Best Picture, Best Director, Best Actor, and Best Actress. Other movies released were *Jaws, Nashville, Dog Day Afternoon* and *Barry Lyndon*. Notable deaths included those of Aristotle Onassis, Haile Selassie and Casey Stengel. The population of the world was 4.086 billion.

My life took a different direction in 1972 with the beginning of my nursing diploma in October of that year. Arriving in Sydney at the end of 1971 or beginning of 1972, I was off all drugs and was not having any psychiatric treatment. The work I had in Sydney with Grace Brothers Removals in furniture removals was hard work; made harder by the fact that all the trucks were owner operated; but I loved it. What I loved most about it, was that I was getting paid for my labour. Coming from a background of hard physical work on the land, I found hard work second nature. Lugging pianos, refrigerators, washing machines, etcetera, up and down stairs, I got very fit. I got as strong as a bull and most of the owner drivers wanted me to work for them. Whilst there I was 'bullied' by another one of the permanent staff, a bloke that was a little bit older than myself. I can't remember his name but by now I had extreme anathema about being bullied. I wasn't the smallest boy in the school anymore and resented being treated that way. I called him out in front of everybody one day and wanted to settle it the old way with the Queensberry rules, like we used to do at boarding school. He didn't want to fight but the bullying stopped and generally the men were on my side in the argument. It is really interesting that some people, fortunately not too many, sense that some people can be bullied because of their appearance and manner. They think that just because they are easy going and agreeable that they are weak, but usually that is not the case, and they get it very wrong; to their detriment. They confuse kindness and geniality with weakness. This was such a case. Sometimes they do it because they are in a position of authority and they just enjoy seeing someone being humiliated and put down in front of others like my Overseer did when I was a Jackaroo. I saw so much of that in the cops and you can imagine whose side I was on. I stayed with Grace Brothers Removals for about nine months until I was accepted to study at the Prince of Wales Hospital. I was a bit sorry to leave there actually as I loved the hard work; the pay was good and the men were generally good fun to be with. Whilst it was hard work, it was nothing compared to shearing those wrinkly jumbucks (merino sheep) on 'The banks of the Condamine.' Now that I was off all the medication, working hard, sleeping well and enjoying my work, I was looking good. I was now starting to have some success with the ladies and for most of the time that I was working at Grace Bros Removals I was going out with a very nice and attractive girl from the North Island of NZ.

I mentioned to you earlier that I went back to school in 1963 because I wanted to go to university and make my parents happy and proud of me. The real reason may have been that I was believing all the negative criticism that was being directed towards me about my future so it might have been more of an appeasement reaction. Mum wanted a son who would be successful and not someone 'just like his father.' She was absolutely sure that I could be whatever I wanted to be because the teaching clergy had told her so. All I had to do was to apply myself. Mum was more or less indirectly influencing me into going back to school. She would have loved to have had a son who was a priest and if not that, then a doctor. At that time I decided I wanted to become a doctor so that would indicate that

I had an interest in the health field. I knew one thing was for sure. I didn't want to be a cocky and a shearer for the rest of my life. With this in mind I decided to do a diploma in nursing. I was aware that this field was dominated by women and that most of the men that were nurses were gay but I wanted to do it anyway. I do have a compassionate and humanitarian streak in me, especially for the more unfortunate in our society. I think I mentioned earlier that people that have suffered tend to have more empathy with other people that suffer. Plus of course, there was the motivation that my mother had badgered me over the years about never being able to do what the girls had done. I could never do it because I didn't have any staying power; basically because I was a 'useless damn coot'. Certainly when I started the course I quickly found out that I hated it and Mum's negativism about me did motivate me to finish it. It really did keep me going and in retrospect I'm only half pleased that I did. I couldn't bear the thought of giving her the satisfaction of proving that she was right. In a sense, Mum unknowingly did me a favour. I really did have an interest in medicine. So I went out to the Prince of Wales hospital at Randwick in Sydney and filled out all the forms, had the interviews, and was accepted.

Wow, it was a cultural shock for me. I had gone from the very macho environment of removing furniture, shearing and the like, and now I was in a women's world. Of course, there were some benefits to that and I'll go into that later. There were some really profound negatives as well. In those days student nurses were overwhelmingly women and accommodation was provided for them, but not for men. We were all being paid a paltry $38 per week at the time and I can tell you that even a simple purchase like buying a beer was a rarity. At first I stayed with a Greek family in their house in Kensington that I had sourced through the accommodation section of the UNSW (University of New South Wales). The hospitals were the teaching hospitals for the UNSW and we were able to use their services. The Greek accommodation didn't suit me as I was basically cooped up in a room so I started to look around for something more suitable. I answered an advertisement in the local Randwick rag. Two medical students were looking for a flat mate and they wanted $12 a week for the room in Dutruc Street, Randwick and I replied to the advert. Can you believe $12 per week? (1973). These fellas were in their final year of medicine and in those days medicine was a six year course before you became an intern at a hospital. I think at the time you could only get into medicine if you were in the top 3% of the state in the Higher School Certificate (NSW). That does seem odd as you could have been anybody but all you had to be was intelligent. My understanding was that there were no interviews to determine suitability or anything like that. When I went to see the boys about the spare room, one of them said to me at the interview, quote, "Well mate, I have only one question for you. Are you a poofter?" Nothing like calling it as it is. His name was Justin and I became very good friends with him. I told him I wasn't and he was happy for me to move in. The other bloke Gary concurred, so I moved in with these final year medical students and it was great. They were great blokes.

Gary spent his life studying and every night he would be burning the midnight oil. Justin was the opposite. This unit was one of about six in this very big old mansion that used to be the Randwick's Mayor's house. We lived very cheaply and paid $9 per week for our meat. The local butcher would put a bit together for the 'boys' and we could collect it every Saturday. I loved living there. My depression was much better but the obsessional thinking and anxiety increased. I think that might have had something to do with my aversion to nursing and the social interaction with all those women. I really did not like it. I have learnt that it tends to be worse in stressful situations which makes perfect sense. I was finding it hard to adjust to a women's world. In the main the nursing sisters were good to me, but some of them made it clear I was not wanted. I recall in the last ward I did before I finished the three years, this young lesbian Sister made me clean all the pans and bottles. This is normally nothing much but it was the infectious disease ward and a fairly demeaning job for a graduate nurse. I struggled throughout but the severe depression did not come back. In fact, it never has. Many of the male nurses were gay and it was generally considered that if males did nursing they would most probably be gay. That was not quite right but having said that, many were. I think there were about eight males in our class and only one or two were gay; maybe our class set the trend for change. These days there are many dedicated married men that have successful careers in nursing and we think nothing of it but at the time, it was a bit of a deal.

I think that if I didn't have Justin and Gary as company away from the hospital for that first year, I wouldn't have made it. Socially, I was constantly having to explain why I was a nurse. Some bloke would say to me in a social setting, "What do you do Max?" I'd tell them that I was a nurse and they would say, "What, a male nurse?" After a while, I used to tell people I was a fireman. It was a lot easier. Earlier I mentioned I gave up smoking in 1973 and doing that is one of the best decisions I have ever made. Giving up smoking is very hard. You have to be a strong minded person to be able to do it. I found out that I had the mental strength that hitherto I did not believe I had. I was smoking at least forty cigarettes per day, every day, and with my medical exposure I knew I would end up with many severe medical conditions if I did not give up. One night I was having a drink and I decided that now was the time. I went cold turkey and have never had one since. Would you believe that's forty-three years ago? There were a number of catalysts stimulating the need to quit smoking but the nail in the coffin was probably when we were given a lecture by one of the pathologists in the morgue. One day a group of us attended a post mortem. I don't know how that came about but one of the nurses organised it. The cadaver was an elderly person who had died from lung cancer. After the pathologist had opened up the chest cavity and surrounding areas, he cut out a piece of the lung and showed us. He asked us for a show of hands on how many of us smoked. Most of us put our hands up and he told us that whilst he could not guarantee that if we smoked we would die from one of the many causes of smoking (lung cancer, emphysema, chronic obstructive pulmonary disease, heart disease, stroke, asthma, diabetes, blindness, cataracts and age-related macular degeneration) he could guarantee that if we smoked, our lungs would look like the piece of lung tissue he had in his hand and it looked awful. It was more black than pink and it was a very effective way for the pathologist to make his point. That sealed it for me. It was that night at the Prince Henry Golf Club that I gave up smoking. Earlier in the book I did the maths on what I have saved from not smoking. It really is a staggering figure but even more importantly, is that smoking impinges on your quality of life and will most likely lead to a premature death.

I was training with the University of New South Wales Rugby Club at this time and the Club had arranged a tour to go to New Zealand on a rugby tour. The hospital made a bit of mileage out of letting it be known that one of their student nurses was going on a rugby tour in NZ. In the trial match at Port Hacking I lasted ten minutes. You would not believe it; my shoulder popped out again. I was devastated. The putti platt operation was twelve years ago and I had been assured by one of the best orthopaedic surgeons in Brisbane that it was very unlikely to happen again. First game of rugby in the first few minutes of the game and it came out. No NZ rugby tour for me and to think, the Matron was going to let me go as well.

After six weeks in a sling I went back to my studies and work. I had now decided to join the AIF (Australian Infantry Forces) Reserve Commandos. They were stationed at Georges Heights near Mosman. To get in, I had to pass the fitness tests which were of a fairly high standard. I couldn't get fit smoking forty cigarettes a day and I have told you how I eventually managed to get on top of this. I saw the evidence on a daily basis what it was doing to people. What I did not mention when I addressed the smoking issue was how badly I was addicted to it. I had been smoking since I was 13. You will remember how I told you about Brother Higgins catching me with a sack of tobacco in my pocket and gave me an almighty backhander that knocked me to the ground. One of the great delights I used to have, was to roll a cigarette and have a smoke. I loved it but knew it was killing me. When I was working in the wards I was forever ducking off to the toilet mid-way through the shift to have a smoke, which was forbidden. You could have a smoke in the break in the staff room but nowhere else. I found that the last thing that I would do of a night before switching off the bedside lamp would be to put out a cigarette and the very first thing I would do in a morning before getting out of bed would be to have a smoke. I developed a chronic cough and I knew that if I did not do something about this addiction I would ultimately pay the price for it. I had a strong support base. Justin and Gary never smoked so there was no smoking at home and Geoff (another new flat mate) and I, along with a few of his friends, started running. We would usually do that at Centennial Park and I started to get pretty fit; fit enough to be accepted into the Commandos. When I had to do the medical, the army Doctor asked me about the putti platt scar but I assured him that it was fine and that I had not had any problems since the operation in 1960-61. I neglected to tell him that it had recently 'popped out' during a game of rugby. That could have been a big mistake because part of the exercises that we carried out at the Commandoes was parachuting and well, you can imagine the dire circumstances that could arise if it 'popped out' whilst doing a jump.

I was now at the end of my first year of nursing and generally speaking I 'hated' it. One night, when I was on night duty at the Prince Henry I was five minutes late for a shift. Bearing in mind I had to catch a bus from Randwick to Little Bay, it might have been reasonable that I could be late. That was not the case with the hospital hierarchy in those days. I had to report to the Matron's office the following day. The Matron gave me a stern dressing down and told me that I was very lucky that she was approving my promotion which she subsequently did. I was now a first year student nurse, aged 29, and had two years to go. It meant that I could now get one stripe on my uniform. I suppose that was better than being institutionalised in a mental hospital; but only marginally I'd suggest.

Life continued to be good at the flat. Justin was an extremely intelligent man, probably in the genius class. You wouldn't think so though. He never studied and wore jodhpurs and R. M. Williams riding boots. All he wanted in life was to be a cocky: own some cattle and sheep and live the life of a farmer and grazier. His father was a respected solicitor in Wollongong and had a small farm on the outskirts of town. We had a fire place at Dutruc Street and I got it into my mind that the girls might find sitting around the fire a romantic activity. I asked Justin if he had any dead timber on the farm. He said it was everywhere and as an added bonus, he had a utility car and a chain saw. Remember St Brendan's and how we used to get all the wood for the school. Well, we did the same here except we used a chainsaw instead of an electrical circular saw. We filled up his ute with sawn logs from the farm and got the fire going at home in our flat. We had some great times around that fire and I can tell you that I put paid to Justin's fears that I might be a homosexual, multiple times over. Many nurses (female) would come around, we told yarns, recited a bit of Australian poetry, played some of the fashionable music of the 70s and drank around the fire at Dutruc Street. Of course, some of these nurses stayed the night with me. It was on one such occasion that I met this young nurse who was 18 I think, and she let me sleep with her. I mentioned earlier I was starting to find my feet with women now and did not have the inferiority complex that plagued me during my teenage years. Well, I thought that I was in heaven and found the experience so exhilarating I kinda fell in love with her. She went home to her nursing quarters the next morning and I thought that we might be able to get things going again so I rang for her a number of times but she was never in. Finally I woke up that she had decided to ditch me after just one night. This hit me very hard indeed and I was not mature enough to deal with it effectively. She was in the same class as me during our training and we had to regularly go to the Nursing Education Centre for our formal lectures and learning medical theory. This could go on for several weeks, several times a year. I never spoke to her again, even though we were in the same class. That is the way that I dealt with rejection at this point in time and it further endorsed my view that women generally could not be trusted. I think it was about this time and after this innocuous incident, that I made a conscious decision that I would never fall in love again. I need to explain that. I mean the type of love that makes you a slave to the other person. It is all encompassing and for someone like me with my type of personality, it was just too dangerous a path to do down. The fear of rejection and abandonment was just too great for me and that was clearly demonstrated with the Pauline incident in 1966/1967.

My one night stand with this 18-year old nurse showed again how immature I was with handling this type of love. It really upset me that she could dump me like that and I took it badly but in the longer term, she did me a great favour. That was when I resolved that in any future love affairs, I would have more control and make sure that I did not become psychologically dependent on my partners. I resolved that if they walked away from it, I would be ok and would not breakdown. That is what I have done for the rest of my life and it worked. It was that way when I got married and it was that way when I entered into my existing long term partnership. I loved them both but in a different, less encompassing and dramatic way. I did not crack up when my wife left me and handled it well. If my present partner left me, I would not breakdown. I'd be sad for sure, but I could deal with it. No more Romeo and Juliet type romances for me after this incident with the 18-year old nurse beauty.

Oddly enough Justin thought it was not right that we sleep with women before marriage. Of course after the first girl stayed with me, there were plenty more women and we kept the fire going so to speak. Justin also never touched alcohol. He had very high moral principles and he would not get involved in that side of things. Nor would Gary; he had a lovely girlfriend who he later married and had five children with. In a moment of weakness once, Justin did ask me for my little black book with the names and phone numbers of women that I knew (there weren't that many), but he didn't go through with it. I mentioned that another chap joined us from Wollongong - Geoff Bright. He was doing a Diploma of Education at the University of New South Wales (UNSW), as a post graduate course to be qualified as a high school teacher. The four of us got on well and we never had any problems. Geoff was on a scholarship at the UNSW and he would get more on that scholarship than I would in wages from the hospitals. It was the age of promiscuity and one of the benefits of working as a Nurse in a big city teaching hospital was the availability of sex. Apart from Gary and Justin, I now had a circle of friends and had to some degree lost my introversion and feelings of inferiority. I suppose it was more about moving on from the depression. I had quite a few girls come around and it became of bit of a source of conversation with my male friends. One time I arranged for a group of them to come up to Moonie Park at Tara in my Holden station wagon. To help pass the kilometres (945 of them), we tried to work out how many women we had all 'screwed' in the last twelve months. I can't remember what the tally was for the other boys but I remember that I got up to about 12 or so; averaging one per month. I look back on that and wonder what we were all about, and the conclusion I come to is that we were just a bunch of juvenile prats.

Justin went on to become a highly respected specialist in Gastro Intestinal (GI) medicine and set up shop in Texas, USA; Austin I think. I have not caught up with him for probably near forty years but I don't think he ever got that farm he so dearly would have liked. Gary became a specialist in Cardiology and he also is highly respected in his field in NSW. I still see Geoff fairly regularly. He gave away teaching, realising that this was not the way to make real money and went into selling photo copying machines. He made a lot of money doing this. He married, had three children and now lives on the North Shore in Sydney. We all stayed together until Gary and Justin had to go to do their internships at different hospitals.

In my second year of nursing, I spent most of my time at the Prince Henry Hospital (now defunct). At one stage, I worked in the Police ward and found out that I got on very well with the

Police patients. I had been toying with the idea of giving nursing away and applying to join the Police. I was worried about the past history of mental illness and knew that they would not take me if I told them about it; that's common sense. I knew then that I would not tell them about it but thought that there would be a real possibility that they would uncover it when they did their investigation into my background. Naturally when they found out, they would reject me. I am not sure that I was that immature at this time not to give nursing away just because of Mum's taunts; but it helped, definitely. That did act as a motivating tool. You often read where coaches take some negative comments out of the paper and pin them up in the dressing sheds to remind the boys what the opposition think of them or something like that. I saw it as something similar to that. In those days the Police promotion system was based on seniority, not merit. Consequently, the earlier you joined the quicker you would get promoted. I spoke about it with the cops in their ward (Ward 2 at Prince Henry) and they generally reckoned that it was better to get in sooner rather than later. I hesitated but did go in to Police Headquarters in College Street, Sydney and applied.

The day that I went in to be considered would have been sometime in early 1974. There were about sixty or seventy other applicants there. They started off by giving us an English test by reading an editorial out of the Sydney Morning Herald. They would then mark that and something like half of the applicants failed. Off they went, just like that. Than we got onto simple mathematics and they marked that. That cut it down further until there were about ten or so of us left. I can't remember what the next test was but I do remember that at the end of the tests, there were only three of us left standing. The next step in the chain was that we three would have to come back at an appointed time and do our medical. If we passed that, we would than go before a selection panel of three senior Police. So, you can see it was no easy feat to get into the Police Force. In those days, gays were not accepted and although it wasn't official, nor were Aboriginals or Asians. They also didn't encourage women but they had to let some in. I went back to my contact at Police

HQ and he said that he had discussed my application with one of the Senior Superintendents. They felt that I should finish nursing, get the qualification and they would send me to the Police Rescue Squad. Of course, none of this was official. I procrastinated about it and eventually decided to stay in hell for another eighteen months. The Police Rescue Squad really appealed to me as it was one of the few squads in the force that the people respected and it had an approval appeal to it. The Police knew that I would be a qualified paramedic and that was unheard off in those days, that you would find paramedics outside the ambulance service. For example, say in cliff rescues which the rescue squad was originally set up for, I would be able to be lowered down to the victim and could legally do electrocardiograms and/or give them intravenous injections and perform other life-saving procedures such as defibrillation. You could imagine the public relations that the Police could get out of this and I warmed to this thinking. This fitted into my personality characteristic of seeking approval by others. This would give the public a much more positive image of the Police Force. They felt that the Highway Patrol were giving the Police a bad name and they needed initiatives like this to balance it out. Of course, they would never admit any of this but we discussed it. The Senior Superintendent all but guaranteed that if I was willing to do this, he would ensure my safe passage through the application process. Even if I hadn't, and wanted to join straight away, I would have been accepted.

By now the flat had disbanded because Gary and Justin had graduated. About this time, I joined the Nursing Union and there was talk of a strike. In those days we were paid a pittance and everybody knew it. Our slogan was 'a fair go for the nurses'. We did not strike but we did have a stop work meeting and a march in the CBD which ended at the town hall. I used to have a photo of myself with a group of fellow nurses standing on the steps of the town hall with this very long banner, perhaps held by about fifteen to twenty nurses. It said, 'THE PUBLIC BLUDGERS ON US'. This made the front page of the next day's newspapers. Wow, we got on the front page and ended up getting better pay and conditions. The Nursing Union had by now secured accommodation for men and I moved into the nursing quarters at Prince Henry Hospital. My academic results at the Nursing Education Centre were terrible. The senior Nurse Educator spoke with me about it and she suggested that if I was so desperately unhappy with what I was doing (nursing), I should leave. It was clear that I was not going to pass my exams. But I wouldn't leave. Quite apart from not wanting my mother to have the satisfaction of telling me 'I told you so'; I felt that it was time I finished something. I was now thirty and needed some stability. I dug my heels in, recognised I had made a mistake doing nursing in the first place and hated it but needed to prove to myself that no matter how rough it got, I could get over the finishing line; sort of like running a marathon or maybe more so, like climbing Mt Everest. Of course, there was also the very strong incentive of my going to the Police rescue squad once I finished. I don't know that I would have kept going if I did not have that incentive. I adopted the same attitude as I did with giving up smoking, stop talking about it and just do it. I was really starting to hate it more and more now, and not surprisingly the obsessional thinking and associated anxiety was now my constant companion. Some of the nursing sisters loved me, some hated me. When I got into a ward with the latter, they made life pretty miserable for me. But to my credit, I kept going and there were some good times I have to say.

I was fascinated with surgery and was lucky enough to be deployed to both the operating theatres at Prince of Wales (POW) and Prince Henry (PH) hospitals. I think the PH was first. I saw and assisted (in a student nurse lackey role mind you), in some major operations. I remember Dr. Gonsky performing an incredible neurological operation at PH. I think it was on a woman from country NSW. She had a double tumour in her brain and the surgery was the only way that her life might be saved. One of the tumours was embedded deep into a part of the brain sitting on top of the pituitary gland that was very difficult to operate on. Dr. Gonsky was one of the best. After taking the first tumour out, he said to me, "Max, are you a religious man?" I said that I was because I knew he was Jewish and I didn't want to offend him. He then said, "Well, you better start praying now because I am going after the second one. It's a 50/50 thing if she can survive". So, I crossed myself and he saw that and maybe appreciated it. It was truly amazing what he was about to do; the way he navigated all the nerves and blood vessels. The end result was that he got it. The women not only survived but went home shortly thereafter. I dare say she probably lived a fruitful life. These surgeons do truly amazing work and I greatly respected them. On another occasion they were doing open heart surgery and in 1974 this operation was not all that common. It was just unbelievable the skill level of these surgeons. They took the heart out of the body and the patient was put on a heart lung machine. This machine would move blood away from the heart so the surgeon could operate on it. They do this by cutting through the patient's breastbone with a saw. Then they took a healthy vein, in this case from the leg and graft it onto the heart so that it would bypass the diseased artery. It was major surgery but the patient would be up in a few days and home not that much longer after that. Where else would one at my level be lucky enough not just to see it but to actually participate in it? A whole lot different to shearing the rams I'd venture to suggest.

It was while I was working in the cardio-thoracic theatres at Prince Henry that Dad passed away. It was November 26, 1974. I was shocked. We never thought of Dad as ever getting sick and thought that he would live forever. I told you that he never used to go and see a doctor. When I got the news I was out with one of the nurses in my class and she was around at my place. I got the call from my cousin Neil McCosker in the early hours of the morning and just couldn't believe it. He had not been sick and it just came out of the blue. The Charge Sister of the Cardio Thoracic ward was a real bitch, especially to me. The hospital gave me three days bereavement leave. I flew up to Queensland, attended the funeral and came back on time. I mentioned earlier that the whole town came to Dad's funeral, such was his popularity. There was no suggestion that I would leave the hospital to go home and help Mum with the property.

She sold it a bit over a year later and the new owners took possession of it on 17 January 1976. She held an auction, sold everything very cheaply and went to live in Childers, which is near Bundaberg in Queensland. When I got back to the ward, the first job this charge nurse gave me was to clean and sterilise all the walls and equipment in the recovery ward. She never mentioned anything about my Dad and never offered any condolences. I continued my journey with nursing. At this time, I had not taken any medication for three years but as I have said the stress of nursing did little to reduce the anxiety centred around the obsessional thinking. I think it is clear now that the obsessional thinking was an unconscious defence mechanism protecting me against having to continue with the nursing. I think it (the OCD) did its best to get me to stop but I wouldn't have it. Nothing on God's earth was going to stop me from completing my diploma, such was the level of my obstinate determination.

I have to tell you about when I assisted a plastic surgeon with a sex change operation; again in a student nursing role. It was all fairly new then and controversial. I hate repeating it but you have to admire the skills of the surgeons. I can tell you this, they really have to know their anatomy and physiology; well anatomy anyway. People who elect to have sex reassignment surgery from male to female (which is the one I was involved in) have to have their genitals reshaped into a functional vagina and female genitalia. To qualify for this, they have to have extensive psychiatric assessments and then go on a hormone replacement therapy regime. They also usually have breast augmentation and a host of other medical requirements. Anyway, the surgeon said to me, just as he was about to start, "How big do you think I should make the incision Max?" I told him he shouldn't make it too big; that his boyfriend might appreciate that. I got a very disapproving look from the Charge Theatre Sister over that one but what could she do. The surgeon asked me and I gave him an honest answer. Make no mistake about it. In the operating theatre, the surgeon is king. He certainly thought it was funny and had to stop for a little while to gather himself. In that particular operation it got even a bit squeamish for me when the urethra was dissected from the shaft of the penis. I admit I had to look away at this point. There were many other interesting operations I was involved in. Understand that my role was a fairly insignificant one but nevertheless, I was fortunate to have seen all of this. I saw other very fascinating operations. We all had to do a case study in the hospital that involved surgery for our final hospital examinations. For my case study, I was working in a surgical ward at the time at the POW and took on a case of a morbidly obese man (about 160 kgs) who was about to have, from memory, a duodenal switch surgery. An individual is considered morbidly obese if he or she is forty-five kilograms over his/her ideal body weight, has a BMI of 40 or more and is experiencing obesity-related health conditions, such as high blood pressure or diabetes. There was a lot of blood and guts in this one. It was everywhere and the amount of fat they had to cut through was something that will stay with me forever. I followed his case before, during and after surgery and really got into it. My paper was so good that I was told it had a major impact on my hospital finals results. I went from the bottom of the class and believe that by the end I was in the top three of the hospital finals. This patient got well and I spoke with him before he was discharged. The POW hospital had the world's first micro-surgery reconstruction centre. When I was there a 3-year old child came into the emergency Department with his index finger amputated cleanly. Doctor Owen replanted the child's index finger successfully by using updated new techniques in microsurgery. It was the talk of the hospital and the POW was starting to get an international reputation for micro-surgery.

Perhaps the saddest thing I came across whilst doing my training was the death of a young professional footballer (soccer). I was working the night shift at the POW, A&E ward (accident and emergency). The ambulance bought in this chap who had been involved in a car accident, just near his home in Coogee. We admitted him and regularly monitored his vital signs, blood pressure, pulse, that sort of thing. He seemed to be fine and was talking normally with us. Everything was stable until suddenly his vital signs changed. We went from an emergency to a crisis. The medical crisis response team responded and they worked on him for ages. Unfortunately he passed away on the bed in the emergency ward right in front of me. He was in his early to mid-twenties and I think that he was a professional footballer from Scotland or maybe northern England. He had everything to live for and died literally in our hands. It is an awful feeling when you lose a patient that you felt you should not have. This is one of the major psychological issues that doctors and nurses have to deal with. I wondered for some time after that if the emergency medical staff had done enough, quickly enough, to try and save this chap's life. Perhaps they did but were fighting a losing battle.

One of the most unusual matters I had to deal with was couple of weeks out from the rugby league grand final. A well-known rugby league player came in and wanted to know if we could discreetly X-ray his hand. He thought that his hand might be broken but didn't want the coach to know about it so he came quite late at night. He wanted to see what the damage was and he would do his own risk assessment. He was worried that if he told the coach, the coach would rule him out straight away. Could he play with it if they got to the grand final in other words? I spoke with the boss of A&E and he arranged with the radiology Department to do it. It was broken but not badly and from memory it was not a bad fracture, most probably a hairline fracture. We did the mandatory splint on him and told him that medically the right thing to do was to rest it and not play but that was not our decision. He thanked us for our discretion and went off and ended up not telling the coach about it. He played a blinder in the grand final which they won. He was one of Australia's best rugby league players and a really good decent humble sort of a bloke.

Whilst I was nursing I had a part time job driving a truck around Sydney. I was really only living a subsistence life on the wages the hospital paid me; so I got this part time job on my days off. It was great. I'd drive this truck around Sydney delivering goods to various places. I told you that when Dad died, Mum sold the property and sold all the equipment at auction. Of course, the usual carpetbaggers came and cleaned her out. When I learnt that she was going to sell everything, I rang her and asked her if she would 'lease' Dad's truck to me. I would be able to pay for it from the contract money I would earn. The truck was a good one, only a few years old. You wouldn't believe it, after all that exploitation of my labour, she said no. I couldn't believe it and felt that her level of bitterness and vindictiveness ran deep. I did see her when she came to Sydney and stayed with us for a few days. My wife Sue wanted to mend the bridges and she made a big effort to do that. Sue felt that the kids needed to know their grandmother. I couldn't argue with that. She went up and saw them in Queensland with our young baby, Dan. When she came back, she wished that she had not made the effort.

There were a couple of other times I saw her. One time she came to Sydney after Dad passed to go on the Indian Pacific from Sydney to Perth. She was becoming quite the traveller but she had messed up her booking to get a sleeper. I took her to Central Station and it was not until she was to board, that she was told that she did not have a sleeper. I was in the cops at the time and this was just one more occasion when I used my Police warrant card to solve a non-Police matter. Mum was quite distressed about it so I asked to see the most senior person that was connected to that particular train. I told him that Mum had to have a sleeper because she had an embarrassing medical condition that required a high level of privacy and flashed my warrant card. I was quite a good negotiator in those days and got Mum her sleeper. Mum never found out that I told him about the fictitious medical condition.

Unfortunately as my brother John had so aptly put it many years later, there was no love in our family. Mum was just not the sort of person to say sorry and I think found it very difficult to admit to any wrong doing. I think that she would have considered that as a sign of weakness to say sorry, even if she felt it. Mum did all sorts of things after she sold out and to a degree it was proper that she did. I think this included three trips to England to see Margaret and tour around Ireland, Wales and Scotland and then over to the Continent. She and Margaret lived together for a while in London, and by now there was no contact between us. Years later John asked me where Mum's money went from the sale of 'Moonie Park.' I suggested that travel may have eaten a part of it but the bulk went into buying properties, horses and cattle. There were times when individual members of my 'family' would come through Sydney but they never contacted me. It didn't bother me. Both my sisters followed suit with their mother and there was virtually no contact for the next fifteen to twenty years. I recall that when I had my first year's holidays from nursing, I drove from Sydney to go and see my cousins up in central Queensland. That is a distance of over 1,460 kilometres. I went up through an area just north of Goondiwindi called Moonie. In fact my parents property was a short distance from the turnoff, off the Moonie Highway but I had already decided that I was not going to call in and see them. My journey more or less took me past their front gate. I knew that if I did call in there would be the usual disharmony and unpleasantness; so I kept driving.

It's awful to think back and realise just how bad the relationship was between my parents and myself, even though it had improved significantly from the Torrendorra Capella days. You must have a clear picture of how bad it was then, but I still feel that I am not sufficiently versed with words to articulate how bad it was in those early days. It was more or less the same for my brother John, perhaps even worse, but that hostility did not start until after we moved to Tara. In my case, it did get better after I did my nine months stint there in 1971 and managed to get off all the drugs. In John's case it turned very bitter and he stills feels that way. I think that story in itself indicates how fractured the relationship was between we boys and my parents. Interestingly, and not surprisingly, Mum had a great relationship with her daughters.

I mentioned the CMF (Citizens Military Forces) Commandos. I joined them around about late 1973. I now got fit enough being off the cigarettes, and passed the selection criteria. I was doing nicely with this mob. I was close to getting my green beret but had to do the Army's induction course in Sydney. It lasted for two weeks and all CMF troops were collectively thrown into it from all over Australia. You have to admire these men and women that give up a lot of their spare time to serve their country. We weren't paid much and we had to give it a lot of our spare time. I think it was one night a week, one weekend a month and two weeks per year. Not much you might say, but a lot when you are fully employed somewhere else. A very unusual incident happened during the induction course with the army. We all had to go into a big hall and fill out a psychological questionnaire. After filling out the questionnaires, a corporal came around and collected them. There was one missing. The captain asked everybody in the room if they knew where the missing questionnaire was. There were about three to four hundred troops there. I quickly realised that he was going to make sure that he found the missing questionnaire. I was the one who took the missing one. I didn't realise at the time of taking it, that the blank questionnaire would be considered such valuable property by the army. I took it because I wanted to take it back to the hospital and show it to a hospital clinical psychologist I knew. I wanted to ask him what it was all about. I stood up and admitted to it straight away. The Captain went berserk and in front of everybody, got stuck into me. There were only two commandos in the whole group. He told me that we commandos all thought that we were better than anybody else and he was going to put me in my place. He did. During the course, the troops were given half of Saturday and Sunday off, mid-course. At the final parade before dismissing us, the Captain told me that my leave would be cancelled and I was to be given guard duty. I thoroughly deserved it and it was a stupid mistake on my part but there was no malice in it. It reminds me a bit of when we took the council grader but this was different. I really did not think it was a big deal but the captain certainly made it one. I just thought that I was being clever but got caught out. Towards the end of the course we did helicopter familiarisation work. The idea was that helicopters would come to pick up the troops but not have to touch the ground. They would hover about a foot off the ground. You had to jump into the helicopter for a quick take off. It was all about the training for Vietnam soldiers. In fact at this time all Australian troops were out of Vietnam. When these choppers were coming to land to let you off, you would jump off the helicopter when it started hovering and only after you were given the order to jump. I went before the order and jumped too soon. When I hit the ground I got tangled up with the rifle and very badly damaged my left shoulder. It was a total dislocation with fractures of the shoulder. Jesus, the pain was just unbearable. I couldn't move. Almost immediately the medics arrived. They injected me intravenously with 15 milligrams of morphine. That made me as high as a kite and I started talking rubbish. I went from inexpressible agony to a state of total euphoria within ten-seconds. Morphine is a synthetic version of heroin; so for me, it was the same as having a shot of heroin. I was telling the medics not to worry about it. Just let me get my rifle and I would be fine to get back on the chopper. Of course, they were used to this as they had been medics in Vietnam. This was a major disappointment as I had very high hopes with the Commando Unit.

Now I had to be strapped up for six weeks and then have extensive physiotherapy. I went and saw a wonderful man who I knew from the Prince of Wales hospital. His name was Professor Ron Huckstep. Ron was the Professor of Traumatic and Orthopaedic Surgery at the University of New South Wales. I had worked with him in the POW theatres where he used to do orthopaedic surgery. He arranged for me to immediately be scheduled for another putti-platt operation. Ron understood that I required a shoulder that would not pop out if I was to do the parachuting course. He reckoned he could fix me up so in mid 1975 I had the operation. I was off work altogether for three months; six weeks immobilised and six weeks of intensive physiotherapy. This proved to be a double-edged sword. On the negative side, I had to make up the three months to graduate, which was originally October 1975. Now it would be January 1976. I can tell you that having to spend an extra three months at the hospitals was really difficult. On the positive side, because I couldn't do anything manual, I started studying. I spent three months studying. It is my nature that once I start doing something I believe in, I give it everything. When we did the hospital finals the Nursing Education Centre were amazed at my improvement and pleased with my academic transformation. I ended up getting high distinctions in the hospital finals and credits in the state finals. I completed my nursing course in early January 1976. I have to admit that when I walked through the gates of Prince Henry hospital for the last time I turned around and gave it the finger. Perhaps a bit immature but I can tell you that I had a really good drink that night. To think I didn't have to go back nursing anymore and I imagine it would be like being released from prison. I have never nursed since. I really wish I could express it in better words what a relief it was to finish nursing. For three years and three months I put up with the low wages, the night shifts, the weekend shifts, the menial duties, the draconian hospital environment, the bitter lesbian Charge Sisters and the awful autocratic female hierarchy that prevailed at the time. Most of all I had to put up with the low opinion some people had of male nurses. One time I told a medical student at rugby training that I was a nurse and he wouldn't believe me. He thought that I was joking and just could not imagine a man like me being a nurse and to think that this fella was going to be a Doctor.

At this time I was living with my cousin Neil McCosker who had come back to school in his late twenties. He wanted to go onto university and get a degree, which he did. Neil was very helpful whilst I was incapacitated. I couldn't have a shower and had to be very careful getting into the bath tub. Neil helped me with all this. Even simple things like doing up shoe laces was out of the question. It wasn't just not having the use of both arms, but the pain that went with movement. Eventually that eased and I got out of the strapping after six weeks. The physiotherapy started by putting my fingers on the wall and trying to take my hand upwards, crablike by crawling up the wall. The last time I did that was when I broke my arm in 1958/59. Eventually I got there and then Ron started me on swimming. There was a lot trepidation initially doing that but that also went well. Sometime after the physiotherapy was finished I went and had my medical at Police HQ in College Street. I saw the Police Doctor and he asked me about the scar on my shoulder. I told him it was an old scar from an operation many years ago in 1960. The Professor had cut over the old incision and only at the bottom of the scar, so you would you not that there were two. It is perfectly reasonable that the Police Doctor would not have noticed it. He told me that normally they would not take people that had this operation. However, he put me through a series of exercises and I could do all of them to his satisfaction. He would not have accepted me if I told him the first one was unsuccessful and that just months before my medical examination, I had another putti-platt. That is for sure. Did I lie? Before I can answer that, let me first tell you about the depression side of things. Of course, the Police were very in-tune at this period in time with not recruiting people in the Police Force that have a history of mental illness. Perhaps it's different now but certainly at that time, it was standard. They just didn't take them; full stop, end of story. You can understand that they don't want to issue firearms to mentally ill people. That could prove to be fatal mistake; literally. I knew that but I never said a word about it. I answered no to all the questions about mental illness and rest assured, they asked them. There was no suspicion on their part. Why would there be? You can get very skilful at covering up your mental issues. The Police Doctor told me that I was one of the fittest men he had through there in all of his years in the Police Force. I was 183 centimetres and weighed 84 kilograms. After all that commando training, I was very fit, in-spite of the injury. There was no negligence on the Doctor's part. He believed what I told him and as I have reiterated, why wouldn't he? What is a lie? Remember the lie I told Br Higgins; that was a lie. The legal definition of a lie is an intentionally false statement to a person made by another person who knows it is not wholly the truth. So on that basis, I lied. But there was no malice in it. I didn't hurt anybody and was only pursuing what I felt I had the right to pursue. I just knew that if I had been truthful about either the depression and the recent injury, I would not have been accepted. This is the first time that I have ever mentioned this to anyone. I never felt guilty about it so perhaps I was making headway on this guilt complex thing. I left the Police Force with a good record of distinguished service. I think that it does raise some interesting questions about the stigma associated with mental illness. If I had told them about it, I would not have got in. We have established that. However, I am now posing the question that should people like me be discriminated against in the employment area? When I tell you about my career in the Police, you will see that I was a really good cop and did very well. I wonder where you draw the line. I know from my Police service that I was as good as any of them in a tight situation.

Some stage during my last year of nursing, Mum came to Sydney on some religious thing and stayed with us. There you go, we must have had some sort of a relationship and we got on reasonably well. Whilst in Sydney, she got me to sign a piece of hand written paper accepting $10,000 as my share of the inheritance. Given my wages as a student nurse, you can imagine that this was too hard to turn down. She did not say that this is all that I would get, but this is what she was prepared to give me at the moment. I believe that she might have done the same for John. I don't know what Mum got from the sale of Moonie Park but its present day value is somewhere between two and a half to three million. There was a lot of stock and equipment as well. I told you about the truck. When Dad passed, I assumed everything would be passed on to her and never queried it. When Mum passed, I was never contacted my sisters about her will. It has never been mentioned to me by either of my sisters. You might say, well why don't you ask them? I don't know the answer to that. Good question, why didn't I? Perhaps I was waiting for them to do what I saw as the right thing, but I don't think that is in their makeup, to be truthful. Even though I had been assured many times that the property would be split evenly between the four of us, it never happened. So not only was I not paid (except that one time in 1971) for the years of labour I gave them, Mum left my brother and I out of the will. I thought that maybe a fair swap might have been Dad's truck for my John Shearer plough. John also did a lot of free work for them but not to the extent that I did, but still he did a lot. One year he went share farming with Dad and John paid for all the seed out of his own pocket and did all the work. This was about 1971 and things got so bad for him at home. He was at war with Mum and my sisters about silly little things. I don't know when John's poor relationship with his mother first erupted but Mum developed a terrible set against John. It was alleged by the girls he had made some malicious and possibly defamatory remarks about Mum that I am not prepared to write about in this book. True or not I don't know, but I would be very dubious as to their authenticity and if that is right, John has much to answer for. If John is right, well! Best to let sleeping dogs lie I think. One thing led to another and John packed up and left long before harvest. John's star had certainly started to fade dramatically. The harvest was a bumper one and they did very well out of it. Dad and Mum never gave John anything for his work because he was not there for the harvest but he did everything else. They didn't even give him the money back for the seed. My sisters looked after Mum for the latter part of her life and nursed her when she became an invalid. Of course they should be left something. The other side of the coin is what about all the work that John and I did gratis at Capella and to a lesser extent at Tara? This turned out to be a great injustice, particularly to me but I'm deviating a bit here. I'm supposed to be taking about my nursing days.

I had now been off all medication now since 1971; a period of four years. As a nurse, I had access to some very learned Psychiatrists who were willing to talk with me about my demons and not charge me. At one time I was referred to a leading Psychoanalyst in Macquarie Street, Sydney for long term consultation and it was terrible. The way it worked was that when I went to see him I had to do all of the talking, or nearly all of it. He would just sit there and occasionally, very occasionally nod his head and say something. After a couple of sessions I found myself repeating over and over what I had already said. I think the treatment was based on the techniques developed by

Sigmund Freud called psychoanalysis. Freud believed that people could be cured by making conscious their unconscious thoughts and motivations, thus gaining insight into their problems. It is commonly used to treat depression and anxiety disorders so I thought that when I first went there that this might be the answer. The theory sounded good at least but the bottom line is that it didn't work.

So my nursing days had come to an end. Whilst I have said a number of times that I hated it, in the end I believe that it was good for me. Hitherto I had been a loner, drifting from job to job, like a rolling stone. Nursing for all its faults made me settle down and try and find some stability in my life. Previously I was all over the place but that was largely because I had this terrible mental illness and I was very much on my own. The fact is that I lost over a decade of my life because of it. I stopped being aggressive on the drink and became a different person. Even when I did drink heavily I was fairly subdued and never carried on like I did when I was in New Zealand, doped up with the madness, drugs and booze. The best thing that I did during this time was to find some stability and I can thank nursing for that. After I graduated I never nursed again, although there was a group of people that I refer to as my 'druggie group' when writing about my Police days that thought that I was doing specialist work as a graduate nurse. That was my alibi when I was with them working as an undercover cop and I go into detail about that in the Police section. After the good doctor passed me medically fit to join the Police Force, I fronted the three wise men on the selection panel of commissioned officers and they rubber stamped it. I never went to my nursing graduation ceremony and am not sure why, nor have I kept in touch with the many friends I made in nursing. Again, I don't know why.

The next big challenge in my life was to see what I could do in the NSW Police Force.

Chapter Eight: The NSW Police Force
1976 - 1981

In 1976 - Khmer Rouge leader Pol Pot became Prime Minister (and virtual dictator) of Cambodia after Prince Sihanouk stepped down. Israeli airborne commandos attacked Uganda's Entebbe Airport and freed 103 hostages held by pro-Palestinian hijackers of Air France plane. US Supreme Court ruled that death penalty is not inherently cruel or unusual and is a constitutionally acceptable form of punishment. US celebrated Bicentennial. Mysterious disease struck American Legion convention in Philadelphia, eventually claiming 29 lives. Jimmy Carter elected US President on 2 November. Viking I landed on Mars. The US Navy tested the Tomahawk cruise missile. The movies, *Rocky*, *Taxi Driver*, *Network* and *All The President's Men* were released. Alex Haley released the book *Roots*. Notable deaths included those of Agatha Christie.

In 1977 - Deng Xiaoping, the purged Chinese leader, restored to power as Gang of Four is expelled from Communist Party. Nuclear-proliferation pact, curbing spread of nuclear weapons, was signed by 15 countries, including US and USSR. First woman Episcopal priest ordained. Scientists identified previously unknown bacterium as cause of Legionnaires Disease. The neutron bomb was developed. The space shuttle Enterprise made its first test glide, from the back of a 747. Paul MacCready (US) developed the Gossamer Condor, the first successful human-powered aircraft. Lasers were first used to initiate a fusion reaction. Movies released included *Saturday Night Fever*, *Star Wars*, *Annie Hall*, *Close Encounters of the Third Kind* and *Julia*. Notable deaths included those of Charles Chaplin, Bing Crosby, Groucho Marx, Vladimir Nabokov and Elvis Presley.

In 1978 - Rhodesia's Prime Minister Ian D. Smith and three black leaders agreed on transfer to black majority rule. Former Italian Premier Aldo Moro kidnapped by left wing terrorists, who killed five bodyguards; he was found slain. Pope Paul V1 died aged 80. New Pope, John Paul I, 65, unexpectedly died after 34 days in office; succeeded by Karol Cardinal Wojtyla of Poland as John Paul II. Jim Jones followers committed mass suicide in Jonestown, Guyana. Sony introduced the Walkman, the first portable stereo. Balloon angioplasty was developed to treat coronary artery disease. Louise Brown, the first test-tube baby, was born at Oldham Hospital in London. Recombinant DNA techniques were used to produce human insulin. The movies *The Deer Hunter, Midnight Express, Heaven Can Wait* and *Coming Home* were released. Notable deaths included those of Hubert Humphrey and Anastus Mikoyan.

In 1979 - Vietnam and Vietnam-backed Cambodian insurgents announced the fall of Cambodian capital Phnom Penh and collapse of Pol Pot regime. Shah left Iran after year of turmoil; revolutionary forces under Muslim leader, Ayatollah Ruhollah Khomeini, took over. Conservatives won British election; Margaret Thatcher became new prime minister. Iranian militants seized US embassy in Teheran and held hostages. Soviet invasion of Afghanistan stirred world protests. Allan McLeod Cormack (US) and Godfrey Newbold Hounsfield (UK) won the Nobel prize in Medicine, for developing computed axial tomography (CAT scan) X-ray technique. The movies released included *Apocalypse Now, All That Jazz, Kramer vs. Kramer* and *Breaking Away*. Notable deaths included those of Arthur Fiedler, John Wayne, Charles Mingus, Jean Renoir and Nelson Rockefeller.

In 1980 - Six US embassy aides escaped from Iran with Canadian help. The US broke diplomatic ties with Iran. Eight US servicemen were killed and five injured as helicopter and cargo plane collided in abortive desert raid to rescue American hostages in Teheran. Ronald Reagan elected US president in Republican sweep. John Lennon of the Beatles shot dead in New York City. Ted Turner launched CNN, the first all-news network. The movies released included *Raging Bull, Ordinary People, Coal Miner's Daughter, The Elephant Man* and *Tess*. Notable deaths included those of William Douglas, Erich Fromm, Alfred Hitchcock, John Lennon, Jesse Owens, Jean Piaget and Mae West.

In 1981 - US-Iran agreement freed 52 hostages held in Teheran since 1979; hostages welcomed back in US. Egyptian President Anwar el-Sadat was assassinated by Islamic extremists during a military parade in Cairo. Ronald Reagan took oath as 40th President on 20 January. President Reagan wounded by gunman, with press secretary and two law-enforcement officers. The US Supreme Court ruled to allow television cameras in the courtroom. The book by Salman Rushdie, Midnight's Children appears. The AIDS virus was first identified. IBM introduced its first personal computer, running the Microsoft Disk Operating System (MS-DOS). The 236-m.p.h., TGV, Europe's first high-speed passenger train, began operating out of Lyons, France. The FDA approved the use of the artificial sweetener aspartame (NutraSweet). Movies released included *Raiders of the Lost Ark, Chariots of Fire, On Golden Pond, Reds* and *Atlantic City*. Notable deaths included those of Joe Louis, Anwar Sadat, Bobby Sands and Bill Haley. The population of the world was 4.529 billion.

I started at the Academy on 11 January 1976, class No 150. Up until this book was written, I have never told anybody about the 'little fibs' I told to get into the Police. Now you know a couple more of my skeletons. I stayed in the Police Force until April 1981. In those days, the Police Academy was at the Bourke Street barracks in Redfern. Redfern is an inner city suburb that borders the Sydney CBD and at that time, there was a large Aboriginal community there as well as subsidised government housing. Consequently it was a high risk crime area and maybe the ideal place to have a Police academy. The Mounted Police section and 21 Division were also based there. The boss of the academy at that time was Inspector Cecil Abbott, who later became the Commissioner of Police. The initial training course went for ten weeks before we were assigned a station to start our career in the Police. I was still very fit from my nursing/ commandos days so found the physical training easy enough. Most of the time, we spent in the classroom studying things like the law, Police procedures, powers of arrest, the use of lethal force, etc. I made some great friends there; blokes like Frank and Allan, who I used to train with and there were no significant events that occurred during the probationary training. I and everybody else passed and we had our passing out parade. I think I was the only one there that did not have parents or relatives attend but I was well used to that now but I did have one of the cops I nursed in the Police ward come. His name was Harry (Father) Devine. Harry never rose past the rank of Senior Constable as he never did the examinations and ended up becoming a wireless car operator. He had this reputation as being a pretty good bare knuckle fighter in his youth and he was one of those older quintessential type of coppers from the old days. It was said he'd offer to fight anybody out the back of pubs, bare knuckle. Apparently, according to him, he made quite a bit of money doing it. But you know, stories get blown out of proportion over time and it would probably end up only being the truth in part. They say never let the truth get in the road of good story. This was quite common in the Police Force, often in the witness box! I first met Harry when he was a patient at the POW hospital and we became friends. He was a really good bloke and as it turned out he was mates with one of the most senior Superintendents in the Police, so apart from our friendship, it was a very valuable connection to have. The training at the academy was much the same as it was in the army. You had to do a lot of drill work and I was forever getting out of step with the marching and I'd get bawled out over it all the time but it didn't bother me. When it came to all the physical training stuff I was one of the star recruits and that held me in good stead with the academy staff. After all, that's what they wanted to churn out; people that could look after themselves and more importantly look after members of the community.

The boss of the drill section was a 'bull' of a man and a fitness fanatic. Bejesus, this fella epitomised what human physical strength was all about. He could bench press an incredible weight and could, and did, intimidate all of the recruits, or so he/we thought. All different types join the Police Force and some of them are pretty rugged individuals themselves. There are a lot of first grade footballers from both league and union that are cops and these blokes are often fairly tough individuals as you could imagine. I found the Police, as opposed to army personnel, to be more individualistic people and they didn't need the leadership that the military service people generally require. They have to go out on the streets and make split second decisions that could have life or death implications. There are many incidents that Police have to deal with where there is no standard operating procedure for it and they have to come up with something fairly quickly, or the consequences could be catastrophic. One day he was showing us some good wrestling/judo holds as part of our unarmed combat training on how to restrain violent, aggressive people. He actually got me to show the class some unarmed combat moves that I had learnt in the commandoes and that went over pretty well with the recruits. Well, one time he made a mistake and picked on the wrong fella. He asked him to come out on the mat where all this took place and told him to disarm him. He was holding a Police truncheon and told this recruit it was a knife and he was going to attack him with it. Well, this young recruit within the blink of an eyelid had him on his back and the truncheon out of his hand. He and all the rest of us got the shock of our lives. Once he had regathered himself, to his credit, immediately told the recruit that he had done a good job and that is what he wanted us to do, out on the streets. It was a classic response on his part about thinking quickly on your feet and he avoided what could have been a very embarrassing situation for him. Frank, Alan and I used to go to the gym during our lunch breaks and I would show them the unarmed combat moves and Alan would show us some karate moves. Alan was a black belt karate expert so he was not one to fool around with. He was a redhead like me and like most redheads, I think he had similar hang ups about bullying as I did. What is it about red headed men? Frank was a boxer. Probably not as good a one as he thought he was but he won a few fights with the Police boxing team. He was Italian and he had this almost exact style of another Italian fighter, Rocky Marciano. They used that crouching style; probably because they weren't tall men. Anyway we (our little group) got to know this fella who sat Brian on his ass pretty well but I don't really remember his name. We did some training with him and we were no match for him. I mean between us we had a black belt karate expert, a boxer and myself, an unarmed combat exponent but this fella could have beaten us all up by himself I do believe. It turned out that he was a champion amateur wrestler and was good enough to be considered for the Olympic Games but had not told the academy about it because he feared he might be singled out. He wasn't that big, but bejesus he was strong, fast and very skilful. He swore us to secrecy and we honoured that. Years later I learnt that our PT Instructor rose to the rank of Superintendent and when he got diagnosed with terminal cancer, he committed suicide. I was very sad to hear it because he was good bloke and deep down cared a lot about his recruits. I heard that he put the muzzle of the .38 Smith and Wesson into his mouth and ended it all. I personally got on very well with him and we kept in contact for a number of years. In fact, when I went into plain clothes at 21 Special Squad (21 Division), we were stationed at the academy and I used to train with him down at the academy gym. The most important thing we learnt at the academy was when, and more importantly when not to, discharge our firearms. In those days we all took our guns home and there are many stories about Police getting into trouble with their revolvers.

At the time Police were issued with .38 Smith and Wesson six shot revolvers. I can assure you that I would have trouble hitting a bull anywhere at thirty meters with this thing, but definitely could at five to ten meters, which is what Police mainly have to do. They drilled it into us how very important it was to make sure that you only used it when you absolutely had to, as a very last resort and you had exhausted all other options. In those days we never had the capsicum or pepper spray, tasers and the like. You have to remember that some of these Police were only nineteen years of age. It is an awesome responsibility for a young nineteen year old to have to carry on his shoulders. Who else has the legal right to shoot somebody dead? A judge can't. The smartest lawyer in the land can't. The Prime Minister can't but a nineteen year old cop can. I made some great friends at the Police Academy and unlike nursing, I fitted in well with them and I think at last I had found a group that I was comfortable belonging to. The Police became my gang, my brotherhood and I felt that I belonged there.

When I graduated from the Police Academy, I was posted to No 10 division, headquartered at Waverley in the eastern suburbs of Sydney. The division covered all of the eastern suburbs from Coogee in the South, to Watson's Bay in the North, with the affluent suburbs of Vaucluse, Rose Bay, Double Bay and Bellevue Hill. We used to refer to Rose Bay as Nose Bay; Double Bay as Double Pay, and Bellevue Hill as Belljew Hill. I suppose that was a reference to the big Jewish population that lived there! The suburb that got most of our attention was Bondi. In the mid-70s, this is where the kiwi expatriates used to live and Bondi has this magnificent beach that is recognised worldwide. It was also a major drug hub at that time and the hard drug of choice was heroin. The very first night I was on the job I went with another probationary constable and our leader was a First Class Constable. I'll call him Fred and Fred was out to impress us. As we were out patrolling, a call came over via VKG radio that there were persons on premises and that required urgent action. Well, Fred put the siren on and put this ford falcon through its paces. He was driving like a maniac, weaving in and out of traffic, crossing medium strips and the like. We got to the location and it turned out there was no one there. He could have got us all killed. Worse still, killed an innocent civilian, who happened to be in the wrong place at the wrong time. That is the very first job I did in the Police Force.

I can tell you people have to learn quickly in this job. When I first walked into the Waverley Police station, the old Sergeant got me aside and told me to forget what I had learnt at the academy. The advice he gave me went something like this – "Them c**** at the Academy would not know if you were f****** them up the a**. Things are done f****** differently at this f****** station mate," he told me in no uncertain terms, whilst drinking a can of VB. It seemed every second word he used was f***. He advised me to "keep my f****** eyes open, keep my f****** mouth

f****** shut, and listen to every f****** thing. You f*****
understand and one more thing, don't trust any c*** that doesn't
drink." I told him that he had made himself perfectly clear. Pretty
good advice I would say for a fella starting out and that's pretty
much what I did. Most of our work was police general duties
stuff and I used to love it. It beat washing bed pans that is for
sure. You'd go to work not knowing what was going to happen
on your shift as in general duties Police work and anything can
happen at any time. One minute you might be doing a traffic
accident and the next thing you could be at a murder scene.

I learnt more of less straight away that there were a few
perks in the job for the boys. For example we did not have to pay
full price for our meals at McDonalds. They wanted a Police
presence and for us going there, they considered that it was a
worthwhile investment on their part. I rarely went to McDonalds
as I was very fit individual at this time and would not eat junk
food. On the night shift, our vehicle had to go around and pick
up the bread from the bakery and it was all free. Just little things
like that. Now and again the boss would tell us to go around to
the bottle shop in the Police paddy wagon and pick up a couple
of cartons of beer. We never paid and never asked any questions.
I well remember on one such occasion we were picking the beer
up and as I was putting it into the back, Warren Mitchell said to
me "Enjoy the drink boys". You may remember that Warren was
the British actor who played the part of Alf Garnett in the leading
role in the 'Till Death Us Do Part' series which was a well known
sitcom at the time. I guess you could call these little
misdemeanours corrupt practises but I do not think that anyone
would get offended by them. It graduated to the next level when
you'd 'cop a quid' for notifying a tow truck operator when you
went to an accident and made sure that his company got the job.
I don't remember how much but it was a pittance. It was the
same thing with reporting that a cadaver had to be collected and
you'd arrange for the government contractor to come around and
pick up the body to take it to the morgue at Glebe. When I first
started, I reported that some windows had been smashed in a
retail outlet in Bondi Junction and I contracted the leading glass

repair people to come around and fix it. We stayed there until they did and when I ended my shift, the desk sergeant put something like $30 in my hand and told me it was for the glass. That was my very first experience of actually receiving anything.

It was common knowledge that corruption in the Police Force was rampant at the time and everybody knew it. Nevertheless, when I went to plain clothes I never got involved in any form of corruption mainly because I did not have the opportunity to. I was too junior in rank and I go into detail about this later. Generally speaking however it was well known that 21 Division was controlling all the illegal gambling in the state (all of it) as well as working with the Vice Squad with drugs and prostitution. People were forever talking about how much rent the SP (starting price) bookies and illegal casinos were paying to 21 Division who were said to be the bagmen for all the distribution of all the money. This money allegedly went to some high profile people in the political, judicial and Police organisations. I know that it's all hearsay but it was certainly something you heard a lot about but I never actually saw it happening. It was generally believed to be true that deals were done between the Police and the lawyers for some defendants. It was easy enough to change the brief of evidence and leave crucial parts out in exchange for dollars. Sometimes quite a lot and you can add to that giving false evidence.

The second day on the job I made my first arrest. This bloke had assaulted a taxi driver in Cooks Road, Centennial Park. The offender was a young English bloke out to see the lucky country but his luck ran out. He put up a bit of a scuffle at the scene but I had his right arm locked behind him before he knew what had happened and put the cuffs on him. We took him back to the station to carry out the charging process for common assault. When I was taking him down to the cells he was begging me not to give him a flogging. He was almost urinating himself with fear. He was absolutely certain that he was about to get a Police bashing; a sort of summary justice scenario. I think he may have been through all this before in his home country but in different circumstances. Maybe he had been arrested at Darlinghurst (Darlo). I didn't belt him and had no intention to but I let him stew on it just the same. I told him if he came back we would give him a 'father of a hiding' so he better start behaving himself and learn how to handle the booze. I told him this forcefully enough and he believed me. He had no doubt that if he came back to the Bondi Police Station he would get a belting that he would never forget and I reminded him that we had plenty of telephone books on hand. The implications were clear and he got the message. When we went to court he pleaded guilty and apologised to the court for what he had done. He even came up to us afterwards and shook our hands telling us we had done him a big favour. He turned out to be an ok sort of bloke and I doubt that he would have offended again. I wondered if he was going through the same sort of trauma that I did when I was in NZ in those 'days of darkness.' I think this is one of the things that set me aside from other Police. I knew what dark places were like and had empathy with people that were 'doing it tough' mentally. Most Police didn't.

Our job was to keep the peace and sometimes you might have to think outside the box and do some creative thinking. Some of the general duties were traffic matters like accidents and directing traffic at major sporting events. A lot of our time was taken up with domestic disputes and some of them could get very ugly. The general duty Police are usually the first at the scene of a crime, so you really had to be careful all the time. You couldn't let your guard down for a second; you just didn't know what was around the corner. We all knew that the uniform was a target and most of us acted accordingly. There have been cases where Police have responded to a call where there is a domestic dispute taking place inside a house. The Police go there, the fella opens the door and fires without a word. Anything can and does happen in the Police Force and some Police were so averse to the risk of getting into trouble, they just didn't respond to emergency calls. Other cops just could not get enough of it; the more dangerous the better. I suppose it's a reasonable risk strategy —

if its looks iffy (dangerous), avoid it. Not much good for the public though!

I'm just making the point that operational Police that are out on the front line face the possibility of having to face a person with a dangerous weapon every day they are on duty. You can therefore understand that some of them get a bit paranoid about it and when faced with dangerous situations, their judgement can be impaired. It is very well for our judicial and civil liberties people to go on about Police brutality. I wonder how they would act in similar circumstances. I was watching a true life crime story recently on TV about a woman who murdered her partner in the town where I first went to boarding school - Aberdeen. After she killed him, she hung him up in the hallway. This woman was good with a knife as she had previously worked as a boner in the Aberdeen meat works. Then she cut off slices of his glutes (backside), cooked them and served them up for dinner, represented as a steak dinner. When the cops got there they found the gutted body hanging up from the hall ceiling, in much the same way that you would see an animal carcass that had been slaughtered. The head was missing and when the cops went into the kitchen there was a big saucepan on the stove and they knew straight away what was in it. This of course is a very extreme case but it does highlight the scenarios that Police can be and are exposed to. The investigating Police went on to explain how it had affected them later on in life with recurrent nightmares and PTSD (post-traumatic stress disorder). Just imagine having to deal with something as horrific at this.

It didn't take me long to work out what the Police culture was at this time. Cops generally are suspicious people and not trusting of the general public. They were mostly conservative in politics and generally liberal voters. That made me different to start with. They were generally very prejudiced towards minorities and ethnic groups and did not like change. This was another point of difference with me. Abuse of alcohol was rampant and I became as bad as anybody else. They were very resistant to change and you'd often hear, "We have been doing it this way for 100 years, why change it now?" You can imagine the problems the old fellas had with the advent of computerisation. This was just starting to come into Police operations at the time and the old timers reckoned it was rubbish; their defence mechanism of course? I often worked with plain clothes Police on the drunk truck at 21 Division and you would forever hear them decrying different groups of people, poofters, the drunks, the unemployed (bludgers), the wogs, the Asians', and so on. Some of them thought that the Asians did not need to attack us militarily; they were invading us successfully through the migration system. Who knows, that might prove to be right. Yet I'd go out and work with these fellas and the first three to four hours of our shift was spent drinking in some club or pub somewhere. They wouldn't work and generally they were all the things that they were accusing others of. I'd put this at a 50-50 ratio with Police that were doing their jobs properly. Some cops were fantastic workers, some were totally lazy. I'll say some things about Justice Wood's comments on Police culture later.

Nevertheless I liked the job and one of the reasons for that is that it gave me a sense of worth. Hitherto, I had a hard time of it as I have outlined to you. I'd always looked upon myself as a nobody and now I felt that I was at least getting some respect and recognition. I had been degraded to varying degrees at all the schools I attended and to a lesser extent that happened at the hospital as well. I had never known what it was like to feel good about myself and I had never known what it was like to feel important. The Police gave me a sense of importance and purpose, but more importantly it made me feel valuable and of belonging. It was the first time I had ever really experienced a sense of being valued, worthwhile and respected. I was starting to get some self-esteem, something I had never had. The Police work was exciting and you never knew what the next day was going to bring. The authority I had never went to my head. I was still the same easy going self-effacing humble bloke that I have always been. If I could do a good turn for a member of the public, I'd do it. I will say that even though I had been entrusted with this new power, it never changed me as a person. I never became a bully and as I will talk about later, I always had something for the down trodden, the not so fortunate. There are a thousand stories I could tell you about my work in the Police Force and there was never a dull moment. After a few months I asked for and was given a transfer to Bondi Police Station. Bondi was a sub-station of Waverley. Surprisingly, I met with a fair amount of hostility when I first went there and verbal bullying was a part of the culture. Some of the cops just did not trust me. These sub-stations usually didn't have a lot of troops so they developed cliques. If you were in the clique, which of course you aren't when you are new there, you might find it difficult. The Police in those days were in the main homophobic, very much so. They were also xenophobic. They were also racists and racial vilification was rampart in the Police Force at the time. The Police were so homophobic that homosexuals were barred from the Police Force. To be fair to the Police, they really only represented the society in which they lived and operated. Society in those days was all of the above as well, generally speaking. The Police just enforced the law, whether they agreed with it or not. Some of them thought that because I was a nurse before I joined that I must have been a 'poofter' but that didn't hang around long. You can surely see the flawed rationalisation and bigotry in play here.

One night I was working with this Sergeant who was an ex-detective. He had 'hit a hurdle' and been sent back to uniform. He was a great bloke and had this lovely girlfriend. He asked me if it was ok if we had an easy night as his girlfriend had invited him over for dinner and she had told him that I could come to if I wanted. She said that she would have a friend there as well for me. I told him that it was too good an offer to refuse and that I thought it was a great idea as long as we covered our tracks. All my good Sergeant did was to leave a six pack with the Station Sergeant (which we got for nothing at the local bottle shop) and gave him the number where we would be if it was urgent. It turned out that we spent the entire shift at their flat in Bondi, eating, drinking and ended up sleeping with these girls. After we eventually did leave and went back to the station, I got a call that I had left behind my registered number. You have to wear this number on your Police uniform so that people can identify you and it can be quite serious if you lose it. We went straight back and carried on with the party but I made sure I never left anything behind this time. My good Sergeant told me that both of the girls were former prostitutes for some escort agency and he had really fallen in love with his girl. Guess what? We claimed overtime and got it.

Then some of the boys at the station (not the good Sergeant) decided that I was a plant for internal affairs. This is an example of the paranoia that I referred to earlier. Internal Affairs (IA) was a special squad within the Police Force that was manned by normal Police. Their brief was to investigate complaints about fellow Police Officers. Usually the complainant would contact the Ombudsman and lodge an official complaint and the Ombudsman would direct IA to investigate it. Apparently because I used to like taking photos of where I'd been and what I'd done (within reason of course), they formed this opinion. That blew over after a while as well and I eventually got on well with most of them but there was a bit of bullying at the beginning and it unnerved me a bit. At this station there was a distinct ratio of work attitude and ethics of different individuals. As I was a Probationary Constable you had to work with whoever you were assigned to. Your enjoyment of the shift would very much hang on who that senior person was. Sometimes I'd score a worker and we'd run-arse first, as we f***** and cursed (recognise it), and we'd be flat out the whole shift, often doing overtime and making some good money. Sometimes you'd score a shift with the laziest bloke you'd ever meet. Sometimes you'd score a socialiser, like my good Sergeant mate I just told you about. Sometimes you'd score an absolute drunk. One night I worked with a Senior Constable who was so drunk he could not walk, but drove the Police car. We went to a scene of a traffic accident and when he got out of the Police car he fell over. I covered it up with a story that he was diabetic and was suffering from a bout of hypoglycaemia. I knew how to explain all that and I got my man to sit in the back of the car and I handled the accident. I took him back to the station when I had finished getting all the details and never mentioned a word of it to anybody. In cases like this you are half expecting to get a call from IA about a complaint made by a member of the public that the Police were drunk and were this and that; whatever! We didn't so there was no complaint made which means the members of the public had probably accepted my story about him having an attack of hypoglycaemia. Christ, once we got back to the station (I'm the driver now) he wanted to go up to the Sergeants mess at South Head Naval base and continue with the drinking. That is how we spent the shift. He was a good bloke but dangerous, a hopeless alcoholic and we his fellow workers, covered up for him. That too was very much a part of the Police culture that Justice Wood referred to and I will agree that this is an example of misguided loyalty. You just put loyalty above everything else and even though this fella was completely unsuitable to be carrying a firearm and driving a police car, we covered for him. It is a matter of opinion as to whether or not we should have. As it turned out he died not that long later and we did not have to cover for him anymore. No second guesses as to what he died from; cirrhosis of the liver.

On the other hand there were fellas like the Fred I told you about. He would set a cracking pace at the beginning of the shift and work flat out for the whole duration. We'd be lucky to stop for a meal break. He was tough on the public as well and would not take any s*** from anyone. Most times that I worked with Fred, we would get overtime. He'd stop the car outside a pub, any old pub, didn't matter to him where it was, and we would get out and go through the pub liked we owned the place. If it was closing time we make sure that they were all out ten minutes after the last drink, then stay at the pub and have a couple of beers ourselves. So you had these two very different attitudes to work.

The Police Force was a mixture of everything and it made the job very interesting. One thing they were all united on was the welfare of a fellow cop. Woe betide anybody who hurt a cop, especially if he was a criminal. You might be able to use your imagination as to what might have happened when they got them back to the station. I'll leave that one to you. There was a definite brotherhood in the Police that you wouldn't find in any other job. I recall another night when I was the senior man and went out with a new Probationary Constable on his very first night on the job. After telling him how quiet it generally was, we attended to one attempted suicide and two successful suicides in one night. Unbelievable! The first attempted suicide was when a chap was going to jump off the Gap. We grabbed him by his belt and pulled him back. We then had to take him to Callan Park, which was a psychiatric hospital in the inner west of Sydney at the time. The Gap is the short version for Watsons Bay Gap, which is at Watsons Bay on the eastern shoreline of Sydney and it is the site of many suicides. It is estimated that about fifty people commit suicide there every year. A nice place to die I suppose but a gruesome way of doing it. Then in the same night we went to a heroin overdose, which might have been a suicide in Bondi. Who knows, it might even have been murder. I often wonder how many murders are written off as heroin overdoses. A nice and quick way to clear up a murder I should have thought; just write it off as a suicide. To cap the trifecta, we went to a third one at Birrell Street in Waverley where a bloke had blown off a side of his head with a shotgun. Christ, talk about blood and guts, but I was de-sensitised to it to some degree. Plenty of it in the bush in the animal form and lots more of it in the hospital in the human form. It is however not right to say that you get used to it; you never do. While I was at Bondi I attended a number of other suicides there as well as attempted suicides. It saddened me but cops have to learn to deal with tragedy. Perhaps that is why they drink so much; have such a high rate of divorce and they themselves have a high rate of suicide. They also have a very high rate of mental illness but most of this is covered up. It's a stressful job and at times you are dealing with the scum and dregs of society. By this time my depression had largely dissipated but I still had the anxiety related to the obsessional thinking. But it is fair to say that when the depression got better, so did the anxiety and obsessional thinking. One time whilst working at Bondi I had to go with a Sergeant and tell a lady that her son had died of a heroin overdose and that it may have been suicide. I can tell you that this is the hardest part of Police work. As soon as they open the door and see you with your caps off, they sense something is wrong. To see the sorrow a mother has when she learns of her son's (or daughter's) death is heart rending. I had to participate in this a couple of times and I dreaded it. In fact all cops do and this is a big thing to ask a young 19 year old to do.

Most of the cops in my time were bigots and some were hypocrites. Aren't we all you might say? Maybe! I gave you the definition earlier of what a bigot is but what is a hypocrite? I think that such a person is one who pretends to have virtues, morals and principles, etc., that he/she does not actually possess, especially a person whose actions belie their stated beliefs. I would say that most police in my days did not fit this category, except the ones in high office. Some of them were master hypocrites. They would say one thing in public and do something very opposite in private. Something they have in common with our modern day politicians. Many of them had conveniently forgotten their past when they became commissioned officers. Once they became officers, the crooks of the past became the moral and ethical guardians of the future.

I learnt at Bondi first-hand what summary justice was, but the good news is that it was not a lynching. I was working with another Sergeant one night on the beach promenade that runs parallel to Campbell parade. There were some young fellows playing up there; that was not altogether unusual — more skylarking than anything else! When we approached them they high tailed it away but one young fella was too slow off the mark. He had been urinating in the park but it was night time and I did not think that he was offending anyone. In any event he ended up in our hands. When we were speaking to him the Sergeant delivered him a vicious left punch, right below the solar plexus. He followed it with a thunderous right to the left kidney area. Well, the young fella dropped like a sack of potatoes. It took him a while to regather himself. The Sergeant told him that he was an idiot and that this was his punishment for pissing in a public place. He then told him we were not going to arrest him. I don't know if he thought that was a good deal or not, but of course he accepted it. He really couldn't believe we were letting him go and probably thought that he was going to get more of the same when we got back to the Station. The Sergeant told me that when I was working with him we were never going to arrest anybody. He generally thought it was a waste of time arresting them, bailing them and then putting them before a court where they would more than likely plead not guilty. They would often plead not guilty and on and on it would go. Mostly (though not always) they were as guilty as sin but the courts were far too lenient on them. This trait of always pleading not guilty became a bone of contention with me later on in my Police career and was one of the reasons that I left. This particular Sergeant felt that we should be the judge, jury and executioner. This is not the legal route of course, but under a given set of circumstances, it could have some merit. I bet that young fella thought twice before urinating in a public place again. You are crying vigilante with this story and that's what it was. I'm not saying I agree with it but I am suggesting that there may be some method in its madness. However imagine if the two blows he had received had done some damage even though they were to the body. Just imagine what our predicament, or more pertinently mine, would have been if he had collapsed and died. Where would that leave me? They could charge me with being an accessory and than I'd be forced into having to lie to protect my mate. General duties were often lined with minefields and this story is just one of the many examples I could give you; like Fred and his maniacal driving. Like the Senior Constable who got out of the Police car and fell over in a drunken stupor. Young coppers should not have to work with blokes like this because they are putting him/her in harm's way and then when the shit hits the fan, you have to front up and protect them and if necessary, commit perjury. I can tell you there was plenty of this sort of madness at 21 Division when I was there.

Sometime in 1976 when I was a uniform cop I was deployed to attend a student demonstration at the UNSW (University of New South Wales) in 1976. Sir John Kerr came to the University and the students were very irate that he had the audacity to come to their campus. This was compounded by the cops being on the campus to protect him and the demonstrations were fairly fierce. Many people were very upset about it. When Kerr came to where we were, we had to surround his Government Rolls Royce to protect him. This little old lady who was very well dressed, yelled through the inner cordon of Police at Kerr, quote, "You f****** c*** Kerr" and that is the absolute truth. There were a couple of cops on the front or third page of the following day's newspaper and I was one of them. We were shocked and I think so was she, but we didn't arrest her. That story kinda highlights the depth of feeling towards the Governor General at that time. That little old saintly lady epitomised the depth of feeling that many people felt. Sir John Kerr died in 1991 and Gough Whitlam died in 2014 so he outlived Kerr by fifteen years. I would speculate that this would have been the first time in her life that this little saintly lady used such foul language. She just totally lost it, such was her anger at him.

I mentioned xenophobia in the Police Force. I have said they hated just about all groups of people. Blacks, Asians, wogs, gays, lesbians, lawyers, Jews, politicians, reporters, and so on. I did not fit into this character description. The Catholics hated the Masons and the Masons hated the Catholics. I did not have any prejudice towards anybody. There were many incidents that occurred whilst I was in uniform at Bondi that are worth talking about and I will mention just a couple. I was doing the night shift in the middle of winter on a cold and rainy night. About 5 am we got a call via the Police VKG radio that a woman could hear what sounded like a person moaning outside her unit, which was just off Campbell Parade in Bondi. We went around to the back of the block of units using torches to guide us. We than saw what the lady had reported. There was a male person dying/dead on the ground near the fence, with his chest caved in. I went over to assess if there was anything that we could do but he was too far gone. In fact he was dead and had probably died just before we got there. In those circumstances where there is an unnatural death, the law requires there has to be a coronial inquest. It turned out that he was a 23 year old NZ white man who was well known to the Police. He had form (history) for BE&S (break, enter and steal) and drug offences. What they determined was that he had been attempting to break into a unit on the fourth floor during the early hours of the morning and slipped on the balcony (because of the rain). He fell right onto the boundary fence and the force caved his chest in. Obviously he didn't die instantly because the woman heard him moaning. It makes you think. What was he doing out at 4 a.m. on a cold windy wintery morning, trying to break into a unit? To steal of course, but why was he that desperate? Was he doing it to buy drugs? Who knows, but this is another example of what young nineteen year old cops have to deal with. It's also an example of how desperate drug addicts can get and the lengths that they will go to get a 'score'.

During my uniform time I was also selected to work with the close protection team of the NSW Police for the protection of Queen Elizabeth II and Prince Phillip. They came to Sydney on the Royal ship 'Britannia' and that's where I was posted to protect her and the good Duke. I had to stand at the end of the gangway on the wharf and look after the one and only legitimate access point to the ship. It was berthed at Circular Quay so I can actually say that I met the Queen and would be telling the truth. In 1982 my wife Sue and I did a trip to Europe and we stayed in a B&B guesthouse at Russell Square in London. The landlady was a bit of an English snob and thought that we were just some simple colonials. You still get those types in England who think that they are still the colonial masters, but it's getting rarer as time moves on and we live in a more enlightened world with the information revolution that has taken place. Anyway, in conversation one night she was kinda boasting that she had seen the Queen once and proceeded to tell us that the Queen actually came to her son's school in Kent. I told her that I had actually met the Queen on more than one occasion. I also told her I'd met and spoken with the Duke of Edinburgh. She was speechless; she just could not believe it but I convinced her it was true and it was. From then on her attitude and demeanour towards us improved significantly. Previously to that we used to get rather small portions for our breakfast but that improved greatly after I informed her of my social network!

Naturally, like any disciplinary body, there were times when we were asked to do things that did not sit well with us; Christmas Eve in 1976 was one such time. The boss of Bondi sent us down to book all the cars that were illegally parked on the beach promenade front at Bondi beach. We went and inspected the vehicles and of course, some had extended their time slot and could have been booked. As we were inspecting the vehicles, this assertive (but not very bright) young woman reprimanded us for not showing the true Christmas spirit and said we should show a little consideration. Well, little did she know that this is what we were doing but we didn't tell her that. In fact my mate told her to "f*** off you f****** whore and mind your own f****** business or else she would end up back at the station in the cooler". She got the message but I was shocked that he would speak to her like that. I really didn't like that but let it drop. We worked out the shift and came back to the station empty handed; that is that we had not written any infringements. We told the boss that the motorists were unusually well behaved this day and we did not have to book anyone. Well, he got stuck into us and told us that we were bullshitting him. He knew we were not being upfront but let it go. Perhaps he was showing some Christmas spirit! This is the sort of Police behaviour (on our boss's part) that really gets the public offside and it is easy to understand why.

During this year one of our boys committed suicide. One night he sat on the end of his bed, put the service revolver into his mouth and pulled the trigger. He was not very senior in rank and probably one of the nicest cops at Bondi. He had just been given the flick by his girlfriend and he could not deal with the rejection. Remember the Pauline story. After it became clear that she was not going to come back to him, he committed suicide.

We went to his funeral at the Sacred Heart Church at Randwick. That was a fairly bleak day for all of us. Police funerals can be very sad affairs, especially if one is killed on duty. Another chap that I worked with at No 21 Division had an unfortunate accident in a car where he hit a pedestrian with his own car when he was off duty and killed him. The problem was his instincts kicked in and he left the scene before the Police arrived. It didn't take long for them to track him down and he admitted it. He agreed to be interviewed, went to a room to get ready to go with the Police and put the Smith & Wesson into his mouth and pulled the trigger. Is it a case of only the good die young? Another one was my Instructor at the Police Academy who shot himself. I sometimes think that the Smith & Wesson service revolvers killed more Police by suicide than they did vicious violent criminals. Whilst at 21 Division, one of our boys was killed in a Police car on his way back to our HQ at the academy. He was driving and the car hit a pole in South Dowling Street after trying to avoid a collision in front of him. He was a really good bloke and I liked him. They had a Police funeral for him at Waverley because he had been killed whilst he was on duty. There is something very special and sobering about Police funerals. When the lone piper plays the last lament it is difficult not to shed a tear. Another cop friend of mine got killed in an Anzac parade going home in the early hours of the morning. He was driving a van towards Maroubra, hit a wooden fence and a rail impaled him through the neck.

It is worthwhile mentioning the high incidence of mental illness in the Police Force; especially PTSD (Post Traumatic Stress Disorder). It was not commonly known in my day but knowing what we know now, I can identify quite a few cases of Police that were suffering from it when I was in the job. My research on PTSD included finding out that the new figures reveal an Australian Police Officer is taking their own life every 9/10 weeks or so. Experts in the field of PTSD management say that Police are more prone to PTSD than combat soldiers are because of the types of stressful situations that Police can be subjected to on a regular basis. Of course I'm not talking about Police that sit in offices all day but rather the general duties Police on operational duties. Most of these cops that kill themselves are aged between 30 to 49 years and they use firearms, which of course they'd have handy. I have just dealt with three that I knew personally and worked with. In my case I had my demons long before I joined the force and now seemed to have this capacity to handle tragic events. There were many tragic events I had to deal with as a junior Policeman. A bloke who left most of his brains on a wall in an apartment in Waverley; a homicide of a young boy which was particularly violent and gruesome; terrible car accidents where you would see badly mangled and decapitated bodies, mainly of young people; drug overdoses; people that had been viciously assaulted; victims of fire (one with 90% of his body burnt with 3rd degree burns, he died (of course); the list goes on. You'd often go to a 'dead-un' (dead person) where the victim had died days or even weeks before and you'd have to deal with it. One case we went to, was an older person who had slipped in his shower and banged his head violently on the tiled floor and killed himself. Nobody knew about it until neighbours complained about a foul smell coming from the apartment. Of course, who do they call? The Police naturally, and the Police are the ones that are exposed to this type of thing regularly. You can imagine finding badly decomposed bodies with all sorts of distressing things happening to it such as maggots crawling in and out of every orifice. I think you can understand why cops drink so much, why they have a high rate of divorce, mental illness and suicide.

It is very easy for me to understand the stress that operational Police can be subjected to as I was on the front line for all of my Police service. I was also exposed to it in my nursing days. In fact, the first dead person I ever saw was a toddler that was bought into the A&E of the Prince of Wales hospital when I was on duty. I will never forget the distraught parents and I can clearly understand how some people could not cope with that. Some of the surgical operations I witnessed were very gruesome. One in particular comes to mind where this chap had major abdominal surgery and his insides were all over the operating table. Just for the record he did survive. In fact, he was the one that I did my case study on for the hospital finals.

There were no major crimes that I was involved in that year. Most of it was petty crime, although there was one case of attempted rape. He pleaded not guilty but we got up on that one. I did a lot work with a particular sergeant I got on well with. He would entertain me with stories emanating from his detective days. He was one of those old school cops who was hard but always fair. One night we got this call about a mentally disturbed person behaving erratically in the street at Bondi Junction. After we detained him, it became clear that we would have to take him to the mental hospital and have him scheduled under the Mental Health Act. This bloke was really 'off his rocker'. We didn't have a car and for some reason, the other cars were not available; so we took him out in the paddy wagon. The good Sergeant drove and I had to sit in the back with this fella in case he hurt himself, but left my service revolver in the front. For reasons I can't remember we could not handcuff him but didn't feel it was safe leaving him alone in the back. You can well imagine the ramifications if he should die or even injure himself whilst in Police custody. On the journey he started getting aggressive so I had to subdue him and I did that by giving him a couple of sharp punches to the solar plexus. I then had to wrestle him and pinned his arms behind his back. I ended up hand cuffing him. We go out to Rozelle and he is screaming with his arms cuffed behind his back. My work mate didn't know any of this was going on. Putting handcuffs on mentally disturbed people can have negative legal consequences. Putting him in the back on his own could have had negative consequences. Putting him in the front was an absolute no, no. This bloke was roaming the streets next day in Bondi Junction. Talk about a waste of the taxpayers resources. When he got to the hospital he started yelling that the cops (me) were trying to rape and kill him. He told the staff that I had belted him (true), robbed him (false) and wanted him to give me a blow job (very false). Fortunately the staff did not take any notice of him but they could have and I'd have found myself before the Ombudsman. I understand that when they checked him in they were surprised that he only had a five dollar note in his wallet. So! He had told them that I took about $300 and told him that, "You'll need $5 to get home with and if we have to deal with you again, I will give you the father of all hidings, you c***."

Lots of stories go around about Police transferring a problem from one area to another. I'm not admitting I took part in it and I'm not denying it either, but I knew for a fact that it used to go on. Stories abounded that Police would take a cadaver to another division because they got it late in their night shift and wanted to avoid all the paperwork. There is a mountain of that in these sorts of cases. Once having secreted the body in some lonely place like a park under the cover of darkness, they'd make a call from a local telephone box and tell the unlucky station that they are so and so and they saw a body in the park or wherever whilst they were taking their dog for an early morning walk. Other similar stories go that 21 Division used to fill the truck up with 'warbs' (homeless alcoholics/mentally ill) and take them out to the outer western suburbs. They'd give them a rough ride out there and just let them go in some park in the early hours of the morning. They than became somebody else's problem. It was very advisable to not get caught doing this type of thing but take my word for it, it used to go on. I wonder if it still does?

Domestic violence is one of the most common tasks that uniform Police have to attend to. I went to lots of them and some were not pretty. I learnt pretty quickly that there are always two sides to a story. In the main however Police gravitate towards taking the side of the woman and it was usually the man who got the raw end of the deal. One such case I remember was a row that started over the wife flirting with one of the tradesmen. She was flaunting her body by wearing flimsy clothing when the workmen were doing the renovations and was focused on one of the young good looking tradesmen. She had made it clear to him that he was the chosen one and when the husband caught her flirting (by coming home unexpectedly; you know, the same old story), a verbal fight ensued. The husband called the Police and that's how we got involved in it. In these cases we would separate the warring couple and get each side of the story. The Sergeant believed the woman; I believed the tradesman. The problem was the Sergeant was the boss. She was saying that the tradesman was coming on to her without any cue from her but the tradesman denied this. When we got there we noticed her attire and it certainly did not leave too much to the imagination. There was no doubt about that but you know, the woman can wear what she likes as long as it is socially acceptable. Some of that doesn't leave much to the imagination! You can imagine how difficult these things can be to deal with. In this instance it was agreed that the young tradesman would be relocated on another site and that the woman was to keep away from the men working on the house. Even though we settled everything down temporarily I am sure that married couple would have encountered problems down the track with her behaviour.

Domestic violence cases can be explosive and many murders are committed because of them. Police have to walk a thin line dealing with domestic violence. You can be damned if you do, damned if you don't. You can see how important it is for Police in general duties to show good judgement. We did follow up with the contractor about a week later and he had relocated the bloke somewhere else and all seemed to be well. The renovations were continuing but the lady was not wearing provocative clothing anymore. As it turned out I think we handled it properly. On another domestic matter, I recall that on one night shift my partner and I when we were doing general duty work in uniform had to go down to the city morgue at Glebe on some Police matter. I don't remember what it was but whilst we were there another team bought in a body from a domestic dispute in Newtown. The victim was an elderly man, around about eighty. I asked them what had happened and they told us that the wife of the victim had been suffering physical abuse from her husband for years and had reported it to the Police previously. On this occasion she got the kitchen knife to defend herself and somehow she had struck him in the upper thigh. Unfortunately the knife hit the femoral artery and he bled to death. She was reluctantly charged with murder but was exonerated at trial. I had another very serious domestic dispute at Waverley. The lady (the victim) had tried to terminate her relationship with this bloke and he had threatened to kill her. When we interviewed her she was adamant that he would, given the opportunity. We judged it to be serious enough to pass it onto the Detectives. Because it was late at night we had to take her to Waverley Police Station and call the wireless car for the eastern suburbs zone. At the time the CIB had a number of cars manned by three detectives each that used to patrol the metropolitan areas of Sydney in the early hours. They were sort of a motorised detective unit and the concept proved to be successful. They were also very successful with their social life and the shifts became known as the cocktail shifts; but they did a lot of good work as well. In these cases you can take out whatever restraining order you like but if he says he is going to do it, he might and to hell with the consequences. Some of them think along the lines, if I am not going to have her, no one else will either. That can be their thinking. I never followed up what happened but at least we put her in the right hands. I have never seen a person more terrified in my whole life, before or since and I really felt for her. In these situations women are often in dire circumstances and to this day I still think about her.

I mentioned earlier when I was talking about the abuse that I suffered at St Brendan's that in my adulthood I had developed a severe abhorrence towards brutality towards children. There was one time at Bondi my work mate and I went to a domestic dispute in their semi detached house in Waverley. The husband had assaulted his wife after she had thrown some food at him. Both of them agreed with that, but in the melee the young boy aged about ten, was struck by the father when he tried to intervene on his mother's behalf. He was not badly hurt but did have a black eye where his father had hit him. I suggested to my workmate, a Senior Constable, that I take the man outside and get his version of events and that he interview the wife inside the house. That was a normal tactic to employ in these situations but unknown to the Senior I had ulterior motives. He agreed and the father and I went outside. I told the bloke to hit me like he had hit his son but he wouldn't, so I slapped him and told him he was a weak c*** to hit a child and I then threw the set of car keys (for the Police car) into his face to distracted him. I grabbed hold of his hair and pulled his head down and bought my right knee up under his solar plexus as hard as I could. That sorta put him on the ground and then I kicked him in the groin. He was big fella and in a fair fight he may have beaten me but I had been trained to engage in unarmed combat with the Commandoes. It really hurt him and I told him that we ever came back to this house again we would f****** kill him, not for hitting his wife, but for hitting a defenceless child. I told him that if he decided to report me to IA I would say that he attacked me first and would tell whatever lies were necessary. In my eyes, when it came to physical child abuse, all gloves were off. The bloke never said a word when we went inside and his injuries were not visible. He apologised to his wife and said that after talking it over with me he did not want to press charges against her and she in turn reciprocated. As a result of this accord we did not make any arrests and left. My work mate smelt a rat and asked me what happened out in the back yard. I told him the bloke felt really bad about hitting his son and was grimacing. The grimacing part was true but that was from the pain I had inflected upon him. I have never told this story to anyone until now and the strange thing is that I never felt guilty about it. Should I? He got what he deserved and it could have been worse. We could have arrested him and charged him with 'assault with actual bodily harm' on a child and a Magistrate could very well have sent him to prison for it and I told him this. It was the only time, before or since, that I have ever attacked somebody maliciously like that. Sure I got into fights, especially at 21 Division but they were in the main trying to effect arrests. I don't think you have to be a psychoanalysis to figure out what the catalyst was in this event. How would I have explained this one to IA? Child abuse was my Achilles heal but even in this instance I never lost my cool. I had it planned while we were still inside and decided unlawfully that I would be Judge, Jury and Executioner on this rarest of occasions.

A tragic example of how dangerous uniform Police work can be is the following story. You may remember the murder of two young uniform Police in Melbourne in 1988. These were referred to as the Walsh Street Police murders. One cop was 22 and the other 20. A call had come over the radio about an abandoned car in Walsh Street, at South Yarra in Melbourne. It happened about 5 a.m. so you can imagine how easy and cowardly it was for the offenders to ambush them. The cops didn't stand a chance. A group of at least four blokes, maybe six, were waiting for them in the dark for an ambush. They were heavily armed with shotguns and the like. They just gave it to the cops whilst they were having a look at the abandoned car. Imagine how the parents, brothers, sisters and friends of these two young innocent cops felt. Young blokes just trying to make society safer and they were murdered in cold blood. I think a couple of suspects were shot dead by Police and four others went to trial. They were acquitted by a jury. Just because they were acquitted does not mean they were not guilty. So, anyone thinking of joining the Police Force should be fully aware of the risks.

My year for being a Probationary Constable was nearly finished. I had to go back to the Academy for my secondary training in January 1977. I think the course went for about six weeks. It was during this course that the Granville Rail disaster occurred. At 8.10am on Tuesday 18 January 1977, a crowded Sydney-bound commuter train travelling from the Blue Mountains derailed near the western suburbs station of Granville, and carried away piers holding up a road bridge which then collapsed on the train; 83 people died and more than 200 were injured as a result of the accident. A subsequent inquiry into the disaster found the primary cause of the accident was the bad condition of the fastening of the track where the train derailed. All of us were seconded from the academy to the disaster area. It was chaos. There was a Police Superintendent with a loud speaker who took control of the disaster response. The bridge had collapsed and I would say on the carriages after the first two. The concrete bridge flattened the carriages that were full of people. Many of them were killed outright but there were many more that were trapped in a concrete tomb. The medical teams were performing surgery out in the open to try and save people's lives. My job, probably because they knew about my medical training, was to take the body bags to the make-shift morgue on site. God, it was a truly gruesome job. Some of the bodies were just a mass of pulped bone and flesh. In most cases you could not recognise they were human remains. It could just as easy have been a bag of bones and meat left overs in a butcher shop. The bodies were just like that; it was just horrific. I thought, I didn't join the Police Force to do this but accepted that it was part of the job. I don't remember how long we were at the scene but I think it was about three days. I will never forget the Granville Rail Disaster. You can just imagine ordinary people catching the early morning train from the Blue Mountains to go to work and this happens. Countless thousands of trains had gone this way before and nothing happened. Maybe it's true that when your time is up, it is up and there is no explanation. For quite some time after this accident, I used to have unpleasant dreams about the bodies that we had to take to the make-shift morgue. I think it's easy to understand that. After time they dissipated and I never had to seek any counselling about it. I will tell you that for years after I finished nursing, I used to have dreams that I had to go to work at the Prince Henry hospital on the night shift. That particular dream hung around for years and it is fair to say that this effected me more than the Granville rail disaster.

I finished secondary training and got confirmed as a Constable in February 1977.

Around about this time, the powers to be thought that I would make a good addition to the permanent staff of No 21 Special Squad at the Criminal Investigation Branch that had a fairly tainted reputation. They were commonly known as 21 Division and they were a motley crew. Well, that came out of the blue and I got a bit of a shock. I had just been in the force for less than a year and here they are sending me into plain clothes. This was very unusual. I saw it as a massive endorsement of my work at Bondi and accepted the offer. I found out later that one of the tough nut permanent Sergeants at 21 Division, a bloke by the name of Eric Murdock (the big E), found out about me from one of the detectives at Bondi and liked the idea that I was an ex-shearer, an ex-commando and a trained nurse. He set up a meeting with one of the legends of the NSW Police Force, Detective Inspector Noel Morey. Noel was a no-nonsense sort of a bloke and didn't waste much time with small talk. He asked me if I could adapt to the culture of the CIB - boozing, protecting your work mate, all that sort of thing and that was about it. I was transferred to 21 Division not long thereafter. My work mates at Bondi were as taken aback as I was and wondered whose palm I was greasing to get this transfer. Then one of them even bought up the old chestnut about me being a plant for Internal Affairs. When I got to 21 Division that was the first thing that I had to deal with. 21 Division's primary functions were to look after all the illegal betting in the state; serve as a training squad for people wanting to be designated detectives and assist with the policing of drug and vice, particularly prostitution. You can add some more to that: teach trainee detectives to become alcoholics; learn to type perfectly while drunk; f*** whoever and whenever you could; fit into the CIB culture (e.g., lying in court); bash a few heads if necessary; get a divorce and generally have a good time whilst they were stationed there.

In the squad they had a section specifically devoted to the gaming industry. The boss told me that I was never going to work with them. I knew the real reason and that was that I had not been vetted to determine if I could be trusted with the corruption side of things. Then there was the general duty part of the squad and that was to go around and pick up the drunks or go to known trouble spots and get stuck into the hoodlums; all that sort of thing. All crews were given carte blanche to do whatever criminal work they wanted but the hard heads didn't want to do any. That might mean they would have to arrest someone, get a not guilty and have to front court. That was not their idea of work. Their idea was lock up a few drunks, fill in a couple of CIRs (criminal intelligence reports), often make them up and then get on the piss and generally have a good time. That was the shift. If you didn't like it, you could go back to uniform. Then there was a section of Detectives. They numbered about five and were usually rejects from the other squads. They had what we used to refer to as 'having hit a hurdle' and were only one more step from going back to uniform. Some of them were really good detectives but had been caught 'copping a quid' or something like that. They accepted their role at 21 Division because they did not want to go back to uniform. Initially they had me on the drunk wagon and you did not have to be a genius to work the drunk truck. You'd work with a lazy Sergeant (usually, although not always) and drink for the first four or five hours of your shift. Then the good Sergeant would declare that it was time for dinner and sometimes he treated us to a very nice restaurant – no questions asked and no explanations given. After a couple of hours for dinner with wine, we would go to the Haymarket down near Central Railway Station or the Matthew Talbot hostel at Woolloomooloo and grab a few drunks and take them to Central for charging; that was the shift. Often we were drunker than the people we were locking up but that didn't matter. We were in a sense, 'Princes of the city'. We could do what we liked and often did. I have to admit that I had a lot of fun with these blokes. There was never a dull moment and take it from me, once you are accepted into the inner circle, you go for a ride and have a very interesting and fun life. More about that later!

One night at 21 Division I worked with a team on the drunk truck. The good Sergeant, much more than half drunk himself, asked this bloke if he'd rather a belting or an arrest. I think he was another 'pisser'. He chose the arrest and I think he made the right decision. At 21 Division it was not unusual for us to be asked to clean out known trouble spots, usually from someone in the Government or the Church. Often a complaint by a concerned citizen would end up going to a Member of Parliament or even a Minister about hoodlum behaviour in certain areas. They would complain about the behaviour of patrons at particular venues. It didn't matter what was going on in the venue that we were targeting. If we were told to go and clean it up, that is what we did. 'Mine is not to reason why; mine is to do and die'. Our purpose was to send a message to the broader community that the Government wasn't going to put up with hoodlum behaviour and if there was some collateral damage that was unfortunate but the job still had to be done. The problem with this strategy was that it could, and often did, target the wrong people. The Sergeants didn't care. On one such occasion we were sent to the street level bar at a hotel in the Cross. One of our boys was sent in; the smallest one and his job was to start an argument with a group and instigate a fight. That's what happened and of course the publican would call the Police. We were waiting just around the corner and expecting the call. When we got there, there was a brawl going on. The cops (us) just went in there and started hauling patrons out and putting them in the paddy wagons. It didn't matter if they were fighting or not; in they went. It was the classic case of being in the wrong place at the wrong time. On this occasion I was asking an Aboriginal man to get in the back of the truck. He was totally bewildered, sober and reasonably well dressed. He wanted to know why and I told him we were cleaning the pub up and he happened to be in the wrong place at the wrong time. I told him to just get in and not to make a scene in the street and I would let him go when we got to Darlinghurst Police station. I told him if he didn't get in, he'd end up being charged with additional charges of resisting arrest and assaulting Police. He got in. I told the sergeant what arrangements I had made with this bloke and we were going to let him go. Unfortunately the sergeant had a thing about the 'Abos' as most racists cops did. He reprimanded me and told me that since I had arrested him he had to be charged with something. That we could not let him go or else he might sue the Police Department with wrongful arrest. So, we charged this decent citizen with drunkenness and he spent four hours in the cooler. I was upset that I'd broken my word to him that I actually went down and saw him in the cells. I told him what had happened and sincerely apologised. He told me to f*** off in no uncertain terms and assured me that if he ever saw me in the street again, there would be a reckoning. Naturally no one knew this. If the sergeant had found out, I could easily have been sent back to uniform. They would have thought that I was not tough enough to be a plain clothes Policeman. The truth is I was tough enough but I had a real thing about charging decent law abiding people when they have done nothing wrong and 21 Division did plenty of that.

There was another case at 21 Division with mixture of white blokes and aboriginal men that I am ashamed to admit to; although I didn't instigate it. We were out on patrol in the late hours and we were in a drunken state, which was almost the norm. We came across a group of blokes that was misbehaving (just skylarking) in a park in Redfern. It was just silly alcohol fuelled stuff and we decided (that is the Sergeant decided) that we would not lock them up but give them one hell of a fright. He gave them the choice of being arrested or being given a sporting chance to escape. What he proposed to them was that they could make a run for it. He would count to ten and then we would fire our revolvers at them. They had a bit of a conference and decided that they would take the escape opportunity. On the count of one they started running and they ran with the 'speed of startled gazelles'. After ten-seconds they were easily out of sight but the good Sergeant fire two shots in the air anyway. Bejesus, imagine if they had complained. How would we explain that one but rest assured it would have been defended robustly and a neat little story would have been hatched that would have exonerated us. If it's any consolation I did not want the Sergeant to do it but he wanted to have what he thought was just a bit of fun. Of course he was never going to shoot them and in their half drunken state, they didn't know that. I have to confess reluctantly that it did have me in stitches but am ashamed to admit to it now.

Another time, with the same Sergeant, he just hauled someone off the street and threw him in the paddy wagon. When I asked him what we were going to charge him with he said, 'Let me think about it mate'. Ok, so after a few minutes he thought about it and said that we would charge him with unseemly words under the Summary Offences Act. When I asked him what unseemly words the bloke was alleged to have used, the good Sergeant said, 'put in the charge that he called the sergeant a big fat c***'. At least the Sergeant was right about that part of it so we took him back to Central Police Station to charge him with unseemly words. The bloke got really angry when we got to Central and became aggressive. He wasn't handcuffed and he started throwing punches claiming he was being arrested unlawfully which was true, he was. Now we had to charge him with assault Police as well. I thought, here we go again, another not guilty. But to my surprise, he pleaded guilty. When I registered my surprise with the Sergeant, he just looked at me and said, "Mate, I have been in this business a long time. I knew he would plead guilty; he f****** knows the rules". He did not elaborate what he meant by that and I left it at that. It would never have crossed my mind to make a complaint about any of my colleagues, even the scumbags, but I could not abide the idea of charging innocent people. The thing we had to do was 'when in Rome do what the Romans do'.

Sometime during my time at 21 Division there was a changing of the guard at the top level of management. The Government of the day under the premiership of Neville Wran (Nifty Nev) from 'Balmain boys don't cry' fame, was getting a lot of flak in the press about police corruption and in particular the illegal casinos and the SP (starting price) bookies that operated on every street corner. Every Tom, Dick, and Harry knew that they were only allowed to operate on the provision that they paid the rent. The rent was a certain amount to the Police every week. I don't know what that figure was and I have told you that I did not have anything to do with the gaming. It was generally thought that 21 Division was the bagman who collected all the 'rent' and took the money higher up. It was speculated that this system could not operate so openly and brazenly if the corruption money was not being shared with higher authorities in both the judiciary and the government. The newspapers of the day were accusing the government of being involved in this enterprise and that went right up to the top of the tree. Whether or not it is true I don't know but a lot of people believed it was. Illegal gambling consequently became a hot potato so Nifty had to do something about it. At least show the electorate he was proactive. One of the initiatives that was implemented was to bring a fella by the name of Mervyn Beck to take over the management of 21 Division. He had a reputation of being untouchable, tough and willing to take these fellas on, whoever they were. The illegal gambling was controlled by organised criminals and generally they did a fairly good job of it. Most people thought that there wasn't anything wrong with having an SP bet at the local pub or going to an illegal casino and playing blackjack or whatever. It was seen as harmless and not really hurting anyone. The trouble was the government was not getting its share of the betting revenue through its TAB systems and that was not making them happy. There were no legal casinos in Sydney at that time and organised crime was getting all that business. It was generally considered that the system was allowed to flourish because 'hands were being greased' all the way up the ladder. This system had been in place for many years and it seemed to keep most people happy, especially the cops. It all became politically explosive and the government had to act. The 'fly in the ointment' was that organised crime was not just into the illegal gambling (which the day-to-day bloke accepted) but they were also the Mr Bigs of the illicit drug trade, especially heroin, and that was not acceptable to the man in the street. Corruption from a little bit of gambling and whoring was not seen as anything too bad but to overlook the distribution of heroin was not politically expedient. It was even worse when the Police allegedly got involved in it as well; so something had to be done. Nifty appointed Beck to clean up the gambling side of it and to a large extent he did, momentarily. It didn't take any special detective work to do this. All you had to do was go into the pub, grab the SP bookie and charge him. He would soon realise that the game was up and either go underground or get out of it.

One day when I came to work on normal duties, Beck called me into his office. I was well dressed in a suit and I had my wife's carry-on bag with an airline logo written on it. She was a former hostess with that airline and I had taken her bag with my gym gear in it to work. Beck ordered me to go out to the airport, get a taxi and ask the taxi driver to take me to an illegal game. So I went out to the International terminal in a Police car and came out of the terminal like I had just got off a plane. I caught a taxi and told him that I had never been to Sydney before but would like to go to one of Sydney's famous casinos. Initially he was sceptical and asked me a few questions. I gave him some money and convinced him that I was genuine and so he said that he would take me to a game on the North side. He told me where it was but I made out that I had no idea where to go. It happened to be in Crows Nest. Well, this taxi driver took me all over the place to get to Crows Nest. Instead of heading for the city he headed to La Perouse, which is in the opposite direction. From there he ended up in Bondi and came into the city via New South Head Road, over the bridge and eventually to Crows Nest. I think the fare was double what it should have been but of course, I couldn't say anything. He dropped me at the address and pointed upstairs to where the casino was operating. I stayed for a while, had a few bets and then caught a taxi back to the Remington Rand building in Liverpool Street where 21 Division was now housed. I gave Beck my report and he told me that he was already aware of this place but that I had done a good job. That is the full extent of my work with the gaming Police and I only did that because I was carrying my wife's airline bag.

I did take the number plate of the taxi and the next day I rang the taxi company telling them that I was on official Police business and wanted the name and address of the taxi driver. I did not give the company my correct details. In those days they always gave the Police whatever they wanted so I got his telephone number as well. I rang him and introduced myself (under a different name), told him I was from the Police and asked him about the bloke that he took to the illegal casino the previous evening. Well, he almost s*** himself. I told him that the bloke he took had been critically bashed and robbed outside an illegal casino in Crows Nest and was on the critical list at the

Royal North Shore hospital. He was very likely going to die and then we could be investigating a murder. I went onto to tell him that I needed to interview him. I told him to come to the Homicide Squad office for a formal interview at such and such a time, gave him the address, told him not to speak with anybody else about it and not to be late. The Homicide Squad was just a couple of floors above us at the Remington Rand building in Liverpool Street. I than told him that if he didn't come we'd come and arrest him and I left it at that. I made sure that I was outside the building with a cup of coffee 10-20 minutes before he was due and would you believe, I saw him get out of a taxi and go into the building. I did not feel guilty about doing this because I reckoned that this taxi driver was a scumbag ripping a member of the public off like that and he got what he deserved. I toyed with the idea of calling him and telling him that I was the cop he had ripped off and that he was a c***. However in the end I thought there was the possibility that he might report it to Internal Affairs and best to let sleeping dogs lie. I really got pissed off with him doing what he did and I felt that I had squared the ledger. I told you that most Police are paranoid and sometimes it pays to be. I have another story about a run in I had with a taxi driver and will tell you about that later.

I've got to say I had some great times with these hard heads at 21 Division. They'd been around the block and knew what was going on. I now got exposed to the hookers, the drug dealers and addicts around Kings Cross, as well as some fairly well known criminals. We worked in teams of three. The hookers knew when they were going to be arrested so it was all organised. We would pick them up and take them to Central. We'd charge them and the uniform cops would take it from there. They would either bail them or they could stay for a few hours in the can and appear at the Central Court of Petty Sessions in the morning. The Magistrate would fine them $80 (this is what it was at the time). The whores were always first on the list and of course they always pleaded guilty. This was a good system, a win-win for everybody. The tax payer was getting some revenue going into the government coppers. The cops were getting the arrest numbers they wanted. The girls thought it was fair and just looked upon it as a bit of rent they had to pay. It let the criminal world know who really was in charge and of course, the corrupt few, those faceless men, were making a mint out of it. Those that were running the hookers (and the drugs) needed to know that the Police were really the ones in charge and had to be reminded every now and again. They were happy with this arrangement and it all worked hunky-dory as they say. I think that this was the message that my old Sergeant was giving this fella when we falsely arrested and charged him with unseemly words that I told you about.

I have always had an affinity with the underdog in society. Some cops wanted to persecute black fellows. Some zeroed in on ethnics and all of them zeroed in on gay people. Remember this was still only 1977 and gays were not welcome in the Police Force. Some people thought that I was too nice to be a cop. Of course, those that knew me knew that was not right. Many years later, I was drinking in the piano bar of the Mandarin Hotel in Hong Kong with my boss at that time. I'll tell you a lot more about that period later but suffice to say at this point in time that one of his cohorts told him that he felt that I tried too hard to get people to like me. Interesting isn't it? The truth is that I am one of the few fellas I know that really doesn't care that much about what people think of me. I wouldn't be writing this book if I did. Naturally I was surprised to hear that and took note of it. I did an executive training course once entitled, 'To see yourself as others see you' when I was at The Regent Sydney. The results were very interesting, (I will tell you more about that later). I did however stick up for the underdogs. I used to say things like, "Why are we picking on the Abos. What have they done?" The answer was usually, "Nothing mate, they are black, isn't that enough?". With the gays when I stuck up for them, they reckoned I was one. They'd say they all knew I was just a poofter nurse trying to be a cop. We'd end up having a laugh about it. Talk about bigots. When they met Sue, they changed their mind. I felt that Police resources were not directed where they should have been and that is in criminal operations.

The state spends so much money on the Highway Patrol who spend a lot of their time 'picking' on the public. The rationale for that was that it was such a good revenue stream for the government that it was considered a real champion; which of course it was in the revenue sense. Don't get me wrong. A lot of these Highway Patrol people are very decent human beings. It's the system that gets them and at an early impressionable age. I was over thirty when I joined and perhaps not so easy impressed. Some of us used to call the Highway Patrol the Gestapo. In their uniforms, they even looked a bit like the Gestapo. At times their behaviour warranted that title as well. You will recall I wrote about the Police hierarchy wanting me to go to the Police rescue squad to offset some of the negative publicity that the highway patrol were giving to the Police Force.

Like everybody else I read the newspapers and all sorts of allegations were being made at the time. If you believe the newspapers, corruption went to the highest levels in NSW. It seems that the Police, the judiciary and the politicians were all up to their necks in it. Talking about the judiciary, I went and saw Chief Stipendiary Magistrate (CSM) Murray Farquhar to get my Justice of the Peace certificate. I often had him in matters at the Central Court of Petty Sessions and always found him to be good to the Police. The Big E arranged for me to see him and all I had to do was swear in front of him that I was a decent and honourable man and would uphold the office of Justice of the Peace in accordance with law. That was it and then I was sworn in as one. This turned out to be a very valuable tool to have because it gave me the legal right to sign search warrants, even my own and that is what I did when I was working undercover drugs. I used to sign the search warrants for any searches that I organised for the detectives at 21 Division. It worked a treat and was perfectly legal. It turned out that Murray was really quite a crook and ran afoul of the law. He was sentenced to 4 years jail in 1985. Fancy that, going from the Chief Stipendiary Magistrate to prisoner number XXXX out at the Bay. They proved that he was in a conspiracy to pervert the course of justice but I liked him and thought that he was a good bloke. This was this same year

(1977) 'that famous photo' was taken of Farquhar, Freeman and Paltos.

The transition from Bondi uniform to plain clothes at 21 Division was a cultural shock. I had now given away the idea of going the Police Rescue Squad and decided that my future with the police was in criminal investigation. I think I had been a do-gooder for long enough and had done my time so to speak. However, at 21 Division I could only get involved in the periphery of it but that was better than nothing and at least I was now knocking on the door so to speak. It was clear that the specialist squads handled crimes within their particular areas of expertise. Homicide - murders; Armed Hold Up Squad - armed robbery; etcetera. The divisional detectives handled all the crime in their divisions. 21 Division was essentially what I explained before; looking after gaming, peripheral drug and vice, hoodlum control, and a vetting squad for would-be detectives. It was formed during Police Commissioner McKay's term of office as a type of flying squad for trouble shooting in any areas requiring attention throughout New South Wales. I had made inquiries about being allowed to become a designated detective by doing the Detectives 3-month designation course. Unfortunately I was too old. The cut-off age point was thirty and I was now thirty-three. If I wanted to get involved with criminal investigation, 21 Division was it for me, or so we thought at the time. Sometimes we would be seconded to work with other squads when they were down on numbers. I got to meet a lot of detectives and found that I had an affinity with them. I felt at home in their company and felt like one of them. I think now I had found where I wanted to be and where I belonged. Seldom was I now bothered by the depression and the OCD thing at this stage. It felt like it was a thing of the past. It was as if I had never had it in the first place.

I also met a lot of well-known criminals. People that come to mind were Abe Saffron, the King of Kings Cross. Another was Jimmy Anderson, also a Kings Cross identify. I think the most violent criminal I ever met was Arthur Stanley Smith, commonly known as Neddy Smith. It's a strange thing but I kinda liked him. I met him in the pub a couple of times with other detectives socially. He was a big fella, about my age. He was charming and oddly enough had a lot of charisma. He was polite and when I met him he showed no signs of his violence. Of course he wouldn't would he? But rest assured he was very violent. He was a major heroin dealer and armed hold-up merchant in Sydney. He committed numerous armed robberies and was known to have murdered X number of people. He eventually got life for the murder of Ronnie Flavell in Coogee Bay Road. Neddy was convicted of killing him with a knife over a road rage incident. It was rumoured at the time that Neddy had been given the green light to conduct his criminal enterprises by Roger Rogerson and that was confirmed later by Neddy in his book of the same name. The idea was that he would work in cahoots with certain detectives in the Armed Hold-Up Squad and they would all share in the 'spoils of war.' Neddy talks about this a lot in his book and it was the subject for the television drama, 'Blue Murder'. I don't know where the truth lies but I am sure that much of what Neddy says in his book is true. I was just a very junior Policeman at the time and happened to be with my senior partner in a pub where they were. That's how I met him and 'Abo' Henry as well with other detectives. They were all drinking together and appeared to be great mates, which is what they were I suppose if Neddy was given the green light. You could tell they were really hard men but if you did not know their antecedents, you'd probably think they were just successful businessmen. But the fact remains, they were very violent criminals.

I met Roger Rogerson a couple of times; just briefly over a beer with other detectives at the old Bourbon and Beef Bar in the Cross. He was a very impressive man to me. Not a big tough fella but really, really switched on. I would have loved to work with such a man but I need to qualify that. I mean that I would have loved to work with him within the boundaries of the law. In no way can I condone what it was later found out that he had done. In point of fact Roger became a vicious violent criminal. He was known to be probably the best detective in the Police Force at the time. Not many people realise that Roger was one of the Police most decorated Police Officers in NSW, having received at least 13 awards for bravery, outstanding Police work and devotion to duty including the Peter Mitchell Trophy, the highest annual Police award. They accused him of murdering a drug dealer, Warren Lanfranchi in 1981. He was also alleged to have been involved with the well-known Melbourne criminal who migrated to Sydney and set up shop as a paid hit-man with the slogan, Mr Rent-A-kill, Chris Flannery. The story goes that Roger had approached Mike Drury, an undercover Policeman at the Drug Squad that I knew a bit, to accept a bribe of $30,000 to get the charges against a Melbourne drug dealer, Alan Williams, dropped. Mike was to give damning evidence in an upcoming trail which would probably have convicted Williams. Apparently Mike rejected the offer and Williams later claimed that he agreed to pay Rent-A-kill and Roger, $50,000 each to murder Mike. On the 6 June 1984 (D-day), Flannery allegedly carried out the attempted hit. He went to Mike's home at Chatswood in Sydney and shot him through the kitchen window, critically wounding him in his own house in front of his family. It was only a miracle that Mike lived.

In May 2014 Roger was charged with the murder of Sydney student Jamie Gao, allegedly after a drug deal had gone wrong. The following January Roger and his co-accused Glen McNamara (also a former Police detective) were committed to stand trial over the alleged murder and also for possession to supplying 2.78 kilos of 'Ice' (methamphetamine). Wow, this just does not look like having Roger's handprint on it? What an incredible fall from grace. In 2009 his book, The Dark Side, was launched by Alan Jones at the Iron Duke Hotel in Zetland. This is quite a feat on Roger's part as Jones was the No 1 radio commentator in Australia. Jones was known to have said at the book launch that if only more cops today were like Rogerson, the streets would be a lot safer. Of course that is partially true but the price to pay for such security was far too high. Roger's conviction for the murder of Gao ruined his legacy and myth.

Previously he had been seen as just a bit of a larrikin who used 'unusual' methods to catch his man but now he is seen, probably for what he is, as a vicious violent criminal. However the fact remains that he was a great detective and it's a pity he turned rogue. It's interesting how cops of the style Rogerson left their mark and had some influence over Police like myself. Take out the bad part and you can see that they did an incredible job in keeping our streets safe, albeit using 'different' methods. Of course they operated on the edge and lived their lives that way. The fact remains that during their time, the streets were a lot safer. Does the end justify the means? An interesting question; I am ambivalent on this one.

Well, I guess we might have had a bit of a different culture in the NSW Police Force. Might it be a throw-back to the Rum Corps days of early settlement? Maybe! I can see how effective their modus operandi were and it achieved the end game — putting violent dangerous criminals where they should be. If they were to operate within the rules, some of the violent criminals might well have gone on to commit more violent crimes (probably would have) where people were killed. Does that not sound like the end justifies the means? So they did all these illegal things that came out of the Royal Commission like verbals, commit perjury, load criminals up with evidence and so on. The other side of the coin could be that the rules are there to make sure that the evidence against an alleged suspect is strong enough to convict him/her without the addition of manufacturing evidence. 'He who asserts, must prove' but within the confines of the law. I don't know. As I said, I am ambivalent on it. Maybe something they could debate on the ABC's *Q&A*. When I was working in NZ for the earthquake commission (which I have yet to talk about) I met a couple of NZ ex-detectives and we had a yarn about this over a beer one night. Both of them were adamant that they would never do anything like this to secure a conviction.

Roger is now 75 so he will die in prison but in typical Rogerson fashion, he is appealing and will take it to the bitter end. I find it difficult to understand how he could be so non professional. It is hard for me to imagine him being involved in something like that. I don't condone the illegality of what Rogerson did; nor am I saying I am a friend of Rogerson. I doubt that he would even remember meeting me. I am just bringing up the question about old ways versus the new ways. Which is better or more importantly, more effective? The New Zealand ex-detectives told me that they would never think about loading someone up, or verbalising them, or bashing them or whatever to get a conviction. They explained to me that it was just not in their DNA and it would never cross their mind to do it. That sounds pretty reasonable to me. However I wonder that it they are not prepared to operate outside the law, how do they get their difficult not guilty cases over the line.

Another criminal I met but did not talk with was another Smith - Edward 'Jockey' Smith. We had to escort him out to Parramatta jail after he had been to the District Court up in Darlinghurst. Four of us in a CIB vehicle, shadowed by the dogs (Observation Squad) in another vehicle would take him back to Parramatta jail. I was in the back with another cop and we had him in the middle, all handcuffed up. He never said a word to us. His form was impressive. He had committed armed robberies; break, enter and steal offences; drug offences and murder. Jockey hated the Police with a pathological passion and you could sense it sitting next to him. He was later shot dead by a uniform cop at Creswick in Victoria in 1992. That's another thing about these high profile criminals. They don't seem to live long lives unless they spend most of their life in prison.

Sometime around about 1978 there was a strike at Long Bay Jail. I don't remember what it was all about but all the warders went on strike. In these circumstances the cops have to man the prison and I was deployed to work in Katingal. This is the place I mentioned that Russell Cox escaped from. It was a fascinating place. I can't remember if it was before it was closed down or still had prisoners there. I know that they closed it down around about mid-1978. It was designed to house terrorists, as well as the most dangerous prisoners. People referred to it as an electronic zoo because everything inside was controlled electronically. The idea was to deprive prisoners all contact from the outside world. There were no windows and no natural light. It had forty prison cells and they all operated electronically. The exercise yard Cox exercised in was situated at one end of the complex. There was the design flaw that Cox spotted with the blind spots for the cameras and the rest is history. Out of all the criminals that I met or indirectly had something to do with, Russell Cox is the one that I admired the most. Now of course, Police are never meant to say anything good about a criminal but you have to admire daring, intelligence and courage when you see it; not matter what form it takes.

I recall on one shift a woman had told us that there were two men in a gay bar in Oxford Street, Paddington that were definitely Cribb and Munday. At the time the whole State, not just the Police Force, was looking for these two. John Cribb had committed rape on Valda Connell in 1978 and he then murdered her and her children Sally and Damien. After his arrest, he went to Morisset Hospital for the criminally insane and he escaped from there with Billy Munday. This was a dangerous combination and only trouble could come out of it and it did; big time. From there they committed numerous armed robberies before kidnapping two seventeen year old schoolgirls from outside the Hakoah Club in Bondi. The Hakoah Club is the club that caters to the Jewish community and I used to go there from time to time when I worked uniform at Bondi. Here they held them hostage and repeatedly raped them over nearly two days. It was during this escape period that we were looking for them. I was working with a fairly switched on fella. We didn't know whether to take this woman seriously or not. We decided that we would go into the wine bar and have a look before calling for back-up. The bar was very dimly lit. I suppose that this was intended to create an atmosphere of warmth and intimacy for the gay boys. They did look like Cribb and Munday but we were only going from photographs and it was hard to see. In the final wash-up we bailed them up very discreetly in the corner of the bar and they knew that we were armed. It wasn't them. They were just a couple of gay lovers. Well, we managed to pacify them and eventually got them to understand the stress that we under to catch these two blokes. They understood and accepted this. We bought them a drink confident they would not report us to the authorities. We didn't want to have another trip to Internal Affairs and fortunately we never heard any more about it. Cribb and Munday were caught a short time later and I understand will die in prison. Make no mistake, there are blokes like this running around our streets and you need somebody who is prepared to take them on.

At 21 Division I did sometimes get shifts in the car where we could get out and do some criminal investigation. On one such occasion we acted on information received and visited a flat on Campbell Parade, Bondi (everything seemed to happen in Bondi). The occupier let us come in and he was pretty friendly and we told him that we had received information about illegal drugs being on the premises. He said there wasn't and invited us to have a look and so we did. We didn't find any drugs but we found a photo of him with a lot of what appeared to be marijuana on a table. It was so much he could barely get his arms around it. He was shocked when we showed him the photo. He admitted it was him; he could hardly deny it. He also admitted that it was marijuana but said that it was for his own use. He then went on to say that he had used it all. We knew that he was lying so we arrested him, did a record of the interview in which he made no admissions to drug trafficking but he admitted the obvious - ownership. We charged him with supplying and used the photograph as evidence as well as an 'expert' opinion as to what weight it might have been. When he went to the lower court he pleaded not guilty. To cut a long story short, the Magistrate accepted our version and we won. He agreed with us that he could not have smoked that much by himself and that made him a trafficker. Can't remember if he went to the big house or not, but it was interesting that we won that case based only on the photographic evidence and suggested weight of the drug itself.

Digressing just a little whilst taking about drug convictions, you may remember the execution of two Australians, Barlow and Chambers, in Kuala Lumpur (KL) in 1986. They were caught and convicted of trafficking heroin. These executions were carried out at a place called Pudu prison, which is not that far from the centre of KL. When I was doing some work in KL, I found the time to go to Pudu prison. It had ceased operating as a prison and was now open to the public. I had a good look through it and that included the execution chamber. I was actually able to see the death row cells and to stand on the trapdoor where these two boys were hanged. Let me tell you that it's a real sobering experience. They only had 142 grams of heroin on them when they were caught. In many countries they still have corporal punishment and this is done by flogging the offender with a rattan. The rattan is a flexible bamboo rod that can be delivered with great force to the buttocks area of a human, causing excruciating pain. Amnesty International had condemned caning in South East Asian countries for punishment as cruel, inhuman and degrading. I have not seen it being given other then watching a video at Pudu prison. The offender is tied to a standing tripod and is strapped in so that he cannot throw his head back or move about. Then they put a type of padding around his lower back and thighs, exposing only the buttocks and the blows are delivered. It seemed to me the flogger was using as much force as he could. You could see the skin disintegrating as the cane came in contact with the flesh and then it starts to bleed. People that have been flogged describe the pain as 'beyond description and excruciating'. After the flogging the offender is released from the tripod and treated with antiseptic lotion. It beggars belief that some countries still do this. I have had many discussions with my fellow expatriates in Asia when I was living there about capital and corporal punishment and I have a definite stand on it. I am against both of them but most of my fellow Australian compatriots feel the opposite. They feel that this is what keeps a society in order and would like Australia to take a much tougher stand on criminals. Most would like to see both corporal and capital punishment reintroduced. I am sure it is very unusual for a cop, or ex-cop, to think the way I do. However that has always been my view on it. Maybe those floggings given by the nuns and brothers in the 1950s were not so bad after all! I only mention this because the fella we got convicted on drug trafficking based on the photographic evidence might have been executed in many SE Asian countries, but definitely would have been in Singapore. Food for thought!

A typical working night when we were rostered on the hoodlum shift (5 p.m. - 1 a.m.) at 21 Division would go something like this. Down to the Gladstone Hotel in Regent Street for a beer, then another and another, until about 8 p.m. or 9 p.m. We would then go for dinner. If we were working with a Sergeant, more than likely we would end up in the Cross and go somewhere for a good meal with some wine, usually gratis. The Sergeant looked after all that and we never asked any questions. By this time, it might be about 11 p.m. or so and we would hit the streets. Maybe we'd picked up a few hoodlums and/or drunks, take them down to Central Police and charge them. If we were really ambitious and felt like doing a bit of work, we might go and start a fight somewhere and clean up the mess. Than we would knock off and end up going to some club somewhere; often the Mandarin Club in Goulburn Street. Life was good. I was still young but not so fit anymore. By now I was over 100 kilograms (remember I joined at 84 kgs). It was a fun job and you were working with a lot of interesting fellas. There's no doubt Police are interesting people. They have been around the block and generally know what's going on. I told you earlier that one of 21 Division's function was to act as a screening squad for potential detectives. They wanted to make sure that you would fit into the culture of the CIB. They wanted to know if you were a man that could be trusted and would be there when needed. The old heads believed that generally speaking you could not trust a man who did not drink. Nor could you trust a man who had deep religious convictions. I recall once that one of the boys was deeply religious and did espouse his beliefs to others on the job. He did not last long and was transferred fairly quickly and quietly back to uniform 'in the middle of the night' so to speak. I remember one of our esteemed leaders giving us a briefing before we went out. He told us that we could do what we liked 'within reason'. Sydney was our oyster he said but whatever you do, there are three things he would not abide. One was to not submit any type of report at the end of a shift with any typographical errors. The second one was not to smash the Police car and the third one was to make sure that we did not get into any situations that we could not handle. We made sure that we adhered to these three directives but pretty much did everything else.

A lot happened for me in 1978. I'd say it was one of the best years of my life, before and since. I was now 34 years of age and was largely free from mental illness. I bought my first house that year, in Carrington Road, Randwick and paid $34,000 for it. It was a three bedroom semi with a good size back yard but in need of a complete renovation. I loved it. I had made friends with the Westpac Bank Manager in Randwick and I put down $6000 deposit. His name was Stewart Honey and he was a really good bloke. Stewart had a close call with an armed robbery merchant and never got over it. He was ready to close the bank one day but had one appointment left to finish. The fella came into his office in a calm and relaxed manner and started off telling Stewart that he was thinking about opening a business in Randwick and wanted to talk about a loan. When Stewart had both his hands on the desk, the bloke put a gun on the table and told him not to move his hands or do anything with his feet that might trigger an alarm. He told him to remain calm and if he did, he promised he too would remain calm and no-one would get hurt. He ordered Stewart to go out into the work area once the bank was shut and instruct all staff to empty the cash into a bag and not to be silly and push any alarms. It went off without a hitch for the armed robber and he left the bank with Stewart as a hostage. When they got outside he told Stewart to walk ahead of him and not to look behind. At this point Stewart thought that there was a strong possibility that he was going to be shot dead. Thankfully he wasn't and that's how I came to meet Stewart. Interestingly enough there was another robbery of this bank by a fella named Phillip (Mad Dog) Weston who was later shot dead by Police in Avoca in 1976. Just across the road from the bank is a laundromat that is still there. It was just outside this laundromat that a well-known criminal and ex-boxer, Roy Thurgar was shot in the throat at point-blank range with a 12-gauge sawn-off shotgun while waiting in his car for his wife to finish work in 1991. So the bank and its surrounds where I did my banking business used to see plenty of action and had some colourful criminal history.

I did most of the renovations myself and quickly learnt how to be a handyman. Some things of course you can't do, like electrical or plumbing. I was making a lot of contacts now because of the Police and it was not difficult to get good discounts as I now had a good discount card with my Police warrant card. I completely did the place up. Put in a new kitchen, new bathroom, outdoor laundry, new hot water system, new wiring, painted it completely inside and out and put new carpet throughout the three bedrooms, hallway and living room. I was a bit worried when it came to bricklaying and thought that I should get in qualified tradesmen to do that. I was working with Bilko (Sergeant Kevin Roberts) at the time. Bilko was one of Sydney's top rugby league referees and was very well known. He was an old South Sydney boy so he had grown up in the lower socio-economic part of town. He was a really good bloke and he arranged for some bricklayer mates of his to come around and do the work for me — for cash of course. They did a great job and I was very happy with them. I do remember one of Bilko's stories fairly well. He was controlling a game between South Sydney and some other team in the early '70s I think and he gave a penalty against South Sydney. The captain of South Sydney, George Piggins objected and they got into an argument. I don't know if it was during the game or after it but George allegedly told Bilko that there were two types of people that he really hated: football referees and cops and that he was both.

Once I had made the house liveable I got in a couple of fellas to pay rent and things were good. I had not been on any medication since 1971 and felt that I was doing pretty well. I had a good secure interesting job and now, for the first time, everything that I did was moving forward for me and I was really getting rid of that guilt complex that so burdened me. I now had my own house; or at least the bank and I did.

In 1978 I met a lady named Sue. You may remember I told you that I lost all of my friends in NZ because of the bad behaviour whilst on the booze and drugs. To my knowledge none of them knew about the mental illness and because I was so ashamed of it, I never discussed it with anybody. Well, Sue rang me at the squad one night and told me she was engaged to one of my kiwi mates; a fella named Ron. Well, I really was not interested in a woman that was engaged but she wanted to meet me, so I agreed. She was an air hostess and was on her way to Singapore to do some shopping. I thought I would go and have a drink with her and find an excuse to leave but I ended up staying the night. She took an immediate liking to me and let it be known. What about the engagement I queried! She said that she made that up just so I wouldn't hit on her. Let me tell you, Sue was a really good looking woman. She was about 178 cm and weighed about 63 kilograms. It wasn't that hard to stick around and she went to Singapore the next day. I thought that was that but about four or five days later I got a call from her asking me if she could move in with me 'for a little while' and I agreed. I was with Sue one afternoon at Louis at the Loo with some work mates of mine. This was a really interesting pub down in Woolloomooloo in Sydney and I mentioned it before that we used to go down there for choir practice after the end of night shifts when on general duties at Bondi. It was said at the time to be the one place where the cops, the criminals and the whores could all go and have a drink and not bother each other — neutral territory sort-of. There was tacit agreement that a ceasefire would occur whilst we were all there. You could get a great steak at Louis for just over three dollars. On the weekends, usually Saturday afternoon, they had this great ragtime band. It used to really heat up and the publican allowed us to store our guns in his safe. Maybe in hindsight that might not have been such a good idea. One time Sue and I got into a fairly decent conversation with a well-known Sydney criminal, who was no mug either. I'll call him Harry. Sue got pissed as she usually did after a couple and took her eye off the ball. She asked Harry to come home for dinner and to bring his wife. He said he'd like to do that one day but he was just being polite. Sue persisted and wanted to nail him down to a specific time. He had to tell her in the end, "Look Sue, I really appreciate you asking me, but you need to know that there is this line between Max and me. If I came to your home I'd be crossing that line". Sue continued to labour the point and I had to tell her to stop. We had a good afternoon with Harry and to tell you the truth, I never saw him again, but believe me he was top class criminal with an impressive criminal resume.

You will recall me telling you that in my early days I had a terrible time with girls/women. They just didn't find me attractive. I was awkward, lacked confidence and self-esteem and was a lanky redhead with freckles. Consequently I experienced a lot of rejection but it started to change when I went nursing. I realised I was not so bad after all and started to get a bit of confidence and the results came. Sue moved in and did not move out until eighteen years later. When I would come home with some of the blokes from 21 Division, they all noticed her. They just couldn't believe that I could manage to find someone as attractive as Sue and naturally enough, coming from the position I have so aptly described, it did marvellous things for my ego. I liked these compliments and in the end they decided that I must be like Flynn - 'well hung'. I'm not but that's Police logic for you. One night one of my mates in the squad took me to one side and said, "Max, you know that we are mates. I just want to know something. How come such an ugly looking bastard like you can get such an attractive girl like that?" I told him that he was wrong on two counts. One, I was not that ugly and two, she wasn't that good. I had a lot of good times with Sue but there were some things I kept from her that I will deal with shortly.

Every night I wasn't on the hoodlum shift, we would go out to some restaurant. I had a good Lebanese mate who had a little restaurant up in Avoca Street, Randwick, just around the corner from the bank I was telling you about. His name was Roy and he was a terrific bloke and a great entertainer. I really loved his food and we started going up there most nights. I was drinking fairly heavily, eating lots of Lebanese food and the fitness training took a bit of back seat. The difference with my drinking at this time is that I never went silly. I think the main reason for that is I didn't have any of that heavy medication inside me. I had completely changed and the more I drank the more passive I became. Roy and I would have no trouble in drinking two bottles of Scotch whisky between us and we did it on more than one occasion. I just had this great capacity to drink a lot, provided it was not beer; I could never drink much beer. I started to put on the weight and it was not long before I was 110 kilograms. Sue and I got married on her birthday (October 11) in 1979. She had previously delivered an ultimatum to me. Either I marry her and give her my name or she would go back to New Zealand. I consulted with some work mates over drinks down at 'Louis at the Loo' and asked them what they thought I should do. It was a very different relationship to the one that I had with Pauline. This time around it was more of being with somebody that I really got on well with and enjoyed being around. There's no doubt that I loved Sue but it wasn't that all encompassing Romeo and Juliet type of love. I mentioned earlier that I had decided I was not going to put myself in that vulnerable position again, ever. My colleagues told me I'd be a fool to let her go; they knew her by now. Mate they said, an ugly c*** like you will never get this opportunity again. I agreed to marry her and even agreed to have it in the Catholic Church. She was a Catholic and wanted to do that, mainly for her parent's sake. To me it made no difference. I did not want any ceremony. Just do the religious bit she wanted, sign the necessary papers and that would be that. We had to have two witnesses each, so I asked some cops, Dave and Frank to do it for me. Roy was another and Phil, a doctor friend of mine from my nursing days came. That's how we got married at St Joseph's Church at Kogarah on 11 October 1979.

The Police Chaplin performed the service and I threw him a few bob his way for doing it. I rang my mother; one of those rare occasions I did and told her that I had got married. I explained that it was just a simple Catholic ceremony with only the necessary witnesses attending. She thought that it was a great idea to do it the way we did and wished me all the best in the years ahead. I never went to either my brother's John or sister's Patricia weddings. My younger sister Margaret never married. At my wedding, I made it clear that I did not want a reception but Roy had arranged (behind my back) to close his restaurant for the night and put on a big party there for us. It turned out to be a great night and I'm really pleased he did it. I thought that we were just going up to his restaurant just to celebrate with him but Roy had organised about 30-40 people to come. People from the cops and some from my medical days came to wish us well.

I had to deal with a potentially explosive situation for Roy one day. Roy was sort of on the fringe of the criminal world. He might be what you'd call a wanna-be crim. He used to get involved in SP betting and may have dealt a bit in cannabis. He wasn't a well-known criminal and was not on the Police databases but he knew a lot of criminals and he was a compulsive gambler. He and some of his Lebanese friends had lent some money to another Lebanese bloke living in the Cross. This fella had more or less reneged on paying it back within the agreed time frame and Roy and his mates were very angry about it. Well, these fellas are pretty hot headed blokes and it doesn't pay to cross them; even worse when you are one of them. Unbeknownst to Roy this fella was in the underworld himself and he had his connections as well. He was also a drug addict and was addicted to heroin. To support his habit he became a small time heroin supplier and he claimed to know the big shots in the heroin supply chain, intimating I suppose that he had their protection, which he didn't as it turned out. One early morning Roy and a few of his mob kidnapped him as he was walking to his unit in the Cross. Maybe they had some experience with kidnapping in Lebanon! Anyway they tied him up with wire around his wrist and threw him in the boot of Roy's car and drove over to Roy's restaurant, a distance of about five kilometres. There was talk that if he didn't pay them back they were going to kill him. Roy panicked and rang me to ask me to intervene. As I told you by now I was more or less a free agent at that time doing the undercover work and could do what I liked, within reason of course. When I got there I gave Roy the father of all lectures reminding him that kidnapping was a very serious offence and that he was not living in Lebanon anymore. The victim was petrified as you could well imagine, but the good news was he was alive and apart from the abrasions around his writs where they had tied the wire, he was unhurt. The first thing I told them to do was to untie him and give him some water. I told Roy to tell me what they were owed and then to let me take it over. Remember Roy was the best man at my wedding and I felt compelled to help him. I finally got this bloke to agree to pay the total sum back. I told him that even though I was a cop, we did not want to make this a Police matter. I wanted to resolve it here and now so that everybody could settle down a bit. He fully cooperated and not only that, he was prepared to do it straight away. Wow, I'm now in the debt collection business! I told Roy and one of the others to go with him to such and such a bank and let him draw it out. Fortunately all this happened during the day so the banks were still open. I knew that I couldn't go in because if something happened, it would all be picked up on camera. I did warn the bloke I wouldn't be able to help him now or in the future if he attempted to pull out of it. He assured me he would not and I think that he still believed that they might do him in if he reneged. They gave him an incentive not to do anything silly by taking his apartment keys and one of them went there and waited for the phone call to say that everything was ok. They told him that if he 'did a runner' they would ring the bloke they had in his apartment and tell him to burn it. I still believe to this day that they would have done it. If he got the Police involved by informing the bank staff, Roy's mob would be charged with kidnapping and he would be charged with drug trafficking. He withdrew the full amount and paid them. It was not that much and if memory serves me correctly, about $5,000. They came back to Roy's restaurant and he gave them the money. They let him go and he sincerely apologised and they all made up. We all had an arak on it. That fella did not know how lucky he was Roy rang me. I probably saved his life. If Roy had not have rung me I don't know how it would have panned out. I guess everything conspired to make it work out. I think that on this particular day the Gods were with us; fortunately for all concerned. Imagine if I had been implicated in a kidnapping and murder!

I referred this bloke onto one of the contacts I had in the Drug Squad and he began working as an informant for him — so the Police got something out of it as well — a win-win situation. I understand that he became a very good informant and the Police were given valuable information about the importation of hashish out of Lebanon. The only one who didn't get anything out of it was me. Roy offered me a few hundred but I didn't want it. Of course if IA had got wind of it, it would have been curtains for me. There is no doubt about that but I took some risks with this one and was glad when it was all over. Nevertheless, I went out on a limb for Roy and took the risk. I can tell you one thing for sure I really got stuck into Roy and told him not to do anything so stupid again. Not only was he putting himself (and his family) into a precarious position, he was also putting me into one.

Bejesus, I could have been in a lot of trouble with this one but in the end it all turned out ok for all of us. Not surprisingly, this is the first I have ever spoken about it outside of those that were involved. There is a photo of me when I was doing my undercover work 1979/80 in the photo section. It is actually a Police photo and was taken (unbeknownst to me) by the Special Branch who were taking photographs of interested people at a political demonstration outside the Police Headquarters in Liverpool Street, Sydney. They could not figure out who I was and how I might be connected to the demonstration and only found out when one of them recognised me from No 21 Division. My boss had sent me down there to find out what was going on; so now I was on the Special Branch database!

These three photos were taken when I was about 5 or 6. On the left an altar boy; in the middle dressed as a girl and on the right as a boarder at St Jospeh's in Aberdeen. Mum had me destined to become a Catholic priest.

The train station at Capella where I used to have to catch the train to go to St Brendan's College at Rockhampton. It was the scene of a lot of trauma - separation, rejection and abandonment.

Opposite is the most interesting place I ever worked - The Anantara Resort - Maldives. Note the 4 seperate islands with the channels that are dredged to allow for boats to move about and go into the vast Indian Ocean - a truly remarkable place.

Where so much damage was done to me by the Christian Brothers - 1957-1958. This is where Dad dumped me in 1958.

Lowson House on the right when I was given ECT in the late sixties.

My children Toni and Dan - 2011

My Guide in the Golden Triangle Thai/Burmese border - 2006

My car covered in snow - NZ 2011

Poonam and I at Luang Prabang
in Laos - 2013

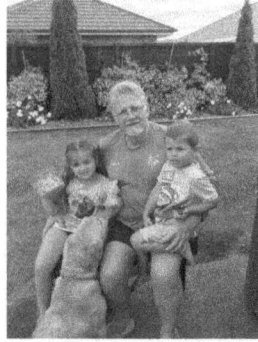

Grandpa Max with Brooke
and Hunter - Xmas 2015

The tiger cages for Vietnam
prisoners - Phuc Che - Saigon

That famous tank at Presidential
Palace - Saigon

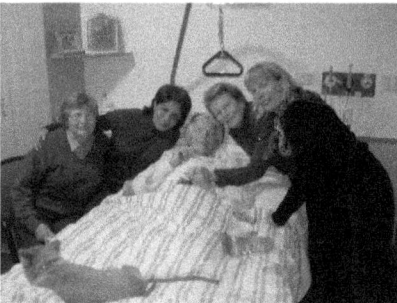

Mum in hospital - 2010. From left,
sister Patricia, partner Poonam,
sister Margaret and cousin Anne
Barker.

Being a good Dad - son dan 2010
with their first born, Brooke

Chapter Nine: A Gun and a Pound of Heroin

When I am asked what the most memorable moment for me in the Police Force was, my memory doesn't hesitate but I do hesitate to talk about it, even now. This incident happened some 38 years ago so not surprisingly I don't remember the people involved. I don't even remember who my work mate was. But it did illustrate to me in basic pragmatic terms how powerful the Police Force really could be and how that potential has never really been released. One day my partner and I were working the Cross and we had taken someone back to the detective's offices in Darlo (Darlinghurst) for an interview. It was just one of those times that the interview room was occupied by other detectives and we had to interview our man out in the main office where all the detectives worked. Darlo was a very busy station and there was never a dull moment working there. That was fairly normal for us as that is what we would usually do. It also turned out that another team of detectives were interviewing somebody else in the main room and I checked with them if it was ok for us to stay and do our work. He asked me where we were from and gave me the go-ahead. About half way through our interview, I saw the lead detective give this bloke a real hard backhander and then began to flog him with a telephone book. Then he got him back up onto the chair and said to him, "Mate, you better start telling us the truth or we are going to load you up with a gun and a point of f****** heroin, f*** you". With that, he stuck an unloaded revolver into the criminal's hand (the one that was not cuffed) and put a packet of white powder on the table. Well, the criminal went white and he knew that they were fair dinkum about it. He started 'singing like a canary' and told them everything about multiple break and enters he had been doing in the area and also turned informer by turning in people that he knew were involved in the drug trade in the Eastern Suburbs of Sydney. He was even telling them about break and enters that they were not aware off. They got their man because he knew what the consequences of being charged with a gun and a pound of heroin were and he figured correctly I think, that the cops were not bluffing. I found out later that the criminal pleaded guilty to all charges and 'copped it sweet.' He had admitted to everything that he had done and I thought about this incident for a long, long time and pondered a lot about it of. The legal part of it was quite straight forward enough. There's also no doubt about the professional standards — there weren't any. It spits in the face of all those decent values and norms that we believe in and live by. On the other hand I thought that this was a very effective way to get somebody to tell the truth and clear up an appalling house breaking rate in the area as well as gaining valuable information about drug trafficking. To me it's a kind of damn if you do, damned if you don't kinda thing. Inducement I think they call it but if they had not have used these very effective measures to nail him, he would not have given them much at all. I'm inclined to think that there are times where the end justifies the means. Society can be all sanctimonious and righteous about it but above all else, citizens have to be protected against criminals otherwise you will have anarchy. Some would respond to this by saying that citizens also need protection from the Police and that too is correct.

It's an interesting debate and raises a lot of questions about how far do individual cops want to go to make sure that they get their man and make the streets safe. For cops to do this sort of thing means they really have to have 'balls'. It's very high risk behaviour and I believe that the cops had a genuine concern about citizens houses and wanted to get this bloke off the streets. There was nothing in it for them other than getting crime cleared up. The cops weren't demanding to know where any loot was; they were demanding he tell them about the crimes he had been committing. The cops just wanted to clear up this major problem and they knew they had their man but unless he admitted to it, they would not have been able to get a conviction. So they set about making sure that not only did he admit to it, but also to tell them about others break and enters that the cops never knew about. I walked away from that and thought, f*** these blokes don't f*** around. Maybe there is method in their madness. It begs the question doesn't it? What would you do if you knew a bloke had say (we will pick a heinously emotive crime) raped and murdered a young child and you thought you knew who it was but you couldn't prove it. You needed him to tell you in a signed record of interview how it all went down but he wouldn't do it. What would you do? Would the end justify the means? As we passed them on the way out, the lead detective said to me, "You didn't see or hear anything did you?" I told him I did not know what he was talking about.

I never got involved in this type of thing myself mainly because I had no reason to but I often wondered if I had pursued my CIB career, if I would have gone down this path. I suspect I might have. I do think that this story highlights the extraordinary power that the Police can wield. They can stop you in the street, arrest you and take you back to the Police station for interview. There they can 'load you up' with whatever they like (e.g., drugs), do an unsigned record of interview and charge you with indictable offences that will put you away in prison for a very long time. There is bugger all you can do about it. Get a smart lawyer (who aren't really half as smart as they think they are), pay him a fortune but at the end of the day, it's the criminal's word against upstanding Police Officers. I think from this you can see how easy it was for Police to manipulate the system. They talk about having the means to commit a crime, the motivation and the opportunity. If the cops want to put you away there is nothing to stop them from doing it. My work mate and I had committed an offence for not reporting it but there's no guilt on my part for that. It does raise a serious ethical question for the working detective — do I or don't I? For me to report a fellow cop, it would have to be something extremely serious. Something like murder or rape, depending on the circumstances. I definitely would report a cop if I knew he was a pedophile but a cop dealing in drugs would not do it for me. Loyalty for me would be a more important value to uphold than see a cop lose his job over something that in the overall scheme of things that is relatively insignificant. I am not saying that it is right to do the illegal things that some Police did but what I am suggesting is that the loyalty value could override the need to report it. I mentioned earlier that Justice Wood described that as misguided loyalty. I told you about where the cop was driving the car but could not stand on his own two feet it was clearly a case of misguided loyalty, but I still would never report him. Yet he could have killed someone in his drunken state. The most I could do would be to have a discreet word with the boss and tell him to get him off the streets. A lot of people disagree with me on this point and many Police do. I actually told my two colleagues at the NZ-EQC (who I mentioned previously) the story about the gun and a pound of heroin and they were horrified.

Many cops join the Police at 19 and could be in plain clothes by the time they are 22 or so. I think that they could be designated detectives by 25 so you can see that if they get in with a certain group, it is not difficult to understand how many of them cede to the temptation. Look at it this way. Let's say you execute a search warrant at a house; you search the house, find some illegal drugs and a heap of money. Let's say $30,000. There are three of you and the leader of the offenders come to you and says that you can keep the money and they won't say anything. Just charge them with a summary offence whereby they will not go to prison. You have a number of choices with this scenario.

1.   Keep the money and charge them anyway with the full amount of the drugs.
2.   Another option is to charge them with the full amount of drugs and add the money in the charges as well and enter it as an exhibit.
3.   You could keep the money, flush the drugs down the toilet and let them go.
4.   Finally you could charge them with a lesser offence, keep the money and the drugs and resell the drugs cheaply to one of your dealer informants.

If you go the right path (point 2), they will most likely plead not guilty. Ultimately you might win the case after a lot of work and court sessions, and the Judge gives them a few years with a non-parole period. It is something to think about isn't it?

Another experience I had with Roy just shows you how careful you need to be when speaking with people you don't know. This incident occurred when I was working undercover. I was up at Roy's restaurant having a few drinks one day. Roy and I had an understanding that he would never tell anyone that I was cop and I would in return, would not interfere with any of his customers. Fair deal I thought. I needed to have a place I could go to where Sue and I felt safe and would not be hassled. We were just chilling out, having a drink; it was mid-afternoon and he didn't have any customers. This bloke came in and Roy knew him. He was an academic from the University of NSW but I can't remember his name. Let's call him Jason. Jason had a drink with us and then another and another. The subject turned to drugs. He picked me as a drug supplier, which is what I wanted people to think at the time. He started telling us (Roy already knew) about how much he was selling and wanted to know if I was interested in buying any from him. I told him that I was a seller, not a buyer. He expanded the conversation and left us in no doubt that he was a dealer of some significance. He started dropping names and was really interested in doing some business with me. Roy played a straight bat the whole time but was wishing he'd shut up. At one stage he got up and went to the toilet which was outside the restaurant. Roy and I had a chat and we agreed that when I went to the toilet Roy would tell him I was a cop and to get out, quick smart. I wouldn't renege on my agreement with Roy and vice versa. About twenty minutes or so after he came back I got up and went to the toilet. When I came back he was gone. I could really have gone somewhere with this fella under different circumstances. The caveat there of course is whether or not he was telling the truth but I think he was. He was well dressed, well spoken, educated and definitely not a drug addict. I knew I was not doing my job but felt loyalty was more important; still do. If he had been a pedophile or something like that it would have been a different story. All bets would be off in that scenario. Roy told me he came back that night a very worried man. Roy told Jason not to worry about it. He would guarantee that he had no problem. Roy sort of enjoyed playing the role of a Godfather. He told him that he should be a lot more careful with his mouth and to keep it shut in future. He also told him that he was not interested in any drugs going through his restaurant. Roy just liked crooks but was careful what he got involved in. I did not even ask Roy his surname. Should I have gone after him? No doubt he was selling the drugs to his university students and I got the feeling that he was more than a low level dealer. He should have been charged but I felt that I was bound by my agreement with Roy and never pursued it. To some degree, I regret that. You don't know where these things can lead and you should not let opportunities slip by. Again I would have been in trouble if my supervisors had found about it. Of course, there's another way to look at it. He could have been an undercover cop. That's food for thought.

For some reason, we had to vacate the house in Carrington Road for a while. I can't remember why. I put an advertisement in the SMH (Sydney Morning Herald) offering to mind somebody's house for six weeks. We got a reply from a high flyer up at Pymble. He was a senior executive with one of the big four banks. They were going on an overseas trip and he had no one to look after his extensive garden of orchids. He needed someone there to turn on his water irrigation system at certain times, keep the weeds out and generally look after the place. In return we could stay there and have full run of the house and gardens. It had a grand entrance with established trees on either side of the driveway which was about 50 meters long. There was a swimming pool and a tennis court. I thought that the boy from the bush was now doing fairly well. I can tell you that we completely looked after this place for these good people and they were very pleased with everything when they came back. I would not have it any other way. If I give my word to someone, I try very hard never to break it. Something it seems that some Police seem to have trouble doing. By this time I think I probably had the best job in the Police Force. I was still only a constable with two and a half years' service. I was able to take a Police car home overnight and very few cops are allowed to do that. I did not have to report to my OIC (Officer in Charge) every day before work. I could go where I liked in the metropolitan area and do what I wanted to do. Just get results was all my OIC (Officer in Charge) wanted and I did. I set up quite a few drug busts which in turn gave the trainees some exposure to executing search warrants, putting briefs together and then having to go to give evidence at court if they pleaded not guilty. I touched on earlier how going to court created a great deal of anxiety within me and that manifested itself as the OCD. The sort of unpleasant thought that you might get could be that you would tell the Magistrate or Judge that he could go and get f*****. You probably recall me telling you about the priest in the pulpit. Whilst you know that you won't do it, you can never be 100% sure. If you know you will never do it, why think it? The most learned Psychiatrists in the world can't answer that question. When I was doing the undercover work, I never had to go to court for obvious reasons and we had a lot of success with this system.

Sue had been badgering me for some time now that she wanted to see the morgue. It was just a fascination thing on her part. For my part, the less I saw of the morgue the better. At any rate I thought that I would get it over and done with. I had a contact at the City Morgue down at the Glebe Coroners Court. I knew that when push came to shove, she would back out. One day when we were out and about, I told her we were going to see somebody I knew in Glebe. Instead I drove to the City morgue. We were all but there before she woke up to what was going on. I told her that I had arranged for her to view the morgue and that this was highly unusual. She couldn't back out now so we went. It was an extraordinary experience for her and I doubt very much if she would want to do it again. She actually viewed the body of a person that had been murdered and they were getting ready to do the autopsy. She also saw all the bodies, viewing room, dissecting tables, and refrigeration. She was shocked and probably leant more about life and death in one hour that most people learn in a lifetime. This just highlights again the types of exposures that Police have to deal with. You can imagine why mental illness is so prevalent in the Police Force. Some Police have a lot of difficulties in dealing with this part of the job. Quite some time after I left, a uniform cop found a human head in the microwave and suffered a complete nervous breakdown as a result. I understand that he had to be medically discharged over it and required long term intensive psychiatric help.

I was sitting at my desk in the detectives office one day and got a message that the Internal Affairs wanted to interview me and that I was to report to them at such and such time and date stated. I had no idea what it was about but no operational Police want to go to IA. As it turned out another cop (in fact one of my mates from the Academy) and I had arrested a petty criminal at the el-Alamein foundation in Kings Cross one night who had been supplying amphetamines to minors. His clientele were usually young male prostitutes, around the fourteen years of age mark and he was their pimp. We took him to Darlo Police Station, charged him and left the bailing to the desk Sergeant as that is his responsibility. We went back to work and thought nothing more of it. Let's call the offender Jack. Jack had gone to IA and made a complaint against both of us and the desk sergeant. He alleged that I told him he was a despicable c***; that I had grabbed him by his belt and lifted him out of the dock and threw him head first in the rubbish bin; that xxxxxx (my work mate) urinated on him; that the desk sergeant came around and started beating the side of the bin with his baton; that xxxxxx pulled him out of the bin and smashed the top of the bin into his face and that he suffered both broken collarbones and sustained other injuries. That is what we were supposed to have done. Those facts would substantiate a charge of assault with GBH (grievous bodily harm). He went on to tell IA that we told him that he was the scum of the earth and he should be shot dead. That people like him that sold drugs to young male kids were bad enough but his criminality was compounded a thousand times over by acting as a pimp for them and to sell themselves for sex to pay for the drugs. We also allegedly told him to get out of the Kings Cross or we would see to it that he wouldn't be around for long. In other words, he claimed that we threatened to kill him.

Pretty serious allegations wouldn't you say? I wasn't worried at all because it was a complete fabrication. The problem for Jack was that he had not made the allegations for a few days after the arrest. He presented to St Vincent's Accident and Emergency ward days later with the injuries. If you had sustained two broken collar bones in an incident at a Police station why would you wait for days before you saw medical people about it? I don't think so and neither did IA. He thought it too good an opportunity to have a shot at the cops and the Ombudsman dismissed the allegations. Strangely enough though, we never saw Jack around the Cross again. He just disappeared off the radar. Just for the record, we had nothing to do with his disappearance. He was of British descent and maybe he went back to his mother country. I had a few other trips down to IA. It was not unusual for working Police to have to go down to IA from time to time. It went with the territory of being an operational cop as the criminals could say what they liked. They had to be listened to and the complaints investigated. Many criminals are not fools and they know how to work the system. If you can discredit the Police, so much the better; your defence team can work to get you off the charges, even if you are 100% guilty. It's a reasonable strategy for criminal defence lawyers to adopt. If they can demonstrate that the prosecuting Police have lied under oath just once, it can, and probably will, destroy your case.

The cops that worked at 'Darlo' were a great bunch of blokes. Generally tough bastards who would not put up with any bullshit. One of the toughest I met was Frank 'Bumper' Farrell when he was the Chief Inspector there. There are many stories floating around about Bumper but I reckon he was great man. One of the allegations made against him was that he allegedly bit part of the ear off a St George player, Bill McRitchie during a Rugby League match in Sydney during 1945 when he was Captain of Newtown. I believe it but I don't think he ever admitted to it. In fact he was exonerated at a hearing and that was the end of it. If the walls of Darlinghurst Police Station could talk, I think that there would be a lot of cops running for cover but I loved it. There was never a dull moment there.

One time I was ordered to attend IA to be questioned about another allegation. I can't remember which one this was so it could not have been too significant. In any event I was interviewed by a Detective Inspector and a Detective Senior Constable, who did the typing. They did a record of interview (ROI) with me and I told them that I would refuse to answer any questions, which I felt was my right. I told them that criminals and any member of the public have that right and that meant that I must also have it. "Not so" the Inspector said. He said that as an Officer in the NSW Police Force and under section such and such of the Police Regulation Act, he had the right to order me to answer questions, whether I wanted to or not. I accepted that he knew his law but I wanted him to include in the ROI that I was answering questions under duress and against my own free will. It seemed strange to me that everyone else has the right not to answer questions by Police but the Police themselves do not. That seems to be a bit unfair? Anyway, I asked him if it was their intention to charge me and he said, "Not at this stage of the investigation." I complied with his instructions and answered all the questions and we completed the interview. Then I told him I wouldn't sign it. He then went through his rigmarole with the Police Regulation Act and directed me to sign it, which I did. They gave me a copy of it and off I went back to work and thought no more about it. I knew I had not done anything wrong and felt that there was no way that IA would set me up. Not that long afterwards two things happened. Firstly, I got a letter from the Ombudsman that I was exonerated of any wrong doing in relation to the allegation. That is what I expected. Secondly, and more importantly, I got word back through one of the Detectives in our squad that I was looked upon even more favourably with the detectives designation course because of the manner in which I stood up for myself at the interview. Somehow that information had filtered back to the Chief of Detectives at 21 Division and he passed it onto me. There you go — every cloud had a silver lining.

Another interesting job that came up during this period was our involvement in the 'Great Beer Robbery.' This one was a lot of fun. The Detectives had received information that many of the staff working in the brewery (I think it was the Reschs Brewery in South Dowling Street in Redfern) were stealing cartons of beer. They were simply putting cartons of beer in the boots of their cars, taking them home, keeping some, but mostly selling some cheaply to mates and their associates. We did some surveillance and yes that was what they were doing. So the Chief of Detectives got a big group of us and gave us our orders. From a central command and control post at the brewery, he would direct each Police vehicle to follow one of the offenders. This would always happen at the end of their shift so it was easy to coordinate. The command centre had a visual on them loading up their vehicles and would let us know when they were exiting the building. These fellas (the workers) did not have a clue we were onto them. My workmate and I had to follow a car somewhere to the outer western suburbs of Sydney. He had no idea we were following him as all the vehicles were unmarked. When he pulled into his home to his garage, we put the strobe light on and pulled in behind him. Crikey, he almost dropped dead from fright. At least he knew we were the Police and were not going to hurt him, all things being equal. We asked him to open the boot of his car. He complied and there were four or five cartons in there. We than asked him to open his garage and it was nearly full of beer cartons and there was no way he could have parked his car in there. We asked him if he had any in the house and he took me in and showed us some more. He was a migrant who lived by himself but spoke reasonable English. We did not harass him and I think he appreciated our softly, softly manner. He admitted that he had stolen it all and said they all regarded it as just one of the perks of the job. I counted the cartons inside and made sure I took longer than I should have so that my mate could slip a few cartons into the back of our Police car. After checking inside thoroughly we moved to the garage and counted what was there and noted it all in our Police notebooks as contemporaneous notes. We then arrested him and charged him at Redfern Police Station. This same scenario was taking place all over Sydney with the other Police crews doing the same thing although they might not have been loading their own vehicles up. It became the lead story for the following morning newspapers and they called it 'The Great Beer Robbery'. After we were finished we took the beer back to my apartment and left it with our friendly neighbour by prearrangement. There were ten cartons of beer for us and they keep us supplied in beer for quite a while. Maybe a case of robbing Peter to pay Paul? I'm not too ashamed of this one.

Sometime in 1978 we went to Bathurst for the motorbike races that were held every year up at Mt Panorama. This year the Police hierarchy were serious about maintaining law and order. Bikers came from all over Australia to attend. Our squad sent up seven or eight vehicles, with three man crews. All motorbikes coming into Bathurst from any direction were stopped and searched for weapons and drugs. The riders and passengers were all checked for any outstanding warrants. All registration and licence details were vetted. They knew now, even before they got into town that we were serious. Generally they were good. We were billeted at the Family Hotel in Bathurst. At one stage a call came over the radio that the bikers had kidnapped the publican and his family at a hotel about half an hour's drive from Bathurst. I think it was on the way to Oberon. Although we were all armed with standard Police appointments, we also had pieces of timber in our vehicles, in case things got ugly. I was working with Big E and he was not one to put up with any rubbish. Anyway we got out to this pub and there was no kidnapping. Plenty of bikers there though, but they were behaving themselves. Our boss, Detective Inspector Noel Morey asked to speak with the Sergeant-at-Arms and they had a pow wow. Morey told him what he wanted. Name checks, warrant checks, etcetera. If any of them was wanted, they had to come with us. The Sergeant-At-Arms agreed and we checked them all out. One had warrants and he came back to Bathurst in one of the Police paddy wagons. It gave me my first hands-on insight into the radical bike gangs. The three groups I recall that were there were the Comancheros, the Gypsy Jokers, and the Mob Shitters. One of the Gypsy Jokers had the name tattooed on the inside of his lips. It seemed to me that they didn't bathe at all and were a very dirty scruffy lot. They were not like they are today. Although many of them were on drugs, they were not at the time heavily involved in trafficking them. I'll say this; they were very different to us. Make no mistake, they were scary and potentially very dangerous but we were ready for them. Mutual respect was shown on this occasion and nothing untoward happened. A couple of years after I left the Force, there was a biker shootout at Milperra. Milperra is in the outer southern western suburbs of Sydney. It happened on Father's Day in 1984. There was bad blood between two of the major biker gangs, the Bandidos and the Comancheros. They had a shootout — much like the OK Corral shoot out in the old American west. When the dust had settled, seven were killed and twenty-eight injured. It would take a lot to convince me that they are not dangerous. These days they are supposed to be major drug traffickers and into many aspects of crime. It is probably correct but I really wouldn't know.

I explained to you that part of the structure of 21 Division included a detective section of five people. As an adjunct to that, there was a drug and vice group of two people that worked with the detectives. These two left and the detectives wanted to change it a little and just bring over one man. This man would take two trainee detectives with him for a month and teach them some of the ropes. That man turned out to be me. Now I had my own Police car I was more of less working undercover. I was issued with a short version of the .38 Smith & Wesson. It was a five shot and a lot smaller than the standard six shot version that Police are issued with. They also gave me some rolls of money, or at least what looked like rolls of money. On the outside there would be a real note but all the others were blank except the edge of the note. It gives the appearance that you were carrying a lot of money when in fact you only had $100 or $50. I was told to be very careful and not to take unnecessary risks. I grew my beard and looked the part. I could go pretty much where I liked in the metropolitan area. All I had to do was get results and show that we were doing the business. It worked really well for me and the squad. We did do a lot of good work now because I could call the shots. I am by nature a worker and we got stuck into it and the trainee detectives loved it. We would work hard, play hard and most importantly of all, have a lot of fun. We never got into the big stuff. I knew better than to tread on anybody's toes; especially the blokes down at the Drug Squad. We executed a lot of search warrants and put people before the courts, mainly drug offences. I remember once we executed a search warrant in a place in Coogee and there were only four small marijuana plants there. We still charged them and had to go through all the formalities in doing that. The offenders just could not believe that Police resources were tied up in dealing with such an inoffensive matter. I thought here we go again, a complaint to the Ombudsman but it never happened. The detectives liked what I was doing and I was making them look good as well. My team and I would do a lot of the surveillance work, get the intelligence from informants (which I often did alone) and the detectives would carry out the busts with other trainee detectives.

At this stage of my Police career, I used to do a yearly cruise on the cruise ships in the Pacific area. The water Police had some arrangements with the cruise companies whereby Police would keep the peace on the ship. In return the ship would give us a free cruise plus $10 per day to buy booze. That was quite a bit then because the booze was duty free and cheap. I did three cruises in 1978, '79 and '80. We started off on the P&O Arcadia; then the CTC Line, MS Taras Shevchenko and the last one was the Sitmar Line, TSS Fairstar. It was not all beer and skittles. On the Tara Shevchenko we had a lot of trouble. It was a Russian ship and therefore flew the hammer and sickle. On this particular cruise it was top heavy with young men and there were not enough women. The women that were there did not want to go with these young fellas because they drank too much and did not look after them the way they felt they should. Instead they went for the officers in their nice white uniforms and foreign accents. This really was adding fuel to the fire. The young blokes reckoned they were the paying customers and the officers should not be mixing with the guests. A fair point I suppose. In any event we had trouble the whole trip. The Captain who could not speak a word of English, closed the discotheque after just three or four days out. Young Aussies and Kiwis were throwing beer cans at one another and they closed it. More incidents occurred. One young fella from Wollongong came into the dining room one night with just a bow tie around his neck and absolutely nothing else. Another was caught urinating on the dance floor. The Russians could not believe it and were really angry about it. Matters came to a head one day when it was discovered that thirteen deck chairs went overboard. Unfortunately for the offenders an officer had seen them do it (or said he did). We had to handle this one delicately. Remember we are in the middle of the Pacific Ocean and there are just two of us. There were scores of them. In the end we were able to negotiate with a group of the young fellas and they admitted the offence. We told them that we believed we could persuade the Captain to accept x number of dollars in restitution for the chairs. They agreed on a figure of about $150 from memory and so, through the Purser we put it to the captain and he accepted the offer. We gave them the money and that was the end of it. Before we left the ship when it got back to Sydney, the Captain asked to see us up in his cabin. That is very rare. Again through the Purser, he wanted to thank us for saving what he saw as a potential riot on his ship. He gave us each a medal of the 'Tomb of the Unknown Soldier' and a bottle of pure Russian vodka. I kept that medal for many years. The purser told us that the behaviour of the young Aussies and Kiwis showed why so called democracy did not work and further enforced his view on Communism. Perhaps he had a valid point there.

One month when I was about to get my new team, one of them approached me. I'll call him John. John was a lot senior to me and that was the first thing we had to deal with. I told him it was my gig and that I had the confidence of the detectives. If he didn't like it he could arrange to go back to the drunk truck. He then went on about his concern that he might be asked to get involved in some of the well documented Police malpractices. Things like 'verbalising' offenders in court; planting evidence; taking bribes; working with solicitors to pervert the course of justice and corruption generally. Wow, that's a handful. I spent time with John explaining that he did not have to concern himself with any of these things. That this is not the way we operated and he accepted that. To cut a long story short, years later when I was working as a Director of Security at the Regent Hotel in Sydney, I was reading the Sydney Morning Herald one morning. Guess what was on the front page; a story about John. He had gone out into one of the divisions and was working as a divisional detective. They arrested somebody for assaulting his wife and they told him he could get off it for $4,000; two each for the detectives. He agreed but said he didn't have the money on him and would have to go to the bank and they made arrangements to meet him back at his house later in the day and they would do the business. You can probably guess what happened. This fella went to the IA instead. He got wired up and a trap was set that involved cameras and listening devices. They were caught cold and that was the end of his Police career. So what happened to him and his high standards of ethics and values? It's an interesting question. Why is it that some of the blokes went down this track instead of focusing on staying within the law? What changed him from an honest cop into a crooked cop? I think there are two main factors, greed and a sense of entitlement. The greed one is obvious and self-explanatory. The second reason is not so obvious and this is entitlement. Many see themselves doing the dirty work and putting in the hard yards. Then they see the criminal lawyers making a lot of money out of it but they are not. Many detectives feel they are entitled to more. They are the ones that take all the physical risks dealing with the angry violent men, the armed offenders, the spaced out drug addicts; and for what — a reasonably small wage in the overall scheme of things. They also rationalised that the judiciary were far too lenient towards criminals and they wondered why they were doing what they were doing for relatively small wages. Cops are not stupid and some of them felt that they were entitled to a 'piece of the pie'. I'm guessing that is what happened with John and if you want to, you can rationalise anything and justify your unlawful actions. All I can say about John is that he should have stayed true to the values he had when he was working with me at 21 Division. At least he would not have gone to prison.

I developed another relationship with an informant. He was up to it in heroin and was going to help me get some people that he reckoned had cheated him out of some of his share of it. It did not bother me what his motive was. I just happened to run into him at the right time when he has a real set against this group that he was involved with. I did a fair bit of the reconnaissance and surveillance work on the information he had given me. One night I was to meet with him in Bondi and had a bit of a bad feeling about it. Because I had the 'sixth sense' they often talk about, I went to the agreed rendezvous an hour earlier in a different vehicle and sat off the place. It turned out that my 'sixth sense' was wrong and we had our meeting. He gave me some very good information and I passed that onto the detectives who went to work on it and they got some significant arrests. You do get quite paranoid with this type of work and you never know what might be in front of you. There was one time that I thought there was a distinct possibility that I would be shot. I had been doing surveillance on this drug dealer for quite some time and I had it down pat what his MO (modus operandi) was. He would come out his apartment, get into his car which was always parked on the same side of the street as his apartment block, do a U-turn and go down left on a major arterial road. I had seen him doing it countless times. When I set it up with the detectives to carry out the bust, my informant told me that he would be at such and such a place at a certain time where he would meet with his dealers and they would buy the heroin from him. It was to be all done in a secluded part of a public park. My job was to notify our people at the park when this was to happen and they would arrest not just the low level dealers but the major supplier as well. I saw him come out of the unit, get into his car but this time he drove straight ahead. I was about 100 metres away and as soon as I saw this happening I threw myself on the floor under the dashboard of the van I was in. His car roared past and then did a U-turn and stopped directly next to my van. I thought for sure and certain I had been spotted and I knew this bloke's history. He was a killer and I was in an extremely vulnerable position. To be perfectly honest I actually wet myself with fear but sometimes 'something' or 'someone' is on your side and inexplicably he just drove off. He went to the park, distributed the drugs and was arrested along with a number of his dealers. When he was being interviewed he asked the interviewing detective if that white van (mine) was a Police vehicle and he told him it wasn't. Perhaps this was an example of the criminal's 'sixth sense' and on this occasion he should have trusted it but thankfully he didn't. I have no doubt that if he had, I would have been shot dead. Think about that for a moment!

A lot of the work during this time was basic undercover work. Not deep undercover, but deep enough! This was probably the most interesting, exciting and scary period of my short Police career. I started doing this in mid 1979 and continued until the end of 1980. About eighteen months in total. I'd had no contact with any of my family since 1971 except at Dad's funeral in 74, but I was doing well. I was a married man now and Sue had some interesting jobs. She was in the sales and marketing sector and worked for Kwik-as-Air, selling air freight. She also worked for East West Airlines and Budget Rent-a-Car. She had her own car, her own job and there were no children. We had agreed as part of our marriage agreement that we would not have children. I claimed that I did not think it was much of a world to bring children up into and used the threat of nuclear war as the basis for my reasoning. I didn't want children to have the upbringing that I had. You will recall that I never mentioned my illness to anyone. No one knew except my 'family' and they were so ashamed of it they would never tell anyone. I felt it better not to mention it and still believe it was the right strategy. I felt that it could be thrown back at me. Besides, I was going along at one hundred miles an hour now. People change their view if they know that you have had the sort of treatment I outlined earlier. I saw myself as a 'has been' case. Let sleeping dogs lie.

I exposed myself to a world of difference. I began to mix with druggies and fell in with a particular group of 'druggie intellectuals'. I felt like I was becoming one of them. I devised a strategy whereby I had two bottles of Seconal. A real one and a fake one! Seconal is a barbiturate and a very strong one at that, a bit like the Mandrax but even stronger. They work by depressing the central nervous system causing sleep, depending on the dose. If you take too many barbiturates, you will die; simple as that! Druggies found them easy to get. Just go to an unscrupulous doctor and you could get a script for them and that's how I got them. I emptied the capsules and put flour in those in my fake bottle. They looked the same. The druggies used to take Seconal and resist the sleeping effects and that would give them the high they were looking for. They knew me as a fella that used Seconal; but unbeknown to them I wasn't. I was using the flour substitutes only. In that way I fitted in. I used to eat hash cookies with them and to be truthful, was having a great time with them. They'd smoke the grass/hash but I told them that I had given up smoking and did not want to start again. I never sold them any drugs but I used to give them my hash cookies which were always a hit. It cemented my relationship with them. I'd give Roy some hash and get him to make them in his restaurant. In fact Roy and I would sometimes have a session eating the cookies and drinking arak. You could imagine how high we used to get. Sue did not know anything about this and I imagine that the first she would have heard about it will be when she reads this book. Sometimes I used to take amphetamines with the flour capsules. These were stimulants that would give you a reasonable high and I loved them when we were playing Bob Dylan. One of the girls was the supplier for them and naturally I never inquired as to where she got them from. I used to make sure that I did not take too much of the 'speed'. I was concerned that with all the booze, the hash cookies, and the speed, I could get myself into trouble, so I was very careful and always took less than my friends thought that I had. I'd pop a Seconal but it would be one of the flour ones. Then when I gave them one, it would be the real thing. Then sometimes I'd pop a 'speed' tablet. That is potentially dangerous stuff and as a trained nurse I was well aware of that. Seconal to make you sleep; speed to have the opposite effect. I was also worried that the effects of the drugs would interfere with my mental health, given my background. One night I got it wrong with the Seconal — fortunately not long before I was due to leave anyway. I inadvertently took one from the wrong bottle and only realised it when I started to get really sleepy. It was not long before I realised my mistake and I had to get out of their place quick smart. I caught a taxi, gave him my address and he took me home. I never gave the taxis my right address and always got one in a different street just around the corner from where I lived. I was asleep in the taxi when we got there and he had to wake me up. I staggered home and collapsed on the couch downstairs in the TV room. I told the taxi driver I had just drunk too much and gave him a good tip. I was worried he might report me to the Police. I did not want to go to IA with a please explain but nothing happened. I got back in contact with the group the following night and we continued on. They were anything but big time; just a bunch of people that really lived as squatters in derelict houses along Bourke Street. I got to like them and knew right from the start that this was a big mistake. They knew me as Max Sands. You may remember the movie 'Nevada Smith' with Steve McQueen in it. Max Sands was the main character. This way when someone called me Max, it didn't get confusing, especially when I was bombed out on the drugs. I had them believing that I was a trained nurse (which was true) and that I trained at a hospital in Melbourne (which wasn't). Truth is they didn't care who I was, as long as I was not a cop. I cemented my cover by telling them that I did casual work through a specialist nurse agency in various locations around Sydney. This was perfectly feasible as that is what many graduated nurses do. If we had a job on at a particular time at 21 Division, I simply told them I was working. When they used to ask me what job I had just finished it was easy for me to answer. I'd just talk about somebody that needed specialised nursing like geriatrics, people that have had major surgery, people that needed nursing care 24/7 and so on. I even used to wear my nursing uniform sometimes when I met them. They never suspected me to be anything else other than what I told them. I have never told anyone about them until now, not a single soul. This one is perhaps my biggest skeleton and the one I feel most ashamed about. I was a cop and ended up sharing heroin with druggies. What had happened to my sense of righteousness? The group used to have these incredible discussions and because I was as high as a kite sometimes, I got totally fascinated with it all. I was the designated man to talk on medical matters. At that time, I had recently graduated with high distinctions so I knew a lot about medicine. They used to call me 'the Doctor'. Strange isn't it. Initially the Police had me down for the Rescue Squad because of my medical training and I ended up using my medical training to break the law with a bunch of drug addicts. Nothing to be proud of and in the end I really beat myself up about it. I'm a bit of a history buff and one of the group had studied modern history at university. He was a bit of an expert on the French and the Russian Revolutions. He (Dave) used to talk about the Bolsheviks and knew all the henchmen from that time on until Stalin died in 1953. He had an extraordinary memory about the persecution of the Kulaks and the different leaders of the Secret Service. The first time I heard about the Katyn massacres was from Dave. That massacre pales into insignificance when you compare it with Stalin's genocide in the Ukraine. Stalin organised through his henchman a set of circumstances designed to create a famine of biblical proportions in the Ukraine in 1932-33. It is estimated that over 7,000,000 Ukrainian people died in the farming areas of that country. All he did was take away all the food (wheat grain) for Russian consumption and literally starved them to death. This was as bad, or worse, than the extermination of the Jews under Hitler. Can you believe it? 7,000,000 souls dead in a little over a year. Stalin was an even bigger monster than Hitler. Just as a matter of interest, Stalin shared something in common with our own former Prime Minister Tony Abbott. They were both studying to become Catholic Priests in their earlier lives. I'm not suggesting that Tony Abbott is a monster. I just find it interesting to make the comparison.

Dave knew all this with the names without referring to any books and he was usually doped up to the eyeballs. In my heightened state of euphoria, I became a devotee of Dave's and his history lessons. I'd listen to him for hours in my drug induced state. Even though he was high there was nothing wrong with his memory. All this was done sitting around a dilapidated table in the middle of the room in a squatters' dwelling with candles burning. It was a real hippie culture and I loved it. When Dave got started on the French Revolution, he was just incredible. He would talk about the period from 1789 onwards (BTW - one year after Australia was settled - 1788). He told us about the storming of the Bastille on 14 July 1789. I remember this date well as I was in Paris in 1981 for Bastille Day. Remember Fredrick Forsyth's book, 'The Day of the Jackal?' After Dave's talk about the revolution, I just had to see Paris and where all this happened; especially the period known as the 'Reign of Terror.' This was the birth of democracy as we know it. I tried to figure out why these intelligent people did not want to fit into mainstream society. As near as I can figure it, they saw our leaders as bigots and hypocrites. I'm not sure that they were wrong about that. The main area to vent their spleens was the Vietnam War. All the way with LBJ was something that Dave in particular, could not get his head around. He just generally thought that the western world was run by politicians that were usually lawyers and narcissists. I am sure that there would be many that would agree with that.

I was gravitating more and more to the group. There was another bloke (Steve) who had studied political science at Sydney University, or so he said. Crikey, what he did not know about Australian politics was not worth knowing. There were three girls in the group. They would have been attractive if they had looked after themselves but that was not part of their culture. Sex was easily available; it was after all a free love environment. The conversation would get more in depth and loose, the more hash we ate, the more pills we popped, the more we drank booze (cheap wine), and of course the Seconal. Sometimes they took heroin when they had money but that was not that common. I knew better than most the dangers of heroin and was initially reluctant to use it. I wrote about my experience with it (morphine) when I was in the Army and had the helicopter accident. However, it must be clear now that I was not adverse towards risk taking and I wanted to know if heroin was as good (or bad) as it was painted out to be. One night I brought in my own needle and syringe and actually injected myself with some of this 'rubbish'. I was careful to gauge how much I took and made sure that I took from a batch that one of the girls had already used. It did not kill her so I figured that it would not kill me either. I got an even higher high than when the army medics gave it to me. The feeling was one of total euphoria. I think it is near impossible to describe how beautiful it was. If one could live in this state all the time, life would be just so wonderful. The truth is that I could not wait to do it again and a short time later, that is exactly what I did. The only precautions I took were that I never used anybody else's needle and only used from a batch that the others had used before. The other thing is that I always paid for it and it was very expensive. The experience was the same; an incredible high followed by an incredibly bad low. I knew that travelling down this path was very dangerous for me. Not just because it was illegal but even more so because of its addictive power. I got hooked on cigarettes badly as I have told you and ended up smoking over forty every day. That indicated to me that I might have a bit of an addictive personality. The other major concern was that it might take me back to the dark days of depression and that is absolutely the last thing I wanted. I had to make a decision. Take it but control it (which deep down I knew I couldn't), or don't take it at all. I weighed everything up and decided the smart thing to do would be to stop taking it and that is what I did. I would say all in all I probably injected myself with heroin about seven times and each time it got harder to resist it. I used to hang out wanting to get back to the druggie joint to have some more. I'm pleased with the fact that I had the experience and that I had the good sense and will power to stop it when I did. Having said that I am ashamed of my incredible poor judgement at that time. I just could not believe that I was doing the things that I did as a fairly junior cop. Hitherto I had never done this sort of thing before. Looking back I find it difficult to fathom how I could lead this high risk lifestyle with these criminals. I took heroin with them; I slept with them; I broke bread with them and I think that I was in love with them. All this whilst I had Sue and was working as a cop. I think that it was a matter of me breaking the law, sinking deeper into the world of a drug addict and showing extremely poor judgement.

The big catch with these heavy drugs (and heroin is the heaviest) is that the high doesn't last long and therein lies the catch; you want more. The experience was so good and all you could think off was doing it again ASAP. I gave it up because I felt that I would not have the strength to resist it and would end up becoming a heroin addict. At the time most of the heroin addicts ended up in the morgue or prison. The depression afterwards was tough and I struggled with it for a couple of days but it was nothing like it was in 1967. Once the drug wore off, so too did the depression. Each time I took it, I knew that would be the end for me if I continued doing it. It was just so incredibly illuminating and exhilarating. After the last time I took it, I gave the group a rest for a couple of weeks to get myself together. I believe that I was now within an inch away from becoming addicted to it and that would have ruined my whole life. I also felt very guilty about it and I knew what guilt could do to me. I didn't know where they got their money from to buy their drugs; I didn't ask and they didn't volunteer. I suppose the girls were prostitutes and the boys, well they could have been up to anything. The squatter's houses were on the edge of the red light district of Sydney (Kings Cross) and the area was loaded with drug dealers. It would have been a simple matter to get the drugs. I really had to look seriously at what I was doing. Imagine if the cops had busted us? What the f*** was I thinking at that time? What about my mental health? What about my wife? What about my comrades?

I used to look forward to being with them and in different circumstances I could easily have been one of them but that would have been a disaster. What I liked most about them was that they were a peace loving group and had no time for violence; the exact opposite of the Police Force. I had them completely fooled about me and they would have died if they had known I was a cop. Sue never knew about them, the boss never knew and I never told anybody about them. I never carried Police identification when I was with them, nor did I carry my five shot snub nose .38 Smith and Wesson. To all intents and purposes I was just another druggie but not an addict. In conversations with them, I was careful not to make them suspicious and never queried them about where they got their drugs or money from. I did have an exit strategy in place in the event we were busted but that was on the proviso that I was not doped up myself, especially with heroin. If they caught us all doped up, there is no way I could contact my boss. I decided that if we were busted and I was doped up, I would go in the paddy wagon with them to Central or Darlo, give false particulars and go through the charging process. Later on fingerprints would have shown up who I was and then I would have some explaining to do, which I would be able to after I got bail. It would not have been difficult to clear all this up with the boss. In fact, we had talked about an exit strategy in the event of an arrest and this was pretty much what it was. The fly in the ointment was me being on the drugs myself. That was not part of the discussions I had with him and naturally there was no way the Police would sanction me taking illegal drugs. If I wasn't high, I would ask the cops if I could talk to my lawyer but in fact, it would have been a phone call to the office at 21 Division. Remember there were no mobile phones in those days. They would have made the necessary arrangements. The group would have thought that I had just received bail like they would have. In any event that never happened so it didn't become an issue. If I was questioned about my relationship with the group all I had to say was that they were giving me information and were valuable informants. If they made allegations against me after they found out my true identify I would deny them and I felt confident that IA would believe me. After all, who would believe a bunch of drug addicts against a serving Police Officer? I tell you at the end of the day it was all about survival and after a while you became really skilled at it.

It was usually a group of five, never anymore, and they accepted me totally. To me they were normal and just disagreed with the way the country was being run. We frequently talked about politics and often the Police came up in conversations. Some of them had been arrested a number of times and they told me about the bashings they got. They also talked about how the Police robbed them of any money they had and they also claimed that some Police offered not to charge them if they could come up with a drink (money). All I ever commented on when they told me this was to say, "What c****." I never let them see me show much interest in the Police. I told them I had never been arrested and did not want to be. I told them that my reason for being with them is that I liked them; that I liked their conversation, the history lessons, the drugs and music. I was now living in three social structures — my domestic life with Sue (we were not married at this time — thank God); my Police life and my druggie life. I saw a lot of heroin affected people in my work and the vast majority of them were in an absolute physical and psychological mess. At the time most of the prostitutes working the Cross were on it; in fact one of them told me once that she could never have done her work unless she was under the influence of the drug. She just hated herself for the fact that she was selling her body so she could pay for her habit and she had a terrible opinion of herself, something that resonated with me. I did get information in general conversation from the group indirectly that led to other things. I would then feed that information onto the detectives but never told them where it came from. They would then arrange the search warrants and carry out their execution. My job essentially was to get the information and we did get some good arrests for drug trafficking.

Eventually I divorced myself away from the group but I often thought about them, even now. Where they are? What happened to them? I wonder if any of them settled down to what we call a normal life. It took me a long time to get over them and I missed them. I fact I'd say that I still do. It took me years to get over the heroin 'effect'; it was that good. I believe that under different circumstances I would have stayed with them and could have ended up in the morgue I suppose. I was now married to a great girl and doing well in the Police. Giving up the group and the drugs was a bit like giving up smoking; terribly hard to do but ultimately I was a lot better off doing it. The group was definitely a very high risk for me and I decided that when I left them I would not give them up (inform on them). First of all if I did and they found out it was me, they would tell the cops all about my involvement and I probably would have been charged myself and would have gone to prison. However I'd like to think that my main reason for not giving them up was that I liked them, that I was one of them and I could not do a Judas on them. Maybe this is where the power of rationalisation comes into play. I wrongly rationalised that they were not doing anything to hurt anyone else, only themselves. The reality was that they were taking hard drugs and must have been committing crimes to get the money. They were breaking the law; every day in fact and my job as a cop was to uphold the law. I wonder if Dave and Steve did anything with their incredible knowledge and intellect or did they end up in the morgue or in prison. I wonder what happened to the girls. Did they eventually drift off to suburbia, get married and raise a family? It's hard to imagine it. I always had this concern that when I went back into normal plain clothes I would run into them and have to act upon it. Fortunately that never happened, although most of my work was centred around the Darlinghurst and Kings Cross areas. I would say that if I had not stopped taking the heroin when I did I would have ended up in a very quickly becoming a complete drug addict. It was that good when you were high on it; life was beautiful. They say that timing is everything. However at the end of the day I had to fully accept responsibility for what I was doing. I could not blame the church, my parents or anybody else for this one. The heroin experience was a two-edged sword. On the one hand I had shown a human frailty in doing it but on the other hand, I had the strength to stop it and accept responsibility for my behaviour. Isn't it interesting the many challenges that we have to face up to in just our normal day to day living? I guess more-so working in undercover drugs.

I had an informant that worked the wailing wall at Darlo. I don't know why we called it the wailing wall but I suppose it is in reference to the real wailing wall in Jerusalem. The wailing wall in the old city of Jerusalem is a section of the ancient wall of Herod's Temple, the second temple built on that spot. Anyway, the wailing wall in Darlo was part of the old gaol in the middle of Darlo that was built around about 1840. They say there are plenty of ghosts from the number of people that have been executed there. It is surrounded by a large wall and it is the wall on the eastern side that I am referring to as the 'Wailing Wall'. There are some interesting facts about Darlinghurst Jail. I should mention before I tell you about my informant. Henry Lawson was an inmate there. He did time for non-payment of alimony and drunkenness. He even wrote a poem about it and named it 'One Hundred and Three' after his prison number. He referred to the jail as Starvinghurst Jail because of the meagre rations that were provided for inmates. The jail used to do public executions and a total of 79 inmates were executed there and there were some notable names amongst them. Captain Moonlite, the bushranger was hanged there in 1880. Incidentally that was the same year that Ned Kelly was hanged in Melbourne. Jimmy Governor from the 'Chant of Jimmy Blacksmith' was hanged there in 1901. The last woman hanged in NSW was Louisa Collins and she was hanged there in 1889.

My informant was working as a male prostitute at the wall. They all had their spot there and my man used to tell the others that he had Police protection, which was not quite true, but it probably stopped others from taking his spot. I went to see him one night and he was not there. I asked one of the other male prostitutes about him and apparently he had run foul of a client. What I could gather was that he went with a client who not only ripped him off but brutally raped him and gave him a terrible beating. I believe that it was touch and go as to whether or not he would live. These sex workers live in an environment that is very high risk. They are exposing themselves to constant danger and it is their perpetual companion. I never heard from him again. I thought that he might have called me at 21 Division but he didn't. The funny thing is that I never knew his real name which might have been a bit of a slip-up on my part. I should have done my homework on him but didn't. He gave me a bit of useful information about what was going on in the area and strangely enough I kinda liked him as well. He even told me about my druggie group. He told me I could f*** him for nothing if I wanted to, but as I have said, I never went down that track; pardon the pun. For my part in return for his information, I had to help him if he got into trouble. Well, I didn't because I never knew about it, until it was all too late. That's my little bit of history emanating from Darlinghurst Jail in 1979.

One particular time I had dealings with a well-known violent criminal from the Cross. I knew what he had done, and he knew I knew. It was a fraud matter. This fella was a man that you wouldn't fool with. He was not a druggie, far from it. He was a stand-over man in the protection business. We had him on some relatively minor fraud charges. He had been given up by an informant and I carried out surveillance on him. I knew for a fact that the information was correct because I had seen it happening. The interviewing detectives made it clear to him what would happen if he didn't tell the truth. The fact was that all the evidence the cops had, was my word that I had seen him doing it, but they did not want me to go to Court, for obvious reasons. Faced with the threat of being verbalised and maybe even loaded up on more serious charges (e.g., a gun and a point of heroin) he admitted it, and pleaded guilty when he went to Court. Just the threat of being verbalised and charged with more serious offences was enough to sway him to tell the truth. The cops in return for the criminal's co-operation, might enter into a cop-informer relationship and sometimes something quite sinister well beyond that.

I think I mentioned before that I wanted to become a designated detective but was too old. You had to be 30 or under to go on the course. To be selected you had to do some years in plain clothes starting with what they called the 'A list' with the Divisional Detectives, then go to 21 Division and learn to become a drunk and all the other misdemeanours we used to get up to. Then you would go back to the Division and work with the Detectives for maybe a couple of years before being selected for the designation course. The boss of 21 Division and the Chief of the Detectives were lobbying hard for me to go on the detective's designation course. They now had a fair bit of ammunition to support my suitability and really put in a big effort on my behalf. I was told that I was a good cop and would make a good detective. Eventually the boss of the CIB relented on the age thing and relented to make my case an exception to the rule. The Commissioner of Police agreed and I was put down to go on the next course. It was all set that after I completed detective training I would be sent to the Drug Squad. Then something happened that really came out of the blue. I resigned and gave three months' notice. You can really imagine how pissed off they were with me. They had stuck their necks out for me and really supported me with the detective application. It was unheard of to turn down an opportunity to become a designated detective, but I did. I knew how they felt and thought it was completely understandable. I had really let them down but I had my reasons. I got put back on the drunk truck for the remaining couple of months of my service and left the Police in April 1981. I don't hesitate to say that the Police Force was the best job I ever had and in my short time in it, I crammed an enormous amount of experience into my life and you have just read about some of that. So the question arises, if I liked it so much why did I leave at such a crucial point? They had (the CIB hierarchy) broken with many decades of tradition at the CIB and allowed me to do the course. They had just never done this before and they could not understand why I would turn it down.

Why didn't I go through with it? I'll tell you why. For a start, I did not like the promotion system in the Force. In those days, it was promotion by seniority not merit. I was working with some Senior Constables and Sergeants who were very incompetent and lazy. They were secure in the job and didn't want to create any waves. A lot of them, like the Sergeant who used to dish out summary justice I told you about at Bondi, did not want the stress of court cases. Many cops do not like going to court and being cross examined by the defence. So they avoid it by doing nothing. Consequently you often found yourself working under people that were incompetent drunkards and lazy and that can be very demoralising. Secondly, most offenders were now pleading not guilty to any arrests. Generally they were as guilty as sin but criminal lawyers were making a lot of money getting them to plead not guilty. I had heard that many of the cops did business with some of these lawyers. Thirdly, I knew that they would send me to the Drug Squad. I felt that the temptations to become corrupt there would be much greater and that I would become part of the corruption system. I did not know, but suspected that I might not have had the strength to resist it. I like a dollar as much as the next man and thought it would be freely available. I did not want to end up shaming my family or worse still, going to prison, nor did I want to be responsible for any other cops going there. Finally and by far the most important point is that I had a very big concern about the trust issue. Could I trust some of my fellow Police Officers? I knew that I couldn't. There are a lot of good blokes in the job and you could trust them with your life. Equally, there are others who were absolute scumbags and snakes. I knew that I would only be a Detective Constable first-class at the Drug Squad and would be the junior man on a team. That meant that I would not be able to make decisions by myself and that a situation could arise where I would have to make a decision about corruption. As I have said I felt that I could be corrupted, but that was not the big issue. The big issue was that I had a deep fear, a very deep fear that others would 'rat' on me to save their own hide and I could not take the risk. Some would sell you down the drain in a second to save their own hide. The trick is to be able to pick who's who and that was easier said than done. We heard so much about that with the Royal Commission into the New South Wales Police Service. That is why I have mentioned the *Prince of the City* book and movie. Bob Leuci betrayed all of his workmates because he had suddenly developed a conscience and wanted to do the right thing by his family. This value outweighed his loyalty to his best friends and workmates in the drug (narcotics) squad. They committed all these wrong-doings and he was at the forefront of it. Then in a moment of conscience he betrayed them all. Which is the greater good; betray your best friends to save your own skin or to stick by them once you have to committed yourself to them? I know what it would be for me. I would never betray them but I knew that some of my colleagues, pushed into a corner would do it and I was not prepared to take that risk.

So I pulled the pin on the best job I ever had, before or since. Do I regret it? Sometimes I do, but not generally. I probably would have made Detective Chief Inspector or maybe even Detective Superintendent and these are choice jobs in the force. So, in order to simplify it and put it into one short sentence, the main reason I left the Police Force was that I did not have trust and confidence in some of the men that I would be working with and I felt that this was a risk that I didn't have to take. I had already demonstrated a willingness to operate outside the law with my druggie group. I did not oppose corruption and malpractice for any moral reasons. I understand 'verbalising' a known offender under a given set of circumstances. I understand the question of loading a known offender up under a given set of circumstances. I understand fabricating evidence to get a conviction of a known offender for a violent serious crime. I understand copping a quid in a given set of circumstances. I make the point that many cops turned against their former work mates during the Royal Commission to save their own hides. I mentioned earlier and it is worth repeating that loyalty is a very strong value with me as I have demonstrated to you and I saw a lot of disloyalty in the job. It's a question that all Police have to answer at some point in their career. If you know that an offender, say a child molestation case, is guilty but you lack evidence, what do you do? Taking this hypothetical case, you might have to 'help' it adding some evidence which is not true. For example, you may say the offender told you something that he didn't. You get up in Court and swear it on the good book. You win the case and put the child offender away; but you did it in an illegal manner. Did you do the right thing? The punishment for perjury can be incarceration and must be taken seriously. The justice system is based on telling the truth in Court. Do you think the criminals are telling the truth? Do you think the lawyers are telling the truth? I take the view that there are times you might have to bend the rules to get a conviction but there would not be one cop in the state who would publicly agree with me but privately most would. It is the same with the judiciary and the same with the politicians. That's a good example of their hypocrisy!

Whilst I was in the Police Force I moved houses from Carrington Road and bought a four bedroom semi at St Paul's Street, Randwick. That cost me $100,000 in 1978. That means that in one year I had doubled my money. The same modus operandi followed in that it needed a complete renovation. When I was living there with Sue, I had a very unusual accident. One day I was sitting/lying on a bean bag and Sue ran over playfully and jumped on my right knee. It was a total dislocation of the patella. A freak accident! Well, I was in so much agony I could not move. They got the ambulance and I was taken to Prince of Wales hospital to my old work place, the A&E ward. Remember the story I told you about with the Rugby League player and the broken hand — same place. They put it back using the muscle relaxant, valium. I always thought that valium was just a sedative but it can also be used as a powerful muscle relaxant but has to be injected intravenously. When you have a dislocation, your muscles around the joint go into spasms and lock everything into place; a sort of physical defence mechanism. The pain is shocking if it is a total dislocation. Once they are able to unlock the spasms with a strong muscle relaxant, it will slip back into place. Now I had to be in plaster for the next six weeks. It's strange how simple accidents like that can happen.

After living in St Paul's at the Spot for a year or so, we moved down the road to Canberra Street in Randwick. We paid $200,000 for a free standing house, owned by a gay couple. They had it looking great and we bought it straight away. I also bought two units, one at Kensington and another at Merrylands, as investments. Some people, including my mother, wondered where I got the money from. That reminds me of Bob Leuci's parents in the *Prince of the City*. It was all borrowed from my good friend Stewart Honey at the Westpac Bank in Randwick. At about this time, I started sweating profusely at night time in my sleep. I had a chat with my GP about it and he referred me to the POW for some tests. There are a multitude of reasons for night sweating, some quite serious. The main ones that I remember from my nursing days were lymphoma and tuberculosis. The tests proved to be negative. When the specialist was taking to Sue and I about it, he asked if I was under a lot of stress at the time. As soon as they say that, you know you have not got a physical problem. I told him that I had borrowed a lot of money to buy my real estate portfolio which now included a live-in house, a unit in Kensington and a unit at Merrylands; all in Sydney. He asked me how much I had to pay per month and I remember it was well over $2,000. This was in the late 1970s. He asked Sue what she was doing. Sue told him that at the moment she was not working and was in between jobs. Sue is a terrific worker and laziness is not part of her DNA. It just so happened that it was one of those rare occasions when she wasn't working. Well, the specialist blurted out, "No wonder you are sweating at night. You are paying back all this money and your wife is not working". He told her she had to get a job and help me. Wow, that upset Sue who is a very sensitive person. I did not hear the end of that for ages. I did well with my real estate investments and ended up buying a house down near Centennial Park in North Randwick. We paid $300,000 for that one at an auction in 1989. It's worth about $3,800,000 now (2016). That's an amazing jump over twenty-six years. Unfortunately I lost it in bankruptcy which we will talk about later on. At the time I bought it, Sue turned to me and said on the fall of the hammer at the auction, "Have you gone f****** mad?" Within weeks, after her friends had told her what a good buy it was, she took the credit for it. Women! Women are from Venus, Men are from Mars.

There are some legendary stories that have been around for years in the cops. They may be true, they may not be. However, we must never let the truth get in the road of a good story. The first one that comes to mind is the story of a well-known Detective Sergeant, sometime in the late 1960s. They were driving up Oxford Street, en-route to Darlinghurst Police Station. This cop spotted a well-known criminal walking in the same direction. He told the other two detectives that were with him, to wait in the car. He was going to arrest this known criminal because he reckoned it was time he went to the big house again. They took him up to Darlinghurst and charged him with possession of an unlicensed concealable weapon and produced that weapon in court as evidence. That's a pretty strong case but it was all a complete fabrication. The gun had been planted inside a newspaper by the Police that the criminal had been carrying. The Lower Court established a prima facie case and sent the matter to the District Court for trial. At the trial the criminal pleaded guilty. The good Detective Sergeant couldn't believe it. Why would he plead guilty? The criminal completely outsmarted him. He told His Honour (the learned Judge) that yes, he did have the gun and that he was on his way to Darlinghurst Police Station to hand it in. He told the Court that he had taken it from a young relative earlier in the day. Even though he was a habitual career criminal himself, he did not want this boy to go down the same path. So he back handed him and took the weapon off the boy. That's what happened. His case was dismissed. That's the story and I have heard it many times. The old hard heads in the cops swear it is true.

Another case involved three detectives interviewing a criminal in a fairly serious matter at a suburban station. The criminal would not make any admissions and told them all to get f*****. One of the detectives got a ukulele (a musical instrument) and started playing it in the interview while another detective starting dancing in his underwear. When it went to trial the criminal told the truth; that is that he had not made any admissions. The cops had lied he said. They tended a record of interview where he made lots of admissions but would not sign the record of interview. The Crown Prosecutor questioned the criminal about what were the Police doing during the interview. He (the criminal) told them that one detective was playing the ukulele and another was dancing around the room near naked. The Court broke out into fits of laughter and the poor old criminal got convicted. His credibility was shot to pieces by the truth. The Police were lying in their interview but no-one would believe the criminal. True or not true? Again, as with the previous story, there are a lot of old coppers who insist it is. I don't know, but I do know that some would be well capable of this sort of thing.

The other one that does the rounds of the traps is when the cops interviewed a very well-known violent criminal at Darlinghurst. This fella was dangerous and the cops wanted him behind bars. They fabricated a record of interview and wanted him to sign it. Of course, a signed record of interview will carry a lot more weight than an unsigned one. Naturally he wouldn't sign it. They threatened to belt him. He told them to give him all they had, he could take it and I'm sure he would have. Make no mistake, some of these criminals are very tough men. Well, when he wouldn't sign, the story goes that they hung him out of the window on the second floor of the station and threatened to let him go head first if he did not sign. He agreed to sign it and signed in his own language, which was one of those from the Balkan States. The matter went to Court and the record of interview was tended as evidence. The defence asked the lead detective to tell him the name on the signed record of interview. The detective said the full name of the defendant. The defence then asked a court interpreter who knew the language well, to read what was on the record of interview. The interpreter said that it read as 'The Police are lying'. Case dismissed. True or not true? I don't know but legend has it as being so.

Another hard man I had a fair bit to do with was a chap named Tim Bristow. I first met Tim when I was still in uniform at Bondi in 1976. I had decided to take a pacific cruise for a bit of a holiday. Well, even before we were out of the heads of Sydney Harbour, I heard about Tim. He had got on the ship at the last moment because his wife/partner/girlfriend was on board. She was running away from him. He found out where she was and he screwed up her holiday for her. He made it clear very early on in the piece that no was man was to go near her. I kinda made friends with Tim. Everyone on the ship was frightened by him but he was a real interesting bloke. He talked a lot, mainly about himself. When the ship berthed, I used to go ashore with him as I was on my own. I had a bit in common with him. He was an ex-Policeman but got kicked out; I think for assault. He became one of the State's most famous/infamous private investigators and specialised in divorces. He knew a lot of people and was very well connected. He offered me a job when I left the Police but I knew better than to get involved with Tim. He was interviewed once; I think it was on 60 minutes about his role in the building industry. In that interview he made the famous statement, quote, "I can't help it if people have accidents on building sites" or words to that effect. He claimed to be the original model for Chesty Bond. He certainly had the build and looks for it. After a few days out on the cruise, things settled down and Tim would hold court on the upper deck. People were fascinated with his stories. He was full of it, no doubt, but a lot of it would have been true. He had this reputation for being able to handle himself. He got jail time for 18-months for assault and later got five years for supplying drugs. He was well-known at the Newport Arms Hotel and he was in charge of security there. It was part of his legend that he was never beaten and would fight anyone who fancied himself. Apparently they came from near and far to try him on but he beat all comers, but that sounds a bit far-fetched to me. He gave evidence against a number of Chatswood Police about how they threw out about fifty packets of heroin from the window of the Chatswood Police Station and he caught them and loaded them into his car. Problem was they all got caught and Tim did some time. Tim did brag a lot. He did this, he did that and not all of it would have been true. But he was a good story teller and I liked him. I kept in contact with him and went up a couple of times to the Newport Arms and had a beer with him. I remember him clearly telling me that he had been bribing Police for a long time and that he found the higher the rank, the lower the morals and the higher the bribe. Tim thought that applied to the judiciary and politicians as well and he would have known. He was a big man with a big heart. He told me that if I ever needed help, all I had to do was call him. He had this reputation for doing a lot of work for life saving on the northern beaches in Sydney and helping young life savers obtain their certification. Another unsavoury string he had to his bow, was that he was allegedly barred for life from playing rugby after he stomped on someone's head. He was a tough nut Tim, but I'm pleased I ran into him.

I don't believe that my morals and ethics are fundamentally any better than most other Police. I think it the height of either hypocrisy or nativity (or both) to think that you wouldn't get involved in a given set of circumstances. What people need to realise is that there is an awful lot of money involved in the drug business. It is also easy to understand why cops get a bit cynical about the judicial system. They arrest these blokes, put them before a court and the court often delivers them a very soft custodial sentence or no sentence at all. The cops think, well what the f*** did we go to all that effort for, just for him to get a couple of months and he'd be back out on the street in no time, doing exactly the same thing. I found many of the people sitting on the bench naive about criminals and many of them were played off a break by them. I think this became one of the motivating forces behind a lot of cops saying. "well if this is the way that it works, we might as well make a quid out of it".

If I stayed in the Police I would have been a designated detective within three to six months and most probably in the drug squad, doing what I was good at and loved doing. I was now 37 years of age and had a great life; great job, well paid (plenty of overtime in those days), a great wife, my own house and investment properties and good health. I think that when I resigned from the Police I could see the writing on the wall. I think I somehow sensed that there would be a day of reckoning for the NSW Police Force; it just couldn't go on like it was indefinitely. When that day of reckoning came, I did not want to find myself before a Royal Commission answering questions or being grilled. I had to make a decision: to leave or not to leave.

The decision was made easy for me in the end. One day (I remember it was a Saturday) we executed a search warrant in the Bondi area and caught this fella red-handed with hard evidence of heroin dealings. He had the scales with residue on them, a few small packets of heroin and it was not looking good for him. I had two new trainees with me at the time and we took this fella back to Waverley Police Station and were going to do a record of interview with him. Once that was done our plan was to charge him with an indictable drug trafficking offence. Before we got started, I got a call from a bloke who said that he was a Superintendent from the CIB headquarters. He did not give me his name so I really did not know who I was speaking to. He knew about the fella that we had arrested so news travels fast. He told me that he did not want me to charge him as he was working with the drug squad as an informer on some very 'big' matter. Of course anyone can say that and I told him so. On the other hand it could be 100% correct and I would not want to do anything that might jeopardise the success of a major drug inquiry. I told him I could not just let him go because somebody had called and told me a story without any proof. It was quite normal for some drug informers to be allowed to carry on their nefarious activities because they were supplying important information to the Police on the understanding that they would not be busted and could continue to make a quid. He asked me to accept what he was telling me was the truth. I told him I needed some proof and he must have pre-empted that he would need to do that. He told me that he had my Police desk diary in front of him and told me to ask him for any day as to what I had done and he would read it out to me. Snooker. I knew than that not only was he connected to the CIB but at a very high level because the only way that he could have my Police diary would have been to go to our office and get it or have someone in the office deliver it; most likely the later. Nevertheless, I asked him for a couple of days activities and he read them out exactly as I had written them. Based on that, we only charged the bloke with a summary possession charge of heroin; a charge that he would not get a sentence for. My two trainees were not party to the conversation and they were convinced that I had 'copped a big quid' for it and that was why we were basically letting him go. This is another thing that I have never mentioned before. That really sealed it for me to make the decision to leave the NSW Police Force.

I had one more thing to do before I resigned. I knew that I was giving up a lot and I spoke with a well known experienced detective friend of mine, who worked at Darlo. I went through it with him and told him my biggest fear was being betrayed. I had a real thing about it and my diary incident reinforced that. Police have this incorrigible will to survive and the motto right from day one, was to look after number one — yourself. I asked him how I could mitigate this risk but we both agreed that I'd be going to the Drug Squad and would not be the senior man and in that sense, I would have to go with the flow. We talked about committing perjury, loading offenders up, verbalising them and so on, but the really thorny issue was the one of trust. I wrote earlier that there were some real snakes amongst the cops (apologies to most who don't fall into this category) and at the end of the day, I decided not to take the risks. I also mentioned earlier the other reasons, but this is the one that most 'stuck in the belly.'

Shortly thereafter I resigned.

Chapter Ten: The NSW Police Royal Commission

Things got so bad in the cops that something had to be done about it; so the Government set up the Royal Commission into the NSW Police Service. This was conducted between 1995 and 1997. The Commission's main terms of reference were to determine the existence of and the extent of corruption in the NSW Police. It wanted to determine if the corruption and malpractice were systemic and entrenched. Having determined that the Commission then had to make recommendations on how to address it.

One of the Royal Commission's recommendations was the establishment of a permanent Commission to investigate serious Police misconduct. This came into effect in January 1997. After reading about the findings of the Royal Commission I felt that I had made the right decision in 1981 not go on the detectives training course and instead resigned. The Commission opened a can of worms and exposed the systemic and entrenched corruption in the NSW Police Force. People often ask me firstly if I was involved in it and secondly if I wasn't, did I see what was going on around me. Remember I was a junior rank and to a very large degree I was kept at arm's length in that respect. It was considered that we had not yet earned our stripes, so to speak. The sort of behaviour described in the Commission's report, was not at my level. It was more centred round the rank of Senior Constable and upwards. All the types of malpractices described in the report were common knowledge but all hearsay. Remember when I first went to Division 21, they thought that I might be a plant from Internal Affairs? To cap it off, I came as a trained nurse and that put another serious sexuality question mark about me. It would be quite some time before I was accepted. The hearsay centred around activities like the manipulation of the evidence; the abuse of Police powers; the theft of drugs; verbals; planting evidence on suspects; assaults on suspects and/or offenders; opportunistic theft; consorting socially with known criminals; corruption and bribes; interfering with due the judicial process and protecting criminals in their drug trading business.

These are activities that have been well documented and portrayed in numerous books, television dramas and the like. The point is that because I was so junior in rank, I was not so exposed to it but knew about it. At that time I had not really done the hard yards and earned the trust of the hard heads. I felt that now that I had been accepted into the ranks of detectives (or would have been) and served my time at 21 Division, the corrupt detectives would have viewed me as one of them. When we were working the vice at 21 Division, we'd often drive the sergeant to a certain place and he would tell us to go and speak with a few criminals, find out what they were doing, submit the CIRs (Criminal Intelligence Reports) and meet him at the same spot in an hour. We didn't know where he went and of course, never asked. There was always a lot of talk but that's all it was, talk. You learned to be discreet. If we went for a handsome dinner that night, somewhere in a fancy restaurant, you reckoned the good sergeant had a good day at the races. There was always this tacit agreement that you went with the flow and kept your nose clean. So not only was I not involved in corruption, I never really had the chance to be. I knew that would change once I got my designation. I think that my stories relating to my undercover work and in particular my druggie group, would indicate that I was not immune to walking on the wrong side, so to speak. Actually I really don't know how you could become a good detective if you were not prepared to bend the rules significantly to be perfectly honest.

You need to understand the culture in the Police Force at that time. I have no idea of what it is like now but I am told it is very much around informing on your colleagues if you know they are committing even the slightest infraction. I think if that is true, that is a terrible shame. Justice Wood from the Royal Commission summed up the culture in my time this way. He said, quote, *"Police formed a distinct 'occupation culture'. They set their own set of values, perspectives, norms and craft rules which*

influenced their conduct. These often have little bearing on the Police regulations and guidelines, as taught at the Academy." I told you what the good Sergeant told me at Waverley when I first went there; "forget what you f****** learnt at the f****** Academy he said, we do things f****** differently here". Justice Wood wrote what he called the Police Officer's 'working personality' and he said it was characterised by the following traits. I am including it so that you can understand that the culture in the Police is distinct and probably quite different to any other sector of society. Maybe that is why I liked it so much. Some of these cultural characteristics were as quoted by Justice Wood:
• *a sense of mission about Police work;*
• *an orientation towards action;*
• *a cynical or pessimistic perspective about the social environment;*
• *an attitude of constant suspiciousness;*
• *an isolated social life coupled with a strong sense of solidarity with other Police Officers;*
• *a clear categorisation of the public between the rough and the respectable;*
• *a conservative stance in politics and morality;*
• *a machismo outlook that permits sexism and glorifies the abuse of alcohol and heterosexual indulgences;*
• *a prejudiced attitude towards minorities; and*
• *a pragmatic view of Police work which discourages innovation and experimentation.*
I think he hit the nail on the head there.

For each one of these points, I could give you many practical examples. In relation to Police having a machismo outlook that permits sexism and glorifies the abuse of alcohol and heterosexual indulgences, I was involved (regrettably) in three separate 'gang bangs' while in uniform, which was only for one year. Don't misunderstand me. These were totally consensual and I was as much to blame as anyone else but hate myself for doing it now. Nobody held a gun to my head and said I had to do it. I wanted to. The best example I can give you is that there was this woman, actually a very attractive woman, who just loved men in uniform. We could go to her place at night time and get it whenever we wanted, by arrangement of course, which was easy to do with a phone call. The method she used was to bring out a pack of cards. Say there were three of us, she would get each one of us to take a card from the pack. The one with the highest card went first and so on. Imagine what the neighbours must have thought. My memory is very hazy about this woman. I cannot remember anything about her other than what I have written. I don't remember where we used to go to see her, what her name was or even what the house looked like. One time we went there we took a portable radio with us. We were wanted back at the station to interview somebody from a previous traffic accident so we told the operator that we were involved in a domestic matter (which was true I suppose) and could not come back for an hour or so and we asked the operator to tell the station we would be another hour and for him to wait for us. We finished what we were doing and went back to the station for the interview. Now as an older, wiser and more mature man, I understand how irresponsible this was but these were the times. I think this might fit into Justice Wood's assertion of *a machismo outlook that permits sexism and glorifies the abuse of alcohol and heterosexual indulgences.*

Another time, one of the boys at a suburban station found this girl in town who was keen to 'entertain' the boys. She too loved men in uniform and she too, was attractive. She took on about seven of us, one after the other, in the Police meal room at the back of the station. She was not intoxicated, was not on drugs, did not want money and did not appear to be mentally ill. I think I would question that now. One of the boys was the desk sergeant whilst all this was going on and he had to deal with the public at the front desk. He had to come out a couple of times and tell us to quieten it down at bit or else we might get caught. While one was having sex with her, the others drank beer and watched the performance until each had his turn; all this whilst on duty and members of the public were just a couple of rooms away. If that is not sexism and total disrespect to women, I don't know what is. I am really ashamed of myself for being involved in that today but obviously wasn't at the time. It hurts me to admit doing this but I suppose it was the behaviour of a bunch of cops that were immature and deep down had little respect for women. It's hard for me to reconcile that on the one hand we respected women yet treated them like this. Perhaps it was a matter of compartmentalisation.

We had a staff member at 21 Division who had this obsession with arresting homosexuals. He hated them with a passion and he and his team would prowl around the public toilets, parks and known gay areas until he had a truck full of gays. Sometimes he would send in one of his men into a known gay area and ask some gay bloke who was soliciting if he wanted sex. When he said yes, they would arrest him. I heard that it was not usual for the offender to get a bit of a hiding as well back at the station but fortunately I never worked the 'poofter' truck. I think also the truck ride back to the station could have been quite hazardous for the fellas locked up in the back. The system not only allowed them to do it; it tacitly encouraged it. We need to remember that this was the mid-70s and many people had no problem with Police dishing out a bit of summary justice to 'poofters'. I recall when I first went to Waverley Police station there was a uniform cop there that seem to be a bit different. It turned out that he was gay and that was completely unacceptable to the Police hierarchy. He actually was made to resign and it was not spoken about at the station. He really just disappeared. It is encouraging that gays can now join the Police Force but I have told you earlier that I never had a sense of homophobia against them and never found myself persecuting them when I was in the cops. If memory serves me correctly, homosexuality was a crime up until the mid-eighties so the cops were just enforcing the law. The summary punishment and the rough truck rides were not part of that law though.

Justice Wood talked about Police having a conservative stance in politics. He's 100% right. He included two traits that really go hand in hand. An isolated social life coupled with a strong sense of solidarity with other Police Officers and an attitude of constant suspiciousness. In my time, only part of my social structure was centred around other Police and their families. I had a fairly strong social structure before I joined the Force but I was 30 at the time. Most people join when they are nineteen so have not had the chance to do that. Police generally felt that it was them against all others and viewed outsiders with suspicion, but I think that it was fair to say that most Police fitted well into society. Naturally we gravitated towards our own because they would understand the trials and tribulations that Police work with every day; especially if you are doing something wrong, like verbalising offenders or dishing out a bit of summary justice. That's hardly something you could go down to the local RSL club and talk about with members of the public. Many Police thought that they had a moral legitimacy, if not a legal one, to do some of the illegal things they did to effect convictions and I have just explained that. You generally would not expect the man in the street to understand but I would think that most Australians at that time would have supported the Police. An orientation towards action is what people join the Police for, at least when they joined. Many of them after a few short years of service had an orientation for non-action and I have explained why. In those days if you asked one hundred Police if they liked their job, ninety-nine would say, "I love it". Justice Wood hit the nail on the head with his summary of Police traits and that was the way we were. On the rare occasion that I hear from the Police these days they tell me "Mate, the job's f*****". When I ask them why, they tell me that young people going through the academy are encouraged to 'snitch' on other Police if they see them doing something wrong. The problem appears to be that this 'snitching' seems to relate to matters that are sometimes very insignificant in nature and I alluded to this before. If that is right, I think it a great shame and one thing is for sure and certain, I would not fit into in the present day environment.

Justice Wood went on to say quote, "*These characteristics are sometimes understood as functional to the survival and sense of security of officers working under frequently dangerous, unpredictable and alienating conditions. As such, the 'group loyalty' aspect of Police culture is not in itself negative, however, the associated 'siege mentality' and 'code of silence' have been often linked to the proliferation and concealment of Police corruption. The Mollen Commission identified the main ways in which these aspects of Police culture facilitate corruption: First, they encourage corruption by setting a standard that nothing is more important than the unswerving loyalty of officers to one another — not even stopping the most serious forms of corruption. This emboldens corrupt cops and those susceptible to corruption. Second, these attitudes thwart efforts to control corruption. They lead officers to protect or cover up for others' crimes — even crimes of which they heartily disapprove.*

The strong sense of loyalty and the code of silence among Police has frustrated many inquiries into Police corruption, including those conducted by Police services themselves. Nevertheless, the tendency in some accounts to use the concept of Police culture as a primary tool for understanding Police corruption is overly simplistic, having regard to:
- *the fact that there is no single Police culture, significant differences existing, for example, between the cultures relevant for uniformed beat Police, detectives and senior command, and between different jurisdictions;*
- *a pragmatic view of Police work which discourages innovation and experimentation."*

Did I make the right decision in hindsight to leave the Police Force? Maybe I might never have got involved in the malpractice culture and went smoothly through the ranks. Who knows what might have happened? One thing is for sure and certain, I would never again have a job that I enjoyed so much and have many fond memories off. The Royal Commission did their job well. There were a total of 284 cops that were adversely named and the Commission sent forty-six briefs to the Director of Public Prosecution for consideration for possible criminal charges. By 2001 nine cops had pleaded guilty to corruption charges and seven Police were given jail sentences. A further fourteen cops had charges against them dismissed because of irregularities with the management of search warrants but they were all probably guilty. In other words the good blokes stuffed it up. We all know that most Detectives are pretty smart blokes and the Commission was unable to 'nail them to the wall' but wanted to. The 'new' Police Force came up with a brilliant piece of legislation (depending how you look at it). They came up with the introduction of what is known as section 181D of the Police Service Act. This Act allowed the Police Commissioner to give notice to any cop, any one at all, that he (the Commissioner) did not have confidence anymore in the cop's suitability to continue as a Police Officer. If a cop received this, he would then have to show cause as to the unfairness of the direction and advocate why he should be able to keep his job. If he/she was then dismissed, they could appeal to the Industrial Relations Tribunal. A number of very senior Police ended their careers in disgrace including an Assistant Commissioner and a Chief of Staff had his contract torn up. Twelve Police that were caught up in the web of the Commission committed suicide.

As I write this book (2017) I do some part time work out at the Sydney Cricket Trust and Sydney Football Stadium. My official role is being a Crowd Controller which really is being a security guard. It's something I do to bring in some badly needed cash and also provides me with something to do in my retirement. Sometimes I get to see the games so that is an added bonus. One day I was speaking to a couple of coppers at a game and one of them was a Chief Inspector. We were just chit chatting about nothing in particular, but when I realised that he was a Chief Inspector I thought that he might be about my vintage so I told him that I used to be in the job. He asked me what class I was in and when I said 150, he just looked at me in an incredulous manner and asked me what my name was. When I said Michell, he said, "You are not Max Michell are you?" When I replied in the affirmative, he said that he had been looking for me for thirty years. In fact he had been told by another former class member that I had died. I thought Jesus, what have I done? It turned out that Michael (the Inspector) was in my class and that it was me who talked him into joining the Commandos. He said that every time that he did one of his many parachute jumps (he did well over 100) he thought about me. I actually caught up with him later and we attended our 40-year class anniversary dinner. I regularly see the Police that come and work at the Sydney Cricket Ground and Sydney Football Stadium and I often speak with them. I get the impression that they are more professional than we were in the 1970s, better educated and definitely fitter. The Senior Constables and Sergeants don't seem to have the Sperm-whale figure characterised in the Choir Boys. Maybe the alcohol fuelled nights at the station are a thing of the past. Maybe they don't even do the choir practice anymore. They are a lot more approachable than we were and it seems to me that they have more of a service culture to the public generally. They present to me as a group of people that are fairly impressive so perhaps the Police Force has gotten its act together and may present a good career for any young person who might want to join. The story I told you about with the women and her sex system with the cards epitomises the extraordinary lack of discipline, low moral standards, sexism and very ordinary supervision within the Police at the time that I was in it. I'd be very surprised if a group of cops these days could do something like that but perhaps even more pertinently they would not want to anyway. The thing that would not sit well with me on the modern day Police Force in NSW would be, if it is correct, the culture of 'snitching.' I could never abide that. Maybe they are NSW finest now, but leave the part out that money can buy.

Footnote: A large part of the success of the Royal Commission into the NSW Police Force was that they were able to get a detective in the Kings Cross district to 'rollover' and work for them. Let's call him Bob. I had met Bob a number of times and he seemed to be a good sort of a bloke to me. He was coerced into working undercover for the Commission for months carrying a wire and working with videotaped evidence. His work exposed many corrupt police and other criminals that went all the way up to the rank of Chief Superintendent. The Commission acknowledged that the subsequent success that they had, was achieved in a large part to the work that that been done by him in collecting the evidence, helping putting the briefs together, and than giving evidence it in Court. He did this against police that he considered good friends.

This is exactly what I was writing about when I talked about the issue of trust and betrayal. I am only speculating now but I'd suggest that the Commission had Bob over a barrel and he was looking at a jail sentence if he did not cooperate. This is almost a double of what Bob Leuci did as written in the non-fiction book *Prince of the City*. All the prosecutors have to do is to detect your weakness, assess your knowledge in criminal activity and give you an incentive to 'sing like a canary'. In Leuci case, it may have been that he felt that he had dishonoured his family and he wanted to rectify that. In Bob's case, I'd suggest that he felt that this was the only way he could survive. But he was wrong. A better way would have been to go to jail and 'cop it sweet'. In other words, man up to it and take his medicine.

In an interview that Bob did he admitted that he had made a big mistake working with the Royal Commission and subsequently betraying his police friends. He said that if he had his time over again, he would have preferred to go to jail rather than do what he did. Bob went on to say that he probably would only have got a few years sentence but now he says that has a life sentence. Once they had no further need for him, not surprisingly, they dumped him. That should not surprise anyone. Another case that epitomises betrayal was during the Fitzgerald Royal Commission in police corruption in Qld. At these proceedings, it was established that one of the most senior police figures in 'the joke' (police corruption), who was an Assistant Commissioner, rolled over for the Commission and betrayed his fellow 'Joke' comrades to save himself.

I think I will rest my case on the issue of trust and betrayal.

Chapter Eleven: The International Hotel Business
1982 - 1989

1982 - Britain overcame Argentina in Falklands war. Princess Grace 52, died of injuries when her car plunged off mountain road. Lebanese Christian Phalangists killed hundreds of people in two Palestinian refugee camps in West Beirut. Leonid Brezhnev, Soviet leader, died at 75. Yuri V. Andropov, 68, chosen as successor. John W. Hinckley, Jr. found not guilty because of insanity in shooting of President Reagan. The books Schindler's List and The Colour Purple came onto the market. MRI (magnetic resonance imaging) diagnostic machines were introduced in Britain. The movies released included *ET – the Extra-Terrestrial, Tootsie, Gandhi* and *The Verdict*. Notable deaths included those of Ingrid Bergman, John Belushi, Leonid Brezhnev, Grace Kelly and Satchel Paige.

1983 - Benigno S. Aquino, Jr., 50, political rival of Philippines President Ferdinand Marcos, was assassinated in Manila. South Korean Boeing 747 jetliner bound for Seoul apparently strayed into Soviet airspace and was shot down by a Soviet SU-15 fighter after it had tracked the airliner for two hours; all 269 aboard were killed. Terrorist explosion killed 237 US Marines in Beirut. "Crack" cocaine was developed in the Bahamas, and soon appeared in the United States. The movies released included *The Big Chill, Terms of Endearment, Fanny and Alexander*, and *The Right Stuff*. Notable deaths included those of Tennessee Williams, Joan Miró and Jack Dempsey.

1984 - Three hundred slain as Indian Army occupied the Sikh Golden Temple in Amritsar. Indian Prime Minister Indira Gandhi assassinated by two Sikh bodyguards; 1,000 killed in anti-Sikh riots; son Rajiv succeeded her. Toxic gas leaked from Union Carbide plant in Bhopal, India, killing 2,000 and injuring 150,000. President Reagan re-elected in landslide with 59% of vote. Apple introduced the user-friendly Macintosh personal computer. The movies released included *Amadeus, The Killing Fields, A Passage to India* and *The Pope of Greenwich Village*. Notable deaths included those of Indira Gandhi, Francois Truffaut, Truman Capote and Count Basie.

1985 - Soviet leader Chernenko died at 73 and was replaced by Mikhail Gorbachev, 54. Under the slogans of glasnost and Perestroika, Gorbachev initiated a broad program of reform and liberalisation. Two Shi'ite Muslim gunmen captured TWA airliner with 133 aboard, 104 of them Americans; 39 remaining hostages freed in Beirut. Terrorists seized Egyptian Boeing 737 airliner after take-off from Athens; 59 dead as Egyptian forces stormed plane on Malta. Rock Hudson died of AIDS at age 59. Michael S. Brown and Joseph L. Goldstein (both US), won the Nobel prize in Medicine for their work, which has drastically widened our understanding of the cholesterol metabolism and increased our possibilities to prevent and treat atherosclerosis and heart attacks. The movies released included *Kiss of the Spider Woman, Out of Africa, Prizzi's Honour* and *The Colour Purple*. Notable deaths included those of Louise Brooks, Marc Chagall, Rock Hudson and Frank Oppenheimer.

1986 - President Reagan froze Libyan assets in US. US planes attacked Libyan "terrorist centres". President Ferdinand Marcos fled Philippines after ruling for 20 years; newly elected Corazon Aquino succeeded him. Union Carbide agreed to settlement with victims of Bhopal gas leak in India. Major nuclear accident at Soviet Union's Chernobyl power station alarmed the World. Space shuttle Challenger exploded after launch at Cape Canaveral, Fla., killing all seven aboard. The first genetically engineered vaccine, for hepatitis B, gained FDA approval. The Voyager 2 probe passed Uranus in January, returning images and data on its moon, rings, atmosphere, interior, and magnetic field. Halley's Comet yielded information on return visit. The movies *Platoon, Hannah and Her Sisters, The Colour of Money* and *The Mission* were released. Notable deaths included those of Harold Macmillan and Duchess of Windsor.

1987 - William Buckley, American hostage in Lebanon, reported slain. Iraqi missiles killed 37 in attack on US Frigate Stark in

Persian Gulf; Iraqi president Hussein apologised. Prime Minister Thatcher won rare third term in Britain. Prozac released for use in US by Eli Lilly & Company. AZT won FDA approval for use in the treatment of AIDS. An International treaty signed in Montreal called for a 50% reduction in the use of CFCs by the year 2000. The movies released included *Moonstruck, Wall Street, The Last Emperor* and *Fatal Attraction*. Notable deaths included those of Toni Morrison, 'Beloved' William Casey (CIA), Andy Warhol, Rudolf Hess, John Huston and James Baldwin

1988 - Benazir Bhutto became the first Islamic woman Prime Minster, chosen to lead Pakistan. Pan-Am 747 exploded from terrorist bomb and crashed in Lockerbie, Scotland, killing all 259 aboard and 11 on the ground. US Navy ship shot down Iranian airliner in Persian Gulf, mistaking it for jet fighter; 290 killed. Republican convention nominated George Bush for President and Indiana Senator Dan Quayle for Vice President. NASA scientist James Hansen warned congress of the dangers of the global warming and the greenhouse effect. The movies released included *Rain Man, Mississippi Burning, A Fish Called Wanda* and *Bull Durham*. Notable deaths included those of Roy Orbison, Chet Baker, Luis Alvarez Edgar Jean Faure and Nora Astorga.

1989 - Iran's Ayatollah Khomeini declared author Salman Rushdie's book 'The Satanic Verses' offensive and sentenced him to death. Tens of thousands of Chinese students took over Beijing's Tiananmen Square in rally for democracy. More than one million people in Beijing demonstrated for democracy; chaos spread across Nation. Thousands killed in Tiananmen Square as Chinese leaders took hard line toward demonstrators. Mikhail S. Gorbachev named Soviet President. P. W. Botha quit as South Africa's President. Deng Xiaoping resigned from China's leadership. After 28 years, Berlin Wall was opened to the West. President Ceausescu and wife executed. US troops invaded Panama, seeking capture of General Manuel Noriega. Ruptured tanker Exxon Valdez sent 11 million gallons of crude oil into Alaska's Prince William Sound. First World Wide Web server and browser developed by Tim Berners-Lee (England) while working at CERN. The movies released included *Glory, Born on the Fourth of July, My Left Foot, Sex, Lies, and Videotape,* and *Field of Dreams.* Notable deaths included those of Jim Backus, Lucille Ball, Samuel Beckett, Salvador Dali, Bette Davis, Ferdinand Marcos, Billy Martin, Laurence Olivier and Sugar Ray Robinson. The population of the world was 5.190 billion.

It had now been over a decade since I had taken any medication for depression and anxiety. I had gone from being a loser to being a winner; at least that is how I saw it. In this space of time I had completed and graduated with a nursing degree with high distinctions in my hospital finals. I had also completed six years as one of NSW's finest and left with distinguished service. I now had my own house, two investment properties and a wife who was a working professional. We each had late model cars and both of us had a wide circle of friends. If you can recall my position when I described my second trip back to Lowson House in Brisbane in 1967/68 you will understand that my current situation was a major reversal for someone who was curled up in the foetal position severely depressed in a locked psychiatric ward in 1967 and could not see the point in living. Or even earlier when I was thinking about using the .45 colt to end my life, such was the torment and pain. Sue and I lived the life of middle class Australians and wanted for nothing. We had an overseas trip every year and most nights of the week, we went out and life was good.

One day I caught a taxi a couple of months after I left the Police. Nothing out of the ordinary about that, except I left my hand bag in the cab which contained well over $1,500 in various notes; plus all my personal details. I was still fairly switched on and figured out what taxi company it was by the type of hand piece they used for their radio. I spoke with a detective mate of mine who agreed he would do the charging if we found him. It was very much a needle in the haystack type of scenario but you have to try. However there was one distinguishing feature of the driver in that he wore a French beret and I thought that he was probably Lebanese. I drove around for a couple of weeks on the off-chance that I would see him. You would not believe it but as luck would have it, I spotted him one day driving his taxi. So I now knew the number plates of the taxi and passed them onto the detective who was going to investigate. He picked me up along with his workmate and we went out to this bloke's place in the South east suburbs. The taxi was parked outside his house so that meant he was probably home. The Detectives left me in the car and went to the house to speak with him. He denied everything. As part of the inquiry, he was asked if they could have a look inside his cab. An innocent man is always going to say yes and he did. Amazingly, he had left the bag in the boot of his car with everything in it, except of course the money. All he had to do was to get rid of it and he failed this very basic pub test. He insisted that he did not know how the bag got into the boot of his car and said he was as shocked as we were to see it there. Not surprisingly, the Detectives did not buy his story and he was charged. At court, either being stupid or acting on his stupid lawyer's advice, he pleaded not guilty. He should have had it explained to him that possession is nine-tenths of the law. He never made any allegations against the Police such as they must have planted it in his car. He was quickly found guilty by the Magistrate and ordered to pay me what he stole (the $1,500) plus the extra Court costs including the fine. Now if I wanted to be a real c***, I could have put any figure on what was actually stolen. I could have for example said it was $10,000 and he would have been convicted of that and made to pay me that amount. But I am not like that and I don't have that nasty streak in me that would allow me to do anything like that. However, I think some of my former colleagues wouldn't have hesitated to have done it and it was suggested to me as to why I didn't.

You will remember my story about the taxi driver who ripped me off taking me to the illegal casino. That was very different and I did not have any trouble teaching him a lesson but of course in the eyes of the law, it was wrong what I did. What is it about me and taxis? One time I was catching a taxi from JFK airport outside NYC into 44th street and he had the meter on. When we got to the hotel I paid him what was on the meter and took it to the nearest dollar. The taxi driver was an Indian gentleman and he started being rude to me and told me I was a very mean man. He added that in the US it was normal to add on 10%. I told him that I was not an American and if he had explained that to me when I was paying, I might have co-operated. As it was I told him he could go and get f***** and go back to Bombay where he was probably making nothing. That is very unlike me as I normally wouldn't react like that but something about this fella really put a bee in my bonnet and I let him know what I thought about him. Perhaps something to do with the 8 + hour economy flight from Frankfurt and the 12-hour flight from Singapore. Another time, I think it was in Phnom Penh in Cambodia, I caught a taxi into town. There was no meter, the driver did not understand one word of English and the car itself was a rust bucket. You could see the road through the floor boards as we were driving along; that's not unusual in many of the developing countries. When we got to the hotel he said X number of dollars. I knew what the correct fare should have been. Blokes like me in the security risk management business do their homework when travelling and we are very in-tune with this sort of thing. However I did not hesitate and paid him what he was asking for. The bigger risk for me would have been to end up in an argument with him as there could well be some retribution later on. Right is not always might!

There's another hand bag story when I was in the cops. I had relatives over from New Zealand and we went to the Eastern Suburbs Leagues Club for lunch. I had this habit of taking my hand held bag with me. The reason for this was because of the high rate of break, enter and stealing offences that occurred in the eastern suburbs so I didn't like leaving it at home. I figured it was safer to have it on my person. Inside the bag were things that should not have been. Firstly my Police identification badge and secondly, the fake money that I told you about. Thirdly there was the bottle of Seconal. Finally, some foils that looked like heroin foils but were in fact flour. I got distracted and left the bag on the seat in the canteen at Easts. Within thirty-seconds I realised that I had forgotten my bag. When I rushed back in to where we were sitting it was gone. It could not have been more than a minute. I just couldn't believe that I could do such a dumb thing but kept my cool. I knew now that I would be in serious trouble with the Police once I reported it. I thought that I would probably be sacked over it. This happened on a Friday and I really sweated over it on the weekend. I didn't tell my superiors and was going to wait for a couple of days; I was buying time and I knew that I would have to report it Monday. I have told you previously that I am not a religious man but if there is a God, he came to my aid in spite of all the crimes I have committed against him. On the following Monday morning I was going to fess up to my boss and tell him what happened and brace myself for the inevitable. Incredibly as I came out of my house to catch the bus to the office there was an express post envelope at our front door; my heart missed a few beats. I opened it and there is was with everything intact, except of course the money. That was the least of my worries. Now it was not in my interest to know who took it so I could not get the fingerprint section involved. I still often reminisce how lucky I was that day. Naturally I never said anything about it to the cops. It was my fault and a major embarrassment to me that I could be so negligent. I often wonder what motivated the thief to return it and can only surmise that he/she must have panicked when they saw the Police badge and the drugs. They must have thought, Christ who is this bloke, what is he doing with all this gear? I think they would have realised pretty quickly that they had a 'hot potato' in their hands and had to act on it. Whatever the reason Sue and I were overjoyed and I tell you we really celebrated that night up at Roy's and had a bit more arak than normal.

I had some time off after leaving the Police and felt that I should do something useful. I bought an existing laundromat in Belmore Road Randwick, near the Prince of Wales hospital from a dodgy Indian bloke; maybe a former taxi driver from NYC! It was fairly ordinary but I worked hard there. I used to do all the ironing that clients wanted and I really don't like ironing. I built the business up enough to sell it and made some money out of it, but not much. The business was all cash and my police mates used to reckon that I was laundering my ill-gotten gains from the Police Force; but it was nothing like that. I worked a lot harder than I did in the Police and made a lot less but it did serve as a transition for me. After I sold the laundromat Sue and I did a trip to Europe. Sue was able to get 10% fares because she worked for an airline so off we went. Sydney to Singapore, Bahrain, London, Amsterdam, Maastricht, Brussels, Paris, Montreux, Vienna, Munich, Amsterdam, London, Bahrain, Singapore and back to Sydney. I loved Paris and have been back there a couple of time since. I always think about Dave from my druggie group when I am there. I liked Amsterdam a lot as well. Unusual for an ex-cop but I loved the liberal society and found the red light area fascinating. Little did I know then when we transited in Singapore overnight that I would later go on to spend over fifteen years there. When we got back to Sydney I had to start looking for a job. There was an advertisement in the Sydney Morning Herald looking for a House Detective-Security Officer at the Hilton Hotel in the city. I applied and got it. I did not have a clear understanding of the shift work involved and Sue was not happy being on her own at home whilst I was working night shift there. It turns out the night shift was a lot more than I had been told so I took it up with the Security Manager. I told him I would have to leave if we could not do something about it. He could not and so I left. I did the right thing and stayed until they found my replacement and had him trained up to do the job. I then applied to work at the new luxurious hotel at the Rocks. It was called The Regent Sydney and it was the first truly five-star hotel in Australia. I was offered and accepted a job as a Security Officer. This was the beginning of my hotel career and I was now 38.

I did some good things at the hotel whilst I was doing security for them and that bought me to the attention of the General Manager (GM). The hotel was fairly big; thirty-six stories with 620 rooms and suites. It was the biggest hotel in Australia at the time and certainly the best. It was at the other end of the spectrum to the ones I shared with the group in the squatter's houses on Bourke Street that is for sure. It was very luxurious, something I was not used to and never experienced before. The Regent Sydney was really the first hotel in Australia to introduce silver service across the board, even for room service. There was also a fair amount of security work to do there. In my time there (1982 - 89) I met some well-known people (Celebrities). To name some that I remember - Sean Connery, Pavarotti, Mel Gibson, Jack Thompson, John McEnroe, Martina Navratilova, Michael Jackson, Sophia Loren and Dan Quayle. Of course the meetings were brief but nevertheless, I did meet them. Sometimes as an Assistant Manager, I had to solve problems for them. The hotel had this policy that we would not cash cheques and staff were under strict instructions not to. Martina Navratilova came down to reception one night and wanted to cash a cheque. The Receptionist could not do it so she called the Assistant Manager(AM), which is proper procedure. I met Ms Navratilova and she said to me that she felt that I might know who she was. I confirmed that I did and allowed the cheque to go through. Just little things like that. There was one international celebrity I had to ask to keep the noise down in his room — twice. On the second time, I told him he would have to leave the hotel if I had to come back a third time. Fortunately he complied but if he had not, I would have made him leave the hotel in the middle of the night. Imagine the headlines and I did allude to that the second time I had to go back. I told him that it was in both of our interests not to have an incident that would probably hit the press and he agreed. Dan Quayle had a lot of security men with him so I did not actually meet him but I met Michael Jackson. He was a very nice man and his entourage occupied the entire 34th floor. He had his own security and chef. The security men were all big well-dressed black men and they were at all entrances and exits to the floor and I must say they were very professional. For Michael Jackson, the Housekeeping staff had to dismantle one of the bedrooms so that Michael could put his dance floor in there. I'm told that he would practice for hours on the dance floor in that bedroom. I met Sophia Loren and she left us a little memento of her visit. She planted a kiss on a napkin and the hotel kept it as a souvenir in the display cabinet.

Whilst still a Security Officer, I solved a couple of theft cases that had an impact on my hotel career. There had been a theft of a gold ladies watch from one of the rooms. The victim was a senior executive from a high profile US financial institution. The watch had great sentimental value for her, as well as a hefty price tag. At that time hotels were protected by the Innkeepers Act which extended their liability to just a couple of hundred dollars in the event of a theft. This law was unfair and one sided and I believe that it is still the case. This woman was beside herself with disappointment and very angry. She made it very clear that the hotel would lose all of her company's business if this watch was not found and returned to her. She saw it as a personal affront that she checked into a high profile hotel and then this is what happened. I was assigned the case but we all knew that it was like a case of 'finding a needle in the haystack'. In any event my partner, Stan Oldknow (since deceased - I'll tell you about him later) and I started searching the haystack. We knew for a fact who had been in the room; the maid who cleaned it; the houseman who delivered the sheets and supplies and the floor supervisor; all Housekeeping staff. The victim had not ordered any room service so we discounted that. It could also have been one of a number of staff that had to carry a master key to perform their day to day duties. For example, engineering staff had to have them to carry out their duties. However officially no one had been in the rooms except the three persons mentioned. I did something on a hunch and banking on a great deal of luck. I did not have a clue who stole the watch but interviewed each of the three Housekeeping staff separately. I told each of them that I knew who took it but was not interested in having that person charged. I just wanted to get the watch back. I told them that I did not want them to tell me if they took it or not. They must have thought that I was crazy. I explained if they didn't tell me they stole it, I couldn't charge anybody. Just to return it to the Chief of Security office and he would give it to me. I really emphasised how important this was for the hotel as a lot of business was riding on it. If we got her watch back, we may be able to salvage that business. What I then did was to give the three of them, three different ways to return it. As luck can sometimes fall your way, it was returned via courier on the following Monday from the Paddington Post Office. I then knew straight away who had sent it; it was the Houseman. I interviewed him and thanked him for returning the watch. He told us that he had a fight with his girlfriend and he stole the watch. He added that he gave it to her in an effort to placate her and make up. He said that after I had emphasised how important it was he felt very guilty and made the decision to return it. True to our word we did not call the Police into it but we did dismiss him. The GM just couldn't believe that we had solved the case (nor could I). He said that in all of his time in hotels, he had never seen anything like it. As a reward, he invited Sue and I to come and stay in a junior suite in the hotel and to have dinner in the hotel's fine dining restaurant Kables. I thanked him but also asked, "What about my workmate?" Stan got the same deal but not in a junior suite and not in the fine dining room. Sue and I joined Stan and his wife in the downstairs Lobby restaurant for dinner and forsook the fine dining. We were beginning to understand what luxury was all about. The 'Who's Who' of Sydney used the Regent Sydney as their number one hotel and you were forever seeing well-known Sydney social identities at functions, high tea or in the fine dining room. It really was a 'classy' hotel and if you wanted to be seen, this was the place to go.

Whilst I was working at the Regent Sydney, our son Dan was born. Even though Sue had promised me that we would not have children, there was not much I could do to stop her and when she announced that she was pregnant; I supported her. Dan was born at St Margaret's Hospital in Darlinghurst on 29 June 1986. I attended the birth of both of our children and was aghast at the pain that Sue had to go through for her first child in particular. I had no idea that it would be such a painful ordeal and if memory serves me correctly she was in labour for about twelve hours. Given that I had a bit of medical training, I asked the Doctor why Sue could not have an epidural to relieve the pain and assist her with the delivery. I recall one woman in the ward screaming out so loudly that everybody could hear her 'to get this f****** thing out of me' and that she could not stand it anymore. Let me assure you that the first time a woman has to give birth, it can be a very painful occurrence and husbands need to be with them to get them through it. In any event, the obstetrician agreed to give her the epidural and that settled things down a lot. An epidural is the insertion of a catheter into the lower back of the woman. It is done by an anaesthesiologist and he/she injects the area with numbing medicine and carefully guides the needle into the lower back. It delivers a continuous pain relief to the lower part of the body while allowing the patient to remain fully conscious. It significantly decreases the pain sensation but doesn't result in a total lack of feeling. I made sure that when Toni was born that Sue had an epidural; so much for having natural births. On both occasions, the obstetrician asked me if I wanted to cut the umbilical cord and I am happy to say that I took him up on it.

There is an interesting story around naming of the hotel's fine dining restaurant, Kables. The hotel is located at the end of George Street in The Rocks area of Sydney. The Rocks was the site of the first settlement in Australia in 1788 (one year before the French revolution). The story goes that the first white man to set foot on Sydney Cove was a convict named Henry Kable. He had been a butcher in his native country (England) and committed burglary. Initially he was sentenced to death but that was commuted because of his young age (18) and he was sentenced to penal servitude for fourteen years in Australia. He was originally meant to go to America but because of the American War of Independence, Britain had suspended convict transportation there. Well, they had to, didn't they? Instead he was sent to Australia and came out on the very first fleet. Because he was a big strong young fella he was selected to carry Governor Phillip from the row boat to the shore, so that the good Governor would not get his feet wet. That's the story and could well be right. Henry went onto become a model citizen and became a wealthy man in the new Sydney town. The restaurant was named after him because that is where he and his wife Susannah built their house and raised a family. A good friend of mine, Bill Kable is a direct descendant of Henry and Susannah Kable. There is an interesting book written about them entitled, 'The Raking of the Embers' by June Whittaker. Another interesting fact about Henry Kable was that he was the first convict to successfully sue a British Naval Officer. Henry came out on the first fleet on the ship, 'Alexander' and he, along with his future wife Susannah, sued the Captain, a bloke by the name of Duncan Sinclair for stealing their possessions during the voyage to Australia. The Court, under Governor Phillip's control, found in favour of Kable and the Captain was ordered to pay restitution to Henry Kable. Remarkable when you think about it. This was at a time in Sydney when people were being hanged for simple stealing offences and it was common for convicts to be lashed severely. Yet Phillip saw fit to make sure that even the convicts had their rights. Perhaps also he was a pragmatic man. He knew that at this time, the vast majority of the white inhabitants were white convicts and it may have been that he used this as leverage to keep law and order by showing that everyone was equally accountable to him under the law.

I had another interesting case with a staff member who committed a misdemeanour when I was an Assistant Manager. He was a room service waiter on the overnight shift and this night he was servicing one of the butler's suites on the 33rd level. The occupants had hired some hookers and they were having an orgy. They wanted him to be part of it. They offered him $1,000 (1983 currency) to service their room dressed only in a bow tie. He agreed to do it. Unfortunately for him, a butler spotted him and reported it to security, who reported it to me. He was a really good bloke but showed very poor judgement on this occasion. Something we all have done at some stage of our lives. He told me that the offer was too good to refuse. I didn't want to fire him but knowing the butler had spotted him, I had to. The correct procedure for firing was that we would send them home and have them come back the next day to the Human Resources Department. He did that and his dismissal was upheld. I took him aside on the way out and told him that if he wanted a verbal reference I would support him. I did get a phone call from another hotel and they wanted to employ him. They said that he had given me as a reference. I was after all an Assistant Manager of the hotel. I never mentioned the naked incident and told them he did a good job whilst he was employed at The Regent Sydney (which was true). When they asked me if I hire him again I said yes, definitely. That too would have been true. Just as well they did not ring the Human Resources Department for their reference check.

I mentioned my work mate, Stan Oldknow earlier. Stan was a super bloke but well past his prime. He migrated to Australia from Rhodesia and made a model citizen. One night I was talking with him when I was the AM on duty. He was very happy because he was going for his annual leave the following day. He had everything packed and even had his fishing rods on the top of his red falcon car. Later in the shift I got a call from the security office that they had an emergency. I immediately went there with our trainee manager, Gordon Fuller. The emergency was that Stan had collapsed in the security clerk's office and was cold stone dead on the floor. His body was positioned in such a way that staff could not see him on the way out. The Security Officer on duty had dropped his bundle temporarily so we had to settle him down and tell him what to do. It was about 4 a.m. We called the Police and arranged to inform his wife. I actually went out to their house and we informed her of the bad news. I told you before that this was the worst part of Police work and it was no different now. Naturally she took it very badly so we had to make provisions for her as well. The Executive Management of the hotel and all of the security Department, except those on duty, went to his funeral at Rookwood cemetery in western Sydney. Stan was only in his late 40s and died of a massive heart attack. He was very overweight and a heavy smoker; I doubt that he experienced any pain. This was almost a replica of the death of Ricky May that I also had to deal with.

As a footnote to this story, there was an incident in the Grand Hyatt Hotel in Hong Kong. In late 2007 cleaning staff found two male bodies in one of the rooms. The deceased men were Americans and the legal occupiers of the room. At first the Police suspected foul play but it turned out that they had taken overdoses of cocaine. They brought in a couple of hookers but the girls got out of there quickly once they saw that the men were frothing at the mouth. I was working in Hong Kong at the time and rang the hotel to try and make an appointment to sell them my security risk management services. I had a meeting with the chief of security and learnt who the GM was. I rang him and had coffee with him. He told me about first seeing the bodies in the room and his mind immediately flashed back to the death of the Security Officer when he was a Trainee Manager at the Regent Sydney. The GM was Gordon Fuller. Small world isn't it.

I made it known at the Regent Sydney that I felt that I would like to have a career in the international hotel business. It didn't fall on deaf ears. After about six months as a Security Officer I was called in to see the GM. He asked me if I would like to be an Assistant Managers(AM). The hotel had four Assistant Managers that covered the hotel 24/7, 365 days per year. The main function of the AM was to represent the GM when he was not there and often when he was there. Any problems, get the AM seemed to be the hotel's motto. We were the sort of Mr Fixit people. They offered me the job over an army of young people that were university graduates from the hotel teaching centres around the world. This put quite a few noses out of joint. They were young, mostly good looking and fitted into the image the hotel wanted to project and highly educated in hospitality management. People were querying my qualifications for such a reasonably high profile middle management job. They saw me a big fat ex-cop who did not have the smarts when it came to dress and style. The hotel had a newsletter for the staff and the GM felt that they should know why I was appointed. He wrote that I was appointed because I had demonstrated on a number of occasions, a clear sense of judgement in unusual situations and knew how to solve problems. That was the end of any disquiet and now I was a Hotel Assistant Manager. I couldn't believe it.

This new position exposed me to the day-to-day operations of the hotel. I grabbed the opportunity with both hands. I started doing internal and external courses. I learned as much as I could. I got a certificate in rooms division management from the Institute of the AH&LA (American Hotel and Lodging Association). I did an internal trainee management course in my own time. Part of that training exposed me to all parts of the hotel, including the kitchens and restaurants. I was fascinated by how the kitchens could churn out so many meals so quickly. I spent time with the fishmonger, the butchers, the cold kitchen, pastry chefs and so on. I learnt about portion control, menu planning, rostering, cleaning and sanitisation, cost control, purchasing, quality service and so on. Before too long, I was beginning to understand the 'game'. I also learned a great deal about the front office. How to check people in, how to check them out. I learned a lot about reservations and how to maximise the ARR (average room rate) and maximise occupancy levels. That is a real art that the Front Office Manager had to know; he had to get every room full without running into the problem of not having rooms for guaranteed reservations. He would often oversell by twenty rooms or so; banking on a certain number of non-guaranteed rooms not fronting. Sometimes he would even sell a guaranteed room which was poor form. In that situation the hotel would not only get the no-show guaranteed full rate, they would also get the full rate they sold the room for; 'double dipping' if you like. But business is business and they were trying to get every dollar they could and they did. Some people are very good at it.

One night when I was on duty, the hotel was completely full and a guaranteed reservation turned up and we obviously could not accommodate him. The thing is by law we had to because he had paid for a guaranteed reservation. If he had not turned up, the hotel would still be paid. I had to take the brunt of this bloke's fury and he was very angry. In these situations, you have to make arrangements to accommodate them in something comparable somewhere else. This situation had developed because of the Front Office Manager's oversight (and stupidity I believe). I managed to get a booking in a suite (which was an upgrade for him) at the Sydney Hilton and offered to have the hotel's Rolls Royce take him the short distance to the Hilton. He settled down and accepted my offer and withdrew his threats of taking legal action against us. At the beginning of the conversation he was most definitely going to do that and had every right to. It was just a matter of the hotel being too revenue aggressive and throwing the dice and losing.

Another time I had to deal with an American bloke who was not allowed into the Don Burrows Supper Club because he was dressed in jeans (designer jeans). Crikey, this fella really lost it so the staff called the Assistant Manager. I was always against the dress standards of the club thinking that they were not realistic to the needs of the hotel clientele. Nevertheless, the GM had determined that the strict dress code would stay in place and that was the end of it. I took along a Security Officer with me as I had been told that the client was being aggressive. I spoke with him and he really got stuck into me and was very personal. He told me that the jeans he was wearing would be worth more than the cheap s*** I had on and that his shirt and tie were whatever they were. This is the approach he took and I knew that there could only be one outcome with all of this. He was totally unreasonable and crossing the line, but he was not drunk. He was just so offended so I explained the fact that I did not have the power to change hotel policy and I could not ring the GM at this time of night over a dress code incident. I told him that I was willing to refund his room costs and he could make a booking in another hotel. Normally I would offer to do that but he was so rude to me, I decided that I wouldn't do anything more for him. I assured him that dressed as he was, he would not be going into the Club. Eventually after a fair amount of time he walked off and most likely went back to his room. These were the sorts of things that we regularly had to deal with and my Police training had me well equipped for it.

One New Year's Eve, we were fully booked as you would expect for a hotel on the harbour. Sydney is known for its NYE fireworks and this bloke came into reception and demanded a room. He fought with the male receptionist and they had to call me into it. He was another obnoxious bloke who felt that money could get whatever he wanted. You know, the nouveau riche type! He just could not believe that a hotel with 620 rooms did not have a spare room and he offered us, the receptionist and myself, $1,000 to get one for him. I was telling him the truth, we literally did not have a spare room, all 620 of them were occupied. His bribe offer didn't work and I ended up telling this fella that he would have to leave the hotel now as he was becoming too aggressive towards us. He told me to f*** off and I told him if he didn't go immediately, I would call the Police. You get this sort of thing a lot in hotels; the more upmarket the hotel is, the more likely you are to have to deal with this type of behaviour. The hotel was doing fabulously well and it was the talk of the town. The GM was a great marketer and promoter; not just promoting the hotel, but himself as well. He was regarded as the foremost leading hotelier in the country. As an Assistant Manager I would attend the DOMs (daily operations meetings) and the weekly DHM (Departmental heads meeting). It was a great learning curve for me and I was making serious in-roads into hotel management.

It wasn't all glamourous. Assistant Managers were constantly bombarded with problems. In those days we did not have the necessary software to write all our reports online. It all had to be done by handwriting in the AM log book. When we were on duty in the absence of the GM or the Hotel Manager (HM), we had to meet VIPs and personally escort them up to their rooms. On more than one occasion I would have to attend ballroom functions on behalf of the GM and thank the client. On one such occasion, I received a plaque from one of Australia's war ships that was having a formal dinner for about 600 people. It was no problem for me to get up on stage and do the thank-you bit. Probably because I am a rugby league buff, the following was one of my favourite meetings. The Queensland State of Origin team were staying in the hotel. That was very rare as the Regent Sydney normally did not take sporting teams because of the potential trouble they can give. The executive management were satisfied that the assurances given by the QRL (Queensland Rugby League) were adequate and they went ahead and sanctioned the booking. I was the AM on duty for the evening shift the night they stayed. They had just won the match in Sydney and clinched the series for 1984. I met with the team management and they discussed with me about having a private function in one of our function rooms. I am going back thirty-two years now and I may have some names wrong. I met firstly with the team Manager, Des (maybe Rod) Morris and Paul (maybe David) Green, the Captain of the Wynnum Manly team from Brisbane. I was taken aback with their good manners and courteous behaviour towards me. I spoke with Des for a couple of hours. David asked me if he could introduce the Queensland team to me, one by one. That's what we did. They all lined up and I shook hands with each one. When he came to Greg Dowling, Mr Dowling told me that he was Steve Ella (who was also with them). Of course Mr Dowling wouldn't think I knew the difference. He probably thought that I was just some 'full of himself' hotelier in my three piece tailor-made suit and he was just having a bit of a lark. I told him quote: "It's my pleasure to meet you Mr. Dowling". He must have wondered how I would have figured that out. I'd been watching them play for years but he didn't know that. The team was excellent and gave us no trouble at all. The only member of the team that I didn't meet was the King himself, Wally Lewis.

At some stage during my Assistant Manager's tenure, the position of Chief of Security came up. The GM wanted me to apply. I told him that I did not want to get out of hotel operations so we agreed that I would do a dual role - Chief of Security/ Assistant Manager. A condition on my taking the job was that the hotel would have to take away the guns from the security staff. It is difficult to believe that the security staff at that time were armed with concealable revolvers. I was very concerned about a number of issues with that. They did not have the proper training in the use of a firearm; nor did they have special powers to use them as Police do. Most of them had never been in a situation where the use of a firearm might be appropriate. I was also concerned that the firearm could be taken off them and turned against them. Most of all, I was concerned that they could shoot a member of the public without due course. The GM had an American attitude towards firearms and felt that the security staff had a right to be armed. It took me a great deal of time to convince him that the hotel's high profile positive image was at risk should a Security Officer discharge his firearm in the hotel. I think the point where I explained how the hotel's reputation and image could be seriously damaged with such a scenario won the day. He relented and much to the disappointment of some of the security staff, I got the job. On the very first day, within the first hour of that day, I issued a memorandum to the staff that from this point on whilst I was the Chief of Security, staff were not to carry firearms. They were to hand them in immediately. I think at the time the inventory was three revolvers. I locked them in a safe deposit box and made provisions for their license to be revoked. I told the GM that we should get rid of them and we did. I guess it's hard for many Americans to get their head around our view of guns generally and the GM needed to make that change now that he was in Australia.

Many things happened during my tenure as Chief of Security. One of the problems with security staff generally is that they become bored with the mundane duties they have to perform. That leads to a non-motivated staff and generally an unrewarding work environment that lacked imagination and creativity. I got the staff together and told them I wanted to upgrade the Department using our existing resources and make us more valuable to the hotel. I put a type of blueprint to them that had never been seen in a hotel in Australia previously. The initiatives were:

• That the security Department should take over the management of lost and found property from Housekeeping (that is actually a very big job);

- That the security Department should take over the control and ongoing management of all of the keys within the hotel, including all master keys from the engineering Department;
- That the security Department should set up a fire safety committee and the Chief of Security should chair these meetings;
- That the security Department carry out an audit of all life and fire safety equipment within the hotel at least once per week;
- That the security Department would work towards conducting a full scale emergency evacuation exercise of the hotel once per year;
- That the Security Officer on duty on the night shift would become the Night Manager (this one caused a few sighs from the management staff);
- That all security staff would be encouraged to do cross training in front office procedures to prepare them for the night manager's role;
- That random bag searches of staff would be carried out at least once per week;
- That the Chief of Security would conduct covert fire alarm exercises on the overnight shift without the knowledge of the Security Officer, now Night Manager on duty;
- That the Chief of Security would undertake formal training for the security staff in criminal investigation and incident reporting.

I presented this blueprint to the GM. As I expected, it got a lot of resistance from some of the conservatives but in the end the progressives (mainly the GM) won the day and I got it approved and moved forward with it. Initially some members of the Executive Committee were sceptical about the security staff becoming Night Managers so it was agreed that we would trial it over a period of three months. The security staff responded very positively to it. A couple had left because they did not accept my gun policy but they were easily replaced. Once the Security Officer became the Night Manager, they really got motivated and the Department was now seen as much more than 'a necessary evil'. We managed to turn an unrewarding work environment into a rewarding one and many of them went onto becoming security managers in other hotels. Luxurious five-star hotels generate their own stories and there are countless ones I can tell. Perhaps one of the saddest, apart from the death of Stan Oldknow, was the death of Ricky May. Ricky was an incredible jazz singer. In June of 1988 he had just done a performance in our Don Burrows Supper Club. When he got into the lift after the performance, he collapsed and died of a heart attack. He was only 44 and had only just recently become an Australian citizen.

During my tenure we also had a homicide of one of our staff, fortunately not in the hotel. Her name was Johanne Hatty. Johanne was one of our hostesses in the Kables restaurant that I mentioned before. After she finished work in the early hours of 18 February 1984 she said goodbye to the security staff and drove home to her apartment at Kurraba Point on the North side. Sometime after that she was strangled to death, sexually assaulted and left in a nearby reserve. An inquest confirmed she had been strangled with a rope, robbed and then sexually assaulted. This shook all of us to the core. We all knew her well and she was highly regarded. I liaised with the Homicide squad on a regular basis as we thought that the killer might have been a member of the staff. The case went cold for 21 years. We were all disappointed as the Police put in an incredible amount of work into it but got nowhere. In 2005 I was reading the SMH online in Singapore and read that the Police had made an arrest in relation to the case. I couldn't believe it. They had arrested a bloke by the name of David Graham Fleming. His DNA was found in a sperm swab taken from Johanne's body. Fleming had been a suspect at the time but the Police could not get any evidence to support a charge. He was living in a boarding house just 600 meters from Johanne's place. The Police believe that he strangled her as she got out of her car. He may have raped her after death. Fleming had form. He had been in prison in Queensland for rape and somehow had been accidentally shot. Unfortunately for the Police, DNA testing at the time was not sophisticated enough to identify Fleming. But they kept the swabs anyway in the right environment. He was convicted and sent to prison for 21 years.

It was during this period that I decided to take a trip to Cairns on my own in mid 1983 and all I wanted to see was the Great Barrier Reef. I had no contact with any of my family for years now but I did get an abusive letter from John many years before and he told me that he never wanted to have anything to do with me again. It's a shame I never kept the letter but basically he levelled a number of allegations against me but I really can't remember what they were. It did not bother me as I was now pretty much resigned to living my life with little to no contact with my 'family'. When I was in Cairns I saw a man with two little children at a phone booth on the wharf. I looked at him and said to myself, "It couldn't be could it?" I thought it might be John. He had a big red beard and was very overweight. I'd heard that he was living in the Cairns area and that he had separated from his wife. This man fitted the profile of a man who might have custody of the children for the weekend. I noted that he was calling from a pay telephone box of the type that is not enclosed. I got close enough to hear him speaking. Once I heard his voice I knew that it was John. I was not going to approach him, given his last correspondence to me years earlier. Fate intervened. We both got on the same boat to go to the same coral reef that turned out to be Michaelmas Cay. Once on the boat I had made a decision to approach him but wanted to do it delicately. I told the Captain of the boat what I was going to do and asked him to keep an eye on me as I approached this bloke. I went and sat down on the bench opposite him. I initiated some small talk, about the weather and things like that. He was quite relaxed with me talking to him so I said to him, "Have we ever met before?". He politely said, "Yes, I think I have seen you around". He didn't have a clue who I was. Then I told him, "I'm your brother Max". All he said was, "Bugger me, are you?" He shook my hand and it was clear that his earlier animosity has gone. I met his two children, Lisa aged 11 and Nigel, aged 9. We had a few beers and I stayed in Cairns an extra couple of days to spend time with him. We have more or less kept in contact ever since. He told me that Mum had told him certain things about me that upset him and that's why he wrote the nasty letter. To be fair to Mum, she may not have but that was his explanation.

Another successful case I was involved in when I was Chief of Security was the uncovering of a gang that were stealing large amounts of food and beverages from the hotel. Nobody in the hotel knew it; actually that was not quite right as it turned out. I had a phone call from an anonymous female who told me about a gang that were systemically stealing from the hotel and that hotel staff were involved. She would not give me any personal details about herself but the information appeared to be solid. Their modus operandi were that on selected Saturday mornings, they would drive a panel van into the loading dock of the hotel. One of the gang had a job at the hotel as a store man. Because it was Saturday the receiving dock would be very quiet with just a couple of deliveries of perishable items. What was happening was that the store man was taking expensive items out of the inventory stores and putting them on the loading dock. It was an ingenious system. No one would suspect him as this was his job; the only difference was it was going out instead of coming in. In those days it was rare for hotels to have cameras so there was no way to watch sensitive areas and besides the loading dock was closed on weekends. Once the store man had stockpiled what they were going to steal he would inform the other two members of the gang that it was all systems go, then he would lift the roller shutter and they would drive into the loading dock, fill up the vehicle and leave as casually as they liked. They had a cockatoo posted outside the hotel who had a clear view of the loading dock and the adjacent streets. A cockatoo is a colloquial Australian term for a person that is used as a lookout. I posted one of our men on an upper level floor and kept another with me in my office. This office was just around the corner from the loading dock, about a 25 meter sprint. I was to wait for the lady to call me when they were going to pull it off. She did that and our man on the upper floor had a clear view of the panel van entering the loading dock. We did not want to make our move until they had actually loaded the van and were in the process of leaving. He let us know that and we sprinted around to the dock and got them just as they were about to get on the street. My first reaction was to whip the keys out of the ignition. They were so startled that they did not react quickly enough. We arrested them and called The Rocks detectives. They had about $4,000-5,000 worth of stock in the vehicle (wholesale prices) and they admitted to us that they had been doing this for a while. They were selling the goods at a local pub at greatly reduced prices and had no problem getting rid off all the stuff they had stolen. They were all charged with the appropriate offences. The case was so watertight that they all pleaded guilty but there were aftermath ramifications. I will credit the crooks with having good taste and they at least knew quality when they stole it because the haul in the recovered items included bottles of Dom Perignon champagne, caviar, expensive wines and Cuban cigars. From that day on the Financial Controller developed a set against me and he was part of a group that eventually got rid of me, but that's for later. The GM was once again overly impressed with me and Sue and I got another free night at the Regent Sydney and dinner at Kables. He was very happy with me as his Chief of Security and he told me and others that I was the best Security Chief he had ever worked with. It was a great shame that I was later to have a falling out with him.

One of the threats that always concerns me in a high rise building is the risk of an uncontrolled fire. I rated it at the time as the highest security risk we had to deal with. The hotel had all the updated life and fire safety equipment in place. The Engineering Department used to test the emergency generator every week to make sure that all the life and safety equipment would work. Systems like the water pumps, communications, alarms, smoke detectors, sprinklers, UPS (uninterrupted power supply), etcetera, all had to be tested. We were fanatical about this. So much so, that I would come into the hotel in the early hours of the morning and with the permission of the city fire Department, trigger a smoke detector. I would always pick a high rise floor. I wanted to make sure that the Security Officer would attend in a timely manner. This meant that he had to be able to read the panel (which meant a run down to the basement), locate the alarm and go to the site to see if it was actually a fire or false alarm. We had all the procedures in place in the standard operating procedures manual. Having it on paper and actually doing it, are two very different things. At the beginning the responses were hopeless. In some cases it was ten minutes before the officer arrived; far too late in an actual fire situation. But over time, we improved and got the response down to under two minutes to anywhere in the hotel. Sometimes it was quicker. Once the staff knew that covert audits were taking place, they made sure they knew what to do. Collectively, we conducted the first emergency evacuation training exercise for an international hotel in Sydney; at least that is what the City Fire Department told me. With them over-seeing it, we carried it out but did not involve the guests. The evacuation procedures were full of details and 'the devil is in the detail.' Each area of the hotel had to carry out a set of procedures. An example of that was say in the kitchens; they had to turn the gas off. You could imagine a fully fledged fire raging in the hotel with the gas still on. The exercise went well and we were fully supported by the City Fire Department. I got another letter from the GM with an invitation for Sue and I to stay at the hotel and have dinner at Kables. These letters were mounting up and it was becoming a bit of a habit. What a shame that I did not keep all those references.

I knew that formal qualifications coupled with 'on the job' training was one of the key elements required for my hotel career to develop. Apart from doing an internal trainee management course with the hotel's Training Manager, I did courses with the American Hotel and Lodging Association. In my spare time, I would go to a Department and get hands-on experience. One day I worked with the fishmonger and all I did all day was peel prawns and by the end of it, I thought that I would be happy never to see a prawn again. This particular fishmonger was from Portugal and it was just amazing what he could do with a fish, especially his way of filleting them. I spent time with the cleaning stewards, front office reservations, accounts receivable and payable, the operations analyst, banqueting, valet, worked as a Commissionaire, cross trained in engineering, and so on. I really had a good look at all of the hotel's operations.

The good, the bad and the ugly stay at these luxurious hotels. I'll add one more to that — the mentally ill. On a number of occasions I had to deal with people that suffered from manic depressive psychosis. This is a very serious illness but can be controlled with lithium medication; if the patient takes it. The problem is that the patient feels so good that he/she decides they don't need it any more. Two cases come to mind. One was of a lady who had checked into one of the butler's suites. She had met the credit criteria and everything was in order, or so we thought. She started ordering several bottles of Dom Perignon champagne with plates of rock oysters. The thing was she was by herself so that raised a red flag and that's how I got involved in it. She was going through the 'manic' stage where the world is your oyster (literally in this case) and nothing is impossible. When someone is manic, they can feel energised like they are on an upper. They talk really quickly and everything speeds up. They can get involved in high risk activity and don't care about the consequences; like over-spending. That's as much as I know about it and I had this woman pegged as suffering from this unfortunate disease. I knew from my nursing and Police days that these people can become violent, especially when you try and stop them from doing something. I spoke to her in the company of a female guest relations officer and asked her why she wanted so much champagne and oysters. She said that was her business and indeed it was. I told her we had a 'duty of care' to our guests and suggested to her that she might be needing some medical help. Oddly enough, she told us that she had just been released from a psychiatric hospital and was celebrating. I think one of the reasons for my being appointed an Assistant Manager was that I could recognise the red flags and this was one such case. I knew that this lady was in serious trouble and that in turn, could lead to trouble for us. I told her the account had to be settled immediately and that once it went above a certain figure, it would again have to be settled. I also told her that even though I was not a medical professional, I thought she should get help. She thought that was a preposterous proposition. I needed a catalyst to do something for her. It came in the form of her credit card being rejected. I knew that when I told her this, she would behave very negatively; potentially violently. I had security on standby. She did react violently but we were ready for her. We restrained her as gently as we could and called the Police. They took her back to the hospital and from our perspective, the problem was solved.

The other case also involved a woman. I got a call that there were missing shoes that had been put out for the shoe-shine man to polish overnight; a common practice in deluxe hotels. It was in the early hours of the morning so I went up there with a Security Officer to investigate. The only thing that appeared out of the ordinary was noise coming from one of the rooms, at 3 a.m. I checked the guest folio and found out that it was a single older lady staying in the room. Because of the noise, we had an excuse to knock on the door. She opened it and was stark naked. We were of course taken aback by this; but not for long. She started coming towards us into the guest corridor. I told her abruptly to get back in her room and fortunately she did. I then instructed the Security Officer to quickly get one of the female front office staff up to the floor, which he did. This time she would not open the door so we opened it with a master key. She also got violent but we restrained her. Imagine restraining a completely naked woman in her luxurious room. In a situation like this, you'd better have your facts right as you are leaving yourself wide open to very serious allegations that she could have made; hence the reason for having the female staff member with us. This time we called our hotel doctor and the Police. The doctor administered a drug to sedate her and the Police scheduled her under the Mental Health Act. Not altogether surprisingly, the missing shoes were in her room.

The biggest problem we had for the hotel in security was hoodlum behavioural problems at the Rocks on Friday and Saturdays nights. We had to man the front of the hotel with up to six security people. I hired some detectives from Manly who were moonlighting on their nights off. They were excellent and at that time, the Police Force allowed off-duty Police to do this. They knew the law, what you could do and what you couldn't. If things were going the wrong way for them, all they had to do was tell the hoodlums they were from the Police. That usually did it. The hoodlum problem got so bad that we formed a committee with some of the Rocks businessmen and tried to do something about it but nothing really happened. There were often fights outside the front of the hotel and it didn't look good for our image. One day I met a former international boxer of some repute, who was friends with the GM; who wasn't? He was a great bloke and very charming. He reckoned he had the solution to my problems with the hoodlums. He told me that he would take on the job of controlling the door (which was actually three doors) on Friday and Saturday nights by himself and that I could get rid of everybody else. I didn't doubt him for a minute. He said that the hotel could pay him what it paid the other six security guards. Now the thing is I didn't know if he was serious or just having a joke with me. I had a chat with the GM about it and he quickly dismissed it. It was not in keeping with the image he wanted projected. I reckon this bloke could have kept the peace without too much trouble. I could see the headlines now, 'Former Champ assaults patrons at The Regent Sydney Hotel'. I just could not imagine that it would be the other way around, 'Hoodlums assault former Champion Boxer'. I think the GM was right; too much of a risk both for the hotel and the former champ. Having said that, I would have loved to have done it. Maybe he could have taught all my security staff how to fight properly.

One of the ugly ones I had to deal with was when a patron in the DBSC (Don Burrows Supper Club) attacked the Manager of the club. It was a busy Saturday night and this half drunk patron punched the Manager, Chris Stafford, on the jaw. I received a message about the assault but by this time the offender had left the club. He was close to exiting the hotel. I had a security chap with me and we bailed him up in the front driveway. This thug thought he could do the same with us but he got that wrong. In the ensuring struggle he was pinned down head first, with his face down on the bonnet of one of the luxury cars in the driveway. As it was a Saturday night, there were a lot of people about and as it so happened, even the GM. He and his party of senior managers, who happened to be in the lobby atrium, watched all this as it unfolded. Once we had subdued this bloke we took him up to the security office. He was a reasonably big fella but not really good with the rough stuff, when push came to shove. I think just another bully pushing vulnerable people around. We were in the office no more than a couple of minutes when I got a call from a detective asking us to be lenient with him. He used the usual argument. That he was helping them with some inquiry. Of course I knew that wouldn't be true. I bought Chris into it and gave him the option of charging this fella with assault or to leave it. I explained to Chris the pros and cons of doing that. I told him that it could get ugly and that blokes like him make all sorts of false allegations and he might be subjected to some stiff cross-examination. But on the other hand, the bloke should not be allowed to get away with it. In the end, Chris elected not to press charges and we let the bloke go. I didn't care one way or the other. We recorded it in our contemporaneous notes for possible future reference and made it clear to the bloke not to come back to the hotel ever again. I think he was fairly embarrassed that we had handled him relatively easy when he was supposed to be a big tough criminal. However, don't get me wrong. Some of these big tough criminals are big tough criminals but he wasn't one. This is an example of the type of incident security staff have to deal with from time to time. It is regrettable that it had to be on display in main driveway but we really did not have any other alternative. Incidentally the club was named after Don Burrows who was an outstanding jazz and swing musician who won the Handel Music Prize. It's interesting that we had a fine dining room named after a convict and a supper club named after a world famous jazz musician. I used to go and listen to him when he was playing at the DBSC and he was quite outstanding. I loved his music.

Many years later I audited some hotels in Singapore for the Singapore Government. Of course I am not about to comment on any of the findings in the audit as that would be unprofessional and also breaching confidentiality. This particular hotel was the hotel of choice that the Police used when they had high profile guests staying in Singapore. The President of the USA used this hotel when he was in South East Asia. It was generally considered the hotel with the best security for this type of assignment. When I summarised all of the hotels within the assignment, this was also my conclusion. There was an interesting case at the hotel that bears mention whilst talking on the subject of guest room theft. It is a public matter, easy to read on the internet and nothing to do with my audit. A female American multi-millionaire sued the hotel believing that a $220,000 diamond ring had been stolen during her stay at the hotel in 2009. She gave evidence that she put the ring on the dressing table of her bedroom after she let two hotel staff come into the room — a massage therapist and her assistant. She added that she went into the en-suite to change for the massage and whilst she was doing this, the assistant set up the massage table and left. The masseur left after finishing the massage. A couple of hours later a butler delivered her room service while she was in the shower. Sometime after that she discovered her ring missing. She blamed the loss on negligent hotel staff and made the accusation that one of the hotel staff had stolen the ring. The matter went to a Singapore Court after the hotel refused to accept liability. She lost. The presiding Judge found too many discrepancies and inconsistencies in her evidence and there was no compelling evidence that she even brought the ring into Singapore. The Judge also explained that the hotel would only have been liable for a maximum claim of $500 under the Innkeepers Act which limits liability. The fact that she lost the case does not mean that what she was saying was not true. Maybe she just did not have enough evidence to prosecute it. All the Judge can do is rule on the evidence presented. She just did not have a strong enough case. In law is it always a case of 'he who asserts must prove'. This case shows that an allegation of room theft is a two-edged sword.

There are many cases of guests making false claims in order to obtain insurance payouts and/or get some form of compensation. The most common one is that guests will claim that something was stolen from their room, usually cash (when it wasn't). To avoid litigation and adopting a policy of appeasement, the hotel will often waive all their costs for the stay. To make a complaint like this is considered a 'good con'. On the other hand, it could be a genuine claim; like the lady I told you about with the gold watch that was stolen from her room. How do you determine if they are telling the truth or if it is a 'con'? It can be difficult and requires a competent investigator who can find an inconsistency or a discrepancy in the victim's statement. During my tenure we had a number of hyperbolic claims where we just did not believe the guest's story and refused to give them any sort of a payout. Their option was then to report it to the Police for insurance purposes and we would facilitate that if required. The other scenario was where guests would honestly believe they were telling the truth but they were confused. We had a lady who was connected with a major luxury cruise line that used the Regent Sydney for their stopover in Sydney. You can imagine the hundreds of rooms these high end travellers would use. They were very important guests and the cruise line was a highly regarded client. Certainly one we would not want to lose. This lady claimed that a number of traveller's cheques were stolen from her suitcase in the room and used the usual threat that she would withdraw future business if she was not compensated. She really got very angry about it and left the hotel in no doubt that she would take it to the highest level. When I was interviewing these people I would let them know that I was a competent trained investigator and that I formerly worked with the state Criminal Investigation Branch. I wanted them to know that we would do our best for them. She later (after one day out to sea) contacted the hotel to tell us that she had found the missing cheques in another part of her cabin. She had temporary amnesia and had just forgotten she had transferred them to a safe haven. Thank goodness, she had the decency to let us know.

I did have a case when I was working security for the cruise lines whilst in the cops and forgot to mention it before. One time, I think it was on the Sitmar line, this family reported that a valuable camera was missing from their cabin. Their assertion was that the room steward must have taken it. The wife was very distraught and because of that the husband was aggressive and demanding action. I interviewed them and asked when did she last see the camera? She told me that she clearly remembered carrying it on board so that she could take photos of their departure. I asked her how she carried it on board and she said that she had it on her left shoulder. Her husband and both of her children confirmed this. They then went to their cabin, left all their luggage there including the camera and when they came back it was gone. Seems simple enough but these things are never as simple as they may seem to be. Then I had an inspired thought. I asked them if they had their photo taken when they were boarding the ship like most people do. It's a bit of a racket for the photographer but all above board (pardon the pun). They said that they had but had not yet received the photos. I told them that on the basis of what they had told me thus far, the photo would show that she was carrying the camera. I had no doubt that this would be the case and told them so. But we investigators have to do our homework and make sure we uncover all of the pertinent facts. We looked at the photos upstairs that had just been put up and there was this lovely photo of them boarding the ship at the top of the gangplank. You can guess the rest. I was able to debunk their story about her carrying it on board at least in the manner they had said she had. It gets even more interesting. I borrowed a magnifying glass from the photographer and we were able to see the strap mark over the left shoulder of her jacket where something had been hanging. Then the penny dropped for the lady who said, "Oh my God, I must have left it in the taxi." I telexed the Pillage Squad (Water Police), gave them the details and asked them to follow up. They did this very quickly and were able to report that the driver of the taxi had handed it into lost and found property for the taxi company. These people just could not believe how this panned out. They were very embarrassed and totally apologetic. The Captain of the ship told the Purser to waive our drink accounts for the trip. For that little job, we drank free for the whole journey. I often tell this story when I am giving my lectures on hotel security. What appears to be cut and dried is not always so and investigators need to look at all the angles. This family just could not believe how I solved this case but when you think about it, isn't it just common sense?

Most International branded hotels these days take the view that they provide adequate security and don't accept liability. They have initiatives such as electronic locking systems on guest room doors; double deadlocks, in-room safes and safe deposit boxes at reception. It's worthwhile to note that somebody on the hotel's staff holds a key to the in-room safe in the event you forget the combination. That is a security vulnerability and if the hotel does not provide safe deposit boxes, a potential victim would have a stronger case. An in-room safe is not a safety deposit box. As an Assistant Manager the problems with the air conditioning was the most common complaint that we had to deal with. To compound it, there wasn't a great deal that we could do about it. The rooms did not have individual air conditioning units. They were all serviced by a central cooling system and an individual room could not adjust it if they wanted to make it hotter or colder, whatever the case may be. We were forever having to deal with this. Of course, all these design flaw matters have long ago been dealt with but at the time, it was difficult to deal with as an Assistant Manager. We bore the brunt of it.

One of the more interesting matters that I dealt with was the way that an individual cashier could extract money from departing guests. He would ask the guest when they were settling their account, if they wanted to leave a gratuity 'for the staff'. The words 'for the staff' became highly significant when the s*** hit the fan. This bloke was extraordinary at extracting these tips. You can imagine that many of the accounts may be for a couple of thousand dollars. He would just talk to the guests like it was normal for tips to be left 'for the staff'. Often they would, especially the Americans. However when I got wind of this, I wanted to stamp it out and get rid of him. To me he was like that taxi driver that ripped me on taking me to the illegal casino. The senior management were not too perturbed about it.

They argued that he wasn't doing anything illegal but they accepted that it was unethical. This fella was making a fortune and he wasn't sharing the tips with anybody. Talk about Police corruption. I did win the day in the end. I argued that it could backfire on the hotel and tarnish our reputation. That is always a key selling point. He was told to leave in the end but never gave any of the 'tips for the staff' to anyone but himself. He could make hundreds of dollars a day, just like that.

On the domestic front all was well. By 1986 I had been free from depression and off medication now for fifteen years and had not spoken to a Psychiatrist since I had left nursing in 1975. I was doing well and talked with the Human Resources Department about career development. The Regent International hotel group only had twelve hotels worldwide, so corporate promotion was unlikely. I felt that I had to get into operations full time. I took a demotion to the role of Assistant Executive Housekeeper and worked with a very fine Executive Housekeeper, Ellen ter Hoven, a Dutch lady. She taught me the ropes. Housekeeping is by far the largest Department in the hotel. If you can imagine the hotel running at 100% occupancy, which it often was, that meant that there had to be 620 rooms and suites cleaned every day. Each room had king size beds with three sheets and four pillows on them. These had to be changed every day, irrespective of how long the guests were staying. This is what 5-star plus standards are all about. Then at night time we had to provide a turn down service for all the rooms. We had an internal laundry so you can imagine how busy that was. Having to wash and iron 1,800 sheets and a similar number of pillows cases every day. All the towels were terry towelling and there were four in each room, plus two bathrobes. I think we had about 150 staff and I do remember we had a $10 million operating budget. Ellen left not long and her position became available. Then they had to decide who to replace her with. In the end, they decided to run with me and I became the Executive Housekeeper in 1987. There was a lot of debate around my promotion to this position by the executive committee (ExCom). Just to make it easier to understand, the ExCom consisted of the GM, HM, the

Director of F&B, the Director of F&B, the Director of Human Resources and the Financial Controller. The GM was backing me but had little support from the rest of the committee. They argued that I did not have the necessary experience and that it was essentially a job for a woman or a gay man. In the end the GM had his way and I got the job.

Now I ran the biggest Department in the hotel which was the largest and most luxurious hotel in Australia. The Regent Sydney consistently won the nation's tourism award for best accommodation. It was only five years previously that I started as a Security Officer with no hotel experience at all. The Housekeeping Department's main responsibilities were:

- The cleaning of all the guest rooms;
- The turn down service for all guest rooms;
- The laundry for all of the hotel's linen;
- The valet service for all of the hotel guest's dry cleaning and staff uniforms;
- The maintenance of all of the hotel's linen and uniform room inventory;
- The cleaning of the hotel's public spaces;
- Liaising with all of the relevant service providers servicing the hotel;
- Responsible for the ongoing maintenance of the guest rooms with engineering;
- Responsible for the human resource management of approximately 150 staff;
- Submission of the monthly profit and loss statements;
- Conducting stocktaking of all of the hotel's linen and uniforms;
- Submitting five rooms per day for executive inspections;
- Conducting interviews with potential employees;
- Preparing productivity reports;
- Overseeing procedures to ensure OH& S standards were maintained;
- Working towards maintaining quality and quantity standards;
- Providing support for special projects, (room renovations).

Submitting five rooms per day for inspection was an interesting one. Every weekday, a group of us would meet just before 2 p.m. at a designated place for guest room inspection. The group consisted of the GM and/or the HM; the Chief Engineer; the Assistant Manager on duty, the Front Office Manager(FOM), the Executive Housekeeper and the Floor Housekeeping Supervisor. Just prior to the meeting the FOM would take five rooms that were showing VC status (vacant clean) out of the system and change the status to OOO (out of order). These would be the five rooms that we would inspect and nobody knew beforehand which ones they would be. We would contact the Floor Supervisor and ask her to join us on the inspection. The room was gone through in an obsessional detail. If anyone could find a speck of dust, it was noted. Any minor defect was observed. Everything was checked. Were the right creases in the bed; was the teaspoon at the right angle on the saucer; were the guest supplies X number of inches from the wall; were the towels hung so that they were in a complete straight line, etcetera. It was overly obsessional and of course, Housekeeping took the brunt of it. I had seen a number of occasions where the Floor Supervisor would start crying. When I think back, it was unfair. You had all these management staff trying to impress the boss and that usually did not augur well for the Housekeeping staff. It did however maintain the very high quality standards the hotel became renowned for. It did nothing to improve the high turnover of staff and staff morale generally. Anything but perfect was not good enough. That was all very well for those who were not scrutinised. The Housekeeper in a sense was the punching bag of the hotel and was often discredited and marginalised unnecessarily. I found this out to my detriment when I took over the role.

You can see that the Executive Housekeeper role is a very demanding role. The Housekeeping Department of a large international hotel is the busiest and least appreciated Department in the whole organisation. If you can run a large Housekeeping Department, you can run anything. Initially everything went well and the GM was able to say to the members of ExCom, "I told you so". At the end of the first year, I had my yearly appraisal with the HM which was also vetted by the GM. My appraisal was rated as a good performance and I was given a pay rise. Not long after that things started to go wrong. I mentioned earlier that I liked the rugby league. Housekeeping was no nine to five job and I regularly used to come in on Saturdays. I felt that there would be no harm in me watching the game in an out of order room. Sometimes if it wasn't too busy I would watch a game on a Saturday afternoon. One time the gay AM on duty found out about this from another gay fella in Housekeeping and reported me to the GM. You see, these gay guys can be worse than women if they have a mind to be. The GM had a chat with me and talked about the boss setting the standards. He told me that I needed to adjust my culture to fit in more with the hotel environment. If it was not good enough for a staff member to do it, it wasn't good enough for the manager. Fair enough, so that put an end to that. In future all I did was go home earlier and watch it at home or I'd get Sue to videotape it. You can appreciate in a hotel with the profile that the Regent Sydney had, it would also have a great deal of political manoeuvring going on.

The GM wanted me to do a feasibility study on the possibility of providing fine dining room service to the Butler's suites on the 33rd and 34th floors. He suggested that I stay at the Royal Suite with Sue and Dan (our new little boy). The Royal Suite was the next step down from the Presidential Suite and was really luxurious. So, we checked in and I arranged with Kables fine dining Restaurant to set up dinner in the suite, as if it were room service and I would do an evaluation of it. Well, it did not go according to plan. Sue was a very gregarious person, with an engaging personality and liked a drink. She invited a couple of people in and did her usual trick with the booze — drank too much. Dan was sick on a very expensive rug. One of our guests went to sleep on the toilet. By the time dinner arrived, everybody except me, was under the weather and it ruined what should have been a nice romantic weekend. The food standard and service was excellent and I reported that to that to the GM. I was

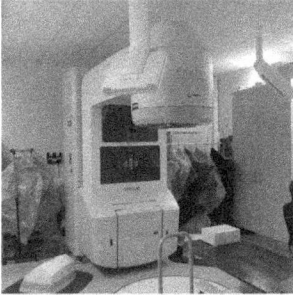

The linear accelerator for my EBRT Treatment

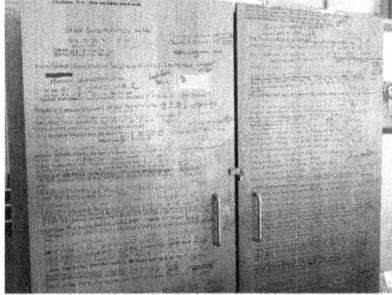

A historical monument at the SCG where I worked.

MM as a Doorman on the Indian Dressing room in 2016

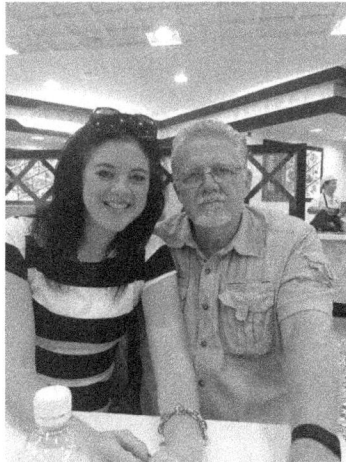

Daughter and Father in Singapore 2015

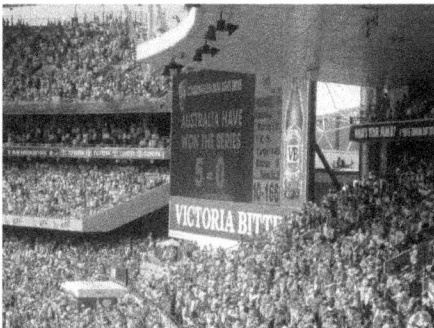

What a great day! Australia wraps up the Ashes 5-0 at the SCG 2014. I had to work with the Barmy Army. They were great.

really disappointed that it turned out this way. I told the GM that I didn't think it was a good idea to offer fine dining as a room service option because of the logistics involved and the multiple options that the hotel offered for dinner anyway.

During this time I was approached by Professor John Cox from Hawaii. Chris Stafford had been a student of his at the hotel school in Hawaii many years earlier and Chris bought us together. He interviewed me and we discussed my career aspirations in the hotel industry. He was a really good bloke and I thought it would be great to work with him. He offered both Chris and I jobs in separate hotels. Chris was offered the GM of the Radisson Hotel in Cairns. I don't know why he did not take it but I think it was for domestic reasons. I was offered the Executive Assistant Manager's role at the Radisson in Port Douglas. That would have made me number two in the pecking order after the GM. It really was a great opportunity and I had been to Port Douglas and really liked it. The hotel would have provided us with excellent villa fully furnished accommodation with all the benefits. I can't remember the wages but in these positions, you get good perks. Things such as free meals, free laundry, entertainment account, discounted prices for beverage, free car parking, free valet service and heavily discounted room rates in their hotels for the whole family when travelling, either domestically or overseas. I discussed it with Sue and she was dead-set against it. We had recently bought a new home and she loved it there. She did not want to leave her job. Most of all, she did not want to work in the tropics where she was convinced that everybody there suffered from diseases relating to the excessive heat and humidity. She quoted malaria, dengue fever, cholera, typhoid fever, etcetera. I lost the argument and did not accept the offer. John basically dumped me after that and I don't blame him. If I had gone ahead with it, goodness knows how far up the chain I might have gone. At the very least I would have been a GM of one of their hotels worldwide within five years. Radisson is a strong global player in the 5-star hotel market and a very strong brand. It was an opportunity lost. This happened before all the covert political rubbish at the hotel became overt. At this point in time, I was still riding high and doing well. Bottom line is that I should have taken that job offer and I deeply regret that I didn't. They say you should not have any regrets but I think that's balderdash. This is certainly one of mine that rates highly. It was an opportunity that would only come once to me and I did not take it.

One Saturday I was in the hotel late in the day because the ironing roller had broken down in the laundry. I was not watching the rugby and I didn't want to go home until it was fixed. Whilst I was waiting I asked the Assistant Manager on duty to join me at the Lobby restaurant for dinner. His name was Ron and he used to work with me in security. He accepted the offer and we met in the Lobby restaurant. One thing led to another and we had a bottle of Yellow Glen wine. As a Departmental head I was able to drink in the hotel and get 50% discount, in fact so was he, but not while he was on duty. The conversation flowed and so did the wine. Ron was getting louder and louder. We ended up drinking four bottles between the two of us. Ron was now intoxicated on duty. I was not on duty and not drunk, but setting a bad example in front of the staff. The GM was a teetotaller and did not like his troops drinking too much in the hotel, even when they were off duty. I went to check that the ironing roller had been fixed and thought no more of it. I got a call on Sunday from the HM telling me that he wanted to see me the next day in his office. I suspected it was about our drinking in the restaurant on Saturday. I rang Ron and he told me he was fired on the spot on Sunday morning when the HM came to work. Now, I felt that they might have to be consistent and fire me as well. I found out later that this is just what he wanted to do but the GM wouldn't let him. I saw him on Monday and he asked me why he should not fire me. I told him it would not be right and I would consider it an unfair dismissal. I argued that I was not Ron's keeper and therefore not responsible for what he might or might not do. I also argued that I was entitled to drink in the hotel and that I was not drunk. He asked me how was it possible to drink four bottles of wine and still be sober. I told him it was easy. That I was a seasoned drinker and in the Police we used to drink much more than that and still do our job. I also told him I drove home. He decided that I would be given a written warning but not sacked. He didn't tell me that it was not his decision. So now I had lost the support of the number two and three in the management pecking order: the Financial Controller and the Hotel Manager.

They had a system in the hotel whereby they would invite guests to comment on the hotel, good or bad. Naturally, it was usually the Housekeeping Department that got the most negative comments. Complaints like the water was not hot enough; the maid knocked on her door when the guest was still in bed; there was a speck (almost microscopic) of dust in the bathroom; the public toilets did not have enough towels, etcetera. You get the idea. The GM would read the guest comments out at the weekly operations meetings and of course, I had to face the music. Sometime later the HM sent me a stinging letter, outlining what things I was doing wrong and basically telling me to get my act together. It was only months before that he had done a very good appraisal of me. He was constantly complaining about the cleaning contractors and the standard of cleaning in the public areas of the hotel. I took that to mean he was not happy with the existing contract cleaners. Whilst he was away, the Director of F&B took over his role and she was a really nice lady. I discussed his ongoing complaints with her and told her that the contract was now expired and we had the opportunity to have a look at others. She agreed and I went about the business of finding a new contract cleaner for the hotel. I did and recommended my findings to her in her acting HM role and she approved it. Now it gets political. The CEO of the now fired contract cleaners had a strong connection with the GM like everybody else did. The GM went into bat for him and made me rescind the contract. I was very unhappy with this and did not want to do it. Well, that is one I was sure to lose wasn't it? I did. Now I had lost the support of the GM. I knew that my days were numbered and resigned on a matter of principle. I had gone through the right channels for the new contract and did not do anything that was not in the best interests of the hotel. Rumours floated around that I had been bribed but they were way off the mark. The company that I gave the contract to spoke with me about it when the contracts expired and he asked if they could 'throw their hat in the ring.' I told him he could, why not? Soon after that, I resigned and gave three months' notice.

It was bad timing for me. Sue had just given birth to our second child Toni on 24 March 2009. We had bought a new house in North Randwick and were saddled with a hefty mortgage but I resigned anyway. I was not going to go back on my word and told them that. My assassins were delighted. I now had no job. My career development plan had come to a sudden halt. Just a couple of short months before, I had turned down a golden opportunity with the Radisson Group up in beautiful Port Douglas. The Regent Sydney taught me a great deal; some of which I have put into practice since. I do feel that the GM himself lost his way in the end before he went back to his home country. In his prime he was an outstanding hotelier, probably the best in the country and a staunch supporter of me (except at the end). I think I'd prefer to remember him for that.

The HM got the Housekeeper he wanted. Things didn't go right, right from the start. The feedback given to me, plus what I read in the newspapers, was that the new Housekeeper had a very different style to me and one thing lead to another. I don't know really what happened but the staff went on strike for a few days and the proverbial s*** had now really hit the fan. Unfortunately, the ExCom staff thought that the strike had my imprint on it. There's that political rubbish again. Nothing could have been further from the truth. Once I had left the hotel, I really had lost contact with everybody that worked there. The reasons for the strike were entirely internal and I had absolutely nothing to do with it. It must have been a serious embarrassment for the hotel and I understand that, but don't put the blame on me. The strike was plastered all over the news but eventually peace was restored. However in the process I was defamed, a couple of times. The GM said on national radio that the new Housekeeper had inherited a lot of problems. That could only mean that she had to clean up a mess left by her predecessor and that was me. A Barrister cousin of mine rang me and told me he had heard it. He also said he thought it might be defamation. The GM said that staff resented the new Housekeeper's approach to installing quality standards and her form of discipline. I saw a specialist defamation lawyer and he told me that it was his view that I had been defamed. I got a second opinion and he also thought the same. The problem was my inherent distrust of lawyers and their sometimes mercenary approach to practicing the law. I had seen a lot of them when I was a cop so I had a fair handle on them. He was willing to take it on at $300 per hour and remember this was 1989 rates. I had a long think about it but at the end of the day, I did not have confidence in the lawyers; also I was now with no job, a new baby and a big mortgage. I really was not in a financial position to go down the long and uncertain track of defamation. Defamation is essentially the domain of the wealthy but I think in all probability if I had pursued it, the GM would have settled out of court for an amount that might have compensated me but I couldn't risk it. I balanced everything up and decided not to proceed with it. It was the right decision. Imagine if I had lost but than again, imagine if I had won!

This was more or less the end of my hotel career. I had done exceedingly well in such a short time but hit this hurdle on my career path. I spent seven years of my life at the hotel. As I told you, the GM told me that I was the most competent Chief of Security he had ever worked with so it was very disappointing for me to leave on such a sour note. I wonder where I would have been today if I had stayed as the Chief of Security. I could well have been the global head of security for a major hotel corporation. I certainly have it in me to do that. However, after letting the defamation die, I did move on and started up a contract cleaning company in Sydney in 1990. Overall I enjoyed my time at the Regent Sydney and had a great time there. I have developed something that Chris and I call 'the briefing box'. It's a management program that allows senior hotel management to keep their finger on the pulse in relation to maintaining all of the quality standards throughout the hotel. It includes quality standards relating to service, cleanliness, safety & security, maintenance, human resources and image. When I was presenting it to Chris to take out into the market place (April 2016) I told him how lucky he and I were to have worked at the Regent Sydney because it was there that we learnt the true value and culture of a 5-star establishment that really did have fantastic quality standards across the board. We really had the GM to thank for that. I was proud to be part of a team that went through the opening of the hotel and during the time that I was there, I held four senior management positions: Assistant Manager, Chief of Security, Assistant Executive Housekeeper and Executive Housekeeper. The political rubbish was a shame but that's life I suppose. The truth is that I have never been a very good politician.

As part of the management team, I had to attend a top team seminar every year. The most notable one was when we all went to Peppers up in the Hunter Valley. There were about twenty of us and no expenses were spared. We ate the best foods and drank the best wine. This particular seminar centred around exploring how other people saw you and it was entitled, 'To see yourself as others see you'. Before we went on the seminar, each member of the team would be evaluated by ten (or was it 5) members of the staff. The staff were not chosen by the management team member and could be anybody in the hotel. All up, including the part time staff there were about 800 staff members. The staff filled in their questionnaires which were based on questions that gave five options, e.g., excellent, good, fair, ordinary and bad. These questionnaires went sent off to America and the results were computer generated but not shown to us until the seminar. Basically the seminar facilitator said that we all fitted into one of four types of personality. We may have characteristics of all of them but we were predominately one. The four types were a promoter, a supporter, an analyser and a controller. Broadly speaking the promoters were seen as the outgoing, gregarious types who were found in the sales and marketing fields, the people that were good at selling something.

The supporters were people that liked to help other people and they could be found in the roles of secretaries and the like. The analysers were the thinkers, the people that pay attention to detail and these can be found in finance and cost control. The controllers were the people that liked to be the boss and were ambitious and you saw these in junior to senior management positions. Of course it's much more than that but that is a broad outline of the personality types we were looking at.

The matrix looked at the good and negative points of each type and the idea was that when you were interacting with each other, you knew basically what turned them on and what turned them off. If for example you were dealing with a promoter, it was a good idea to tell them good things about themselves. They wanted praise and wanted to be seen as the people that drove things. Fill all those rooms up every night for example. It was always good to tell them how good they looked, they loved being noticed; nothing wrong with that. The big negative for the promoter was that they could be perceived as having too much bulls*** in them and were false. The supporters wanted to be seen as 'I'm always there for you, all you have to do it ask'. The overwhelming positive was that once given a direction, they'd get it done. The negative was that they needed to be liked too much and spent their life making sure they did not offend anybody. Remember the hidden compulsions I talked about when I was describing pure obsessional disorder. The analysers were seen as those people getting things right, especially financial statements and paying a lot of attention to detail. The negative was that they spent too much time on the detail and it took forever to get a decision from them and that stifled creativity and innovation. The controllers were seen as people that got things done quickly and were very decisive people. They were result driven and not frightened to have a crack at difficult assignments. The negative was that they could be too overbearing, too impatient and too demanding. Well, I had to fit into one of these. The facilitator saw me as a supporter but the staff results showed differently. I came out as a controller. The measurement was from 1-20 on the matrix; 1-5 was a promoter,

6-10 a supporter, 11-15 an analyser and 16-20 a controller. I was rated an 18. There was only one other person in the group that had a higher score and he was 19. Guess what? He was the HM. It seems that the law of physics that like repels and unlike attracts applies to human relationships as well. The best combination was a controller with a supporter and a promoter with an analyser. The second part of the exercise was to determine your level of flexibility. That was rated from 1-4, with one being very inflexible and upwards to highly flexible. On this, the staff rated me as highly flexible. So that was it and I was the only one that got that rating, which could be both good and not so good depending on how you looked at it. So I was a flexible controller which surprised me a bit and I might have picked up some of those controlling characteristics from my mother and the flexibility bits from my Dad. The GM told me after the seminar not to be too flexible. He didn't want his Chief of Security going too soft on the staff. I assured him I wouldn't.

We all have our regrets, even those that say they don't. After over seven years at The Regent Sydney, I left with a wine decanter as a present and no extra pay. I realise how important it is to be able to communicate and network effectively and to always try to exude self-confidence. The Regent Sydney was top class (I hate using that word class) hotel and its senior management were people that were international, very well dressed, stylish, exuded confidence, were well mannered and behaved in a bit of a superior manner without being rude or condescending to others. When I look back, I now realise that I did not fit into the mould of the senior executive of a large luxurious international hotel. I just didn't have that certain panache required for this type of position. That is not to say that I could not have obtained it. In some areas I was better at the social graces than they were. The other area I outshone them was my impeccable table manners. You will remember me telling you how Mum used to drill that into me day after day after day in the early years about the need to have good table manners. I had the ability but at the end of the day, I did not have the image that was required. Nor did I have the confidence when dealing with people in authority or people that were celebrities and I alluded to that in detail earlier when dealing with depression but I was getting much better with that and I have no doubt now that I would have succeeded, even on the confidence front. I suppose deep down I felt that they were better than me and that reflected in the way I dealt with them. The thing is that I should not have thought that because it isn't true and never has been. I think that was a real shame. It's very hard to put into words. I felt very comfortable in the company of cops, because I felt like one of them. I did not feel comfortable when I was in the company of the top hotel executives at the start but as I said, I was getting much better. I was aware that I did not dress as well as they did; that I did not have the style they did; that I did not have the hotel experience that they did and I did not have that most important quality of all that is required at the top level, supreme confidence, but I was getting it. It is not to say for a moment that they were better people than me, far from it, but they were more suited to the international hotel business than I was. Maybe some of those social phobia elements would come out in these situations.

Confidence is the huge thing or at least appearing to be confident. I am talking about confidence in dealing with people. I am not talking about confidence in my ability to do the job. I had plenty of that but it is more about confidence in relationships with other people, especially people in authority. If you are confident, it will show and people will gravitate towards you much more readily and have more confidence in you. If you are not confident, that will also show in a negative way. I know I carried with me the sins of the past and at times it showed that I was introverted, unassuming and lacked confidence. I had an inherent distrust of people generally and I'm sure that this came through in my relationships with executive management. I guess I did not feel like that I belonged to this group of people. Fair enough if that were so; at least I would understand that.

I can be specific about that because Toni was born in March and I was at the hotel then. As I said, it was a shame that it ended the

MM as the PT Instructor
on SS Arcadia - 1976

The World Trade Centre in NYC
from the 5th floor of the Hilton
on my visit there in 2007

A border crossing between
Burma and Thailand

A damaged house beyond
repair from the 2011
Christchurch. I estimate that I
assessed over 500 houses

The fastest train I have ever
been on; to the airport at
Shanghai in 2006 - 431 Kph.

The front row in my bar at
Singapore in 2002.

Our Team for the Beijing Olympics, that's me, second front right - 2008.

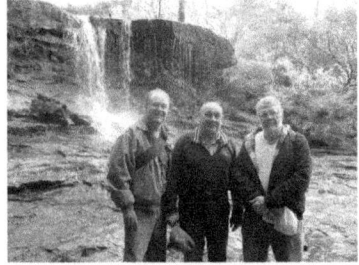

My enduring guardians, Geoff Bright middle and Bill Kable on the left - 2015

Our team building an electric fence at Johor in Malaysia-2010

MM in the Commandos 1975

The best friends any man could have. Poonam on the left, Chris Stafford on the right

The TurkishAmbassador
and MM during the Anzac
day services at Kranji War
Memorial Services in 2001

The French Guillotine had
extensive use in Vietnam -
Saigon - 2014

I shed a few kilos on these
stairs - Bukit Timah Nature
Reserve - Singapore

Poonam on one of the few trips
to Svdnev 2014

Poonam and I hot air
ballooning Over the rice
paddies of Chiang Mai in
2013.

way that it did and if I had been a lot smarter, I could have avoided it. I believe that I could have negotiated a transfer back to Chief of Security, when the position next became available and who knows where that could have lead me to. When I got the stinging letter from the HM, I should have sat down with him and spoke about. When the FC turned against me, I should have been smart enough to win him back. As I wrote earlier, it would have been conceivable that I might have become the Global Head of Security for a big multi-national hotel brand like the Hyatt, Hilton, Sheraton, Marriott, Four Seasons, and so on. After spending seven years at the Regent Sydney and holding down four separate management positions I left with nothing. If I had been dismissed, they would have had to pay me at least 3 months in wages. At least I can say that I left with my personal reputation and integrity intact. That's got to be worth something; something special perhaps, but it doesn't pay to be too idealistic.

Footnote: On a genuine sad note, the GM suffered a severe stroke when he was flying between Canada and China (2012) and you'd be hard pressed to find a worse place to have one than 30,000 feet in the air. The results were devastating and my understanding is that he has been permanently ensconced in a nursing home in Sydney ever since. When I balance up all the good things that he did for me against the negatives, I think the positives will win out. I started at the Regent Sydney as a Security Officer and within six months I was promoted to an Assistant Manager. I was probably the most rapidly promoted person at the hotel during this time and this was all because of the GM. In spite of my 'assassination,' it does not stop me from singing his praises and I am quite sad to learn of his medical demise. You just never know what is just around the corner.

I left The Regent Sydney about the middle of 1989

Chapter Twelve: The Holy Trinity
1990 - 1995

In 1990 - General Manuel Noriega surrendered in Panama. The Communist Party relinquished sole power in Soviet Government. South Africa freed Nelson Mandela who was imprisoned for 27½ years. Iraqi troops invaded Kuwait, setting off the Persian Gulf War. East and West Germany were reunited. Lech Walesa won Poland's runoff Presidential election. The Hubble Space Telescope was launched. The movies released included *Dances with Wolves, Goodfellas, Henry and June* and *Reversal of Fortune*. Notable deaths included those Greta Garbo, Sammy Davis, Jr. and Le Duc Tho.

In 1991 - South African Parliament repealed apartheid laws. Boris Yeltsin became first freely elected president of Russian Republic. Lithuania, Estonia, and Latvia won independence from USSR and the US recognised them. US indicted two Libyans in 1988 bombing of Pan Am Flight 103 over Lockerbie, Scotland. The Soviet Union broke up after President Gorbachev's resignation; Constituent republics formed a Commonwealth of Independent States. The FDA approved the use of Bristol-Meyers' DDI (didanosine) in the treatment of AIDS. The first cholera epidemic in a century sickened 100,000 and killed more than 700 in South America. The movies released included *The Silence of the Lambs, Beauty and the Beast, JFK* and *Thelma and Louise*. Notable deaths included those of Miles Davis, Theodore Seuss Geisel, Frank Capra, Leo Durocher and Graham Greene.

In 1992 - Bush and Yeltsin proclaimed a formal end to the Cold War. General Manuel Noriega, former leader of Panama, was convicted in a US court and sentenced to 40 years on drug charges. US forces left The Philippines, ending nearly a century of American military presence. UN approved US-led force to guard food for Somalia. Four officers were acquitted in Los Angeles of the beating of Rodney King and afterwards violence erupted in Los Angeles. Bill Clinton was elected President and Al Gore Vice President. Compact discs surpassed cassette tapes as the preferred medium for recorded music. The movies *Unforgiven, The Crying Game, Howard's End, Glengarry Glen Ross* and *The Player* were released. Notable deaths included Alex Haley, Anthony Perkins, Isaac Asimov, Willie Dixon and Lawrence Welk.

In 1993 - Twenty-two UN troops killed in Somalia. Yeltsin's forces crushed revolt in Russian Parliament. Clinton agreed to compromise on military's ban on homosexuals. Federal agents besieged Texas Branch Davidian religious cult after six were killed in raid. Fire killed 72 as cult standoff in Texas ended with federal assault. Five arrested, sixth sought in bombing of World Trade Center in New York. According to the World Health Organization (WHO), tuberculosis threatened to kill more than 30 million in the next decade. First humans cloned. Cells taken from defective human embryos that were to be discarded in infertility clinic were grown in vitro and developed up to 32-cell stage and then were destroyed. The movies *Schindler's List, The Piano, Philadelphia, Six Degrees of Separation* and *In the Name of the Father* were released. Notable Deaths included those of Anthony Burgess, Frank Zappa, Arthur Ashe, Dizzy Gillespie, William Golding, Audrey Hepburn and Cesar Chavez.

In 1994 - Serbs' heavy weapons pounded Sarajevo. Many hundreds of thousands died in Rwanda massacre. South Africa held first inter-racial national election; Nelson Mandela elected President. IRA declared ceasefire in Northern Ireland. Ulster Protestants declared ceasefire. US sent forces to Persian Gulf. Russians attacked secessionist Republic of Chechnya. Aldrich Ames, high C.I.A. official, charged with spying for Soviets. Four convicted in World Trade Center bombing. Clinton accused of sexual harassment while Governor of Arkansas. O. J. Simpson arrested in killings of wife, Nicole Brown Simpson, and friend, Ronald Goldman. Kurt Cobain killed himself; he was 27. Steven Spielberg won his first directing Oscar for Schindler's List. Tom Hanks won his second consecutive Best Actor Oscar. Dr. Ned First (US) cloned calves from cells of early embryos. The movies *Forrest Gump, Pulp Fiction, The Shawshank Redemption, Quiz Show* *and Nobody's Fool* were released. Notable deaths included those of President Nixon, Cab Calloway, Burt Lancaster, John Candy, Jacqueline Kennedy Onassis, Tip O'Neill and Jessica Tandy.

In 1995 - A nerve gas attack in Tokyo subway killed eight and injured thousands. France exploded a nuclear device in Pacific; wide protests ensued. Israelis and Palestinians agreed on transferring West Bank to Arabs. Israeli Prime Minister Yitzhak Rabin was slain by a Jewish extremist at a peace rally. Scores killed as terrorist's car bomb blew up block-long Oklahoma City federal building; Timothy McVeigh, 27, arrested. Los Angeles jury found O. J. Simpson not guilty of murder charges. The movies *Babe, Braveheart, Leaving Las Vegas, The Usual Suspects* and *Dead Man Walking* were released. Notable deaths included those of Jerry Garcia, Rose Kennedy, Howard Koch, Mickey Mantle and Ginger Rogers.

In 1996 - Britain alarmed by an outbreak of "mad cow" disease. Israel elected Benjamin Netanyahu as Prime Minister. Iraqis struck at Kurdish enclave; after warning, US attacks Iraq's southern air defences. Militant Taliban leaders seized Afghan capital of Kabul. Clinton approved plan for UN-backed relief mission for 1.2 million Hutu refugees starving in eastern Zaire. F.B.I. arrested suspected Unabomber. Clinton appointed Madeleine Albright as first female US Secretary of State. Global warming climbed to record levels. Scientists analysing a Martian meteorite claimed that it may provide evidence for the existence of ancient life on Mars. Dr. Ian Wilmut and his team cloned the world's first sheep from adult cells. The lamb born in July 1996 was named Dolly. The movies *The English Patient, Fargo, Jerry Maguire, The People vs. Larry Flynt, Shine* and *Sling Blade* are released. Most notable deaths included Ella Fitzgerald, Spiro Agnew, George Burns, Gene Kelly, Timothy Leary, Marcello Mastroianni and Carl Sagan. The population of the World was 5.760 billion.

I refer to this time as the period of the Holy Trinity. I had to deal with three potentially catastrophic incidents simultaneously. After the unfortunate Regent Sydney hotel incident, I formed a company with two other chaps; one who was Chris Stafford. Remember I told you about the assault at the Don Burrows Supper Club; Chris was the one assaulted. He left the Regent Sydney because he was disenchanted with not being able to gain meaningful promotion within that group. The other bloke was Alan somebody. I don't remember his family name but he was a Lebanese fella I had made a connection with. I put it to Chris and Alan that we should form a contract cleaning company. I saw this as an opportunity to put into practice part of what I had learnt whilst at the hotel in relation to contract cleaning. We did quite well for a while but in the final wash-up, we lacked the sales and marketing skills to really grow. We got good cleaning contracts but nothing like an international hotel. You only need one of them. We did get the contract to clean the Orient Hotel at The Rocks in Sydney. This is a well-known pub with three levels and I worked this one myself with the help of three Koreans. Chris came sometimes. We used to get to the hotel at about 4 a.m. 7 days per week. It was back breaking work and we worked just as hard (maybe harder) as our workers. We would sweep and mop the floors, polish the brass and clean the toilet cubicles that were always filthy but especially so on the weekends. It was a total clean every day and by the time we had finished it looked magnificent. Once a week we used to wash the sandstone floor with a special washing machine and we made it sparkle. We held that contract for quite some time until someone came in and undercut us. That's business! Nevertheless, we were not hitting the big league that I thought, with our experience, we should have. We got various small contracts and many of them I did myself. We had the Gladstone Hotel at Leichhardt and a couple of office blocks at Chippendale and Double Bay. Chris got a job offer in Tahiti as General Manager of a Resort, so I was left on my own. Alan had a young family and was snapped up by a big contract cleaning company. I was able to sell of all the contracts over time and ended up making some money, since we did not have to pay to get the contracts in the first place.

So for a number of years, I survived by contract cleaning. I found I was not able to get suitable employment in the hotel industry and was deeply suspicious about the reasons for that. Eventually I branched out into the steam cleaning of carpets. Like most cleaning this was hard work but financially more rewarding. I met a fella named John Rogerson who got me started with it. John is a very interesting man who was a contract cleaner with no formal education. He had done very well for himself and he was probably one of the hardest workers I have ever worked with. He was also a bit of a genius with electronics. He designed and built a steam cleaning machine that he called the green machine. This portable green machine could do all and more, than a truck mounted machine. Without going into the technical side of things, he was able to offer clients the same product but had the advantage of going anywhere with it. I got the first green machine and made a lot of money with it doing thousands of hours of cleaning carpet. John would get these big contracts and it was not unusual for him and I to go into say, a big retail outlet like Target and clean all the carpet on all the floors. We would do this overnight. Security would lock us in and off we'd go. I'd start at one end and he'd start at the other. We worked really hard but made good money. The problem for me of course was I didn't get any of that money, not a cent of it and will explain later why. The first machine that John got off the 'assembly' line he sold to me and I now started to get some good jobs. For very big jobs, I'd get somebody to help me and we could just keep this machine going until we had finished. We did jobs like all the carpet in the bars of the old Sydney show grounds at Moore Park and numerous functions rooms around town. I never ventured into the residential area as I considered it was too much work for the money you could make. Otherwise I was prepared to go anywhere at any time and do any job, not matter how tough. I can tell you some of the pubs we did were in terrible shape. In many cases the waste water coming out was as black as black ink. The publicans were amazed that we could get it so clean and for a relatively low cost. This business was growing for me. I got a good contract in the city in one the luxurious high rise apartments. This apartment complex was now being managed by my old mate Ron. Remember Ron from the Yellow Glen story at the Regent Sydney? He was giving me regular work and also arranged for my company to do all the window cleaning. Because it was run like a hotel, all the windows had to be cleaned regularly. I didn't know how to clean windows and realised that window cleaning was very skilful and needed a professional. I spoke with a fella who I had met before that was a professional window cleaner. He was fantastic at it and we struck up a deal. I can't remember the details of that but he would give me a percentage of his invoice and I didn't have to do anything else. The client would ring him direct when they wanted windows cleaned and that was at least once every week. I used Ron as a check and balance method to ensure that the window cleaning sub-contractor was being honest with me and as I expected, he was very honest and honourable in his dealings.

There was a fly in the ointment. Sue was embarrassed that her husband was a contract cleaner. When she married me, I was one of NSW's finest, working at the Criminal Investigation Branch. She was very proud of me and loved the life that we used to lead at that time. Later when I rose rapidly up in the ranks at the Regent Sydney, she was even more prouder of me. When it all went belly up and I ended up doing whatever I could get; she faltered. I am a bit ambivalent about it. On the one hand I didn't really blame her; on the other hand I felt that she could have stuck by me and supported me. It was reasonable for her to have achievable high expectations and she felt that I was not putting in the effort to get out of the 'cleaning rut'. That was not the case but that is the way that she saw it. She began to complain a lot and felt that I could have done a lot better for myself and more importantly, for her of course. I think this was the starting point of when she wanted a divorce but that's getting ahead of myself.

During this time, I undertook a course that would give me certification to become a fitness instructor. Part of the deal was that you had to do thirty hours of practical training taking fitness classes. At this time I got down to just over 90Kgs and was really fit again. All the fat from the Police Force and the Regent high-life had gone. I had a number of people that I was doing personal training with. One of them was the husband of one of the girls I trained with at the hospitals. His name was Johnny King. I say was, because he died in 2012. Johnny had a stroke in the 1980s and it changed his attitude to just about everything. He lost all his drive and initiative. He put on an enormous amount of weight and smoked heavily. He just didn't care anymore but Betty, my classmate and Johnny's wife, wanted him to do something about it. So, for next to nothing, I used to take Johnny for long walks and gradually got to the stairs at the Football Stadium. He could climb maybe twenty of so but then I would stop him. I knew it was too hard for him and was worried that his heart would give out. I told Betty that we were pushing him to do something that he really did not want to do and it would be better if he didn't do it. She agreed. After I went to Singapore, I got the sad news that Betty had died of a brain haemorrhage whilst on the treadmill at a gymnasium. It's strange how things work out. In 2012, Johnny was admitted to the Prince of Wales Hospital with cirrhosis of the liver and died shortly afterwards. I was lucky enough to be in Sydney at the time and caught up with him before he passed. They had three children and we knew them well. One of them, Danny, had always wanted to be a boy. In 2001 he had the sex change operation and became a man. I caught up with him when Johnny was in hospital. He is a delightful bloke and very happy with his new life. He is an upholsterer, married and has a son. Of course all funerals are sad affairs and Johnny King's, wasn't any exception. There were a couple of hundred people there and many of them from his surf life saving club at South Maroubra. I noted with interest that he had the South Sydney Rabbits scarf on his coffin and I think from memory his ashes were place alongside Betty's at the cemetery.

For a long time, I mean years, I'd been looking up the Sydney Morning Herald classifieds for coffee shops for sale. It is just something I wanted to do. In 1995 I found one that I thought was ideal. It was on the North Shore of Sydney. To finance it I had to take out a second mortgage on the house, which was now officially valued at $550,000. This shot my mortgage up to well over $400,000. I got the finance through one of these 'questionable' mortgage brokers. Interest rates were exorbitant at that time. I think the rate was about 13% but I had to pay more than that because it was a second mortgage. Just after I bought the business the rates started to escalate even further. I got a friend of mine who is a hospitality consultant to help me do my due diligence. We looked at it in detail (or so we thought) and I bought it. It had a very busy lunchtime trade with take-away food and this was complemented by a fairly brisk catering trade. I thought here is my chance to make a couple of thousand per week without having to bust myself like I was doing with the cleaning. That was the plan; but you know with plans; "the best laid plans of mice and men often go awry". They did, catastrophically.

I knew within one week, I had made a terrible decision. I was losing money from day one. By this time Sue and I were estranged and she would not have anything to do with me or with the business. She was adamant that I had made a wrong decision and how right she proved to be. She claimed later that I coerced her into signing the necessary documents to get the loan. Just after I bought the business, we lost a major customer who represented about 20% of the revenue. It came from the workers on a building site that was not visible from the shop, but just around the corner. The seller did not mention this to me when we were doing our due diligence but he would have known. After the trial period he gave me the keys and left. Although I did not realise it at the time, I had been misled. 'Buyer beware' as they always say. Within two weeks I was down to the bank asking for an overdraft just so I could pay the wages. It's a very simple formula. More money was going out than coming in. Originally I wanted to work the cash register but couldn't. I found myself working as the kitchen hand as no one else would do it and I could not afford to hire anybody. Nor could I afford to lose any staff. For nine months I slaved in that kitchen and lost $2,000 per week for the pleasure of doing so. I was now in very big trouble. It was like being caught in quicksand. The more you fight it, the more you sink but you sink more slowly. I rang John Rogerson and he gave me some carpet cleaning. I used to work in the business from 6am until 4pm and often go carpet cleaning after that for most of the night. I was a physical and mental wreck. All the money that I made carpet cleaning went into the business. Sue's animosity was getting worse and she asked me to move out of the main house. Part of our house had a granny flat and we had a tenant in it. He used to work for me at the Regent Sydney and was a really nice chap, whose name was Eric Tomkinson. I told Eric he'd have to go as I had been 'thrown' out of my own house and needed somewhere to live. He went and I moved into the granny flat. I stayed there for a few months until she demanded I leave there as well. I was under the impression at that time, that if your wife wanted you to leave the family home, you were legally obliged to do so, and so I did. My understanding now is that I did not have to do that and it now seems that I was acting under a false impression. Sue was getting her advice from a network of female friends that she had and unfortunately for me, and ultimately for her, she put a lot of importance on their advice. I moved out and went into rental share accommodation in North Sydney when I really could not afford it. I was now in desperate financial and domestic trouble. I could not get my head around having to leave my own home, especially the granny flat part of it and it got to me. To me it all seemed to be profoundly unfair. I bought the house but I was the one that had to leave.

Things came to a head one day. Sue told me that she was thinking of taking the children to New Zealand for a holiday. She told me this on Father's Day of 1995. I broke down and screamed at her and told her that I had never hated anybody as much as I hated her at this point in time. I also told her I thought that she was the scum of the earth. This was all in front of the children. I wanted to know how any decent person could do what she was doing, given my financial circumstances. Even in this state, it never occurred to me to become violent. It just broke my heart. I was up to my eyeballs in debt, couldn't possibly work any harder than I was, had lost ten kilograms and was just about coming to the end of my tether. Sue's attitude was the last straw and I sort of had a mini temporary breakdown. That night I rang a mate of mine from my fitness class and asked him if I could come and stay at his flat until I got organised and he agreed. I really was now in deep trouble, financially, domestically and socially. It seemed things couldn't get any worse but they did. The good news was that I did not get a return bout of the clinical depression I had from 1967-1971. However it is fair to say that I felt hopelessness and severe anxiety at this stage and I thought that I was going to go under and lose everything. I also thought that everything that I had worked and saved for from 1975 until 1995 was going down the tube; twenty-one years for nothing. The worst fear however was that I realised that the children could 'lose a roof above their heads'. It's and understatement to say that things were desperate for me.

I will divert momentarily and tell you about a friend of mine, Bill Kable. Bill ran into trouble with his marriage in April of 2001. He had no inclination that there was anything wrong until his wife told him one day that she wanted a divorce; just like that. When he asked her what was her reason, she insisted that he already knew that and refused to discuss the matter any further. She chose immediate separation rather than counselling. They lived in an upmarket suburb named Killara on the upper north shore and Bill went to live in an attached garage/granny flat. At the time they had two little kids, one boy aged ten and a girl aged four. They would come and see Bill from time to time in the granny flat but the wife put an end to that and stopped them from continuing it. She was adamant the divorce would go through as soon as possible and wanted to sell the house and assets as soon as possible. Bill was perplexed with the alienation. Even though he was a corporate lawyer, there seemed little he could do against the onslaught against him. He found that in spite of his legal training and networking contacts, he was not given any favourable treatment in the Australian family law court system. The divorce itself was simple and he did not even go to the rubber stamping exercise at the family court. Bill told me that the divorce was granted by the Judge who made no inquiries as to the welfare of the children, nor for that matter, his welfare.

But the worst was in front of him. The real problems were in the area of property settlement, child custody and continued welfare. With respect to the property, he had his life savings on the line. His now ex-wife had stripped the house of all the more valuable possessions she wanted and some of these items included presents that Bill had received from his family and friends over the years. She put a ridiculously low value on everything including the new Kawai grand piano Bill had recently bought for her exclusive use. Bill's lawyers advised him that he could engage his own valuers but that would be expensive and probably would not amount to much if they refused to negotiate and it had to go to court.

But the attack on finances were only starting to warm up. His ex-wife immediately applied for child support and also maxed out any credit cards that he had not cancelled thinking that she might need money in an emergency. He certainly made an error of judgement thinking that he could trust her with his credit cards. She took them to their absolute limit. Not a lot of pride there. So confronted with the assets gone, Bill's income saddled with an impost of 29% on top of tax, the financial hole was deep with steep sides but then the worst blow was yet to come.

Despite the consent agreement stipulating the time to be spent with his children his ex-wife immediately breached the terms of the agreement and made it as difficult as she could for him to see the children. This was done while disparaging him at every opportunity while she lived temporarily with her mother. This was demonstrated when one of the children said that they could not afford breakfast anymore because Bill did not give enough money to their mother. It was not long after this, probably about four months after the separation, his ex-wife set her sights on a new man in her life. This led quickly to her moving in with him to a rented home on the northern outskirts of Sydney. This was followed by another move in the same area and then by a move to the town of Taree 300 km north of Sydney. Bill was told subsequently by this new man that she had promised him that the move to Taree would get Bill out of their lives. We (Bill's friends) always thought that Bill was not telling us the full story; that there must have been something that he had done to make her so angry and bitter. Why would she suddenly become so vindictive and acrimonious towards him and carry such bitterness. I rationalised that he was probably caught out sleeping around, in other words, cheating. When Bill came to one of his visits to Singapore with his work, I put that to him. He vehemently denied it and swore on a stack of bibles that he didn't and I believe him. So what had he done? He was at a complete loss as to why and to this day, does not know. She never told him. In my own case, my wife accused me of not loving her anymore and never ventured any other explanation. She felt that was enough to go for a divorce. Perhaps Bill's ex had a similar explanation, but because it was so superficial, she never put it out there.

What was disconcerting to Bill was that he was never told about these moves until after they happened. In every case there was a delay of a week or more when Bill did not know where the children were. Imagine not knowing where your children were. In the case of the move to Taree she eventually called on a mobile and let the kids speak to Bill on the phone. Bill then had to put on his investigators hat and find out where they were going to school. That was simple enough as Taree is a relatively small town with a population of about 20,000 people. All he had to do was ring the schools in the area to see if the children had been enrolled. He hit pay dirt when he found that they were at the Baptist school but the Principal was reluctant to tell Bill anything as they had been enrolled in the ex-wife's new boyfriend's name. The children continued to be known by that name at the school even in breach of direct orders from the Family Court. The school also did everything it could to frustrate Bill's time with his children, although by this time only the younger child was prepared to see him. He still does not know why the school took this adversarial stance against him and can only think that they had been influenced unduly by the ex-wife's propaganda. When

Bill left his full time employment in 2006 he moved to the Taree area to be near the children, but the Family Court would still only allow him limited time with his children even though he was never even accused of anything unbecoming. The highest amount of time allowed was five days out of fourteen but usually it was one or two days. Under the orders the child still seeing Bill had to be collected on the farm where they lived and so the ex-wife made this as confrontational and unpleasant as she could. By this time, the older child, a boy, had disassociated himself from his father and there was not a thing that Bill could do about it. It seems that the boy had been indoctrinated with such negative and allegedly untruthful information that he just did not want to have anything to do with his father.

The younger child, a girl, followed suit a few years later. After some years of strong parental alienation the younger child started saying that she did not want to see Bill. When Bill was due to pick her up after school she went off unannounced in the school bus. This led to Bill searching all over Taree for her and he was almost on the verge of calling the Police to report her missing. This, as all parents know, is a parent's worst nightmare. However the ex-wife said she had arrived home and was not going back to Bill's place. This was one of numerous occasions when Bill travelled 300 km to see his daughter only to be refused contact so he had to drive home again. On the last two occasions Bill saw his daughter, the child ran away causing enormous trauma to him. He just could not understand why and it was this that was causing the most hurt and anxiety. He kept asking himself, what had he done to deserve this?

The end of this saga was that Bill did not see his son for over ten years and his daughter for seven years. Miraculously contact was re-established in 2014, but nothing will ever make up for so much lost time. Maybe it wasn't a miracle. Maybe it was because Bill's mother had recently passed and he had come into a reasonable inheritance. Whatever the case, his kids came back to him and I think Bill deserves an explanation from them. If not from his ex-wife, then from his children! Bill was lucky in a sense that he formed a relationship shortly after his separation with a wonderful lady by the name of Kathryn who gave him such incredible support during this tiring time. I wonder if most people understand what it would be like for a father to lose his children. I am telling Bill's story because during the latter part of 1995 and 1996, I had this real fear that I could lose my children. Like I said before, I could cope with losing everything (which I did) and then some, but not my children. One day I went to the house when I knew no one was there and took my son's passport; such was my fear. After a week or so, I put it back, having had a change of heart and Sue never knew about that. I spoke to a detective friend of mine and he said that if it were him, it is just something that would never happen. When I pushed him on it, he left it hanging by saying that his wife knew what would happen if she did that to him. This is a very strong emotive issue. Bill is a bit like me, in that he is a reasonably mild mannered person, not given to fits of violence but rather a person who likes to negotiate settlements. As I write this (December 2016), there is a lot of talk about domestic violence. Before I go down this road, let me say that it is my view that violence is never warranted against a woman in the domestic sense; not under any circumstances. There has been 62 women who have died in Australia (from 1/1/15 until 12/9/15) by the hands of a man they were related to. What's my point! I wonder if in any of these 62 cases, if the issue of child custody was an instigating factor? I'm not for a minute, even a second, condoning violence even if the law is grossly unfair to the man; that he resorts to violence. What I would suggest is that the Family Law Courts get their act together and look after men a lot better than they do. You only have to listen to Bill's story, to understand how little the law did to protect his rights. Perhaps if they took a more balanced and fairer approach to men's rights in family law, there would be fewer acts of wanton violence towards women.

I mentioned before that during the 'Holy Trinity' period Sue was taking her advice from the network of friends. They were telling her she could not make a clean break whilst I was living in the granny flat. I had to leave there just when things were hitting rock bottom. I took whatever came my way and fought it. I never had to have any medication, nor see any medical people about depression during this period. I have written that during this period I lost 10 kilograms so you can see, every cloud has a silver lining. I tried everything to improve the business. I increased the catering revenue and maintained our lunch time trade. People would be lined up three deep waiting for their coffee, meals and sandwiches. Where was all this cash going? Later when I went through all this with my accountant, he was very firm in his opinion that I was being ripped off 'fearsomely' by the staff. That was probably right. You could see by the numbers coming in that I was not getting the cash that the cost of sales should have represented. The business was all cash and if I had challenged the staff about it, they would have walked out en-masse and I couldn't let that happened. They had me corralled in the kitchen and there was nothing I could do about it. I had absolutely no one I could call for help. No family, no friends, nobody! The year was 1996. Physically I was enervating and there had to be a time limit to how long I could keep this up; but I did keep going. The second half of 1995 and the first half of 1996 was my second 'Annus Horribilis'. You will remember the first was 1967/68. I did not know how much longer I could keep going but interestingly enough mentally I never wavered. I think the thought that I would leave my children in a very precarious position unconsciously made me realise that I just could not afford to get ill, either physically or mentally. Getting ill was not an option for me under these difficult circumstances. I had to stay on my feet and keep going.

Eventually, I thought that I had found the solution. The business broker that had sold the business to me in the first place had a buyer that was very interested. Oh my god, I thought, my nightmare is coming to an end. He bought this lovely Greek couple around and they were very interested. They came a number of times and could see the business was generating good revenue. They did not know that I was not getting all of it but that was not their problem. This is exactly what the business needed; one of them on the cash register, the other on the front counter. They were satisfied that it was making what I said it was (it wasn't) but that was probably due to the staff stealing, or so I reasoned. I offered them a trial period and the deal was done. The contract was going to be exchanged the next day. I was offered about $30,000 less than I paid for it. I told them that even through the business was making money I did not like working it and wanted to leave, even with a loss. I was so happy. Christ, I thought my hell on earth was coming to an end. I compare it with a climber who has almost reached the top of Mt Everest and only has a short number of meters to go. Imagine the sense of repose and exhilaration I felt. Then disaster struck. The broker rang me at the end of the day to tell me that the buyer had pulled out at the very last moment. I was devastated, totally gutted. I thought how much more of this do I have to endure. Using the same analogy, it was like I had slipped and fallen all the way back to base camp. At this time an epiphany came to me and I thought about the time that my Dad had lost a very valuable wheat crop overnight and how he reacted to it. The crop in question was probably the best that he had ever had and just before the harvest a severe hale storm came and completely wiped it out. I recall how he responded to this major setback and decided I had to do the same. He didn't go to pieces and didn't curse or blame anyone. All he did was to tell me that we had to start cultivating as soon as we could and get ready for next year. He showed tremendous doggedness and fortitude and I decided that I had to do the same and that is what I did.

I spoke to a chap who was a client of mine in the carpet cleaning business. I got on quite well with him and told him all about the business. At the end of the day he was happy to inject money ($30,000) into the business for a share of it. Of course, I was not going to turn that down. He knew of a couple that could run it. She was a chef and the husband could work the cash register and make coffee. This seemed to be a good solution and I was starting to find a 'second wind'. Unfortunately it all went belly-up. The couple could not manage it properly and the revenue dropped even more after I left. I knew I had to get some more money somewhere just to keep the business afloat. I had exhausted all the avenues with the bank. They would not extend the overdraft and I had already taken out a second mortgage to secure the business in the first place. So I decided to let this couple run the place and I would get a job. The money I earned from a full time job, plus some carpet cleaning, would all go into propping up the business. I thought that with this new initiative I could at least keep paying the two mortgages. I got a job as the Security Manager at a major hotel in Sydney. However it became clear after a short time that the married couple were hopeless and were not the solution. Business was dropping and my fellow shareholder reckoned he had the answer and brought in a chap who was reputed to be an expert in this type of business. Naturally I was willing to try anything. For a multitude of reasons, this also failed. I knew that no matter what happened, I had to meet those mortgage payments. The bank had the first and second mortgage over my house and they were a secured creditor. The hotel had given me a flat to live in for next to nothing and I ate in the hotel canteen, also for nothing. I owed over $420,000 just to the bank (this was in 1995) and those monthly payments just had to be made; or else they would take possession of the property. Apart from that there was about $200,000 owed to creditors. I had really got myself in a mess.

Everything I tried to do to resurrect the business failed. My accountant and I went into the city to see the lawyers acting for the owners of the building renting the business to me. We went with the express purpose of trying to find a solution to keep the business going. The lawyer was sympathetic and even gave us a cup of tea. Unbeknownst to us, whilst he was talking and drinking tea with us, he had arranged for people to go out and secure the place by putting chains and locks on the two entrance doors. He never mentioned anything about this to us at the time and left us with the impression that we could work towards a collective solution. What a scumbag! We left there believing that we could give it one last shot. That lawyer had deceived us. They had taken possession of the shop and everything in it. That included a fully stocked kitchen with all the perishables items and of course all the operating equipment. When I contacted him about what to do with all the perishables, he simply said that nothing would happen until I paid the unpaid rent. They were prepared to let a lot of good food rot rather than let me into the premises. I asked him why he couldn't have discussed it with me the previous day when we were in his office. He simply said, "I thought it better not to". Maybe one day I will write a book about my experiences with lawyers. They truly are a mercenary lot. Maybe one of the problems with our current political system is that too many of our leading politicians are lawyers. You may recall the line from Shakespeare's play *Henry IV*, "The first thing we do, let's kill all the lawyers". I think I agree with Shakespeare.

When I went flat hunting after I was shunted from my home, I found a share accommodation in Crows Nest. I answered an advertisement in the Sydney Morning Herald. This very attractive lady was looking for a flat mate to help her share the rent. She was a really good looking woman and she wanted somebody that wasn't going to hit on her. She picked the right man. I could not have done anything even if I wanted to. I did meet a lovely lady on a fitness course that I had done earlier. She came home with me one day but I could not get an erection. This is not surprising given the stress that I was under. One day I brought the kids over and my little girl Toni, accidentally dropped a bottle of wine on the carpet. I screamed at her. Now I had to replace that area of the carpet that was damaged and I just didn't have the money to do it. Toni mentioned this to me years later. She has a clear recollection of me screaming at her when she was five years old. You see what impact parents can have on their children. What she also realises now, that she could not have done then, was that I was on the verge of becoming a completely broken man; I had lost my home, my wife, my children, all my assets, my business and was just hanging on by the barest of threads. The most profound emotion that I had at this time was I was completely on my own. There was no one I could turn to for help.

It was at about this time that Sue had decided to take the children to NZ for a holiday. I was OK with that and went with them to see them off. Unfortunately, as they were about to leave me I completely broke down in front of everybody in the airport departure lounge and sobbed uncontrollably. It passed and from memory I composed myself relatively quickly. Both of my children have a clear recollection of this. This is what mental and physical exhaustion can do to you. I was a wreck, but I kept going and just would not give up; like the way that I stuck out the nursing. This was an extraordinary difficult time for me and very hard to articulate just how difficult it was. The rent at the flat became too much for me and I moved in with a fella who had a run-down house in Northbridge in Sydney. His name was David and David became my friend and my accountant. In fact he still is. My mental and physical exhaustion was beyond belief. I was now working full time at the hotel and cleaning carpet on my time off. All the money I earned from both of these endeavours went to keeping the house and business afloat. If you had asked me to come and have a beer with you I would not have because I simply could not afford either the time or the money.

With respect to the hotel, we had a big problem with hoodlum behaviour which is not surprising because it was in a big profile tourist area. To deal with this, I had a team of about ten bouncers who were all big, strong young fellas. When I first got to the hotel there was a culture amongst the bouncers, that it is better to be safe than sorry. They strongly believed what we believed in the Police Force. Do unto others as they would do to you, but make sure that you do it first. That meant that they sometimes became physical when there was no need to be. If there were any signs of trouble they'd get the trouble makers out. That was good and that's what we were paying them to do, but the problem was that sometimes they would inflict a bit of summary justice on them. I was very concerned about this and worried that the hotel was being exposed to an unnecessary risk of litigation and reputation damage; not to mention criminal charges being laid against the bouncer. I related to them a situation that I was very familiar with where the 'bouncer' of a hotel in Bondi asked a young fella to leave and the young bloke wouldn't. An argument developed and the bouncer hit him once in the head and killed him. The bouncer was subsequently charged with murder which was later scaled down to manslaughter. I told my blokes that I never wanted to see that happen to them. I discussed it with the General Manager and recommended that I begin a series of lectures on the law as it relates to them and at the conclusion of those lectures, I would have them sign off on it. I also had it noted in their contract of employment that a condition of their employment was that they must adhere to the new set of guidelines for using physical force against patrons. The idea was that they needed to know what the legal exposure was for them when they started roughing people up, which they saw as a necessary part of their work. To some degree that was correct, but I emphasised that force could only be used as a last resort and only if absolutely necessary. I wanted the hotel protected against any wrong-doing on the part of the bouncers. I also wanted the bouncers to have some protection so I clarified the whole thing for them. That really was my job; to protect the hotel, its assets and reputation. The strategy worked really well. They enjoyed the lectures and had a far deeper insight into what their roles and responsibilities were within the organisation. They responded very positively to it. We cut down the number of 'assaults' dramatically and the blokes were taught some communication skills in handling people that were 'difficult'. There was a period of adjustment but full credit to them, they adjusted very well. You may recall that at The Regent Sydney, my first assignment as Chief of Security was to get rid of the guns. At this hotel, it was to stop the doormen using what I regarded as unreasonable force with patrons. I think in both cases, I left my mark.

Chapter Thirteen: The Lady in the Sauna
1996

Things just could not get any worse for me. I had been evicted from my own house; now I had been evicted from my business. I still had five years left on the business lease at $1,300 per month. Work it out — $78,000 (1996). There was one important thing I hadn't lost. I continued my membership with the Sydney Cricket Ground Trust as the fees were not due until October of each year. The acrimony with Sue had reached fever pitch and we could barely speak with one another. She felt that she still had what it took to get a good relationship going with somebody of means who could give her the life she was accustomed to and was not prepared to give up. Fair enough I suppose. I could certainly understand she did not want to be married to a carpet cleaner; I didn't want to be a carpet cleaner either. She started going out with blokes and I knew that it would not talk her long before she found someone to replace me. Besides we were separated so she had every right to do that,

One evening I was in the gymnasium at the football stadium and after finishing my workout I went to have a sauna, as was my custom. At this time there was a very attractive lady in there. Her name was Amanda. I had seen her from our circuit training group so we sort of knew each other. At the time I probably looked pretty down and you would not have to be a genius to see that something was seriously wrong for me. Amanda told me that I looked down and probably if there had been someone else in the sauna, she wouldn't have said anything. A few tears started to come to my eyes and I told her that I was on my knees and could not see the light of day. As luck would have it no one else came into the sauna so we were able to talk. I told her that I was copping it on all fronts; that I had been trying to sell the house for four years now and could not move it. The house needed a lot of renovations but was in a premier spot near Centennial Park in Sydney. I told her that I could not declare bankruptcy because they would take the house away and the kids would have nowhere to live. I also told her how my wife was treating me and how bad my financial position was. I ended up by telling her that I really was now struggling to cope as the physical and mental pressure was taking its toll. She said to me, "So that's why you have lost so much weight." She asked me if I could sell the house, would I than be OK? I told her that this would be like a gift from heaven; if I could at least get the price that the house was valued at or somewhere near it.

She asked me to meet her after we got showered and dressed for a coffee in the gym cafe. As it transpired Amanda had some really good real estate agent connections. She told me that she knew an agent in the Double Bay area that might try and sell it for me. I told her to forget it as I would not be able to afford any of the fees associated with putting it on the market and advertising it. I mentioned that a carpet bagger from a local agent in Randwick had made an absurdly low offer of $420,000. Sue insisted that I accept that. She told me that I had buggered up her life, our children's lives, and to just give her what was left over and she would make her own way. It would have paid the mortgages but there would be little left for her and the children. Sue is a New Zealander and I was worried that she would take the children back to New Zealand and that her family would rally around her and she would get by that way. At least she had a family! The children were now nine and six and I couldn't and wouldn't allow that to happen. As I have said I was prepared to lose everything, but not my children. I would not accept the $420,000 and wouldn't sign anything to endorse the sale. I knew if I could continue to service the mortgage repayments, which were about $1,250 per week (a fortune in those days), I could keep the house going. If I stayed at the hotel and continued with my moonlighting as a carpet cleaner with the green machine, I could stay afloat. This was a time that I had to be really strong as two little children depended on me. It was not a time to weaken as that would have destroyed everything. I knew that there was a time limit to being able to work this hard, so something had to happen soon. I believed I was at my best now; dealing with what really was a catastrophic personal crisis. Amanda told me that she would speak with the Double Bay agent and ask him if he would take it on, without any expense to me. She would tell him that I had to get $550,000. Remember, we had been trying for years to sell it and never even got a serious offer. She said she would ask him to take it on; on the basis of a double commission fee if he sold it and got the full asking price. If he could not get it, he would receive nothing. Not surprisingly I agreed, believing that I had everything to gain and nothing to lose. A few days later I had not heard from Amanda and I thought that she had not been able to discuss it with the bloke. A few days after that I saw her at the gymnasium. I figured that if she had good news she would have called me, so I was fairly dejected about that. She came up to me before our class started and told me he had accepted the offer and that lifted my spirits for the night. I bought Amanda a drink after the class that I could really not afford and she said that she would keep me informed. In my heart I did not believe that the bloke would be able to sell it for the asking price as for years it never attracted any worthwhile offers so I really did not expect much to happen. Such was my luck (and negativism) during this stage of my life.

My God, you wouldn't believe it. He sold it within six weeks for the full asking price and they exchanged contracts. I went to a quiet little corner on my own and uncontrollably and unapologetically totally broke down and wept. This time it was not weeping because of despair, it was weeping out of sheer relief. I had finally got there; I had climbed my Mt Everest. In my eyes I had done the impossible. To emphasise how I felt I would say that the sense of relief would be like an innocent person who has been charged with say murder, being found not guilty. You can image the sense of relief. It felt like an enormous weight had been taken off my shoulders. I had not received a single penny in support from anybody during this period, including any type of welfare. I had no friends who were willing to put their hands in their pockets to help me out. Actually that's not quite true, one did. Chris Stafford up in Singapore told me that if I ever needed some money just to get by all I had to do was ask him. However, I never did but if it had got even more desperate, perhaps I might have had to. In this position, I for one, would never ask for financial help it but if a friend of mine was in a similar position, I would not hesitate to offer it. I think in these types of circumstances your 'friends' take on a philosophy that if you make your own bed you sleep in it. The concept of my family helping me out was so far fetched I did not even think to ask. They never offered any help in the 'days of darkness' period so it would be unrealistic to think they would now. Later I will tell you all about the so called 'friends' that went to see Sue in hospital. The sale of the house was a major turning point for me and I now saw my road to redemption. Sue owned half of the house and I felt that she was not responsible for any of the losses I had incurred so it was clear the proceeds of the sale of the house, after the banks had been paid, would all go to her. It was hers and I was left now with what to do with the unsecured creditors. One weekend shortly after the contracts were exchanged, I went around the house to see Sue to discuss these and other matters. The kids were over at my friend's Geoff Bright place, so it was a good opportunity for me to go through things with her. I was not interested in getting back together and neither was she but we needed to sort out the logistics.

Sometime prior to this, Sue had decided to celebrate her new found freedom and planned to celebrate by throwing a party at 'her' house. Of course quite naturally I would not be invited since it was all about her letting all our friends know that she was now a separated 'desirable' woman. Many of the friends that she invited were really friends of mine that Sue had met as a result of being with me. I was doubtful that my close friends would take part in celebrating my demise and fall from grace; but I was wrong. I could not believe it; they went to this party and I felt slighted about it. I did mention it to a couple of the more important ones and they were certainly able to see my point of view. I guess it depends on how you see things and whose set of glasses you are looking through.

In any event, when I went around to see Sue we opened a bottle of wine to celebrate the good news. We now both knew that we were going to pull through this financial hell. I must say at this point that Sue never denied me access to the children before or since. She promised me she would not renege on her undertaking that she would not take the children out of Australia to live until they were 16. The only thing that Sue ever levelled at me was that I didn't love her anymore but I think the money (or rather, lack of it) was more likely the cause. It turned out that Sue had been going out with a bloke who also had a couple of children and I think it was a reasonably new relationship. She told me that she had to go to the shops to get something for when the kids came home from the Brights. When she did not come back, I got concerned. I waited a couple of hours and the house phone rang; it was the Police. The young Constable told me that Sue had been taken to the A&E ward at the Prince of Wales; my old stomping ground. I was shocked. It turns out that she didn't go shopping for the children after all, but instead went to see her new man to pronounce her new found freedom. She told him that she was now a free woman and indicated this by taking the ring off her finger and showing it to him. She also told him that he could have her now. He responded by telling her that it was far too early in the relationship for him to commit to anything. Everyone has their breaking point and Sue's pressure cooker blew. She suffered a complete breakdown. I was asked by the emergency ward staff at POW to look after her in a room until they could get to her. She was in a very distressed and agitated state. I had no difficulty restraining her but it seemed like hours that I had to do it. Patients of this nature don't get priority in A&E wards of the big public hospitals, especially on busy weekend days. This was the same ward where I had done my training and told you about how we lost that young footballer from Coogee and the same ward I arranged the X-ray for that well known Rugby League player. If it were not for my medical training I would have found it hard to comprehend how she had got to this stage but I knew from my nursing days that if you put enough pressure on anybody, they will breakdown. That applies to every human being in my view. She did not know who I was at this time and kept asking me if my name was Kevin. I think he was the man of the moment. She had been through a terrible time with my financial collapse. She had two little children, a 'no hoper' husband, no money, and was now being rejected by a potential suitor. Sue stayed in hospital for about three weeks and responded well to the treatment. During the treatment stage, I moved back into the house to take care of the kids, got them off to school, fed them, and all the other motherly chores. I told the GM at the hotel about it and he was great. He allowed me to come in when the kids were at school and gave me carte blanche to run my own race at the hotel. He understood that my first duty was to my family and helped me a great deal.

During Sue's stay in hospital only one of Sue's friends went to see her. Her name is Helen and she was visibly upset to the point of crying when she saw Sue. Other than Helen, not one of Sue's many so-called friends and advisors went to see her. They were full of advice to her about getting rid of me and evicting me out of my own house and even the granny flat. But when the s*** hit the fan, they were nowhere to be seen; they were found wanting. On the weekend this happened, I have told you the kids were over at my friend Geoff's place on the North side. They had a big house and I thought maybe they could help me out for a couple of days until I could sort things out. This all happened after the business had been taken away from me so I had time to do this; I just needed a settling back period. I came over to see Geoff to pick up the children and was going to discuss it with him. He met me at the front gate of his house and told me that they would not be able to cope with having to look after their own three and my two. I was shocked and disappointed but didn't say anything. I thought that Geoff was a good friend of mine and would help me in this unusual situation but this proved to be a bridge too far. I took the kids home with me and made do.

So much for all that we hear about women forming close and protective relationships. That was not my experience. As I have said, they all went missing except Helen. They wanted to know her when she was the life of the party but certainly not in her present condition at the Prince of Wales Hospital. It was shortly after this time that Dan started to get double vision and I was worried about him. He was seeing two of everything so that when he went for example to get on a bus, he would see two doors; that type of thing. I was thinking it could be some sort of neurological condition and took him to the Prince of Wales hospital to see a Neurologist. They did a series of tests on him and they all came back negative, which was good. The Consultant Doctor asked him if there was anything that was seriously worrying him and it came out that he was suffering from the effects of our separation and all the acrimony that went with it. Once that was established, he responded quickly and got back to his former self. It does point out how badly children can be affected by the separation of their parents. It must be very hard from them to witness the acrimonious fights that invariably come with divorce and they have to come to grips with Dad not being around for them. I think in Toni's case, she saw it more as me leaving them and it was not until much later in life, when she came to Singapore in 2015 that I explained to her what really happened. Up until then, she didn't know.

When Sue came home from hospital she demanded I leave immediately; so I did. Within months she had a relapse. This time it was worse than before. Dan was at a day care centre in Bronte at the time and had to be picked up by 6 p.m. I don't know where Toni was but suspected that she may have been staying with Jack and Marg, our next door neighbours. I got a call from her friend Helen whilst I was travelling to work at the hotel. She told me that Sue had called her crying in some hotel room and that she was suffering from a broken heart. She did not tell Helen which hotel it was but that it was in the Eastern suburbs. I immediately came back knowing that Dan had to be picked up. I checked the hospital but they had not heard from her. That didn't offer much of a clue for me. I managed to pick Dan up by 6 p.m. and confirmed with the next door neighbours that Toni was there and they had not heard from Sue. Dan and I drove around the Eastern suburbs of Sydney for a couple of hours looking for her. He was eight at the time. You might be able to imagine what a profound effect that might have had on him. After we failed to find her, father and son went to the Randwick Police Station and reported her missing. They were very helpful and eventually they found her at the A&E of the POW hospital. She was in the company of one of my training partners from the City Tattersalls Club in the city. Wow, that caught me off guard. We were relieved that she was found and now in good care. This time she stayed longer and was being treated by a specialist Consultant, Dr Jacobs, from Bondi Junction. I came back home (again) and looked after the kids. Of course I was concerned about the long term effect this might have on the children. I loved my children and loved being with them. Even though Sue was not well, the medical staff were optimistic about the prognosis and thought that she would make a full recovery. She was put on suitable medication and slowly recovered. She had now reconsidered her marriage with me and wanted to reignite it. I was ambivalent about it but given the set of circumstances we found ourselves in, I agreed to attend marriage guidance consulting. We had been to one years before but Sue walked out during the first session. This time it would be conducted by Dr. Jacobs himself. We did that for a number of weeks after she was discharged and we agreed that we would try and get the marriage working again and I moved back to the house. It was about this time that the house had to be transferred to the new owners so we rented a place in Rainbow Street, Randwick. She was very down at this point in time, not able to work and doing it really tough. I would say this is now about November 1996.

For myself, I had weathered the storm. I just had one major matter to deal with before I went to Singapore. Naturally I could not pay my creditors. David arranged for me to go and see Max Donnelley at Ferrier Hodgson about what to do. Max advised that I should make a note of all the creditors; every single penny of it and gave it to him. He recommended that I enter into a deed of arrangement with the creditors, rather than declare bankruptcy. He told me that if I declared bankruptcy, I would not have to pay the creditors anything as I didn't have any money or assets with which to be able to do that. However, I wanted to do what I could do to pay the creditors and saw the Deed of Arrangement as a means of achieving this; at least in part. Max set up a meeting with them. If memory serves me correctly, I think it was on the 6 January 1997. He had told me that for it to succeed I had to obtain the support of 75% of the creditors and 75% of the amount owing. He told me that I must not get the landlord or the bank offside. I then realised that it was just as well that I did not seek retribution against the landlord's lawyer who had deceived me. As a matter of interest, Max was also the trustee in bankruptcy for Christopher Skase. The difference between Skase and me (apart from the amount involved) is that I did not run away from my creditors. I went to the meeting and spoke to the creditors. I sincerely apologised and spoke from the heart. I told them that I felt very sorry for what had happened and told them that things started badly, right from the start. I told them that I had been mislead about the takings of the business in the first instance; that I lost a major customer after only two weeks; that interest rates had gone up three times during my tenure and that they were at an all-time high; that some staff were stealing cash and I could not control it. I added that I was going through an acrimonious divorce and that I had zero support from my family and friends. I admitted that I had made mistakes and that I should have got a professional to do a more in depth due diligence that might have picked up that the business was not taking what was being represented in the financial statements. In relation to the stealing I told them that I was locked into a situation whereby I could not operate the business if certain staff walked out on me. I suspected that stealing was taking place but I couldn't put into place resources to establish that. I had no money to do that and I told them that I had inadvertently been corralled into doing the kitchen hand's job and did not generally serve at the front counter. No one else would do it and I could not afford to employ anybody to do it for me. I was already losing $2,000 per week as it was. I told them that I had lost 10 kgs and was under extraordinary pressure with the business failing badly, my marriage was very acrimonious and I was living in dire circumstances throughout most of this period.

I did not mention my wife's illness to them but did tell them that I got no support from family or friends during this 'Holy Trinity' period. In short I said that the whole thing was a major disaster and I was genuinely sorry for the unsecured creditors. I told them that I was operating under Murphy's Law, that what could go wrong, did go wrong, or so it seemed. I explained that I was able to generate new business but not enough of it to serve what was now an accumulating overdraft. I went through with them how all the money I made from the security management work and the carpet cleaning was all funnelled into the business and I made sure to tell them there was no cash tin hidden in the back yard. I compared my work in the business to being in quicksand; the more I struggled to survive, the deeper I went down under but when you struggle it takes that little bit longer. All the fighting did was slow the process down. In retrospect it would have been better for me if the business collapse had come earlier instead of me trying so hard to fight my way out of it. I mentioned that my accountant felt that the stealing was on a much bigger scale than I had reckoned but there was no way of proving that now. The major customer I lost was always going to happen. I also told them that at the end of the day it was my responsibility and asked them to support me in a deed of arrangement. I added that if they sent me bankrupt, they would probably get nothing. All but one supported me. This will be very difficult to believe but the one that didn't, sold me some cookies on one occasion. I owed him $80, the smallest creditor. Max drafted the agreement and thereafter managed the whole thing. We had agreed that over three years I would pay them twenty cents in the dollar and the debt would be settled. I never missed a payment.

Even now, some twenty years later, I don't know how I got through this period. To lose everything at 53 years of age is just execrable, abysmal and absolutely demoralising. You hear a lot about people going bankrupt but I'm not sure that there are too many people like me that literally lost everything and then some. I'm told that people siphon cash off the business and put it in a tin in the back yard (so to speak). They transfer assets to family members and so on. None of that for me; I lost everything and never recovered financially. It took me years to pay back the creditors, and at the same time look after Sue and the kids in NZ. It was my experience that when you are down and out, friends are few and far between; take my word for it.

The marriage consulting had its ups and down. Dr. Jacobs set the ground rules from the start. He told both of us that when one of us was speaking, the other was not to interrupt. That was more of a problem for Sue than it was for me. He also laboured the point that we should respect one another and that when we finalised things, he would draw up a written agreement for both of us to sign. It was at one of these sessions that he asked both of us how long we thought the marriage had been 'on the rocks'. Sue thought that everything was fine up until Toni had been born (1989). You may remember we got married in 1979. When he asked me I said that I thought we had about 3-4 good years and it started to slide after that. Well, Sue couldn't contain herself and heatedly said, "Are you saying that you were only happy within our marriage for three years?" I told her that was right. She got very upset and started to abuse me but Dr. Jacobs reminded her of our agreed rules. I was asked to explain further what the problem was and I said it was one of communication. I could never sit down and discuss things with her and if there was any hint of a criticism about her she would get very defensive very quickly and has always been like that. I told her that I had been trying for years to get her to listen to my point of view, even if she disagreed. At the end of the sessions, we agreed that we would get together again and try to make it work. A short time later, I went to Singapore. Sue and the kids went to Christchurch to their new home, new school and new environment. All of them have benefited greatly from that move all those years ago (early 1997). I had been in contact with my friend Chris who was now in Singapore managing a group of pubs. Chris offered me a job in Kuala Lumpur (KL). This offer was made in early to mid-1996. I accepted it, flew up to meet Chris and the owner of the company. We went to KL as well as

Jakarta and I signed the contract to start in January 1997, for about $100,000 per year. I was starting to turn the corner.

Sometime in December 1996 I caught a flight to Christchurch and stayed with Sue's brother, Tony Bastings, Margo and their family; wonderful people. I flew over on a Friday and back on a Tuesday. In that time I had bought a house for Sue in joint names, arranged a $100,000 line of credit with the bank and enrolled the kids into the local Catholic primary school. That included having to be interviewed by the parish priest and I had to tell him a mistruth about being a practicing Catholic. You do whatever it takes, right? Whatever I told him it worked and the kids got enrolled. I gave Sue an undertaking that I would send her $2,000 every month and try and come down from Singapore three times a year. I ended up doing both of those things for quite a few years.

I went to Singapore on 11 January 1997. All I owned was the bag that I was carrying with its contents and $200. I was nearly 53 years of age. The good news was that I had been free of clinical depression and medication for 22 years and had a contract of employment for SGD$100,000 per year for one year, to be extended another year if both parties agreed. The bad news was I had lost everything (I mean everything: wife, children, friends, house, car, business investments, operating equipment, superannuation and all cash). I was now to embark on the next challenge of paying off the deed of arrangement to the bankruptcy trustee, plus sending Sue $2,000 per month, as well as my own rent of $1,500 per month and perhaps $500 living expenses. In addition to that I had given the undertaking to go to Christchurch three times per year so you could add on another $5,000-7,000 in total for that. That left me with approximately $2,000 per month whilst I had the contract to start saving for my own future. In terms of financial savings, that would equate to me starting all over again, as if I were a 21 year old. In other words, I had to start from scratch. The house that I lost in Sydney is currently worth close to four million dollars so that gives you an idea of the financial significance of the losses. The thing that stands out for me the most was that I had to do it on my own. There would never be any suggestion of any family support from my mother or kin; no matter how dire the situation would be, they would never help. They proved that when I had the terrible business in 1967/68. It is embedded in their DNA and I have already explained to you that even though I worked for years for nothing on their properties they would never help me and I would never ask them to. I do know that a man without a family is isolated and vulnerable. He can walk a very lonely road, sad and often paved with social isolation, depression, alcoholism and loneliness but I was determined that this would not happen to me again. I pointed out earlier that I did not consider that I ever had a family (other than my own) and in a paradoxical way, this may have made me a stronger person.

My kids now had a secure home in Christchurch NZ. It was a lovely two story, three bedroom house with a big back yard where the kids could play. It had a double lock up garage and internal heating to deal with the very cold winters that Christchurch can have. I paid NZD$200,000 for it and all Sue had to do was pick up the key from her brother Toni and the house was hers. The kids almost immediately started school at St Patricks and it turned out to be a good school so I don't think too much long term damage was done. Sue's house was wedged in-between her mother's house on one side and her brother's on the other. If she found out she was not coping, she had family support on her doorstep. For Sue, this must have been a very tough time for her. Just years before we were flying high and leading the good life. She must have had a dreadful sense of loss and disappointment. I take my hat off to her for the way that she has come back from her illness to bring the children up on her own and at the same time rehabilitate herself. For me personally beating the 'holy trinity' turned out to be my finest hour. I dealt with Sue's illness, our acrimonious separation, the incredible hard work and my financial catastrophe all at the same time and never wavered and I eventually won. The kids never lost that roof over their heads and I was able to get them firmly established in New Zealand and supported them for a long time thereafter.

Sue was able to generate a lot more support of her plight than I was for mine. Perhaps in our society the support naturally gravitates towards the female and I touched on that when I wrote about us having to deal with domestic abuse in the Police Force. In fact, the first time Sue came out of hospital my sister Patricia and her husband Ian came down from Queensland to help her. It wasn't to help me but I appreciated it anyway. Many men really are on their own in a crisis and my case study is a classic example of that. Perhaps this is why the suicide rate is much higher with men than it is with women. I don't think that I can articulate to anybody just how catastrophic it was for me over that 1995/96 period. I have attempted to but feel that I have fallen a bit short on it. I did wish that I'd had a family or even friends that I could have called upon for support but I was alone, make no mistake about that. I had an associate in Sydney who went bankrupt but before he did he signed over his multi-million dollar apartment to his wife and I would have no doubt, siphoned off a great deal of money from the cash businesses he had. I think I have described to you what real bankruptcy is and believe me, it is just about the worst thing that can happen to you. We know that about seven Australians commit suicide every day and that the ratio of men to women is roughly 3:1. I would feel certain that many of these men commit suicide because of financial hardship, believing that it has destroyed their lives and that it is too big a burden to carry.

I also ponder at times what would have happened to my family and myself if I had not have had that conversation with 'the lady in the sauna.' For once, I was in the right place at the right time. I often tell people in a social setting that God had decided that he had punished me enough for my sins of the past and he decided to give me a break by introducing me to the 'lady in the sauna.'

Chapter Fourteen: South East Asia
1997 - 2015

In 1997 - Israeli Government approved establishment of Jewish settlement in East Jerusalem, a setback in the Middle East peace process. Hong Kong returned to Chinese rule. Khmer Rouge held trial of long-time leader Pol Pot. Timothy J. McVeigh sentenced to death for Oklahoma City bombing. Two convicted in New York Trade Center bombing. Scientists at Oregon Regional Primate Research Centre (US) created the first primates — two rhesus monkeys named Neti and Ditto— from DNA taken from cells of developing monkey embryos. US spacecraft began exploration of Mars. US company launched first commercial spy satellite. The movies released included *As Good as It Gets, The Full Monty, Good Will Hunting, The Ice Storm, LA Confidential,* and *Titanic*. The book by Charles Frazier, *Cold Mountain* was also released. Notable deaths included those of Jacques Cousteau, John Denver, Princess Diana, Mother Theresa, James A. Michener, and James Stewart.

In 1998 - Good Friday Accord was reached in Northern Ireland. Irish Parliament backed peace agreement. Europeans agreed on single currency, the Euro. Indonesian dictator Suharto stepped down after 32 years in power. US embassies in Kenya and Tanzania bombed on 7 August. President accused in White House sex scandal; denies allegations of affair with White House intern, Monica Lewinsky. Titanic became the highest-grossing film of all time, raking in more than $580 million domestically. The FDA approved the male impotence drug Viagra. Dow Corning Corporation agreed on $3.2 billion settlement for tens of thousands of women claiming injury from manufacturer's silicone breast implants. Titanic captured a record-tying 11 Academy Awards, including those for Best Picture and Best Director (James Cameron). The American Film Institute announced its list of the top 100 films of all time. *Citizen Kane* topped the list. The movies *Affliction, American History X, Elizabeth, Shakespeare in Love* and *There's Something About Mary* were released. Notable deaths included those of Gene Autry, Sonny Bono, Frank Sinatra and Junior Wells

In 1999 - Nelson Mandela, first black President of South Africa, stood down and Thabo Mbeki took over. War erupted in Kosovo after Yugoslavia's President Slobodan Milosevic clamped down on the province, massacring and deporting ethnic Albanians. NATO began Operation Allied Force on March 24, 1999, launching air strikes against Belgrade for 78 consecutive days until Milosevic relented. Magnitude 7.4 earthquake killed more than 15,600 and left 600,000 homeless in Turkey. Students Eric Harris, 18, and Dylan Klebold, 17, stormed Columbine High School in Littleton, Colorado, killing twelve other students and a teacher, then themselves. The movies released included *Blair Witch Project, American Beauty, Three Kings* and *The Sixth Sense*. Notable deaths included those of Joe DiMaggio, King Hussein II and George C. Scott.

In 2000 - Concorde crash killed 113 near Paris. US sailors on Navy destroyer Cole died in Yemen terrorist explosion. Mad cow disease alarmed Europe. "I love you" virus disrupted computers worldwide. Human genome deciphered; expected to revolutionise the practice of medicine. Abortion pill, RU-486, won US approval. The movies released included *Chocolat, Crouching Tiger, Hidden Dragon, Erin Brockovich, Gladiator* and *Traffic*. Notable deaths included those of Victor Borge, Sir John Gielgud, Alec Guinness, Walter Matthau, Jason Robards, Charles Schulz and Pierre Trudeau.

In 2001 - Former Yugoslav President Slobodan Milosevic was delivered to UN tribunal in The Hague to await war-crimes trial. Without US, 178 nations reached agreement on climate accord. FBI agent Robert Hanssen was charged with spying for Russia for 15 years. Oklahoma City bomber Timothy McVeigh executed. Terrorists attacked United States. Hijackers rammed jetliners into Twin Towers of New York City's World Trade Centre and the Pentagon. A fourth hijacked plane crashed 80 miles outside of Pittsburgh on 11 September. The movies released included *Ali, A Beautiful Mind, Bridget Jones's Diary, The Fellowship of the Ring,*

Harry Potter and the Sorcerer's Stone, The Majestic, Monsters, Inc., Ocean's 11, Pearl Harbor, Shrek and *Vanilla Sky.* Notable deaths included those of Christiaan Barnard, George Harrison, Jack Lemmon, Robert Ludlum, and Anthony Quinn.

In 2002 - Tamil Tigers and Sri Lankan Government signed a ceasefire agreement, ending 19 years of civil war. India's worst Hindu-Muslim violence in a decade rocked the state of Gujarat after a Muslim mob fire-bombed a train, killing Hindu activists. Hindus retaliated, and more than 1,000 died in the bloodshed. Terrorist bomb in Bali killed hundreds. President Bush's first State of the Union address vowed to expand the fight on terrorism and labels Iran, Iraq, and North Korea "an axis of evil". Snipers preyed upon DC suburbs, killing ten and wounding others between October 2–24. The movies released included *Harry Potter and the Chamber of Secrets, Lord of the Rings: The Two Towers, My Big Fat Greek Wedding, About Schmidt, Far From Heaven, Adaptation, The Hours, Chicago,* and *Gangs of New York.* Notable deaths included those of Milton Berle, Rosemary Clooney, John Gotti, Peggy Lee, Princess Margaret, Dudley Moore, and Billy Wilder.

In 2003 - US and Britain launched war against Iraq. Baghdad fell to US troops. Libya accepted blame for 1988 bombing of flight over Lockerbie, Scotland agreed to pay $2.7 billion to the families of the 270 victims. Saddam Hussein was captured by American troops. Space shuttle Columbia exploded, killing all 7 astronauts. The movies released included *Lost in Translation, Pirates of the Caribbean, The Lord of the Rings: The Return of the King, Finding Nemo, Mystic River, Cold Mountain, Master and Commander: The Far Side of the World, Freaky Friday, House of Sand and Fog* and *Seabiscuit.* Notable Deaths included those of Johnny Cash, Katharine Hepburn, Bob Hope and Gregory Peck.

In 2004 - A. Q. Khan, founder of Pakistan's nuclear program, admitted he sold nuclear-weapons designs to other countries, including North Korea, Iran, and Libya. Spain was rocked by terrorist attacks, killing more than 200. Al Qaeda took responsibility. Chechen terrorists took about 1,200 schoolchildren and others hostage in Beslan, Russia; 340 people died when militants detonated explosives. Yasir Arafat died in Paris. Enormous tsunami devastated Asia; 220,000 killed. The movies released included The *Aviator, Collateral, Eternal Sunshine of the Spotless Mind, Friday Night Lights, The Incredibles, Kinsey, Maria Full of Grace, Million Dollar Baby, Sideways,* and *Spider-Man* 2. Notable deaths included those of Marlon Brando, Ray Charles, Estee Lauder,Tony Randall, Ronald Reagan, Christopher Reeve and Peter Ustinov.

In 2005 - Mahmoud Abbas won Presidency of the Palestinian Authority in a landslide. London hit by Islamic terrorist bombings, killing 52 and wounding about 700. It was Britain's worst attack since World War II. Cancer replaced heart disease as No. 1 cause of death for people aged 85 and under. The movies released included *Brokeback Mountain, Capote, Charlie and the Chocolate Factory, The Chronicles of Narnia: The Lion, the Witch and the Wardrobe, Crash, Good Night and Good Luck, Harry Potter and the Goblet of Fire, The History of Violence, Madagascar, Match Point, Munich, The Squid and the Whale, Star Wars: Episode III-Revenge of the Sith, Walk the Line,* and *The War of the Worlds.* Notable deaths included those of Anne Bancroft, Johnny Carson, John Paul II, Arthur Miller, Richard Pryor and William Westmoreland. The population of the world was 6.4 billion.

Chris Stafford picked me up at Changi airport on my arrival in Singapore on 11 January 1997 and had arranged for me to stay with him and his family for a few days until I could get organised. I had been to Asia a number of times before, but never lived there. When I was in the cops, a group of us went to Pattaya in the south of Thailand for holidays in 1978. I had heard all these stories about the sex trade in Thailand from returning cops and just didn't believe the stories we were being told. It couldn't be as easy as they were making it out to be, could it? Not only the sex side of things being attractive, we were told stories about how you could get wonderful clothing made for next to nothing, food was cheap and that Thailand was a man's paradise. You could have a beautiful young woman for the night for something like $20. There was sex for sale everywhere. We stayed in a hotel on the beachfront in Pattaya, probably about 1-2 stars. It was owned and run by an American veteran from the Vietnam War. He told us he was not a deserter but many of them were and they had made their homes in Thailand, mostly Chiang Mai. I would see old 'farangs' (foreigners) who could barely walk with the most beautiful girls hanging off their arms. It didn't matter how old they were, how ugly they were, or where they came from; as long as they had cash. 'no money, no honey' was the girls slogan. They spoke little English. Their standard three questions were, "What your name? Where you from? How long you be here?" They were doing their own marketing research and summing up whether or not they can make a good quid out of you. To tell you the truth after a short while when the novelty wore off, I was more interested in the Thai culture and their history. I wasn't even interested in drinking much so I kinda drifted away from the group and did my own thing. In fact I came back a bit earlier than the rest of them. I understood that the girls were mainly from the impoverished north and were simply finding a way to send money back to their homes. Even so! I did have a relationship with the receptionist at the hotel, which I did not have to pay for. I can't remember her name but she came back to BKK (Bangkok) with me and we stayed in a hotel for a couple of days. Even though I was not paying her I think it more than likely that she was looking for a husband to take her away from Thailand. Many of them are like that. They mainly want to get away from the impoverishment of the rural areas. Then I came back to Sydney with a bag full of new clothing and plenty of memories.

I'd also been through Singapore when Sue and I toured Europe in 1981; so I was a bit familiar with it. I went there again for my job interview and signing of contracts in 1996 and also went and stayed in Jakarta and Kuala Lumpur as well. Sometime in the 1980s a group of us went to the rugby sevens in Hong Kong so I had seen a bit of Asia. Singapore was now my new home. There is nothing backward about Singapore and it surely is a first world developed country. Singapore is very strict on illegals. If they are caught they get three months' imprisonment, three strokes of the cane and are then deported. Interesting that even though they know they are going to deport them they give them a flogging first. A gentle reminder perhaps! I know that to be a fact because I was in court one day when the Judge was handing down the sentences. He was dishing them out like jelly beans. I was not officially on Harry's books until I had my EP (employment pass) that took a few weeks to come through. When I did get my EP I set up arrangements with the bank to send Sue her $2,000 monthly and Ferrier Hodgson (the bankruptcy trustee) whatever I had to pay them every month. I liked Singapore right from the start. The government was well led by the PAP (People's Action Party) and as a general statement they did not put up with any nonsense. They had an overwhelming mandate from the people to govern the way they saw fit. When I attended court and saw all the illegals being sentenced I was there to support my boss, Chris Stafford. He had been summoned to attend court to explain why Harry's Bar should not have its licence revoked because we were allowing patrons to throw the empty peanut shells on the floor. It had been a long standing tradition at the bar where we supplied patrons with shelled peanuts whilst they were drinking. Other bars caught up with it and many of them started doing the same. The MOE (Ministry of Environment) argued that it presented a health hazard and wanted it stamped out. We were successful in being able to argue that it was a firmly established practice that had been sanctioned by the MOE for many years and only now had they raised an objection to it. We represented ourselves and won the case. Nevertheless, it is not good business to raise the ire of the Singapore Government so we stopped the practice, not wishing to antagonise the MOE anymore and getting on their hit list. Make no mistake, if they want to get you they will, so it paid to be humble and diplomatic when dealing with them.

Singapore is particularly tough on drug offenders; unreasonably so. In Singapore, the punishment for drug trafficking is death by hanging. The Judge has no discretionary power and he has no choice but to issue the mandatory death penalty (it is possible that this may have been changed very recently). What constitutes trafficking? You will be shocked to learn that if you have in your possession more than 15 grams of heroin; 30 grams of cocaine or 500 grams of cannabis, you are deemed in the eyes of the law to be trafficker. Singapore has (or had) the highest per capita execution rate in the world. I disagree with the death penalty, but that's irrelevant. When I was there the death penalty would be given for drug trafficking, murder, kidnapping and wait for it, possession of an unlicensed firearm. It's not illusory, it's the way it is. Little wonder that Singapore is considered one of the safest countries in the world. It's a sobering thought and lends a lot of weight to the argument that is often espoused that tough penalties are warranted if you want to clean up crime. It certainly works in Singapore and the Government makes no apologies for it. Most airline companies inform their passengers just before landing at Changi airport in Singapore that the death penalty applies for drug trafficking. It is also written on the immigration disembarkation card with the following warning, 'Death for drug traffickers under Singapore Law'. It is naturally no defence to claim that you did not know the penalties.

The strictness of Singapore did not bother me. They allow you to make a good money, allow drinking and sex and that was good enough for me. After a while I met this real estate agent and lawyer, Anne. Anne was Chinese and was a great woman. I think she was a first generation Singaporean with her parents coming from mainland China. She was doing well in her chosen career. The expatriate men used to talk about local women that had the big five Cs. Cash, car, condo, credit card, and career. Anne lived in what they called a HDB flat that she owned. The HDB concept (Housing Development Board) was one of Lee Kwan Yew's great innovations. He wanted Singaporeans to have their own home, so he developed this concept. It goes something like this. Firstly he developed the CPF scheme. CPF stands for Central Provident Fund. It is like our superannuation fund, but much better. Every Singaporean had to put 20% of their wages into a CPF account which naturally enough is managed by the Government. Here's the good part. The employer has to match that and put in 20% as well. So every month the citizen is getting 40% of their wages put away into a secured guaranteed government account. They are then allowed to buy one of these affordable HDB units with this money as well as low interest loans. It shows the genius of Lee Kwan Yew. The HDBs were not as good as the condominiums, but nevertheless they were more than adequate. I would have no trouble in living in one and for a time I lived with Anne in one of these HDBs. Anne wanted some permanency with our relationship but that was far too early for me after the recent dramas of my relationship with Sue. I had to find a way out of it without hurting her too much. On my birthday, I made other arrangements to celebrate. I did not know that she had arranged something special for me (but if I am going to be truthful I thought she would) and I went to Chris's place for dinner without telling her. She went bananas. She even threatened to jump off the tenth floor of her apartment block. That really ended our affair and she suggested we have a three-month hiatus. I agreed. When we talked about getting back three months later, I told her that I had met another local woman, also Chinese. She told me that I could not have two girlfriends. I told her I loved both as much as each other and could not give up either. Of course the second one was all fictitious. I made it all up and predicted with some accuracy how she would respond. She gave me the flick and of course, that is what I wanted.

To keep fit I used to regularly walk the Bukit Timah Nature Reserve. This nature reserve is about 400 acres and pretty much in the middle of Singapore, so was considered a bit of a gem by bush walkers. It is Singapore highest point but still only 163 meters high but it had one of the country's biggest rainforests and was declared an ASEAN Heritage Park in late 2011. I figured the bush walking was a way to keep my weight in check which I have battled with nearly all my adult life. Parts of the walk were quite difficult and one of the tracks there had about 600 steps. You could imagine trudging up these stairs in temperatures above 30 degrees Celsius with the humidity sometimes running at 90%. It is after all only a bit over a hundred kilometres from the Equator. At one part of the track there was a continuous set of two hundred and thirty stairs. One of the questions I used to ask at trivia nights under the geography sessions, was whether Singapore was in the northern or southern hemisphere. Most people got it wrong. The answer is that it is in the northern hemisphere. Sometimes I'd take people with me but usually they did not come back for second doses. It was not unusual to come across snakes, including the deadly king cobra snakes. You had to be careful and make sure you stayed on the track and kept an eye out all the time. This was their natural habitat and you certainly would not want to get bitten by one. One day I had Chris with me and I went within a meter of a king cobra that was in the upright position. It frightened the life out of me and I thought every time I went trekking I was taking a risk getting bitten by one of these deadly snakes, but it didn't deter me and I still kept doing it.

Work had its ups and downs at Harry's Bar. It was a very busy, predominantly expat bar. I had been hired to start a new bar in Kuala Lumpur but the owner pulled the pin on it. He wanted to rescind my contract before I even started to work for him but Chris more or less made him honour it. So instead of going to KL, I was made General Manager of Singapore. The problem was they already had one. The owner was against me from day one because of this and understandably there is only one outcome when the boss doesn't like you, and that is that he is going to win. When my contract came up for renewal a year later, he told Chris not to renew it. That was fair enough. He did not undertake the expansion program he hired me for. He was paying expensive expatriate wages, when he did not have to. I was at Harry's for one year. During that time the owner leased the building next door. Like Harry's, it was a large two storey Chinese shop house, owned by the UOB (bank) in Singapore. The owner had a dream one night that he would like to start up a Cajun style restaurant. You have to be careful about following up on your dreams. Chris was all for it but I advised against it. I told them that we should do another pub. Of course, we ended up doing what the owner wanted; it was his money. He and Chris flew to New Orleans and went to Bourbon Street to get a taste of it. They came back very enthusiastic about it all. We went ahead and built a very nice cajun food restaurant and at the time, it was the only one in Singapore. We named it Bourbon Street. Unfortunately for whatever reason the concept did not take off but it was little consolation in my saying, 'I told you so'. The owner had to wrap it up and consequently wrap me up as well. He was a high wealth individual so he could easily carry the loss financially. A short time after I left, Chris also handed in his resignation but probably would have been sacked even if he hadn't.

We had a client at Harry's that bears an interesting story. His name is Michael Townsend. Actually that turned out to be an alias. His real name is Michael McCrea and we got to know Mike well. He was a big spender and worked his own business as a financial adviser. When I opened up my own bar later on, he used to frequent it. We knew that he was a man we had to keep our eye on because of his fearsome reputation of being very violent when he lost it. One night in 2002 in a fit of rage, Mike murdered his driver and the driver's girlfriend in his apartment. Apparently his girlfriend Audrey Ong helped him get rid of the bodies. It was all over an argument when the driver made a derogatory remark about Audrey in his native mandarin. Mike lost it, again. He started punching the driver who fought back. Mike got the better of him but just had to go that one step further and strangle him. Then he strangled the driver's girlfriend as well. After that Mike and Audrey disposed of the bodies and left them in the boot of a car at the 'four floors of whores' building. The building's real name is Orchid Towers. They have made it a tourist attraction where the first four floors are full of whores, lady-boys and what have you, plying their trade. Mike and Audrey then left Singapore for London on January 5. The bodies were found on January 7. The driver's body was stuffed into a wicker chest in the back seat of the car and his girlfriend's body was found bundled in cloth in the boot of the car. They were arrested in Melbourne in June 2002 and Ong was deported by the

Aussies back to Singapore. She got twelve years in Changi prison for helping Mike dispose of the bodies. However the Australians would not deport Mike because of Singapore's archaic law where the death penalty would be mandatory. It took something like three years of negotiations between Australia and Singapore before Australia would send Mike back for trial in Singapore. The authorities in Singapore had to agree that he would not be hanged for the murders. Singapore honoured this agreement as you would expect them to. In 2006 he was sentenced to 24 years in prison. That was the maximum he could be given under the circumstances. I heard later on that Mike was doing it tough in prison and was slowly going insane. Mike appealed against the severity of the sentence but of course, it was rejected. In fact, I think it was increased to 28 years.

I'll give you an example to show you how tough they are on drugs in Singapore. There was this expat bloke who used to have a drink with us when we watched the rugby sometimes. He was in a high position in his company so he was no mug. We liked him but looking back there was something different about him. He was the most unlike gay fella I have met. I would never have picked it. His problem however was not being gay, but having a dip with ICE every now and then. The Police caught up with him with half a tablet of ice on him. Half a tablet! They gave him 18 months in Changi prison. When he did his time, they took him straight to the airport and deported him. Now compare that with what might happen in Australia. Singapore makes no apologies for its tough stance on drugs.

During my year at Harry's Bar, I climbed Mt Kinabalu in Borneo. Mr Kinabalu is the highest peak in South East Asia rising up to 4095 meters. After I broke it off with Anne, I went and lived with an English expatriate, Peter Hogg. Peter was an ex British Army Officer and had a nice older style colonial black and white unit up in Mt Faber. He wanted a flat mate so I moved in. We split the rent of $3,000 per month. Sometimes we caught up for a drink at this neat little bar in Chinatown named Beaujolais. I was also managing this as well as Harry's but it was just a sideshow for the owner. One night Peter Hogg and I were having a drink with a friend of his, Peter West (Westie). Westie bought up that he'd like to climb Mt Kinabalu. Westie was an Australian but had this very pronounced educated English accent. He was more English than the English. Over the following weeks we tossed it around and decided we would do it. It just so happened we met a couple of blokes in the bar a few nights later who had just recently done it so now we could get it from the horse's mouth. They advised us to get some level of fitness first as it was a bit tough in parts; that turned out to be a bit of an understatement. Westie shrugged this off and we three went to Kota Kinabalu which is in Malaysia Borneo. We were all enthusiastic and felt that we could handle this without too much trouble. The first bit was straight for a couple of hundred meters but thereafter, it was up all the way to the summit. Bejesus, talk about tough. Peter and I were reasonably fit but not Westie. He was a heavy smoker and drinker and it was no picnic for him. Hogg and I got to the shelter at the 11,000 feet mark in about three hours and Westie was nowhere to be seen. We had decided (or rather Peter did) that he shouldn't slow us down and he could catch up with us at the overnight shelter. He came puffing and panting a couple of hours after we got there. There was some sort of a local food hawker staff there so we filled up on rice and whatever and bunked down on the floor for the night. At 2.30 am the following morning we took off for the three kilometre climb to the summit. My, this was getting really tough now. It was almost vertical (or so it seemed) starting with steep wooden steps and then coming onto steep granite slabs. For the granite slabs they had guide ropes. We had found out the previous evening that a large group of Koreans were going to leave at 3 am. We did not want to get stuck behind them. It was pitch black going up and Hogg had a torch and I had nothing and had not prepared properly for this trip. We got to the stage where we would climb maybe 30 meters, rest and then do it again. Hogg was starting to get headaches so we paced it carefully. It never seemed to end but eventually after a lot of hard work we reached the summit whilst it was still dark and it was freezing. The other striking thing about the summit was that there were rats everywhere; big, fat rats. What on earth did they feed on? We did not know where Westie was at this stage and I was feeling guilty about leaving him behind; but Hogg was adamant. He had to either keep up with us or do it in his own time. I guess that's the British Army Officer bit coming out of him. It was a great sense of achievement and we had climbed it essentially in just over five hours. We saw the sun come up over the South China Sea and it was very special because it was a really clear morning and we could see a great distance yonder. After quite a long time, we saw Westie at the bottom of the summit. I climbed back down a few hundred meters and I was shocked when I saw him. He was totally exhausted, dehydrated and did not think he could put one leg in front of the other. I slowly encouraged him forward and he reached the summit. Looking back, I think it was a much greater achievement for him than for us. He did it much tougher than us but still made it. He said later that if he could have called a helicopter to come and get him he would have, no matter what it might have cost. We adopted the same strategy for the descent. We would set our own pace and meet back at Timpbohon (the starting point). Hogg and I lost sight of Westie fairly quickly and got back down in not much over an hour. For me it was no problem but Hogg had bad knees and coming down was hurting him but we got back together. Then we waited for Westie. He eventually came with two other climbers. They literally had to take him one on each shoulder and help him down. He was gone. He had nothing left and he got stuck into us for leaving him. That night we celebrated but he had to sit down the entire time and he could barely walk. When he walked we had to assist him wherever he wanted to go. We came back to Singapore the next day and the climbing of Mt Kinabalu became the subject of conversation for quite some time at our little bar *Beaujolais*. When people asked me how hard it was to climb, I told them it was 'bloody' hard and to make sure you are fit before you take it on. My quads were sore for at least a week aterwards. Westie took a long time to get over it and in hindsight, I think we were all negligent and very naive. We should not have taken him. I look back on that and realise that he could quite easily have had a heart attack and died. He looked bad and we were not showing a 'duty of care' that we should have done.

During one of my visits down to see my family in Christchurch, I worked with Dan to settle his future. He was not doing well at school and was considered a disruptive influence on the other children. Dan had always been well liked but he just didn't like school and his grades reflected this. He was going to a good school at St Bede's which was controlled by the Marist Clergy. I spoke to them about Dan attending boarding school. I was satisfied that they were treating the boys well and that he would not have to suffer the way that I did all those years ago at St Brendan's. It seems that the Catholic schooling system had changed completely and that corporal punishment was out. Sue did not agree that Dan should go to boarding school as she righty pointed out, home was just around the corner. In the end the Marist clergy wouldn't take him as a boarder anyway for reasons undisclosed. I spoke with Dan about his future and asked him what he wanted to do. Like most 16 year old kids he said that he didn't have a clue. With that platform he and I went into town to see a vocation guidance professional. She was an excellent young lady and took Dan through a series of Q&As. In the final wash-up, it was agreed that Dan would be best suited to outdoor work that was physically demanding and did not require complex technical knowledge. When he went through the options for apprenticeships, he chose carpentry. Not long after that, he commenced a 9-month course at the Christchurch Technical College to learn all the theory. He then commenced a 4-year apprentice course with a well-known respected builder in the district. Sue's brother Tony Bastings arranged it and for that I will always be deeply indebted. Today Dan is married with three children and has quite a thriving building business. He is regarded highly and well respected within the building industry. He is affectionately known in NZ as 'Ozzie'. One of a number of his achievements was to win a grand final in the Canterbury district rugby league. He played for the Kaiapoi Bulldogs and they won the 2010 premiership. He has the mandatory tattoo to reflect that on his leg. As this book goes to print (July 2017), Dan has a staff of six and has sold his first batch of homes that he built in partnership with his accountant as speculation homes. It makes me very happy to know that he is doing well and the only negative (isn't there always one) is my concern about his gambling but he assures me that he has it well under control. He certainly does have some amazing wins but they say that gamblers only tell you about their wins and keep their big losses to themselves. The fact is that he has turned out to be a really good man. His wife Becks (Rebecca) had their third child in September (2016) and named him Luke. So he has three little ones with all the positives and negatives that entails. At the time of publishing this book, his seven year old daughter Brooke is doing very well at school and his five year old son, Hunter is in day care and doing well also. Luke is now 10 months old. I am very proud of Dan and am pleased that I can share my life with him and Toni in this book. Yes, even the negative parts. Actually, especially the negative parts.

Toni is three years younger than Dan. She was born just as I was being assassinated by the three wise men at the Regent Sydney. They were both born at St Margaret's hospital in Darlinghurst; Dan on 29 June 1986 and Toni on 24 March 1989. Toni was a really good kid, and when I last went back to Christchurch Sue showed me some of the old school reports and it was clear that Toni was a studious and well behaved child at school. I still worry that our separation may have impacted more adversely on Toni than Dan and left deeper scars on her. Toni adapted well in NZ and after St Patrick's primary school in Kaiapoi she went to Marion College in Christchurch. She did very well there and at one stage was Captain of their senior netball team. If she had not damaged her knees from playing she might have gone on to bigger and better things; maybe even professional. She proved to be more scholastic than Dan and went to Canterbury University and graduated with a Degree in Education. Toni knew my financial position and she insisted that she pay her own university fees and over three years obtained her degree. Toni has a history of handling separation badly. I can't remember if I told you the story how she left her passport behind at my unit in Sydney one time to avoid having to leave. Just in case I didn't and risking duplication, we (Dan, Toni and I) got picked up by Geoff to go to the airport. When we got in Geoff's car after we just left, I asked them to check that they had their passports. Toni didn't have it. We had to go back and I found it underneath the telephone. I think there is a chance that she may have done that deliberately and if so, that may explain the anxiety that one can suffer with separation. Remember the story about my catching the train to Aberdeen around about 1950. When she had to leave to go to London, Sue and I were concerned that she would have a lot of trouble saying goodbye but she handled it well. After graduation she went to London and taught in a primary school there. This was a stepping stone to teaching at an International school in Dubai. Toni was only five at the time of our separation and her mother's illness (Dan was eight). They must have been affected badly by what was going on. I feel that she may have it in her mind that I rejected them by going to Singapore and leaving them. It must be difficult for little kids to understand all the acrimony involved with divorce and financial collapse at such a young age and it could not do anything but adversely affect them. Toni has travelled much of the world now and would probably fall into the 'trendy global jet-setter' category. Just as I am proud of Dan, I am also proud of Toni. Both of them had to do it tough after Sue and I separated and I, more than most people I would suggest, would understand and have a great deal of empathy for people that have been scarred by separation anxiety.

I left my mark when I first came to Singapore. We (the western expatriates) could not watch the international rugby. Star Sports only had cable connections in the HDB flats for the local population. One of my colleagues at Harry's Bar and later future partner, Baljit Singh lived in an HDB flat. Once I found this out, we arranged for the game to be video recorded. When the first half was finished we would have a taxi on standby to bring in the video. We would then start showing the game in what was now an absolutely packed bar and function room. We timed it so that we would have the second half in before the first had finished.

We had the mandatory ten minutes half time between the tapes so that everybody could load up on drinks. Sometimes we would extend that to twenty minutes but any longer and our customers would start to get a bit agitated. Of course there were some time management skills involved but we did it and we did it successfully. We were the first bar in Singapore to do this and it greatly increased the trade. It made the business a lot of money but the owner never acknowledged it. It wasn't long however before cable became available to commercial business and condominiums. Once that happened, most of the bars started showing the rugby. I used to market it quite heavily as 'The game they play in Heaven.'

After my sacking at the end of 1997, I needed to sort out what I was going to do to make sure that I could meet my financial commitments that I have described to you. I had met another woman and we were starting to go out quite a bit. On the business front I had two things going for me. Firstly, I thought that it would be a good idea for me to do my own bar. The question was how I would do that with very limited money and no partners. I discussed it with my Operations Manager Baljit (Harry's Bar) and my Manager at Beaujolais, Jackie Stevens, a Dutch girl. I also invited Chris Stafford into the group. I put the idea to them about us doing our own bar. We had the expertise, networking and would find a way to get the money. I was the driver of it all and explained to them that to start up a company suitable for this endeavour in Singapore, we would need $100,000 paid up capital. I managed to get them to all agree to put in $25,000 each. The paid up capital would be used to build the bar and we could all get employment passes. The Singapore Government is very business friendly and they bend over backwards to assist new business ventures. On the day I called all of them to put their money in, my good friend Chris reneged citing financial hardships. I was disappointed with him over this and thought that he could have discussed it with me much earlier. Now I had to find another SGD$25,000. I asked Sue to let me take $25,000 from the line of credit that I had arranged in New Zealand when buying the house for her and the children. It was arranged in the event that she might need it for a rainy day. Sue was totally against it and got very emotional about it. She reminded me in no uncertain terms what had happened last time I went into business and was sure that the same thing would happen this time. In the end I persuaded her to lend it to me and I got the money I needed. I promised Sue I would have it back within one month. I honoured that promise and Sue had it back in three weeks. I did not want her exposed to any stress as that could trigger another 'breakdown'. At this stage of her life she had lost the will to fight and was very fragile, so it was very important to have her in a relatively stress free environment.

We hired an English expatriate Julian Coombs, who was both a customer and an interior designer. We had the bar built within one month and Julian did a great job. Some of this was happening whilst I was in NZ and they all got together and decided to call is Bisous. Bisous is a French word meaning, wait for it, kiss. I did not like it at all, still don't, but democracy prevailed and I lost. We now had a bar in Tanjong Pagar, Singapore. Tanjong Pagar is on the fringe of Chinatown and still has many of the older style Chinese shop houses. Our bar was one of these and Julian really made it look good. My two partners were just fantastic. They told me that I had done my job and all I had to do was sit back and relax. Operationally they would do all the work and that suited me. They really thought that I was not up to it when it came to service. Julian was also a part time artist and we commissioned him to paint a picture of Lawrence of Arabia that would serve as a talking point. 'El Orance' dominated the bar, with the painting holding down a strategic position. Of course we had to explain to our Asian customers who 'El Orance' (Lord Lawrence) was. It was a very well accepted bar and Julian had created a warm, inviting, sophisticated atmosphere and the expatriate customers loved it.

One of the many celebrity guest speakers that I was able to get to the bar to speak with expatriate rugby buffs like myself was Sean Fitzpatrick (former All Black World Cup Captain). He signed an All Black jersey for me that I gave to Dan (my son) but

I don't think Dan kept it for too long. We sponsored a local expatriate rugby team named the Bedok Kings and they went on to win the local grand final in our first year of sponsorship. Other rugby guest speakers were Mark Ella, Tim Horan, Anthony Herbert and Stu Wilson. Baljit and Jackie made sure that service standards were high and they had a great rapport with the customers. The bar was well received and we recuperated our original investment within five months. For that to happen, it had to be firing on all cylinders from day one and it was. We opened it in October 1998. One of our customers was an advertising guru and he developed postcards gratis to promote the bar. He had inscribed on the post cards the following: "What does a Dutch girl, an Indian Sheik and an ex-Cop from Sydney have in common?" Answer, 'Bisous Bar in Singapore'. Last time I was up in Singapore (June 2016) I saw Jacky and business wise she is doing very well but had just recently lost her mother. It turned out that her mother had chosen euthanasia as a form of passing as she had terminal cancer and towards the end she was in a lot of pain. It was distressing to have Jacky relay the sequence of events to us and the impact that it had on her being there to witness it. I assured her that if I was in a similar circumstance I would do the same but of course, it is still illegal in Australia. Jacky was having a dreadful time dealing with it and was really only just hanging in there. I also caught up with Baljit and he was managing a couple of Lebanese restaurants in Arab Street in Singapore.

I did a number of other assignments in 1998. I was asked to oversee a large development in Perak, Malaysia. Perak is one of the thirteen states of Malaysia. I became the Consultant General Manager of the development, Bukit Merah Laketown Resort, not far from the town of Taiping in Perak. The Laketown complex had a themed water park, a hotel and there were large developments for residential property. Whilst I was there for the 3-month assignment, they were starting to develop an eco-island for the orangoutangs. I believed that I left behind my imprint. I got the staff fairly motivated and they wanted me to stay. However, the owners had signed a contract with another

Australian before I came and they had to honour it. They were seriously considering not doing it. The hotel side of things was not working for them and it needed a professional sales and marketing team. I arranged a sales team and we would go out into the regional areas and promote the property. The town of Ipoh was one of my favourites for these excursions. It had these great Chinese restaurants and the most beautiful women I have ever seen. One of the things I remember most about Taiping was its close proximity to a war cemetery. One of the staff told me about it and I asked him to take me there. This particular cemetery is the final resting place for allied personnel who were killed during World War II, the Malayan Campaign and the Japanese occupation of Malaya. Servicemen who died after the war or during their postings in northern Malaya prior to the Malayan Emergency were also interred here. The cemetery was erected and maintained by the Commonwealth War Graves Commission. There are more than 850 World War II casualties commemorated in this cemetery, including more than 500 who remain unidentified. I left this assignment with a great affection for the Malay people.

As part of the business development program with my consulting work, I arranged with a couple of ex-US Government men to go to Phnom Penh in Cambodia. I went there for a week in September 1999. At the time Cambodia was a very backward developing country with a tragic recent history and I related earlier the story about my taxi ride from the airport to the hotel. I had some meetings with the luxury hotels General Managers. To be honest I was more interested in the history of the place and as always, I made it my objective to find out as much as I could about the Cambodian genocide. The North Vietnamese and Vietcong used Cambodia as a base and transported much of their supplies through it. By 1975, the population had blown out to about three million people, many of them refugees from the fighting in Vietnam. The capital Phnom Penh was taken over by the Khmer Rouge (KR) in April 1975. They forcibly evacuated the entire city and so began the genocide of the Cambodian people by the KR. It was described by one journalist as the greatest caravan of misery he had seen in five years of war. He went on to describe how he saw one man in the march who had neither hands nor feet, writhing along the ground like a worm or the man who had a foot dangling off the end of his leg, held only by skin. I recall that one of the Cambodian maids I had at the Regent Sydney in the 1980s told me that her entire family had been murdered by the KR. They were all forced by the KR into labour camps on rural farms as part of a new indoctrination programs. Pol Pot, the leader of the KR, turned a high school in Phnom Penh named Tuol Sleng into a prison camp called S-21. Pol Pot's agenda was to return the country to an agrarian economy and they murdered their own people that were deemed to be too educated or not politically right for the new order of Government. Many more people were starved to death. Perhaps Pol Pot learnt a lesson from Stalin's Russians in the Ukraine in the late 1930s when Stalin committed genocide on the Ukrainian people by starving them of their wheat crops. Pol Pot did the same with the rice crops by selling them to China for military hardware. I went to the Tuol Sleng Genocide Museum where such terrible brutality and death took place. There was photographic evidence right throughout the museum. I also went to Choeung Ek which is about 15 kilometres from Phnom Penh. This is referred to as the killing fields of Cambodia. Eventually the KR were defeated by the Vietnamese in 1979 and the people that survived the genocide returned to Phnom Penh. Estimates of the total number of deaths resulting from the KR reign, including disease and starvation, range from 1.7 to 2.5 million out of a 1975 population of roughly 8 million. That's one out of every three and a half were murdered and all this happened in our time. We have to ask the question, "Where was the United Nations?"

I was deeply moved by what I saw in Cambodia and developed a real affinity with the Cambodian people. I went to the temple region of Siem Reap and toured through Angkor Wat. The place is riddled with history and well worth seeing. All in all, I stayed in Cambodia for two weeks but did not see much of the countryside. However I saw enough to leave an indelible impression upon me. I have been meaning to watch the film *The*

Killing Fields but have not yet got around to it yet. While I was in Phnom Phen, I stayed at a little motel that had been recommended to me by friends in Singapore. It was ok and had good security. When I was taken up to my room by the receptionist, a pretty young Cambodian woman, she asked me if I would like her to stay with me for the night. Rather than show no interest at all, I asked her how much it would be. She said that USD$15 would be fine. Pushing it a bit further I asked her what she would do for me and she told me that she would do whatever I wanted. Just for the record, I never took her up on the offer and felt a bit sad for her that she had to make extra money this way. I imagine that she would have slept with many of the hotel's customers. Another assignment was organised by my friend Chris. An expatriate chap had this theme bar in Kuala Lumpur (KL). He wasn't doing too well so he got Chris up as a Consultant. Chris in turn wanted me there to do all the dirty work. It was an experience. The trade was reasonable but much of the money was not going into the till. In Asia, if you take away a man's rice bowl, it can be dangerous and one has to tread very carefully. There was this criminal system in place that operated a protection racket. Each area had a particular criminal protecting it; protecting it from what I don't know, perhaps other criminals. The man that looked after this one was a bloke Chris and I called Black Joe. Black Joe would put one of his men in the bar and he would sit at the counter all night keeping an eye on things. Chris decided that he wanted to go to the Greek Islands with his new beautiful Japanese girlfriend to get married, just after we started. It was left to me to finish it. The owner could not get a License to operate the bar and had been trying to get it for a couple of years. Even though he did not have a License, he continued to operate as if he did. The police would come around in a big police truck with Police sitting in the back every week. The boss would come in the bar in full uniform and that was that. I never saw the money transacted but that is what the owner told me was happening. I was not going to do anything about it. Nor was I going to challenge Black Joe's authority. This was their domain and I went along with it in the interest of personal safety. When in Rome, do what the Romans do. The owner was just not cut out to be a restaurant/bar operator. He had it because he wanted kudos and to have a good time. He was a nice enough fella but in the wrong business. One day I came to work and the front door was open, as well as the door to the cellar. It looked like someone had a key to gain access because there was no evidence of forced entry. Once I got in there, I found the cellar open but nothing obviously missing but there was an empty bottle of French champagne. I immediately told the owner about it and he fessed up that it was him. He had met some Malaysian beauty and taken her back to his bar. Part of the seduction course was to ply her with French champagne. Apparently it worked for him but he left everything open on his way out. I had made up my mind that I would terminate the agreement. He had made up his mind he was going to sack me/us. He got in first. When he told me I replied to him that he had just beaten me to the punch. I was intending to tell him we would be leaving immediately; so he made that part of it easy for me.

When I was doing the assignment in Kuala Lumpur, I used to take the weekends off and go and see my partner in Singapore. I'd travel by train as I have always had an affinity with rail travel; perhaps a throwback to my boarding school days. The distance between KL and Singapore via rail is about 350 kilometres and the train takes about seven hours. That's averaging 50 kph, not too flash but I always enjoyed it. The seats were comfortable and they had a dining car (sort of) that was cheap. The food was local fare with things like nasi lemak, chicken curry, beef rendang; that sort of thing. One of the negatives of the trip could be breakdowns; they were not all that uncommon. One time we had to get out of the train, get on a bus, travel for half an hour and then get back on the train. It turned out that there had been a land slide and the track was covered. Another time, the air brakes were not working so they had to stop and fix them. On this trip, I got out to see what the maintenance men were doing under the train and to stretch my legs. There was an elderly white man also observing procedures and I struck up a conversation with him. He was a Dutch businessman and like me, he enjoyed travelling by rail if he had the time. At that time I think he was the Dutch Consul for Burma. After we got talking for a while he told me that he had a daughter who owned a bar in Singapore. Well, the penny dropped straight away. How many Dutch girls own bars in Singapore? It had to be Jackie, my partner, and as it turned out, it was. Here in the middle of the rain forests of Negri Sembilan on a broken down Malaysian train, I unwittingly met Jackie's Dad. Small world isn't it? He rang Jackie and told her he was with somebody that she might know. You can imagine the surprise Jackie got when I got on the phone. I think it would be a great idea if Singapore, Malaysia and Thailand got together and built a VFT (very fast train) from Singapore to Bangkok. It takes about two hours to fly from Singapore to Bangkok. Allowing for an hour and a half both ways for immigration, waiting, etcetera, that's five hours but a VFT would take maybe two to three hours and it would be from Central to Central. They really should think about it like the Chinese have done with the VFT from Shanghai to Beijing.

In 1999, soon after we got Bisous Bar going, I was offered an assignment from one of our customers. Baljit knew him fairly well and he mentioned to Baljit that he was thinking of starting up a night club in Singapore. Baljit recommended me and used our bar as a reference for what I was capable of doing. The owner came from a well-known wealthy Singaporean Chinese family that had a lot of influence in local business. In that sense he was born with a silver spoon in his mouth but he was a reasonably humble bloke who did not flaunt his wealth. He was American educated and from real wealth. After interviewing me, I was given the assignment to oversee the building of the night club and getting it ready for operations. The first step was to secure a location. Location is important for bar and restaurants, but critical for night clubs. As luck (and perhaps good work on my part) would have it, I found out that probably the number one night club location in Singapore where a famous night club was located, was folding up. The owners of the location decided they wanted a new tenant and were on the lookout for one. They say that timing is everything and I found this out the very day that the Board had made the decision. When I informed my client about this, he knew I had found the perfect location. It is located in downtown Singapore and you just could not get a better location and the owners were delighted to think that they could get a tenant from such a respected family. I worked closely with the project management team and we built the club in three to four months. I arranged some things for the club that they just would not have got if it were not for my hotel training. I knew that a night club had to supply a food menu of some sort but it did not have a kitchen and there was no space to provide one. I arranged with the hotel that food orders from the club's point of sale go directly to the kitchen above the club on the first level of the hotel. When the order was completed, a blue strobe light would come on and the orders would be sent down in a dumb waiter. With this arrangement the hotel shared in the revenue. I don't remember the terms we agreed to but it solved the problem of being able to supply top class finger food prepared by the chefs of the hotel, who were world class. Not a bad initiative on my part. I also managed to get the hotel to agree to a nominal basic rent, plus a share of the revenue. To make the hotel feel secure I arranged for the club's point of sales registers to be linked directly to the hotel main frame computer. That way we all knew what was being received as revenue. It was not in my client's make up to want to cheat his business partner and another reason why I enjoyed working with him. We didn't know yet if the bar would be successful and needed to have an exit strategy in the event that it wasn't. We also arranged to have what they call a diplomatic clause in the leasing contract so that he had an out if things went south. As well as these key points, I liaised closely with the hotel's engineer to make sure that all the critical infrastructure was up to date. He even allowed us to put work that needed to be done on an on-going basis on his hotel maintenance program which was carried out by hotel staff and paid for by the hotel. I told my client that he would make more money if he put in another corner bar that only sold hard liquor. If patrons wanted beer they would have to get it at the main bar, but the big profits are not in beer but in spirits and cocktails. This proved to be another master stroke and that is what we did. It worked really well. We hired the General Manager and once the club had been built, we had our opening. It was successful right from the start. My client never had to use the monies put aside for initial operating costs. The club was self-supporting right from the start and he had his original investment back within 4-5 months. For this assignment I was paid SGD$40,000. As well as this, I was now getting $3,000 from my own bar as a monthly dividend. It is generally agreed that bars have a minimum of two years to get back their original investment. Both the bars that I was Project Manager for paid back the investors within five months. I felt that with both of these assignments I had performed admirably and was seriously looking at setting myself up as a food and beverage Project Manager; but I never did. If ever I had this self-doubt about my competency, it began to dissipate with these types of successes. I was getting close to settling all debts under the 'Deed of Arrangement' that I had entered into in January 1997 and expected to be able to meet the deadline of having it settled within three years. I managed to do that and this was another major turning point for me. At the same time, I never missed a payment to Sue and the kids.

One of our clients at the Bisous bar was a bloke who was a mortgage broker for one of the Australian banks. His name was Jerry Kane and unfortunately Jerry passed in 2004 from testicular cancer. Jerry was a really good quintessential Aussie fella and not surprisingly we struck up a friendship. I eventually got around to telling him about my financial troubles and felt that it would be many a moon before I could own real estate in Sydney again. He said, "No worries mate, I can fix that up. You don't need any money". He arranged a loan with the overseas branch of an Australian Bank, before you could blink your eye. Poonam (my partner) helped me with the deposit. At that time, the SGD dollar was on par with the AUD. All of a sudden I (well the bank really) owned a one bedroom luxurious unit at the York Apartments in York Street, Sydney. It was a very smart unit and was rented out as a hotel apartment. The rent obtained essentially paid for the mortgage. Soon after property prices in Sydney boomed but not in the CBD. After about five years there had been no capital appreciation on this property. Unbelievable! I had really been banking on that as my way back but it just didn't happen. The unit was now running at a loss with the high strata and body corporate fees and a declining market. I made a decision to sell it and it went for what I paid for it, $375.000. The management wanted to upgrade all the units at a cost per unit of AUD$40,000, and I just didn't have it. I suppose the good news is that I got out of it without a loss. I had this thing that every man has to have his 'shed'. A man thing about having something you could call a home. I bought a two bedroom unit in an up market part of Cairns with the money I got from the York Street unit. I paid about AUD$130,000 and had it in my mind that I would live in Cairns and commute to Singapore. Unfortunately I did not like Cairns for a multitude of reasons. The main one was that it was too humid, too hot and I found, too boring. So, I sold that one as well and made a bit of money on it, maybe about $10,000. The next unit I bought was on the Gold Coast at Runaway Bay and paid $310,000 for it in 2010. I still own it and simply put it out on the rental market. Not long after that the Aussie dollar took off so I got the timing right with that one, but that was luck and not any great financial planning on my part. Not that long later the AUD outstripped the USD and then dropped as the AUD always does eventually.

I was a member of a group of blokes that used to meet the last Friday of every month for a luncheon. The name of the group was the CRAFT Club. CRAFT stands for 'can't remember a f****** thing'. The idea was that we would meet in the cellar of the upmarket Grand Hyatt Hotel and do the boys thing; drink excessively, get drunk, smoke cigars, tell yarns and generally have a good time. Sometimes we would do a trip somewhere and do the same thing there. Usually these trips were to 'exotic' places where there were plenty of cheap women to have some fun with. Just boys being boys really! They say that many men never grow up and I think the Craft Club was a good example of that. Once a year we had a black tie dinner with wives/ girlfriends and at these special functions none of the boys would go for a 'tub and rub' afterwards. At this time I was drinking fairly heavily and I used to come home from these things 'drunk as a skunk' and would take the usual two days to get over it. But they were good times and I have fond memories of them.

It was now 24 years since I had any contact with psychiatric personnel or had any medication. Sue and I had amicably agreed that the marriage was finished but we could remain friends and we did. She met a really good bloke by the name of Ken Cassidy. He was also a humble bloke like me and ideal for Sue. He has a quiet demeanour whilst Sue maintained her gregariousness and liveliness. He was the perfect match for her as he was much more patient than I am.

I had now been going out with Poonam for a year or so and we really got on well. That must have been the case because we are still together eighteen years later. Poonam helped me a great deal and I don't think that I can ever repay her for the many things that she has done for me. When the kids came to see me in Singapore Poonam would put them up, provide us with a car and generally help me take care of them. When I bought the unit in Sydney (2000) Poonam helped me with the deposit and also helped me with the deposit for my Gold Coast unit (2010). We had many good times together and I would venture to suggest that Poonam was the best friend I ever had. My children adore her as do the vast majority of people that have a connection with her. There is much, much more I could say about my time with Poonam but perhaps that might be best left for another occasion. I could write a book about the 15-years that I spent with Poonam but fear that it would have much too much negativity in it, so I have chosen to leave that part of my life out of it. Nevertheless, having said that Poonam played a major supportive role for me from 1998 until 2012 and I will always be deeply indebted to her. When I am having a conversation with people about the problems I had with my own mother, I tell them that I wished that I would have had a mother like Poonam. Under different circumstances I am sure that we would have got married. As I have written and it is worth repeating, Poonam is the best friend I have ever had.

We kept our bar in Tanjong Pagar until 2002 but toward the end it was losing its appeal. Bars can be a fickle business. We had some good accounts for Christmas parties coming up that would fix up the problem with the cash flow but then we had the 11 September 2001 terrorism attack in NYC (New York City). All the Christmas functions we had on our books were for American companies such as JP Morgan and CISCO and they cancelled. This was the final nail in the coffin for us. The key is to get the location right like we did with Bar None and it should, with good management, survive long term. Harry's Bar for example is still going strong after twenty years because it is situated right on the edge of the Raffles financial district of Singapore at Boat Quay. How could it not do well? Bisous captured the imagination for a while but the market ultimately rejected it because of its location. Parking was the biggest issue. I talked with our beer supplier APB (Asian Pacific Breweries) about the way forward. We were given a small sponsorship to start up Bisous and had a good relationship with them. I had several meetings with them and in the end I was able to negotiate a $100,000 sponsorship deal. That was, if I might say, a job well done on my part. We actually were able to sell Bisous for about $20,000. We had no trouble getting the bond back from the Landlord which I believe was about $15,000. These figures might not be completely accurate but not far off the mark. I found a site that I thought would be good. It was located on the fringe of Raffles CBD, adjacent to Citibank, so the market was there. This bar had a fully equipped restaurant and consisted of three Chinese shopfronts. This was a big step up for us but Baljit and Jackie were up for it. By this time we had two other partners. They were two expatriates that had executive positions and were regular patrons of the bar. I put it to them to join us as equal shareholders as we were wanting to expand. They did and ultimately that was a very bad decision on my part. The partnership folded in 2003 and there was a great deal of acrimony around that. We built the bar and it looked great and business was good. We continued our sponsorship of the Bedok Kings and our bar became the talk of the town.

We needed to make close to $80,000 per month to break even. We were getting the business established when along came the Bali bombings in October of 2002. Our bar was near empty for a couple of weeks and that really hurt us. On 12 October 2002, 202 people, including 88 Australians, died when a bomb went off at the Sari nightclub in Bali's Kuta district. A further 209 people were injured. Some of those killed were customers of ours. Later we held a benefit night for the injured victims and raised $160,000 in one night from an auction and a percentage of the trade went towards the benefit. A Mars bar went for over $1,000. The highest item of the night was an All Black's jersey that fetched close to $10,000. People were right behind the idea and never flinched when it came to making a bid. In the end, the bombing made many people think twice about going to expat bars in Singapore for some time and it greatly affected our trade. We were an expat bar that relied heavily on the expatriate market. The shareholders I mentioned were looking to get back their original investment, sooner rather than later. They were not businessmen and did not fully understand the risks that investors take when investing in hospitality outlets. The next hurdle came in March 2003 when Singapore got hit by the pandemic, SARS (severe acute respiratory syndrome). In Singapore, 238 people were infected and 33 died. Our bar came to a near halt. This was worse than the Bali bombings. People were wearing masks; taxis were at near standstill and people were dying. If anybody coughed or even sneezed on public transport, everybody would give them the evil glare and it was reported that people would get off the bus or train from embarrassment. Fear really spreads in this type of environment and in my mind there will be another pandemic in the not too distant future that will be far worse than SARS.

Interestingly enough, I have been to the place where SARS originated. When I was in Hong Kong one time I caught the KCR train from Kowloon to Shenzhen, which takes about fifty minutes. KCR stands for Kowloon Canton Rail and Canton was the former name of the capital of Guangdong but it is now called Guangzhou. In Shenzhen there are the Dongmenwai wet markets and they are a sight to behold. You can buy pretty much anything there that lives and breathes; rats, dogs, cats, monkeys, all types of fish, snakes, what have you. In this part of the world one of the rare delicacies at the markets for the locals is something called the masked palm civet. It is a type of weasel and lives in the surroundings forests and parks. People like to eat them freshly cooked so the buyers had to generally take them back to their restaurants and present the live product to the customer to guarantee its freshness. Than take it out the back, kill it, cook it and serve it. To cut a long story short, somehow it was discovered that the civet was carrying the SARS virus in its saliva and faeces. In 2002 the virus transmitted from the civet to some workers at the wet markets and the rest is history. The medical people had never seen this particular virus before and people presented with flu like systems which could develop into pneumonia. People that were infected often did not know they were carrying the virus and travelled, especially to Singapore, Canada and Vietnam. It took off, but despite this, a visit to the Dongmenwai markets is really worthwhile. I don't know if they still sell the masked palm civet. Another interesting item for sale was a snake that is the main ingredient in another one of their delicacies called the Hundred-Pace Viper soup. As a dog lover it distressed me to see all the dogs that were ready to go on the chopping block but that is just the way it is and they have been doing it for thousands of years like this.

Things were getting really tough at the bar and for a number of weeks we had no revenue at all during the SARS period. You have fixed costs that still have to be paid and this set us back by tens of thousands of dollars. In spite of this we did recover to the point where we were meeting all our commitments to our creditors. It was just that we were not paying shareholders dividends. We had taken on another two shareholders with an agreement that each would inject $30,000 into the business. One of these shareholders was to take over the management of the outlet. It proved to be disastrous. Things came to a head with the shareholders and the relationship became irreconcilable. My overtures of conciliation were met with scorn. Soon after I accepted $10,000 for my shares as final settlement. Jackie left soon after with a $5,000 payout. She has been very successful since in her own operations in Singapore. The proof is always in the pudding isn't it? I had longed since moved on to other and better things. Overall we had a lot of fun in the bar. We used to conduct a Trivia night every Tuesday night and I was the Quizmaster. I'd ask ten questions on six subjects. These subjects were generally centred around History, General Knowledge, Geography, Arts, Music, and Literature. We would give the winner a free pass for the night. Sometimes a member of the audience would be the Quizmaster and Poonam and I really enjoyed the company and the quiz. It is truly amazing what some people know. We also had a strong rugby following and showed all the rugby games. At one stage we were the top sports rugby bar in Singapore. Some of these nights would go on into the early hours of the morning and it was not unusual for me to drink a couple of bottles of wine on my own, plus a pint of beer just to get it started.

APB, the makers of Heineken beer, sent a group of us on an incentive trip to Europe in 2002. It was a great trip and they did not spare the expenses. We flew business class with Singapore Airlines from Singapore to Zurich, then caught a train down to Montreux. What a truly beautiful country Switzerland is! We stayed at a top class hotel and attended much of the yearly jazz festival that was taking place at the time. We stayed about five days there and probably the highlight for me was the night out at Harry's Bar. It is probably the best bar that I have ever been to. Everything about it was first class, the food, the beverage, the entertainment and decor. If I ever have enough money again, I would instruct the project management team to build me a bar just like Harry's Bar in Montreux. Running a close second was the train trip to Rochers-de-Naye. The trip from Montreux to Rochers-de-Naye takes about an hour and from the top it was breathtakingly beautiful. Actually I had been there before when Sue and I did our European trip in 1981, from Montreux we flew to Amsterdam. What an interesting city this is and I was so happy to be revisiting it. The last time I had been there was also in 1981 when Sue and I were there. I just loved the culture and the liberalisation of the Dutch; especially coming out of Asia. The red light area has to be seen to be believed. Not to mention that you can buy hash in some of the cafes, legally. What a cultural change from Singapore! I recall that I went to a bar with a couple of Singaporeans and we got the proprietor to show us how the hash operation works. These blokes were absolutely gob-smacked and could not get their heads around that what you did legally in Holland, you would be executed for in Singapore. APB sent me on another trip during my tenure at Bisous. This time it was to the Australian Open Tennis. Unfortunately the final was a mismatch. Agassi beat Schuettler in three straight sets, 6:2, 6:2, 6:1. Not much more to say about that other than whilst in Melbourne the temperature reached 43 degrees Celsius and in Adelaide at this time it reached 47.

During the 1999 period Chris Stafford was finding it hard to get work. To tide him over I hired him to do some consulting work for us. He was instrumental in arranging for the International rugby player of the year, Tim Horan to come to our bar to do a Sportsmen's Lunch. Tim was passing through Singapore with Anthony Herbert, another Wallaby. Justin (Sambo) Sampson was coach of the Bedok Kings and also worked for Star Sports. We knew Sambo fairly well from our sponsorship of the Bedok Kings and Chris was able to get him to arrange to have these two blokes come to the bar as guest speakers. It was an outstanding success. Tim and Anthony got behind the bar for an hour and did a Q&A session with Anthony asking the questions. We arranged this as a luncheon and used it as a way to further endorse that we were the rugby bar of Singapore. There is a very strong rugby culture in Singapore that centred around the expatriates, but many of the local schools now play it as well. There is a national team that plays in an Asian round-robin tournament with Malaysia, Sri Lanka, and Indonesia. At the 2019 Rugby World Cup to be hosted by Japan, in addition to the nine venues located in Japan, one venue each from Singapore and Hong Kong have also been proposed to host five matches respectively. The one thing that stops the Asian teams from competing in the World Cup (apart from Japan) is that they simply are not big enough. That's all it is. Chris left soon after this to take up a position with the Minor Group in Thailand as General Manager of their 5-star resort in Hua Hin. Hua Hin is a coastal town about 2-3 hours' drive south of Bangkok and its main attraction is that this is where the King of Thailand lives. Chris has lived in Thailand ever since. In fact he chose a delightful educated Thai lady for his third wife and is becoming a Thai citizen. He now speaks fluent Thai which means he can speak five languages fluently - English, Swedish, German, French and Thai. Not bad, I struggle to speak one. When I went to Beijing to work at the Olympic Games I tried to learn some Mandarin but I was hopeless and was the 'dunce' of the class which was a little bit embarrassing.

After Chris got settled into his hotel in Hua Hin he invited me to come up with my children, Dan and Toni for a holiday. Of course I could not normally afford this type of thing for all the reasons I have explained. However, Chris could arrange free accommodation, both in Bangkok and Hua Hin. We actually stayed in his apartment adjacent to the resort. They had these magnificent landscape gardens that really gave the place something special and the kids loved it. We used to go into town on the tuk tuks and explore the Thai culture. They met lady boys and saw how very different life was in this developing country. We did quite a few things, like riding elephants, scuba diving, getting massages, eating Thai food in local restaurants and generally trying out anything Thai. After Hua Hin we went back firstly to Bangkok and did some exploring there; then onto Poonam's in Singapore. We saw the night safari and I took them to the Kranji war memorial, the bird sanctuary, the snake farm, and other tourist destinations. I have a photo of Dan with a python wrapped around his neck. Crikey, I could never do that. Poonam lent me her car, provided totally for them and they had a holiday they would not forget. Dan and Toni came up numerous times after that but generally separately and I made a point of going down to Christchurch at least twice per year.

Soon after my departure from the bar business in 2004 I started a security consulting business, named Safe and Secure Hotels Consulting. It was going along well enough. I did some assignments in Phuket for Six Senses, the Hilton and the Crown Plaza. These were all done in December of 2004. As a courtesy, I rang them all just before Christmas instead of sending a Christmas card. I told them I hoped that the work that I had done for them would assist with their on-going security risk management program. Hotel security risk management is an area that I am really strong in. Well, you can guess what happened. The Boxing Day tsunami hit them on 26 December 2004. I did risk assessments for my clients but never mentioned tsunamis. I mentioned earthquakes but not tsunamis. When I first saw it on CNN I just couldn't believe it. I felt a little guilty about not having raised it in my risk assessments. They all felt that it was understandable as they had never had one before. The damage done by the Boxing Day tsunami was staggering and resulted in at least 227,898 deaths.

One of my first clients in my new venture was my old mate, Chris Stafford. He had been sent from Hua Hin in Thailand to a resort that his boss was developing in the Maldives. He was given the brief to develop three hotels on three separate islands. Chris got me over to audit the fire and life safety systems and procedures; food safety and hygiene and a general audit of safety and security. It was an incredible experience. He was living like Robinson Crusoe. He had this hut on one of the islands with a thatched roof and everything else made of wood. He would often paddle his canoe from his office (which was on a fourth island) to his little hut. The islands were almost at sea level with the highest point being just over a meter. You can imagine what happened when the tsunami paid a visit. What actually saved them was that the outer reef served as a barrier which surrounds the islands, plus there was a very deep crevice in the ocean. When the water came it did not have the impact that it did say at Banda Aceh, which claimed 173,981 fatalities. The whole of the Maldives recorded 82 deaths. The Maldives is southwest of Sri Lanka, right on the equator. The four islands I was working on were all linked together by channels that had been dredged out of the coral atoll and you can clearly see these on the photo I have inserted on the photo pages. If you wanted to travel anywhere it had to be by water. On the fourth island, apart from the administration offices, there was the entire infrastructure. The atoll with its four islands, had to be completely self-sufficient. The islands could be walked around in ten minutes so that gives you an idea how small they are. The infrastructure included four massive generators for electricity; a huge diesel storage tank; a desalination plant to convert salt water to normal water, potable water supply, water treatment sewerage plant, telecommunications tower, etcetera. They are on their own, out in the vastness of the Indian Ocean and they needed to plan for emergency management. Nearly all of the luxury villas were made of timber with highly flammable thatched roofing. They can get category 5 cyclonic weather with rising sea tides. There is a lot that potentially could go wrong. One of things I did for Chris was to give him an emergency evacuation plan. If they had a tsunami like the one on 26 December 2004, they might get up to two hours' notice before the tsunami reached the islands. That would give them time to evacuate everybody to a safe place on one of the other islands. A central key to making it successful was to make sure that they would get a timely warning from the Pacific Earthquake Centre at Hawaii. Then they had to have a system to notify all guests that they'd have to evacuate immediately and tell them where to go and what to do. They must be able to make sure that there are enough vessels to transport the people to the safe place. They must also be able to ensure that the safe place had enough shelter, light, water, food, clothing, blankets and toilets, etcetera. All this needed to be part of a plan that had been tested with simulated exercises.

It was truly a beautiful place and you can imagine how remote it was. In my emergency evacuation plan, I recommended that they transport all of the people to one island and house them on the second level of the administration building until the water receded. The method of communication I suggested was to place a siren on the middle front island with a public address system as part of it. I felt confident that if a tsunami visited them again, they would have a plan and know what to do. You will note that they had to dredge the atoll to allow boats to come to the individual resorts.

Although the Maldives is one of the most beautiful places I have ever been to, it does have its dangers. Many of the villas are built over the water and you can dive into the ocean from your verandah. The water is so clear that you can see the fish, including baby sharks, swimming around. The most dangerous fish however, is the stonefish; it's highly venomous and tends to hang out on rocks where it looks, as its name suggests, like a stone. It is well camouflaged and its venom is usually fatal, so people must take extreme care where they put their feet when snorkelling, swimming or scuba diving amongst coral reefs. There was a terrorist bombing in 2007 that killed twelve foreign tourists, so it does happen. The thing that worried me the most was travel to and from the different islands or to Male airport by boat. Safety standards are often different from what you may expect in a Western Country. In my security review for Chris I found that the main boat transporting passengers to and from Male had the safety life jackets stowed away in the engine room. When I asked the attendant where they were he didn't know. He had to go and ask the Captain. There could have been another disaster if the boat had needed them in a critical emergency.

Around about 2003, I got a call from Chris that he wanted to recruit me to go to Sri Lanka to be a member of his elephant polo team. Chris was the President of the Elephant Polo Association in Thailand and I think he found himself at the last moment without any players. They formed this elephant polo competition, got major sponsors like Chivas Regal and Mercedes Benz as sponsors and raised money for the welfare of elephants in Thailand. The project had the King's blessing and it has become a huge International success. I tried to convince Chris and explained that I had never ridden an elephant, let alone played polo on one. He would have none of it and offered to pay my expenses for the trip. What could I do other than to help an old mate out; so I accepted and we flew out from Singapore to Colombo. At the airport we met the third member of our party; a Chinese lady by the name of Mae who lives in Washington DC. Chris had arranged a car at Colombo airport. The city was in a state of heightened alertness with the military conflict between the Tamil Tigers and the Sri Lankan Armed Forces. We made our way south, past Galle and settled into a hotel that was near Weligama Bay, a beautiful part of the world, at the southernmost part of Sri Lanka. On our first night we went to a restaurant at Matara and negotiated with a tuk tuk driver to take the three of us back to our hotel, about 11 pm. It was quite a way, perhaps 10-15 kilometres. About five kilometres, the driver stopped his tuk tuk and wanted to renegotiate the terms of our fare. He had us by the 'short and curlies'. We were in the middle of nowhere and certainly there was no other traffic on the road. So, we capitulated and gave into his demands. How would we know he didn't have a team waiting for us if we didn't cough up? About 3-5 kilometres on, he stopped again and argued that he did not know it was so far. We renegotiated again and sought a firm undertaking that he would not stop again until we reached the hotel. He of course agreed but to make sure he didn't, I told him that there would be a good tip if he did the right thing. Obviously our aim was to get back to the hotel in one piece. He could easily have stopped at a strategic location and knew he had support there 'somewhere in the dark'. I told Chris and Mae that we should give him what he wanted and so we did. When we did get back to the hotel and were now safe, he asked me about the tip. I told him I now wanted to renegotiate that and decided that there would be no tip because of his 'extortion'. Interestingly enough he knew what extortion meant.

That reminds me of another story that could have proven disastrous for a mate and I when we went on pacific island cruise many years earlier, perhaps sometimes in the 1970s. We had berthed at the capital of Samoa, a town named Apia. Greg Chapman (my mate) and I decided we'd go for a walk through town and visit the grave of Robert Louis Stevenson, who wrote the novel 'Treasure Island'. Stevenson lived in Samoa and died at

44 years of age in 1894. As we were walking towards the grave, a utility stopped and offered to give us a lift. There were about five or six blokes in it, all big fellas and they were drinking beer. We told them no thanks as we were almost where we wanted to go. On the way back they passed us and stopped again, with the same offer to take us back to our ship. We more or less could not refuse as they were insisting they show us some Samoan hospitality. We got in the back but instead of going to the ship, they took us out into the jungle for a drink. Both Greg and I were on alert and we knew something sinister was going on, possibly setting us up for an assault and rob or worse. We all got out of the vehicle and the 'boss' man made some small talk and thrust a beer into our hands. Some quick thinking was required so I did not let on we suspected anything but suggested to the boss that it was such a pretty place to have a party that I had an idea. What about we go back to the ship, get some of the girls we knew, bring back some grog and we could all have a party. The only conditions I put on it was to ask them to wait at the gangway for about half an hour to let us arrange it and to make sure that we got back in time for departure. The 'boss' thought about it and I could sense he was tossing up whether to bash and rob us now or to wait until we got the girls, then they could have it both ways. Eventually he said that was a good idea and we went back to the ship to get our 'supplies'. Wow, what a relief that was. Greg and I watched them waiting for us at the bottom of the gangway. We both knew that we had just had a lucky escape and Greg bought me a beer that night thanking me for the quick thinking. Stories like this really make you understand how vulnerable women are to predators.

Coming back to Sri Lanka, the island of Taprobane where the elephant polo was to be played is located about 180 meters off the southern coast of Sri Lanka in the centre of Weligama Bay. This makes it about 30 minutes south of the provincial capital of Galle, a town designated by the United Nations as a World heritage site. Taprobane was only about an acre in size, like a small rock in the ocean. They had built this three storey colonial open house on it with a lot of rattan and colonial type furniture.

It looked great and in fact, the island can be rented out to anybody who has got the money to pay for it. I think from memory it had about five or six bedrooms and would be ideal for a group wanting to do something different. You walked from the beach through the water to get to the steps of the house. I truly loved it. The island of Taprobane was owned by an English/ Australian chap who was a key figure in the elephant polo. To be honest I forget his surname but remember his first name was Geoffrey. He was a throwback to the old colonial days; they all were.

They saw themselves as the modern day colonials and lived accordingly; spoke with plum English accents, dressed up in the old school style and had impeccable manners and speech. I liked it as it was a bit different for me. It was such a great few days. I can't say that I enjoyed riding the elephants as they would not do what the mahouts wanted them to. I felt that I had no control over them and felt a bit insecure whilst on them. I learnt later that everyone was unhappy with the elephants as they were not trained and were no comparison to those in Thailand or Nepal. That part of it was not much fun for sure, but everything else was great. We travelled around the country a bit and I found generally that the Sri Lankans were not all that subservient. They gave me the impression that they were not going to be pushed around. Galle was an amazing place. We went to the oval where they play test match cricket and of course, the locals were all too familiar with the Aussie cricket team. Galle has an incredible history. The history of Galle started in 1502, when a small fleet of Portuguese ships, under the command of Lourenço de Almeida were blown off course by a storm and ended up in Galle. In 1640, the Portuguese had to surrender to the Dutch East India Company. The Dutch built the present fort in 1663. They built a fortified wall, using solid granite, and built three bastions, known as "Sun," "Moon" and "Star". After the British took over the country from the Dutch in 1796, they preserved the Fort unchanged and used it as the administrative centre of the district. So they firstly had the Portuguese, then the Dutch and then the British. The Sri Lankans took it over on 4

February 1948 when they gained their independence from the British. I went to other elephant polo tournaments in Thailand and always enjoyed them. In fact I had a hand in Chris getting the All Blacks (the world champion rugby team) to have a team of former players each year in Thailand. They also now have a team with only transvestites in the team and Chris tells me they are 'bloody' hard to beat. You can imagine what some might have thought when the Transvestites beat the All Blacks, which they always do. Good on them!

Not long after Sri Lanka, I joined Chris on a trip to Chiang Rai (CR) in the far northern part of Thailand. In fact, Chiang Rai is the most northern city in Thailand. Chris had the Anantara Resort up there under his wing and wanted me to have a look at the safety and security aspects of it. It was a short distance away from the Mekong River and overlooking Burma and Laos. He was just starting an elephant camp there that was run by an Englishman named John and I used to call him the elephant man. I think the resort became part of the Four Seasons portfolio. The idea was to bring guests, usually well-heeled ones, to the camp and have a type of safari holiday centred around the elephants. Of course it was all five star and the guests were not expected to experience any discomfort. When I went there, I again showed a keen interest in the country and what was happening there. We drove further north and went for a hike, with a guide, through where the mountain people live. These people had a history of growing poppies that produced heroin and were right in the heroin growing area of the Golden Triangle of Asia. The Queen of Thailand took the initiative and introduced these people to growing coffee and macadamia nuts to replace the opium. It was called the Doi Tung project and it was just one of many initiatives undertaken by the Royal Family in Thailand. The project rents out coffee trees for half a baht (that's about 1 cent) per tree per year. That gives the farmers a sense of proprietorship. That in turn creates pride and motivation. The more they produce, the more money they make. They have their own factory, roast their own beans and sell the coffee under the Doi Tung brand. They have cafes throughout Thailand, and sell the roasted beans internationally, mainly to Japan. We saw all this on our hike and this is the sort of thing a normal tourist would not do. We were sort of trailblazing to see if it was something that Chris could offer his guests. We concluded that the trek was feasible, but if they were to do the hike, they would have to be fairly fit. We were basically standing in the world's premium spot for the growing of opium but saw no opium plants. During this stay I took a trip to Burma and went to a casino. I can't recall the name of the immigration crossing but it was a very different way of doing it. You had to cross a river in a little tin motor boat to go from Thailand to Burma. The river was about 50 meters across (say the length of a swimming pool) and the cost was only a couple of hundred baht (about AUD$8). A bus would take you to the resort which was only a couple of kilometres away. I wanted to at least set foot in Burma and that is actually my only experience in Burma. That night Chris introduced me to a group of Swedish people that were staying at the hotel. They were all senior executives from Stockholm and they had a real affection for Australia and they were quizzing me about why we were so successful with sport. We were all a bit pissed and I told them that it was something that was in our natural drinking water. For a while there I had them believing me, but when they found out I was a fraud, they made me sing *Waltzing Matilda* for them. One of them asked me what a jumbuck was and I told him it was a very venomous snake. Wow, he could not believe that a homeless man would grab hold of a snake and stash that into his food bag. Again they found out I was a fraud and this time I had to recite an Australian poem and if you have been following my story so far, there are no prizes for guessing what it was. Yes, it was the Shearer's Dream. There were no women present so I could recite it verbatim. I had them in stitches with laughter and could barely contain my own. It was a great night and a good way to end the trip to Chiang Rai.

I did a trip to the Death Railway in Thailand. I travelled from Hua Hin to Kanchanaburi. This is the town where the war cemetery is and there are many Australians buried there. The railway was built by Coolies, mainly Chinese, Malays and

Indonesians. Plus of course, POWs captured in Singapore after the 15 February 1942 British capitulation. The railway is 420 kilometres long and goes from Ban Pong in Thailand to Thanbyuzayat in Burma. The Japanese wanted it done quickly so that they could transport essential supplies to their military operating in Burma. Japanese engineers estimated that it would take five years to construct but it was built in sixteen months. The line has since been cut to run from Nong Pla Duk and Nam Tok in Thailand. The original bridge on the River Kwai is no longer there as the Americans bombed it but we did cross a bridge over the River Kwai on the train when we travelled on the Death Railway. I can definitely say that I left 'something' different when I was on this train. More than 180,000 Asian civilian labourers and 60,000 Allied prisoners of war (POWs) worked on the railway. Of these, estimates of the Coolies who died are thought to have been about 90,000 and 12,621 Allied POWs died during the construction. The dead POWs included 6,904 British, 2,802 Australians, 2,782 Dutch, and 133 Americans. After the end of World War II, 111 Japanese and Koreans were tried for war crimes because of their brutalisation of the POWs and 32 were sentenced to death. The construction of the railway has been the subject of an award-winning film *The Bridge on the River Kwai* with Sir Alex Guinness and William Holden as the lead actors and I haven't meet too many people that have not seen it.

I did quite a few assignments whilst I had Safe and Secure Hotels but I lacked the sales and marketing skills to really take it to the next step. About this time a fella from Hong Kong was looking for a country representative for Singapore. His name was Derek Elmer and his company was called I-onAsia ltd (IOA). The Captain of the Bedok Kings had heard that Derek was looking for somebody and he told them about me. I had an interview with Derek (I call him Del) at the Four Seasons in Singapore. He told me that he had seen my resume and did not think I had the experience that he was looking for in their core business. That was mainly due diligence work on companies and individuals; a sort of corporate private eye. Del thought that he'd liked to have a hotel safety and security branch and asked me if I'd like to set it up for him. He just spotted an opportunity and zeroed in on it. I went to Hong Kong a few days later and signed a contract with I-OnAsia. One of my last assignments with Safe and Secure Hotels was to conduct a workshop entitled 'Managing Terrorism - A Total Approach' run by the Singapore Hotel Association.

The first thing I learnt working for IOA was the Del was a very generous man, a big man with a big heart. He used to hold court down at the Mandarin Oriental Hotel in Hong Kong in their piano bar and his drinking sessions were legendary. Nothing was too expensive. I am a red wine drinker and he made sure that I could order the best red wine they had in the house and that applied for everybody else as well. He would take most of the staff down to this very upmarket bar and we'd drink and eat all night — on him. It wasn't a one off thing. He'd do it at least once every week, sometimes two or three times a week. Like all of us I suppose, Del was far from perfect. He was a bit of a bully, no doubt about that and suffered fools lightly. I recall on one occasion when we were at the Mandarin for one of these drinking session, a young Chinese staff member from the accounts department approached Del about an unpaid bill. He presented Del with an outstanding account and asked him to settle it, right there in the bar in front of everybody. Talk about 'loss of face'. Del snapped the invoice out of the staff member's hand and started eating it in front of him. He then spat it out and the staff member got a real verbal in Cantonese from Del about embarrassing him like this in front of his staff and making him 'lose face'. Fair enough I thought. It was very poor judgement on the part of the employee who was Chinese and should know better than anyone what 'face' is all about. It is such a very big thing in Asia and particularly with the Chinese. Del was a very important customer, a good payer, and to be treated like this was just totally unacceptable. He almost left the bar after that but the Manager of the hotel squared it up with him, apologising profusely. Del was not a man to get offside with.

Chapter Fifteen: I-OnAsia, Hong Kong
2006 - 2009

In 2006 - The International Atomic Energy Agency reported to the Security Council that it has found traces of highly enriched uranium at Iran's Natanz facility. UN Security Council resolution banned the Iranian import and export of materials and technology used to enrich uranium. North Korea test fired missiles over the Sea of Japan and exploded a nuclear device in the North Korean Mountains. More than 200 people died and hundreds more were wounded when a series of bombs exploded on commuter trains in Mumbai, India during the evening rush hour. Saddam Hussein was convicted of crimes against humanity by an Iraqi court and hanged in Baghdad. A group of scientists reported finding the fossil of a 375-million-year-old fish that had early signs of limbs. The fossil suggested the missing link between fish and land animals. The movies released included *The Departed, Casino Royale, Blood Diamonds, Pirates of the Caribbean: Dead Man's Chest* and *The Illusionist*. Notable deaths included those of Gerald R. Ford, Milton Friedman, Saddam Hussein, Steve Irwin, Slobodan Milosevic and Caspar Weinberger.

In 2007 - The International Court of Justice ruled that the slaughter of some 8,000 Bosnian Muslims by Bosnian Serbs in Srebrenica in 1995 was genocide. A commission that investigated 2006 war between Israel and Lebanon said Israeli Prime Minister Ehud Olmert was responsible for "a severe failure in exercising judgment, responsibility, and prudence." Former Pakistani Prime Minister Benazir Bhutto arrived in Pakistan after eight years in exile. She was later killed in a bombing at a campaign rally in Rawalpindi. Australian Prime Minister John Howard lost to the Labor Party's Kevin Rudd. A UN panel, composed of several of the world's top scientists on climate change, found that Earth's climate and ecosystems were already being affected by the accumulation of greenhouse gases and warned that without immediate action to slow the buildup of such emissions, droughts, flooding, and the extinction of species were imminent. The movies released included *No Country for Old Men, Into the*

Wild, American Gangster and *Ocean's 13*. Notable deaths included those of Ingmar Bergman, Betty Hutton, Lady Bird Johnson, Deborah Kerr, Ian Richardson, Arthur Schlesinger, Sidney Sheldon, Kurt Waldheim and Boris Yeltsin.

In 2008 - Dmitri A. Medvedev, a former aide to Russian president Vladimir Putin, won the presidential election in a landslide. Zimbabwe's Morgan Tsvangirai, of the opposition Movement for Democratic Change, said he won 50.3% of the vote in March 29's Presidential election, defeating Robert Mugabe, who had been in power since 1980. April 14: Radovan Karadzic, the Bosnian Serb President during the war in Bosnia in the 1990s, was arrested outside Belgrade and charged with genocide, persecution, deportation, and other crimes against non-Serb civilians. Karadzic orchestrated the massacre of almost 8,000 Muslim men and boys in 1995 in Srebrenica. A truck bomb exploded outside the Marriott Hotel in Islamabad, Pakistan, killing more than 50 people and wounding hundreds. A previously unknown group, Fedayeen Islam, took responsibility for the attack. More than 170 people were killed and about 300 wounded in a series of attacks on several landmarks and commercial hubs in Mumbai, India. Indian officials said ten gunmen carried out the attack. It took Indian forces three days to end the siege. Days after a ceasefire between Israel and Hamas expired, Hamas began launching rocket attacks into Israel, which retaliated with airstrikes that killed about 300 people. Israel targeted Hamas bases, training camps, and missile storage facilities. Sen. John McCain accepted the Republican Presidential nomination. Democratic Senator Barack Obama won the Presidential election against Sen. John McCain, taking 338 electoral votes to McCain's 161. Obama became the first African American to be elected President of the United States. The Academy award for best picture was won by *No Country for Old Men*. Notable deaths included those of William F. Buckley, Bobby Fischer, Charlton Heston, Heath Ledger, Paul Newman, Sydney Pollack, Yves Saint-Laurent and Roy Scheider.

In 2009 - The worst wildfires in Australia's history killed at least 181 people in the state of Victoria, injured more than a hundred, and destroyed more than 900 homes. H1N1 (swine flu) killed as many as 103 people in Mexico, most likely the epicentre of the worldwide outbreak. In the worst aviation disaster since 2001, Air France Flight 447 disappeared somewhere off the Northeast coast of Brazil with 228 people on board, en-route from Rio de Janeiro to Paris. Baitullah Mehsud, the leader of the Taliban in Pakistan, was killed by a CIA drone strike in South Waziristan. After allegedly striking a flock of geese, US Airways Flight 1549, en-route from La Guardia Airport, New York City, to Charlotte, N.C., was forced to land in the Hudson River. All 150 passengers and 5 crew members survived. The pilot, Chesley B. "Sully" Sullenberger III, was hailed as the "Hero of the Hudson" for his quick thinking and deft landing of the plane. Michael Jackson, lifelong musician, pop singer, and superstar, died at age 50. He was found unconscious in his home, then rushed to a Los Angeles hospital where he was pronounced dead. A shooting at the Fort Hood army post in Texas killed 13 and injured 29. Ten of those killed were military personnel, while one was a civilian. Maj. Nidal Malik Hasan, an army psychiatrist, was the alleged shooter. Movies released included *Avatar, New Moon, the Blind Side, Inglorious Bastards, 3 Idiots* and *Public Enemies*. Notable deaths included those of Walter Cronkite, Michael Jackson, Edward Kennedy, Frank McCourt, Robert McNamara and Patrick Swayze.

At I-onAsia (IOA) Del encouraged me to run the hotel plan myself and to start off planning road trips. I put together a comprehensive document outlining all of the potential targets that we could target. I then did road trips to Macau, Shanghai, Kuala Lumpur and Beijing. I found that I still did not have the sales and marketing support that I needed. Any work that I got, I got myself from word of mouth. Nevertheless, briefs came in and I did work for many great hotels throughout the world. During my nearly four years with I-OnAsia I travelled to Tokyo, Seoul, Beijing, Shanghai, Hong Kong, Macau, Manila, Jakarta, Bali, Kuala Lumpur, Singapore, Bangkok, Phuket, Hua Hin, Doha,

Dubai, Amman, Johannesburg, Bloemfontein, Durban, Cape Town, Pretoria, Barcelona, Marbella, Zurich, London, Paris, New York, Toronto, Vancouver, Chicago and Sydney. There are lots of stories that I could tell you about the pitfalls that can cross your path when travelling and I can well imagine how people, especially young people, can get banged up aboard. There are two that come to mind for me and both happened in Bangkok, the city of angels. The first one happened at the beginning of the major political crisis that was engulfing Thailand at the time. There was an ongoing conflict between the People's Alliance for Democracy (PAD) and the National United Front of Democracy Against Dictatorship or the UDD. The PAD members usually dressed in yellow because that signified the King's colours and the UDD dress in red and became known as the Red Shirts. The red shirts were the supporters, and some would say were controlled by the deposed former Prime Minister Thaksin Shinawatra. I think I had just finished an assignment at Hua Hin, which is about a three hour drive south of Bangkok. I came up to the Bangkok International Airport to catch a plane to go to the next assignment, which was on the island resort of Phuket. I had a 5 p.m. Air Asia flight so got there in plenty of time in case there were any hiccups; not that I was expecting any but in Thailand you never know what is going to happen. I booked in, went through immigration as you do and went down to the departure lounge to await my flight. I thought that it was odd that there were no boarding calls and at about ten minutes to five I asked the Air Asia Attendant if there was a delay and if so, why weren't we told. She said in her broken English, "No flight today, problem in Phuket". I asked her what was the problem but she didn't know. Of course now I was frustrated and took it up with her. Eventually she told me that we could not fly to Phuket because demonstrators (yellow shirts I think) had taken over the runway of the airport and no one was allowed to take off or land. Well, to be truthful, when you are in Thailand you learn to expect the unexpected and this was one such occasion. She told me, "You come back tomorrow, maybe go then". So, I went back to Bangkok and come to the airport the next day. When I went to check in again, the lady started laughing and said that there would be no flights today. I got irritated with her laughing and asked her why she was finding it so funny. She assured me that she was not laughing and that it was just a custom of some Thai people when they are trying to deal with difficult situations. The Phuket airport was still being occupied by protesters so I couldn't go. To cut a long story short, I managed to get a refund from Air Asia and caught a flight to Singapore, vowing never to come back to Thailand again. I rescheduled the appointment with the client in Phuket and went a couple of months later. In my role as a security risk management consultant, I never forgot to add in my reports, the risks associated with international travel, especially in developing countries.

The other story was a mishap with my passport. This happened in 2015. I had to go to Bangkok to do some presentations for a friend of mine who was starting up a new hospitality services company in Thailand. I stayed with him in his luxurious apartment at Chong Nonsi, which is in Bangkok. In his guest room where he put me there was no reading light so if you wanted light you had to get out of bed and throw the switch at the entrance door. One night before I went to bed I took a drink out of a plastic water bottle and put it on the bedside cabinet. During the night I woke to take a little water and knocked the bottle over and it didn't have the cap on it. It did not bother me as only a small amount came out and flowed to the back of the cabinet, or so I thought. The next day when I went to get my passport, I discovered that the water had flowed into my shoulder bag that was carrying my passport. The shoulder bag was leaning against the side of the bedside cabinet. The passport was badly damaged but I thought that there may be a chance it would pass once I got the hair dryer on it and dried it up. So off I go to the airport but Jetstar (the carrier) would not check me in. The attendant wanted my ongoing ticket to Sydney from Singapore, my driver's licence and my passport. She photographed them and said that she was sending them to Singapore Immigration to find out if they would accept me and would have to wait for a reply. I waited an hour for her to get one and she said that Singapore Immigration would assess it once they saw the hard copy of my passport when I landed. So, now I knew that I could get to Singapore but the Jetstar attendant did warn me that they may not let me in and then I would have to fly to Sydney. My problems with the Thai side of things didn't stop there. I was pulled up when I went through at Immigration and interviewed by the 'boss'. He did not want to let me through but I persuaded him to speak with the Jetstar girl who had been in touch with Singapore. Fortunately I had the presence of mind to pre-empt that this might happen and took the hand phone number of the girl at the Jetstar counter that I had been dealing with. To my relief he agreed to do this and after a long conversation he stamped my passport and wrote underneath the stamp 'Jetstar airline has certified for this case'. I rushed to the departure lounge and was only just in time to catch my flight to Singapore. At Singapore, I had to be interviewed by their 'boss' and after quite some time, they gave me a special pass that would only allow me to depart on a certain day (the date on my ticket) and I was not allowed to leave Singapore until that time. The problem doesn't end there. When I was leaving I had no trouble with Singapore Immigration but did have with Qantas when I went to the departure lounge. There they got an Australian representative from Immigration to come and see me. She rang Canberra, asked me some personal questions e.g. 'What was my mother's maiden name' and again, after quite some time, they let me board the plane to Sydney. So, that's what can happen when you damage your passport. In Sydney I had to go through the procedure of getting a new passport which entailed having to go to the Department of births, death and marriages and getting a birth certificate (AUD$44). Then I had to go to a Post Office and have photographs taken and have them certified by a guarantor and then fill in submit the application. That took fifteen working days and cost another AUD$250. All in all it taught me a valuable lesson. That is to always keep your passport in not only a secure place but also, as it turned out, a safe place.

I went to Barcelona with Del and stayed there for nearly a week. We attended the Leading Hotels of the World (LHW) annual conference there. I had just been successful in having them sign us up as the preferred supplier of security risk management services for their hundreds of hotels worldwide. I had the big one that I was looking for, or so I thought. We were all excited and Del spent quite a bit on making sure we meet all the big players of the LHW in Barcelona. We took a booth and got quite a few inquiries. However, what we found was that hotel people generally just did not want to spend money on security risk consulting. They had this thing about only dealing with the big multinational risk management firms like Kroll, Control Risks, Hill & Associates, and the like. Consequently that initiative did not work for us and that was a big disappointment. We were invited by Fairmont Hotels and Resorts to tender for their upcoming worldwide security risk management contract. One of my colleagues (and another boss) James Tunkey, put his heart and soul into the preparation for this. James is a very intelligent man and a workaholic to boot. He could smell that we had a good show with this one. He did all the tender documents and presented them to Fairmont. At this time he had established a good working relationship with a chap by the name of Dick Huddak. Dick had been a Captain in the US Army in Vietnam and a former FBI operative. Before working with us, he was the global head of security for Sheraton Hotels Worldwide. James bought me over to New York to meet with Dick and himself to plan our strategy for the upcoming meeting with the Fairmont hierarchy in Toronto. Dick is an alumnus of Harvard University so he was able to get me booked into the Harvard Club on 35 West 44th Street in mid-Manhattan. It was fantastic and I enjoyed my time there. James, Dick and I flew up to Toronto and stayed at the Fairmont Hotel. At Toronto airport, it was the only time in my travels that I have ever really been 'turned over' by Customs. They kept Dick and I for at least an hour, in separate rooms. They did a full body search of me and went through my luggage thoroughly. When I asked one of them what it was about, he abruptly told me that he was the only one that asked the questions. I wasn't worried because there was no need to be. I just took it in my stride but wondered what was going on. I told the Officer that we were booked to have lunch the following day with one of the city's top Police Officers, which we were, but that didn't soften his approach; it didn't seem to make any difference. After they finally finished with us Dick told me that there had been some bad blood between the US and Canada about border crossings and he felt that might have something to do with it since Dick was a former FBI man.

James more than made up for our little inconvenience. That night he took us to the Canoe restaurant on top of the Dominion Bank building in Toronto. That put us all in the right frame of mind for the next day's meeting with Fairmont Executives. We had our meeting and it seemed to go well. One of them (the most senior one) asked us what we would do if one of their remote hotels required a total evacuation. James was more or less honest with his answer and admitted that we wouldn't have been able to do very much at all. I felt that with that answer, we were not going to get it. I would have preferred that he told them that to provide this particular service, we would partner with a reputable company to provide it. But he didn't. We knew that one of our competitors Control Risks was also in the mix. Control Risks provide a 24/7 global call centre, contactable any time and can put into motion immediately the procedures for mass evacuations. I felt that when he asked this question, this was a major concern for them. A week later James called Fairmont and was told we did not get it. Another setback! He put enormous effort into it; not to mention the costs involved in getting us all to New York and then to Toronto to present.

On a positive note for me, I loved New York City (NYC). When we came back from Toronto I spent an extra week to have a good look around NYC. I was lucky enough to be able to catch up with Gus McKay who was the captain of our rugby team in Singapore. Gus had moved to NYC with his family and I went out and had dinner with them in upper Manhattan. I saw quite a bit of NYC and went to all the boroughs and can still remember them; Manhattan, Queens, Brooklyn, the Bronx and Staten Island. I went to the level 87 of the Empire State Building and also went to the Statue of Liberty on Liberty Island. The statue was designed by a French sculptor and dedicated on 28 October 1886, as a gift to the people of the US United States from the people of France. Other places of interest I visited were the Brooklyn Historical Museum; Maddison Square Garden; Broadway; Wall Street; Ground Zero (where the World Trade Centre used to be); Solo, Greenwich and Ellis Island. I really liked NYC and would like to go back there one day and spend a couple of weeks there. I flew back to Singapore direct from Newark in economy class. As a matter of interest that was the longest direct flight in the world at the time, eighteen and a half hours non-stop, covering 15,343 kilometres.

Whilst I was doing these assignments, the contract called for the client to provide accommodation and expenses. This meant that I stayed in the hotels for the duration of my work and was fully provided for. Sometimes I would do assignments that were not hotel related. Tiffany's from New York (as in Breakfast at Tiffany's) wanted me to go to Tokyo and undertake a security assessment of the Tokyo Metropolitan Teien Art Museum. Tiffany was thinking of doing a jewellery and accessories exhibition and this was just part of the site selection process. The museum was situated between Meguro and Shirokanedai stations and this proved to be a very exciting job for me. I felt honoured to be working for such a strong and reputable brand. The Japanese curators were very good to me and I'd say that they are the most polite people I have ever met. Impeccable manners! I found that wherever I went. I did however have trouble getting around in Tokyo. I always used the train services in the cities I went to but found it very difficult in Tokyo. The problem was that none of the names of the stations were written in English; only in Japanese. In China for example and as a point of reference, the names are in both Mandarin and English. I knew that I would have trouble meeting with the client in town when I finished the assignment. That meeting was to be held at Tiffany Ginza Flagship store in Ginza. I felt uneasy so I did a reconnaissance run the day before and just as I predicted, I got lost on the rail system. When I got back to the Radisson Hotel where I was staying I went through the train system with the concierge, who did speak English. They taught me how to use the colours for the different lines. I just had to make sure I got on the right colour line, counted the stations, got off onto another colour line and counted the stations. Then I was in Ginza. The rest was easy from there on and I was fifteen minutes early for the meeting. It shows you the value of doing your reconnaissance work well. The client was very happy with my work. I regret that I did not have more time in Japan to get to see more of it.

Shortly after that I was sent to New Delhi in India. James had an American bio-medical company there that was thinking about taking over offices in New Delhi. My job was to go there and make an assessment of the safety and security of the building that they had chosen. I did that and there was nothing untoward that warranted any change in their plans. The brief took me 3-4 days but I decided that I would stay in New Delhi for a few more days and have a good look around. I hired a car and driver from the hotel. I can't remember what it cost, but it was not much. I wanted someone who could speak English. Actually that is not hard in India as most people I met in India spoke English. The driver took me around and I saw many places of interest. Starting with the Red Fort we than went onto see Shahjahanabad which is the old Delhi. The level of poverty I saw in the slums shocked me. I knew it was bad; but not this bad. I remember reading Bob Hawke's memoirs (former Prime Minister of Australia) when he stated that when he went to India he was a Christian. When he came back to Australia, he became an Atheist. He felt that no God could inflict such inhumanity onto fellow man. He has maintained that position ever since. Other areas I saw were the Jama Masjid, Chandni Chowk, Humayun's tomb, India Gate and Ghandi Smriti. Chandni Chowk is the main street of old Delhi and it is the antithesis of New Delhi. It is paradoxically both captivating and sad. It is one of the oldest and busiest markets in India but my driver told me to move with caution. He would not let me go anywhere in Chandni Chowk without him by my side. Buyer beware! Naturally, you can't talk about India without mentioning the great man himself, Mohandas Karamchand Ghandi. At the Ghandi Smriti (which means remembrance) I saw where Ghandi spent the last 144 days of his life. It is here that he was assassinated by a militant Hindu nationalist on 30 January 1948. He was shot at very close range with three bullets in the chest. If you go there you can see the exact spot at the Martyr's column where he was gunned down.

It must be clear by now that when I went somewhere to do an assignment, I would stay for extra days at my own expenses to get more of a feel for the place. I could have got the prearranged car from the airport to the hotel, driven to the building I had to go to or stay in the hotel, do the assignment and leave. Sometimes I'd do an assignment and it was clear that certain staff just did not want me there. One such assignment was at a very well known resort. This was a truly magnificent resort. Certainly the best that I had ever been to. The resort is almost entirely reliant on its own resources in how to deal with emergencies and disasters such as fire, hydrometrical disasters, medical and other emergencies. The resort needed to be self-sufficient and stand on its own before, during and after a crisis. Talk about risk management! At this particular resort I met with a lot of resentment particularly from some of the Departmental Heads. They just did not want me there minding their business and they made it clear to me right from the start. They resented an outsider coming in and even suggesting to them that, even though things were good, there was always room for improvement. I was just calling it the way that I saw it, but a couple of the management did not like it and as a consequence, did not like me. Given that our reports are always confidential, I need to leave it at that.

I did a number of assignments for a major resort group, headquartered in Thailand. These were beautiful resorts. Each of them had something unique about them but all had the impeccable high standards that the corporation maintained. I remember that the General Manager at one of the resorts told me that he got up one morning and opened his front door to find that a bullet had been left at the entrance to his villa. I think it had something to do with his procurement policy. Remember this is Asia and in Asia it is unwise to take away a man's bowl of rice. There was one resort I did an assignment at that I experienced an interesting example of Murphy's Law. There are lots of variations to this law but I use this one, 'If there is a possibility of several things going wrong, the one that will cause the most damage will be the first one to go wrong'. I was doing a fire safety and life support systems and procedures audit on this property and found an interesting discrepancy. I asked the General Manager how the water supply was transferred to the fire hydrants that were situated outside the accommodation section. He told me that the water was pumped up by a diesel pump from the resort's man-made reservoir. I had already done my homework and knew the pump was not there. When I told him this he said, "Oh that right, it has been sent to − − −for repairs. I thought it was back". It had been gone for a month. He then told me that it was not a problem because they had a secondary supply of water that could come from the landscaping water truck. This was a truck like a petrol tanker. Again, I had done my homework. I asked him what if the truck was inoperable? He said that that would not be the case as they had to water the landscape every day. I actually got on well with this General Manager and asked him to come with me to the truck. He did. I asked him to get one of his men to start the truck. He gave the order and it would not start. There was no battery in it and I knew that. It was away being recharged. Now we had no water supply in the event of a fire emergency and the risk there I think is self explanatory. You could imagine the precarious and embarrassing situation that would place the General Manager in if they did have a fire crisis and human life was injured or lost. The court would tear him to pieces and it would create terrible damage for the brand. He congratulated me on finding this out and said that this is the very type of thing that he needed me to uncover. I use this story in my seminars but quite rightly I don't tell the delegates where it was. I do remind delegates that as far as crisis planning goes, they should think of Murphy's law, 'what can go wrong, will go wrong'. We have to cover all bases and plan for whatever could happen. We have a plan A, if that doesn't work, plan B. In some circumstances, we may need to have a plan C. This was such a scenario. The pump represented plan A; the truck plan B; and Plan C would have been to make sure that the truck was always operable. Have a spare battery on stand-by that can be installed immediately if it is for a life support system. The staff knew the truck was not working and had sent the battery off for recharging, fair enough. But, well I think you get the picture. I recently watched a documentary on the History Channel about how the American Navy Seals shot dead Osama Bin Laden. It was a really good study into how they planned the attack on the compound in Abbottabad on 2 May 2011 in Pakistan. Without going into all the details, the Commander of the raid, Vice Admiral Bill McRaven spoke about the planning of the attack and how they had to have a plan A, plan B, plan C and even a plan D. It was full of what ifs.

I went to Manila and did an assignment for the Peninsula Manila hotel. This is one of the best hotels in Manila. I did a food and beverage audit and followed that up with a one day training seminar. Both were very good and the hotel had great standards. Whilst there I learnt about an incident the hotel had experienced. On the morning of Thursday 29 November 2007 the hotel was taken over by a group of army rebels and as part of the military counter response, they drove an APC (armoured personal carrier) into the lobby of the hotel followed by well armed infantry soldiers and bought the siege to an end. Imagine coming down for breakfast and you find an APC and hundreds of soldiers in the lobby. Interestingly enough I found out that I used to work with the General Manager when he was in the accounts Department at the Regent Sydney in the 1980s. The global hotel world is a small one indeed.

Sometime during this period I visited our office in Amman, Jordan. I had conversations with our representative there, Geoffrey Beaumont. Geoffrey was an ex-Colonel in the British Army and was an MBE. He knew the Middle East backwards. I wanted to work with him on the bombings of those three hotels in Amman and use that as a platform to generate business for I-onAsia. Del thought it was a good idea. On 10

November 2005 terrorists attacked three hotels simultaneously, killing 57 people and wounding about 110. The first blast was at the Grand Hyatt, followed by the Radisson SAS where the blast went off at a wedding taking place in the function room. The third hotel was the Days Inn. At this hotel the security guard challenged a person entering the hotel. He fled and then detonated his vest bomb outside the entrance of the hotel, killing some visiting Chinese delegates. Talk about being in the wrong place at the wrong time. The bombings were carried out under the leadership Abu al-Zarqawi, who was the leader of Al Qaeda in Iraq. He himself was killed in a US airstrike at Hihib in Iraq on 7 June 2006. Geoffrey had been in a bombing himself and could quite easily have been killed. On 19 August 2003 a truck bomb exploded outside the UN headquarters in Baghdad. The top envoy for the UN in Iraq, Sergio Vieira de Mello was killed. The explosion was said to be so powerful that it broke windows over a kilometre away. At the time, Geoffrey was working for the UN and was in the building when the bomb detonated. I don't believe that he was physically badly hurt but imagine being in an explosion like that just doing your job.

Geoffrey and I went to all the hotels that were bombed and talked to various people who were in Amman at the time. Subsequent to that, he organised for both of us to give a group of Hotel Executives a 2-hour seminar on how to deal with the threat of terror. It was very well attended by about forty people. As one General Manager said to me, "We are hoteliers, not bloody counter terrorism experts". They were all very anxious about the future and much of the talk was about bomb blast mitigation measures. In Amman at the time nearly all of the hotels, restaurants and bars were guarded by soldiers armed with automatic weapons. There was a surreal atmosphere throughout the city. When could they expect the next attack seemed to be the conversation of the day? I stayed there for a week with Geoffrey, who was a great host. He took me to the 'hot' spots around town and I must say that the women were beautiful. The following day I coaxed him into taking me to the Dead Sea and the River Jordan. There I saw where it is written that John the Baptist baptised Christ. This was just north of the Dead Sea and I got goose pimples when I was reading the inscription. I felt; imagine standing on the same ground where Jesus and John the Baptist once stood. I don't need to remind you that I am an atheist but I retain a deep interest in the historical aspect of Jesus life. At the time of writing this book, I have not been to Jerusalem and seen where Jesus was crucified and buried but I do intend to do that. I had a swim in the Dead Sea and it is true that you can float on it. This is because of the high salt content in the water. In fact, when you start floating it is a bit difficult to correct yourself. What an extraordinary part of the world! You could see the West Bank on the other side of the River Jordan and from the Dead Sea. I had the mandatory mud bath and no doubt felt a lot better after it. I couldn't stop thinking about 'Swing Low Sweet Chariot' the English Rugby theme song. Geoffrey took me to the airport from there and I flew back to Singapore via Qatar.

Sometime after the Amman visit, I went back to the US. Dick had arranged for me to be a guest speaker at a Security Executive Conference for the AH&LA (American Hotel and Lodging Association), held in Chicago. So I planned again to do my eighteen and a half non-stop flight from Singapore to NYC in economy class, and then went to Chicago. The flight left Singapore at 10:30 pm (or so I thought). I had arranged to meet Dick in NYC at a certain time. The timing centred around the conference in Chicago so naturally I had to be there on time. When I got to Changi airport I found out that the departure time was 10.30a.m. not 10.30p.m. My mistake and one that any traveller can easily make. It was the first time I made it and hopefully my last. The next flight was not due out until the following day and that would have left me too late for the conference. SIA offered me a flight to Frankfurt and then on to JFK in NYC, leaving at 11p.m. so I took that. Keep in mind I had been up all day, I now had to fly to NYC via Frankfurt, and once at NYC, fly onto Chicago. That would mean that I would be up for near enough to two days without any sleep. All my travel was done in economy class and we all know how tiring that can be. Anyway I got to Chicago in one piece and booked into the JW

Marriott at 151 West Adams Street. There I met Dick, had a few drinks, and planned to go to the conference the following morning. A tight schedule but I made it. At the conference there were about 40-50 people. They were all senior security executives from the major hotel corporations so it was a good opportunity for me to network with the decision makers. My presentation was on 'Food Safety and Bioterrorism'. I spoke to them about what we do in the area of food safety and water contamination. How easily it would be for terrorists to attack the food chain and/or use weapons of mass destruction. I went onto talk about examples of bioterrorism and zeroed in the history of bioterrorism weapons and used the following four examples of bioterrorism.

1. In the 1760s the British at Fort Pitt gave blankets from the smallpox hospital to Delaware Indians as a form of germ warfare. The idea was to wipe them out.

2. The Japanese Unit 731 WMD (weapons of mass destruction) program in 1938 when they murdered 250,000 people; many of them by using them for experiments with deadly germs. The Japanese had perfected the art of delivering bioterrorism weapons by the end of the war.

3. The 1984 Rajneeshee bioterror attack was the food poisoning of 751 individuals in The Dalles, Oregon in the US, through the deliberate contamination of salad bars at ten local restaurants with salmonella. A leading group of followers of Bhagwan Shree Rajneesh (later known as Osho) had hoped to incapacitate the voting population of the city so that their own candidates would win the 1984 Wasco County elections. The incident was the first and single largest bioterrorist attack in United States history.

4. Finally I spoke about the gassing of the Kurds in Iraq by Saddam Hussein killing between 3 - 5000 people in 1995 in the city of Halabja.

This is just to give you an idea of what I talked about at the conference in Chicago. In relation to point 2, I told them that the Japanese were on the verge of attacking the USA and now had the capability of attacking the US using planes loaded with infected bubonic fleas in bombs. The plan was to put an aircraft onto a submarine that could be catapulted off it and loaded with bubonic plague fleas. They planned to sail the submarine to San Diego, catapult the deadly loaded plane off and release the infected fleas over the city. I asked the delegates to tell me what stopped them from doing it. To my surprise no one answered so I did it for them. I told them that the dropping of the atomic bombs on Hiroshima (6th) and Nagasaki (9th) in August 1945 ended the war and therefore ended any further ambitions of Unit 731. Imagine if they were given the opportunity to carry out their plans. They were 'within an inch' of doing it.

In June 2008, Dick Hudak and I went sent to Spain to do a couple of hotels in Marbella for the LHW. Marbella is situated on the Costa del Sol on the Mediterranean in the province of Malaga. What a great job this one was! For nearly a week I lived in the very well-known Marbella Club Hotel. Our assignment was to do a complete audit of the safety and security of this hotel, as well as its sister hotel, the next door Puente Romono Hotel. This hotel was named after the 2,000 year plus Roman Bridge that you can still walk across on the grounds of the hotel. These hotels were magnificent and part of the agreement was that we were fully catered for. There certainly wasn't much wrong in the areas of safety and security. The hotels had that well under control. Whilst we were at Malaga, Dick came with me to Gibraltar, which is about a one hour bus ride south. We spent the day here and took a tour that took us up to the Rock. When they asked the inhabitants of Gibraltar at a referendum in 2002, whether Spain and the UK should share sovereignty of Gibraltar, more than 98% of Gibraltarians said it should remain British. Dick had an interesting hobby and that was to souvenir stones from various notable parts of the world so we picked up a small stone from the Rock of Gibraltar for his collection.

James had won a contract to provide security for a high profile US financial company who were undertaking a trip to Hong Kong and Beijing. The group was Orthodox Jews and they were being rewarded with an incentive tour for a job well done. My job was to make sure that they came to no harm whilst in

Beijing. The starting point for me was to first go up to the selected hotel and do a safety and security risk assessment of it. I did that over a couple of days and reported that there was no reason why they could not stay at the St Regis Hotel in Beijing. Later on I had to go back there with the group and stay in this luxurious hotel for ten days. Beijing is a relatively safe place so I had little to do. However I was still suffering from the chronic sinusitis that I had developed there when I was working for the Olympic Games. I was taking a steroid as well as a broncho dilator puffer but just could not shake it. To some degree that took the enjoyment out of it. The brief stipulated that I had to go wherever they went. I would find out beforehand where they were going that night and go and see the establishment beforehand. I was doing my own reconnaissance and checking out the safety systems in place and looking for any potential hazards that might interfere with their well-being. We went to the Great Wall of China; the Forbidden City; the Summer Palace; Lama Temple; Nanluoguxiang; Temple of Heaven; Houhai and Tiananmen Square. I had been to most of these places before but they were well received by the American Jews. The event went well from a security point of view, and they were happy with what I did. We did have a decision to make at the beginning. The 2009 flu pandemic or swine flu had reared its ugly head in Mexico just about the time that the group was coming. We had a meeting about whether or not to cancel the trip but decided not to, for a number of reasons. The swine flu was an influenza pandemic, and the second of the two pandemics involving H1N1 influenza virus (the first of them being the 1918 flu pandemic), albeit in a new version. It turned out to be the right decision. The highlight of that trip for me was when we all went to the Forbidden City for a farewell banquet opera that was held privately on the inside grounds of the city. A truly remarkable event! The President of the company addressed everyone and in that address he thanked me for the work that I had done. He said that it was the first time they had taken a security man with them and that this might be standard operating practice in the future. I felt that vindicated their decision to take me in the first place. The shame of it was that I had this sinusitis problem that took much of the pleasure out of it. In a very indirect way the Forbidden City had a profound effect on me. I was watching a documentary with Poonam about Pu Yi, the last Emperor of China. In fact, I think they made a movie about it. Pu Yi was the last of the Manchu Emperors. He succeeded to the throne as a boy of two in 1908. When he was 19 he escaped to the International settlement at Tientsin to take shelter in the welcoming arms of the Japanese. The Japanese used him. When they took control of Manchuria in 1931, they proclaimed Pu Yi as Emperor of Manchukuo (Manchuria). He was quite rightly viewed as a traitor by his own people. After the war he tried to fly to Korea and on to Japan, but he was caught by Soviet troops at Mukden airport. He was flown to Siberia where he was kept captive until 1950 when the Russians handed him over to the Communist regime in China under Moa Tse Tung. Pu Yi was sure he would be executed but the Chinese put him in a management centre for war criminals along with some of his family and ex-Manchukuo officials and army officers. He was prisoner number 981 and tended to the prison vegetable garden. After several years of 'rehabilitation' he was accepted as a genuine convert to communism and a loyal Chinese citizen and was formally pardoned. He worked part-time as an assistant gardener at the Beijing Botanical Gardens and in 1962 married his fifth and last wife, a hospital nurse, who survived him. He was sometimes trotted out and shown to visiting foreign dignitaries as an interesting curiosity until his death of kidney cancer at the age of 61 in 1967. At one time Pu Yi had 1000 personal servants. 1000! Can you imagine that? Even though he was a traitor Mao Tse-Tung saw more gain in keeping him alive as proof of how the communist system works. Pu Yi himself said before he died that when he was working as an assistant gardener at the Botanical Gardens he had never been happier in his entire life. He had at last found peace and freedom. An extraordinary story and for some reason it deeply resonated with me.

When I was watching it and this last scene came up where he was tending his garden and spoke about his happiness, I completely broke down. I just went into an uncontrollable state of sobbing my heart out. I have no idea why; well maybe I do. It lasted for about ten minutes and I was absolutely fine after that. I have tried to analyse it and think it has something to do with my own father. This type of 'breakdown' had happened once before. I was watching a movie called Shenandoah; one of Jimmy's Stewart's best movies. At the end there was a scene where his youngest son, who they thought had been killed in the American Civil War, limped into the church and came face to face with his father in the church. Again, I went into this uncontrollable state of sobbing. It would appear to me to have something to do with a father son relationship and I have explained to you before how inadequate my relationship with Dad was. Again I was over it in ten minutes or so and just returned to normal. These are the only two times this has happened to me. I understand the trigger but don't know why. I suppose it doesn't really matter why. When I tell these two stories my mind automatically goes back to a little 5-year old boy waiting to catch the steam train to Aberdeen. The other image is of me being dumped on the front steps at St Brendan's by my Dad at the beginning of 1957 and left to my own devices when I was 13. I feel in my heart it is something to do with abandonment and separation and I have gone into detail about that earlier in this narrative.

I went to Lebanon in June 2009 to oversee the security for the CFA examinations that were going to be held at the American University at Beirut. There exams were run by the CFA Institute out of the US. It was a very volatile time in Lebanon as the country was about to have elections to elect a new Parliament. This was a part of my executive summary in my final report.

"Part of the assignment (the observation of the actual examination) was not completed. This was because the xxxxx representative determined that the security threat level was too high to stay for the exams because of the elections that were held on Sunday 7 June 2009. This decision was made by assessing the current on-ground intelligence; current Ministry of Education decrees; consensus local opinion; historical data; general observations; various western government travel warnings and up to date International threat assessments (e.g., International Crisis

Group). Of particular concern to the xxxxx representative was the risk of the road to the Rafiq Hariri International Airport being closed by Hezbollah militants who control it; thus potentially closing down International air traffic. They in fact did this on May 7 last year and as a result, the airport was closed for two weeks. A general prevailing opinion within the local community was there was a 50-50% chance of violence around the election period. Decrees were sent out by the Lebanese Government that all schools and universities should close for Saturday 6 June (exam day) and the following Monday. After the American University of Beirut (AUB) made representations and at the last moment, the Ministry of Education granted a special dispensation for the AUB to hold the CFA examinations, which they duly did. There is an audit trail of correspondence that pertains to these decrees. As it turned out, there were no significant reports of violence, before, during or after the elections. However most International security threat experts see a bleak picture, given that Hezbollah lost the elections".

On the one hand I regret that I did not stay and finish the project, since nothing untoward had happened. On the other hand, I think it was the right thing to do. I did not want a situation where I would be saying, "If only". That is what security risk management is about. Better to be safe, than sorry.

The big assignments I did whilst I was at IOA were in major sporting events. Del realised that the hotel thing was not working as well as we both wanted and was not meeting the heights that we expected. He asked me to go to Beijing and take up the position of Olympic Games Security Co-ordinator. I spent the latter part of 2007 and most of 2008 in Beijing. When I went there it seemed that nobody spoke English, other than in the international hotels. I never met a taxi driver that did and I caught taxis every day that I was there for about nine months. Beijing is about six hours' flight from Singapore so every now and again I would pop down to see Poonam but only for short periods. The vast majority of the time I spent in Beijing. James had won a great contract with the American giant, McDonalds. McDonalds were a major partner with the Beijing Olympic Games Committee; one of ten. They were going to bring 1,500 people to the Games on an incentive trip. These people were either staff of McDonalds or franchise holders from all parts of the world. The Chairman and Board of Directors were also coming. The brief was enormous. We had to assess any accommodation venues, transport companies and service providers. In addition to that we had to source local security staff, drivers, cars, buses for these people and all of these people had to be accredited. Remember we are dealing with a totalitarian and Communist State and you had to be humble and sincere in your dealings with these people. I generally had a lot of success with them because it is my nature to be humble and sincere. They were the bosses; it was their country, and you needed to never lose sight of that. There could never be a hint that you were telling them how it should be done. A brief summary of what of my responsibilities as the Olympic Games Security Coordinator were:

- Country and Site specific Threat and Risk Assessments
- Travel Security Programs
- Emergency Evacuation Planning
- Intelligence Reporting
- 24/7 Security Operations Centre (SOC)
- Venue and Hospitality Security Risk Assessments
- Cultural Awareness Training
- Executive Protection/Close Protection and Security Guards Personnel
- Accreditation and Licensing Programs
- Crisis Management Planning

This was a good test for my psychological well-being. I have explained to you how I suffered from a type of anxiety attack (as opposed to panic attack) when I was in my early twenties. You may recall I told you about how I could not stay on the property overnight and that the darkness had some profound effect on me. In Beijing I was virtually on my own. Although we had the office, I did not see any of these people outside of work. They knew that I was on my own but never asked me to go anywhere with them; let alone to where they lived. It was fairly clear to me that the Manager of the office did not want me there. I didn't take that personally. I felt that she would not want any white foreigner there as she considered it her domain. I was no threat to her but she didn't see it that way. I rather tended to think that Chinese people generally are very suspicious. They are very good at hiding their feelings. You really never know what they really think. They could hate you but kill you with kindness. They could really like you but keep you at a distance. I lived in this massive four bedroom unit on my own for months. Throw this on top of people not being able to speak English and I had a challenge on my hands. I had no trouble with it. I used to enjoy going to the local eating houses and pointing at menu items. Taking a punt on what they may be. In one of these particular restaurants, I just loved the steam boat method of cooking food at the table and I became quite good at it. I'd set myself up with my iPod; listen to Bob Dylan; take my mind back to my druggie group in the 1970s; have some beer, and generally enjoyed it. It was only a short walk from the apartment so I became a regular visitor there. The apartment I lived in was located in the Fulicheng Gardens of the Chaoyang Central Business District and our office was just opposite the CCTV Tower which was on East Third Ring Road, in the Beijing CBD. This tower is a 44-storey building that has this extraordinary design. Near this group of restaurants at Fulicheng there was a massage parlour that only used blind masseurs. They were very good and worked on feel, rather than sight (obviously). I'd say that these were the best massages I had ever had and I used to go at least once a week for the whole time I was in Beijing. I don't remember how much a massage was but it was very reasonable. For my exercise I used to walk home from the office to the apartment. It was about a 40 minute very brisk walk. When I first went there it was winter time and the temperature would drop to minus 6 degrees Celsius. Then there was the chill factor coming off the Siberian wastelands. That would go straight through you. Paradoxically I liked it. Bob Dylan kept me company and I used to walk to and from the office every day. That is from the CCTV towers to Fulicheng Gardens and back again. There were many things I had to adapt to, but two stood out. One was the custom of spitting in the street. It was culturally acceptable to spit in the street and you had to make sure that you were not in the line of fire. I'd frequently see spit on the street with blood in it. A sure sign of the pollution doing its damage. To us spitting in the street is repulsive, to them it was acceptable. A good example of a cultural difference! The other thing was the traffic. The drivers had no respect for the pedestrians. You might well have the green light and be on a pedestrian crossing, but that did not mean you could cross. I developed a very good strategy for dealing with the spitting and the traffic chaos. I always positioned myself to be walking with the wind. For example if it was a westerly wind I would put myself on the western side of the people and only change that when we came to a set of lights. I wanted to be on the right side of the pedestrians as we were crossing so that if a vehicle did come through, I would not be the first to cop it. I saw lots of traffic accidents, many of them involving pedestrians. At the time there were an estimated 3,000,000 vehicles in Beijing, so you could imagine. Many of the drivers did not know the rules and just went for it. I used this as an example of risk mitigation when I was briefing the McDonalds security people. Use the pedestrian crowd as a barrier. I told them that it was like the running of the bulls in Pamplona in Spain. They could see the funny side of it but I told them to advise people of the perils for pedestrians. The traffic was horrendous. I thought it was bad in Bangkok and Manila, but this was much worse. It could take us a couple of hours to go ten kilometres. I know that I could walk home from the office quicker than one of our staff who took a taxi.

We had to provide security staff 24/7 for the hotels our clients were staying in. That is accommodation for about 1,500 people. We also had to provide cars, local drivers and our own staff to act as interpreters for the Chairman and the Board. In addition to this, we had to set up a 24/7 call centre with an immediate response team. I gave cultural awareness training to some of the clients and had the evacuation plan in place well before the Games started. It was truly an incredible experience for me. When I first went there, I was basically on my own.

Before the beginning of the Games and the arrival of the McDonalds group, the whole IOA crew came up from Hong Kong and we set up shop in rented apartments and the office. The Office Manager did not make life easy for me and it almost ended up in my leaving. In the end, we made it work and the whole operation turned out to be a huge success.

The starting point for me was to do a 'Threat Assessment and Risk Analysis' for the client. Doing one of these compels you to research many avenues of the country's functions; especially the infrastructure, judicial and political environments. This in turn helps you have a clearer understanding of the way ahead. Most people thought of terrorism as the major security threat to the Games but I had rated it way down the scale. I reasoned that the PRC (People Republic of China) armed forces would have this well covered with millions of people at their disposal. I told our major client that the No 1 threat was Air Pollution and gave them all my research material to back it up. It turned out to be correct. I rated the other major security threats as:
• Air pollution;
• Identify theft and cyber-crime;
• Transport and vehicular traffic;
• Pandemic;
• Food poisoning/Water contamination;
• The Police and the Judicial system;
• Crime;
• Terrorism;
• Political violence;
• Protests and boycotts;
• Communications infrastructure;
• Fraud and counterfeiting

The pollution was so bad that on some days you could not see high-rise buildings 500 meters away. There was a real fear amongst the Games organisers that major events like the marathon would have to be cancelled. Miraculously a couple of days before the Games started I saw blue skies for the first time I had been in Beijing. It was generally accepted that the PRC government had induced clear skies by chemical means. Consequently there were no disruptions to the Games because of air pollution. It did play havoc with many of our client's customers on the trip. To mitigate the risks of causing a medical health problem or exacerbating an existing one, McDonalds brought out their own medical team, which I had strongly recommended. They set up a clinic on the top floor of the hotel with three Doctors and were open 24/7. I myself became a client of the clinic. I just loved the way the Americans dealt with problems — 'just do it' is their motto, no matter what the problem was. If you have the solution, just do it.

We leased two four bedroom apartments, about a half hours walk from our office. The office naturally enough became the 24/7 call centre for the games and unbelievably for the entire period of the games, we never had one emergency call. The response team did not have to respond to one incident. That is an outstanding result and good luck played just as important a role as good management. We imported extra beds and bedding to accommodate the staff and I think that with the eight bedrooms we were able to put everybody up. We bought in our own cooks and each unit had a cook. Our security staff had to man the hotel 24/7 with one on every shift. There were three McDonalds restaurants near the main stadium we had to be manned for 14 hours per day. Then there were the limousine services we provided for the Chairman and Board of Directors who stayed at the Grand Hyatt Hotel. I did an assessment of that hotel months before they came. The one thing I remember most about this hotel was the incredible swimming pool that was located in the bowels of the hotel . We were concerned that there could be some sort of political backlash against Americans and/or American corporations during the Games and on the second day of the Games an American couple were attacked. A Chinese man wielding a knife stabbed the couple in the Forbidden City, killing the man and seriously wounding the woman before jumping to his death from an ancient tower. We did not know at this stage if this should be viewed as a one-off incident or even if the attacker knew that his victims were American. The offender was seriously deranged and the consensus of opinion was that he was insane. Our intelligence people did not think that the threat level should be increased because of the incident and that ultimately proved to be correct. Just as a matter of interest, we knew about this long before it hit CNN or BCC. We had good intelligence gathering sources with the PSB (Public Service Bureau) and for the rest of the Games there were no further noteworthy security incidents.

It was interesting to meet security people from all around the world. The Americans were at top of their game. I was invited to the US Embassy in Beijing to attend a talk by the US Ambassador on the formation of the JOC (Joint Operations Command). JOC's function was to provide a one stop security group that could provide up-to-date security information and advice to all its members and it had all the major US security services involved. These included the CIA, the FBI, the State Department, Secret Service, Diplomatic Corp, and others. We were provided with the latest intelligence that was available and if we wanted more than that, we could approach the particular Department and solicit their help. I found the Americans fantastic and the intelligence reports we were getting every day from the State Department were of immense help to us in providing our client with an up-to-date intelligence reports. Of course it was in their interest that we be successful since most of the people we were looking after were Americans. Nevertheless, the JOC proved to be a great initiative on the part of the US government and the American security people were great to work with. They always made themselves available if I needed to talk with them.

James had sent a specialist in major event security to Beijing to consult with me on what I was doing and give his constructive views on it. His name was Ray Mey. Ray had spent most of his life with the FBI and looked after their counter terrorism division; so he was well credentialed and very connected. He was a great bloke, down to earth and he had plenty to do with Aussies when he was involved in the Sydney

Olympics Games. Ray came with me to visit the hotels and our office. He viewed the work I had done on the emergency evacuation plan and felt that it was more than adequate. I wanted to make sure that I was on the right track with converting the office to a 24/7 SOC (Security Operations Centre). He gave it all the thumbs up and we struck up a bit of a friendship. Ray was employed by Johnson & Johnson as a full time Consultant for the Games. I was fortunate to be invited to his briefing to J&J executives on their crisis management plans for the Games. You could sense the professionalism of it all and I picked up a lot of good pointers. Ray and I keep in contact from time to time. At one stage we did look at doing something together but it never eventuated. I spent a lot of time doing the emergency evacuation plan for this group (McDonalds). The question we had to answer was how would we get 1,500 people out of China immediately should a 'situation' arise. It becomes even more challenging should the PRC government close the airports. They might very well do that in a given scenario, say a pandemic. Without going into too much detail, I went with our Office Manager to see a commercial air charter company outside of Beijing and discussed with them if they would be prepared to have a commercial passenger plane on standby for the duration of the Games for our client; and if so, at what cost. Of course, for a premium service like this, the cost was exorbitant. Nevertheless, I wanted the client to know that at least there were other options and that we were always working with their interests in mind. After consultations with the client with the emphasis on our risk analysis, it was decided not to pay the retainer fee that the airliner was asking for. It turned out to be the right decision. McDonalds had their own private jet aircraft for the Chairman and Board of Directors so looking after them was no issue, providing the airports were not closed.

The PRC government initiated a lot of their own strategies to deal with the issues of pollution and traffic congestion. Beijing, like most large metropolitan areas, had more than its fair share of transportation issues. They tackled this by doubling the size of its metro-subway system; adding a second airport expressway, revamping the airport and arranging a number of official transit routes that transported people to the various Olympic venues. Beijing's International Capital Airport received the bulk of international flights to China for the Olympics. A new terminal was added with extensive means for expediting visitors. Just like that! They constructed 31 different venues it employed for the Olympics.

Since they were expecting a huge rush during the Games, Beijing's subway system underwent a major expansion, which increased its capacity to more than double. The existing system was composed of four lines and 64 stations. They added three complete new lines and more than eighty new stations; including a direct link to Beijing Capital International Airport. At the airport itself, eleven unmanned trains, each transporting a maximum of 83 passengers, expedited the movement of people throughout the new terminal building. Most of them operated from 30 June 2008, one month before the beginning of the Games. In January 2007, the BOCOG announced that the Metro cars would be fitted with video screens showing the latest news and events during the Games. Additionally, cell phone signals were made available, so that people could use their communication devices in the metro stations or underground. The Chinese are amazing at getting things done. I just couldn't believe it. They don't have to consult with unions or anybody else for that matter. They do away with all the red tape and bureaucracy that stalls things in the western world. None of that in China! If they need to knock down thousands of houses to make way for a new expressway, they do it. Anybody dissenting is dealt with quickly (which I don't agree with). They brought in a system whereby during and before the Games, that on a particular day only vehicles with an odd numbers could be on the road. The next day it would be even numbers. In one easy decision, half of the 3,000,000 vehicles were taken off the road. Just like that and nobody complained. They told factories that were emitting dangerous pollutants within a certain distance of Beijing to shut down their operations months before the Games began. Just like that! Imagine trying to do things like this in a western country.

There is no such thing as democracy in China and it was fascinating for me to view this as an outsider. If there is one thing I took away from China was their incredible ability to get things done, and done quickly.

During my nine months in Beijing preparing for the Olympics Games, I did do a couple of noteworthy trips in China. One of them was to go and see some of the construction of the Three Gorges Dam. The Three Gorges Dam is a hydroelectric dam that spans the Yangtze River in Yiling District of Yichang which is in the Hubei province of China. The Three Gorges Dam is the world's largest power station. I caught a train from Beijing to Yichang that took about eight hours and then from there, a bus that took me to the Three Gorges. I don't think that I have ever seen anything so big before. The massive project sets records for number of people displaced (more than 1.2 million), number of cities and towns flooded (13 cities, 140 towns, 1,350 villages), and more than six hundred kilometres of reservoir length. During the security threat assessment (STA) that I undertook, I concluded that there was a concern by foreign people (especially European and American) that China had a history of corruption, human rights abuses, damaging environmental issues and resettlement difficulties for displaced persons. That appeared to be no more so in my research for the STA than the Three Gorges Dam. It is often stated that well over one million people were displaced as a result of the construction of the Dam. That may or may not be so but certainly people were aware that China had these difficulties and challenges well before being awarded the Olympic Games. All I can say is what I have said before; the Chinese are great engineers and have a wonderful capacity for getting things done. If they say something is going to be ready by a certain time, you can bet it will be

The other place of interest I went was Nanjing. Nanjing is about three hundred kilometres from Shanghai and I caught a train from Shanghai to get there. I wanted to see this city because I had read the book *The Rape of Nanjing* and what I read was horrifying. Nanjing is a beautiful city but one with a very ugly history. Of all the atrocities committed by the Japanese during World War II, the Nanjing massacre stands out as the worst and most brutal. The cruelty inflicted on Nanjing's citizens over just a six weeks' period is worse than what the Nazis did in Auschwitz. It beggars belief and defies comprehension. Out of control Japanese troops killed Chinese people indiscriminately. Prisoners were executed en-masse. Many were mowed down by machine guns; others experienced far more horrifying deaths. Some were beheaded. Some were used for bayonet practice. I saw photos of this at the memorial where Japanese soldiers had used prisoners for bayonet practice and beheadings. Some were buried or burned alive. Thousands of bodies were dumped into ponds and moats, as well as into the nearby Yangtze River, where corpses washed up along the banks like driftwood. If it was possible, Nanjing's women suffered an even worse fate. Thousands were raped and murdered, sometimes on the streets in broad daylight, victims ranging from young girls to grandmothers. Soldiers looted and burned nearly every quarter of the capital. The official Chinese estimate is that 300,000 people were murdered. I was deeply touched by going to Nanjing, and understand full well why the Chinese have so much anger about what happened there in the late 1930s and about the Japanese refusal to apologise for it. On the memorial there is written 'Victims Three Hundred Thousand' and that says it all.

Shanghai is also a very interesting city. I spent a couple of weeks there and particularly liked the old Shanghai area and what used to be the French Concession areas. I think when I was in Shanghai (2008) it was considered the country's biggest city and its global financial hub. At the centre is the Bund and that is where we did all our socialising. This is a waterfront promenade that is lined with colonial-era buildings, many of them French. Across the Huangpu River from the Bund you can see the incredible growth that has and is taking place. Shanghai is much more beautiful than Beijing but Beijing is where the Olympics Games were so that is where I had to be. I have a photo of myself on a train that goes from Pudong (Shanghai) to the airport that runs on magnetic tracks and I clocked it at 431 kph. The only other cities that I went to in China were Guangzhou, Macau and Hong Kong.

James and I had discussions about where we could go with major event security. There was no doubt that the Beijing Olympics was good for IOA and we did a good job of it. James thought that this could be used as a blueprint to get more involved in major global sporting events. He set his sights on the 2010 football World Cup in the Republic of South Africa (RSA) and the Vancouver Winter Olympics. My next assignment was to go to the RSA to undertake reconnaissance of the venues; meet with potential security service providers; assist in the preparation and presentation of a proposal to Adidas, the major partner with FIFA for the World Cup.

I have never been to a place like the RSA. I travelled there from Singapore and stayed in Dubai for a few days at the Movenpick Hotel and did my customary tourist thing. I reckon that Dubai was the hottest place that I have ever been to. I thought that you could probably fry an egg on the tar road, such was the heat. It was a very interesting city with all the new buildings going up. They were in the final stages of completing the world's tallest building, the Burj Khalifa and that is a site to behold. It is 829.8 metres tall with 163 stories. That is not far short of one kilometre. Imagine a building shooting up into the sky that is close to one kilometre high. I also saw the incredible Burj Al Arab Hotel which is the ultimate in luxury. Of course, I didn't stay there. I also saw the Jumeirah Zabeel Saray Resort. This was also interesting as it is modelled on the old palaces of the Ottoman Empire period with its unique design and architecture. The other point of interest I recall was the World Islands. This is an artificial archipelago of various small islands constructed in the shape of a world map, located just off the coast in the Persian Gulf. Everything seemed to be new in Dubai and it reminded me a lot of Singapore. It's just amazing what a small group of elite people, coupled with the oil dollar can do and Dubai is proof of that. Singapore is commonly referred to as the air conditioning city and I can't imagine that Dubai would be far behind it. From

Dubai I flew with Emirates to Johannesburg. Now I was in a different world. I could feel the tension as soon as I got into the airport lounge. Arrangements had been made for someone (a black man) to pick me up and take me to my arranged accommodation, which was in a house on the outskirts of the CBD that belonged to our local security partner. I arrived about 11pm and had done quite a lot of research about Johannesburg and knew what a dangerous place it was. It was well known to security people that staff at immigration would alert criminals who were waiting outside the airport of potential targets they could rob and sometimes murder. A few of the immigration officers were involved in this racket. When you came through immigration, they (the crooked ones) would make an assessment of what valuables you might have with you by studying what you might be wearing, what you are declaring and so on. If they assessed you were a worthwhile target to rob, they would contact part of their gang that would be waiting outside the airport and maybe car jack you on the way to town. It was not uncommon for that to happen so I was on my guard the moment I stepped off the plane.

Apart from the reconnaissance and intelligence gathering brief, I was sent to the RSA to attend the Confederation Cup in June 2009. This is a prelude competition that enables the host country to 'iron out' any problems that they feel they might have for the World Cup. The Confederation Cup is held one year out from the World Cup. Eight teams competed; Brazil, Italy, NZ, Egypt, USA, Iraq, Spain and the RSA. I had never been a fan of football and in my country we call it soccer. I had seen a game at the Beijing Olympics but apart from that, I had never seen any games in person. Now I had to go and see a few of them and I can tell you that I have seen the best soccer teams in the world and this never changed my mind. It is amazing that I cannot get into the most popular game played in the world. The World Cup is the biggest global television event there is. Just to give you an idea of the security issue in the RSA, I was billeted in this house that was considered to be in a 'safe' suburb. It had an electric fence completely surrounding it and it also had a guard at the front 24/7. All doors and windows had steel bars fitted to them and there was a roving patrol of the area by a security company that were all armed and they had German shepherd guard dogs. The security company gave me a car and the black driver to use as I wanted to. My first port of call was the German Embassy in Pretoria. That was because we were making a pitch for the Adidas contract and Adidas is a German company. Adidas were the major sponsor of the World Cup and we put everything into getting this contract. James had been working on it for months. I met with the RSO (Regional Security Officer) at the German Embassy in Pretoria and gained a good understanding of what assistance the German government would be giving generally to any German company or citizens in the RSA. I did my usual thing and set to work on researching information for a security threat assessment and getting ready to help James do the pitch to Adidas. We did that but unfortunately we were unsuccessful with our bid.

I got my driver to drive me around Johannesburg and surrounding areas. It was on one such occasion that I told him I'd like to buy some beer from a bottle shop. Unfortunately I can't remember the name of the suburb but I went into this bottle shop and bought some beer. I knew that James was coming and I wanted to have something on hand for his arrival. As a security professional I am inherently cognisant of situational awareness, and I did notice that I was probably the only white person in the vicinity and that the black people were eyeing me up. That's a definite red flag. Having got out of the car and gone into the bottle shop, I decided that I should act normally and not show any concern, even though I was concerned. Call it a sixth sense if you like. I bought the beer and we left without incident. When we got back to base the security team asked where I had been, what we had been doing, just general chit chat. I told them we bought some beer and they asked me where. I told them and they got very angry about it. Not at me but at my driver! So much so, they fired him. It turned out that he had taken me to a 'no-go' area and put me at great risk by simply being there, so my intuition was right. I got a new driver after that and he explained the whole thing to me. There were a number of areas in and around Johannesburg that white people just would not go to. Naturally enough I needed to know as much as I could about these 'no-go' areas so I could advise potential clients not to make the same mistake that my driver had made, although unwittingly but it cost him his job.

As I have said the RSA is a very dangerous country. The one figure that sticks in my mind most is that there are thought to be about 50 murders per day in the RSA. Wow, that's really something to think about. The safety of the individual was our major concern. Violent crime was out of control. It is easy to see that if you have an unemployment rate of 40% with an HIV rate of infection at 30%, something has got to give. All of this is what made the RSA interesting for me. I went to the other major cities in the republic and they were just as bad. In fact Cape Town was worse. We had a lecture given to us by the FBI in Johannesburg and he told us that Cape Town was the second most violent city in the world at that time. I was speaking to a real estate agent one day as part of my research (not that I was thinking of buying there) and he told me that when they were in the conceptual stages of planning gated communities, mainly for whites, the absolute No 1 consideration was security. It did not matter how luxurious they were or even what price they were. What mattered most was how safe they were. This meant that developers had to make sure that the gated community was surrounded by two fences; one a normal aesthetic fence with an inside electric fence. The fence had to be fitted with infra-red motion detection cameras that were all hard wired back to a central control guardhouse. As well as this, they should be connected to the hand held devices that security guards carried. Sometimes they required that the entire perimeter fence was fitted with automatic sensory lighting. That was still not enough. There also had to be a 24/7 armed security patrol of the premises. Only then could they sell these upmarket properties.

James came over and he stayed with me in the house we were leasing from the security service provider. We spent a lot of time doing our reconnaissance and attended a couple of football matches; to get a feel for it. One of those games was Brazil vs Italy. I think it was at the stadium in Johannesburg. I just could not get into it even though these were the two best teams in the world at the time. We drove down from Johannesburg to Bloemfontein for a match and did similar reconnaissance. After the game, which was a night match, we drove back four hours to Johannesburg and arrived back about 2 am. We talked to the Police, the emergency services people and the medical staff at these events to find out what they would do and how they would do it, in an emergency. Once they knew who we were, they were very co-operative and willing to share the information with us. They were professional and felt that they were ready for the FWC the following year.

My driver took me to Sun City and I made special note of the route there as I thought that if we won the contract, it would be certain that the clients would want to go there. Sun City is about 200 kilometres from Johannesburg and is probably the No 1 tourist destination in the RSA. Jack had never been there and was just as amazed as I was; maybe more so. Jack was a really good bloke. I took him with me to the casino and he had never seen a slot machine before, let alone played one. I gave him ten dollars and told him to go make his fortune. He was back empty handed in what seemed a few short minutes. Maybe he, like me, lost his taste for gambling. I couldn't be bothered putting one coin into a machine. Then we went to the Palace of the Lost City; what a place. Jack had also never been to anything like this so I made a point of going into the lobby with him and we sat down and had high tea. He just loved it. I was really starting to gravitate to Jack. I didn't keep in contact with him but that seems to be my MO throughout my life and I regret it. I did meet his girlfriend and went to his house and met his family. They lived in a modest but well kept, clean house and I was very impressed with the whole family. In the many hundreds of kilometres we travelled, Jack taught me the four languages of the RSA national anthem. The first two lines are sung in Xhosa and the last two in Zulu. After the Xhosa bit, it is sung in Sesotho and then in

Afrikaans. By the time I left the RSA I knew how to sing all of it. Now I have forgotten it all.

I also made friends with some of the white security staff from our potential security service provider. One in particular used to manage the security operations centre, which was adjacent to the house I was living in. His name was Albert and I think by the end I had persuaded him to go and live in Australia. Albert invited me to come and meet his wife and come for Sunday lunch. So Jack and I went to his place, had a great lunch and some fine wine. Albert explained the gun culture. He had two automatic pistols in his house and both he and his wife were proficient in their use. He told me that he kept a pistol under his pillow every night and showed it to me. I believed him. His wife was often alone in what we call a town house, and she needed to feel secure. This was the general environment in the RSA. There was another chap at the lunch who was a hunter. He wanted to take me up to Kruger National Park and show me how to hunt. Even though I did not take him up on it as hunting and killing animals is abhorrent to me now, I did go to the park a couple of weeks later. I went on a dedicated tour out of Johannesburg and it was really fascinating. It is about a 4-5 hour driver from Johannesburg and we did it in relative comfort. The park was founded by Paul Kruger in 1898, so that is where it gets its name from. In 2002 it became part of the Great Limpopo Transfrontier Park that links Kruger with the Gonarezhou National Park in Zimbabwe to the North, and with the Limpopo National Park in Mozambique to the East. There is always a lot of talk about seeing the big five; the leopard, lion, black rhino, the buffalo and elephant and we saw three of them — the lions, buffalo and the elephants. It definitely seduces you with its natural landscape, wildlife, history, African culture, and sense of adventure.

Everybody I met in the RSA felt this insecurity and I could not help but think what great countries Australia and New Zealand are. The South Africans seem to live in a constant sense of danger even though some don't admit it. Albert never went anywhere without his pistol, nor did his wife. He told me that he was shot once when he was riding his motor bike and showed me where the bullet hit him in his left shoulder. He told me that one of his very good friends was moving furniture out of his house to move into a new (safer) place that he had just bought. Because he was regularly coming in and out of the house, he left the front door propped open. Two black men came in and shot him and his white helper, dead, in broad daylight, because they were white. Just like that. He let his guard down just once and paid the ultimate price for it. When I was watching the trial of Oscar Pistorius, I noted that the defence used this heightened state of alertness to danger in his defence. That didn't surprise me. There could well be this mentality of shoot first, ask questions later. It's all a question of about how best to survive, although I don't believe that is the scenario in Pistorius case.

James left after a week or so and I continued on. Prior to leaving we gave our presentation to Adidas. We were given a fair hearing but at the end of the day, we didn't win the contract so there was no need for me to go back for the FWC. I went down to Cape Town and did my tourist thing. What a fascinating city this one is! Take about the good, the bad and the ugly. This had everything. I went up to the Table Mountain via the Table Mountain Aerial Cableway and that gave me a bird's eye view of Cape Town. I also saw the Cape of Good Hope and thought about those early convict ships that made their way to Australia between 1788 and 1853. What a perilous journey that must have been. Taking about convicts and prisons, I went to Robben Island. It's only about 7 kilometres off the coast of Cape Town. It's the RSA version of Alcatraz. Nelson Mandela spent eighteen years there as a convict before the end of apartheid in RSA. It was just another prison but naturally had this great historical added value, so I had to see it. The Cape Town region is well known for its great wine and I went on a Stellenbosch wine tour and sampled some great wines and saw some quite beautiful country. I would like to go back to the RSA and see the Kruger National Park again and the Victoria Falls. From what I hear the RSA is still a dangerous, violent place. From the RSA I went back to Singapore. In relation to safety and security, Singapore is the antithesis to South Africa.

My next assignment was not long coming. This time the workaholic James wanted me to go to Vancouver. He had won the contract to supply security services for the major sponsor of the Vancouver Winter Olympics in 2010. He may not have got Adidas but got a good one with Bell Canada. Historically, Bell Canada has been one of Canada's most important and most powerful companies. In 1975 it was listed as the fifth largest in the country. The company is named after the inventor of the telephone, Alexander Graham Bell, who also co-founded Bell Telephone Company in Boston, Massachusetts.

The plan was that I would take on the same role in Vancouver as I did in Beijing. I would go there, do a reconnaissance and feasibility study of what was to be done and then, in conjunction with James, work out how to do it. We had agreed that we would use the same successful model as we did for the Olympic Games in Beijing. I went to Vancouver and found that nothing yet existed to service the Bell account. No office, nowhere to stay, no staff, and so on. I found a reasonable hotel near the CBD and met with the client at their offices in downtown Vancouver. The starting point for me was always to do a security threat assessment and then to move onto assessing the security threats for the hotel they were going to stay at as well as the main restaurants they were going to use. The hotel was the Westin Grand, part of the Starwood chain. I met with the chief engineer and he went through with me all of the safety features of the hotel. I assessed the hi-rise security, protection of critical infrastructure; guest rooms security; the fire life safety systems and procedures; emergency generator; emergency evacuation plan; elevator safety; the CCTV system; telecommunications systems, access control; perimeter security, security operational and administrative procedures and standard operating procedures. I also looked closely at the food safety and hygiene management program. As I would expect from a Starwood hotel, I found that it was all in good shape and there were no concerns. Near the Westin, was a restaurant named the

Chophouse. This was going to be the main restaurant used by guests so I had a good look at its safety and security features. There were some very high profile people included on the guest list, so security and safety were major concerns for Bell Canada, as you would expect. Like the Westin Grand, it was all in good order. Canada is a first world developed country and it would be expected that their safety and security standards would be equal to any in the world and that was the case.

It became clear to me that things had been left to the last minute and that I was expected to sort it all out in a very limited time. James had decided that we would not use the Beijing model when we used our own staff. He did not want to contract it out to a local service security provider either. The problem was that we were only a few short months out from the Games and we had not yet put together a security team to carry out the brief. Alarm bells were ringing for me. I had it in my mind that James had already organised a local service provider who would have fully accredited staff, ready to go. This was not so. James wanted me to recruit, train and get accreditation for about fifty staff in just a couple of months. I told him I couldn't do that. In all probability any staff that were suitable had already been snapped up. We argued over this point and I felt that I was walking into a hornets' nest. I felt that rather than not wanting to do it, I felt that I couldn't do it. James was adamant that we would move in this direction. I was adamant that I wouldn't take responsibility for it. I resigned over it. I didn't want to as I enjoyed working with Del and James but I felt that I had been left like a shag on a rock and was between a rock and hard place with this one. I was asked to reconsider but unless they were willing to use our staff or at least a local contractor, I couldn't change my mind. I think for them it came down to an economic decision. If they had negotiated with a local contractor, their profit margins would have been diluted and the global financial crisis impacted upon their decision making. Wages in Canada are a very different animal to wages in China. I had a drink with James in Singapore about a year later at the Grand Prix, and he admitted that I was probably right and said that this was the hardest assignment he has ever had to deal with.

I didn't see much of Canada and would have loved to explore the Rocky Mountains area and eastward of that. All I ended up doing was going from Vancouver to Victoria Island and back. The ferry only takes one and a half hours but it is an interesting trip. I was there as winter was starting to come and I'm not really good with the cold weather. After that I came back to Singapore and that finished my tenure with IOA. For the most part I enjoyed it and had a lot of fun with Del and his Asian team. It was a bit of a disappointment that it ended the way it did but I felt vindicated when James told me I right about the security plan. Del is a larger than life character and I'm sure that under his tutelage the company continues to do well. I saw a lot of the world whilst I was with IOA and experienced a lot of different cultures that otherwise I would not have done, if I wasn't working for them. Overall I have very fond memories of IOA.

Chapter Sixteen: Malaysia and Singapore
2010

In 2010 - A 7.0-magnitude earthquake devastated Port-au-Prince, Haiti. The death toll was 200,000 people. A Picasso painting sold for a record-breaking $106.5 million at a Christie's auction. First of 33 trapped Chilean miners were rescued after spending 68 days trapped in a mine half a mile underground. The percentages of Americans living below the poverty line, or $10,830 for an individual and $22,050 for a family of four, reached 15-year high in 2009, according to the US Census Bureau. Over 44 million people, or 14.3 percent of Americans, were considered living in poverty. US scientists estimated that the BP oil spill, which occurred after the April 20 explosion on the Deepwater Horizon Rig, had leaked 5 million barrels of oil into the Gulf Coast, making it the world's largest oil spill of its kind. The virus in monkeys that predated HIV in humans had been affecting monkeys for over 32,000 thousand years, scientific researchers discovered. The movies released included *Toy Story 3, Alice in Wonderland, Iron Man 2, The Twilight Saga: Eclipse, Inception, Harry Potter and the Deathly Hallows, Despicable Me, Shrek Forever After, How to Train Your Dragon and The Karate Kid*. Notable deaths included those of Tony Curtis, Miep Gap, Alexander Haig, Alexander McQueen, Lyn Redgrave and Jean Simmons.

After I finished with I-onAsia, I went back to my consulting business based in Singapore. Poonam and I were able to spend some time together. I did some hotel risk management consulting work and prepared some briefs for international risk management companies. One such brief was to go to Kuala Lumpur (KL) and do an assignment for a large multinational corporation. This company is one of the world's largest offshore drilling contractors. The company rents floating mobile drill rigs, along with the equipment and personnel for operations, to oil and gas companies. They had quite a few people in KL and many of them were provided accommodation packages that included housing. The incident that sparked off the inquiry was when the wife of one of these executives was assaulted in her home whilst he was away. The offenders came in through the back door by forcing it open. She came down stairs to investigate and one of them held a knife to her throat. That's pretty scary stuff. Their motive was robbery and they proceeded to carry it out. She was not physically hurt but you can well imagine the mental trauma she might have suffered. This and other break-in incidents, raised the fear that expatriate homes were being seen as easy targets by break and enter merchants. The company contracted a risk management company to come to KL and assess the security of twenty-three dwellings and that company gave the assignment to me. I completed it in about 5-6 weeks and came up with a long list of recommendations.

Malaysia is an interesting place, not the least because it might be a hotbed for potential terrorism. The country is very much on the radar as a source for inspirational terrorist leaders (who were also bomb makers) for the Jemaah Islamiyah terrorist group who operated mainly out of Indonesia. They were/are affiliated with al-Qaeda and their stated aim was to form a regional Islamic caliphate in South East Asia; not dissimilar to the caliphate in Syria and north-west Iraq. Top of the list of terrorists during my time in SE Asia was Noordin Mohammad Top and until his death, he was Indonesia's most wanted Islamist militant. Noordin was believed to have masterminded the 2003 JW Marriott hotel bombing in Jakarta, the 2004 Australian embassy bombing in Jakarta, the 2005 Bali bombings and the 2009 JW Marriott - Ritz-Carlton bombings, and may have assisted in the 2002 Bali bombings. You will recall that we had a benefit night for the victims of the 2002 Bali bombing at our bar and raised SGD$160,000. Dr. Azahari bin Husin was also another inspirational leader from Malaysia and he was believed to be the technical mastermind behind the 2002 Bali bombing. He was killed in a police raid on his hideout in Indonesia in 2005 and he carried the dubious nickname of the "Demolition Man". These were just two of the Malaysian leaders of JI and the western world now needs to face the possibility that there is a new terrorist threat emanating from Malaysia, Indonesia and the Philippines. The Police in Malaysia have arrested hundreds of

Malaysians because of their links to ISIS. Many of these were people that work for the government in the civil service and the country's security forces. Apparently most of these people are recruited online and only recently the authorities identified two Malays in a video of a beheading in Syria. So it is very serious and on Singapore's doorstep, so to speak. I have spoken to a lot of people in the intelligence field about what is likely to be the forecast for ISIS in SE Asia and they all generally seem to agree that there will be an escalation of terrorist activities, especially in Indonesia. My own view is that terrorism will be with us for a very long time yet and I am constantly reminding people that for there to be an end to it, we have to address the root causes. Other intelligence people take the view that no matter what we do, they will not stop until their brand of Islam dominates global religion. Maybe! I hasten to add that I am not an expert on global terrorism.

I mentioned before about going to Pudu prison and seeing where Barlow and Chambers were executed. KL is a fairly exciting place and even though a Muslim country, it is fairly liberal. There was a bar near the hotel I stayed at called the Beach Bar Cafe. It was loaded with prostitutes who seem to be etching out a decent sort of living from it. I used to go there for dinner, drinks and some 'sightseeing' sometimes. Some of the girls were very attractive and it would have been easy to take up with one but as a risk management consultant, I know it is very unwise to hook up with a prostitute in these third world countries. Prostitutes are generally only interested in how much money you have so it was easy enough to take your pick. It's also easy pickings for them. I have always found in my Asian travels that prostitutes usually mean trouble and I give them a wide berth. Because I wasn't a buyer, I got to meet quite a few of these girls and made it my business to find out whatever I could about them without arousing suspicion. They were from everywhere - Philippines, Thailand (of course), Vietnam, Cambodia, Indonesia, Burma, Laos, China, HK, and so on. There were even lady boys from North Thailand. I'm mentioning this because Malaysia is a Muslim country and generally you would not expect to see such liberal behaviour, but obviously the Police are not too concerned about it. One girl from Vietnam told me that she comes to Malaysia on a 1-month visa and when that is expired, she goes down to the four floors of whores in Singapore for another month. When that was finished, she be off to HK and she told me that she makes quite a lot of money. She had two children in Saigon (Ho Chi Minh) and they stayed with her parents in the countryside. This girl was absolutely beautiful. It's a way of life in Asia and not frowned upon the way we do in the West. I went back to give a 1-day seminar to the company staff at the Mandarin Oriental Hotel and went through with them the risk mitigation measures I had reported on when doing the security risk assessments.

There is a development called Leisure Farm Resort (LFR) that I did work for during this period. Leisure Farm is in the state of Johor that is at the southern-most tip of Malaysia. This puts it very close to Singapore. Johor Bahru, the capital of Johor State, is only separated from Singapore by the Causeway bridge. Many Malay people work in Singapore and many Singapore people live in Johor. I had a friend who had a house at LFR and he and his neighbours were concerned about a recent spate of armed robberies in their homes on the estate. These people, as you would expect, were well heeled and were looking for that peaceful serenity that the brochures promised. They formed a committee and my friend asked me to address the committee and make recommendations as to the way forward to achieve a decent level of security. Nothing much came out of it as the homeowners thought, probably quite rightly, that the development should provide a level of security consistent with its promises when they bought their properties. It was supposed to be a gated community but it was far from that. However a couple of the owners approached me about their individual houses and asked me to do the security for them.

We found that the 24/7 response centre out of Singapore was not always responding to alarms. In those severe electrical storms that you get in this part of the world, you can get a lot off false alarms. The automatic sensory lighting was not proving effective as the light bulbs kept blowing and it became unrealistic and expensive to keep changing them. The owner needed more as he was having sleepless nights knowing that his family was vulnerable. I had previously spoken with him about an electric fence but that was rejected out of hand. On further reflection, he decided that the electric fence might be the way to go. I got in touch with a contractor in NZ and the client and I did all the negotiations via phone from his office in Singapore. The contractor flew up with all the equipment and we went to my client's home in Johor to install my first electric fence. During the installation process the client moved out and we lived in his house.

We worked for a week and did a good job. It is no easy task building an electric fence, let me tell you. People always want to know if they are dangerous and can electrocute you. The answer is yes and no. If they are built to international standards, then no they can't, but if they are not, then yes they can. I won't go into the technical side of that but there are rigid safeguards to prevent this scenario. The client was very happy with what we had done. The fence was designed to blend in with the natural rainforest surroundings that were the norm in this part of the world. The fence posts were jungle green and the wires were barely visible. Take my word for it, they work. They give a shock that would prevent any human from coming back for seconds, but won't kill them. That is the theory anyway. To my knowledge, the client still has the fence all these years later and when I last spoke with him, he was very happy with it.

I also did work for one of the homeowners on an adjacent development, Ledang Heights. They were building this magnificent home but all this business at Leisure Farm had unsettled them. They felt that since they had not yet started construction they had the opportunity to get it right from the start. I spoke with them in detail about having the glass protected so that potential robbers could not smash the glass in with a baseball bat, or jemmy, or the like. They were really receptive to this idea. I sourced a supplier of tempered glass in Singapore and took the clients there to discuss it with the supplier. Of course, there was some scepticism about how effective tempered glass was so the client wanted to test it. He came with his video and a few bricks. At different distances he threw these bricks with all his might at four samples of glass. One of the samples never budged. It was clear now that we had found the glass necessary to mitigate the robbers trying to gain forced entry by smashing the glass windows. I did not finish this assignment as they were way behind in their timeframe and I moved onto other things. Next time I go back to Johor I will call in to see them and see how it all turned out.

I did an interesting brief for a risk management company in Singapore during 2010. Singapore has a very proactive government. It doesn't wait for bad things to happen but rather tends to identify what major events could seriously damage them. They certainly learned their lesson to be independent after the Japanese invasion in February 1942. During the ensuring Japanese occupation, some 50,000 Singaporeans were murdered by the Japanese. So it is easy to understand why Singaporeans are so security minded. They are obsessed with the security of their little Island nation and the threat from terrorism. Not without cause I am sure you'd agree. They came within an inch of having a major terror attack in December 2001. Jemaah Islamiyah (JI) had a radical cleric in Singapore who had a group of followers he had radicalised. In 1997 they started carrying out reconnaissance of potential targets such as the Yishun MRT (train service). At this time the Internal Security Department (ISD) did not know. The plan was to bring in 17 tons of ammonium nitrate and divide this into six trucks and attack six targets simultaneously. Those targets were the British, USA and Australian Embassies which are all next to each other, as well as the Israel Embassy. The other two targets were the US Naval base at Sembawang and Admiralty Road. After the World Trade Centre attack on 11 September 2001, one of the members of the radical group called the ISD and told them about the plan. The ISD then started to make the arrests and the attacks were thwarted. Imagine what might have been if the ISD didn't get that phone call. It is therefore very understandable that the Singapore counterterrorism people are diligent and vigilant about terrorism. Given the history of attacks on hotels, they do their best to make sure that the hotels understand their responsibilities with respect to the threat from terror. They have lots of initiatives to keep people focused on it. Now that it appears that ISIS is gaining a foothold in Malaysia and Indonesia, the Singaporeans will be on an even higher state of alert. Malaysia and Indonesia are Singapore's closest neighbours and both are major Muslim countries. There are close to 200 million Muslim people in Indonesia alone, making it the most concentrated Muslim population on earth.

It may surprise a lot of people to learn that a former Prime Minister of Israel was once a terrorist; or as some might put it, a freedom fighter. During my seminars I talk about hotels that have been attacked by terrorists over the past few decades. An interesting case was the bombing of the King David Hotel in the then Palestine. This hotel was the site for the British Military Headquarters in Palestine. In June 1946, a Jewish terrorist group named Irgun attacked the hotel because they wanted to destroy documents that the British had earlier taken from them. They used seven milk-churns, each containing 50 kilograms of explosives and attached them to pillars in the basement of the hotel. They were all dressed as Arabs. The van with the bombs stopped at the side entrance of the hotel and the terrorists went into the hotel's loading dock. They overpowered the guards and assembled the workers in the restaurant kitchen. They then returned to the van, brought the bombs into the hotel's restaurant and placed them beside supporting pillars. The leader of that group was Menachem Begin. 91 people were killed and 45 injured, Jews were also amongst the casualties of the attack. Begin went on to become the sixth Prime Minister of Israel from 1977-1983. Make of it what you will.

Getting back to my assignment in Singapore, my job was to assess the security levels of the twenty-four hotels that were nominated. This process was between the Singapore Police Force (SPF) and the Singapore Hotels Association (SHA). I was allocated two days for each hotel. Basically one day on site, interviewing the Departmental heads (especially the Director of Security) and inspecting the hotel. The second day I compiled my report of each hotel. I can say that all of them had high standards of security awareness that would be the envy of other countries in the ASEAN group. They understood that hotels were being targeted by terror groups because they were seen as 'soft' targets where Westerners stay and meet. I found the Singapore Police excellent to work with and admired their proactive approach to meeting challenges. I made some friends with the Directors of Security and unfortunately some, not so good friends. I found out later from one of the hotels that there was a group of Security Managers that resented my intrusion into their worlds. They claimed that I questioned them about areas that did not come under their control and that caused them embarrassment. Examples of that were where I felt that security overlapped into engineering matters. This is particularly so when taking about the protection of critical infrastructure. Critical Infrastructure covers areas like the main frame computer room, the emergency generator, the automatic gas cut off sensors, water reservoirs, boiler rooms, ventilation/exhaust units, telecommunications, CCTV, the internet, etcetera. I felt that whilst the Chief Engineer is responsible for these areas, it is security's responsibility to protect them. If I asked a question for example, "How do you turn off the main gas supply in the event of a fire?" I would expect a Security Manager to know and that all his security staff should as well. Another example might be, "What temperature should the computer room be kept at?" I don't know what came out of it other than I was not invited back. A couple of weeks after I finished I gave a presentation at the annual Hotel Security Conference in Singapore, outlining my findings collectively. It was clear even then that some of them were hostile to me. It is unusual for Asians to show their hostility as they have other ways of letting you know they are displeased. It spite of this it was a real experience for me and I was left with a very positive view of the standard of security in the hotels in Singapore. It's typical Singapore really. I would say that the hotel security that I saw in Singapore would be better than any other country per se that I have seen.

The Chinese (Singapore is 75% Chinese) are great at getting things done as I have explained to you before when we were talking about the Olympic Games in Beijing. They leave us behind in this regard; there is no doubt about it. We would be arguing about the pros and cons of every single detail. A great example of that in Australia is the building of Badgerys Creek airport outside of Sydney. Successive governments have been talking about this for decades yet nothing has happened. The Chinese would have done it thirty years ago. Another example we saw was with the High Court rejecting the proposal of the Carmichael mine up in Queensland over some very minor environmental issue that was almost insignificant. That would never happen in Singapore or China - they would just do it and not put up with environmental activists or militant unions interfering. I am not saying that this is right; I'm just pointing out how efficient they are at getting things done.

Singapore was a major part of my life from 1997 until I left permanently in mid 2012. I often tell people that the Singapore Government should hire me as a travelling ambassador as wherever I go I nearly always sing the praises of the country. There are things I don't like and top of the list is their capital and corporal punishment. However I have to admit that Singapore is a safe country; there is no argument there. It is also the place where I undertook my financial rehabilitation process and began my long road back to recovery after suffering the holy trinity of financial ruin, marriage breakdown and family loss and my wife's serious illness. I have a lot to be grateful to Singapore for. None the least was the time that I was able to spend with Poonam.

Singapore will always be special to me.

Chapter Seventeen: New Zealand Earthquake
2011

In 2011 - The Arab Spring movement began in Tunisia when demonstrators took to the streets to protest chronic unemployment and Police brutality. Similar protests broke out in Egypt. Feb. 11: Egyptian President Hosni Mubarak announced his resignation and handed power of the country over to the military. Feb. 16: In Benghazi, Libya, thousands of protesters demanded that Col. Muammar al-Qaddafi step down. US troops and CIA operatives shot and killed Osama bin Laden in Abbottabad, Pakistan. Norway was hit with consecutive terrorist attacks; first, a bomb exploded in Regjeringskvartalet, the government quarter of Oslo. The second explosion happened right outside the Prime Minister's office, killing eight people and wounding several others. Two hours later, a gunman disguised as a Policeman opened fire at a camp for young political activists on the island of Utoya in Tyrifjorden, Buskerud. The gunman killed 68 campers. Japan was hit by an enormous earthquake that triggered a deadly 23-foot tsunami in the country's north. The movies released included *Harry Potter and the Deathly Hallows Part II, Transformers: Dark of the Moon, Twilight Saga: Breaking Dawn Part 1, The Hangover Part II, Pirates of the Caribbean: On Stranger Tides, Thor, Rise of the Planet of the Apes* and *Captain America: The First Avenger*. Notable deaths included those of Osama bin Laden, Warren Christopher, Betty Ford, Joe Frazier, Muammar Gaddafi, Steve Jobs, Kim Jong-Il, Elizabeth Taylor and Amy Whitehouse.

After I finished with the Singapore hotel assignment, I applied to work as a Loss Assessor in Christchurch. My ex-wife Sue whose house had been damaged put me onto it. She told that there were a lot of former Australian Police working with the earthquake commission assessing the damage to the houses during the February 2011 Christchurch earthquake. This was all handled by an organisation named the Earthquake Commission of New Zealand or NZ-EQC. What made this 6.3 earthquake all the more damaging was that it hit close to the surface within three miles (5 km) of central Christchurch on 22 February 2011. The population of Christchurch was 367,700; yet we had to deal with over 400,000 claims. The EQC faced a massive recovery effort from the earthquake and it was estimated that it would eventually cost $NZ40 billion to repair the city. Christchurch and the surrounding Canterbury region suffered a magnitude 7 earthquake in September 2010 that damaged homes and roads, with no loss of life. The 22 February 2011 earthquake struck killing 185 people and wrecking much of the city centre, including its major sports stadium and largest high rise buildings. About 100,000 homes were damaged and 7,000 were condemned. Seventy percent of the shops, hotels and office buildings in the heart of the city were damaged. People left the city after the disaster and the 7,930 aftershocks that followed. The population fell to 363,100 in June 2012 from 376,700 two years earlier. Fletcher Construction was the company used by the EQC to manage the residential rebuild arising from the earthquake damage to houses in the range from $10,000 to $100,000. Claims below the threshold were settled by way of lump sum payments to the homeowner and claims in excess of $100,000 were settled by the homeowner's insurer. In other words the government, through its EQC arm, put up the first $100,000.

The indigenous people of New Zealand, the Maoris, refer to the country as Aotearoa, or 'the land of the long white cloud'. It is also often referred to as the Shaky Isles. This term originated from New Zealand's frequent seismic activity. The islands lie on the margin of two colliding tectonic plates, the Pacific and Indo-Australian Plates. Earthquakes are common in NZ, particularly in the southwest of the South Island and in the central North Island, and the North Island's scenery is marked by several active and dormant volcanoes. There have been some decent earthquakes in NZ. The worst in terms of loss of life was a 7.8 magnitude that occurred on 3 Feb 1931 in the Hawkes Bay area of the North east of New Zealand that killed 256 people. I mentioned that when I was talking about hitchhiking around NZ. Even though the standards of construction in New Zealand are considered world class, the 6.3 magnitude earthquake was centred only two kilometres west of the Christchurch port town of Lyttelton and ten kilometres south east of the centre of Christchurch. The 2010 earthquake that hit Christchurch in September would have seriously weakened structures and in that sense, the February 2011 6.3 magnitude earthquake finished the job. Although the 2010 earthquake was stronger there were no fatalities. My son Dan was working on a construction site in the CBD area of Christchurch when the 2011 earthquake hit and he told me that he narrowly escaped being hit by an air conditioning unit that came hurtling down the side of the building that he was working on missing him by about a meter. He honestly believed that he was going to die and he told me that all he could think of was how his family would cope when he was gone.

The EQC were looking for Loss Assessors with building experience (obviously). I had no building experience but applied anyway. They wrote back that I would be put on a waiting list. I knew that they were desperate for staff and that I might have a chance because I was a former Australian cop. When the next big tremor hit, I wrote to them again and the lady in Human Resources wrote back and told me not to contact her again. If I was wanted, they would contact me. Well, I thought that was the end of that; I may have pushed too hard and screwed up the opportunity. Another tremor struck and I was more than surprised to get an email asking me when I could start. I knew that I was walking into a minefield because of my lack of knowledge in building and construction generally, but I needed assignments and at that time and none were coming in. I got down to Christchurch from Singapore in March 2011 and immediately joined a group of builders and assessors on a three day seminar. I was a 'fish out of water' but typically I never showed it. The truth is that I didn't know what they were taking about. I was the only one in the room who did not have building experience. When they started taking about stud heights, cornices, concrete rings, piles, concrete slabs, retaining walls, this and that, I was lost and naturally that created a certain level of anxiety. As the Assessor, I was in charge of a builder and we would go on site and inspect the damage to the houses. You were really supposed to know the building game before you could comment on the damage. Makes sense doesn't it? It was true you had a builder as part of your two man team, but on site you mostly worked independently. The builder simply did not have the time to explain everything to you. So I had to learn, and learn quickly. As I have mentioned, I have a son in Christchurch who is a builder and I was in his ear all the time for the first couple of months as well as researching the net every night. Gradually I started to get the hang of it without embarrassing myself. I had skills many of them did not have. I was fairly good at writing reports and that was an important component of the job. Another vital ingredient for a loss assessor was to be able to speak with people in a manner that was conducive to getting positive results, both for them and the EQC. They felt that ex-Police were good in this area and I believe that proved to be the case. Some builders are not the most patient of men and can quickly call a spade a spade. When we went on site, the builder would mostly come in with me and we would use a laser beam to take the slope measurement of floor of the house. We wanted to establish as a starting point if the house was sloping too much, at any part of it. Then the builder would go outside and make an assessment of the outside walls, the land, the roof, underneath the floors and inside the roof. My job was to measure all the internal rooms and record the damage done in each room. Once that was done, I would sit down with the claimant and take their relevant history and details, including insurance details. I would have to establish if there were any building issues that required immediate attention. If there were, I'd discuss it with my builder and acting on his advice, submit an emergency repair form to EQC contractors, Fletchers.

When we first started we had to do two houses a day and write up a full description. I remember on one of the first houses we did, the owner was asking me my views on the expansion of concrete walls during an earthquake and at what width did I consider it was unrepairable. F***, I thought. I got around it by saying it was not a straight forward question and there were many variables to consider. I think I actually convinced him I knew what I was talking about but I didn't have a clue. The descriptions we had to give were very detailed, with drawings outlining distances, heights and widths. It was at this stage that the builder had the lion's share of the 'technical' work. There were many occasions that we did not have time to have a proper meal break. It was no picnic. These claim statements started with a description of the property. How old it was; what footprint it was (e.g. rectangular, T shape, L shape); what the foundation was (it could be wood piles, concrete piles, concrete skirt, concrete slab, other); floor construction, (concrete, other, particle board, timber (what sort?), T&G; external wall construction, (brick veneer, fibre cement, stucco, weatherboard, other); roof materials, (clay tiles, concrete tiles, metal tiles, rolled metal, other); Storeys, (one, split level (1), two, three, four); bedrooms, (no bedrooms, one, two (and so on). That's just the inside; outside you had to look at the internal garage, sheds, carports, paved driveway, retaining walls, sewerage piping, water piping, electrical cabling and all external buildings. This is all under property description before you get into identifying damage, assessing the damage and then pricing it. Property description was the easy part.

Then the Loss Assessor had to go and get all the details about ownership, mortgage repayments, any land damage, insurance details and put it all on a file note. Naturally enough some of the claimants were milking it for all that it was worth. I had to fill in any details if there was land damage and any contents damage that they were claiming. In relation to assessing the damage, we would break up the internal house into three areas, the walls, ceiling and floors. They all had to be measured, the type of cladding (e.g., stucco on ceiling, wallpaper on walls and carpet on floors) and what the actual damage was. We had to do every room in the house individually. Once the damage was assessed, we'd work out the repair strategy for every single repair needed. Then back to the office and work out how much all of it would cost. This was the most difficult part. Sometimes the claimants had no insurance, were behind in mortgage payments that put them in conflict with their banks before the earthquake. Sometimes the recommended repair strategies involved lifting the house off the foundation and replacing the foundation. You could understand the challenges I had as a non-builder in being able to not just work out how to do it but how much it would cost. I consider it as one of my great achievements that I ended up being able to do this and do it well. All our work was gone over with a fine tooth comb by the supervising estimator (a highly qualified builder) before it was submitted to EQC HQ. He was a hard task master and told me our work was good. The paperwork was horrendous. Even working with the builder, we would spend hours trying to work out the cost of repairs and we had no technological assistance. But we got there, somehow. I was forever in the ears of the builders asking them this, asking them that, and they were generally pretty helpful but they were under the gun also and to my mind, had the lion's share of the work. Then we had a major breakthrough with updated technology.

At some point, perhaps a couple of months after starting, EQC went on line and issued us all with an iPad. The iPad was synchronised between the builder, his loss assessor and EQC administration; both at our local base and EQC HQ in Wellington. This now meant that the supervisors knew exactly what you were doing, when you were doing it and how long it was taking you to do it. It was as if they were at the house with you. This upped the ante considerably. Now we had to do four a day but the good thing for me was that the technology allowed for all the repair strategies to come up on a screen once you had put in what the damage was. You no longer had to know the repair strategies. It would basically tell you what it was and once you had your measurements in, it would automatically cost if for you. It was great stuff, especially for people like me that were not builders and I remember telling Bill English, the then Deputy Prime Minister how efficient it was. For example, if there was say a 10 mm crack in the gyprock in one of the bedrooms, say two meters long across the ceiling. Once you put into the system the type of ceiling it was, it would offer as one of the repair options, to rack out, scrape, fill and paint. All I had to do was put in the measurements and click Ok. It would add that cost automatically to the final assessment. It was brilliant but there was a trade-off. We now had to double our daily quota from two to four. Some of the men had trouble learning the software but they had to; we all had to, and we had to learn it quickly. If you couldn't you'd lose your job, simple as that. Those who were good with it helped those that weren't. We all got there with it and in the end we were doing six houses a day in the latter stages. Imagine that.

I had to 'sack' my first builder. He was a good bloke too but for a number of reasons I asked to be put with another builder within my first week of starting. I knew I was not going to make the cut with my man and he would drag us both down. He needed to be with another builder who was also a Loss Assessor. I needed to be with someone who was good at his job, worked quickly and was willing to share his knowledge with me. They gave me a first rate man and things got much better. His name was Donald (Donnie) Macilquham. I learnt quickly with Donnie and started 'cooking with gas', especially when we went on line. The hardest part of the job for the Loss Assessors was making the bookings for the three week period. When it was only two per day, it was easy. But when it jumped to five, six, it became a real struggle. You had to do this is your own time. So, a typical day would be up at 6.30 am, shower, have breakfast in your room (you prepare it), and be ready to leave at 7.30am and be on site at 8 am. We finished at 6 pm, when we'd all meet to hand in the day's information to base. That was the day for the builders. However, the Assessors had to go back to their rooms and make these appointments. At times it was a nightmare. People would cancel at the last minute or wouldn't be there when you turned up at the agreed time. There was a real skill at getting this part of the job right and it was the toughest part. You could spend up to two hours in your own time making these appointments. It was not good enough to come back to base and tell them you couldn't get the numbers. You had to find a way to get them and we did. We always met our quotas. Not meeting your quotas was tantamount to asking to be fired. The Supervisors used to ride us and not take any excuses from anybody. But at the end of the day, we all got on well and I really liked those kiwi fellas. They were the salt of the earth type blokes. We refer to them as our brothers across the ditch. There were quite a few occurrences during this period that had a human story to it.

I rang up one night to speak to a claimant to make a time to inspect her house. When I told her who I was, she went berserk. She absolutely lost it. She said something like this. "F*** off you f****** c*** and while you are at it, f*** off back to Australia, you f****** convict". Wow, all I said was hello. I don't know how she knew I was an Australian. A guess perhaps! Many of us were. It became clear to me very quickly that I was dealing with a fairly disturbed person who had suffered badly, probably as a result of the earthquake. I let her go at me and started feeling sorry for her. I told her (when I got the chance) that I was sorry that I had upset her and really did not intend to. She started crying and changed tact with me. She was now apologising and said that she was having psychiatric help to deal with her trauma. She said that she had bad experiences with previous EQC staff. She did not want the inspection but was a very different person at the end of the call than at the beginning. We knew there were a lot of people out there that had been severely traumatised so this type of thing could be expected. Nevertheless, that was the only person that was ever directly rude to me, even though it was not face to face. I found generally the Kiwis to be great people and relatively easy to get on with. The people that had suffered significant damage to their property were naturally enough the hardest to deal with. Many of them were just ordinary working class people and their home was really the only real asset they had, so they fretted about it. The EQC was under tremendous pressure to perform, right from the start. They were overwhelmed with the number of claims they were receiving and the recovery effort generally. There were a lot of complaints about the EQC and their failures, especially communications failures. Many times we would go on site and be told of a chronological list of EQC failures before we could even start the assessment. It was, not surprisingly, the Assessor who had to deal with this and I took a very firm approach to it. I'd tell them that I was a contracted employee whose sole job was to assess the damage and costings for particular properties and report that information to headquarters. Anything outside those parameters (such as complaints) were not within my brief and I made that very clear to them. That usually settled the matter and we could get on with our work. The daily newspapers and television talk-back shows were full of complaints about the performance of the EQC and no doubt many of them were warranted.

Another time Donnie and I were doing a house, and it started shaking. Donnie, who had experienced earthquakes (I hadn't) was out of that house with the 'speed of a startled gazelle'. It took me a second to react but as soon as Donnie heard that particular rumbling noise, he knew what it was. The house literally started shaking. Things flew off the shelves and it was just a little one, 5.1 from memory. One day on my week off I experienced it again; worse this time. I was at my ex's place and same story. Everything got very violent and if you are standing up in the house you really have to hang onto something to stay stable. This was a 5.8 one. About an hour later, I was driving along and saw the telephone poles swaying but for that split second it didn't register with me. Then the road in front of me started waving; like little waves on a beach and of course, I knew now what was happening. That was a 6.3. I can tell you they are very scary things. I could not for the life of me imagine what a 9 on the Richter scale would be like. Donnie and I went to a house one very cold frosty morning and the owner started telling us all the things that were wrong with the place. They often did this and sometimes they would wave engineering reports around so that you could not argue with it. Fair enough, it's their house. It was a beautiful sandstone house with a lakefront view and we decided that the engineering report was exaggerated and we put it the way that we saw it. Donnie was adamant that the building was structurally sound and that the owner was over-emphasising what he saw as the damage. This is where your communication skills came into play and also where your report writing skills came into play. You would report (briefly) what the engineering report was saying but express some doubt about it validity. This would give the EQC the option of getting a second opinion, which they very often did with their own engineers. As I said before, there were a lot of people ripping the system off, no doubt about that. They were claiming for damage that was clearly not earthquake related and this created a lot of resentment. You had to handle this very delicately. The good thing about it was that you were not required to show your report to the owner. They would often ask you how much the repair bill would be. I'd have it in front of me, but they did not know that. I'd simply tell them that it had to be worked out at head office. It was a juggling act to determine if it was earthquake related or not. Donnie and I never argued the point with them. I'd just make a note in my report that they needed to be careful with some of the claims they were making and may need a structural engineer to go out and have a look at it.

You met the good, the bad and the ugly in this job. In the time I did this work (nine months) I would have done many hundreds of houses. Most of the people I met were really good kiwi people. A few, not many, weren't. We went to a house one day that was just out of the movie set for Deliverance; they were dead set hillbillies. Ma and Pa and the kids dressed in overalls, missing their front teeth. The house was filthy and there were empty and half full cans of beer all over the place. The house was 100 years old and absolutely filthy and we had to assess the damage. They of course said that the earthquake damaged everything. There were major cracks in the foundation but they had moss growing in them. They would have been there before the earthquake came but when I suggested that, they weren't happy with me. I told them that I would report everything they mentioned but what I didn't tell them was that I had written that their truthfulness was very questionable and this needed to be taken into account when assessing the repair costs. Many people would offer us a cup of coffee with cake or something similar but the truth was we could only do this once a day as time did not permit us to socialise. Some of the houses we had to assess were even more filthy than the hillbillies' house. I had never seen people living like this, even in my police days. We hated having to do these houses, but fortunately there were few and far between. Both Donnie and I carried a small bottle of hand disinfectant cream and frequently used it.

The houses that had red stickers on them were considered as too far gone to be repaired and would have to be demolished. One such house was located on the cliff tops overlooking the Pacific Ocean. It was a magnificent location in a smart upmarket suburb. I learnt a very valuable lesson at this house not to pre-judge people. I was annoyed that the owner was late. I have explained to you how that screws up our timetable. Well, he came in this late model luxurious Mercedes Benz car. I thought, yeah, rich people can do what they like, can't they? F*** you I thought. He told me he was an Architect and had plans for the house. However, because it was a red zoned house, we were not supposed to go in there. He told us that they were in the final stages of negotiating a $2 million payout with the insurance company. Fair enough but no need for us to hang around. It would not count in our quota since we were not going to assess it. I was really angry with him now but trying hard not to show it. He then told me that it was his wife's parents place and that they had been killed in the earthquake. Not in the house but they were in town when the earthquake struck. Now I began to change my attitude. He then told us that he was suffering very badly from Parkinson's Disease. It was so bad some days he said that he could not put the car keys into the ignition. Christ, now I was feeling pretty bad. I had this initial attitude about him and left there thinking not to pre-judge too quickly. That man taught me a very valuable lesson. We thanked him and wished him well. I gave him my number and told him to ring me if he thought I could help him anymore. You learn these things as you go through life experiences I suppose.

Another of the challenges facing Christchurch was the damage done by something called liquefaction. Liquefaction occurs when the strength and stiffness of the soil underneath is reduced by earthquake shaking. Liquefaction events have been responsible for tremendous amounts of damage in historical earthquakes around the world. What happened in parts of Christchurch was that sewerage pipes fractured during the earthquake and the sewerage got mixed up with liquefied soil. This also happened with the water pipes. You can imagine the potential in this scenario if people were drinking liquefied water. The shaking by the earthquakes and aftershocks bought this stuff to the surface. In some areas, whole suburbs had to be red zoned, never to be inhabited again. I think the long term plan is to make parks out of them. There was liquefaction in areas where work could be done. Some of the houses had liquefaction right through all of the rooms of the house, up to 30 centimetres deep. Donnie and I did a house that did not appear to have too much damage. There were cracks in the brick veneer outside and in the concrete ring foundation, but that would be reasonably easy to repair. The concrete ring was about 60 centimetres high and the slope of the internal floor was within acceptable range. The house was owned by a lovely old couple in their retirement and they told us that since the earthquake they were a lot colder in the house. That raised a red flag. Donnie went to look underneath the house through the trapdoor and the liquefaction had come right up to the bottom of the floor, covering the concrete piles. It smelt putrid and we thought that it had been infected with sewerage. We arranged for engineers to go out and determine if it was safe to live there and treated it as a priority.

Not far from that house, this lady showed us how the slope of her house had changed by showing us her bathtub. It reminded me of the Titanic in the process of sinking. When it was full at one end, it was a third full at the other. Clearly a problem with the foundations! These people were using portable loos (toilets) that were stationed out in the streets. They had been using them for many months and they were getting the drinking water from above ground PVC piping supplied by the council. Many of them were in a bad way and winter was coming. Winters in Christchurch can be very cold and get down to below zero. Whilst we were there we had to stop work for three days because the snow was so heavy that roads became impassable. This was quite new for me as I had not lived in the snow before. I loved it. It gave us a good break but the downside of it was that we were not paid as we were contractors. No work, no pay. But the break came just in time for me; I was feeling exhausted.

Writing about wages, the deal was that we would be paid $75 per hour and supplied with a car, telephone, iPad and accommodation. We had to pay for our own meals. The hotel was a very nice four star hotel and did not rattle too much when we used to get the aftershocks in the middle of the night. You were required to work ten hours per day, six days per week for three weeks. Then you would have one week off. I met quite a few coppers who I had worked with in the NSW finest. Some of them had supervisory positions there. Others were assessors like me and we used to catch up from time to time and have a beer. Funny how we should all end up in Christchurch. In the winter time, it was pitch black when we went to work at 7.30 am and pitch black when we came home at 6 pm. Much of our work was outside, so we had to be fairly rugged up for the cold. I got a bout of sinusitis again (remember Beijing) and saw a 24/7 medical centre about it. They put me on a course of antibiotics which remarkably treated it successfully within a couple of days. I wondered why the medical staff in Beijing did not give me the same treatment. It cost me $85 for a ten minute consultation with the Doctor but only $3 for the medication. Apparently in New Zealand no prescription in the general sense is greater than $3. It was during 2011 that they held the Rugby World Cup in New Zealand. The NZ All Blacks are considered the best rugby team in the world and have been for as long as I can remember. Most of the kiwi staff were rugby mad and somewhat parochial; naturally enough. The All Blacks beat the Aussies in the semi-finals and our Supervisors felt pretty good about that. It was always in our interest for them to feel good. In the final, the All Blacks beat France, but it was a near thing. I secretly wanted France to win as it is my nature to go for the underdog as well as my innate desire to see the All Blacks lose. However, I knew that there would be serious ramifications if they did because the

Supervisors would be really pissed off about it and displacement would surely take place. The All Blacks just won 8-7 and were lucky to have done that. It looked very much like France could win it with five minutes to go. So, all our management staff were happy and if they were happy — well you can guess the rest.

You can imagine on these cold winter mornings going to work through these very damaged suburbs was like driving through an apocalyptic scene. They really were in a mess in some areas. A series of suburbs and the CBD that included suburbs like Avonside were so badly damaged they would not be rebuilt. There were many thousands of houses in Christchurch suburbs in the red zone, mainly in the eastern and southern parts of the city. Avonside is on the River Avon to the immediate north-east of the CBD and it was a working class area of public housing and tenants. The roads were cracked and jagged. Dried liquefaction sat in stagnant, crusty pools throughout the red zone area. On one side you would see the beautiful Avon River running along the road with ducks swimming on it. On the other this liquefied mess and destroyed houses. An interesting contrast to say the least. It really did make you feel like you were driving through a war zone. Donnie and I went all over Christchurch doing these loss assessments for the traumatised people of Christchurch. They are a very resilient lot these kiwis and they have always punched above their weight. Little wonder that they are the champion rugby team in the world and were until recently, the number one rugby league team in the world as well. We Aussies think that it must be something in the water they drink. Remember they only have a population of 4.47 million people. That's about the same as Sydney! I finished up with the EQC in November 2011 and made about NZD$130,000 so that helped me a lot to get out of the financial mess of 1996/97. After the NZ-EQC assignment, I went back to Singapore to continue with my security risk management work.

I started negotiating with the Intercontinental Hotel group (IHG) in Singapore. They, like most of the big players in the corporate hotel world, were expanding rapidly. I was dealing directly with head office in London. We had a handshake deal that I would carry out security design engineering for them with new hotel developments in Indonesia. I did a lot of research for this job and was just waiting for the nod. The brief was to work with the project management team and take control of the security design part of the engineering brief. As we came into 2012 and nothing yet had eventuated with IHG, I was starting to think of security for my future. I could stay in Singapore and live with Poonam but I was not comfortable doing that, mainly because I would have been a non-contributor and I did not want to do that long term. I would have suffered from a guilt complex had I stayed and lived off her. I guess that I would never have been very successful as a 'pimp'. I continued the negotiations with IHG believing that it was just around the corner. By mid-year it had not happened so I made the decision to come back to Australia and make a life for myself here. I had been away for fifteen years.

Chapter Eighteen: Home & Reflection
2012 - 2017

I returned back to Australia on 23 July 2012 with plans to prepare for old age and put myself into a situation whereby I would be eligible for the benefits of the national health and aged pension schemes. I knew that the time would come when I would have to receive these benefits and needed to do the ground work to make it happen. The other motivating factor, apart from not wanting to live off Poonam in Singapore, was to find suitable work, even though I was nearly 70. However, much to my disappointment this was easier said than done. In my absence from the country, it had become a very bureaucratic state with rules and regulations that would put Singapore to shame. When I went to my old hotel school where I had been a teacher, they told me that for me to now teach in Australia I would have to have a university degree, at the very least. To teach at this particular school, I would have to have a Masters' degree. Previously I had taught there and all of my students without exception passed their exams and received their hotel diplomas in hotel management. I have travelled the world working as a global security risk management consultant but in Australia I could not even get a job as a security guard unless I was prepared to undergo courses and get the appropriate accreditation, which I ended up doing just to get part time work. It's amazing that I can be an Olympic Games Security Coordinator in Beijing but couldn't work as a security guard in Australia.

I wasn't prepared for it. I thought that I would get teaching work very quickly and that is something that I am very good at but it did not eventuate. So I ended up doing a 2-week security guard training course, coupled with a 1-day first aid course and a 1-day RSA course (responsible serving of alcohol). This was a far cry from being a guest speaker at a senior global hotel executives' security conference in Chicago in 2008, but that's the way it panned out. Beggars can't be choosers! After doing the courses and passing, I got a job in 2013 as a casual

Crowd Controller at the SCGT (Sydney Cricket Ground Trust) and I am still doing it as this book goes to print.

A couple of months after I returned to Australia, I developed what is known in the medical world as AF (atrial flutter). I had to be admitted to the A&E ward at POW hospital (where I worked in 1975) and be treated as an emergency. Not long after this emergency, they found out I had prostate cancer for which I had EBRT (external beam radiotherapy) treatment. In between all of this they found out that I was a diabetic and also had high blood pressure. The EBRT went well but 16-months after I finished the course, I started to bleed and they found out I had radiation cystitis and that is where I am at now. I think it is reasonable that for any person after they pass the three score and ten mark, to expect medical issues. Through all of this I never stopped working and never told them at work that I was having these problems. In fact with the EBRT I had to attend the hospital every weekday for two months. On many occasions I was able to organise it so that I could be on the EBRT table in the morning and working that afternoon and night. I got dependant on getting the money from my work at the Sydney Cricket Ground and I also enjoyed the comradeship of my fellow workers. I think that I would have had a hard time meeting my financial commitments if I did not get this income. They are a great bunch to work for and I enjoyed it more than I thought that I would. Being the humble bloke that I am it didn't bother me that I was just a Security Guard even though I have been a life member of this prestigious organisation for over thirty years. I don't have those sort of superiority issues and I think I went into that when I wrote about my shearing days.

I live in a B&B in Kirribilli which is just down the street from Kirribilli House where the Australian Prime Minister lives when he is in Sydney. At the time of writing I pay $500 per week for bed and breakfast. It is a nice enough place and I have been here now for nearly five years. I get about $440 per week from my aged pension, about $200 net rent from my apartment and about $300 per week on average from the SCGT. That's about

$940 gross per week. My must have expenses are $500 (rent), medication $7 per week, phone $7 per week, food $100 per week and transport $17.50. That adds up to $631, so I have a balance of $250-270 per week for things other than the bare necessities such as clothes, going out for dinner, airfares; all the non essentials. It's not much off course, but it's enough. The house that I told you about that I lost in bankruptcy in 1996 is now worth $4 million dollars so that puts things in perspective. But I have a good roof over my head, it doesn't leak, the room is warm in winter and cool in summer. I have enough food but don't drink much as you would understand. The bulk of the medical bills that I have had, the government paid for and every time I see a person in a wheel chair I think how lucky I am. I have plenty of free time and that is in part what motivated me to write this book. I live the life of a loner now and I seem to be able to cope with that; in fact I have got used to it. I read a lot and have discovered the joys of reading good books. There is nothing like making friends with people like Ernest Hemingway, Joseph Steinbeck, Richard Flanagan, John le Carré, Norman Mailer and Fredrick Forsyth. I don't seek to make friends which I could easily do living in a B&B but I choose not to. That is what I have become and I can live with it. Nearly everywhere I go, I go on my own and do pretty much everything on my own. Occasionally I catch up with my two old friends from the past, Geoff Bright and Bill Kable who I have mentioned earlier. We might catch up for a pub meal and a couple beers every couple months and that is about the extent of my social engagement. Bill has been a big help by picking me up from my various hospital procedures and taking me home to the B&B. Owning a car is out of the question with my income but I'm OK with the public transport. Unfortunately the hospital insists that I get picked up otherwise I would do what I did on Christmas Day 2014 and catch the public transport home from the hospital. I never go to a decent restaurant and it is years since I have worn a tie, let alone a suit. I think the last time I wore a suit was when I gave evidence at the Royal Commission into Child Sexual Abuse. But I have no complaints and am at peace about my present day circumstances.

I neglected to mention in my section on bankruptcy that in the latter stages of my financial catastrophe I did receive some support from Geoff. Although that support was not financial he did try to find ways for me to dig myself out of the hole that I was in and showed an understanding for the predicament I had got myself into. He even did a cash flow analysis on his own spreadsheets to try and help me. At various times he would visit me at the hotel where I was working to keep an eye on me and occasionally arranged for his children and mine to catch up and go somewhere. I mention this at this late stage because all I have mentioned so far in the story was how he was unable to help me when Sue had her troubles and ended up in hospital. It would be remiss of me not to mention the assistance that Geoff gave to me at that time and I needed to address that imbalance. Geoff and Bill are two good blokes and I refer to them as my multi millionaire mates which might be embellishing it a bit in Bill's case.

We (the world) are in for some interesting times now with the election in the USA of Donald Trump (November 2016). He won against all of the polls predictions that showed that Hilary Clinton would win comfortably. In fact Trump won comfortably and it remains to be seen how this very unpredictable, narcissistic man runs the most powerful nation in the world. He won because he had the overwhelming support of the middle aged white working class man who were fed up with the Washington establishment and elite. A similar pattern occurred in Great Britain in June 2016 when the British people voted to leave the European Union. Again it was mainly because of the middle aged white man who were fed up with mainstream politics and would not do anything significant to curb the inflow of migrants who they saw as taking their jobs. As was the case with the US elections, the Brexit polls got it wrong. So, we live in interesting times and who can guess what the future holds.

As I near the end of this book, I find myself more in a reflective mood and I do sometimes wonder how things could have turned out very differently. I was speaking with Geoff and

Bill at the last dinner we had and I told them that I did not think that I had gone anywhere near reaching my potential and saw myself as an underachiever; a bit of a loser. Bill protested and pointed out the many positive and meaningful things I had achieved. He mentioned how I had got high distinctions in nursing; how I had such rapid promotion at the Regent Sydney hotel and how I was recognised as a global expert on hotel security risk management. All that is true but what I was trying to tell them is that I believe that I could have been a very good leader and could have ended up as a CEO or a President of a global company. Geoff understood that and knew what I was talking about. He sees me as a natural leader and after they read this book, they will probably both understand why I never reached the levels of leadership that I think that I am capable off.

I started this book talking about the terrible Michell boys and wonder what impact being sent off to a Catholic nuns boarding school at 5 years of age would have had upon me. I feel that this separation was seen as abandonment by me at a very young age and in my young mind, it may have been the first seed sown that lead to my mental illness that started at 23. I still believe that. I doubt that it was the sole cause but it was one of the foundations blocks. There has to be an explainable reason why my brother John and I did all those mischievous things as little boys but I am unable to explain it and in my psychotherapy sessions the medical people were not able to either. Nevertheless, I see it as some form of pathology and obviously not normal child behaviour. I am deeply suspicious that I may have repressed some 'significant' traumatic event, perhaps of a sexual nature, at this early stage of my life but that is only conjecture on my part.

Probably the best part of my life would have been the time that I spent at Torrendorra in Inverell on the lifestyle block. I have such fond memories of my mother at that time, Bessie and the sulky and Kathy Marsh, my first love at 11 years of age. I think I articulated how agonising it was for me when she left and the terrible state I was in for a few days. Not surprisingly I have always had trouble saying goodbye and the scenes at the Capella railway station when I was being sent back to St Brendan's College were extremely harrowing and painful. I tried to explain how the rot started when we left NSW to go to Queensland when I was 12. I went through with you the appalling levels of abuse that I experienced at St Brendan's College and detailed that to the Royal Commission in 2013. Can you imagine a teaching brother singling me out as a 13 year old 'pretty' boy and humiliating me in front of the entire school by calling me Miss Australia and telling them I should have been a girl? What a f****** c*** he was and to make it many times worse, my parents did nothing about it. I often reflect on what this man did to me and also what the other brothers at this school did to me. I feel confident that I articulated that good enough for you to understand the gravity of it. If you can't understand the importance and impact that leaving home had on me at 5 years of age you haven't got a heart and should crawl back into your burrow. If you fall into this bracket, I'd suggest you don't have children.

Perhaps it not surprising that these demons inside of me surfaced when Pauline rejected me that night we had a fight and she said, "I can never marry you, you could kill me?" She betrayed and rejected me and in my feeble mental state, I could not cope with it. I grew up in a world where you just couldn't trust anyone; not even your own parents.

I reflect a lot of my mother and to lesser extent my father, and I wrote a lot about both of them. I told Mum many years later that I felt that Dad's dogs were treated better than I was. Of course that is a gross exaggeration and maybe a tad harsh, but it was my way of making the point to reflect that period of time. The time that I spent at Torrendorra Capella between 1958 (late) and 1963 was in the main absolutely demoralising and depressing. I articulated just what rural social isolation, parental abuse and slave labour were all about and you may think that I am being unfair to my parents. Being made to feel guilty was the order of the day and it took me a long, long time to understand that I had nothing to feel guilty about. I think it is therefore altogether understandable that I developed mental illness. I write in this book that I saw myself as a victim of a perfect storm with the marriage of my Mum and Dad. I tried to explain why it was me that suffered and not my brother and my sisters. It is what it is, and we have all moved on. Having said that the final act of vindictiveness on my Mum's part was leaving John and I out of her will after having assured us all our lives that it would be split equally. God knows, I could have done with some financial help during and after the 'holy trinity' period but my family would never help me, no matter what the circumstances were. Their creed was 'if you make your own bed, you sleep in it.' I told you the story about my trying to get Dad's truck after he passed and I think that story says it all. All I ever felt that I was entitled to were wages that should have been paid to me, especially for the shearing. Perhaps it is better to let sleeping dogs lie.

Then came the period that I referred to as the 'days of darkness' whereby I admit to my mental illness, being in a locked ward and further admit that I received ECT treatment. At one stage I was told that I would probably be institutionalised for life. The medical 'experts' had a very negative prognosis for me and I myself can only describe this period as one of desolation, melancholia and depression. I don't know how I came out of it alive and sane, but I did both. I dealt with the challenges a person can face with severe depression, obsessional neurosis and anxiety and to date at least, I have won. I think that when I write about the period when I was in Melbourne for three months and working but can't remember anything about it highlights just how debilitating severe depression can be and how much I needed a family. Shortly after this period of melancholy, about one year later in NZ, I really 'ran off the rails' when I started drinking and mixing the alcohol with very strong sleeping pills and other psychiatric drugs. I went crazy and became fearless. I would fight anyone and even jumped on the bar of a popular hotel in Christchurch on a busy Friday night and offered to fight anyone. When no one accepted my offer, I told them they were all a bunch of weak f****** kiwi c****. Can you believe that? It's very hard to believe that especially if you meet me now. It would be almost impossible to pick a fight with me now but at that time, I could just explode and was a deeply disturbed person and very, very angry with the world. It is worth repeating - I really don't know how I survived this period of the 'Days of Darkness'.

Even though I hated the three years that I spent nursing, this period of time did allow me to establish some permanency in my life and I began to recover, albeit it slowly. I found once I was off the strong medication my behaviour was exemplary, even when I was drinking. I learnt during this period, especially when I graduated that I was not a bum, a con man, a no-hoper or a 'useless damn coot' who would never amount to anything and all the other negatives that used to be bestowed upon me. Then came my time in the cops. I try to explain what life was like in the police force and I admit I lied to get into the job and even admit to taking heroin whilst serving as an undercover Police Officer. The cops made me I think. I gained a lot of confidence working as a cop and I reflect on whether or not I should have left when I did. I reckon that I would have made a Detective Chief Inspector at least, but I give my reasons for leaving and chief amongst those was my fear of betrayal by one of my colleagues. I go to great lengths to admit that I would have got involved in the corruption that was occurring at the time and some might even see me as endorsing it. It was during this time period I got myself back to normality, got married, off all drugs, not seeking medical help and really started a fruitful life. When I left the cops, I got into the international hotel scene and did very well (except at the end). I showed my leadership skills and managed my own Department of 16 men as the Director of Security. The senior management were so impressed with me that they promoted me to the Executive Housekeeper where I had a staff of over 150 people directly reporting to me. No one at the hotel would have ever guessed my past and not surprisingly, I wasn't about to enlighten them.

Then came the next biggest challenge I call the 'Holy Trinity' and if it weren't for the lady in the sauna I don't know what would have happened. At this time I had to deal with three major catastrophes simultaneously, namely, bankruptcy, divorce and spousal illness. Paradoxically I performed at my very best as I was not going to let anything or anyone create a situation whereby my children would not have a roof over their heads. If the mental illness was going to come out of remission, this is when that was most likely to happen. I lost everything - my family, my home, my business, my shares, my superannuation, my car, everything. Talk about stress; it just could not have been worse but I showed extraordinary inner strength and character and just refused to buckle. It was my Everest and a very defining moment.

The rest of the book deals with my time in Asia from 1997-2012.

I often sit down over a cup of tea and reflect about all these things. We were a very dysfunctional family and the primary reason for that is the roles of mother and father were reversed. My Dad certainly was lacking in emotional intelligence. To be fair to my mother, she got no real help from Dad in the parenting role. She must have been terribly disappointed with how things turned out for her and needed someone to unload on (displacement). Unfortunately that someone was me. Mum was also partly responsible for my parents getting out of the financial rut that they were in. She did it by buying and selling cattle, raising chickens & turkeys, rearing poddy calves and so on and did quite well out of it. However, I think what helped them the most was that they did not have to pay wages for many years when both John and I were working on the property gratis. I have absolutely no doubt that after I was about fifteen neither of my parents had any love for me; in fact they may even have despised me. Mum saw me developing as a clone of my father and that is the last thing that she would have wanted. The statement, "Why can't you be like your brother John?" is firmly implanted in my mind. On the positive side I will give my parents credit for passing onto me their resilience and strength of character to face adversity. They were tough and resilient people and I needed these qualities to firstly overcome my 'Days of Darkness' and then many years later, the 'Holy Trinity'. I do think I got some of my 'strength of character' from them or else I may have ended up permanently in a mental hospital, and later with the 'Holy Trinity' I may have declared bankruptcy, the easy way out. Dad passed onto me his incredible sense of fair play and his view that the umpire's decision must always be respected. He was a very good man no doubt and Mum was in her own right a good woman; a pioneering woman who had to be tough to survive. Mum had a wonderful relationship with her two daughters but an estranged one with both of her sons. I think Mum was handicapped by her religious dogma, her mercurial temperament and having a husband who lacked emotional intelligence.

I go into the twilight of my life on my own. For me to see my son and grandchildren, I have to go to NZ and I do that every year; maybe twice a year. My daughter lives and works in Dubai and because of my financial situation that I have aptly described to you throughout this narrative, I am precluded to popping over to see her. I really have no extended family and no meaningful contact with my siblings. On my brothers and sisters, I get a call from John now and then and an email a couple of times a year from my older sister Patricia but not from my younger sister, Margaret unless she is replying to me. Perhaps all my siblings have been affected by our dysfunctional family that I write about. Perhaps they too have their demons to wrestle with. I don't harbour any ill feelings towards any of them at all but John puts it right when he says that there was no love in our family. Mum used to say that the family that prays together, stays together. Well, we did plenty of praying but little staying together.

I often go out on the weekends in Sydney and see all the older couples going here and there; sometimes holding hands and enjoying each other's company. I think how wonderful it would be to be able to go home to a wife or partner every night and see your children and your grandkids on the weekends. I'd love to live close to Dan and Toni and maybe go to the footy with Dan now and again, or out to some movie with Toni. These are all the things that I miss out on in my later years but I accept that this is the way it is, and once you accept your lot and lower your expectations, you tend to deal with things better generally. Remember what Marcus Aurelius stated at the beginning of this book.

Finally I have to mention two people that have been extremely good to me and my best two friends. My partner Poonam and my former business partner and boss, Chris Stafford. Poonam is probably the best friend I have ever had and is a truly remarkable decent human being. She came into my life when I was on the road to recovery (1998) and I can't emphasis enough how much she has helped me to recover from the 'Holy Trinity' period. I will always love her and feel deeply indebted to her. In my eyes Poonam would be just the sort of person I would have liked to have had as a mother. She is soft, caring, supportive and loving. Chris is my other true friend. He gave me a job when I was all but destitute in 1997 and if it weren't for him, I doubt that I would have recovered. He stood up to his boss when the bloke wanted to tear up my contract to work in Singapore. These two people are very special people and the world would be a lot better place if more of us were like them. I keep telling Poonam that she is a much better person than I have ever been and it will be interesting to see how Poonam and Chris react to the revelations I have made in this book.

Some of the assertions I have made may be viewed by some as offensive and others may dispute my version of events. It doesn't really matter because all I have done is tell it as I see it. I'm not seeking clarification or endorsements from anybody. I didn't write this book to make friends. I wrote it to put the record straight and leave a legacy for my children and I think that I have done that. I have not set out to hurt anybody or tarnish anybody's reputation. There were pivotal moments in this book whereby I would have preferred to have left certain facts out but I just couldn't because it would deflect from the story's accuracy. However, if I have hurt or embarrassed anybody I sincerely apologise but ask you to consider the context in which it was written. When searching for a book cover it was a toss up between the mango tree or a cover of a little 5 year old boy catching a steam train to boarding school. I settled for the mango tree but it was a close call. Another cover that came to mind was a rural scene that expressed rural isolation, parental abuse, labour exploitation and abject loneliness.

I have written that parents have an awesome responsibility to bring up their children well. I think it is heartless to send a 5 year old to boarding school for whatever reason. Haven't I already said that! I think that boarding school should only be entertained at the beginning of secondary school and only than after having done very strict due diligence. If you have to send them, be sure to still see them regularly so that they know you are there for them. Never abuse your children and certainly never hit them. As much as possible, instil positive behaviour and language and don't tell them how useless they are, how they are not as good as others, or anything of a negative nature. Bottom line I suppose is to "Teach you children well" and be good role models.

I sincerely hope that the Royal Commission into Child Sexual Abuse hands down their recommendation sooner rather than later. I think at this point in time they expect to do it by the end of 2017. I really hope that they do something about the 'sanctuary of the confessional' and 'vicarious liability' of the clergy. Since 1950 in Australia alone, claims of sexual abuse have been made against 597 religious brothers, 188 religious priests, 384 Catholic diocesan priests, 96 religious sisters, 543 lay church workers and 72 who religious status is unknown. I think this is a stain on the image of the Catholic Church that can never be erased. I hope the Catholic Church has its day of reckoning. To not do so, would be a travesty of justice. There is still the matter of Cardinal Pell that has not been settled. Not only must Justice be done; it must also be seen to be done.

www.ingramcontent.com/pod-product-compliance
Lightning Source LLC
Chambersburg PA
CBHW022127020426
42334CB00015B/796